GNU Emacs Manual

GNU Emacs Manual

Fourteenth Edition, Updated for Emacs Version 20.7

Richard Stallman

Fourteenth Edition
Updated for Emacs Version 20.7,
June 2000
ISBN 1-882114-07-8

Published by the Free Software Foundation
59 Temple Place, Suite 330
Boston, MA 02111-1307 USA

Cover art by Etienne Suvasa.

Short Contents

Preface 1

Distribution 3

GNU GENERAL PUBLIC LICENSE 5

Introduction 13

1   The Organization of the Screen 15

2   Characters, Keys and Commands 21

3   Entering and Exiting Emacs 25

4   Basic Editing Commands 29

5   The Minibuffer 41

6   Running Commands by Name 49

7   Help 51

8   The Mark and the Region 59

9   Killing and Moving Text 65

10 Registers 75

11 Controlling the Display 79

12 Searching and Replacement 85

13 Commands for Fixing Typos 101

14 File Handling 107

15 Using Multiple Buffers 143

16 Multiple Windows 151

17 Frames and X Windows 157

18 International Character Set Support 175

19 Major Modes 191

20 Indentation 195

21 Commands for Human Languages 199

22 Editing Programs 227

23 Compiling and Testing Programs 277

24 Abbrevs 289

25 Editing Pictures 297

26 Sending Mail 301

27 Reading Mail with Rmail 311

28   Dired, the Directory Editor 329

29   The Calendar and the Diary 343

30   Miscellaneous Commands 365

31   Customization 391

32   Dealing with Common Problems 425

Appendix A   Command Line Arguments 441

Appendix B   Emacs 19 Antinews 461

Appendix C   Emacs and MS-DOS 463

The GNU Manifesto 475

Glossary 485

Key (Character) Index 505

Command and Function Index 515

Variable Index 527

Concept Index 533

Table of Contents

Preface 1

Distribution 3

GNU GENERAL PUBLIC LICENSE 5
    Preamble 5
    TERMS AND CONDITIONS FOR COPYING, DISTRIBUTION
        AND MODIFICATION 6
    How to Apply These Terms to Your New Programs 11

Introduction 13

1   The Organization of the Screen 15
    1.1   Point 15
    1.2   The Echo Area 16
    1.3   The Mode Line 17
    1.4   The Menu Bar 19

2   Characters, Keys and Commands 21
    2.1   Kinds of User Input 21
    2.2   Keys 22
    2.3   Keys and Commands 23
    2.4   Character Set for Text 24

3   Entering and Exiting Emacs 25
    3.1   Exiting Emacs 25

4   Basic Editing Commands 29
    4.1   Inserting Text 29
    4.2   Changing the Location of Point 30
    4.3   Erasing Text 31
    4.4   Undoing Changes 32
    4.5   Files 33
    4.6   Help 34
    4.7   Blank Lines 34
    4.8   Continuation Lines 35
    4.9   Cursor Position Information 35
    4.10 Numeric Arguments 37
    4.11 Repeating a Command 39

5 The Minibuffer 41

  5.1 Minibuffers for File Names 41
  5.2 Editing in the Minibuffer 42
  5.3 Completion 43
      5.3.1 Completion Example 43
      5.3.2 Completion Commands 44
      5.3.3 Strict Completion 45
      5.3.4 Completion Options 45
  5.4 Minibuffer History 46
  5.5 Repeating Minibuffer Commands 47

6 Running Commands by Name 49

7 Help 51

  7.1 Documentation for a Key 53
  7.2 Help by Command or Variable Name 53
  7.3 Apropos 54
  7.4 Keyword Search for Lisp Libraries 55
  7.5 Help for International Language Support 56
  7.6 Help Mode Commands 56
  7.7 Other Help Commands 57

8 The Mark and the Region 59

  8.1 Setting the Mark 59
  8.2 Transient Mark Mode 60
  8.3 Operating on the Region 61
  8.4 Commands to Mark Textual Objects 62
  8.5 The Mark Ring 63
  8.6 The Global Mark Ring 63

9 Killing and Moving Text 65

  9.1 Deletion and Killing 65
      9.1.1 Deletion 65
      9.1.2 Killing by Lines 66
      9.1.3 Other Kill Commands 67
  9.2 Yanking 67
      9.2.1 The Kill Ring 68
      9.2.2 Appending Kills 68
      9.2.3 Yanking Earlier Kills 69
  9.3 Accumulating Text 70
  9.4 Rectangles 71

10 Registers **75**

10.1 Saving Positions in Registers 75
10.2 Saving Text in Registers 75
10.3 Saving Rectangles in Registers 76
10.4 Saving Window Configurations in Registers 76
10.5 Keeping Numbers in Registers 76
10.6 Keeping File Names in Registers 77
10.7 Bookmarks 77

11 Controlling the Display **79**

11.1 Scrolling 79
11.2 Horizontal Scrolling 80
11.3 Follow Mode 81
11.4 Selective Display 81
11.5 Optional Mode Line Features 82
11.6 How Text Is Displayed 82
11.7 Variables Controlling Display 83

12 Searching and Replacement **85**

12.1 Incremental Search 85
    12.1.1 Slow Terminal Incremental Search 87
12.2 Nonincremental Search 88
12.3 Word Search 88
12.4 Regular Expression Search 89
12.5 Syntax of Regular Expressions 90
12.6 Searching and Case 94
12.7 Replacement Commands 95
    12.7.1 Unconditional Replacement 95
    12.7.2 Regexp Replacement 96
    12.7.3 Replace Commands and Case 96
    12.7.4 Query Replace 96
12.8 Other Search-and-Loop Commands 98

13 Commands for Fixing Typos **101**

13.1 Killing Your Mistakes 101
13.2 Transposing Text 101
13.3 Case Conversion 102
13.4 Checking and Correcting Spelling 103

14   File Handling 107

14.1   File Names 107
14.2   Visiting Files 108
14.3   Saving Files 111
    14.3.1   Backup Files 113
        14.3.1.1   Single or Numbered Backups 114
        14.3.1.2   Automatic Deletion of Backups 114
        14.3.1.3   Copying vs.Renaming 115
    14.3.2   Protection against Simultaneous Editing 115
14.4   Reverting a Buffer 117
14.5   Auto-Saving: Protection Against Disasters 117
    14.5.1   Auto-Save Files 118
    14.5.2   Controlling Auto-Saving 118
    14.5.3   Recovering Data from Auto-Saves............. 119
14.6   File Name Aliases 120
14.7   Version Control 120
    14.7.1   Introduction to Version Control............... 121
        14.7.1.1   Supported Version Control Systems .. 121
        14.7.1.2   Concepts of Version Control 121
    14.7.2   Version Control and the Mode Line 122
    14.7.3   Basic Editing under Version Control 122
        14.7.3.1   Basic Version Control with Locking .. 123
        14.7.3.2   Basic Version Control without Locking
                  123
        14.7.3.3   Features of the Log Entry Buffer 124
    14.7.4   Examining And Comparing Old Versions 124
    14.7.5   The Secondary Commands of VC 125
        14.7.5.1   Registering a File for Version Control
                  125
        14.7.5.2   VC Status Commands............... 126
        14.7.5.3   Undoing Version Control Actions..... 126
        14.7.5.4   Dired under VC 127
        14.7.5.5   VC Dired Commands 128
    14.7.6   Multiple Branches of a File................... 128
        14.7.6.1   Switching between Branches 129
        14.7.6.2   Creating New Branches............. 129
        14.7.6.3   Merging Branches.................. 130
        14.7.6.4   Multi-User Branching 131
    14.7.7   Snapshots................................... 131
        14.7.7.1   Making and Using Snapshots 131
        14.7.7.2   Snapshot Caveats 132
    14.7.8   Miscellaneous Commands and Features of VC.. 133
        14.7.8.1   Change Logs and VC................ 133
        14.7.8.2   Renaming VC Work Files and Master
              Files 134
        14.7.8.3   Inserting Version Control Headers 135

   14.7.9 Customizing VC............................. 136
     14.7.9.1 Options for VC Backends............ 136
     14.7.9.2 VC Workfile Handling.............. 137
     14.7.9.3 VC Status Retrieval................ 137
     14.7.9.4 VC Command Execution............ 138
 14.8 File Directories 138
 14.9 Comparing Files 139
 14.10 Miscellaneous File Operations....................... 139
 14.11 Accessing Compressed Files.......................... 140
 14.12 Remote Files 141
 14.13 Quoted File Names.................................. 141

15 Using Multiple Buffers................... 143
 15.1 Creating and Selecting Buffers 143
 15.2 Listing Existing Buffers.............................. 144
 15.3 Miscellaneous Buffer Operations...................... 145
 15.4 Killing Buffers 146
 15.5 Operating on Several Buffers......................... 147
 15.6 Indirect Buffers 149

16 Multiple Windows...................... 151
 16.1 Concepts of Emacs Windows......................... 151
 16.2 Splitting Windows 152
 16.3 Using Other Windows 152
 16.4 Displaying in Another Window........................ 153
 16.5 Forcing Display in the Same Window 154
 16.6 Deleting and Rearranging Windows.................... 155

17 Frames and X Windows................. 157
 17.1 Mouse Commands for Editing........................ 157
 17.2 Secondary Selection 159
 17.3 Following References with the Mouse 160
 17.4 Mouse Clicks for Menus 160
 17.5 Mode Line Mouse Commands....................... 161
 17.6 Creating Frames 161
 17.7 Making and Using a Speedbar Frame 162
 17.8 Multiple Displays 163
 17.9 Special Buffer Frames 163
 17.10 Setting Frame Parameters 164
 17.11 Scroll Bars 165
 17.12 Menu Bars 166
 17.13 Using Multiple Typefaces........................... 166
 17.14 Font Lock mode 168
 17.15 Font Lock Support Modes 170
   17.15.1 Fast Lock Mode........................... 170

        17.15.2 Lazy Lock Mode 170
        17.15.3 Fast Lock or Lazy Lock? 171
  17.16 Highlight Changes Mode........................... 172
  17.17 Miscellaneous X Window Features.................. 172
  17.18 Non-Window Terminals............................. 172

18 International Character Set Support 175
  18.1   Introduction to International Character Sets 175
  18.2   Enabling Multibyte Characters....................... 175
  18.3   Language Environments 176
  18.4   Input Methods...................................... 177
  18.5   Selecting an Input Method.......................... 178
  18.6   Unibyte and Multibyte Non-ASCII characters 179
  18.7   Coding Systems..................................... 180
  18.8   Recognizing Coding Systems 182
  18.9   Specifying a Coding System......................... 184
  18.10 Fontsets... 186
  18.11 Defining fontsets 187
  18.12 Single-byte European Character Support............. 188

19 Major Modes........................... 191
  19.1   How Major Modes are Chosen 191

20 Indentation 195
  20.1   Indentation Commands and Techniques............... 195
  20.2   Tab Stops 196
  20.3   Tabs vs. Spaces 197

21 Commands for Human Languages 199
  21.1   Words... 199
  21.2   Sentences... 200
  21.3   Paragraphs 201
  21.4   Pages 202
  21.5   Filling Text...................................... 203
        21.5.1   Auto Fill Mode............................ 204
        21.5.2   Explicit Fill Commands.................... 205
        21.5.3   The Fill Prefix 206
        21.5.4   Adaptive Filling 207
  21.6   Case Conversion Commands 208
  21.7   Text Mode 209
  21.8   Outline Mode...................................... 210
        21.8.1   Format of Outlines 210
        21.8.2   Outline Motion Commands................... 211
        21.8.3   Outline Visibility Commands............... 212

       21.8.4   Viewing One Outline in Multiple Views 214
21.9   TeX Mode.. 214
       21.9.1   TeX Editing Commands 214
       21.9.2   LaTeX Editing Commands................... 216
       21.9.3   TeX Printing Commands.................... 216
21.10   Nroff Mode 219
21.11   Editing Formatted Text 219
       21.11.1   Requesting to Edit Formatted Text 220
       21.11.2   Hard and Soft Newlines 220
       21.11.3   Editing Format Information 221
       21.11.4   Faces in Formatted Text 221
       21.11.5   Colors in Formatted Text 223
       21.11.6   Indentation in Formatted Text 223
       21.11.7   Justification in Formatted Text............. 224
       21.11.8   Setting Other Text Properties 225
       21.11.9   Forcing Enriched Mode 225

22   Editing Programs...................... 227

22.1   Major Modes for Programming Languages 227
22.2   Lists and Sexps 228
22.3   List And Sexp Commands 229
22.4   Defuns 230
22.5   Indentation for Programs 231
       22.5.1   Basic Program Indentation Commands........ 231
       22.5.2   Indenting Several Lines 232
       22.5.3   Customizing Lisp Indentation 233
       22.5.4   Commands for C Indentation................. 234
       22.5.5   Customizing C Indentation................... 234
               22.5.5.1   Step 1—Syntactic Analysis 235
               22.5.5.2   Step 2—Indentation Calculation 236
               22.5.5.3   Changing Indentation Style 237
               22.5.5.4   Syntactic Symbols 238
               22.5.5.5   Variables for C Indentation 242
               22.5.5.6   C Indentation Styles 242
22.6   Automatic Display Of Matching Parentheses 243
22.7   Manipulating Comments............................. 244
       22.7.1   Comment Commands 244
       22.7.2   Multiple Lines of Comments................. 245
       22.7.3   Options Controlling Comments 246
22.8   Editing Without Unbalanced Parentheses 247
22.9   Completion for Symbol Names 247
22.10   Which Function Mode............................... 248
22.11   Documentation Commands 248
22.12   Change Logs....................................... 249
22.13   Tags Tables.. 250
       22.13.1   Source File Tag Syntax 250

22.13.2   Creating Tags Tables 252
22.13.3   Selecting a Tags Table 254
22.13.4   Finding a Tag 255
22.13.5   Searching and Replacing with Tags Tables.... 256
22.13.6   Tags Table Inquiries 257
22.14   Merging Files with Emerge 257
22.14.1   Overview of Emerge 258
22.14.2   Submodes of Emerge 259
22.14.3   State of a Difference 260
22.14.4   Merge Commands 260
22.14.5   Exiting Emerge 262
22.14.6   Combining the Two Versions 262
22.14.7   Fine Points of Emerge 263
22.15   C and Related Modes 263
22.15.1   C Mode Motion Commands 263
22.15.2   Electric C Characters 264
22.15.3   Hungry Delete Feature in C 266
22.15.4   Other Commands for C Mode 266
22.15.5   Comments in C Modes 267
22.16   Fortran Mode 268
22.16.1   Motion Commands 268
22.16.2   Fortran Indentation 268
22.16.2.1   Fortran Indentation Commands 269
22.16.2.2   Continuation Lines 269
22.16.2.3   Line Numbers 270
22.16.2.4   Syntactic Conventions 270
22.16.2.5   Variables for Fortran Indentation.... 271
22.16.3   Fortran Comments 272
22.16.4   Fortran Auto Fill Mode 273
22.16.5   Checking Columns in Fortran 274
22.16.6   Fortran Keyword Abbrevs 274
22.16.7   Other Fortran Mode Commands 275
22.17   Asm Mode 275

23 Compiling and Testing Programs 277

23.1 Running Compilations under Emacs 277
23.2 Searching with Grep under Emacs 278
23.3 Compilation Mode 278
23.4 Subshells for Compilation 279
23.5 Running Debuggers Under Emacs 280
    23.5.1 Starting GUD 280
    23.5.2 Debugger Operation 281
    23.5.3 Commands of GUD 281
    23.5.4 GUD Customization 283
23.6 Executing Lisp Expressions 284
23.7 Libraries of Lisp Code for Emacs 285
23.8 Evaluating Emacs-Lisp Expressions 286
23.9 Lisp Interaction Buffers 287
23.10 Running an External Lisp 287

24 Abbrevs 289

24.1 Abbrev Concepts 289
24.2 Defining Abbrevs 289
24.3 Controlling Abbrev Expansion 290
24.4 Examining and Editing Abbrevs 292
24.5 Saving Abbrevs 292
24.6 Dynamic Abbrev Expansion 293
24.7 Customizing Dynamic Abbreviation 294

25 Editing Pictures 297

25.1 Basic Editing in Picture Mode 297
25.2 Controlling Motion after Insert 298
25.3 Picture Mode Tabs 299
25.4 Picture Mode Rectangle Commands 299

26 Sending Mail 301

26.1 The Format of the Mail Buffer 301
26.2 Mail Header Fields 302
26.3 Mail Aliases 304
26.4 Mail Mode 305
    26.4.1 Mail Sending 306
    26.4.2 Mail Header Editing 306
    26.4.3 Citing Mail 307
    26.4.4 Mail Mode Miscellany 308
26.5 Distracting the NSA 309
26.6 Mail-Composition Methods 309

27   Reading Mail with Rmail 311

27.1   Basic Concepts of Rmail 311
27.2   Scrolling Within a Message 312
27.3   Moving Among Messages 312
27.4   Deleting Messages 313
27.5   Rmail Files and Inboxes 314
27.6   Multiple Rmail Files 315
27.7   Copying Messages Out to Files 316
27.8   Labels 318
27.9   Rmail Attributes 319
27.10   Sending Replies 320
27.11   Summaries 322
         27.11.1   Making Summaries 322
         27.11.2   Editing in Summaries 323
27.12   Sorting the Rmail File 324
27.13   Display of Messages 324
27.14   Editing Within a Message 325
27.15   Digest Messages 326
27.16   Converting an Rmail File to Inbox Format 326
27.17   Reading Rot13 Messages 326
27.18   `movemail` and POP 327

28   Dired, the Directory Editor 329

28.1   Entering Dired 329
28.2   Commands in the Dired Buffer 329
28.3   Deleting Files with Dired 329
28.4   Flagging Many Files at Once 330
28.5   Visiting Files in Dired 331
28.6   Dired Marks vs. Flags 332
28.7   Operating on Files 334
28.8   Shell Commands in Dired 336
28.9   Transforming File Names in Dired 336
28.10   File Comparison with Dired 337
28.11   Subdirectories in Dired 338
28.12   Moving Over Subdirectories 338
28.13   Hiding Subdirectories 339
28.14   Updating the Dired Buffer 339
28.15   Dired and `find` 340

29 The Calendar and the Diary 343

29.1 Movement in the Calendar............................ 343
    29.1.1 Motion by Standard Lengths of Time 343
    29.1.2 Beginning or End of Week, Month or Year..... 344
    29.1.3 Specified Dates................................ 344
29.2 Scrolling in the Calendar 345
29.3 Counting Days....................................... 346
29.4 Miscellaneous Calendar Commands.................... 346
29.5 LaTeX Calendar 346
29.6 Holidays... 347
29.7 Times of Sunrise and Sunset 349
29.8 Phases of the Moon 350
29.9 Conversion To and From Other Calendars.............. 350
    29.9.1 Supported Calendar Systems 351
    29.9.2 Converting To Other Calendars............... 352
    29.9.3 Converting From Other Calendars 353
    29.9.4 Converting from the Mayan Calendar 354
29.10 The Diary.. 355
    29.10.1 Commands Displaying Diary Entries 355
    29.10.2 The Diary File 357
    29.10.3 Date Formats 358
    29.10.4 Commands to Add to the Diary 359
    29.10.5 Special Diary Entries 359
29.11 Appointments 361
29.12 Daylight Savings Time 362

30 Miscellaneous Commands 365

30.1 Gnus.. 365
    30.1.1 Gnus Buffers............................... 365
    30.1.2 When Gnus Starts Up 365
    30.1.3 Summary of Gnus Commands 366
30.2 Running Shell Commands from Emacs................. 367
    30.2.1 Single Shell Commands 368
    30.2.2 Interactive Inferior Shell 368
    30.2.3 Shell Mode................................. 370
    30.2.4 Shell Command History..................... 373
        30.2.4.1 Shell History Ring 373
        30.2.4.2 Shell History Copying 374
        30.2.4.3 Shell History References 374
    30.2.5 Shell Mode Options......................... 375
    30.2.6 Remote Host Shell.......................... 375
30.3 Using Emacs as a Server 376
30.4 Hardcopy Output 377
30.5 Postscript Hardcopy................................. 378
30.6 Variables for Postscript Hardcopy 379

30.7   Sorting Text 380
30.8   Narrowing 382
30.9   Two-Column Editing 383
30.10   Editing Binary Files 384
30.11   Saving Emacs Sessions 385
30.12   Recursive Editing Levels 385
30.13   Emulation 386
30.14   Dissociated Press 387
30.15   Other Amusements 388

31 Customization 391
31.1   Minor Modes 391
31.2   Variables 393
        31.2.1   Examining and Setting Variables 394
        31.2.2   Easy Customization Interface 394
                  31.2.2.1   Customization Groups 395
                  31.2.2.2   Changing an Option 396
                  31.2.2.3   Customizing Faces 398
                  31.2.2.4   Customizing Specific Items 399
        31.2.3   Hooks 400
        31.2.4   Local Variables 401
        31.2.5   Local Variables in Files 403
31.3   Keyboard Macros 405
        31.3.1   Basic Use 405
        31.3.2   Naming and Saving Keyboard Macros 407
        31.3.3   Executing Macros with Variations 407
31.4   Customizing Key Bindings 408
        31.4.1   Keymaps 408
        31.4.2   Prefix Keymaps 409
        31.4.3   Local Keymaps 410
        31.4.4   Minibuffer Keymaps 411
        31.4.5   Changing Key Bindings Interactively 411
        31.4.6   Rebinding Keys in Your Init File 413
        31.4.7   Rebinding Function Keys 414
        31.4.8   Named ASCII Control Characters 415
        31.4.9   Non-ASCII Characters on the Keyboard....... 415
        31.4.10   Rebinding Mouse Buttons 416
        31.4.11   Disabling Commands 418
31.5   Keyboard Translations 418
31.6   The Syntax Table 419
31.7   The Init File, '~/.emacs' 419
        31.7.1   Init File Syntax 420
        31.7.2   Init File Examples 421
        31.7.3   Terminal-specific Initialization 423
        31.7.4   How Emacs Finds Your Init File 423

32   Dealing with Common Problems 425

   32.1   Quitting and Aborting 425
   32.2   Dealing with Emacs Trouble 426
       32.2.1   If ⟨DEL⟩ Fails to Delete 427
       32.2.2   Recursive Editing Levels 427
       32.2.3   Garbage on the Screen 427
       32.2.4   Garbage in the Text 427
       32.2.5   Spontaneous Entry to Incremental Search 428
       32.2.6   Running out of Memory 428
       32.2.7   Recovery After a Crash 428
       32.2.8   Emergency Escape 429
       32.2.9   Help for Total Frustration 430
   32.3   Reporting Bugs 430
       32.3.1   When Is There a Bug 430
       32.3.2   Understanding Bug Reporting 431
       32.3.3   Checklist for Bug Reports 432
       32.3.4   Sending Patches for GNU Emacs 437
   32.4   Contributing to Emacs Development 439
   32.5   How To Get Help with GNU Emacs 440

Appendix A   Command Line Arguments 441

   A.1   Action Arguments 441
   A.2   Initial Options 442
   A.3   Command Argument Example 443
   A.4   Resuming Emacs with Arguments 444
   A.5   Environment Variables 444
       A.5.1   General Variables 445
       A.5.2   Miscellaneous Variables 447
   A.6   Specifying the Display Name 448
   A.7   Font Specification Options 449
   A.8   Window Color Options 450
   A.9   Options for Window Geometry 451
   A.10   Internal and External Borders 452
   A.11   Frame Titles 453
   A.12   Icons 453
   A.13   X Resources 453
   A.14   Lucid Menu X Resources 456
   A.15   Motif Menu X Resources 457

Appendix B   Emacs 19 Antinews 461

Appendix C   Emacs and MS-DOS 463

   C.1   Keyboard and Mouse on MS-DOS 463
   C.2   Display on MS-DOS 464
   C.3   File Names on MS-DOS 465
   C.4   Text Files and Binary Files 466
   C.5   Printing and MS-DOS 468
   C.6   International Support on MS-DOS 470
   C.7   Subprocesses on MS-DOS 472
   C.8   Subprocesses on Windows 95 and NT 473
   C.9   Using the System Menu on Windows 474

The GNU Manifesto 475

   What's GNU? Gnu's Not Unix! 475
   Why I Must Write GNU 476
   Why GNU Will Be Compatible with Unix 476
   How GNU Will Be Available 476
   Why Many Other Programmers Want to Help 477
   How You Can Contribute 477
   Why All Computer Users Will Benefit 478
   Some Easily Rebutted Objections to GNU's Goals 478

Glossary 485

Key (Character) Index 505

Command and Function Index 515

Variable Index 527

Concept Index 533

Preface

This manual documents the use and simple customization of the Emacs editor. The reader is not expected to be a programmer; simple customizations do not require programming skill. But the user who is not interested in customizing can ignore the scattered customization hints.

This is primarily a reference manual, but can also be used as a primer. For complete beginners, it is a good idea to start with the on-line, learn-by-doing tutorial, before reading the manual. To run the tutorial, start Emacs and type C-h t. This way you can learn Emacs by using Emacs on a specially designed file which describes commands, tells you when to try them, and then explains the results you see.

On first reading, just skim chapters 1 and 2, which describe the notational conventions of the manual and the general appearance of the Emacs display screen. Note which questions are answered in these chapters, so you can refer back later. After reading chapter 4, you should practice the commands there. The next few chapters describe fundamental techniques and concepts that are used constantly. You need to understand them thoroughly, experimenting with them if necessary.

Chapters 14 through 19 describe intermediate-level features that are useful for all kinds of editing. Chapter 20 and following chapters describe features that you may or may not want to use; read those chapters when you need them.

Read the Trouble chapter if Emacs does not seem to be working properly. It explains how to cope with some common problems (see Section 32.2 [Lossage], page 426), as well as when and how to report Emacs bugs (see Section 32.3 [Bugs], page 430).

To find the documentation on a particular command, look in the index. Keys (character commands) and command names have separate indexes. There is also a glossary, with a cross reference for each term.

This manual is available as a printed book and also as an Info file. The Info file is for on-line perusal with the Info program, which will be the principal way of viewing documentation on-line in the GNU system. Both the Info file and the Info program itself are distributed along with GNU Emacs. The Info file and the printed book contain substantially the same text and are generated from the same source files, which are also distributed along with GNU Emacs.

GNU Emacs is a member of the Emacs editor family. There are many Emacs editors, all sharing common principles of organization. For information on the underlying philosophy of Emacs and the lessons learned from its development, write for a copy of AI memo 519a, "Emacs, the Extensible, Customizable Self-Documenting Display Editor," to Publications Department, Artificial Intelligence Lab, 545 Tech Square, Cambridge, MA 02139, USA. At last report they charge $2.25 per copy. Another useful publication is LCS TM-165, "A Cookbook for an Emacs," by Craig Finseth, available from Publications Department, Laboratory for Computer Science, 545 Tech Square, Cambridge, MA 02139, USA. The price today is $3.

This edition of the manual is intended for use with GNU Emacs installed on GNU and Unix systems. GNU Emacs can also be used on VMS, MS-DOS (also called MS-DOG), Windows NT, and Windows 95 systems. Those systems use different file name syntax; in addition, VMS and MS-DOS do not support all GNU Emacs features. We don't try to describe VMS usage in this manual. See Appendix C [MS-DOS], page 463, for information about using Emacs on MS-DOS.

Distribution

GNU Emacs is *free software*; this means that everyone is free to use it and free to redistribute it on certain conditions. GNU Emacs is not in the public domain; it is copyrighted and there are restrictions on its distribution, but these restrictions are designed to permit everything that a good cooperating citizen would want to do. What is not allowed is to try to prevent others from further sharing any version of GNU Emacs that they might get from you. The precise conditions are found in the GNU General Public License that comes with Emacs and also appears following this section.

One way to get a copy of GNU Emacs is from someone else who has it. You need not ask for our permission to do so, or tell any one else; just copy it. If you have access to the Internet, you can get the latest distribution version of GNU Emacs by anonymous FTP; see the file 'etc/FTP' in the Emacs distribution for more information.

You may also receive GNU Emacs when you buy a computer. Computer manufacturers are free to distribute copies on the same terms that apply to everyone else. These terms require them to give you the full sources, including whatever changes they may have made, and to permit you to redistribute the GNU Emacs received from them under the usual terms of the General Public License. In other words, the program must be free for you when you get it, not just free for the manufacturer.

You can also order copies of GNU Emacs from the Free Software Foundation on CD-ROM. This is a convenient and reliable way to get a copy; it is also a good way to help fund our work. (The Foundation has always received most of its funds in this way.) An order form is included in the file 'etc/ORDERS' in the Emacs distribution, and on our web site in http://www.gnu.org/order/order.html. For further information, write to

Free Software Foundation
59 Temple Place, Suite 330
Boston, MA 02111-1307 USA
USA

The income from distribution fees goes to support the foundation's purpose: the development of new free software, and improvements to our existing programs including GNU Emacs.

If you find GNU Emacs useful, please **send a donation** to the Free Software Foundation to support our work. Donations to the Free Software Foundation are tax deductible in the US. If you use GNU Emacs at your workplace, please suggest that the company make a donation. If company policy is unsympathetic to the idea of donating to charity, you might instead suggest ordering a CD-ROM from the Foundation occasionally, or subscribing to periodic updates.

Contributors to GNU Emacs include Per Abrahamsen, Jay K. Adams, Joe Arceneaux, Boaz Ben-Zvi, Jim Blandy, Terrence Brannon, Frank Bresz,

Peter Breton, Kevin Broadey, Vincent Broman, David M. Brown, Bill Carpenter, Hans Chalupsky, Bob Chassell, James Clark, Mike Clarkson, Glynn Clements, Andrew Csillag, Doug Cutting, Michael DeCorte, Gary Delp, Matthieu Devin, Eri Ding, Carsten Dominik, Scott Draves, Viktor Dukhovni, John Eaton, Rolf Ebert, Stephen Eglen, Torbjörn Einarsson, Tsugumoto Enami, Hans Henrik Eriksen, Michael Ernst, Ata Etemadi, Frederick Farnback, Fred Fish, Karl Fogel, Gary Foster, Noah Friedman, Keith Gabryelski, Kevin Gallagher, Kevin Gallo, Howard Gayle, Stephen Gildea, David Gillespie, Bob Glickstein, Boris Goldowsky, Michelangelo Grigni, Michael Gschwind, Henry Guillaume, Doug Gwyn, Ken'ichi Handa, Chris Hanson, K. Shane Hartman, John Heidemann, Markus Heritsch, Karl Heuer, Manabu Higashida, Anders Holst, Kurt Hornik, Tom Houlder, Lars Ingebrigtsen, Andrew Innes, Michael K. Johnson, Kyle Jones, Tomoji Kagatani, Brewster Kahle, David Kaufman, Henry Kautz, Howard Kaye, Michael Kifer, Richard King, Larry K. Kolodney, Robert Krawitz, Sebastian Kremer, Geoff Kuenning, David Kågedal, Daniel LaLiberte, Aaron Larson, James R. Larus, Frederic Lepied, Lars Lindberg, Eric Ludlam, Neil M. Mager, Ken Manheimer, Bill Mann, Brian Marick, Simon Marshall, Bengt Martensson, Charlie Martin, Thomas May, Roland McGrath, David Megginson, Wayne Mesard, Richard Mlynarik, Keith Moore, Erik Naggum, Thomas Neumann, Mike Newton, Jurgen Nickelsen, Jeff Norden, Andrew Norman, Jeff Peck, Damon Anton Permezel, Tom Perrine, Jens Petersen, Daniel Pfeiffer, Fred Pierresteguy, Christian Plaunt, Francesco A. Potorti, Michael D. Prange, Ashwin Ram, Eric S. Raymond, Paul Reilly, Edward M. Reingold, Rob Riepel, Roland B. Roberts, John Robinson, Danny Roozendaal, William Rosenblatt, Guillermo J. Rozas, Ivar Rummelhoff, Wolfgang Rupprecht, James B. Salem, Masahiko Sato, William Schelter, Ralph Schleicher, Gregor Schmid, Michael Schmidt, Ronald S. Schnell, Philippe Schnoebelen, Stephen Schoef, Randal Schwartz, Manuel Serrano, Stanislav Shalunov, Mark Shapiro, Richard Sharman, Olin Shivers, Espen Skoglund, Rick Sladkey, Lynn Slater, Chris Smith, David Smith, Paul D. Smith, William Sommerfeld, Michael Staats, Sam Steingold, Ake Stenhoff, Peter Stephenson, Jonathan Stigelman, Steve Strassman, Jens T. Berger Thielemann, Spencer Thomas, Jim Thompson, Masanobu Umeda, Neil W. Van Dyke, Ulrik Vieth, Geoffrey Voelker, Johan Vromans, Barry Warsaw, Morten Welinder, Joseph Brian Wells, Rodney Whitby, Ed Wilkinson, Mike Williams, Steven A. Wood, Dale R. Worley, Felix S. T. Wu, Tom Wurgler, Eli Zaretskii, Jamie Zawinski, Ian T. Zimmermann, Reto Zimmermann, and Neal Ziring.

GNU GENERAL PUBLIC LICENSE

Version 2, June 1991

Copyright © 1989, 1991 Free Software Foundation, Inc.
59 Temple Place, Suite 330, Boston, MA 02111-1307 USA

Preamble

The licenses for most software are designed to take away your freedom
to share and change it. By contrast, the GNU General Public License is
intended to guarantee your freedom to share and change free software—to
make sure the software is free for all its users. This General Public License
applies to most of the Free Software Foundation's software and to any other
program whose authors commit to using it. (Some other Free Software
Foundation software is covered by the GNU Library General Public License
instead.) You can apply it to your programs, too.

When we speak of free software, we are referring to freedom, not price.
Our General Public Licenses are designed to make sure that you have the
freedom to distribute copies of free software (and charge for this service if
you wish), that you receive source code or can get it if you want it, that you
can change the software or use pieces of it in new free programs; and that
you know you can do these things.

To protect your rights, we need to make restrictions that forbid anyone to
deny you these rights or to ask you to surrender the rights. These restrictions
translate to certain responsibilities for you if you distribute copies of the
software, or if you modify it.

For example, if you distribute copies of such a program, whether gratis
or for a fee, you must give the recipients all the rights that you have. You
must make sure that they, too, receive or can get the source code. And you
must show them these terms so they know their rights.

We protect your rights with two steps: (1) copyright the software, and
(2) offer you this license which gives you legal permission to copy, distribute
and/or modify the software.

Also, for each author's protection and ours, we want to make certain
that everyone understands that there is no warranty for this free software.
If the software is modified by someone else and passed on, we want its recipients to know that what they have is not the original, so that any problems
introduced by others will not reflect on the original authors' reputations.

Finally, any free program is threatened constantly by software patents.
We wish to avoid the danger that redistributors of a free program will individually obtain patent licenses, in effect making the program proprietary.

To prevent this, we have made it clear that any patent must be licensed for everyone's free use or not licensed at all.

The precise terms and conditions for copying, distribution and modification follow.

TERMS AND CONDITIONS FOR COPYING, DISTRIBUTION AND MODIFICATION

0. This License applies to any program or other work which contains a notice placed by the copyright holder saying it may be distributed under the terms of this General Public License. The "Program", below, refers to any such program or work, and a "work based on the Program" means either the Program or any derivative work under copyright law: that is to say, a work containing the Program or a portion of it, either verbatim or with modifications and/or translated into another language. (Hereinafter, translation is included without limitation in the term "modification".) Each licensee is addressed as "you".

   Activities other than copying, distribution and modification are not covered by this License; they are outside its scope. The act of running the Program is not restricted, and the output from the Program is covered only if its contents constitute a work based on the Program (independent of having been made by running the Program). Whether that is true depends on what the Program does.

1. You may copy and distribute verbatim copies of the Program's source code as you receive it, in any medium, provided that you conspicuously and appropriately publish on each copy an appropriate copyright notice and disclaimer of warranty; keep intact all the notices that refer to this License and to the absence of any warranty; and give any other recipients of the Program a copy of this License along with the Program.

   You may charge a fee for the physical act of transferring a copy, and you may at your option offer warranty protection in exchange for a fee.

2. You may modify your copy or copies of the Program or any portion of it, thus forming a work based on the Program, and copy and distribute such modifications or work under the terms of Section 1 above, provided that you also meet all of these conditions:

   a. You must cause the modified files to carry prominent notices stating that you changed the files and the date of any change.

   b. You must cause any work that you distribute or publish, that in whole or in part contains or is derived from the Program or any part thereof, to be licensed as a whole at no charge to all third parties under the terms of this License.

   c. If the modified program normally reads commands interactively when run, you must cause it, when started running for such interactive use in the most ordinary way, to print or display an announcement including an appropriate copyright notice and a notice that there is no warranty (or else, saying that you provide a warranty) and that users may redistribute the program under these conditions, and telling the user how to view a copy of this License. (Exception: if the Program itself is interactive but does not normally print such an announcement, your work based on the Program is not required to print an announcement.)

These requirements apply to the modified work as a whole. If identifiable sections of that work are not derived from the Program, and can be reasonably considered independent and separate works in themselves, then this License, and its terms, do not apply to those sections when you distribute them as separate works. But when you distribute the same sections as part of a whole which is a work based on the Program, the distribution of the whole must be on the terms of this License, whose permissions for other licensees extend to the entire whole, and thus to each and every part regardless of who wrote it.

Thus, it is not the intent of this section to claim rights or contest your rights to work written entirely by you; rather, the intent is to exercise the right to control the distribution of derivative or collective works based on the Program.

In addition, mere aggregation of another work not based on the Program with the Program (or with a work based on the Program) on a volume of a storage or distribution medium does not bring the other work under the scope of this License.

3. You may copy and distribute the Program (or a work based on it, under Section 2) in object code or executable form under the terms of Sections 1 and 2 above provided that you also do one of the following:

   a. Accompany it with the complete corresponding machine-readable source code, which must be distributed under the terms of Sections 1 and 2 above on a medium customarily used for software interchange; or,

   b. Accompany it with a written offer, valid for at least three years, to give any third party, for a charge no more than your cost of physically performing source distribution, a complete machine-readable copy of the corresponding source code, to be distributed under the terms of Sections 1 and 2 above on a medium customarily used for software interchange; or,

   c. Accompany it with the information you received as to the offer to distribute corresponding source code. (This alternative is allowed only for noncommercial distribution and only if you received the program in object code or executable form with such an offer, in accord with Subsection b above.)

The source code for a work means the preferred form of the work for making modifications to it. For an executable work, complete source code means all the source code for all modules it contains, plus any associated interface definition files, plus the scripts used to control compilation and installation of the executable. However, as a special exception, the source code distributed need not include anything that is normally distributed (in either source or binary form) with the major components (compiler, kernel, and so on) of the operating system on which the executable runs, unless that component itself accompanies the executable.

If distribution of executable or object code is made by offering access to copy from a designated place, then offering equivalent access to copy the source code from the same place counts as distribution of the source code, even though third parties are not compelled to copy the source along with the object code.

4. You may not copy, modify, sublicense, or distribute the Program except as expressly provided under this License. Any attempt otherwise to copy, modify, sublicense or distribute the Program is void, and will automatically terminate your rights under this License. However, parties who have received copies, or rights, from you under this License will not have their licenses terminated so long as such parties remain in full compliance.

5. You are not required to accept this License, since you have not signed it. However, nothing else grants you permission to modify or distribute the Program or its derivative works. These actions are prohibited by law if you do not accept this License. Therefore, by modifying or distributing the Program (or any work based on the Program), you indicate your acceptance of this License to do so, and all its terms and conditions for copying, distributing or modifying the Program or works based on it.

6. Each time you redistribute the Program (or any work based on the Program), the recipient automatically receives a license from the original licensor to copy, distribute or modify the Program subject to these terms and conditions. You may not impose any further restrictions on the recipients' exercise of the rights granted herein. You are not responsible for enforcing compliance by third parties to this License.

7. If, as a consequence of a court judgment or allegation of patent infringement or for any other reason (not limited to patent issues), conditions are imposed on you (whether by court order, agreement or otherwise) that contradict the conditions of this License, they do not excuse you from the conditions of this License. If you cannot distribute so as to satisfy simultaneously your obligations under this License and any other pertinent obligations, then as a consequence you may not distribute the Program at all. For example, if a patent license would not permit royalty-free redistribution of the Program by all those who receive copies directly or indirectly through you, then the only way you could satisfy both it and this License would be to refrain entirely from distribution of the Program.

If any portion of this section is held invalid or unenforceable under any particular circumstance, the balance of the section is intended to apply and the section as a whole is intended to apply in other circumstances.

It is not the purpose of this section to induce you to infringe any patents or other property right claims or to contest validity of any such claims; this section has the sole purpose of protecting the integrity of the free software distribution system, which is implemented by public license practices. Many people have made generous contributions to the wide range of software distributed through that system in reliance on consistent application of that system; it is up to the author/donor to decide if he or she is willing to distribute software through any other system and a licensee cannot impose that choice.

This section is intended to make thoroughly clear what is believed to be a consequence of the rest of this License.

8. If the distribution and/or use of the Program is restricted in certain countries either by patents or by copyrighted interfaces, the original copyright holder who places the Program under this License may add an explicit geographical distribution limitation excluding those countries, so that distribution is permitted only in or among countries not thus excluded. In such case, this License incorporates the limitation as if written in the body of this License.

9. The Free Software Foundation may publish revised and/or new versions of the General Public License from time to time. Such new versions will be similar in spirit to the present version, but may differ in detail to address new problems or concerns.

Each version is given a distinguishing version number. If the Program specifies a version number of this License which applies to it and "any later version", you have the option of following the terms and conditions either of that version or of any later version published by the Free Software Foundation. If the Program does not specify a version number of this License, you may choose any version ever published by the Free Software Foundation.

10. If you wish to incorporate parts of the Program into other free programs whose distribution conditions are different, write to the author to ask for permission. For software which is copyrighted by the Free Software Foundation, write to the Free Software Foundation; we sometimes make exceptions for this. Our decision will be guided by the two goals of preserving the free status of all derivatives of our free software and of promoting the sharing and reuse of software generally.

NO WARRANTY

11. BECAUSE THE PROGRAM IS LICENSED FREE OF CHARGE, THERE IS NO WARRANTY FOR THE PROGRAM, TO THE EXTENT PERMITTED BY APPLICABLE LAW. EXCEPT WHEN

OTHERWISE STATED IN WRITING THE COPYRIGHT HOLDERS
AND/OR OTHER PARTIES PROVIDE THE PROGRAM "AS IS"
WITHOUT WARRANTY OF ANY KIND, EITHER EXPRESSED OR
IMPLIED, INCLUDING, BUT NOT LIMITED TO, THE IMPLIED
WARRANTIES OF MERCHANTABILITY AND FITNESS FOR A
PARTICULAR PURPOSE. THE ENTIRE RISK AS TO THE QUAL-
ITY AND PERFORMANCE OF THE PROGRAM IS WITH YOU.
SHOULD THE PROGRAM PROVE DEFECTIVE, YOU ASSUME
THE COST OF ALL NECESSARY SERVICING, REPAIR OR COR-
RECTION.

12. IN NO EVENT UNLESS REQUIRED BY APPLICABLE LAW OR
AGREED TO IN WRITING WILL ANY COPYRIGHT HOLDER,
OR ANY OTHER PARTY WHO MAY MODIFY AND/OR REDIS-
TRIBUTE THE PROGRAM AS PERMITTED ABOVE, BE LIABLE
TO YOU FOR DAMAGES, INCLUDING ANY GENERAL, SPECIAL,
INCIDENTAL OR CONSEQUENTIAL DAMAGES ARISING OUT
OF THE USE OR INABILITY TO USE THE PROGRAM (INCLUD-
ING BUT NOT LIMITED TO LOSS OF DATA OR DATA BEING
RENDERED INACCURATE OR LOSSES SUSTAINED BY YOU OR
THIRD PARTIES OR A FAILURE OF THE PROGRAM TO OPER-
ATE WITH ANY OTHER PROGRAMS), EVEN IF SUCH HOLDER
OR OTHER PARTY HAS BEEN ADVISED OF THE POSSIBILITY
OF SUCH DAMAGES.

END OF TERMS AND CONDITIONS

How to Apply These Terms to Your New Programs

If you develop a new program, and you want it to be of the greatest possible use to the public, the best way to achieve this is to make it free software which everyone can redistribute and change under these terms.

To do so, attach the following notices to the program. It is safest to attach them to the start of each source file to most effectively convey the exclusion of warranty; and each file should have at least the "copyright" line and a pointer to where the full notice is found.

    one line to give the program's name and an idea of what it does.
    Copyright (C) 19yy   name of author

    This program is free software; you can redistribute it and/or
    modify it under the terms of the GNU General Public License
    as published by the Free Software Foundation; either version 2
    of the License, or (at your option) any later version.

    This program is distributed in the hope that it will be useful,
    but WITHOUT ANY WARRANTY; without even the implied warranty of
    MERCHANTABILITY or FITNESS FOR A PARTICULAR PURPOSE. See the
    GNU General Public License for more details.

    You should have received a copy of the GNU General Public License along
    with this program; if not, write to the Free Software Foundation, Inc.,
    59 Temple Place, Suite 330, Boston, MA 02111-1307, USA.

Also add information on how to contact you by electronic and paper mail.

If the program is interactive, make it output a short notice like this when it starts in an interactive mode:

    Gnomovision version 69, Copyright (C) 19yy name of author
    Gnomovision comes with ABSOLUTELY NO WARRANTY; for details
    type 'show w'. This is free software, and you are welcome
    to redistribute it under certain conditions; type 'show c'
    for details.

The hypothetical commands 'show w' and 'show c' should show the appropriate parts of the General Public License. Of course, the commands you use may be called something other than 'show w' and 'show c'; they could even be mouse-clicks or menu items—whatever suits your program.

You should also get your employer (if you work as a programmer) or your school, if any, to sign a "copyright disclaimer" for the program, if necessary. Here is a sample; alter the names:

```
Yoyodyne, Inc., hereby disclaims all copyright
interest in the program 'Gnomovision'
(which makes passes at compilers) written
by James Hacker.
```

signature of Ty Coon, 1 April 1989
```
Ty Coon, President of Vice
```

This General Public License does not permit incorporating your program into proprietary programs. If your program is a subroutine library, you may consider it more useful to permit linking proprietary applications with the library. If this is what you want to do, use the GNU Library General Public License instead of this License.

Introduction

You are reading about GNU Emacs, the GNU incarnation of the advanced, self documenting, customizable, extensible real-time display editor Emacs. (The 'G' in 'GNU' is not silent.)

We say that Emacs is a *display* editor because normally the text being edited is visible on the screen and is updated automatically as you type your commands. See Chapter 1 [Screen], page 15.

We call it a *real-time* editor because the display is updated very frequently, usually after each character or pair of characters you type. This minimizes the amount of information you must keep in your head as you edit. See Chapter 4 [Basic Editing], page 29.

We call Emacs advanced because it provides facilities that go beyond simple insertion and deletion: controlling subprocesses; automatic indentation of programs; viewing two or more files at once; editing formatted text; and dealing in terms of characters, words, lines, sentences, paragraphs, and pages, as well as expressions and comments in several different programming languages.

Self-documenting means that at any time you can type a special character, `Control-h`, to find out what your options are. You can also use it to find out what any command does, or to find all the commands that pertain to a topic. See Chapter 7 [Help], page 51.

Customizable means that you can change the definitions of Emacs commands in little ways. For example, if you use a programming language in which comments start with '`<**`' and end with '`**>`', you can tell the Emacs comment manipulation commands to use those strings (see Section 22.7 [Comments], page 244). Another sort of customization is rearrangement of the command set. For example, if you prefer the four basic cursor motion commands (up, down, left and right) on keys in a diamond pattern on the keyboard, you can rebind the keys that way. See Chapter 31 [Customization], page 391.

Extensible means that you can go beyond simple customization and write entirely new commands, programs in the Lisp language to be run by Emacs's own Lisp interpreter. Emacs is an "on-line extensible" system, which means that it is divided into many functions that call each other, any of which can be redefined in the middle of an editing session. Almost any part of Emacs can be replaced without making a separate copy of all of Emacs. Most of the editing commands of Emacs are written in Lisp already; the few exceptions could have been written in Lisp but are written in C for efficiency. Although only a programmer can write an extension, anybody can use it afterward. If you want to learn Emacs Lisp programming, we recommend the *Introduction to Emacs Lisp* by Robert J. Chassell, also published by the Free Software Foundation.

When run under the X Window System, Emacs provides its own menus and convenient bindings to mouse buttons. But Emacs can provide many of the benefits of a window system on a text-only terminal. For instance, you can look at or edit several files at once, move text between files, and edit files while running shell commands.

1 The Organization of the Screen

On a text-only terminal, the Emacs display occupies the whole screen. On the X Window System, Emacs creates its own X windows to use. We use the term *frame* to mean an entire text-only screen or an entire X window used by Emacs. Emacs uses both kinds of frames in the same way to display your editing. Emacs normally starts out with just one frame, but you can create additional frames if you wish. See Chapter 17 [Frames], page 157.

When you start Emacs, the entire frame except for the first and last lines is devoted to the text you are editing. This area is called the *window*. The first line is a *menu bar*, and the last line is a special *echo area* or *minibuffer window* where prompts appear and where you can enter responses. See below for more information about these special lines.

You can subdivide the large text window horizontally or vertically into multiple text windows, each of which can be used for a different file (see Chapter 16 [Windows], page 151). In this manual, the word "window" always refers to the subdivisions of a frame within Emacs.

The window that the cursor is in is the *selected window*, in which editing takes place. Most Emacs commands implicitly apply to the text in the selected window (though mouse commands generally operate on whatever window you click them in, whether selected or not). The other windows display text for reference only, unless/until you select them. If you use multiple frames under the X Window System, then giving the input focus to a particular frame selects a window in that frame.

Each window's last line is a *mode line*, which describes what is going on in that window. It appears in inverse video, if the terminal supports that, and its contents begin with '--:-- *scratch*' when Emacs starts. The mode line displays status information such as what buffer is being displayed above it in the window, what major and minor modes are in use, and whether the buffer contains unsaved changes.

1.1 Point

Within Emacs, the terminal's cursor shows the location at which editing commands will take effect. This location is called *point*. Many Emacs commands move point through the text, so that you can edit at different places in it. You can also place point by clicking mouse button 1.

While the cursor appears to point *at* a character, you should think of point as *between* two characters; it points *before* the character that appears under the cursor. For example, if your text looks like 'frob' with the cursor over the 'b', then point is between the 'o' and the 'b'. If you insert the character '!' at that position, the result is 'fro!b', with point between the '!' and the 'b'. Thus, the cursor remains over the 'b', as before.

Sometimes people speak of "the cursor" when they mean "point," or speak of commands that move point as "cursor motion" commands.

Terminals have only one cursor, and when output is in progress it must appear where the typing is being done. This does not mean that point is moving. It is only that Emacs has no way to show you the location of point except when the terminal is idle.

If you are editing several files in Emacs, each in its own buffer, each buffer has its own point location. A buffer that is not currently displayed remembers where point is in case you display it again later.

When there are multiple windows in a frame, each window has its own point location. The cursor shows the location of point in the selected window. This also is how you can tell which window is selected. If the same buffer appears in more than one window, each window has its own position for point in that buffer.

When there are multiple frames, each frame can display one cursor. The cursor in the selected frame is solid; the cursor in other frames is a hollow box, and appears in the window that would be selected if you give the input focus to that frame.

The term 'point' comes from the character '.', which was the command in TECO (the language in which the original Emacs was written) for accessing the value now called 'point'.

1.2 The Echo Area

The line at the bottom of the frame (below the mode line) is the *echo area*. It is used to display small amounts of text for several purposes.

Echoing means displaying the characters that you type. Outside Emacs, the operating system normally echoes all your input. Emacs handles echoing differently.

Single-character commands do not echo in Emacs, and multi-character commands echo only if you pause while typing them. As soon as you pause for more than a second in the middle of a command, Emacs echoes all the characters of the command so far. This is to *prompt* you for the rest of the command. Once echoing has started, the rest of the command echoes immediately as you type it. This behavior is designed to give confident users fast response, while giving hesitant users maximum feedback. You can change this behavior by setting a variable (see Section 11.7 [Display Vars], page 83).

If a command cannot be executed, it may print an *error message* in the echo area. Error messages are accompanied by a beep or by flashing the screen. Also, any input you have typed ahead is thrown away when an error happens.

Some commands print informative messages in the echo area. These messages look much like error messages, but they are not announced with a beep and do not throw away input. Sometimes the message tells you what the command has done, when this is not obvious from looking at the text being edited. Sometimes the sole purpose of a command is to print a message giving you specific information—for example, C-x = prints a message describing the character position of point in the text and its current column in the window. Commands that take a long time often display messages ending in '...' while they are working, and add 'done' at the end when they are finished.

Echo-area informative messages are saved in an editor buffer named '*Messages*'. (We have not explained buffers yet; see Chapter 15 [Buffers], page 143, for more information about them.) If you miss a message that appears briefly on the screen, you can switch to the '*Messages*' buffer to see it again. (Successive progress messages are often collapsed into one in that buffer.)

The size of '*Messages*' is limited to a certain number of lines. The variable message-log-max specifies how many lines. Once the buffer has that many lines, each line added at the end deletes one line from the beginning. See Section 31.2 [Variables], page 393, for how to set variables such as message-log-max.

The echo area is also used to display the *minibuffer*, a window that is used for reading arguments to commands, such as the name of a file to be edited. When the minibuffer is in use, the echo area begins with a prompt string that usually ends with a colon; also, the cursor appears in that line because it is the selected window. You can always get out of the minibuffer by typing C-g. See Chapter 5 [Minibuffer], page 41.

1.3 The Mode Line

Each text window's last line is a *mode line*, which describes what is going on in that window. When there is only one text window, the mode line appears right above the echo area; it is the next-to-last line on the frame. The mode line is in inverse video if the terminal supports that, and it starts and ends with dashes.

Normally, the mode line looks like this:

   -cs:ch buf   (*major minor*)--*line*--*pos*------

This gives information about the buffer being displayed in the window: the buffer's name, what major and minor modes are in use, whether the buffer's text has been changed, and how far down the buffer you are currently looking.

ch contains two stars '**' if the text in the buffer has been edited (the buffer is "modified"), or '--' if the buffer has not been edited. For a read-only buffer, it is '%*' if the buffer is modified, and '%%' otherwise.

buf is the name of the window's *buffer*. In most cases this is the same as the name of a file you are editing. See Chapter 15 [Buffers], page 143.

The buffer displayed in the selected window (the window that the cursor is in) is also Emacs's selected buffer, the one that editing takes place in.

When we speak of what some command does to "the buffer," we are talking about the currently selected buffer.

line is 'L' followed by the current line number of point. This is present when Line Number mode is enabled (which it normally is). You can optionally display the current column number too, by turning on Column Number mode (which is not enabled by default because it is somewhat slower). See Section 11.5 [Optional Mode Line], page 82.

pos tells you whether there is additional text above the top of the window, or below the bottom. If your buffer is small and it is all visible in the window, *pos* is 'All'. Otherwise, it is 'Top' if you are looking at the beginning of the buffer, 'Bot' if you are looking at the end of the buffer, or '*nn*%', where *nn* is the percentage of the buffer above the top of the window.

major is the name of the *major mode* in effect in the buffer. At any time, each buffer is in one and only one of the possible major modes. The major modes available include Fundamental mode (the least specialized), Text mode, Lisp mode, C mode, Texinfo mode, and many others. See Chapter 19 [Major Modes], page 191, for details of how the modes differ and how to select one.

Some major modes display additional information after the major mode name. For example, Rmail buffers display the current message number and the total number of messages. Compilation buffers and Shell buffers display the status of the subprocess.

minor is a list of some of the *minor modes* that are turned on at the moment in the window's chosen buffer. For example, 'Fill' means that Auto Fill mode is on. 'Abbrev' means that Word Abbrev mode is on. 'Ovwrt' means that Overwrite mode is on. See Section 31.1 [Minor Modes], page 391, for more information. 'Narrow' means that the buffer being displayed has editing restricted to only a portion of its text. This is not really a minor mode, but is like one. See Section 30.8 [Narrowing], page 382. 'Def' means that a keyboard macro is being defined. See Section 31.3 [Keyboard Macros], page 405.

In addition, if Emacs is currently inside a recursive editing level, square brackets ('[...]') appear around the parentheses that surround the modes. If Emacs is in one recursive editing level within another, double square brackets appear, and so on. Since recursive editing levels affect Emacs globally, not just one buffer, the square brackets appear in every window's mode line or not in any of them. See Section 30.12 [Recursive Edit], page 385.

Non-windowing terminals can only show a single Emacs frame at a time (see Chapter 17 [Frames], page 157). On such terminals, the mode line displays the name of the selected frame, after *ch*. The initial frame's name is 'F1'.

cs states the coding system used for the file you are editing. A dash indicates the default state of affairs: no code conversion, except for end-of-line translation if the file contents call for that. '=' means no conversion whatsoever. Nontrivial code conversions are represented by various letters—for example, '1' refers to ISO Latin-1. See Section 18.7 [Coding Systems], page 180, for more information. If you are using an input method, a string of the form '*i*>' is added to the beginning of *cs*; *i* identifies the input method. (Some input methods show '+' or '@' instead of '>'.) See Section 18.4 [Input Methods], page 177.

When you are using a character-only terminal (not a window system), *cs* uses three characters to describe, respectively, the coding system for keyboard input, the coding system for terminal output, and the coding system used for the file you are editing.

When multibyte characters are not enabled, *cs* does not appear at all. See Section 18.2 [Enabling Multibyte], page 175.

The colon after *cs* can change to another string in certain circumstances. Emacs uses newline to separate lines in the buffer. Some files use different conventions for separating lines: either carriage-return linefeed (the MS-DOS convention) or just carriage-return (the Macintosh convention). If the buffer's file uses carriage-return linefeed, the colon changes to either a backslash ('\') or '(DOS)', depending on the operating system. If the file uses just carriage-return, the colon indicator changes to either a forward slash ('/') or '(Mac)'. On some systems, Emacs displays '(Unix)' instead of the colon even for files that use newline to separate lines.

You can customize the mode line display for each of the end-of-line formats by setting each of the variables `eol-mnemonic-unix`, `eol-mnemonic-dos`, `eol-mnemonic-mac`, and `eol-mnemonic-undecided` to any string you find appropriate. See Section 31.2 [Variables], page 393, for an explanation how to set variables.

See Section 11.5 [Optional Mode Line], page 82, for features that add other handy information to the mode line, such as the current column number of point, the current time, and whether new mail for you has arrived.

1.4 The Menu Bar

Each Emacs frame normally has a *menu bar* at the top which you can use to perform certain common operations. There's no need to list them here, as you can more easily see for yourself.

When you are using a window system, you can use the mouse to choose a command from the menu bar. An arrow pointing right, after the menu item, indicates that the item leads to a subsidiary menu; '...' at the end means that the command will read arguments from the keyboard before it actually does anything.

To view the full command name and documentation for a menu item, type `C-h k`, and then select the menu bar with the mouse in the usual way (see Section 7.1 [Key Help], page 53).

On text-only terminals with no mouse, you can use the menu bar by typing M-` or (F10) (these run the command **tmm-menubar**). This command enters a mode in which you can select a menu item from the keyboard. A provisional choice appears in the echo area. You can use the left and right arrow keys to move through the menu to different choices. When you have found the choice you want, type (RET) to select it.

Each menu item also has an assigned letter or digit which designates that item; it is usually the initial of some word in the item's name. This letter or digit is separated from the item name by '=>'. You can type the item's letter or digit to select the item.

Some of the commands in the menu bar have ordinary key bindings as well; if so, the menu lists one equivalent key binding in parentheses after the item itself.

2 Characters, Keys and Commands

This chapter explains the character sets used by Emacs for input commands and for the contents of files, and also explains the concepts of *keys* and *commands*, which are fundamental for understanding how Emacs interprets your keyboard and mouse input.

2.1 Kinds of User Input

GNU Emacs uses an extension of the ASCII character set for keyboard input; it also accepts non-character input events including function keys and mouse button actions.

ASCII consists of 128 character codes. Some of these codes are assigned graphic symbols such as 'a' and '='; the rest are control characters, such as `Control-a` (usually written `C-a` for short). `C-a` gets its name from the fact that you type it by holding down the (CTRL) key while pressing a.

Some ASCII control characters have special names, and most terminals have special keys you can type them with: for example, (RET), (TAB), (DEL) and (ESC). The space character is usually referred to below as (SPC), even though strictly speaking it is a graphic character whose graphic happens to be blank. Some keyboards have a key labeled "linefeed" which is an alias for `C-j`.

Emacs extends the ASCII character set with thousands more printing characters (see Chapter 18 [International], page 175), additional control characters, and a few more modifiers that can be combined with any character.

On ASCII terminals, there are only 32 possible control characters. These are the control variants of letters and '@[]\^_'. In addition, the shift key is meaningless with control characters: `C-a` and `C-A` are the same character, and Emacs cannot distinguish them.

But the Emacs character set has room for control variants of all printing characters, and for distinguishing between `C-a` and `C-A`. X Windows makes it possible to enter all these characters. For example, `C--` (that's Control-Minus) and `C-5` are meaningful Emacs commands under X.

Another Emacs character-set extension is additional modifier bits. Only one modifier bit is commonly used; it is called Meta. Every character has a Meta variant; examples include `Meta-a` (normally written `M-a`, for short), `M-A` (not the same character as `M-a`, but those two characters normally have the same meaning in Emacs), `M-`(RET), and `M-C-a`. For reasons of tradition, we usually write `C-M-a` rather than `M-C-a`; logically speaking, the order in which the modifier keys (CTRL) and (META) are mentioned does not matter.

Some terminals have a (META) key, and allow you to type Meta characters by holding this key down. Thus, `Meta-a` is typed by holding down (META) and pressing a. The (META) key works much like the (SHIFT) key. Such a key is not always labeled (META), however, as this function is often a special option for a key with some other primary purpose.

If there is no (META) key, you can still type Meta characters using two-character sequences starting with (ESC). Thus, to enter M-a, you could type (ESC) a. To enter C-M-a, you would type (ESC) C-a. (ESC) is allowed on terminals with (META) keys, too, in case you have formed a habit of using it.

X Windows provides several other modifier keys that can be applied to any input character. These are called (SUPER), (HYPER) and (ALT). We write 's-', 'H-' and 'A-' to say that a character uses these modifiers. Thus, s-H-C-x is short for Super-Hyper-Control-x. Not all X terminals actually provide keys for these modifier flags—in fact, many terminals have a key labeled (ALT) which is really a (META) key. The standard key bindings of Emacs do not include any characters with these modifiers. But you can assign them meanings of your own by customizing Emacs.

Keyboard input includes keyboard keys that are not characters at all: for example function keys and arrow keys. Mouse buttons are also outside the gamut of characters. You can modify these events with the modifier keys (CTRL), (META), (SUPER), (HYPER) and (ALT), just like keyboard characters.

Input characters and non-character inputs are collectively called *input events*. See section "Input Events" in *The Emacs Lisp Reference Manual*, for more information. If you are not doing Lisp programming, but simply want to redefine the meaning of some characters or non-character events, see Chapter 31 [Customization], page 391.

ASCII terminals cannot really send anything to the computer except ASCII characters. These terminals use a sequence of characters to represent each function key. But that is invisible to the Emacs user, because the keyboard input routines recognize these special sequences and convert them to function key events before any other part of Emacs gets to see them.

2.2 Keys

A *key sequence* (*key*, for short) is a sequence of input events that are meaningful as a unit—as "a single command." Some Emacs command sequences are just one character or one event; for example, just C-f is enough to move forward one character. But Emacs also has commands that take two or more events to invoke.

If a sequence of events is enough to invoke a command, it is a *complete key*. Examples of complete keys include C-a, X, (RET), (NEXT) (a function key), (DOWN) (an arrow key), C-x C-f, and C-x 4 C-f. If it isn't long enough to be complete, we call it a *prefix key*. The above examples show that C-x and C-x 4 are prefix keys. Every key sequence is either a complete key or a prefix key.

Most single characters constitute complete keys in the standard Emacs command bindings. A few of them are prefix keys. A prefix key combines with the following input event to make a longer key sequence, which may itself be complete or a prefix. For example, C-x is a prefix key, so C-x and the next input event combine to make a two-character key sequence. Most of these key sequences are complete keys, including C-x C-f and C-x b. A few, such as C-x 4 and C-x r, are themselves prefix keys that lead to three-character key sequences. There's no limit to the length of a key sequence, but in practice people rarely use sequences longer than four events.

By contrast, you can't add more events onto a complete key. For example, the two-character sequence C-f C-k is not a key, because the C-f is a complete key in itself. It's impossible to give C-f C-k an independent meaning as a command. C-f C-k is two key sequences, not one.

All told, the prefix keys in Emacs are C-c, C-h, C-x, C-x RET, C-x @, C-x a, C-x n, C-x r, C-x v, C-x 4, C-x 5, C-x 6, ESC, M-g and M-j. But this list is not cast in concrete; it is just a matter of Emacs's standard key bindings. If you customize Emacs, you can make new prefix keys, or eliminate these. See Section 31.4 [Key Bindings], page 408.

If you do make or eliminate prefix keys, that changes the set of possible key sequences. For example, if you redefine C-f as a prefix, C-f C-k automatically becomes a key (complete, unless you define it too as a prefix). Conversely, if you remove the prefix definition of C-x 4, then C-x 4 f (or C-x 4 *anything*) is no longer a key.

Typing the help character (C-h or F1) after a prefix character displays a list of the commands starting with that prefix. There are a few prefix characters for which C-h does not work—for historical reasons, they have other meanings for C-h which are not easy to change. But F1 should work for all prefix characters.

2.3 Keys and Commands

This manual is full of passages that tell you what particular keys do. But Emacs does not assign meanings to keys directly. Instead, Emacs assigns meanings to named *commands*, and then gives keys their meanings by *binding* them to commands.

Every command has a name chosen by a programmer. The name is usually made of a few English words separated by dashes; for example, **next-line** or **forward-word**. A command also has a *function definition* which is a Lisp program; this is what makes the command do what it does. In Emacs Lisp, a command is actually a special kind of Lisp function; one which specifies how to read arguments for it and call it interactively. For more information on commands and functions, see section "What Is a Function" in *The Emacs Lisp Reference Manual*. (The definition we use in this manual is simplified slightly.)

The bindings between keys and commands are recorded in various tables called *keymaps*. See Section 31.4.1 [Keymaps], page 408.

When we say that "C-n moves down vertically one line" we are glossing over a distinction that is irrelevant in ordinary use but is vital in under-

standing how to customize Emacs. It is the command `next-line` that is
programmed to move down vertically. `C-n` has this effect *because* it is bound
to that command. If you rebind `C-n` to the command `forward-word` then `C-n`
will move forward by words instead. Rebinding keys is a common method
of customization.

In the rest of this manual, we usually ignore this subtlety to keep things
simple. To give the information needed for customization, we state the name
of the command which really does the work in parentheses after mentioning
the key that runs it. For example, we will say that "The command `C-n`
(`next-line`) moves point vertically down," meaning that `next-line` is a
command that moves vertically down and `C-n` is a key that is standardly
bound to it.

While we are on the subject of information for customization only, it's a
good time to tell you about *variables*. Often the description of a command
will say, "To change this, set the variable `mumble-foo`." A variable is a
name used to remember a value. Most of the variables documented in this
manual exist just to facilitate customization: some command or other part
of Emacs examines the variable and behaves differently according to the
value that you set. Until you are interested in customizing, you can ignore
the information about variables. When you are ready to be interested, read
the basic information on variables, and then the information on individual
variables will make sense. See Section 31.2 [Variables], page 393.

2.4 Character Set for Text

Text in Emacs buffers is a sequence of 8-bit bytes. Each byte can hold
a single ASCII character. Both ASCII control characters (octal codes 000
through 037, and 0177) and ASCII printing characters (codes 040 through
0176) are allowed; however, non-ASCII control characters cannot appear in
a buffer. The other modifier flags used in keyboard input, such as Meta, are
not allowed in buffers either.

Some ASCII control characters serve special purposes in text, and have
special names. For example, the newline character (octal code 012) is used
in the buffer to end a line, and the tab character (octal code 011) is used
for indenting to the next tab stop column (normally every 8 columns). See
Section 11.6 [Text Display], page 82.

Non-ASCII printing characters can also appear in buffers. When multibyte characters are enabled, you can use any of the non-ASCII printing
characters that Emacs supports. They have character codes starting at 256,
octal 0400, and each one is represented as a sequence of two or more bytes.
See Chapter 18 [International], page 175.

If you disable multibyte characters, then you can use only one alphabet
of non-ASCII characters, but they all fit in one byte. They use codes 0200
through 0377. See Section 18.12 [Single-Byte European Support], page 188.

3 Entering and Exiting Emacs

The usual way to invoke Emacs is with the shell command 'emacs'. Emacs clears the screen and then displays an initial help message and copyright notice. Some operating systems discard all type-ahead when Emacs starts up; they give Emacs no way to prevent this. Therefore, it is advisable to wait until Emacs clears the screen before typing your first editing command.

If you run Emacs from a shell window under the X Window System, run it in the background with 'emacs&'. This way, Emacs does not tie up the shell window, so you can use that to run other shell commands while Emacs operates its own X windows. You can begin typing Emacs commands as soon as you direct your keyboard input to the Emacs frame.

When Emacs starts up, it makes a buffer named '*scratch*'. That's the buffer you start out in. The '*scratch*' buffer uses Lisp Interaction mode; you can use it to type Lisp expressions and evaluate them, or you can ignore that capability and simply doodle. (You can specify a different major mode for this buffer by setting the variable initial-major-mode in your init file. See Section 31.7 [Init File], page 419.)

It is possible to specify files to be visited, Lisp files to be loaded, and functions to be called, by giving Emacs arguments in the shell command line. See Appendix A [Command Arguments], page 441. But we don't recommend doing this. The feature exists mainly for compatibility with other editors.

Many other editors are designed to be started afresh each time you want to edit. You edit one file and then exit the editor. The next time you want to edit either another file or the same one, you must run the editor again. With these editors, it makes sense to use a command-line argument to say which file to edit.

But starting a new Emacs each time you want to edit a different file does not make sense. For one thing, this would be annoyingly slow. For another, this would fail to take advantage of Emacs's ability to visit more than one file in a single editing session. And it would lose the other accumulated context, such as registers, undo history, and the mark ring.

The recommended way to use GNU Emacs is to start it only once, just after you log in, and do all your editing in the same Emacs session. Each time you want to edit a different file, you visit it with the existing Emacs, which eventually comes to have many files in it ready for editing. Usually you do not kill the Emacs until you are about to log out. See Chapter 14 [Files], page 107, for more information on visiting more than one file.

3.1 Exiting Emacs

There are two commands for exiting Emacs because there are two kinds of exiting: *suspending* Emacs and *killing* Emacs.

Suspending means stopping Emacs temporarily and returning control to its parent process (usually a shell), allowing you to resume editing later in the same Emacs job, with the same buffers, same kill ring, same undo history, and so on. This is the usual way to exit.

Killing Emacs means destroying the Emacs job. You can run Emacs again later, but you will get a fresh Emacs; there is no way to resume the same editing session after it has been killed.

C-z   Suspend Emacs (`suspend-emacs`) or iconify a frame (`iconify-or-deiconify-frame`).

C-x C-c   Kill Emacs (`save-buffers-kill-emacs`).

To suspend Emacs, type `C-z` (`suspend-emacs`). This takes you back to the shell from which you invoked Emacs. You can resume Emacs with the shell command '`%emacs`' in most common shells.

On systems that do not support suspending programs, `C-z` starts an inferior shell that communicates directly with the terminal. Emacs waits until you exit the subshell. (The way to do that is probably with `C-d` or '`exit`', but it depends on which shell you use.) The only way on these systems to get back to the shell from which Emacs was run (to log out, for example) is to kill Emacs.

Suspending also fails if you run Emacs under a shell that doesn't support suspending programs, even if the system itself does support it. In such a case, you can set the variable `cannot-suspend` to a non-`nil` value to force `C-z` to start an inferior shell. (One might also describe Emacs's parent shell as "inferior" for failing to support job control properly, but that is a matter of taste.)

When Emacs communicates directly with an X server and creates its own dedicated X windows, `C-z` has a different meaning. Suspending an application that uses its own X windows is not meaningful or useful. Instead, `C-z` runs the command `iconify-or-deiconify-frame`, which temporarily closes up the selected Emacs frame (see Chapter 17 [Frames], page 157). The way to get back to a shell window is with the window manager.

To kill Emacs, type `C-x C-c` (`save-buffers-kill-emacs`). A two-character key is used for this to make it harder to type. This command first offers to save any modified file-visiting buffers. If you do not save them all, it asks for reconfirmation with `yes` before killing Emacs, since any changes not saved will be lost forever. Also, if any subprocesses are still running, `C-x C-c` asks for confirmation about them, since killing Emacs will kill the subprocesses immediately.

There is no way to restart an Emacs session once you have killed it. You can, however, arrange for Emacs to record certain session information, such as which files are visited, when you kill it, so that the next time you restart Emacs it will try to visit the same files and so on. See Section 30.11 [Saving Emacs Sessions], page 385.

The operating system usually listens for certain special characters whose meaning is to kill or suspend the program you are running. **This operating system feature is turned off while you are in Emacs.** The meanings of `C-z` and `C-x C-c` as keys in Emacs were inspired by the use of `C-z` and `C-c` on several operating systems as the characters for stopping or killing a program, but that is their only relationship with the operating system. You can customize these keys to run any commands of your choice (see Section 31.4.1 [Keymaps], page 408).

4 Basic Editing Commands

We now give the basics of how to enter text, make corrections, and save the text in a file. If this material is new to you, you might learn it more easily by running the Emacs learn-by-doing tutorial. To use the tutorial, run Emacs and type `Control-h t` (`help-with-tutorial`).

To clear the screen and redisplay, type `C-l` (`recenter`).

4.1 Inserting Text

To insert printing characters into the text you are editing, just type them. This inserts the characters you type into the buffer at the cursor (that is, at *point*; see Section 1.1 [Point], page 15). The cursor moves forward, and any text after the cursor moves forward too. If the text in the buffer is 'FOOBAR', with the cursor before the 'B', then if you type XX, you get 'FOOXXBAR', with the cursor still before the 'B'.

To *delete* text you have just inserted, use (DEL). (DEL) deletes the character *before* the cursor (not the one that the cursor is on top of or under; that is the character *after* the cursor). The cursor and all characters after it move backwards. Therefore, if you type a printing character and then type (DEL), they cancel out.

To end a line and start typing a new one, type (RET). This inserts a newline character in the buffer. If point is in the middle of a line, (RET) splits the line. Typing (DEL) when the cursor is at the beginning of a line deletes the preceding newline, thus joining the line with the preceding line.

Emacs can split lines automatically when they become too long, if you turn on a special minor mode called *Auto Fill* mode. See Section 21.5 [Filling], page 203, for how to use Auto Fill mode.

If you prefer to have text characters replace (overwrite) existing text rather than shove it to the right, you can enable Overwrite mode, a minor mode. See Section 31.1 [Minor Modes], page 391.

Direct insertion works for printing characters and (SPC), but other characters act as editing commands and do not insert themselves. If you need to insert a control character or a character whose code is above 200 octal, you must *quote* it by typing the character `Control-q` (`quoted-insert`) first. (This character's name is normally written `C-q` for short.) There are two ways to use `C-q`:

- `C-q` followed by any non-graphic character (even `C-g`) inserts that character.

- `C-q` followed by a sequence of octal digits inserts the character with the specified octal character code. You can use any number of octal digits; any non-digit terminates the sequence. If the terminating character is (RET), it serves only to terminate the sequence; any other non-digit is itself used as input after terminating the sequence. (The use of octal sequences is disabled in ordinary non-binary Overwrite mode, to give you a convenient way to insert a digit instead of overwriting with it.)

When multibyte characters are enabled, octal codes 0200 through 0377 are not valid as characters; if you specify a code in this range, C-q assumes that you intend to use some ISO Latin-*n* character set, and converts the specified code to the corresponding Emacs character code. See Section 18.2 [Enabling Multibyte], page 175. You select *which* ISO Latin character set though your choice of language environment (see Section 18.3 [Language Environments], page 176).

To use decimal or hexadecimal instead of octal, set the variable **read-quoted-char-radix** to 10 or 16. If the radix is greater than 10, some letters starting with **a** serve as part of a character code, just like digits.

A numeric argument to C-q specifies how many copies of the quoted character should be inserted (see Section 4.10 [Arguments], page 37).

Customization information: (DEL) in most modes runs the command **delete-backward-char**; (RET) runs the command **newline**, and self-inserting printing characters run the command **self-insert**, which inserts whatever character was typed to invoke it. Some major modes rebind (DEL) to other commands.

4.2 Changing the Location of Point

To do more than insert characters, you have to know how to move point (see Section 1.1 [Point], page 15). The simplest way to do this is with arrow keys, or by clicking the left mouse button where you want to move to.

There are also control and meta characters for cursor motion. Some are equivalent to the arrow keys (these date back to the days before terminals had arrow keys, and are usable on terminals which don't have them). Others do more sophisticated things.

C-a   Move to the beginning of the line (**beginning-of-line**).

C-e   Move to the end of the line (**end-of-line**).

C-f   Move forward one character (**forward-char**).

C-b   Move backward one character (**backward-char**).

M-f   Move forward one word (**forward-word**).

M-b   Move backward one word (**backward-word**).

C-n   Move down one line, vertically (**next-line**). This command
          attempts to keep the horizontal position unchanged, so if you
          start in the middle of one line, you end in the middle of the
          next. When on the last line of text, C-n creates a new line and
          moves onto it.

C-p   Move up one line, vertically (**previous-line**).

M-r   Move point to left margin, vertically centered in the window (**move-to-window-line**). Text does not move on the screen.

A numeric argument says which screen line to place point on. It counts screen lines down from the top of the window (zero for the top line). A negative argument counts lines from the bottom (−1 for the bottom line).

M-<   Move to the top of the buffer (**beginning-of-buffer**). With numeric argument n, move to $n/10$ of the way from the top. See Section 4.10 [Arguments], page 37, for more information on numeric arguments.

M->   Move to the end of the buffer (**end-of-buffer**).

M-x goto-char
Read a number n and move point to buffer position n. Position 1 is the beginning of the buffer.

M-x goto-line
Read a number n and move point to line number n. Line 1 is the beginning of the buffer.

C-x C-n   Use the current column of point as the *semipermanent goal column* for **C-n** and **C-p** (**set-goal-column**). Henceforth, those commands always move to this column in each line moved into, or as close as possible given the contents of the line. This goal column remains in effect until canceled.

C-u C-x C-n
Cancel the goal column. Henceforth, **C-n** and **C-p** once again try to stick to a fixed horizontal position, as usual.

If you set the variable **track-eol** to a non-**nil** value, then **C-n** and **C-p** when at the end of the starting line move to the end of another line. Normally, **track-eol** is **nil**. See Section 31.2 [Variables], page 393, for how to set variables such as **track-eol**.

Normally, **C-n** on the last line of a buffer appends a newline to it. If the variable **next-line-add-newlines** is **nil**, then **C-n** gets an error instead (like **C-p** on the first line).

4.3 Erasing Text

⟨DEL⟩   Delete the character before point (**delete-backward-char**).

C-d   Delete the character after point (**delete-char**).

C-k   Kill to the end of the line (**kill-line**).

M-d   Kill forward to the end of the next word (**kill-word**).

M-⟨DEL⟩   Kill back to the beginning of the previous word (backward-kill-word).

You already know about the ⟨DEL⟩ key which deletes the character before point (that is, before the cursor). Another key, Control-d (C-d for short), deletes the character after point (that is, the character that the cursor is on). This shifts the rest of the text on the line to the left. If you type C-d at the end of a line, it joins together that line and the next line.

To erase a larger amount of text, use the C-k key, which kills a line at a time. If you type C-k at the beginning or middle of a line, it kills all the text up to the end of the line. If you type C-k at the end of a line, it joins that line and the next line.

See Section 9.1 [Killing], page 65, for more flexible ways of killing text.

4.4 Undoing Changes

You can undo all the recent changes in the buffer text, up to a certain point. Each buffer records changes individually, and the undo command always applies to the current buffer. Usually each editing command makes a separate entry in the undo records, but some commands such as query-replace make many entries, and very simple commands such as self-inserting characters are often grouped to make undoing less tedious.

C-x u   Undo one batch of changes—usually, one command worth (undo).

C-_   The same.

C-u C-x u   Undo one batch of changes in the region.

The command C-x u or C-_ is how you undo. The first time you give this command, it undoes the last change. Point moves back to where it was before the command that made the change.

Consecutive repetitions of C-_ or C-x u undo earlier and earlier changes, back to the limit of the undo information available. If all recorded changes have already been undone, the undo command prints an error message and does nothing.

Any command other than an undo command breaks the sequence of undo commands. Starting from that moment, the previous undo commands become ordinary changes that you can undo. Thus, to redo changes you have undone, type C-f or any other command that will harmlessly break the sequence of undoing, then type more undo commands.

Ordinary undo applies to all changes made in the current buffer. You can also perform *selective undo*, limited to the current region. To do this, specify the region you want, then run the undo command with a prefix argument (the value does not matter): C-u C-x u or C-u C-_. This undoes the most recent change in the region. To undo further changes in the same region, repeat the undo command (no prefix argument is needed). In Transient Mark mode, any use of undo when there is an active region performs selective undo; you do not need a prefix argument.

If you notice that a buffer has been modified accidentally, the easiest way to recover is to type C-_ repeatedly until the stars disappear from the front of the mode line. At this time, all the modifications you made have been canceled. Whenever an undo command makes the stars disappear from the mode line, it means that the buffer contents are the same as they were when the file was last read in or saved.

If you do not remember whether you changed the buffer deliberately, type C-_ once. When you see the last change you made undone, you will see whether it was an intentional change. If it was an accident, leave it undone. If it was deliberate, redo the change as described above.

Not all buffers record undo information. Buffers whose names start with spaces don't; these buffers are used internally by Emacs and its extensions to hold text that users don't normally look at or edit.

You cannot undo mere cursor motion; only changes in the buffer contents save undo information. However, some cursor motion commands set the mark, so if you use these commands from time to time, you can move back to the neighborhoods you have moved through by popping the mark ring (see Section 8.5 [Mark Ring], page 63).

When the undo information for a buffer becomes too large, Emacs discards the oldest undo information from time to time (during garbage collection). You can specify how much undo information to keep by setting two variables: undo-limit and undo-strong-limit. Their values are expressed in units of bytes of space.

The variable undo-limit sets a soft limit: Emacs keeps undo data for enough commands to reach this size, and perhaps exceed it, but does not keep data for any earlier commands beyond that. Its default value is 20000. The variable undo-strong-limit sets a stricter limit: the command which pushes the size past this amount is itself forgotten. Its default value is 30000.

Regardless of the values of those variables, the most recent change is never discarded, so there is no danger that garbage collection occurring right after an unintentional large change might prevent you from undoing it.

The reason the undo command has two keys, C-x u and C-_, set up to run it is that it is worthy of a single-character key, but on some keyboards it is not obvious how to type C-_. C-x u is an alternative you can type straightforwardly on any terminal.

4.5 Files

The commands described above are sufficient for creating and altering text in an Emacs buffer; the more advanced Emacs commands just make things easier. But to keep any text permanently you must put it in a *file*.

Files are named units of text which are stored by the operating system for you to retrieve later by name. To look at or use the contents of a file in any way, including editing the file with Emacs, you must specify the file name.

Consider a file named '/usr/rms/foo.c'. In Emacs, to begin editing this file, type

        C-x C-f /usr/rms/foo.c (RET)

Here the file name is given as an *argument* to the command C-x C-f (**find-file**). That command uses the *minibuffer* to read the argument, and you type (RET) to terminate the argument (see Chapter 5 [Minibuffer], page 41).

Emacs obeys the command by *visiting* the file: creating a buffer, copying the contents of the file into the buffer, and then displaying the buffer for you to edit. If you alter the text, you can *save* the new text in the file by typing C-x C-s (**save-buffer**). This makes the changes permanent by copying the altered buffer contents back into the file '/usr/rms/foo.c'. Until you save, the changes exist only inside Emacs, and the file 'foo.c' is unaltered.

To create a file, just visit the file with C-x C-f as if it already existed. This creates an empty buffer in which you can insert the text you want to put in the file. The file is actually created when you save this buffer with C-x C-s.

Of course, there is a lot more to learn about using files. See Chapter 14 [Files], page 107.

4.6 Help

If you forget what a key does, you can find out with the Help character, which is C-h (or (F1), which is an alias for C-h). Type C-h k followed by the key you want to know about; for example, C-h k C-n tells you all about what C-n does. C-h is a prefix key; C-h k is just one of its subcommands (the command **describe-key**). The other subcommands of C-h provide different kinds of help. Type C-h twice to get a description of all the help facilities. See Chapter 7 [Help], page 51.

4.7 Blank Lines

Here are special commands and techniques for putting in and taking out blank lines.

C-o   Insert one or more blank lines after the cursor (**open-line**).

C-x C-o   Delete all but one of many consecutive blank lines (**delete-blank-lines**).

When you want to insert a new line of text before an existing line, you can do it by typing the new line of text, followed by (RET). However, it may be easier to see what you are doing if you first make a blank line and then insert the desired text into it. This is easy to do using the key C-o (open-line), which inserts a newline after point but leaves point in front of the newline. After C-o, type the text for the new line. C-o F O O has the same effect as F O O (RET), except for the final location of point.

You can make several blank lines by typing C-o several times, or by giving it a numeric argument to tell it how many blank lines to make. See Section 4.10 [Arguments], page 37, for how. If you have a fill prefix, then C-o command inserts the fill prefix on the new line, when you use it at the beginning of a line. See Section 21.5.3 [Fill Prefix], page 206.

The easy way to get rid of extra blank lines is with the command C-x C-o (delete-blank-lines). C-x C-o in a run of several blank lines deletes all but one of them. C-x C-o on a solitary blank line deletes that blank line. When point is on a nonblank line, C-x C-o deletes any blank lines following that nonblank line.

4.8 Continuation Lines

If you add too many characters to one line without breaking it with (RET), the line will grow to occupy two (or more) lines on the screen, with a '\' at the extreme right margin of all but the last of them. The '\' says that the following screen line is not really a distinct line in the text, but just the *continuation* of a line too long to fit the screen. Continuation is also called *line wrapping*.

Sometimes it is nice to have Emacs insert newlines automatically when a line gets too long. Continuation on the screen does not do that. Use Auto Fill mode (see Section 21.5 [Filling], page 203) if that's what you want.

As an alternative to continuation, Emacs can display long lines by *truncation*. This means that all the characters that do not fit in the width of the screen or window do not appear at all. They remain in the buffer, temporarily invisible. '$' is used in the last column instead of '\' to inform you that truncation is in effect.

Truncation instead of continuation happens whenever horizontal scrolling is in use, and optionally in all side-by-side windows (see Chapter 16 [Windows], page 151). You can enable truncation for a particular buffer by setting the variable truncate-lines to non-nil in that buffer. (See Section 31.2 [Variables], page 393.) Altering the value of truncate-lines makes it local to the current buffer; until that time, the default value is in effect. The default is initially nil. See Section 31.2.4 [Locals], page 401.

See Section 11.7 [Display Vars], page 83, for additional variables that affect how text is displayed.

4.9 Cursor Position Information

Here are commands to get information about the size and position of parts of the buffer, and to count lines.

M-x what-page
>   Print page number of point, and line number within page.

M-x what-line
>   Print line number of point in the buffer.

M-x line-number-mode
>   Toggle automatic display of current line number.

M-=
>   Print number of lines in the current region (count-lines-region). See Chapter 8 [Mark], page 59, for information about the region.

C-x =
>   Print character code of character after point, character position of point, and column of point (what-cursor-position).

There are two commands for working with line numbers. M-x what-line computes the current line number and displays it in the echo area. To go to a given line by number, use M-x goto-line; it prompts you for the number. These line numbers count from one at the beginning of the buffer.

You can also see the current line number in the mode line; See Section 1.3 [Mode Line], page 17. If you narrow the buffer, then the line number in the mode line is relative to the accessible portion (see Section 30.8 [Narrowing], page 382). By contrast, what-line shows both the line number relative to the narrowed region and the line number relative to the whole buffer.

By contrast, M-x what-page counts pages from the beginning of the file, and counts lines within the page, printing both numbers. See Section 21.4 [Pages], page 202.

While on this subject, we might as well mention M-= (count-lines-region), which prints the number of lines in the region (see Chapter 8 [Mark], page 59). See Section 21.4 [Pages], page 202, for the command C-x l which counts the lines in the current page.

The command C-x = (what-cursor-position) can be used to find out the column that the cursor is in, and other miscellaneous information about point. It prints a line in the echo area that looks like this:

```
Char: c (0143, 99, 0x63)  point=21044 of 26883(78%)  column 53
```

(In fact, this is the output produced when point is before the 'column' in the example.)

The four values after 'Char:' describe the character that follows point, first by showing it and then by giving its character code in octal, decimal and hex. For a non-ASCII multibyte character, these are followed by 'ext' and the character's representation, in hex, in the buffer's coding system, if that coding system encodes the character safely and with a single byte (see Section 18.7 [Coding Systems], page 180). If the character's encoding is longer than one byte, Emacs shows 'ext ...'.

'point=' is followed by the position of point expressed as a character count. The front of the buffer counts as position 1, one character later as

2, and so on. The next, larger, number is the total number of characters in the buffer. Afterward in parentheses comes the position expressed as a percentage of the total size.

'column' is followed by the horizontal position of point, in columns from the left edge of the window.

If the buffer has been narrowed, making some of the text at the beginning and the end temporarily inaccessible, `C-x =` prints additional text describing the currently accessible range. For example, it might display this:

```
Char: C (0103, 67, 0x43)  point=252 of 889(28%) <231 - 599>  column 0
```

where the two extra numbers give the smallest and largest character position that point is allowed to assume. The characters between those two positions are the accessible ones. See Section 30.8 [Narrowing], page 382.

If point is at the end of the buffer (or the end of the accessible part), the `C-x =` output does not describe a character after point. The output might look like this:

```
point=26957 of 26956(100%)  column 0
```

`C-u C-x =` displays additional information about a character, in place of the buffer coordinates and column: the character set name and the codes that identify the character within that character set; ASCII characters are identified as belonging to the `ASCII` character set. In addition, the full character encoding, even if it takes more than a single byte, is shown after 'ext'. Here's an example for a Latin-1 character A with a grave accent in a buffer whose coding system is iso-2022-7bit[1]:

```
Char: À (04300, 2240, 0x8c0, ext ESC , A @) (latin-iso8859-1 64)
```

4.10 Numeric Arguments

In mathematics and computer usage, the word *argument* means "data provided to a function or operation." You can give any Emacs command a *numeric argument* (also called a *prefix argument*). Some commands interpret the argument as a repetition count. For example, `C-f` with an argument of ten moves forward ten characters instead of one. With these commands, no argument is equivalent to an argument of one. Negative arguments tell most such commands to move or act in the opposite direction.

If your terminal keyboard has a (META) key, the easiest way to specify a numeric argument is to type digits and/or a minus sign while holding down the (META) key. For example,

```
M-5 C-n
```

would move down five lines. The characters Meta-1, Meta-2, and so on, as well as Meta--, do this because they are keys bound to commands (digit-argument and negative-argument) that are defined to contribute to an

---

[1] On terminals that support Latin-1 characters, the character shown after 'Char:' is displayed as the actual glyph of A with grave accent.

argument for the next command. Digits and - modified with Control, or Control and Meta, also specify numeric arguments.

Another way of specifying an argument is to use the C-u (universal-argument) command followed by the digits of the argument. With C-u, you can type the argument digits without holding down modifier keys; C-u works on all terminals. To type a negative argument, type a minus sign after C-u. Just a minus sign without digits normally means −1.

C-u followed by a character which is neither a digit nor a minus sign has the special meaning of "multiply by four." It multiplies the argument for the next command by four. C-u twice multiplies it by sixteen. Thus, C-u C-u C-f moves forward sixteen characters. This is a good way to move forward "fast," since it moves about 1/5 of a line in the usual size screen. Other useful combinations are C-u C-n, C-u C-u C-n (move down a good fraction of a screen), C-u C-u C-o (make "a lot" of blank lines), and C-u C-k (kill four lines).

Some commands care only about whether there is an argument, and not about its value. For example, the command M-q (fill-paragraph) with no argument fills text; with an argument, it justifies the text as well. (See Section 21.5 [Filling], page 203, for more information on M-q.) Plain C-u is a handy way of providing an argument for such commands.

Some commands use the value of the argument as a repeat count, but do something peculiar when there is no argument. For example, the command C-k (kill-line) with argument n kills n lines, including their terminating newlines. But C-k with no argument is special: it kills the text up to the next newline, or, if point is right at the end of the line, it kills the newline itself. Thus, two C-k commands with no arguments can kill a nonblank line, just like C-k with an argument of one. (See Section 9.1 [Killing], page 65, for more information on C-k.)

A few commands treat a plain C-u differently from an ordinary argument. A few others may treat an argument of just a minus sign differently from an argument of −1. These unusual cases are described when they come up; they are always for reasons of convenience of use of the individual command.

You can use a numeric argument to insert multiple copies of a character. This is straightforward unless the character is a digit; for example, C-u 6 4 a inserts 64 copies of the character 'a'. But this does not work for inserting digits; C-u 6 4 1 specifies an argument of 641, rather than inserting anything. To separate the digit to insert from the argument, type another C-u; for example, C-u 6 4 C-u 1 does insert 64 copies of the character '1'.

We use the term "prefix argument" as well as "numeric argument" to emphasize that you type the argument before the command, and to distinguish these arguments from minibuffer arguments that come after the command.

4.11 Repeating a Command

The command C-x z (repeat) provides another way to repeat an Emacs command many times. This command repeats the previous Emacs command, whatever that was. Repeating a command uses the same arguments that were used before; it does not read new arguments each time.

To repeat the command more than once, type additional z's: each z repeats the command one more time. Repetition ends when you type a character other than z, or press a mouse button.

For example, suppose you type C-u 2 0 C-d to delete 20 characters. You can repeat that command (including its argument) three additional times, to delete a total of 80 characters, by typing C-x z z z. The first C-x z repeats the command once, and each subsequent z repeats it once again.

5 The Minibuffer

The *minibuffer* is the facility used by Emacs commands to read arguments more complicated than a single number. Minibuffer arguments can be file names, buffer names, Lisp function names, Emacs command names, Lisp expressions, and many other things, depending on the command reading the argument. You can use the usual Emacs editing commands in the minibuffer to edit the argument text.

When the minibuffer is in use, it appears in the echo area, and the terminal's cursor moves there. The beginning of the minibuffer line displays a *prompt* which says what kind of input you should supply and how it will be used. Often this prompt is derived from the name of the command that the argument is for. The prompt normally ends with a colon.

Sometimes a *default argument* appears in parentheses after the colon; it too is part of the prompt. The default will be used as the argument value if you enter an empty argument (for example, just type ⟨RET⟩). For example, commands that read buffer names always show a default, which is the name of the buffer that will be used if you type just ⟨RET⟩.

The simplest way to enter a minibuffer argument is to type the text you want, terminated by ⟨RET⟩ which exits the minibuffer. You can cancel the command that wants the argument, and get out of the minibuffer, by typing C-g.

Since the minibuffer uses the screen space of the echo area, it can conflict with other ways Emacs customarily uses the echo area. Here is how Emacs handles such conflicts:

- If a command gets an error while you are in the minibuffer, this does not cancel the minibuffer. However, the echo area is needed for the error message and therefore the minibuffer itself is hidden for a while. It comes back after a few seconds, or as soon as you type anything.

- If in the minibuffer you use a command whose purpose is to print a message in the echo area, such as C-x =, the message is printed normally, and the minibuffer is hidden for a while. It comes back after a few seconds, or as soon as you type anything.

- Echoing of keystrokes does not take place while the minibuffer is in use.

5.1 Minibuffers for File Names

Sometimes the minibuffer starts out with text in it. For example, when you are supposed to give a file name, the minibuffer starts out containing the *default directory*, which ends with a slash. This is to inform you which directory the file will be found in if you do not specify a directory.

For example, the minibuffer might start out with these contents:

     Find File: /u2/emacs/src/

where 'Find File: ' is the prompt. Typing `buffer.c` specifies the file
'/u2/emacs/src/buffer.c'.   To find files in nearby directories, use
..; thus, if you type `../lisp/simple.el`, you will get the file named
'/u2/emacs/lisp/simple.el'. Alternatively, you can kill with M-(DEL) the
directory names you don't want (see Section 21.1 [Words], page 199).

   If you don't want any of the default, you can kill it with `C-a C-k`. But you
don't need to kill the default; you can simply ignore it. Insert an absolute file
name, one starting with a slash or a tilde, after the default directory. For
example, to specify the file '/etc/termcap', just insert that name, giving
these minibuffer contents:

     Find File: /u2/emacs/src//etc/termcap

GNU Emacs gives a special meaning to a double slash (which is not normally
a useful thing to write): it means, "ignore everything before the second slash
in the pair." Thus, '/u2/emacs/src/' is ignored in the example above, and
you get the file '/etc/termcap'.

   If you set `insert-default-directory` to `nil`, the default directory is
not inserted in the minibuffer. This way, the minibuffer starts out empty.
But the name you type, if relative, is still interpreted with respect to the
same default directory.

5.2 Editing in the Minibuffer

   The minibuffer is an Emacs buffer (albeit a peculiar one), and the usual
Emacs commands are available for editing the text of an argument you are
entering.

   Since (RET) in the minibuffer is defined to exit the minibuffer, you can't
use it to insert a newline in the minibuffer. To do that, type `C-o` or `C-q C-j`.
(Recall that a newline is really the character control-J.)

   The minibuffer has its own window which always has space on the screen
but acts as if it were not there when the minibuffer is not in use. When
the minibuffer is in use, its window is just like the others; you can switch to
another window with `C-x o`, edit text in other windows and perhaps even
visit more files, before returning to the minibuffer to submit the argument.
You can kill text in another window, return to the minibuffer window, and
then yank the text to use it in the argument. See Chapter 16 [Windows],
page 151.

   There are some restrictions on the use of the minibuffer window, however. You cannot switch buffers in it—the minibuffer and its window are
permanently attached. Also, you cannot split or kill the minibuffer window. But you can make it taller in the normal fashion with `C-x ^`. If you
enable Resize-Minibuffer mode, then the minibuffer window expands vertically as necessary to hold the text that you put in the minibuffer. Use

`M-x resize-minibuffer-mode` to enable or disable this minor mode (see Section 31.1 [Minor Modes], page 391).

Scrolling works specially in the minibuffer window. When the minibuffer is just one line high, and it contains a long line of text that won't fit on the screen, scrolling automatically maintains an overlap of a certain number of characters from one continuation line to the next. The variable `minibuffer-scroll-overlap` specifies how many characters of overlap; the default is 20.

If while in the minibuffer you issue a command that displays help text of any sort in another window, you can use the `C-M-v` command while in the minibuffer to scroll the help text. This lasts until you exit the minibuffer. This feature is especially useful if a completing minibuffer gives you a list of possible completions. See Section 16.3 [Other Window], page 152.

Emacs normally disallows most commands that use the minibuffer while the minibuffer is active. This rule is to prevent recursive minibuffers from confusing novice users. If you want to be able to use such commands in the minibuffer, set the variable `enable-recursive-minibuffers` to a non-`nil` value.

5.3 Completion

For certain kinds of arguments, you can use *completion* to enter the argument value. Completion means that you type part of the argument, then Emacs visibly fills in the rest, or as much as can be determined from the part you have typed.

When completion is available, certain keys—⟨TAB⟩, ⟨RET⟩, and ⟨SPC⟩—are rebound to complete the text present in the minibuffer into a longer string that it stands for, by matching it against a set of *completion alternatives* provided by the command reading the argument. `?` is defined to display a list of possible completions of what you have inserted.

For example, when `M-x` uses the minibuffer to read the name of a command, it provides a list of all available Emacs command names to complete against. The completion keys match the text in the minibuffer against all the command names, find any additional name characters implied by the ones already present in the minibuffer, and add those characters to the ones you have given. This is what makes it possible to type `M-x ins` ⟨SPC⟩ `b` ⟨RET⟩ instead of `M-x insert-buffer` ⟨RET⟩ (for example).

Case is normally significant in completion, because it is significant in most of the names that you can complete (buffer names, file names and command names). Thus, 'fo' does not complete to 'Foo'. Completion does ignore case distinctions for certain arguments in which case does not matter.

5.3.1 Completion Example

A concrete example may help here. If you type `M-x au` ⟨TAB⟩, the ⟨TAB⟩ looks for alternatives (in this case, command names) that start with 'au'.

There are several, including `auto-fill-mode` and `auto-save-mode`—but they are all the same as far as `auto-`, so the 'au' in the minibuffer changes to 'auto-'.

If you type (TAB) again immediately, there are multiple possibilities for the very next character—it could be any of 'cfilrs'—so no more characters are added; instead, (TAB) displays a list of all possible completions in another window.

If you go on to type `f` (TAB), this (TAB) sees 'auto-f'. The only command name starting this way is `auto-fill-mode`, so completion fills in the rest of that. You now have 'auto-fill-mode' in the minibuffer after typing just `au` (TAB) `f` (TAB). Note that (TAB) has this effect because in the minibuffer it is bound to the command `minibuffer-complete` when completion is available.

5.3.2 Completion Commands

Here is a list of the completion commands defined in the minibuffer when completion is available.

(TAB)   Complete the text in the minibuffer as much as possible (`minibuffer-complete`).

(SPC)   Complete the minibuffer text, but don't go beyond one word (`minibuffer-complete-word`).

(RET)   Submit the text in the minibuffer as the argument, possibly completing first as described below (`minibuffer-complete-and-exit`).

?   Print a list of all possible completions of the text in the minibuffer (`minibuffer-list-completions`).

(SPC) completes much like (TAB), but never goes beyond the next hyphen or space. If you have 'auto-f' in the minibuffer and type (SPC), it finds that the completion is 'auto-fill-mode', but it stops completing after 'fill-'. This gives 'auto-fill-'. Another (SPC) at this point completes all the way to 'auto-fill-mode'. (SPC) in the minibuffer when completion is available runs the command `minibuffer-complete-word`.

Here are some commands you can use to choose a completion from a window that displays a list of completions:

Mouse-2   Clicking mouse button 2 on a completion in the list of possible completions chooses that completion (`mouse-choose-completion`). You normally use this command while point is in the minibuffer; but you must click in the list of completions, not in the minibuffer itself.

(PRIOR)
M-v   Typing (PRIOR) or (PAGE-UP), or M-v, while in the minibuffer, selects the window showing the completion list buffer (`switch-to-completions`). This paves the way for using the commands

below. (Selecting that window in the usual ways has the same effect, but this way is more convenient.)

(RET)   Typing (RET) *in the completion list buffer* chooses the completion that point is in or next to (`choose-completion`). To use this command, you must first switch windows to the window that shows the list of completions.

(RIGHT) Typing the right-arrow key (RIGHT) *in the completion list buffer* moves point to the following completion (`next-completion`).

(LEFT)   Typing the left-arrow key (LEFT) *in the completion list buffer* moves point toward the beginning of the buffer, to the previous completion (`previous-completion`).

5.3.3 Strict Completion

There are three different ways that (RET) can work in completing minibuffers, depending on how the argument will be used.

- *Strict* completion is used when it is meaningless to give any argument except one of the known alternatives. For example, when `C-x k` reads the name of a buffer to kill, it is meaningless to give anything but the name of an existing buffer. In strict completion, (RET) refuses to exit if the text in the minibuffer does not complete to an exact match.

- *Cautious* completion is similar to strict completion, except that (RET) exits only if the text was an exact match already, not needing completion. If the text is not an exact match, (RET) does not exit, but it does complete the text. If it completes to an exact match, a second (RET) will exit.

  Cautious completion is used for reading file names for files that must already exist.

- *Permissive* completion is used when any string whatever is meaningful, and the list of completion alternatives is just a guide. For example, when `C-x C-f` reads the name of a file to visit, any file name is allowed, in case you want to create a file. In permissive completion, (RET) takes the text in the minibuffer exactly as given, without completing it.

The completion commands display a list of all possible completions in a window whenever there is more than one possibility for the very next character. Also, typing ? explicitly requests such a list. If the list of completions is long, you can scroll it with `C-M-v` (see Section 16.3 [Other Window], page 152).

5.3.4 Completion Options

When completion is done on file names, certain file names are usually ignored. The variable `completion-ignored-extensions` contains a list of strings; a file whose name ends in any of those strings is ignored as a possible completion. The standard value of this variable has several elements including ".o", ".elc", ".dvi" and "~". The effect is that, for example, 'foo' can complete to 'foo.c' even though 'foo.o' exists as well. However, if *all* the possible completions end in "ignored" strings, then they are not ignored. Ignored extensions do not apply to lists of completions—those always mention all possible completions.

Normally, a completion command that finds the next character is undetermined automatically displays a list of all possible completions. If the variable `completion-auto-help` is set to `nil`, this does not happen, and you must type ? to display the possible·completions.

The `complete` library implements a more powerful kind of completion that can complete multiple words at a time. For example, it can complete the command name abbreviation p-b into print-buffer, because no other command starts with two words whose initials are 'p' and 'b'. To use this library, put (load "complete") in your '~/.emacs' file (see Section 31.7 [Init File], page 419).

Icomplete mode presents a constantly-updated display that tells you what completions are available for the text you've entered so far. The command to enable or disable this minor mode is M-x icomplete-mode.

5.4 Minibuffer History

Every argument that you enter with the minibuffer is saved on a *minibuffer history list* so that you can use it again later in another argument. Special commands load the text of an earlier argument in the minibuffer. They discard the old minibuffer contents, so you can think of them as moving through the history of previous arguments.

UP
M-p   Move to the next earlier argument string saved in the minibuffer
              history (previous-history-element).

DOWN
M-n   Move to the next later argument string saved in the minibuffer
              history (next-history-element).

M-r *regexp* RET
              Move to an earlier saved argument in the minibuffer history
              that has a match for *regexp* (previous-matching-history-
              element).

M-s *regexp* RET
              Move to a later saved argument in the minibuffer history that
              has a match for *regexp* (next-matching-history-element).

The simplest way to reuse the saved arguments in the history list is to move through the history list one element at a time. While in the minibuffer, use M-p or up-arrow (`previous-history-element`) to "move to" the next earlier minibuffer input, and use M-n or down-arrow (`next-history-element`) to "move to" the next later input.

The previous input that you fetch from the history entirely replaces the contents of the minibuffer. To use it as the argument, exit the minibuffer as usual with (RET). You can also edit the text before you reuse it; this does not change the history element that you "moved" to, but your new argument does go at the end of the history list in its own right.

For many minibuffer arguments there is a "default" value. In some cases, the minibuffer history commands know the default value. Then you can insert the default value into the minibuffer as text by using M-n to move "into the future" in the history. Eventually we hope to make this feature available whenever the minibuffer has a default value.

There are also commands to search forward or backward through the history; they search for history elements that match a regular expression that you specify with the minibuffer. M-r (`previous-matching-history-element`) searches older elements in the history, while M-s (`next-matching-history-element`) searches newer elements. By special dispensation, these commands can use the minibuffer to read their arguments even though you are already in the minibuffer when you issue them. As with incremental searching, an uppercase letter in the regular expression makes the search case-sensitive (see Section 12.6 [Search Case], page 94).

All uses of the minibuffer record your input on a history list, but there are separate history lists for different kinds of arguments. For example, there is a list for file names, used by all the commands that read file names. (As a special feature, this history list records the absolute file name, no more and no less, even if that is not how you entered the file name.)

There are several other very specific history lists, including one for command names read by M-x, one for buffer names, one for arguments of commands like `query-replace`, and one for compilation commands read by `compile`. Finally, there is one "miscellaneous" history list that most minibuffer arguments use.

The variable `history-length` specifies the maximum length of a minibuffer history list; once a list gets that long, the oldest element is deleted each time an element is added. If the value of `history-length` is t, though, there is no maximum length and elements are never deleted.

5.5 Repeating Minibuffer Commands

Every command that uses the minibuffer at least once is recorded on a special history list, together with the values of its arguments, so that you can repeat the entire command. In particular, every use of M-x is recorded there, since M-x uses the minibuffer to read the command name.

C-x (ESC) (ESC)
> Re-execute a recent minibuffer command (`repeat-complex-command`).

M-x list-command-history
> Display the entire command history, showing all the commands C-x (ESC) (ESC) can repeat, most recent first.

C-x (ESC) (ESC) is used to re-execute a recent minibuffer-using command. With no argument, it repeats the last such command. A numeric argument specifies which command to repeat; one means the last one, and larger numbers specify earlier ones.

C-x (ESC) (ESC) works by turning the previous command into a Lisp expression and then entering a minibuffer initialized with the text for that expression. If you type just (RET), the command is repeated as before. You can also change the command by editing the Lisp expression. Whatever expression you finally submit is what will be executed. The repeated command is added to the front of the command history unless it is identical to the most recently executed command already there.

Even if you don't understand Lisp syntax, it will probably be obvious which command is displayed for repetition. If you do not change the text, it will repeat exactly as before.

Once inside the minibuffer for C-x (ESC) (ESC), you can use the minibuffer history commands (M-p, M-n, M-r, M-s; see Section 5.4 [Minibuffer History], page 46) to move through the history list of saved entire commands. After finding the desired previous command, you can edit its expression as usual and then resubmit it by typing (RET) as usual.

The list of previous minibuffer-using commands is stored as a Lisp list in the variable `command-history`. Each element is a Lisp expression which describes one command and its arguments. Lisp programs can re-execute a command by calling `eval` with the `command-history` element.

6 Running Commands by Name

The Emacs commands that are used often or that must be quick to type are bound to keys—short sequences of characters—for convenient use. Other Emacs commands that do not need to be brief are not bound to keys; to run them, you must refer to them by name.

A command name is, by convention, made up of one or more words, separated by hyphens; for example, `auto-fill-mode` or `manual-entry`. The use of English words makes the command name easier to remember than a key made up of obscure characters, even though it is more characters to type.

The way to run a command by name is to start with M-x, type the command name, and finish it with (RET). M-x uses the minibuffer to read the command name. (RET) exits the minibuffer and runs the command. The string 'M-x' appears at the beginning of the minibuffer as a *prompt* to remind you to enter the name of a command to be run. See Chapter 5 [Minibuffer], page 41, for full information on the features of the minibuffer.

You can use completion to enter the command name. For example, the command `forward-char` can be invoked by name by typing

    M-x forward-char (RET)

or

    M-x forw (TAB) c (RET)

Note that `forward-char` is the same command that you invoke with the key C-f. You can run any Emacs command by name using M-x, whether or not any keys are bound to it.

If you type C-g while the command name is being read, you cancel the M-x command and get out of the minibuffer, ending up at top level.

To pass a numeric argument to the command you are invoking with M-x, specify the numeric argument before the M-x. M-x passes the argument along to the command it runs. The argument value appears in the prompt while the command name is being read.

If the command you type has a key binding of its own, Emacs mentions this in the echo area, two seconds after the command finishes (if you don't type anything else first). For example, if you type M-x forward-word, the message says that you can run the same command more easily by typing M-f. You can turn off these messages by setting `suggest-key-bindings` to `nil`.

Normally, when describing in this manual a command that is run by name, we omit the (RET) that is needed to terminate the name. Thus we might speak of M-x auto-fill-mode rather than M-x auto-fill-mode (RET). We mention the (RET) only when there is a need to emphasize its presence, such as when we show the command together with following arguments.

`M-x` works by running the command `execute-extended-command`, which is responsible for reading the name of another command and invoking it.

7 Help

Emacs provides extensive help features accessible through a single character, C-h. C-h is a prefix key that is used only for documentation-printing commands. The characters that you can type after C-h are called *help options*. One help option is C-h; that is how you ask for help about using C-h. To cancel, type C-g. The function key (F1) is equivalent to C-h.

C-h C-h (help-for-help) displays a list of the possible help options, each with a brief description. Before you type a help option, you can use (SPC) or (DEL) to scroll through the list.

C-h or (F1) means "help" in various other contexts as well. For example, in the middle of query-replace, it describes the options available for how to operate on the current match. After a prefix key, it displays a list of the alternatives that can follow the prefix key. (A few prefix keys don't support C-h, because they define other meanings for it, but they all support (F1).)

Most help buffers use a special major mode, Help mode, which lets you scroll conveniently with (SPC) and (DEL).

Here is a summary of the defined help commands.

C-h a *regexp* (RET)
:   Display a list of commands whose names match *regexp* (apropos-command).

C-h b
:   Display a table of all key bindings in effect now, in this order: minor mode bindings, major mode bindings, and global bindings (describe-bindings).

C-h c *key*
:   Print the name of the command that *key* runs (describe-key-briefly). Here c stands for 'character'. For more extensive information on *key*, use C-h k.

C-h f *function* (RET)
:   Display documentation on the Lisp function named *function* (describe-function). Since commands are Lisp functions, a command name may be used.

C-h h
:   Display the 'hello' file, which shows examples of various character sets.

C-h i
:   Run Info, the program for browsing documentation files (info). The complete Emacs manual is available on-line in Info.

C-h k *key*
:   Display the name and documentation of the command that *key* runs (describe-key).

C-h l
:   Display a description of the last 100 characters you typed (view-lossage).

C-h m
:   Display documentation of the current major mode (describe-mode).

C-h n   Display documentation of Emacs changes, most recent first (`view-emacs-news`).

C-h p   Find packages by topic keyword (`finder-by-keyword`).

C-h s   Display current contents of the syntax table, plus an explanation of what they mean (`describe-syntax`). See Section 31.6 [Syntax], page 419.

C-h t   Enter the Emacs interactive tutorial (`help-with-tutorial`).

C-h v *var* (RET)
             Display the documentation of the Lisp variable *var* (`describe-variable`).

C-h w *command* (RET)
             Print which keys run the command named *command* (`where-is`).

C-h C *coding* (RET)
             Describe coding system *coding* (`describe-coding-system`).

C-h C (RET)
             Describe the coding systems currently in use.

C-h I *method* (RET)
             Describe an input method (`describe-input-method`).

C-h L *language-env* (RET)
             Describe information on the character sets, coding systems and input methods used for language environment *language-env* (`describe-language-environment`).

C-h C-c   Display the copying conditions for GNU Emacs.

C-h C-d   Display information about getting new versions of GNU Emacs.

C-h C-f *function* (RET)
             Enter Info and go to the node documenting the Emacs function *function* (`Info-goto-emacs-command-node`).

C-h C-k *key*
             Enter Info and go to the node where the key sequence *key* is documented (`Info-goto-emacs-key-command-node`).

C-h C-p   Display information about the GNU Project.

C-h (TAB) *symbol* (RET)
             Display the Info documentation on symbol *symbol* according to the programming language you are editing (`info-lookup-symbol`).

7.1 Documentation for a Key

The most basic C-h options are C-h c (describe-key-briefly) and
C-h k (describe-key). C-h c *key* prints in the echo area the name of
the command that *key* is bound to. For example, C h c C-f prints
'forward-char'. Since command names are chosen to describe what the
commands do, this is a good way to get a very brief description of what *key*
does.

C-h k *key* is similar but gives more information: it displays the documentation string of the command as well as its name. This is too big for the
echo area, so a window is used for the display.

C-h c and C-h k work for any sort of key sequences, including function
keys and mouse events.

7.2 Help by Command or Variable Name

C-h f (describe-function) reads the name of a Lisp function using the
minibuffer, then displays that function's documentation string in a window.
Since commands are Lisp functions, you can use this to get the documentation of a command that you know by name. For example,

    C-h f auto-fill-mode (RET)

displays the documentation of auto-fill-mode. This is the only way to get
the documentation of a command that is not bound to any key (one which
you would normally run using M-x).

C-h f is also useful for Lisp functions that you are planning to use in a
Lisp program. For example, if you have just written the expression (make-
vector len) and want to check that you are using make-vector properly,
type C-h f make-vector (RET). Because C-h f allows all function names, not
just command names, you may find that some of your favorite abbreviations
that work in M-x don't work in C-h f. An abbreviation may be unique
among command names yet fail to be unique when other function names are
allowed.

The function name for C-h f to describe has a default which is used if you
type (RET) leaving the minibuffer empty. The default is the function called by
the innermost Lisp expression in the buffer around point, *provided* that is a
valid, defined Lisp function name. For example, if point is located following
the text '(make-vector (car x)', the innermost list containing point is the
one that starts with '(make-vector', so the default is to describe the function
make-vector.

C-h f is often useful just to verify that you have the right spelling for
the function name. If C-h f mentions a name from the buffer as the default,
that name must be defined as a Lisp function. If that is all you want to
know, just type C-g to cancel the C-h f command, then go on editing.

C-h w *command* (RET) tells you what keys are bound to *command*. It prints a list of the keys in the echo area. If it says the command is not on any key, you must use M-x to run it. C-h w runs the command where-is.

C-h v (describe-variable) is like C-h f but describes Lisp variables instead of Lisp functions. Its default is the Lisp symbol around or before point, but only if that is the name of a known Lisp variable. See Section 31.2 [Variables], page 393.

7.3 Apropos

A more sophisticated sort of question to ask is, "What are the commands for working with files?" To ask this question, type C-h a file (RET), which displays a list of all command names that contain 'file', including copy-file, find-file, and so on. With each command name appears a brief description of how to use the command, and what keys you can currently invoke it with. For example, it would say that you can invoke find-file by typing C-x C-f. The a in C-h a stands for 'Apropos'; C-h a runs the command apropos-command. This command normally checks only commands (interactive functions); if you specify a prefix argument, it checks noninteractive functions as well.

Because C-h a looks only for functions whose names contain the string you specify, you must use ingenuity in choosing the string. If you are looking for commands for killing backwards and C-h a kill-backwards (RET) doesn't reveal any, don't give up. Try just kill, or just backwards, or just back. Be persistent. Also note that you can use a regular expression as the argument, for more flexibility (see Section 12.5 [Regexps], page 90).

Here is a set of arguments to give to C-h a that covers many classes of Emacs commands, since there are strong conventions for naming the standard Emacs commands. By giving you a feel for the naming conventions, this set should also serve to aid you in developing a technique for picking apropos strings.

> char, line, word, sentence, paragraph, region, page, sexp, list, defun, rect, buffer, frame, window, face, file, dir, register, mode, beginning, end, forward, backward, next, previous, up, down, search, goto, kill, delete, mark, insert, yank, fill, indent, case, change, set, what, list, find, view, describe, default.

To list all user variables that match a regexp, use the command M-x apropos-variable. This command shows only user variables and customization options by default; if you specify a prefix argument, it checks all variables.

To list all Lisp symbols that contain a match for a regexp, not just the ones that are defined as commands, use the command M-x apropos instead of C-h a. This command does not check key bindings by default; specify a numeric argument if you want it to check them.

The `apropos-documentation` command is like `apropos` except that it searches documentation strings as well as symbol names for matches for the specified regular expression.

The `apropos-value` command is like `apropos` except that it searches symbols' values for matches for the specified regular expression. This command does not check function definitions or property lists by default; specify a numeric argument if you want it to check them.

If the variable `apropos-do-all` is non-`nil`, the commands above all behave as if they had been given a prefix argument.

If you want more information about a function definition, variable or symbol property listed in the Apropos buffer, you can click on it with `Mouse-2` or move there and type (RET).

7.4 Keyword Search for Lisp Libraries

The `C-h p` command lets you search the standard Emacs Lisp libraries by topic keywords. Here is a partial list of keywords you can use:

abbrev — abbreviation handling, typing shortcuts, macros.

bib — support for the bibliography processor `bib`.

c — C and C++ language support.

calendar — calendar and time management support.

comm — communications, networking, remote access to files.

data — support for editing files of data.

docs — support for Emacs documentation.

emulations — emulations of other editors.

extensions — Emacs Lisp language extensions.

faces — support for using faces (fonts and colors; see Section 17.13 [Faces], page 166).

frames — support for Emacs frames and window systems.

games — games, jokes and amusements.

hardware — support for interfacing with exotic hardware.

help — support for on-line help systems.

hypermedia — support for links within text, or other media types.

i18n — internationalization and alternate character-set support.

internal — code for Emacs internals, build process, defaults.

languages — specialized modes for editing programming languages.

lisp — support for using Lisp (including Emacs Lisp).

local — libraries local to your site.

maint — maintenance aids for the Emacs development group.

mail — modes for electronic-mail handling.

matching — searching and matching.

news — support for netnews reading and posting.

non-text — support for editing files that are not ordinary text.

oop — support for object-oriented programming.

outlines — hierarchical outlining.

processes — process, subshell, compilation, and job control support.

terminals — support for terminal types.

tex — support for the TeX formatter.

tools — programming tools.

unix — front-ends/assistants for, or emulators of, Unix features.

vms — support code for VMS.

wp — word processing.

7.5 Help for International Language Support

You can use the command C-h L (`describe-language-environment`) to find out the support for a specific language environment. See Section 18.3 [Language Environments], page 176. This tells you which languages this language environment is useful for, and lists the character sets, coding systems, and input methods that go with it. It also shows some sample text to illustrate scripts.

The command C-h h (`view-hello-file`) displays the file 'etc/HELLO', which shows how to say "hello" in many languages.

The command C-h I (`describe-input-method`) describes information about input methods—either a specified input method, or by default the input method in use. See Section 18.4 [Input Methods], page 177.

The command C-h C (`describe-coding-system`) describes information about coding systems—either a specified coding system, or the ones currently in use. See Section 18.7 [Coding Systems], page 180.

7.6 Help Mode Commands

Help buffers provide the commands of View mode (see Section 14.10 [Misc File Ops], page 139), plus a few special commands of their own.

⟨SPC⟩   Scroll forward.

⟨DEL⟩   Scroll backward.

⟨RET⟩   Follow a cross reference at point.

⟨TAB⟩   Move point forward to the next cross reference.

S-⟨TAB⟩   Move point back to the previous cross reference.

Mouse-2   Follow a cross reference that you click on.

When a command name (see Chapter 6 [Running Commands by Name], page 49) or variable name (see Section 31.2 [Variables], page 393) appears in the documentation, it normally appears inside paired single-quotes. You can click on the name with Mouse-2, or move point there and type ⟨RET⟩, to view the documentation of that command or variable. Use C-c C-b to retrace your steps.

There are convenient commands for moving point to cross references in the help text. (TAB) (`help-next-ref`) moves point down to the next cross reference. Use S-(TAB) to move point up to the previous cross reference (`help-previous-ref`).

7.7 Other Help Commands

`C-h i` (`info`) runs the Info program, which is used for browsing through structured documentation files. The entire Emacs manual is available within Info. Eventually all the documentation of the GNU system will be available. Type `h` after entering Info to run a tutorial on using Info.

If you specify a numeric argument, `C-h i` prompts for the name of a documentation file. This way, you can browse a file which doesn't have an entry in the top-level Info menu. It is also handy when you need to get to the documentation quickly, and you know the exact name of the file.

There are two special help commands for accessing Emacs documentation through Info. `C-h C-f` *function* (RET) enters Info and goes straight to the documentation of the Emacs function *function*. `C-h C-k` *key* enters Info and goes straight to the documentation of the key *key*. These two keys run the commands `Info-goto-emacs-command-node` and `Info-goto-emacs-key-command-node`.

When editing a program, if you have an Info version of the manual for the programming language, you can use the command `C-h C-i` to refer to the manual documentation for a symbol (keyword, function or variable). The details of how this command works depend on the major mode.

If something surprising happens, and you are not sure what commands you typed, use `C-h l` (`view-lossage`). `C-h l` prints the last 100 command characters you typed in. If you see commands that you don't know, you can use `C-h c` to find out what they do.

Emacs has numerous major modes, each of which redefines a few keys and makes a few other changes in how editing works. `C-h m` (`describe-mode`) prints documentation on the current major mode, which normally describes all the commands that are changed in this mode.

`C-h b` (`describe-bindings`) and `C-h s` (`describe-syntax`) present other information about the current Emacs mode. `C-h b` displays a list of all the key bindings now in effect; the local bindings defined by the current minor modes first, then the local bindings defined by the current major mode, and finally the global bindings (see Section 31.4 [Key Bindings], page 408). `C-h s` displays the contents of the syntax table, with explanations of each character's syntax (see Section 31.6 [Syntax], page 419).

You can get a similar list for a particular prefix key by typing `C-h` after the prefix key. (There are a few prefix keys for which this does not work—those that provide their own bindings for `C-h`. One of these is (ESC), because (ESC) `C-h` is actually `C-M-h`, which marks a defun.)

The other `C-h` options display various files of useful information. `C-h` `C-w` displays the full details on the complete absence of warranty for GNU Emacs. `C-h n` (`view-emacs-news`) displays the file 'emacs/etc/NEWS', which contains documentation on Emacs changes arranged chronologically. `C-h F` (`view-emacs-FAQ`) displays the Emacs frequently-answered-questions list. `C-h t` (`help-with-tutorial`) displays the learn-by-doing Emacs tutorial. `C-h C-c` (`describe-copying`) displays the file 'emacs/etc/COPYING', which tells you the conditions you must obey in distributing copies of Emacs. `C-h C-d` (`describe-distribution`) displays the file 'emacs/etc/DISTRIB', which tells you how you can order a copy of the latest version of Emacs. `C-h C-p` (`describe-project`) displays general information about the GNU Project.

8 The Mark and the Region

Many Emacs commands operate on an arbitrary contiguous part of the current buffer. To specify the text for such a command to operate on, you set *the mark* at one end of it, and move point to the other end. The text between point and the mark is called *the region*. Emacs highlights the region whenever there is one, if you enable Transient Mark mode (see Section 8.2 [Transient Mark], page 60).

You can move point or the mark to adjust the boundaries of the region. It doesn't matter which one is set first chronologically, or which one comes earlier in the text. Once the mark has been set, it remains where you put it until you set it again at another place. Each Emacs buffer has its own mark, so that when you return to a buffer that had been selected previously, it has the same mark it had before.

Many commands that insert text, such as `C-y` (`yank`) and `M-x insert-buffer`, position point and the mark at opposite ends of the inserted text, so that the region contains the text just inserted.

Aside from delimiting the region, the mark is also useful for remembering a spot that you may want to go back to. To make this feature more useful, each buffer remembers 16 previous locations of the mark in the *mark ring*.

8.1 Setting the Mark

Here are some commands for setting the mark:

C-(SPC)   Set the mark where point is (`set-mark-command`).

C-@   The same.

C-x C-x   Interchange mark and point (`exchange-point-and-mark`).

Drag-Mouse-1
            Set point and the mark around the text you drag across.

Mouse-3   Set the mark where point is, then move point to where you click (`mouse-save-then-kill`).

For example, suppose you wish to convert part of the buffer to upper case, using the `C-x C-u` (`upcase-region`) command, which operates on the text in the region. You can first go to the beginning of the text to be capitalized, type C-(SPC) to put the mark there, move to the end, and then type `C-x C-u`. Or, you can set the mark at the end of the text, move to the beginning, and then type `C-x C-u`.

The most common way to set the mark is with the C-(SPC) command (`set-mark-command`). This sets the mark where point is. Then you can move point away, leaving the mark behind.

There are two ways to set the mark with the mouse. You can drag mouse button one across a range of text; that puts point where you release the mouse button, and sets the mark at the other end of that range. Or you can click mouse button three, which sets the mark at point (like C-⟨SPC⟩) and then moves point (like Mouse-1). Both of these methods copy the region into the kill ring in addition to setting the mark; that gives behavior consistent with other window-driven applications, but if you don't want to modify the kill ring, you must use keyboard commands to set the mark. See Section 17.1 [Mouse Commands], page 157.

Ordinary terminals have only one cursor, so there is no way for Emacs to show you where the mark is located. You have to remember. The usual solution to this problem is to set the mark and then use it soon, before you forget where it is. Alternatively, you can see where the mark is with the command C-x C-x (exchange-point-and-mark) which puts the mark where point was and point where the mark was. The extent of the region is unchanged, but the cursor and point are now at the previous position of the mark. In Transient Mark mode, this command reactivates the mark.

C-x C-x is also useful when you are satisfied with the position of point but want to move the other end of the region (where the mark is); do C-x C-x to put point at that end of the region, and then move it. A second use of C-x C-x, if necessary, puts the mark at the new position with point back at its original position.

There is no such character as C-⟨SPC⟩ in ASCII; when you type ⟨SPC⟩ while holding down ⟨CTRL⟩, what you get on most ordinary terminals is the character C-@. This key is actually bound to set-mark-command. But unless you are unlucky enough to have a terminal where typing C-⟨SPC⟩ does not produce C-@, you might as well think of this character as C-⟨SPC⟩. Under X, C-⟨SPC⟩ is actually a distinct character, but its binding is still set-mark-command.

8.2 Transient Mark Mode

Emacs can highlight the current region, using X Windows. But normally it does not. Why not?

Highlighting the region doesn't work well ordinarily in Emacs, because once you have set a mark, there is *always* a region (in that buffer). And highlighting the region all the time would be a nuisance.

You can turn on region highlighting by enabling Transient Mark mode. This is a more rigid mode of operation in which the region "lasts" only temporarily, so you must set up a region for each command that uses one. In Transient Mark mode, most of the time there is no region; therefore, highlighting the region when it exists is convenient.

To enable Transient Mark mode, type M-x transient-mark-mode. This command toggles the mode, so you can repeat the command to turn off the mode.

Here are the details of Transient Mark mode:

- To set the mark, type C-(SPC) (set-mark-command). This makes the mark active; as you move point, you will see the region highlighting grow and shrink.

- The mouse commands for specifying the mark also make it active. So do keyboard commands whose purpose is to specify a region, including M-@, C-M-@, M-h, C-M-h, C-x C-p, and C-x h.

- When the mark is active, you can execute commands that operate on the region, such as killing, indenting, or writing to a file.

- Any change to the buffer, such as inserting or deleting a character, de-activates the mark. This means any subsequent command that operates on a region will get an error and refuse to operate. You can make the region active again by typing C-x C-x.

- Commands like M-> and C-s that "leave the mark behind" in addition to some other primary purpose do not activate the new mark. You can activate the new region by executing C-x C-x (exchange-point-and-mark).

- C-s when the mark is active does not alter the mark.

- Quitting with C-g deactivates the mark.

Highlighting of the region uses the **region** face; you can customize how the region is highlighted by changing this face. See Section 31.2.2.3 [Face Customization], page 398.

When multiple windows show the same buffer, they can have different regions, because they can have different values of point (though they all share one common mark position). Ordinarily, only the selected window highlights its region (see Chapter 16 [Windows], page 151). However, if the variable **highlight-nonselected-windows** is non-**nil**, then each window highlights its own region (provided that Transient Mark mode is enabled and the window's buffer's mark is active).

When Transient Mark mode is not enabled, every command that sets the mark also activates it, and nothing ever deactivates it.

If the variable **mark-even-if-inactive** is non-**nil** in Transient Mark mode, then commands can use the mark and the region even when it is inactive. Region highlighting appears and disappears just as it normally does in Transient Mark mode, but the mark doesn't really go away when the highlighting disappears.

Transient Mark mode is also sometimes known as "Zmacs mode" because the Zmacs editor on the MIT Lisp Machine handled the mark in a similar way.

8.3 Operating on the Region

Once you have a region and the mark is active, here are some of the ways you can operate on the region:

- Kill it with `C-w` (see Section 9.1 [Killing], page 65).
- Save it in a register with `C-x r s` (see Chapter 10 [Registers], page 75).
- Save it in a buffer or a file (see Section 9.3 [Accumulating Text], page 70).
- Convert case with `C-x C-l` or `C-x C-u` (see Section 21.6 [Case], page 208).
- Indent it with `C-x` (TAB) or `C-M-\` (see Chapter 20 [Indentation], page 195).
- Fill it as text with `M-x fill-region` (see Section 21.5 [Filling], page 203).
- Print hardcopy with `M-x print-region` (see Section 30.4 [Hardcopy], page 377).
- Evaluate it as Lisp code with `M-x eval-region` (see Section 23.8 [Lisp Eval], page 286).

Most commands that operate on the text in the region have the word `region` in their names.

8.4 Commands to Mark Textual Objects

Here are the commands for placing point and the mark around a textual object such as a word, list, paragraph or page.

`M-@`	Set mark after end of next word (`mark-word`). This command and the following one do not move point.
`C-M-@`	Set mark after end of next Lisp expression (`mark-sexp`).
`M-h`	Put region around current paragraph (`mark-paragraph`).
`C-M-h`	Put region around current Lisp defun (`mark-defun`).
`C-x h`	Put region around entire buffer (`mark-whole-buffer`).
`C-x C-p`	Put region around current page (`mark-page`).

`M-@` (`mark-word`) puts the mark at the end of the next word, while `C-M-@` (`mark-sexp`) puts it at the end of the next Lisp expression. These commands handle arguments just like `M-f` and `C-M-f`.

Other commands set both point and mark, to delimit an object in the buffer. For example, `M-h` (`mark-paragraph`) moves point to the beginning of the paragraph that surrounds or follows point, and puts the mark at the end of that paragraph (see Section 21.3 [Paragraphs], page 201). It prepares the region so you can indent, case-convert, or kill a whole paragraph.

`C-M-h` (`mark-defun`) similarly puts point before and the mark after the current or following defun (see Section 22.4 [Defuns], page 230). `C-x C-p` (`mark-page`) puts point before the current page, and mark at the end (see Section 21.4 [Pages], page 202). The mark goes after the terminating page delimiter (to include it), while point goes after the preceding page delimiter (to exclude it). A numeric argument specifies a later page (if positive) or an earlier page (if negative) instead of the current page.

Finally, C-x h (mark-whole-buffer) sets up the entire buffer as the region, by putting point at the beginning and the mark at the end.

In Transient Mark mode, all of these commands activate the mark.

8.5 The Mark Ring

Aside from delimiting the region, the mark is also useful for remembering a spot that you may want to go back to. To make this feature more useful, each buffer remembers 16 previous locations of the mark, in the *mark ring*. Commands that set the mark also push the old mark onto this ring. To return to a marked location, use C-u C-SPC (or C-u C-@); this is the command set-mark-command given a numeric argument. It moves point to where the mark was, and restores the mark from the ring of former marks. Thus, repeated use of this command moves point to all of the old marks on the ring, one by one. The mark positions you move through in this way are not lost; they go to the end of the ring.

Each buffer has its own mark ring. All editing commands use the current buffer's mark ring. In particular, C-u C-SPC always stays in the same buffer.

Many commands that can move long distances, such as M-< (beginning-of-buffer), start by setting the mark and saving the old mark on the mark ring. This is to make it easier for you to move back later. Searches set the mark if they move point. You can tell when a command sets the mark because it displays 'Mark Set' in the echo area.

If you want to move back to the same place over and over, the mark ring may not be convenient enough. If so, you can record the position in a register for later retrieval (see Section 10.1 [RegPos], page 75).

The variable mark-ring-max specifies the maximum number of entries to keep in the mark ring. If that many entries exist and another one is pushed, the last one in the list is discarded. Repeating C-u C-SPC cycles through the positions currently in the ring.

The variable mark-ring holds the mark ring itself, as a list of marker objects, with the most recent first. This variable is local in every buffer.

8.6 The Global Mark Ring

In addition to the ordinary mark ring that belongs to each buffer, Emacs has a single *global mark ring*. It records a sequence of buffers in which you have recently set the mark, so you can go back to those buffers.

Setting the mark always makes an entry on the current buffer's mark ring. If you have switched buffers since the previous mark setting, the new mark position makes an entry on the global mark ring also. The result is that the global mark ring records a sequence of buffers that you have been in, and, for each buffer, a place where you set the mark.

The command C-x C-⟨SPC⟩ (pop-global-mark) jumps to the buffer and position of the latest entry in the global ring. It also rotates the ring, so that successive uses of C-x C-⟨SPC⟩ take you to earlier and earlier buffers.

9 Killing and Moving Text

Killing means erasing text and copying it into the *kill ring*, from which it can be retrieved by *yanking* it. Some systems use the terms "cutting" and "pasting" for these operations.

The commonest way of moving or copying text within Emacs is to kill it and later yank it elsewhere in one or more places. This is very safe because Emacs remembers several recent kills, not just the last one. It is versatile, because the many commands for killing syntactic units can also be used for moving those units. But there are other ways of copying text for special purposes.

Emacs has only one kill ring for all buffers, so you can kill text in one buffer and yank it in another buffer.

9.1 Deletion and Killing

Most commands which erase text from the buffer save it in the kill ring so that you can move or copy it to other parts of the buffer. These commands are known as *kill* commands. The rest of the commands that erase text do not save it in the kill ring; they are known as *delete* commands. (This distinction is made only for erasure of text in the buffer.) If you do a kill or delete command by mistake, you can use the `C-x u` (`undo`) command to undo it (see Section 4.4 [Undo], page 32).

The delete commands include `C-d` (`delete-char`) and `DEL` (`delete-backward-char`), which delete only one character at a time, and those commands that delete only spaces or newlines. Commands that can destroy significant amounts of nontrivial data generally kill. The commands' names and individual descriptions use the words '`kill`' and '`delete`' to say which they do.

9.1.1 Deletion

`C-d`   Delete next character (`delete-char`).

`DEL`   Delete previous character (`delete-backward-char`).

`M-\`   Delete spaces and tabs around point (`delete-horizontal-space`).

`M-SPC`   Delete spaces and tabs around point, leaving one space (`just-one-space`).

`C-x C-o`   Delete blank lines around the current line (`delete-blank-lines`).

`M-^`   Join two lines by deleting the intervening newline, along with any indentation following it (`delete-indentation`).

The most basic delete commands are C-d (delete-char) and (DEL) (delete-backward-char). C-d deletes the character after point, the one the cursor is "on top of." This doesn't move point. (DEL) deletes the character before the cursor, and moves point back. You can delete newlines like any other characters in the buffer; deleting a newline joins two lines. Actually, C-d and (DEL) aren't always delete commands; when given arguments, they kill instead, since they can erase more than one character this way.

The other delete commands are those which delete only whitespace characters: spaces, tabs and newlines. M-\ (delete-horizontal-space) deletes all the spaces and tab characters before and after point. M-(SPC) (just-one-space) does likewise but leaves a single space after point, regardless of the number of spaces that existed previously (even zero).

C-x C-o (delete-blank-lines) deletes all blank lines after the current line. If the current line is blank, it deletes all blank lines preceding the current line as well (leaving one blank line, the current line).

M-^ (delete-indentation) joins the current line and the previous line, by deleting a newline and all surrounding spaces, usually leaving a single space. See Chapter 20 [Indentation], page 195.

9.1.2 Killing by Lines

C-k   Kill rest of line or one or more lines (kill-line).

The simplest kill command is C-k. If given at the beginning of a line, it kills all the text on the line, leaving it blank. When used on a blank line, it kills the whole line including its newline. To kill an entire non-blank line, go to the beginning and type C-k twice.

More generally, C-k kills from point up to the end of the line, unless it is at the end of a line. In that case it kills the newline following point, thus merging the next line into the current one. Spaces and tabs that you can't see at the end of the line are ignored when deciding which case applies, so if point appears to be at the end of the line, you can be sure C-k will kill the newline.

When C-k is given a positive argument, it kills that many lines and the newlines that follow them (however, text on the current line before point is spared). With a negative argument −n, it kills n lines preceding the current line (together with the text on the current line before point). Thus, C-u - 2 C-k at the front of a line kills the two previous lines.

C-k with an argument of zero kills the text before point on the current line.

If the variable kill-whole-line is non-nil, C-k at the very beginning of a line kills the entire line including the following newline. This variable is normally nil.

9.1.3 Other Kill Commands

C-w   Kill region (from point to the mark) (`kill-region`).

M-d   Kill word (`kill-word`). See Section 21.1 [Words], page 199.

M-⟨DEL⟩   Kill word backwards (`backward-kill-word`).

C-x ⟨DEL⟩   Kill back to beginning of sentence (`backward-kill-sentence`).
               See Section 21.2 [Sentences], page 200.

M-k   Kill to end of sentence (`kill-sentence`).

C-M-k   Kill sexp (`kill-sexp`). See Section 22.2 [Lists], page 228.

M-z char   Kill through the next occurrence of char (`zap-to-char`).

A kill command which is very general is C-w (`kill-region`), which kills everything between point and the mark. With this command, you can kill any contiguous sequence of characters, if you first set the region around them.

A convenient way of killing is combined with searching: M-z (`zap-to-char`) reads a character and kills from point up to (and including) the next occurrence of that character in the buffer. A numeric argument acts as a repeat count. A negative argument means to search backward and kill text before point.

Other syntactic units can be killed: words, with M-⟨DEL⟩ and M-d (see Section 21.1 [Words], page 199); sexps, with C-M-k (see Section 22.2 [Lists], page 228); and sentences, with C-x ⟨DEL⟩ and M-k (see Section 21.2 [Sentences], page 200).

You can use kill commands in read-only buffers. They don't actually change the buffer, and they beep to warn you of that, but they do copy the text you tried to kill into the kill ring, so you can yank it into other buffers. Most of the kill commands move point across the text they copy in this way, so that successive kill commands build up a single kill ring entry as usual.

9.2 Yanking

Yanking means reinserting text previously killed. This is what some systems call "pasting." The usual way to move or copy text is to kill it and then yank it elsewhere one or more times.

C-y   Yank last killed text (`yank`).

M-y   Replace text just yanked with an earlier batch of killed text (`yank-pop`).

M-w   Save region as last killed text without actually killing it (`kill-ring-save`).

C-M-w   Append next kill to last batch of killed text (`append-next-kill`).

9.2.1 The Kill Ring

All killed text is recorded in the *kill ring*, a list of blocks of text that have been killed. There is only one kill ring, shared by all buffers, so you can kill text in one buffer and yank it in another buffer. This is the usual way to move text from one file to another. (See Section 9.3 [Accumulating Text], page 70, for some other ways.)

The command `C-y` (`yank`) reinserts the text of the most recent kill. It leaves the cursor at the end of the text. It sets the mark at the beginning of the text. See Chapter 8 [Mark], page 59.

`C-u C-y` leaves the cursor in front of the text, and sets the mark after it. This happens only if the argument is specified with just a `C-u`, precisely. Any other sort of argument, including `C-u` and digits, specifies an earlier kill to yank (see Section 9.2.3 [Earlier Kills], page 69).

To copy a block of text, you can use `M-w` (`kill-ring-save`), which copies the region into the kill ring without removing it from the buffer. This is approximately equivalent to `C-w` followed by `C-x u`, except that `M-w` does not alter the undo history and does not temporarily change the screen.

9.2.2 Appending Kills

Normally, each kill command pushes a new entry onto the kill ring. However, two or more kill commands in a row combine their text into a single entry, so that a single `C-y` yanks all the text as a unit, just as it was before it was killed.

Thus, if you want to yank text as a unit, you need not kill all of it with one command; you can keep killing line after line, or word after word, until you have killed it all, and you can still get it all back at once.

Commands that kill forward from point add onto the end of the previous killed text. Commands that kill backward from point add text onto the beginning. This way, any sequence of mixed forward and backward kill commands puts all the killed text into one entry without rearrangement. Numeric arguments do not break the sequence of appending kills. For example, suppose the buffer contains this text:

> `This is a line ⋆of sample text.`

with point shown by ⋆. If you type `M-d M-⟨DEL⟩ M-d M-⟨DEL⟩`, killing alternately forward and backward, you end up with 'a line of sample' as one entry in the kill ring, and 'This is   text.' in the buffer. (Note the double space, which you can clean up with `M-⟨SPC⟩` or `M-q`.)

Another way to kill the same text is to move back two words with `M-b M-b`, then kill all four words forward with `C-u M-d`. This produces exactly the same results in the buffer and in the kill ring. `M-f M-f C-u M-⟨DEL⟩` kills the same text, all going backward; once again, the result is the same. The text in the kill ring entry always has the same order that it had in the buffer before you killed it.

If a kill command is separated from the last kill command by other commands (not just numeric arguments), it starts a new entry on the kill ring. But you can force it to append by first typing the command C-M-w (append-next-kill) right before it. The C-M-w tells the following command, if it is a kill command, to append the text it kills to the last killed text, instead of starting a new entry. With C-M-w, you can kill several separated pieces of text and accumulate them to be yanked back in one place.

A kill command following M-w does not append to the text that M-w copied into the kill ring.

9.2.3 Yanking Earlier Kills

To recover killed text that is no longer the most recent kill, use the M-y command (yank-pop). It takes the text previously yanked and replaces it with the text from an earlier kill. So, to recover the text of the next-to-the-last kill, first use C-y to yank the last kill, and then use M-y to replace it with the previous kill. M-y is allowed only after a C-y or another M-y.

You can understand M-y in terms of a "last yank" pointer which points at an entry in the kill ring. Each time you kill, the "last yank" pointer moves to the newly made entry at the front of the ring. C-y yanks the entry which the "last yank" pointer points to. M-y moves the "last yank" pointer to a different entry, and the text in the buffer changes to match. Enough M-y commands can move the pointer to any entry in the ring, so you can get any entry into the buffer. Eventually the pointer reaches the end of the ring; the next M-y moves it to the first entry again.

M-y moves the "last yank" pointer around the ring, but it does not change the order of the entries in the ring, which always runs from the most recent kill at the front to the oldest one still remembered.

M-y can take a numeric argument, which tells it how many entries to advance the "last yank" pointer by. A negative argument moves the pointer toward the front of the ring; from the front of the ring, it moves "around" to the last entry and continues forward from there.

Once the text you are looking for is brought into the buffer, you can stop doing M-y commands and it will stay there. It's just a copy of the kill ring entry, so editing it in the buffer does not change what's in the ring. As long as no new killing is done, the "last yank" pointer remains at the same place in the kill ring, so repeating C-y will yank another copy of the same previous kill.

If you know how many M-y commands it would take to find the text you want, you can yank that text in one step using C-y with a numeric argument. C-y with an argument restores the text the specified number of entries back in the kill ring. Thus, C-u 2 C-y gets the next-to-the-last block of killed text. It is equivalent to C-y M-y. C-y with a numeric argument starts counting from the "last yank" pointer, and sets the "last yank" pointer to the entry that it yanks.

The length of the kill ring is controlled by the variable `kill-ring-max`; no more than that many blocks of killed text are saved.

The actual contents of the kill ring are stored in a variable named `kill-ring`; you can view the entire contents of the kill ring with the command `C-h v kill-ring`.

9.3 Accumulating Text

Usually we copy or move text by killing it and yanking it, but there are other methods convenient for copying one block of text in many places, or for copying many scattered blocks of text into one place. To copy one block to many places, store it in a register (see Chapter 10 [Registers], page 75). Here we describe the commands to accumulate scattered pieces of text into a buffer or into a file.

`M-x append-to-buffer`
> Append region to contents of specified buffer.

`M-x prepend-to-buffer`
> Prepend region to contents of specified buffer.

`M-x copy-to-buffer`
> Copy region into specified buffer, deleting that buffer's old contents.

`M-x insert-buffer`
> Insert contents of specified buffer into current buffer at point.

`M-x append-to-file`
> Append region to contents of specified file, at the end.

To accumulate text into a buffer, use `M-x append-to-buffer`. This reads a buffer name, then inserts a copy of the region into the buffer specified. If you specify a nonexistent buffer, `append-to-buffer` creates the buffer. The text is inserted wherever point is in that buffer. If you have been using the buffer for editing, the copied text goes into the middle of the text of the buffer, wherever point happens to be in it.

Point in that buffer is left at the end of the copied text, so successive uses of `append-to-buffer` accumulate the text in the specified buffer in the same order as they were copied. Strictly speaking, `append-to-buffer` does not always append to the text already in the buffer—it appends only if point in that buffer is at the end. However, if `append-to-buffer` is the only command you use to alter a buffer, then point is always at the end.

`M-x prepend-to-buffer` is just like `append-to-buffer` except that point in the other buffer is left before the copied text, so successive prependings add text in reverse order. `M-x copy-to-buffer` is similar except that any existing text in the other buffer is deleted, so the buffer is left containing just the text newly copied into it.

To retrieve the accumulated text from another buffer, use the command `M-x insert-buffer`; this too takes *buffername* as an argument. It inserts a copy of the text in buffer *buffername* into the selected buffer. You can alternatively select the other buffer for editing, then optionally move text from it by killing. See Chapter 15 [Buffers], page 143, for background information on buffers.

Instead of accumulating text within Emacs, in a buffer, you can append text directly into a file with `M-x append-to-file`, which takes *filename* as an argument. It adds the text of the region to the end of the specified file. The file is changed immediately on disk.

You should use `append-to-file` only with files that are *not* being visited in Emacs. Using it on a file that you are editing in Emacs would change the file behind Emacs's back, which can lead to losing some of your editing.

9.4 Rectangles

The rectangle commands operate on rectangular areas of the text: all the characters between a certain pair of columns, in a certain range of lines. Commands are provided to kill rectangles, yank killed rectangles, clear them out, fill them with blanks or text, or delete them. Rectangle commands are useful with text in multicolumn formats, and for changing text into or out of such formats.

When you must specify a rectangle for a command to work on, you do it by putting the mark at one corner and point at the opposite corner. The rectangle thus specified is called the *region-rectangle* because you control it in about the same way the region is controlled. But remember that a given combination of point and mark values can be interpreted either as a region or as a rectangle, depending on the command that uses them.

If point and the mark are in the same column, the rectangle they delimit is empty. If they are in the same line, the rectangle is one line high. This asymmetry between lines and columns comes about because point (and likewise the mark) is between two columns, but within a line.

`C-x r k`   Kill the text of the region-rectangle, saving its contents as the "last killed rectangle" (`kill-rectangle`).

`C-x r d`   Delete the text of the region-rectangle (`delete-rectangle`).

`C-x r y`   Yank the last killed rectangle with its upper left corner at point (`yank-rectangle`).

`C-x r o`   Insert blank space to fill the space of the region-rectangle (`open-rectangle`). This pushes the previous contents of the region-rectangle rightward.

`M-x clear-rectangle`

Clear the region-rectangle by replacing its contents with spaces.

M-x delete-whitespace-rectangle
> Delete whitespace in each of the lines on the specified rectangle, starting from the left edge column of the rectangle.

C-x r t *string* (RET)
> Insert *string* on each line of the region-rectangle (string-rectangle).

The rectangle operations fall into two classes: commands deleting and inserting rectangles, and commands for blank rectangles.

There are two ways to get rid of the text in a rectangle: you can discard the text (delete it) or save it as the "last killed" rectangle. The commands for these two ways are C-x r d (delete-rectangle) and C-x r k (kill-rectangle). In either case, the portion of each line that falls inside the rectangle's boundaries is deleted, causing following text (if any) on the line to move left into the gap.

Note that "killing" a rectangle is not killing in the usual sense; the rectangle is not stored in the kill ring, but in a special place that can only record the most recent rectangle killed. This is because yanking a rectangle is so different from yanking linear text that different yank commands have to be used and yank-popping is hard to make sense of.

To yank the last killed rectangle, type C-x r y (yank-rectangle). Yanking a rectangle is the opposite of killing one. Point specifies where to put the rectangle's upper left corner. The rectangle's first line is inserted there, the rectangle's second line is inserted at a position one line vertically down, and so on. The number of lines affected is determined by the height of the saved rectangle.

You can convert single-column lists into double-column lists using rectangle killing and yanking; kill the second half of the list as a rectangle and then yank it beside the first line of the list. See Section 30.9 [Two-Column], page 383, for another way to edit multi-column text.

You can also copy rectangles into and out of registers with C-x r r r and C-x r i r. See Section 10.3 [Rectangle Registers], page 76.

There are two commands you can use for making blank rectangles: M-x clear-rectangle which blanks out existing text, and C-x r o (open-rectangle) which inserts a blank rectangle. Clearing a rectangle is equivalent to deleting it and then inserting a blank rectangle of the same size.

The command M-x delete-whitespace-rectangle deletes horizontal whitespace starting from a particular column. This applies to each of the lines in the rectangle, and the column is specified by the left edge of the rectangle. The right edge of the rectangle does not make any difference to this command.

The command C-x r t (M-x string-rectangle) replaces the rectangle with a specified string (inserted once on each line). The string's width need not be the same as the width of the rectangle. If the string's width is less, the text after the rectangle shifts left; if the string is wider than the rectangle, the text after the rectangle shifts right.

10   Registers

Emacs *registers* are places you can save text or positions for later use. Once you save text or a rectangle in a register, you can copy it into the buffer once or many times; you can move point to a position saved in a register once or many times.

Each register has a name which is a single character. A register can store a piece of text, a rectangle, a position, a window configuration, or a file name, but only one thing at any given time. Whatever you store in a register remains there until you store something else in that register. To see what a register *r* contains, use `M-x view-register`.

`M-x view-register` (RET) *r*
> Display a description of what register *r* contains.

10.1   Saving Positions in Registers

Saving a position records a place in a buffer so that you can move back there later. Moving to a saved position switches to that buffer and moves point to that place in it.

`C-x r` (SPC) *r*
> Save position of point in register *r* (`point-to-register`).

`C-x r j` *r*   Jump to the position saved in register *r* (`jump-to-register`).

To save the current position of point in a register, choose a name *r* and type `C-x r` (SPC) *r*. The register *r* retains the position thus saved until you store something else in that register.

The command `C-x r j` *r* moves point to the position recorded in register *r*. The register is not affected; it continues to record the same position. You can jump to the saved position any number of times.

If you use `C-x r j` to go to a saved position, but the buffer it was saved from has been killed, `C-x r j` tries to create the buffer again by visiting the same file. Of course, this works only for buffers that were visiting files.

10.2   Saving Text in Registers

When you want to insert a copy of the same piece of text several times, it may be inconvenient to yank it from the kill ring, since each subsequent kill moves that entry further down the ring. An alternative is to store the text in a register and later retrieve it.

`C-x r s` *r*   Copy region into register *r* (`copy-to-register`).

`C-x r i` *r*   Insert text from register *r* (`insert-register`).

C-x r s *r* stores a copy of the text of the region into the register named *r*. Given a numeric argument, C-x r s *r* deletes the text from the buffer as well.

C-x r i *r* inserts in the buffer the text from register *r*. Normally it leaves point before the text and places the mark after, but with a numeric argument (C-u) it puts point after the text and the mark before.

10.3 Saving Rectangles in Registers

A register can contain a rectangle instead of linear text. The rectangle is represented as a list of strings. See Section 9.4 [Rectangles], page 71, for basic information on how to specify a rectangle in the buffer.

C-x r r *r*   Copy the region-rectangle into register *r* (copy-rectangle-to-register). With numeric argument, delete it as well.

C-x r i *r*   Insert the rectangle stored in register *r* (if it contains a rectangle) (insert-register).

The C-x r i *r* command inserts a text string if the register contains one, and inserts a rectangle if the register contains one.

See also the command sort-columns, which you can think of as sorting a rectangle. See Section 30.7 [Sorting], page 380.

10.4 Saving Window Configurations in Registers

You can save the window configuration of the selected frame in a register, or even the configuration of all windows in all frames, and restore the configuration later.

C-x r w *r*   Save the state of the selected frame's windows in register *r* (window-configuration-to-register).

C-x r f *r*   Save the state of all frames, including all their windows, in register *r* (frame-configuration-to-register).

Use C-x r j *r* to restore a window or frame configuration. This is the same command used to restore a cursor position. When you restore a frame configuration, any existing frames not included in the configuration become invisible. If you wish to delete these frames instead, use C-u C-x r j *r*.

10.5 Keeping Numbers in Registers

There are commands to store a number in a register, to insert the number in the buffer in decimal, and to increment it. These commands can be useful in keyboard macros (see Section 31.3 [Keyboard Macros], page 405).

C-u *number* C-x r n *reg*
             Store *number* into register *reg* (number-to-register).

C-u *number* C-x r + *reg*
> Increment the number in register *reg* by *number* (increment-register).

C-x r g *reg*
> Insert the number from register *reg* into the buffer.

C-x r g is the same command used to insert any other sort of register contents into the buffer.

10.6 Keeping File Names in Registers

If you visit certain file names frequently, you can visit them more conveniently if you put their names in registers. Here's the Lisp code used to put a file name in a register:

    (set-register ?r '(file . name))

For example,

    (set-register ?z '(file . "/gd/gnu/emacs/19.0/src/ChangeLog"))

puts the file name shown in register 'z'.

To visit the file whose name is in register *r*, type C-x r j *r*. (This is the same command used to jump to a position or restore a frame configuration.)

10.7 Bookmarks

Bookmarks are somewhat like registers in that they record positions you can jump to. Unlike registers, they have long names, and they persist automatically from one Emacs session to the next. The prototypical use of bookmarks is to record "where you were reading" in various files.

C-x r m ⟨RET⟩
> Set the bookmark for the visited file, at point.

C-x r m *bookmark* ⟨RET⟩
> Set the bookmark named *bookmark* at point (bookmark-set).

C-x r b *bookmark* ⟨RET⟩
> Jump to the bookmark named *bookmark* (bookmark-jump).

C-x r l   List all bookmarks (list-bookmarks).

M-x bookmark-save
> Save all the current bookmark values in the default bookmark file.

The prototypical use for bookmarks is to record one current position in each of several files. So the command C-x r m, which sets a bookmark, uses the visited file name as the default for the bookmark name. If you name each bookmark after the file it points to, then you can conveniently revisit any of those files with `C-x r b`, and move to the position of the bookmark at the same time.

To display a list of all your bookmarks in a separate buffer, type `C-x r l` (`list-bookmarks`). If you switch to that buffer, you can use it to edit your bookmark definitions or annotate the bookmarks. Type `C-h m` in that buffer for more information about its special editing commands.

When you kill Emacs, Emacs offers to save your bookmark values in your default bookmark file, '`~/.emacs.bmk`', if you have changed any bookmark values. You can also save the bookmarks at any time with the `M-x bookmark-save` command. The bookmark commands load your default bookmark file automatically. This saving and loading is how bookmarks persist from one Emacs session to the next.

If you set the variable `bookmark-save-flag` to 1, then each command that sets a bookmark will also save your bookmarks; this way, you don't lose any bookmark values even if Emacs crashes. (The value, if a number, says how many bookmark modifications should go by between saving.)

Bookmark position values are saved with surrounding context, so that `bookmark-jump` can find the proper position even if the file is modified slightly. The variable `bookmark-search-size` says how many characters of context to record, on each side of the bookmark's position.

Here are some additional commands for working with bookmarks:

`M-x bookmark-load` (RET) *filename* (RET)
> Load a file named *filename* that contains a list of bookmark values. You can use this command, as well as `bookmark-write`, to work with other files of bookmark values in addition to your default bookmark file.

`M-x bookmark-write` (RET) *filename* (RET)
> Save all the current bookmark values in the file *filename*.

`M-x bookmark-delete` (RET) *bookmark* (RET)
> Delete the bookmark named *bookmark*.

`M-x bookmark-insert-location` (RET) *bookmark* (RET)
> Insert in the buffer the name of the file that bookmark *bookmark* points to.

`M-x bookmark-insert` (RET) *bookmark* (RET)
> Insert in the buffer the *contents* of the file that bookmark *bookmark* points to.

11 Controlling the Display

Since only part of a large buffer fits in the window, Emacs tries to show a part that is likely to be interesting. Display-control commands allow you to specify which part of the text you want to see, and how to display it.

11.1 Scrolling

If a buffer contains text that is too large to fit entirely within a window that is displaying the buffer, Emacs shows a contiguous portion of the text. The portion shown always contains point.

Scrolling means moving text up or down in the window so that different parts of the text are visible. Scrolling forward means that text moves up, and new text appears at the bottom. Scrolling backward moves text down and new text appears at the top.

Scrolling happens automatically if you move point past the bottom or top of the window. You can also explicitly request scrolling with the commands in this section.

C-l   Clear screen and redisplay, scrolling the selected window to center point vertically within it (**recenter**).

C-v   Scroll forward (a windowful or a specified number of lines) (**scroll-up**).

(NEXT)   Likewise, scroll forward.

M-v   Scroll backward (**scroll-down**).

(PRIOR)   Likewise, scroll backward.

arg C-l   Scroll so point is on line *arg* (**recenter**).

C-M-l   Scroll heuristically to bring useful information onto the screen (**reposition-window**).

The most basic scrolling command is C-l (**recenter**) with no argument. It clears the entire screen and redisplays all windows. In addition, it scrolls the selected window so that point is halfway down from the top of the window.

The scrolling commands C-v and M-v let you move all the text in the window up or down a few lines. C-v (**scroll-up**) with an argument shows you that many more lines at the bottom of the window, moving the text and point up together as C-l might. C-v with a negative argument shows you more lines at the top of the window. M-v (**scroll-down**) is like C-v, but moves in the opposite direction. The function keys (NEXT) and (PRIOR) are equivalent to C-v and M-v.

The names of scroll commands are based on the direction that the text moves in the window. Thus, the command to scroll forward is called **scroll-up** because it moves the text upward on the screen.

To read the buffer a windowful at a time, use C-v with no argument. It takes the last two lines at the bottom of the window and puts them at the top, followed by nearly a whole windowful of lines not previously visible. If point was in the text scrolled off the top, it moves to the new top of the window. M-v with no argument moves backward with overlap similarly. The number of lines of overlap across a C-v or M-v is controlled by the variable next-screen-context-lines; by default, it is 2.

Some users like the full-screen scroll commands to keep point at the same screen line. To enable this behavior, set the variable scroll-preserve-screen-position to a non-nil value. This mode is convenient for browsing through a file by scrolling by screenfuls; if you come back to the screen where you started, point goes back to the line where it started. However, this mode is inconvenient when you move to the next screen in order to move point to the text there.

Another way to do scrolling is with C-l with a numeric argument. C-l does not clear the screen when given an argument; it only scrolls the selected window. With a positive argument n, it repositions text to put point n lines down from the top. An argument of zero puts point on the very top line. Point does not move with respect to the text; rather, the text and point move rigidly on the screen. C-l with a negative argument puts point that many lines from the bottom of the window. For example, C-u - 1 C-l puts point on the bottom line, and C-u - 5 C-l puts it five lines from the bottom. Just C-u as argument, as in C-u C-l, scrolls point to the center of the selected window.

The C-M-l command (reposition-window) scrolls the current window heuristically in a way designed to get useful information onto the screen. For example, in a Lisp file, this command tries to get the entire current defun onto the screen if possible.

Scrolling happens automatically if point has moved out of the visible portion of the text when it is time to display. Normally, automatic scrolling centers point vertically within the window. However, if you set scroll-conservatively to a small number n, then if you move point just a little off the screen—less than n lines—then Emacs scrolls the text just far enough to bring point back on screen. By default, scroll-conservatively is 0.

The variable scroll-margin restricts how close point can come to the top or bottom of a window. Its value is a number of screen lines; if point comes within that many lines of the top or bottom of the window, Emacs recenters the window. By default, scroll-margin is 0.

11.2 Horizontal Scrolling

Horizontal scrolling means shifting all the lines sideways within a window—so that some of the text near the left margin is not displayed at all.

C-x <   Scroll text in current window to the left (`scroll-left`).

C-x >   Scroll to the right (`scroll-right`).

When a window has been scrolled horizontally, text lines are truncated rather than continued (see Section 4.8 [Continuation Lines], page 35), with a '`$`' appearing in the first column when there is text truncated to the left, and in the last column when there is text truncated to the right.

The command C-x < (`scroll-left`) scrolls the selected window to the left by *n* columns with argument *n*. This moves part of the beginning of each line off the left edge of the window. With no argument, it scrolls by almost the full width of the window (two columns less, to be precise).

C-x > (`scroll-right`) scrolls similarly to the right. The window cannot be scrolled any farther to the right once it is displayed normally (with each line starting at the window's left margin); attempting to do so has no effect. This means that you don't have to calculate the argument precisely for C-x >; any sufficiently large argument will restore the normal display.

You can request automatic horizontal scrolling by enabling Hscroll mode. When this mode is enabled, Emacs scrolls a window horizontally whenever that is necessary to keep point visible and not too far from the left or right edge. The command to enable or disable this mode is M-x `hscroll-mode`.

11.3 Follow Mode

Follow mode is a minor mode that makes two windows showing the same buffer scroll as one tall "virtual window." To use Follow mode, go to a frame with just one window, split it into two side-by-side windows using C-x 3, and then type M-x `follow-mode`. From then on, you can edit the buffer in either of the two windows, or scroll either one; the other window follows it.

To turn off Follow mode, type M-x `follow-mode` a second time.

11.4 Selective Display

Emacs has the ability to hide lines indented more than a certain number of columns (you specify how many columns). You can use this to get an overview of a part of a program.

To hide lines, type C-x $ (`set-selective-display`) with a numeric argument *n*. Then lines with at least *n* columns of indentation disappear from the screen. The only indication of their presence is that three dots ('...') appear at the end of each visible line that is followed by one or more hidden ones.

The commands C-n and C-p move across the hidden lines as if they were not there.

The hidden lines are still present in the buffer, and most editing commands see them as usual, so you may find point in the middle of the hidden text. When this happens, the cursor appears at the end of the previous line, after the three dots. If point is at the end of the visible line, before the newline that ends it, the cursor appears before the three dots.

To make all lines visible again, type `C-x $` with no argument.

If you set the variable `selective-display-ellipses` to `nil`, the three dots do not appear at the end of a line that precedes hidden lines. Then there is no visible indication of the hidden lines. This variable becomes local automatically when set.

11.5 Optional Mode Line Features

The current line number of point appears in the mode line when Line Number mode is enabled. Use the command `M-x line-number-mode` to turn this mode on and off; normally it is on. The line number appears before the buffer percentage *pos*, with the letter 'L' to indicate what it is. See Section 31.1 [Minor Modes], page 391, for more information about minor modes and about how to use this command.

If the buffer is very large (larger than the value of `line-number-display-limit`), then the line number doesn't appear. Emacs doesn't compute the line number when the buffer is large, because that would be too slow. If you have narrowed the buffer (see Section 30.8 [Narrowing], page 382), the displayed line number is relative to the accessible portion of the buffer.

You can also display the current column number by turning on Column Number mode. It displays the current column number preceded by the letter 'C'. Type `M-x column-number-mode` to toggle this mode.

Emacs can optionally display the time and system load in all mode lines. To enable this feature, type `M-x display-time`. The information added to the mode line usually appears after the buffer name, before the mode names and their parentheses. It looks like this:

  hh:*mm*pm *l.ll*

Here *hh* and *mm* are the hour and minute, followed always by 'am' or 'pm'. *l.ll* is the average number of running processes in the whole system recently. (Some fields may be missing if your operating system cannot support them.) If you prefer time display in 24-hour format, set the variable `display-time-24hr-format` to `t`.

The word 'Mail' appears after the load level if there is mail for you that you have not read yet.

11.6 How Text Is Displayed

ASCII printing characters (octal codes 040 through 0176) in Emacs buffers are displayed with their graphics. So are non-ASCII multibyte printing characters (octal codes above 0400).

Some ASCII control characters are displayed in special ways. The newline character (octal code 012) is displayed by starting a new line. The tab character (octal code 011) is displayed by moving to the next tab stop column (normally every 8 columns).

Other ASCII control characters are normally displayed as a caret ('^') followed by the non-control version of the character; thus, control-A is displayed as '^A'.

Non-ASCII characters 0200 through 0377 are displayed with octal escape sequences; thus, character code 0243 (octal) is displayed as '\243'. However, if you enable European display, most of these characters become non-ASCII printing characters, and are displayed using their graphics (assuming your terminal supports them). See Section 18.12 [Single-Byte European Support], page 188.

11.7 Variables Controlling Display

This section contains information for customization only. Beginning users should skip it.

The variable `mode-line-inverse-video` controls whether the mode line is displayed in inverse video (assuming the terminal supports it); `nil` means don't do so. See Section 1.3 [Mode Line], page 17. If you specify the foreground color for the `modeline` face, and `mode-line-inverse-video` is non-`nil`, then the default background color for that face is the usual foreground color. See Section 17.13 [Faces], page 166.

If the variable `inverse-video` is non-`nil`, Emacs attempts to invert all the lines of the display from what they normally are.

If the variable `visible-bell` is non-`nil`, Emacs attempts to make the whole screen blink when it would normally make an audible bell sound. This variable has no effect if your terminal does not have a way to make the screen blink.

When you reenter Emacs after suspending, Emacs normally clears the screen and redraws the entire display. On some terminals with more than one page of memory, it is possible to arrange the termcap entry so that the 'ti' and 'te' strings (output to the terminal when Emacs is entered and exited, respectively) switch between pages of memory so as to use one page for Emacs and another page for other output. Then you might want to set the variable `no-redraw-on-reenter` non-`nil`; this tells Emacs to assume, when resumed, that the screen page it is using still contains what Emacs last wrote there.

The variable `echo-keystrokes` controls the echoing of multi-character keys; its value is the number of seconds of pause required to cause echoing to start, or zero meaning don't echo at all. See Section 1.2 [Echo Area], page 16.

If the variable `ctl-arrow` is `nil`, control characters in the buffer are displayed with octal escape sequences, except for newline and tab. Altering the value of `ctl-arrow` makes it local to the current buffer; until that time, the default value is in effect. The default is initially `t`. See section "Display Tables" in *The Emacs Lisp Reference Manual*.

Normally, a tab character in the buffer is displayed as whitespace which extends to the next display tab stop position, and display tab stops come at intervals equal to eight spaces. The number of spaces per tab is controlled by the variable `tab-width`, which is made local by changing it, just like `ctl-arrow`. Note that how the tab character in the buffer is displayed has nothing to do with the definition of (TAB) as a command. The variable `tab-width` must have an integer value between 1 and 1000, inclusive.

If the variable `truncate-lines` is non-`nil`, then each line of text gets just one screen line for display; if the text line is too long, display shows only the part that fits. If `truncate-lines` is `nil`, then long text lines display as more than one screen line, enough to show the whole text of the line. See Section 4.8 [Continuation Lines], page 35. Altering the value of `truncate-lines` makes it local to the current buffer; until that time, the default value is in effect. The default is initially `nil`.

If the variable `truncate-partial-width-windows` is non-`nil`, it forces truncation rather than continuation in any window less than the full width of the screen or frame, regardless of the value of `truncate-lines`. For information about side-by-side windows, see Section 16.2 [Split Window], page 152. See also section "Display" in *The Emacs Lisp Reference Manual*.

The variable `baud-rate` holds the output speed of the terminal, as far as Emacs knows. Setting this variable does not change the speed of actual data transmission, but the value is used for calculations such as padding. It also affects decisions about whether to scroll part of the screen or redraw it instead—even when using a window system. (We designed it this way, despite the fact that a window system has no true "output speed," to give you a way to tune these decisions.)

You can customize the way any particular character code is displayed by means of a display table. See section "Display Tables" in *The Emacs Lisp Reference Manual*.

12 Searching and Replacement

Like other editors, Emacs has commands for searching for occurrences of a string. The principal search command is unusual in that it is *incremental*; it begins to search before you have finished typing the search string. There are also nonincremental search commands more like those of other editors.

Besides the usual `replace-string` command that finds all occurrences of one string and replaces them with another, Emacs has a fancy replacement command called `query-replace` which asks interactively which occurrences to replace.

12.1 Incremental Search

An incremental search begins searching as soon as you type the first character of the search string. As you type in the search string, Emacs shows you where the string (as you have typed it so far) would be found. When you have typed enough characters to identify the place you want, you can stop. Depending on what you plan to do next, you may or may not need to terminate the search explicitly with (RET).

C-s   Incremental search forward (`isearch-forward`).

C-r   Incremental search backward (`isearch-backward`).

C-s starts an incremental search. C-s reads characters from the keyboard and positions the cursor at the first occurrence of the characters that you have typed. If you type C-s and then F, the cursor moves right after the first 'F'. Type an O, and see the cursor move to after the first 'FO'. After another O, the cursor is after the first 'FOO' after the place where you started the search. At each step, the buffer text that matches the search string is highlighted, if the terminal can do that; at each step, the current search string is updated in the echo area.

If you make a mistake in typing the search string, you can cancel characters with (DEL). Each (DEL) cancels the last character of search string. This does not happen until Emacs is ready to read another input character; first it must either find, or fail to find, the character you want to erase. If you do not want to wait for this to happen, use C-g as described below.

When you are satisfied with the place you have reached, you can type (RET), which stops searching, leaving the cursor where the search brought it. Also, any command not specially meaningful in searches stops the searching and is then executed. Thus, typing C-a would exit the search and then move to the beginning of the line. (RET) is necessary only if the next command you want to type is a printing character, (DEL), (RET), or another control character that is special within searches (C-q, C-w, C-r, C-s, C-y, M-y, M-r, or M-s).

Sometimes you search for 'FOO' and find it, but not the one you expected to find. There was a second 'FOO' that you forgot about, before the one you were aiming for. In this event, type another C-s to move to the next occurrence of the search string. This can be done any number of times. If you overshoot, you can cancel some C-s characters with (DEL).

After you exit a search, you can search for the same string again by typing just C-s C-s: the first C-s is the key that invokes incremental search, and the second C-s means "search again."

To reuse earlier search strings, use the *search ring*. The commands M-p and M-n move through the ring to pick a search string to reuse. These commands leave the selected search ring element in the minibuffer, where you can edit it. Type C-s or C-r to terminate editing the string and search for it.

If your string is not found at all, the echo area says 'Failing I-Search'. The cursor is after the place where Emacs found as much of your string as it could. Thus, if you search for 'FOOT', and there is no 'FOOT', you might see the cursor after the 'FOO' in 'FOOL'. At this point there are several things you can do. If your string was mistyped, you can rub some of it out and correct it. If you like the place you have found, you can type (RET) or some other Emacs command to "accept what the search offered." Or you can type C-g, which removes from the search string the characters that could not be found (the 'T' in 'FOOT'), leaving those that were found (the 'FOO' in 'FOOT'). A second C-g at that point cancels the search entirely, returning point to where it was when the search started.

An upper-case letter in the search string makes the search case-sensitive. If you delete the upper-case character from the search string, it ceases to have this effect. See Section 12.6 [Search Case], page 94.

If a search is failing and you ask to repeat it by typing another C-s, it starts again from the beginning of the buffer. Repeating a failing reverse search with C-r starts again from the end. This is called *wrapping around*. 'Wrapped' appears in the search prompt once this has happened. If you keep on going past the original starting point of the search, it changes to 'Overwrapped', which means that you are revisiting matches that you have already seen.

The C-g "quit" character does special things during searches; just what it does depends on the status of the search. If the search has found what you specified and is waiting for input, C-g cancels the entire search. The cursor moves back to where you started the search. If C-g is typed when there are characters in the search string that have not been found—because Emacs is still searching for them, or because it has failed to find them—then the search string characters which have not been found are discarded from the search string. With them gone, the search is now successful and waiting for more input, so a second C-g will cancel the entire search.

To search for a newline, type C-j. To search for another control character, such as control-S or carriage return, you must quote it by typing C-q first. This function of C-q is analogous to its use for insertion (see Section 4.1 [Inserting Text], page 29): it causes the following character to be treated the way any "ordinary" character is treated in the same context. You can also specify a character by its octal code: enter C-q followed by a sequence of octal digits.

You can change to searching backwards with C-r. If a search fails because the place you started was too late in the file, you should do this. Repeated C-r keeps looking for more occurrences backwards. A C-s starts going forwards again. C-r in a search can be canceled with (DEL).

If you know initially that you want to search backwards, you can use C-r instead of C-s to start the search, because C-r as a key runs a command (isearch-backward) to search backward. A backward search finds matches that are entirely before the starting point, just as a forward search finds matches that begin after it.

The characters C-y and C-w can be used in incremental search to grab text from the buffer into the search string. This makes it convenient to search for another occurrence of text at point. C-w copies the word after point as part of the search string, advancing point over that word. Another C-s to repeat the search will then search for a string including that word. C-y is similar to C-w but copies all the rest of the current line into the search string. Both C-y and C-w convert the text they copy to lower case if the search is currently not case-sensitive; this is so the search remains case-insensitive.

The character M-y copies text from the kill ring into the search string. It uses the same text that C-y as a command would yank. See Section 9.2 [Yanking], page 67.

When you exit the incremental search, it sets the mark to where point *was*, before the search. That is convenient for moving back there. In Transient Mark mode, incremental search sets the mark without activating it, and does so only if the mark is not already active.

To customize the special characters that incremental search understands, alter their bindings in the keymap isearch-mode-map. For a list of bindings, look at the documentation of isearch-mode with C-h f isearch-mode (RET).

12.1.1 Slow Terminal Incremental Search

Incremental search on a slow terminal uses a modified style of display that is designed to take less time. Instead of redisplaying the buffer at each place the search gets to, it creates a new single-line window and uses that to display the line that the search has found. The single-line window comes into play as soon as point gets outside of the text that is already on the screen.

When you terminate the search, the single-line window is removed. Then Emacs redisplays the window in which the search was done, to show its new position of point.

The slow terminal style of display is used when the terminal baud rate is less than or equal to the value of the variable `search-slow-speed`, initially 1200.

The number of lines to use in slow terminal search display is controlled by the variable `search-slow-window-lines`. Its normal value is 1.

12.2 Nonincremental Search

Emacs also has conventional nonincremental search commands, which require you to type the entire search string before searching begins.

C-s (RET) *string* (RET)
> Search for *string*.

C-r (RET) *string* (RET)
> Search backward for *string*.

To do a nonincremental search, first type C-s (RET). This enters the minibuffer to read the search string; terminate the string with (RET), and then the search takes place. If the string is not found, the search command gets an error.

The way C-s (RET) works is that the C-s invokes incremental search, which is specially programmed to invoke nonincremental search if the argument you give it is empty. (Such an empty argument would otherwise be useless.) C-r (RET) also works this way.

However, nonincremental searches performed using C-s (RET) do not call `search-forward` right away. The first thing done is to see if the next character is C-w, which requests a word search.

Forward and backward nonincremental searches are implemented by the commands `search-forward` and `search-backward`. These commands may be bound to keys in the usual manner. The feature that you can get to them via the incremental search commands exists for historical reasons, and to avoid the need to find suitable key sequences for them.

12.3 Word Search

Word search searches for a sequence of words without regard to how the words are separated. More precisely, you type a string of many words, using single spaces to separate them, and the string can be found even if there are multiple spaces, newlines or other punctuation between the words.

Word search is useful for editing a printed document made with a text formatter. If you edit while looking at the printed, formatted version, you can't tell where the line breaks are in the source file. With word search, you can search without having to know them.

C-s (RET) C-w *words* (RET)
> Search for *words*, ignoring details of punctuation.

`C-r` (RET) `C-w` *words* (RET)
>   Search backward for *words*, ignoring details of punctuation.

Word search is a special case of nonincremental search and is invoked with `C-s` (RET) `C-w`. This is followed by the search string, which must always be terminated with (RET). Being nonincremental, this search does not start until the argument is terminated. It works by constructing a regular expression and searching for that; see Section 12.4 [Regexp Search], page 89.

Use `C-r` (RET) `C-w` to do backward word search.

Forward and backward word searches are implemented by the commands **word-search-forward** and **word-search-backward**. These commands may be bound to keys in the usual manner. The feature that you can get to them via the incremental search commands exists for historical reasons, and to avoid the need to find suitable key sequences for them.

12.4 Regular Expression Search

A *regular expression* (*regexp*, for short) is a pattern that denotes a class of alternative strings to match, possibly infinitely many. In GNU Emacs, you can search for the next match for a regexp either incrementally or not.

Incremental search for a regexp is done by typing `C-M-s` (**isearch-forward-regexp**). This command reads a search string incrementally just like `C-s`, but it treats the search string as a regexp rather than looking for an exact match against the text in the buffer. Each time you add text to the search string, you make the regexp longer, and the new regexp is searched for. Invoking `C-s` with a prefix argument (its value does not matter) is another way to do a forward incremental regexp search. To search backward for a regexp, use `C-M-r` (**isearch-backward-regexp**), or `C-r` with a prefix argument.

All of the control characters that do special things within an ordinary incremental search have the same function in incremental regexp search. Typing `C-s` or `C-r` immediately after starting the search retrieves the last incremental search regexp used; that is to say, incremental regexp and non-regexp searches have independent defaults. They also have separate search rings that you can access with `M-p` and `M-n`.

If you type (SPC) in incremental regexp search, it matches any sequence of whitespace characters, including newlines. If you want to match just a space, type `C-q` (SPC).

Note that adding characters to the regexp in an incremental regexp search can make the cursor move back and start again. For example, if you have searched for 'foo' and you add '\|bar', the cursor backs up in case the first 'bar' precedes the first 'foo'.

Nonincremental search for a regexp is done by the functions **re-search-forward** and **re-search-backward**. You can invoke these with `M-x`, or bind

them to keys, or invoke them by way of incremental regexp search with
C-M-s (RET) and C-M-r (RET).

If you use the incremental regexp search commands with a prefix argument, they perform ordinary string search, like `isearch-forward` and
`isearch-backward`. See Section 12.1 [Incremental Search], page 85.

12.5 Syntax of Regular Expressions

Regular expressions have a syntax in which a few characters are special
constructs and the rest are *ordinary*. An ordinary character is a simple
regular expression which matches that same character and nothing else. The
special characters are '$', '^', '.', '*', '+', '?', '[', ']' and '\'. Any other
character appearing in a regular expression is ordinary, unless a '\' precedes
it.

For example, 'f' is not a special character, so it is ordinary, and therefore
'f' is a regular expression that matches the string 'f' and no other string.
(It does *not* match the string 'ff'.) Likewise, 'o' is a regular expression that
matches only 'o'. (When case distinctions are being ignored, these regexps
also match 'F' and 'O', but we consider this a generalization of "the same
string," rather than an exception.)

Any two regular expressions *a* and *b* can be concatenated. The result is a
regular expression which matches a string if *a* matches some amount of the
beginning of that string and *b* matches the rest of the string.

As a simple example, we can concatenate the regular expressions 'f' and
'o' to get the regular expression 'fo', which matches only the string 'fo'.
Still trivial. To do something nontrivial, you need to use one of the special
characters. Here is a list of them.

. (Period) is a special character that matches any single character except a
            newline. Using concatenation, we can make regular expressions
            like 'a.b', which matches any three-character string that begins
            with 'a' and ends with 'b'.

*   is not a construct by itself; it is a postfix operator that means
            to match the preceding regular expression repetitively as many
            times as possible. Thus, 'o*' matches any number of 'o's (in-
            cluding no 'o's).

            '*' always applies to the *smallest* possible preceding expression.
            Thus, 'fo*' has a repeating 'o', not a repeating 'fo'. It matches
            'f', 'fo', 'foo', and so on.

            The matcher processes a '*' construct by matching, immediately,
            as many repetitions as can be found. Then it continues with the
            rest of the pattern. If that fails, backtracking occurs, discarding
            some of the matches of the '*'-modified construct in case that
            makes it possible to match the rest of the pattern. For example,
            in matching 'ca*ar' against the string 'caaar', the 'a*' first

tries to match all three 'a's; but the rest of the pattern is 'ar' and there is only 'r' left to match, so this try fails. The next alternative is for 'a*' to match only two 'a's. With this choice, the rest of the regexp matches successfully.

+   is a postfix operator, similar to '*' except that it must match the preceding expression at least once. So, for example, 'ca+r' matches the strings 'car' and 'caaaar' but not the string 'cr', whereas 'ca*r' matches all three strings.

?   is a postfix operator, similar to '*' except that it can match the preceding expression either once or not at all. For example, 'ca?r' matches 'car' or 'cr'; nothing else.

[...]   is a *character set*, which begins with '[' and is terminated by ']'. In the simplest case, the characters between the two brackets are what this set can match.

Thus, '[ad]' matches either one 'a' or one 'd', and '[ad]*' matches any string composed of just 'a's and 'd's (including the empty string), from which it follows that 'c[ad]*r' matches 'cr', 'car', 'cdr', 'caddaar', etc.

You can also include character ranges in a character set, by writing the starting and ending characters with a '-' between them. Thus, '[a-z]' matches any lower-case ASCII letter. Ranges may be intermixed freely with individual characters, as in '[a-z$%.]', which matches any lower-case ASCII letter or '$', '%' or period.

Note that the usual regexp special characters are not special inside a character set. A completely different set of special characters exists inside character sets: ']', '-' and '^'.

To include a ']' in a character set, you must make it the first character. For example, '[]a]' matches ']' or 'a'. To include a '-', write '-' as the first or last character of the set, or put it after a range. Thus, '[]-]' matches both ']' and '-'.

To include '^' in a set, put it anywhere but at the beginning of the set.

When you use a range in case-insensitive search, you should write both ends of the range in upper case, or both in lower case, or both should be non-letters. The behavior of a mixed-case range such as 'A-z' is somewhat ill-defined, and it may change in future Emacs versions.

[^ ...] '[^' begins a *complemented character set*, which matches any character except the ones specified. Thus, '[^a-z0-9A-Z]' matches all characters *except* letters and digits.

'^' is not special in a character set unless it is the first character. The character following the '^' is treated as if it were first (in other words, '-' and ']' are not special there).

A complemented character set can match a newline, unless newline is mentioned as one of the characters not to match. This is in contrast to the handling of regexps in programs such as **grep**.

^   is a special character that matches the empty string, but only at the beginning of a line in the text being matched. Otherwise it fails to match anything. Thus, '^foo' matches a 'foo' that occurs at the beginning of a line.

$ is similar to '^' but matches only at the end of a line. Thus, 'x+$' matches a string of one 'x' or more at the end of a line.

\   has two functions: it quotes the special characters (including '\'), and it introduces additional special constructs.

Because '\' quotes special characters, '\$' is a regular expression that matches only '$', and '\[' is a regular expression that matches only '[', and so on.

Note: for historical compatibility, special characters are treated as ordinary ones if they are in contexts where their special meanings make no sense. For example, '*foo' treats '*' as ordinary since there is no preceding expression on which the '*' can act. It is poor practice to depend on this behavior; it is better to quote the special character anyway, regardless of where it appears.

For the most part, '\' followed by any character matches only that character. However, there are several exceptions: two-character sequences starting with '\' that have special meanings. The second character in the sequence is always an ordinary character when used on its own. Here is a table of '\' constructs.

\| specifies an alternative. Two regular expressions *a* and *b* with '\|' in between form an expression that matches some text if either *a* matches it or *b* matches it. It works by trying to match *a*, and if that fails, by trying to match *b*.

Thus, 'foo\|bar' matches either 'foo' or 'bar' but no other string.

'\|' applies to the largest possible surrounding expressions. Only a surrounding '\(... \)' grouping can limit the grouping power of '\|'.

Full backtracking capability exists to handle multiple uses of '\|'.

\(... \)   is a grouping construct that serves three purposes:

1. To enclose a set of '\|' alternatives for other operations. Thus, '\(foo\|bar\)x' matches either 'foox' or 'barx'.

2. To enclose a complicated expression for the postfix operators '*', '+' and '?' to operate on. Thus, 'ba\(na\)*'

matches 'bananana', etc., with any (zero or more) number of 'na' strings.

3. To record a matched substring for future reference.

This last application is not a consequence of the idea of a parenthetical grouping; it is a separate feature that is assigned as a second meaning to the same '\(... \)' construct. In practice there is no conflict between the two meanings.

\d   matches the same text that matched the dth occurrence of a '\(... \)' construct.

After the end of a '\(... \)' construct, the matcher remembers the beginning and end of the text matched by that construct. Then, later on in the regular expression, you can use '\' followed by the digit d to mean "match the same text matched the dth time by the '\(... \)' construct."

The strings matching the first nine '\(... \)' constructs appearing in a regular expression are assigned numbers 1 through 9 in the order that the open-parentheses appear in the regular expression. So you can use '\1' through '\9' to refer to the text matched by the corresponding '\(... \)' constructs.

For example, '\(.*\)\1' matches any newline-free string that is composed of two identical halves. The '\(.*\)' matches the first half, which may be anything, but the '\1' that follows must match the same exact text.

If a particular '\(... \)' construct matches more than once (which can easily happen if it is followed by '*'), only the last match is recorded.

\'   matches the empty string, but only at the beginning of the buffer or string being matched against.

\'   matches the empty string, but only at the end of the buffer or string being matched against.

\=   matches the empty string, but only at point.

\b   matches the empty string, but only at the beginning or end of a word. Thus, '\bfoo\b' matches any occurrence of 'foo' as a separate word. '\bballs?\b' matches 'ball' or 'balls' as a separate word.

'\b' matches at the beginning or end of the buffer regardless of what text appears next to it.

\B   matches the empty string, but *not* at the beginning or end of a word.

\<   matches the empty string, but only at the beginning of a word. '\<' matches at the beginning of the buffer only if a word-constituent character follows.

\>   matches the empty string, but only at the end of a word. '\>'
            matches at the end of the buffer only if the contents end with a
            word-constituent character.

\w   matches any word-constituent character. The syntax table de-
            termines which characters these are. See Section 31.6 [Syntax],
            page 419.

\W   matches any character that is not a word-constituent.

\s*c*   matches any character whose syntax is *c*. Here *c* is a character
            that represents a syntax code: thus, 'w' for word constituent,
            '-' for whitespace, '(' for open parenthesis, etc. Represent a
            character of whitespace (which can be a newline) by either '-'
            or a space character.

\S*c*   matches any character whose syntax is not *c*.

The constructs that pertain to words and syntax are controlled by the
setting of the syntax table (see Section 31.6 [Syntax], page 419).

Here is a complicated regexp, used by Emacs to recognize the end of
a sentence together with any whitespace that follows. It is given in Lisp
syntax to enable you to distinguish the spaces from the tab characters. In
Lisp syntax, the string constant begins and ends with a double-quote. '\"'
stands for a double-quote as part of the regexp, '\\' for a backslash as part
of the regexp, '\t' for a tab and '\n' for a newline.

```
"[.?!][]\"')]*\\($\\|\t\\|  \\)[ \t\n]*"
```

This contains four parts in succession: a character set matching period,
'?', or '!'; a character set matching close-brackets, quotes, or parentheses,
repeated any number of times; an alternative in backslash-parentheses that
matches end-of-line, a tab, or two spaces; and a character set matching
whitespace characters, repeated any number of times.

To enter the same regexp interactively, you would type (TAB) to enter a
tab, and C-j to enter a newline. You would also type single backslashes as
themselves, instead of doubling them for Lisp syntax.

12.6 Searching and Case

Incremental searches in Emacs normally ignore the case of the text they
are searching through, if you specify the text in lower case. Thus, if you
specify searching for 'foo', then 'Foo' and 'foo' are also considered a match.
Regexps, and in particular character sets, are included: '[ab]' would match
'a' or 'A' or 'b' or 'B'.

An upper-case letter anywhere in the incremental search string makes the
search case-sensitive. Thus, searching for 'Foo' does not find 'foo' or 'FOO'.
This applies to regular expression search as well as to string search. The
effect ceases if you delete the upper-case letter from the search string.

If you set the variable `case-fold-search` to `nil`, then all letters must match exactly, including case. This is a per-buffer variable; altering the variable affects only the current buffer, but there is a default value which you can change as well. See Section 31.2.4 [Locals], page 401. This variable applies to nonincremental searches also, including those performed by the replace commands (see Section 12.7 [Replace], page 95) and the minibuffer history matching commands (see Section 5.4 [Minibuffer History], page 46).

12.7 Replacement Commands

Global search-and-replace operations are not needed as often in Emacs as they are in other editors[1], but they are available. In addition to the simple `M-x replace-string` command which is like that found in most editors, there is a `M-x query-replace` command which asks you, for each occurrence of the pattern, whether to replace it.

The replace commands normally operate on the text from point to the end of the buffer; however, in Transient Mark mode, when the mark is active, they operate on the region. The replace commands all replace one string (or regexp) with one replacement string. It is possible to perform several replacements in parallel using the command `expand-region-abbrevs` (see Section 24.3 [Expanding Abbrevs], page 290).

12.7.1 Unconditional Replacement

`M-x replace-string` ⟨RET⟩ *string* ⟨RET⟩ *newstring* ⟨RET⟩
> Replace every occurrence of *string* with *newstring*.

`M-x replace-regexp` ⟨RET⟩ *regexp* ⟨RET⟩ *newstring* ⟨RET⟩
> Replace every match for *regexp* with *newstring*.

To replace every instance of 'foo' after point with 'bar', use the command `M-x replace-string` with the two arguments 'foo' and 'bar'. Replacement happens only in the text after point, so if you want to cover the whole buffer you must go to the beginning first. All occurrences up to the end of the buffer are replaced; to limit replacement to part of the buffer, narrow to that part of the buffer before doing the replacement (see Section 30.8 [Narrowing], page 382). In Transient Mark mode, when the region is active, replacement is limited to the region (see Section 8.2 [Transient Mark], page 60).

When `replace-string` exits, it leaves point at the last occurrence replaced. It sets the mark to the prior position of point (where the `replace-string` command was issued); use `C-u C-`⟨SPC⟩ to move back there.

A numeric argument restricts replacement to matches that are surrounded by word boundaries. The argument's value doesn't matter.

---

[1] In some editors, search-and-replace operations are the only convenient way to make a single change in the text.

12.7.2 Regexp Replacement

The M-x replace-string command replaces exact matches for a single string. The similar command M-x replace-regexp replaces any match for a specified pattern.

In replace-regexp, the *newstring* need not be constant: it can refer to all or part of what is matched by the *regexp*. '\&' in *newstring* stands for the entire match being replaced. '*d*' in *newstring*, where *d* is a digit, stands for whatever matched the *d*th parenthesized grouping in *regexp*. To include a '\' in the text to replace with, you must enter '\\\\'. For example,

M-x replace-regexp (RET) c[ad]+r (RET) \&-safe (RET)

replaces (for example) 'cadr' with 'cadr-safe' and 'cddr' with 'cddr-safe'.

M-x replace-regexp (RET) \(c[ad]+r\)-safe (RET) \1 (RET)

performs the inverse transformation.

12.7.3 Replace Commands and Case

If the first argument of a replace command is all lower case, the commands ignores case while searching for occurrences to replace—provided case-fold-search is non-nil. If case-fold-search is set to nil, case is always significant in all searches.

In addition, when the *newstring* argument is all or partly lower case, replacement commands try to preserve the case pattern of each occurrence. Thus, the command

M-x replace-string (RET) foo (RET) bar (RET)

replaces a lower case 'foo' with a lower case 'bar', an all-caps 'FOO' with 'BAR', and a capitalized 'Foo' with 'Bar'. (These three alternatives—lower case, all caps, and capitalized, are the only ones that replace-string can distinguish.)

If upper-case letters are used in the replacement string, they remain upper case every time that text is inserted. If upper-case letters are used in the first argument, the second argument is always substituted exactly as given, with no case conversion. Likewise, if either case-replace or case-fold-search is set to nil, replacement is done without case conversion.

12.7.4 Query Replace

M-% *string* (RET) *newstring* (RET)
M-x query-replace (RET) *string* (RET) *newstring* (RET)
        Replace some occurrences of *string* with *newstring*.

C-M-% *regexp* (RET) *newstring* (RET)
M-x query-replace-regexp (RET) *regexp* (RET) *newstring* (RET)
        Replace some matches for *regexp* with *newstring*.

If you want to change only some of the occurrences of 'foo' to 'bar', not all of them, then you cannot use an ordinary replace-string. Instead, use M-% (query-replace). This command finds occurrences of 'foo' one by one, displays each occurrence and asks you whether to replace it. A numeric argument to query-replace tells it to consider only occurrences that are bounded by word-delimiter characters. This preserves case, just like replace-string, provided case-replace is non-nil, as it normally is.

Aside from querying, query-replace works just like replace-string, and query-replace-regexp works just like replace-regexp. This command is run by C-M-%.

The things you can type when you are shown an occurrence of *string* or a match for *regexp* are:

(SPC)   to replace the occurrence with *newstring*.

(DEL)   to skip to the next occurrence without replacing this one.

, (Comma)
               to replace this occurrence and display the result. You are then asked for another input character to say what to do next. Since the replacement has already been made, (DEL) and (SPC) are equivalent in this situation; both move to the next occurrence.

               You can type C-r at this point (see below) to alter the replaced text. You can also type C-x u to undo the replacement; this exits the query-replace, so if you want to do further replacement you must use C-x (ESC) (ESC) (RET) to restart (see Section 5.5 [Repetition], page 47).

(RET)   to exit without doing any more replacements.

. (Period)   to replace this occurrence and then exit without searching for more occurrences.

!   to replace all remaining occurrences without asking again.

^   to go back to the position of the previous occurrence (or what used to be an occurrence), in case you changed it by mistake. This works by popping the mark ring. Only one ^ in a row is meaningful, because only one previous replacement position is kept during query-replace.

C-r   to enter a recursive editing level, in case the occurrence needs to be edited rather than just replaced with *newstring*. When you are done, exit the recursive editing level with C-M-c to proceed to the next occurrence. See Section 30.12 [Recursive Edit], page 385.

C-w   to delete the occurrence, and then enter a recursive editing level as in C-r. Use the recursive edit to insert text to replace the deleted occurrence of *string*. When done, exit the recursive editing level with C-M-c to proceed to the next occurrence.

C-l   to redisplay the screen. Then you must type another character
             to specify what to do with this occurrence.

C-h   to display a message summarizing these options. Then you must
             type another character to specify what to do with this occur-
             rence.

Some other characters are aliases for the ones listed above: y, n and q
are equivalent to (SPC), (DEL) and (RET).

Aside from this, any other character exits the query-replace, and is
then reread as part of a key sequence. Thus, if you type C-k, it exits the
query-replace and then kills to end of line.

To restart a query-replace once it is exited, use C-x (ESC) (ESC), which
repeats the query-replace because it used the minibuffer to read its arguments. See Section 5.5 [Repetition], page 47.

See also Section 28.9 [Transforming File Names], page 336, for Dired
commands to rename, copy, or link files by replacing regexp matches in file
names.

12.8 Other Search-and-Loop Commands

Here are some other commands that find matches for a regular expression.
They all operate from point to the end of the buffer, and all ignore case
in matching, if the pattern contains no upper-case letters and case-fold-
search is non-nil.

M-x occur (RET) regexp (RET)
             Display a list showing each line in the buffer that contains a
             match for regexp. A numeric argument specifies the number of
             context lines to print before and after each matching line; the
             default is none. To limit the search to part of the buffer, narrow
             to that part (see Section 30.8 [Narrowing], page 382).

             The buffer '*Occur*' containing the output serves as a menu for
             finding the occurrences in their original context. Click Mouse-2
             on an occurrence listed in '*Occur*', or position point there and
             type (RET); this switches to the buffer that was searched and
             moves point to the original of the chosen occurrence.

M-x list-matching-lines
             Synonym for M-x occur.

M-x count-matches (RET) regexp (RET)
             Print the number of matches for regexp after point.

M-x flush-lines (RET) regexp (RET)
             Delete each line that follows point and contains a match for
             regexp.

`M-x keep-lines` (RET) *regexp* (RET)

> Delete each line that follows point and *does not* contain a match for *regexp*.

In addition, you can use **grep** from Emacs to search a collection of files for matches for a regular expression, then visit the matches either sequentially or in arbitrary order. See Section 23.2 [Grep Searching], page 278.

13 Commands for Fixing Typos

In this chapter we describe the commands that are especially useful for the times when you catch a mistake in your text just after you have made it, or change your mind while composing text on the fly.

The most fundamental command for correcting erroneous editing is the undo command, `C-x u` or `C-_`. This command undoes a single command (usually), a part of a command (in the case of `query-replace`), or several consecutive self-inserting characters. Consecutive repetitions of `C-_` or `C-x u` undo earlier and earlier changes, back to the limit of the undo information available. See Section 4.4 [Undo], page 32, for for more information.

13.1 Killing Your Mistakes

(DEL)   Delete last character (`delete-backward-char`).

M-(DEL)   Kill last word (`backward-kill-word`).

C-x (DEL)   Kill to beginning of sentence (`backward-kill-sentence`).

The (DEL) character (`delete-backward-char`) is the most important correction command. It deletes the character before point. When (DEL) follows a self-inserting character command, you can think of it as canceling that command. However, avoid the mistake of thinking of (DEL) as a general way to cancel a command!

When your mistake is longer than a couple of characters, it might be more convenient to use M-(DEL) or C-x (DEL). M-(DEL) kills back to the start of the last word, and C-x (DEL) kills back to the start of the last sentence. C-x (DEL) is particularly useful when you change your mind about the phrasing of the text you are writing. M-(DEL) and C-x (DEL) save the killed text for C-y and M-y to retrieve. See Section 9.2 [Yanking], page 67.

M-(DEL) is often useful even when you have typed only a few characters wrong, if you know you are confused in your typing and aren't sure exactly what you typed. At such a time, you cannot correct with (DEL) except by looking at the screen to see what you did. Often it requires less thought to kill the whole word and start again.

13.2 Transposing Text

C-t   Transpose two characters (`transpose-chars`).

M-t   Transpose two words (`transpose-words`).

C-M-t   Transpose two balanced expressions (`transpose-sexps`).

C-x C-t   Transpose two lines (`transpose-lines`).

The common error of transposing two characters can be fixed, when they are adjacent, with the C-t command (transpose-chars). Normally, C-t transposes the two characters on either side of point. When given at the end of a line, rather than transposing the last character of the line with the newline, which would be useless, C-t transposes the last two characters on the line. So, if you catch your transposition error right away, you can fix it with just a C-t. If you don't catch it so fast, you must move the cursor back to between the two transposed characters. If you transposed a space with the last character of the word before it, the word motion commands are a good way of getting there. Otherwise, a reverse search (C-r) is often the best way. See Chapter 12 [Search], page 85.

M-t (transpose-words) transposes the word before point with the word after point. It moves point forward over a word, dragging the word preceding or containing point forward as well. The punctuation characters between the words do not move. For example, 'FOO, BAR' transposes into 'BAR, FOO' rather than 'BAR FOO, '.

C-M-t (transpose-sexps) is a similar command for transposing two expressions (see Section 22.2 [Lists], page 228), and C-x C-t (transpose-lines) exchanges lines. They work like M-t except in determining the division of the text into syntactic units.

A numeric argument to a transpose command serves as a repeat count: it tells the transpose command to move the character (word, sexp, line) before or containing point across several other characters (words, sexps, lines). For example, C-u 3 C-t moves the character before point forward across three other characters. It would change 'f⋆oobar' into 'oobf⋆ar'. This is equivalent to repeating C-t three times. C-u - 4 M-t moves the word before point backward across four words. C-u - C-M-t would cancel the effect of plain C-M-t.

A numeric argument of zero is assigned a special meaning (because otherwise a command with a repeat count of zero would do nothing): to transpose the character (word, sexp, line) ending after point with the one ending after the mark.

13.3 Case Conversion

M-- M-l   Convert last word to lower case. Note Meta-- is Meta-minus.

M-- M-u   Convert last word to all upper case.

M-- M-c   Convert last word to lower case with capital initial.

A very common error is to type words in the wrong case. Because of this, the word case-conversion commands M-l, M-u and M-c have a special feature when used with a negative argument: they do not move the cursor. As soon as you see you have mistyped the last word, you can simply case-convert it and go on typing. See Section 21.6 [Case], page 208.

13.4 Checking and Correcting Spelling

This section describes the commands to check the spelling of a single word or of a portion of a buffer. These commands work with the spelling checker program Ispell, which is not part of Emacs.

M-x flyspell-mode
> Enable Flyspell mode, which highlights all misspelled words.

M-$ Check and correct spelling of the word at point (`ispell-word`).

M-(TAB)   Complete the word before point based on the spelling dictionary (`ispell-complete-word`).

M-x ispell-buffer
> Check and correct spelling of each word in the buffer.

M-x ispell-region
> Check and correct spelling of each word in the region.

M-x ispell-message
> Check and correct spelling of each word in a draft mail message, excluding cited material.

M-x ispell-change-dictionary (RET) dict (RET)
> Restart the Ispell process, using dict as the dictionary.

M-x ispell-kill-ispell
> Kill the Ispell subprocess.

Flyspell mode is a fully-automatic way to check spelling as you edit in Emacs. It operates by checking words as you change or insert them. When it finds a word that it does not recognize, it highlights that word. This does not interfere with your editing, but when you see the highlighted word, you can move to it and fix it. Type M-x flyspell-mode to enable or disable this mode in the current buffer.

When Flyspell mode highlights a word as misspelled, you can click on it with Mouse-2 to display a menu of possible corrections and actions. You can also correct the word by editing it manually in any way you like.

The other Emacs spell-checking features check or look up words when you give an explicit command to do so. Checking all or part of the buffer is useful when you have text that was written outside of this Emacs session and might contain any number of misspellings.

To check the spelling of the word around or next to point, and optionally correct it as well, use the command M-$ (`ispell-word`). If the word is not correct, the command offers you various alternatives for what to do about it.

To check the entire current buffer, use M-x ispell-buffer. Use M-x ispell-region to check just the current region. To check spelling in an email message you are writing, use M-x ispell-message; that checks the whole buffer, but does not check material that is indented or appears to be cited from other messages.

Each time these commands encounter an incorrect word, they ask you what to do. They display a list of alternatives, usually including several "near-misses"—words that are close to the word being checked. Then you must type a character. Here are the valid responses:

$\overline{\text{SPC}}$ Skip this word—continue to consider it incorrect, but don't change it here.

r *new* $\overline{\text{RET}}$
          Replace the word (just this time) with *new*.

R *new* $\overline{\text{RET}}$
          Replace the word with *new*, and do a `query-replace` so you can replace it elsewhere in the buffer if you wish.

digit   Replace the word (just this time) with one of the displayed near-misses. Each near-miss is listed with a digit; type that digit to select it.

a   Accept the incorrect word—treat it as correct, but only in this editing session.

A   Accept the incorrect word—treat it as correct, but only in this editing session and for this buffer.

i   Insert this word in your private dictionary file so that Ispell will consider it correct it from now on, even in future sessions.

u   Insert the lower-case version of this word in your private dictionary file.

m   Like i, but you can also specify dictionary completion information.

l *word* $\overline{\text{RET}}$
          Look in the dictionary for words that match *word*. These words become the new list of "near-misses"; you can select one of them to replace with by typing a digit. You can use '*' in *word* as a wildcard.

C-g   Quit interactive spell checking. You can restart it again afterward with C-u M-\$.

X   Same as C-g.

x   Quit interactive spell checking and move point back to where it was when you started spell checking.

q   Quit interactive spell checking and kill the Ispell subprocess.

C-l   Refresh the screen.

C-z   This key has its normal command meaning (suspend Emacs or iconify this frame).

The command `ispell-complete-word`, which is bound to the key M-(TAB) in Text mode and related modes, shows a list of completions based on spelling correction. Insert the beginning of a word, and then type M-(TAB); the command displays a completion list window. To choose one of the completions listed, click `Mouse-2` on it, or move the cursor there in the completions window and type (RET). See Section 21.7 [Text Mode], page 209.

Once started, the Ispell subprocess continues to run (waiting for something to do), so that subsequent spell checking commands complete more quickly. If you want to get rid of the Ispell process, use `M-x ispell-kill-ispell`. This is not usually necessary, since the process uses no time except when you do spelling correction.

Ispell uses two dictionaries: the standard dictionary and your private dictionary. The variable `ispell-dictionary` specifies the file name of the standard dictionary to use. A value of `nil` says to use the default dictionary. The command `M-x ispell-change-dictionary` sets this variable and then restarts the Ispell subprocess, so that it will use a different dictionary.

14 File Handling

The operating system stores data permanently in named *files*. So most of the text you edit with Emacs comes from a file and is ultimately stored in a file.

To edit a file, you must tell Emacs to read the file and prepare a buffer containing a copy of the file's text. This is called *visiting* the file. Editing commands apply directly to text in the buffer; that is, to the copy inside Emacs. Your changes appear in the file itself only when you *save* the buffer back into the file.

In addition to visiting and saving files, Emacs can delete, copy, rename, and append to files, keep multiple versions of them, and operate on file directories.

14.1 File Names

Most Emacs commands that operate on a file require you to specify the file name. (Saving and reverting are exceptions; the buffer knows which file name to use for them.) You enter the file name using the minibuffer (see Chapter 5 [Minibuffer], page 41). *Completion* is available, to make it easier to specify long file names. See Section 5.3 [Completion], page 43.

For most operations, there is a *default file name* which is used if you type just (RET) to enter an empty argument. Normally the default file name is the name of the file visited in the current buffer; this makes it easy to operate on that file with any of the Emacs file commands.

Each buffer has a default directory, normally the same as the directory of the file visited in that buffer. When you enter a file name without a directory, the default directory is used. If you specify a directory in a relative fashion, with a name that does not start with a slash, it is interpreted with respect to the default directory. The default directory is kept in the variable **default-directory**, which has a separate value in every buffer.

For example, if the default file name is '/u/rms/gnu/gnu.tasks' then the default directory is '/u/rms/gnu/'. If you type just 'foo', which does not specify a directory, it is short for '/u/rms/gnu/foo'. '../.login' would stand for '/u/rms/.login'. 'new/foo' would stand for the file name '/u/rms/gnu/new/foo'.

The command M-x pwd prints the current buffer's default directory, and the command M-x cd sets it (to a value read using the minibuffer). A buffer's default directory changes only when the cd command is used. A file-visiting buffer's default directory is initialized to the directory of the file that is visited there. If you create a buffer with C-x b, its default directory is copied from that of the buffer that was current at the time.

The default directory actually appears in the minibuffer when the minibuffer becomes active to read a file name. This serves two purposes: it *shows* you what the default is, so that you can type a relative file name and know with certainty what it will mean, and it allows you to *edit* the default to specify a different directory. This insertion of the default directory is inhibited if the variable `insert-default-directory` is set to `nil`.

Note that it is legitimate to type an absolute file name after you enter the minibuffer, ignoring the presence of the default directory name as part of the text. The final minibuffer contents may look invalid, but that is not so. For example, if the minibuffer starts out with '`/usr/tmp/`' and you add '`/x1/rms/foo`', you get '`/usr/tmp//x1/rms/foo`'; but Emacs ignores everything through the first slash in the double slash; the result is '`/x1/rms/foo`'. See Section 5.1 [Minibuffer File], page 41.

'`$`' in a file name is used to substitute environment variables. For example, if you have used the shell command '`export FOO=rms/hacks`' to set up an environment variable named `FOO`, then you can use '`/u/$FOO/test.c`' or '`/u/${FOO}/test.c`' as an abbreviation for '`/u/rms/hacks/test.c`'. The environment variable name consists of all the alphanumeric characters after the '`$`'; alternatively, it may be enclosed in braces after the '`$`'. Note that shell commands to set environment variables affect Emacs only if done before Emacs is started.

To access a file with '`$`' in its name, type '`$$`'. This pair is converted to a single '`$`' at the same time as variable substitution is performed for single '`$`'. Alternatively, quote the whole file name with '`/:`' (see Section 14.13 [Quoted File Names], page 141).

The Lisp function that performs the substitution is called `substitute-in-file-name`. The substitution is performed only on file names read as such using the minibuffer.

You can include non-ASCII characters in file names if you set the variable `file-name-coding-system` to a non-`nil` value. See Section 18.9 [Specify Coding], page 184.

14.2 Visiting Files

C-x C-f   Visit a file (`find-file`).

C-x C-r   Visit a file for viewing, without allowing changes to it (`find-file-read-only`).

C-x C-v   Visit a different file instead of the one visited last (`find-alternate-file`).

C-x 4 f   Visit a file, in another window (`find-file-other-window`). Don't alter what is displayed in the selected window.

C-x 5 f   Visit a file, in a new frame (`find-file-other-frame`). Don't alter what is displayed in the selected frame.

M-x find-file-literally
            Visit a file with no conversion of the contents.

Visiting a file means copying its contents into an Emacs buffer so you can edit them. Emacs makes a new buffer for each file that you visit. We say that this buffer is visiting the file that it was created to hold. Emacs constructs the buffer name from the file name by throwing away the directory, keeping just the name proper. For example, a file named '/usr/rms/emacs.tex' would get a buffer named 'emacs.tex'. If there is already a buffer with that name, a unique name is constructed by appending '<2>', '<3>', or so on, using the lowest number that makes a name that is not already in use.

Each window's mode line shows the name of the buffer that is being displayed in that window, so you can always tell what buffer you are editing.

The changes you make with editing commands are made in the Emacs buffer. They do not take effect in the file that you visited, or any place permanent, until you *save* the buffer. Saving the buffer means that Emacs writes the current contents of the buffer into its visited file. See Section 14.3 [Saving], page 111.

If a buffer contains changes that have not been saved, we say the buffer is *modified*. This is important because it implies that some changes will be lost if the buffer is not saved. The mode line displays two stars near the left margin to indicate that the buffer is modified.

To visit a file, use the command C-x C-f (find-file). Follow the command with the name of the file you wish to visit, terminated by a (RET).

The file name is read using the minibuffer (see Chapter 5 [Minibuffer], page 41), with defaulting and completion in the standard manner (see Section 14.1 [File Names], page 107). While in the minibuffer, you can abort C-x C-f by typing C-g.

Your confirmation that C-x C-f has completed successfully is the appearance of new text on the screen and a new buffer name in the mode line. If the specified file does not exist and could not be created, or cannot be read, then you get an error, with an error message displayed in the echo area.

If you visit a file that is already in Emacs, C-x C-f does not make another copy. It selects the existing buffer containing that file. However, before doing so, it checks that the file itself has not changed since you visited or saved it last. If the file has changed, a warning message is printed. See Section 14.3.2 [Simultaneous Editing], page 115.

What if you want to create a new file? Just visit it. Emacs prints '(New File)' in the echo area, but in other respects behaves as if you had visited an existing empty file. If you make any changes and save them, the file is created.

Emacs recognizes from the contents of a file which convention it uses to separate lines—newline (used on GNU/Linux and on Unix), carriage-return linefeed (used on Microsoft systems), or just carriage-return (used on the Macintosh)—and automatically converts the contents to the normal Emacs convention, which is that the newline character separates lines. This is a part of the general feature of coding system conversion (see Section 18.7 [Coding

Systems], page 180), and makes it possible to edit files imported from various different operating systems with equal convenience. If you change the text and save the file, Emacs performs the inverse conversion, changing newlines back into carriage-return linefeed or just carriage-return if appropriate.

If the file you specify is actually a directory, `C-x C-f` invokes Dired, the Emacs directory browser, so that you can "edit" the contents of the directory (see Chapter 28 [Dired], page 329). Dired is a convenient way to delete, look at, or operate on the files in the directory. However, if the variable `find-file-run-dired` is `nil`, then it is an error to try to visit a directory.

If the file name you specify contains wildcard characters, Emacs visits all the files that match it. See Section 14.13 [Quoted File Names], page 141, if you want to visit a file whose name actually contains wildcard characters.

If you visit a file that the operating system won't let you modify, Emacs makes the buffer read-only, so that you won't go ahead and make changes that you'll have trouble saving afterward. You can make the buffer writable with `C-x C-q` (`vc-toggle-read-only`).   See Section 15.3 [Misc Buffer], page 145.

Occasionally you might want to visit a file as read-only in order to protect yourself from entering changes accidentally; do so by visiting the file with the command `C-x C-r` (`find-file-read-only`).

If you visit a nonexistent file unintentionally (because you typed the wrong file name), use the `C-x C-v` command (`find-alternate-file`) to visit the file you really wanted. `C-x C-v` is similar to `C-x C-f`, but it kills the current buffer (after first offering to save it if it is modified). When it reads the file name to visit, it inserts the entire default file name in the buffer, with point just after the directory part; this is convenient if you made a slight error in typing the name.

If you find a file which exists but cannot be read, `C-x C-f` signals an error.

`C-x 4 f` (`find-file-other-window`) is like `C-x C-f` except that the buffer containing the specified file is selected in another window. The window that was selected before `C-x 4 f` continues to show the same buffer it was already showing. If this command is used when only one window is being displayed, that window is split in two, with one window showing the same buffer as before, and the other one showing the newly requested file. See Chapter 16 [Windows], page 151.

`C-x 5 f` (`find-file-other-frame`) is similar, but opens a new frame, or makes visible any existing frame showing the file you seek. This feature is available only when you are using a window system. See Chapter 17 [Frames], page 157.

If you wish to edit a file as a sequence of characters with no special encoding or conversion, use the `M-x find-file-literally` command. It visits a file, like `C-x C-f`, but does not do format conversion (see Section 21.11 [Formatted Text], page 219), character code conversion (see Section 18.7 [Coding

Systems], page 180), or automatic uncompression (see Section 14.11 [Compressed Files], page 140). If you already have visited the same file in the usual (non-literal) manner, this command asks you whether to visit it literally instead.

Two special hook variables allow extensions to modify the operation of visiting files. Visiting a file that does not exist runs the functions in the list `find-file-not-found-hooks`; this variable holds a list of functions, and the functions are called one by one until one of them returns non-`nil`. Any visiting of a file, whether extant or not, expects `find-file-hooks` to contain a list of functions and calls them all, one by one. In both cases the functions receive no arguments. Of these two variables, `find-file-not-found-hooks` takes effect first. These variables are *not* normal hooks, and their names end in '`-hooks`' rather than '`-hook`' to indicate that fact. See Section 31.2.3 [Hooks], page 400.

There are several ways to specify automatically the major mode for editing the file (see Section 19.1 [Choosing Modes], page 191), and to specify local variables defined for that file (see Section 31.2.5 [File Variables], page 403).

14.3 Saving Files

Saving a buffer in Emacs means writing its contents back into the file that was visited in the buffer.

C-x C-s   Save the current buffer in its visited file (`save-buffer`).

C-x s   Save any or all buffers in their visited files (`save-some-buffers`).

M-~   Forget that the current buffer has been changed (`not-modified`).

C-x C-w   Save the current buffer in a specified file (`write-file`).

M-x set-visited-file-name
            Change file the name under which the current buffer will be saved.

When you wish to save the file and make your changes permanent, type C-x C-s (`save-buffer`). After saving is finished, C-x C-s displays a message like this:

    Wrote /u/rms/gnu/gnu.tasks

If the selected buffer is not modified (no changes have been made in it since the buffer was created or last saved), saving is not really done, because it would have no effect. Instead, C-x C-s displays a message like this in the echo area:

    (No changes need to be saved)

The command C-x s (save-some-buffers) offers to save any or all modified buffers. It asks you what to do with each buffer. The possible responses are analogous to those of query-replace:

y   Save this buffer and ask about the rest of the buffers.

n   Don't save this buffer, but ask about the rest of the buffers.

!   Save this buffer and all the rest with no more questions.

⟨RET⟩   Terminate save-some-buffers without any more saving.

.   Save this buffer, then exit save-some-buffers without even asking about other buffers.

C-r   View the buffer that you are currently being asked about. When you exit View mode, you get back to save-some-buffers, which asks the question again.

C-h   Display a help message about these options.

C-x C-c, the key sequence to exit Emacs, invokes save-some-buffers and therefore asks the same questions.

If you have changed a buffer but you do not want to save the changes, you should take some action to prevent it. Otherwise, each time you use C-x s or C-x C-c, you are liable to save this buffer by mistake. One thing you can do is type M-~ (not-modified), which clears out the indication that the buffer is modified. If you do this, none of the save commands will believe that the buffer needs to be saved. ('~' is often used as a mathematical symbol for 'not'; thus M-~ is 'not', metafied.) You could also use set-visited-file-name (see below) to mark the buffer as visiting a different file name, one which is not in use for anything important. Alternatively, you can cancel all the changes made since the file was visited or saved, by reading the text from the file again. This is called *reverting*. See Section 14.4 [Reverting], page 117. You could also undo all the changes by repeating the undo command C-x u until you have undone all the changes; but reverting is easier.

M-x set-visited-file-name alters the name of the file that the current buffer is visiting. It reads the new file name using the minibuffer. Then it specifies the visited file name and changes the buffer name correspondingly (as long as the new name is not in use). set-visited-file-name does not save the buffer in the newly visited file; it just alters the records inside Emacs in case you do save later. It also marks the buffer as "modified" so that C-x C-s in that buffer *will* save.

If you wish to mark the buffer as visiting a different file and save it right away, use C-x C-w (write-file). It is precisely equivalent to set-visited-file-name followed by C-x C-s. C-x C-s used on a buffer that is not visiting a file has the same effect as C-x C-w; that is, it reads a file name, marks the buffer as visiting that file, and saves it there. The default file name in a buffer that is not visiting a file is made by combining the buffer name with the buffer's default directory.

If the new file name implies a major mode, then C-x C-w switches to that major mode, in most cases. The command set-visited-file-name also does this. See Section 19.1 [Choosing Modes], page 191.

If Emacs is about to save a file and sees that the date of the latest version on disk does not match what Emacs last read or wrote, Emacs notifies you of this fact, because it probably indicates a problem caused by simultaneous editing and requires your immediate attention. See Section 14.3.2 [Simultaneous Editing], page 115.

If the variable require-final-newline is non-nil, Emacs puts a newline at the end of any file that doesn't already end in one, every time a file is saved or written. The default is nil.

14.3.1 Backup Files

On most operating systems, rewriting a file automatically destroys all record of what the file used to contain. Thus, saving a file from Emacs throws away the old contents of the file—or it would, except that Emacs carefully copies the old contents to another file, called the *backup* file, before actually saving.

For most files, the variable make-backup-files determines whether to make backup files. On most operating systems, its default value is t, so that Emacs does write backup files.

For files managed by a version control system (see Section 14.7 [Version Control], page 120), the variable vc-make-backup-files determines whether to make backup files. By default, it is nil, since backup files are redundant when you store all the previous versions in a version control system. See Section 14.7.9.2 [VC Workfile Handling], page 137.

The default value of the backup-enable-predicate variable prevents backup files being written for files in '/tmp'.

At your option, Emacs can keep either a single backup file or a series of numbered backup files for each file that you edit.

Emacs makes a backup for a file only the first time the file is saved from one buffer. No matter how many times you save a file, its backup file continues to contain the contents from before the file was visited. Normally this means that the backup file contains the contents from before the current editing session; however, if you kill the buffer and then visit the file again, a new backup file will be made by the next save.

You can also explicitly request making another backup file from a buffer even though it has already been saved at least once. If you save the buffer with C-u C-x C-s, the version thus saved will be made into a backup file if you save the buffer again. C-u C-u C-x C-s saves the buffer, but first makes the previous file contents into a new backup file. C-u C-u C-u C-x C-s does both things: it makes a backup from the previous contents, and arranges to make another from the newly saved contents, if you save again.

14.3.1.1 Single or Numbered Backups

If you choose to have a single backup file (this is the default), the backup file's name is constructed by appending '~' to the file name being edited; thus, the backup file for 'eval.c' would be 'eval.c~'.

If you choose to have a series of numbered backup files, backup file names are made by appending '.~', the number, and another '~' to the original file name. Thus, the backup files of 'eval.c' would be called 'eval.c.~1~', 'eval.c.~2~', and so on, through names like 'eval.c.~259~' and beyond.

If protection stops you from writing backup files under the usual names, the backup file is written as '%backup%~' in your home directory. Only one such file can exist, so only the most recently made such backup is available.

The choice of single backup or numbered backups is controlled by the variable `version-control`. Its possible values are

t   Make numbered backups.

nil   Make numbered backups for files that have numbered backups already. Otherwise, make single backups.

never   Do not in any case make numbered backups; always make single backups.

You can set `version-control` locally in an individual buffer to control the making of backups for that buffer's file. For example, Rmail mode locally sets `version-control` to `never` to make sure that there is only one backup for an Rmail file. See Section 31.2.4 [Locals], page 401.

If you set the environment variable `VERSION_CONTROL`, to tell various GNU utilities what to do with backup files, Emacs also obeys the environment variable by setting the Lisp variable `version-control` accordingly at startup. If the environment variable's value is 't' or 'numbered', then `version-control` becomes t; if the value is 'nil' or 'existing', then `version-control` becomes nil; if it is 'never' or 'simple', then `version-control` becomes `never`.

14.3.1.2 Automatic Deletion of Backups

To prevent unlimited consumption of disk space, Emacs can delete numbered backup versions automatically. Generally Emacs keeps the first few backups and the latest few backups, deleting any in between. This happens every time a new backup is made.

The two variables `kept-old-versions` and `kept-new-versions` control this deletion. Their values are, respectively the number of oldest (lowest-numbered) backups to keep and the number of newest (highest-numbered) ones to keep, each time a new backup is made. Recall that these values are used just after a new backup version is made; that newly made backup is included in the count in `kept-new-versions`. By default, both variables are 2.

If `delete-old-versions` is non-nil, the excess middle versions are deleted without a murmur. If it is `nil`, the default, then you are asked whether the excess middle versions should really be deleted.

Dired's . (Period) command can also be used to delete old versions. See Section 28.3 [Dired Deletion], page 329.

14.3.1.3 Copying vs. Renaming

Backup files can be made by copying the old file or by renaming it. This makes a difference when the old file has multiple names. If the old file is renamed into the backup file, then the alternate names become names for the backup file. If the old file is copied instead, then the alternate names remain names for the file that you are editing, and the contents accessed by those names will be the new contents.

The method of making a backup file may also affect the file's owner and group. If copying is used, these do not change. If renaming is used, you become the file's owner, and the file's group becomes the default (different operating systems have different defaults for the group).

Having the owner change is usually a good idea, because then the owner always shows who last edited the file. Also, the owners of the backups show who produced those versions. Occasionally there is a file whose owner should not change; it is a good idea for such files to contain local variable lists to set `backup-by-copying-when-mismatch` locally (see Section 31.2.5 [File Variables], page 403).

The choice of renaming or copying is controlled by three variables. Renaming is the default choice. If the variable `backup-by-copying` is non-nil, copying is used. Otherwise, if the variable `backup-by-copying-when-linked` is non-nil, then copying is used for files that have multiple names, but renaming may still be used when the file being edited has only one name. If the variable `backup-by-copying-when-mismatch` is non-nil, then copying is used if renaming would cause the file's owner or group to change. `backup-by-copying-when-mismatch` is `t` by default if you start Emacs as the superuser.

When a file is managed with a version control system (see Section 14.7 [Version Control], page 120), Emacs does not normally make backups in the usual way for that file. But check-in and check-out are similar in some ways to making backups. One unfortunate similarity is that these operations typically break hard links, disconnecting the file name you visited from any alternate names for the same file. This has nothing to do with Emacs—the version control system does it.

14.3.2 Protection against Simultaneous Editing

Simultaneous editing occurs when two users visit the same file, both make changes, and then both save them. If nobody were informed that this was happening, whichever user saved first would later find that his changes were lost.

On some systems, Emacs notices immediately when the second user starts to change the file, and issues an immediate warning. On all systems, Emacs checks when you save the file, and warns if you are about to overwrite another user's changes. You can prevent loss of the other user's work by taking the proper corrective action instead of saving the file.

When you make the first modification in an Emacs buffer that is visiting a file, Emacs records that the file is *locked* by you. (It does this by creating a symbolic link in the same directory with a different name.) Emacs removes the lock when you save the changes. The idea is that the file is locked whenever an Emacs buffer visiting it has unsaved changes.

If you begin to modify the buffer while the visited file is locked by someone else, this constitutes a *collision*. When Emacs detects a collision, it asks you what to do, by calling the Lisp function `ask-user-about-lock`. You can redefine this function for the sake of customization. The standard definition of this function asks you a question and accepts three possible answers:

s   Steal the lock. Whoever was already changing the file loses the lock, and you gain the lock.

p   Proceed. Go ahead and edit the file despite its being locked by someone else.

q   Quit. This causes an error (`file-locked`) and the modification you were trying to make in the buffer does not actually take place.

Note that locking works on the basis of a file name; if a file has multiple names, Emacs does not realize that the two names are the same file and cannot prevent two users from editing it simultaneously under different names. However, basing locking on names means that Emacs can interlock the editing of new files that will not really exist until they are saved.

Some systems are not configured to allow Emacs to make locks, and there are cases where lock files cannot be written. In these cases, Emacs cannot detect trouble in advance, but it still can detect the collision when you try to save a file and overwrite someone else's changes.

If Emacs or the operating system crashes, this may leave behind lock files which are stale. So you may occasionally get warnings about spurious collisions. When you determine that the collision is spurious, just use p to tell Emacs to go ahead anyway.

Every time Emacs saves a buffer, it first checks the last-modification date of the existing file on disk to verify that it has not changed since the file was last visited or saved. If the date does not match, it implies that changes were made in the file in some other way, and these changes are about to be lost if Emacs actually does save. To prevent this, Emacs prints a warning message and asks for confirmation before saving. Occasionally you will know why the file was changed and know that it does not matter; then you can answer **yes** and proceed. Otherwise, you should cancel the save with **C-g** and investigate the situation.

The first thing you should do when notified that simultaneous editing has already taken place is to list the directory with **C-u C-x C-d** (see Section 14.8 [Directories], page 138). This shows the file's current author. You should attempt to contact him to warn him not to continue editing. Often the next step is to save the contents of your Emacs buffer under a different name, and use **diff** to compare the two files.

14.4 Reverting a Buffer

If you have made extensive changes to a file and then change your mind about them, you can get rid of them by reading in the previous version of the file. To do this, use **M-x revert-buffer**, which operates on the current buffer. Since reverting a buffer unintentionally could lose a lot of work, you must confirm this command with **yes**.

revert-buffer keeps point at the same distance (measured in characters) from the beginning of the file. If the file was edited only slightly, you will be at approximately the same piece of text after reverting as before. If you have made drastic changes, the same value of point in the old file may address a totally different piece of text.

Reverting marks the buffer as "not modified" until another change is made.

Some kinds of buffers whose contents reflect data bases other than files, such as Dired buffers, can also be reverted. For them, reverting means recalculating their contents from the appropriate data base. Buffers created explicitly with **C-x b** cannot be reverted; **revert-buffer** reports an error when asked to do so.

When you edit a file that changes automatically and frequently—for example, a log of output from a process that continues to run—it may be useful for Emacs to revert the file without querying you, whenever you visit the file again with **C-x C-f**.

To request this behavior, set the variable **revert-without-query** to a list of regular expressions. When a file name matches one of these regular expressions, **find-file** and **revert-buffer** will revert it automatically if it has changed—provided the buffer itself is not modified. (If you have edited the text, it would be wrong to discard your changes.)

14.5 Auto-Saving: Protection Against Disasters

Emacs saves all the visited files from time to time (based on counting your keystrokes) without being asked. This is called *auto-saving*. It prevents you from losing more than a limited amount of work if the system crashes.

When Emacs determines that it is time for auto-saving, each buffer
is considered, and is auto-saved if auto-saving is turned on for it and it
has been changed since the last time it was auto-saved. The message
'Auto-saving...' is displayed in the echo area during auto-saving, if any
files are actually auto-saved. Errors occurring during auto-saving are caught
so that they do not interfere with the execution of commands you have been
typing.

14.5.1 Auto-Save Files

Auto-saving does not normally save in the files that you visited, because
it can be very undesirable to save a program that is in an inconsistent state
when you have made half of a planned change. Instead, auto-saving is done
in a different file called the *auto-save file*, and the visited file is changed only
when you request saving explicitly (such as with C-x C-s).

Normally, the auto-save file name is made by appending '#' to the front
and rear of the visited file name. Thus, a buffer visiting file 'foo.c' is
auto-saved in a file '#foo.c#'. Most buffers that are not visiting files are
auto-saved only if you request it explicitly; when they are auto-saved, the
auto-save file name is made by appending '#%' to the front and '#' to the
rear of buffer name. For example, the '*mail*' buffer in which you compose
messages to be sent is auto-saved in a file named '#%*mail*#'. Auto-save
file names are made this way unless you reprogram parts of Emacs to do
something different (the functions make-auto-save-file-name and auto-
save-file-name-p). The file name to be used for auto-saving in a buffer is
calculated when auto-saving is turned on in that buffer.

When you delete a substantial part of the text in a large buffer, auto save
turns off temporarily in that buffer. This is because if you deleted the text
unintentionally, you might find the auto-save file more useful if it contains
the deleted text. To reenable auto-saving after this happens, save the buffer
with C-x C-s, or use C-u 1 M-x auto-save.

If you want auto-saving to be done in the visited file, set the variable
auto-save-visited-file-name to be non-nil. In this mode, there is really
no difference between auto-saving and explicit saving.

A buffer's auto-save file is deleted when you save the buffer in its visited file. To inhibit this, set the variable delete-auto-save-files to nil.
Changing the visited file name with C-x C-w or set-visited-file-name
renames any auto-save file to go with the new visited name.

14.5.2 Controlling Auto-Saving

Each time you visit a file, auto-saving is turned on for that file's buffer
if the variable auto-save-default is non-nil (but not in batch mode; see
Chapter 3 [Entering Emacs], page 25). The default for this variable is t,
so auto-saving is the usual practice for file-visiting buffers. Auto-saving

can be turned on or off for any existing buffer with the command M-x
auto-save-mode. Like other minor mode commands, M-x auto-save-mode
turns auto-saving on with a positive argument, off with a zero or negative
argument; with no argument, it toggles.

Emacs does auto-saving periodically based on counting how many characters you have typed since the last time auto-saving was done. The variable
auto-save-interval specifies how many characters there are between auto-
saves. By default, it is 300.

Auto-saving also takes place when you stop typing for a while. The
variable auto-save-timeout says how many seconds Emacs should wait
before it does an auto save (and perhaps also a garbage collection). (The
actual time period is longer if the current buffer is long; this is a heuristic
which aims to keep out of your way when you are editing long buffers, in
which auto-save takes an appreciable amount of time.) Auto-saving during
idle periods accomplishes two things: first, it makes sure all your work is
saved if you go away from the terminal for a while; second, it may avoid
some auto-saving while you are actually typing.

Emacs also does auto-saving whenever it gets a fatal error. This includes
killing the Emacs job with a shell command such as 'kill %emacs', or disconnecting a phone line or network connection.

You can request an auto-save explicitly with the command M-x
do-auto-save.

14.5.3 Recovering Data from Auto-Saves

You can use the contents of an auto-save file to recover from a loss of data
with the command M-x recover-file (RET) file (RET). This visits file and
then (after your confirmation) restores the contents from its auto-save file
'#file#'. You can then save with C-x C-s to put the recovered text into file
itself. For example, to recover file 'foo.c' from its auto-save file '#foo.c#',
do:

        M-x recover-file (RET) foo.c (RET)
        yes (RET)
        C-x C-s

Before asking for confirmation, M-x recover-file displays a directory
listing describing the specified file and the auto-save file, so you can compare
their sizes and dates. If the auto-save file is older, M-x recover-file does
not offer to read it.

If Emacs or the computer crashes, you can recover all the files you were
editing from their auto save files with the command M-x recover-session.
This first shows you a list of recorded interrupted sessions. Move point to
the one you choose, and type C-c C-c.

Then recover-session asks about each of the files that were being edited
during that session, asking whether to recover that file. If you answer y, it

calls `recover-file`, which works in its normal fashion. It shows the dates of the original file and its auto-save file, and asks once again whether to recover that file.

When `recover-session` is done, the files you've chosen to recover are present in Emacs buffers. You should then save them. Only this—saving them—updates the files themselves.

Interrupted sessions are recorded for later recovery in files named '~/.saves-*pid-hostname*'. The '~/.saves' portion of these names comes from the value of `auto-save-list-file-prefix`. You can arrange to record sessions in a different place by setting that variable in your '.emacs' file, but you'll have to redefine `recover-session` as well to make it look in the new place. If you set `auto-save-list-file-prefix` to `nil` in your '.emacs' file, sessions are not recorded for recovery.

14.6 File Name Aliases

Symbolic links and hard links both make it possible for several file names to refer to the same file. Hard links are alternate names that refer directly to the file; all the names are equally valid, and no one of them is preferred. By contrast, a symbolic link is a kind of defined alias: when 'foo' is a symbolic link to 'bar', you can use either name to refer to the file, but 'bar' is the real name, while 'foo' is just an alias. More complex cases occur when symbolic links point to directories.

If you visit two names for the same file, normally Emacs makes two different buffers, but it warns you about the situation.

If you wish to avoid visiting the same file in two buffers under different names, set the variable `find-file-existing-other-name` to a non-`nil` value. Then `find-file` uses the existing buffer visiting the file, no matter which of the file's names you specify.

If the variable `find-file-visit-truename` is non-`nil`, then the file name recorded for a buffer is the file's *truename* (made by replacing all symbolic links with their target names), rather than the name you specify. Setting `find-file-visit-truename` also implies the effect of `find-file-existing-other-name`.

14.7 Version Control

Version control systems are packages that can record multiple versions of a source file, usually storing the unchanged parts of the file just once. Version control systems also record history information such as the creation time of each version, who created it, and a description of what was changed in that version.

The Emacs version control interface is called VC. Its commands work with three version control systems—RCS, CVS and SCCS. The GNU project recommends RCS and CVS, which are free software and available from the Free Software Foundation.

14.7.1 Introduction to Version Control

VC allows you to use a version control system from within Emacs, integrating the version control operations smoothly with editing. VC provides a uniform interface to version control, so that regardless of which version control system is in use, you can use it the same way.

This section provides a general overview of version control, and describes the version control systems that VC supports. You can skip this section if you are already familiar with the version control system you want to use.

14.7.1.1 Supported Version Control Systems

VC currently works with three different version control systems or "back ends": RCS, CVS, and SCCS.

RCS is a free version control system that is available from the Free Software Foundation. It is perhaps the most mature of the supported back ends, and the VC commands are conceptually closest to RCS. Almost everything you can do with RCS can be done through VC.

CVS is built on top of RCS, and extends the features of RCS, allowing for more sophisticated release management, and concurrent multi-user development. VC supports basic editing operations under CVS, but for some less common tasks you still need to call CVS from the command line. Note also that before using CVS you must set up a repository, which is a subject too complex to treat here.

SCCS is a proprietary but widely used version control system. In terms of capabilities, it is the weakest of the three that VC supports. VC compensates for certain features missing in SCCS (snapshots, for example) by implementing them itself, but some other VC features, such as multiple branches, are not available with SCCS. You should use SCCS only if for some reason you cannot use RCS.

14.7.1.2 Concepts of Version Control

When a file is under version control, we also say that it is *registered* in the version control system. Each registered file has a corresponding *master file* which represents the file's present state plus its change history—enough to reconstruct the current version or any earlier version. Usually the master file also records a *log entry* for each version, describing in words what was changed in that version.

The file that is maintained under version control is sometimes called the *work file* corresponding to its master file. You edit the work file and make changes in it, as you would with an ordinary file. (With SCCS and RCS,

you must *lock* the file before you start to edit it.) After you are done with a
set of changes, you *check the file in*, which records the changes in the master
file, along with a log entry for them.

With CVS, there are usually multiple work files corresponding to a single
master file—often each user has his own copy. It is also possible to use RCS
in this way, but this is not the usual way to use RCS.

A version control system typically has some mechanism to coordinate
between users who want to change the same file. One method is *locking*
(analogous to the locking that Emacs uses to detect simultaneous editing of
a file, but distinct from it). The other method is to merge your changes with
other people's changes when you check them in.

With version control locking, work files are normally read-only so that
you cannot change them. You ask the version control system to make a work
file writable for you by locking it; only one user can do this at any given
time. When you check in your changes, that unlocks the file, making the
work file read-only again. This allows other users to lock the file to make
further changes. SCCS always uses locking, and RCS normally does.

The other alternative for RCS is to let each user modify the work file at
any time. In this mode, locking is not required, but it is permitted; check-in
is still the way to record a new version.

CVS normally allows each user to modify his own copy of the work file
at any time, but requires merging with changes from other users at check-
in time. However, CVS can also be set up to require locking. (see Section 14.7.9.1 [Backend Options], page 136).

14.7.2 Version Control and the Mode Line

When you visit a file that is under version control, Emacs indicates this
on the mode line. For example, 'RCS-1.3' says that RCS is used for that
file, and the current version is 1.3.

The character between the back-end name and the version number indicates the version control status of the file. '-' means that the work file is
not locked (if locking is in use), or not modified (if locking is not in use). ':'
indicates that the file is locked, or that it is modified. If the file is locked by
some other user (for instance, 'jim'), that is displayed as 'RCS:jim:1.3'.

14.7.3 Basic Editing under Version Control

The principal VC command is an all-purpose command that performs
either locking or check-in, depending on the situation.

C-x C-q
C-x v v   Perform the next logical version control operation on this file.

Strictly speaking, the command for this job is **vc-next-action**, bound
to C-x v v. However, the normal meaning of C-x C-q is to make a read-

only buffer writable, or vice versa; we have extended it to do the same job properly for files managed by version control, by performing the appropriate version control operations. When you type C-x C-q on a registered file, it acts like C-x v v.

The precise action of this command depends on the state of the file, and whether the version control system uses locking or not. SCCS and RCS normally use locking; CVS normally does not use locking.

14.7.3.1 Basic Version Control with Locking

If locking is used for the file (as with SCCS, and RCS in its default mode), C-x C-q can either lock a file or check it in:

- If the file is not locked, C-x C-q locks it, and makes it writable so that you can change it.
- If the file is locked by you, and contains changes, C-x C-q checks in the changes. In order to do this, it first reads the log entry for the new version. See Section 14.7.3.3 [Log Buffer], page 124.
- If the file is locked by you, but you have not changed it since you locked it, C-x C-q releases the lock and makes the file read-only again.
- If the file is locked by some other user, C-x C-q asks you whether you want to "steal the lock" from that user. If you say yes, the file becomes locked by you, but a message is sent to the person who had formerly locked the file, to inform him of what has happened.

These rules also apply when you use CVS in locking mode, except that there is no such thing as stealing a lock.

14.7.3.2 Basic Version Control without Locking

When there is no locking—the default for CVS—work files are always writable; you do not need to do anything before you begin to edit a file. The status indicator on the mode line is '-' if the file is unmodified; it flips to ':' as soon as you save any changes in the work file.

Here is what C-x C-q does when using CVS:

- If some other user has checked in changes into the master file, Emacs asks you whether you want to merge those changes into your own work file (see Section 14.7.6.3 [Merging], page 130). You must do this before you can check in your own changes.
- If there are no new changes in the master file, but you have made modifications in your work file, C-x C-q checks in your changes. In order to do this, it first reads the log entry for the new version. See Section 14.7.3.3 [Log Buffer], page 124.
- If the file is not modified, the C-x C-q does nothing.

These rules also apply when you use RCS in the mode that does not require locking, except that automatic merging of changes from the master

file is not implemented. Unfortunately, this means that nothing informs you
if another user has checked in changes in the same file since you began editing
it, and when this happens, his changes will be effectively removed when you
check in your version (though they will remain in the master file, so they
will not be entirely lost). You must therefore verify the current version is
unchanged, before you check in your changes. We hope to eliminate this risk
and provide automatic merging with RCS in a future Emacs version.

In addition, locking is possible with RCS even in this mode, although it
is not required; C-x C-q with an unmodified file locks the file, just as it does
with RCS in its normal (locking) mode.

14.7.3.3 Features of the Log Entry Buffer

When you check in changes, C-x C-q first reads a log entry. It pops
up a buffer called '*VC-Log*' for you to enter the log entry. When you are
finished, type C-c C-c in the '*VC-Log*' buffer. That is when check-in really
happens.

To abort check-in, just **don't** type C-c C-c in that buffer. You can switch
buffers and do other editing. As long as you don't try to check in another
file, the entry you were editing remains in the '*VC-Log*' buffer, and you
can go back to that buffer at any time to complete the check-in.

If you change several source files for the same reason, it is often convenient
to specify the same log entry for many of the files. To do this, use the history
of previous log entries. The commands M-n, M-p, M-s and M-r for doing this
work just like the minibuffer history commands (except that these versions
are used outside the minibuffer).

Each time you check in a file, the log entry buffer is put into VC Log
mode, which involves running two hooks: text-mode-hook and vc-log-
mode-hook. See Section 31.2.3 [Hooks], page 400.

14.7.4 Examining And Comparing Old Versions

One of the convenient features of version control is the ability to examine
any version of a file, or compare two versions.

C-x v ~ *version* (RET)
  Examine version *version* of the visited file, in a buffer of its own.

C-x v =   Compare the current buffer contents with the latest checked-in
          version of the file.

C-u C-x v = *file* (RET) *oldvers* (RET) *newvers* (RET)
  Compare the specified two versions of *file*.

C-x v g   Display the result of the CVS annotate command using colors.

To examine an old version in toto, visit the file and then type C-x v ~
version (RET) (vc-version-other-window). This puts the text of version

version in a file named '*filename.˜version˜*', and visits it in its own buffer in a separate window. (In RCS, you can also select an old version and create a branch from it. See Section 14.7.6 [Branches], page 128.)

But usually it is more convenient to compare two versions of the file, with the command C-x v = (vc-diff). Plain C-x v = compares the current buffer contents (saving them in the file if necessary) with the last checked-in version of the file. C-u C-x v =, with a numeric argument, reads a file name and two version numbers, then compares those versions of the specified file.

If you supply a directory name instead of the name of a registered file, this command compares the two specified versions of all registered files in that directory and its subdirectories.

You can specify a checked-in version by its number; an empty input specifies the current contents of the work file (which may be different from all the checked-in versions). You can also specify a snapshot name (see Section 14.7.7 [Snapshots], page 131) instead of one or both version numbers.

This command works by running the diff utility, getting the options from the variable diff-switches. It displays the output in a special buffer in another window. Unlike the M-x diff command, C-x v = does not try to locate the changes in the old and new versions. This is because normally one or both versions do not exist as files when you compare them; they exist only in the records of the master file. See Section 14.9 [Comparing Files], page 139, for more information about M-x diff.

For CVS-controlled files, you can display the result of the CVS annotate command, using colors to enhance the visual appearance. Use the command M-x vc-annotate to do this. Red means new, blue means old, and intermediate colors indicate intermediate ages. A prefix argument *n* specifies a stretch factor for the time scale; it makes each color cover a period *n* times as long.

14.7.5 The Secondary Commands of VC

This section explains the secondary commands of VC; those that you might use once a day.

14.7.5.1 Registering a File for Version Control

You can put any file under version control by simply visiting it, and then typing C-x v i (vc-register).

C-x v i   Register the visited file for version control.

To register the file, Emacs must choose which version control system to use for it. You can specify your choice explicitly by setting vc-default-back-end to RCS, CVS or SCCS. Otherwise, if there is a subdirectory named 'RCS', 'SCCS', or 'CVS', Emacs uses the corresponding version control system.

In the absence of any specification, the default choice is RCS if RCS is installed, otherwise SCCS.

If locking is in use, C-x v i leaves the file unlocked and read-only. Type C-x C-q if you wish to start editing it. After registering a file with CVS, you must subsequently commit the initial version by typing C-x C-q.

The initial version number for a newly registered file is 1.1, by default. You can specify a different default by setting the variable vc-default-init-version, or you can give C-x v i a numeric argument; then it reads the initial version number for this particular file using the minibuffer.

If vc-initial-comment is non-nil, C-x v i reads an initial comment to describe the purpose of this source file. Reading the initial comment works like reading a log entry (see Section 14.7.3.3 [Log Buffer], page 124).

14.7.5.2 VC Status Commands

C-x v l   Display version control state and change history.

To view the detailed version control status and history of a file, type C-x v l (vc-print-log). It displays the history of changes to the current file, including the text of the log entries. The output appears in a separate window.

14.7.5.3 Undoing Version Control Actions

C-x v u   Revert the buffer and the file to the last checked-in version.

C-x v c   Remove the last-entered change from the master for the visited file. This undoes your last check-in.

If you want to discard your current set of changes and revert to the last version checked in, use C-x v u (vc-revert-buffer). This leaves the file unlocked; if locking is in use, you must first lock the file again before you change it again. C-x v u requires confirmation, unless it sees that you haven't made any changes since the last checked-in version.

C-x v u is also the command to unlock a file if you lock it and then decide not to change it.

To cancel a change that you already checked in, use C-x v c (vc-cancel-version). This command discards all record of the most recent checked-in version. C-x v c also offers to revert your work file and buffer to the previous version (the one that precedes the version that is deleted).

If you answer no, VC keeps your changes in the buffer, and locks the file. The no-revert option is useful when you have checked in a change and then discover a trivial error in it; you can cancel the erroneous check-in, fix the error, and check the file in again.

When C-x v c does not revert the buffer, it unexpands all version control headers in the buffer instead (see Section 14.7.8.3 [Version Headers], page 135). This is because the buffer no longer corresponds to any existing version. If you check it in again, the check-in process will expand the headers properly for the new version number.

However, it is impossible to unexpand the RCS 'Log' header automatically. If you use that header feature, you have to unexpand it by hand—by deleting the entry for the version that you just canceled.

Be careful when invoking C-x v c, as it is easy to lose a lot of work with it. To help you be careful, this command always requires confirmation with yes. Note also that this command is disabled under CVS, because canceling versions is very dangerous and discouraged with CVS.

14.7.5.4 Dired under VC

When you are working on a large program, it is often useful to find out which files have changed within an entire directory tree, or to view the status of all files under version control at once, and to perform version control operations on collections of files. You can use the command C-x v d (vc-directory) to make a directory listing that includes only files relevant for version control.

C-x v d creates a buffer which uses VC Dired Mode. This looks much like an ordinary Dired buffer (see Chapter 28 [Dired], page 329); however, normally it shows only the noteworthy files (those locked or not up-to-date). This is called *terse display*. If you set the variable vc-dired-terse-display to nil, then VC Dired shows all relevant files—those managed under version control, plus all subdirectories (*full display*). The command v t in a VC Dired buffer toggles between terse display and full display (see Section 14.7.5.5 [VC Dired Commands], page 128).

By default, VC Dired produces a recursive listing of noteworthy or relevant files at or below the given directory. You can change this by setting the variable vc-dired-recurse to nil; then VC Dired shows only the files in the given directory.

The line for an individual file shows the version control state in the place of the hard link count, owner, group, and size of the file. If the file is unmodified, in sync with the master file, the version control state shown is blank. Otherwise it consists of text in parentheses. Under RCS and SCCS, the name of the user locking the file is shown; under CVS, an abbreviated version of the 'cvs status' output is used. Here is an example using RCS:

```
/home/jim/project:


-rw-r--r-- (jim)      Apr  2 23:39 file1
-r--r--r--            Apr  5 20:21 file2
```

The files 'file1' and 'file2' are under version control, 'file1' is locked by user jim, and 'file2' is unlocked.

Here is an example using CVS:

```
/home/joe/develop:

-rw-r--r-- (modified) Aug  2  1997 file1.c
-rw-r--r--            Apr  4 20:09 file2.c
-rw-r--r-- (merge)    Sep 13 1996 file3.c
```

Here 'file1.c' is modified with respect to the repository, and 'file2.c' is not. 'file3.c' is modified, but other changes have also been checked in to the repository—you need to merge them with the work file before you can check it in.

When VC Dired displays subdirectories (in the "full" display mode), it omits some that should never contain any files under version control. By default, this includes Version Control subdirectories such as 'RCS' and 'CVS'; you can customize this by setting the variable vc-directory-exclusion-list.

You can fine-tune VC Dired's format by typing C-u C-x v d—as in ordinary Dired, that allows you to specify additional switches for the 'ls' command.

14.7.5.5 VC Dired Commands

All the usual Dired commands work normally in VC Dired mode, except for v, which is redefined as the version control prefix. You can invoke VC commands such as vc-diff and vc-print-log by typing v =, or v l, and so on. Most of these commands apply to the file name on the current line.

The command v v (vc-next-action) operates on all the marked files, so that you can lock or check in several files at once. If it operates on more than one file, it handles each file according to its current state; thus, it might lock one file, but check in another file. This could be confusing; it is up to you to avoid confusing behavior by marking a set of files that are in a similar state.

If any files call for check-in, v v reads a single log entry, then uses it for all the files being checked in. This is convenient for registering or checking in several files at once, as part of the same change.

You can toggle between terse display (only locked files, or files not up-to-date) and full display at any time by typing v t vc-dired-toggle-terse-mode. There is also a special command * l (vc-dired-mark-locked), which marks all files currently locked (or, with CVS, all files not up-to-date). Thus, typing * l t k is another way to delete from the buffer all files except those currently locked.

14.7.6 Multiple Branches of a File

One use of version control is to maintain multiple "current" versions of a file. For example, you might have different versions of a program in which you are gradually adding various unfinished new features. Each such independent line of development is called a *branch*. VC allows you to create branches, switch between different branches, and merge changes from one branch to another. Please note, however, that branches are only supported for RCS at the moment.

A file's main line of development is usually called the *trunk*. The versions on the trunk are normally numbered 1.1, 1.2, 1.3, etc. At any such version, you can start an independent branch. A branch starting at version 1.2 would have version number 1.2.1.1, and consecutive versions on this branch would have numbers 1.2.1.2, 1.2.1.3, 1.2.1.4, and so on. If there is a second branch also starting at version 1.2, it would consist of versions 1.2.2.1, 1.2.2.2, 1.2.2.3, etc.

If you omit the final component of a version number, that is called a *branch number*. It refers to the highest existing version on that branch—the *head version* of that branch. The branches in the example above have branch numbers 1.2.1 and 1.2.2.

14.7.6.1 Switching between Branches

To switch between branches, type C-u C-x C-q and specify the version number you want to select. This version is then visited *unlocked* (write-protected), so you can examine it before locking it. Switching branches in this way is allowed only when the file is not locked.

You can omit the minor version number, thus giving only the branch number; this takes you to the head version on the chosen branch. If you only type (RET), Emacs goes to the highest version on the trunk.

After you have switched to any branch (including the main branch), you stay on it for subsequent VC commands, until you explicitly select some other branch.

14.7.6.2 Creating New Branches

To create a new branch from a head version (one that is the latest in the branch that contains it), first select that version if necessary, lock it with C-x C-q, and make whatever changes you want. Then, when you check in the changes, use C-u C-x C-q. This lets you specify the version number for the new version. You should specify a suitable branch number for a branch starting at the current version. For example, if the current version is 2.5, the branch number should be 2.5.1, 2.5.2, and so on, depending on the number of existing branches at that point.

To create a new branch at an older version (one that is no longer the head of a branch), first select that version (see Section 14.7.6.1 [Switching Branches], page 129), then lock it with C-x C-q. You'll be asked to confirm, when you lock the old version, that you really mean to create a new branch—if you say no, you'll be offered a chance to lock the latest version instead.

Then make your changes and type C-x C-q again to check in a new version. This automatically creates a new branch starting from the selected version. You need not specially request a new branch, because that's the only way to add a new version at a point that is not the head of a branch.

After the branch is created, you "stay" on it. That means that subsequent check-ins create new versions on that branch. To leave the branch, you must explicitly select a different version with C-u C-x C-q. To transfer changes from one branch to another, use the merge command, described in the next section.

14.7.6.3 Merging Branches

When you have finished the changes on a certain branch, you will often want to incorporate them into the file's main line of development (the trunk). This is not a trivial operation, because development might also have proceeded on the trunk, so that you must *merge* the changes into a file that has already been changed otherwise. VC allows you to do this (and other things) with the vc-merge command.

C-x v m (vc-merge)
    Merge changes into the work file.

C-x v m (vc-merge) takes a set of changes and merges it into the current version of the work file. It first asks you for a branch number or a pair of version numbers in the minibuffer. Then it finds the changes from that branch, or between the two versions you specified, and merges them into the current version of the current file.

As an example, suppose that you have finished a certain feature on branch 1.3.1. In the meantime, development on the trunk has proceeded to version 1.5. To merge the changes from the branch to the trunk, first go to the head version of the trunk, by typing C-u C-x C-q RET. Version 1.5 is now current. If locking is used for the file, type C-x C-q to lock version 1.5 so that you can change it. Next, type C-x v m 1.3.1 RET. This takes the entire set of changes on branch 1.3.1 (relative to version 1.3, where the branch started, up to the last version on the branch) and merges it into the current version of the work file. You can now check in the changed file, thus creating version 1.6 containing the changes from the branch.

It is possible to do further editing after merging the branch, before the next check-in. But it is usually wiser to check in the merged version, then lock it and make the further changes. This will keep a better record of the history of changes.

When you merge changes into a file that has itself been modified, the changes might overlap. We call this situation a *conflict*, and reconciling the conflicting changes is called *resolving a conflict*.

Whenever conflicts occur during merging, VC detects them, tells you about them in the echo area, and asks whether you want help in merging. If you say yes, it starts an Ediff session (see section "Ediff" in *The Ediff Manual*).

If you say no, the conflicting changes are both inserted into the file, surrounded by *conflict markers*. The example below shows how a conflict region looks; the file is called '`name`' and the current master file version with user B's changes in it is 1.11.

```
<<<<<<< name
```
 User A's version
```
=======
```
 User B's version
```
>>>>>>> 1.11
```

Then you can resolve the conflicts by editing the file manually. Or you can type M-x `vc-resolve-conflicts` after visiting the file. This starts an Ediff session, as described above.

14.7.6.4 Multi-User Branching

It is often useful for multiple developers to work simultaneously on different branches of a file. CVS allows this by default; for RCS, it is possible if you create multiple source directories. Each source directory should have a link named '`RCS`' which points to a common directory of RCS master files. Then each source directory can have its own choice of selected versions, but all share the same common RCS records.

This technique works reliably and automatically, provided that the source files contain RCS version headers (see Section 14.7.8.3 [Version Headers], page 135). The headers enable Emacs to be sure, at all times, which version number is present in the work file.

If the files do not have version headers, you must instead tell Emacs explicitly in each session which branch you are working on. To do this, first find the file, then type C-u C-x C-q and specify the correct branch number. This ensures that Emacs knows which branch it is using during this particular editing session.

14.7.7 Snapshots

A *snapshot* is a named set of file versions (one for each registered file) that you can treat as a unit. One important kind of snapshot is a *release*, a (theoretically) stable version of the system that is ready for distribution to users.

14.7.7.1 Making and Using Snapshots

There are two basic commands for snapshots; one makes a snapshot with a given name, the other retrieves a named snapshot.

C-x v s *name* (RET)
>	Define the last saved versions of every registered file in or under
>	the current directory as a snapshot named *name* (vc-create-
>	snapshot).

C-x v r *name* (RET)
>	For all registered files at or below the current directory level,
>	select whatever versions correspond to the snapshot *name* (vc-
>	retrieve-snapshot).
>
>	This command reports an error if any files are locked at or below
>	the current directory, without changing anything; this is to avoid
>	overwriting work in progress.

A snapshot uses a very small amount of resources—just enough to record the list of file names and which version belongs to the snapshot. Thus, you need not hesitate to create snapshots whenever they are useful.

You can give a snapshot name as an argument to C-x v = or C-x v ~ (see Section 14.7.4 [Old Versions], page 124). Thus, you can use it to compare a snapshot against the current files, or two snapshots against each other, or a snapshot against a named version.

14.7.7.2 Snapshot Caveats

VC's snapshot facilities are modeled on RCS's named-configuration support. They use RCS's native facilities for this, so under VC snapshots made using RCS are visible even when you bypass VC.

For SCCS, VC implements snapshots itself. The files it uses contain name/file/version-number triples. These snapshots are visible only through VC.

A snapshot is a set of checked-in versions. So make sure that all the files are checked in and not locked when you make a snapshot.

File renaming and deletion can create some difficulties with snapshots. This is not a VC-specific problem, but a general design issue in version control systems that no one has solved very well yet.

If you rename a registered file, you need to rename its master along with it (the command vc-rename-file does this automatically). If you are using SCCS, you must also update the records of the snapshot, to mention the file by its new name (vc-rename-file does this, too). An old snapshot that refers to a master file that no longer exists under the recorded name is invalid; VC can no longer retrieve it. It would be beyond the scope of this manual to explain enough about RCS and SCCS to explain how to update the snapshots by hand.

Using vc-rename-file makes the snapshot remain valid for retrieval, but it does not solve all problems. For example, some of the files in the program probably refer to others by name. At the very least, the makefile probably mentions the file that you renamed. If you retrieve an old snapshot, the renamed file is retrieved under its new name, which is not the name that the makefile expects. So the program won't really work as retrieved.

14.7.8 Miscellaneous Commands and Features of VC

This section explains the less-frequently-used features of VC.

14.7.8.1 Change Logs and VC

If you use RCS or CVS for a program and also maintain a change log file for it (see Section 22.12 [Change Log], page 249), you can generate change log entries automatically from the version control log entries:

C-x v a   Visit the current directory's change log file and, for registered files in that directory, create new entries for versions checked in since the most recent entry in the change log file. (vc-update-change-log).

This command works with RCS or CVS only, not with SCCS.

C-u C-x v a
            As above, but only find entries for the current buffer's file.

M-1 C-x v a
            As above, but find entries for all the currently visited files that are maintained with version control. This works only with RCS, and it puts all entries in the log for the default directory, which may not be appropriate.

For example, suppose the first line of 'ChangeLog' is dated 1999-04-10, and that the only check-in since then was by Nathaniel Bowditch to 'rcs2log' on 1999-05-22 with log text 'Ignore log messages that start with '#'.'. Then C-x v a visits 'ChangeLog' and inserts text like this:

```
    1999-05-22  Nathaniel Bowditch  <nat@apn.org>

         * rcs2log: Ignore log messages that start with '#'.
```

You can then edit the new change log entry further as you wish.

Unfortunately, timestamps in ChangeLog files are only dates, so some of the new change log entry may duplicate what's already in ChangeLog. You will have to remove these duplicates by hand.

Normally, the log entry for file 'foo' is displayed as '* foo: *text of log entry*'. The ':' after 'foo' is omitted if the text of the log entry starts with '(*functionname*): '. For example, if the log entry for 'vc.el' is '(vc-do-command): Check call-process status.', then the text in 'ChangeLog' looks like this:

```
    1999-05-06  Nathaniel Bowditch  <nat@apn.org>

         * vc.el (vc-do-command): Check call-process status.
```

When `C-x v a` adds several change log entries at once, it groups related log entries together if they all are checked in by the same author at nearly the same time. If the log entries for several such files all have the same text, it coalesces them into a single entry. For example, suppose the most recent check-ins have the following log entries:

- For 'vc.texinfo': 'Fix expansion typos.'
- For 'vc.el': 'Don't call expand-file-name.'
- For 'vc-hooks.el': 'Don't call expand-file-name.'

They appear like this in 'ChangeLog':

```
1999-04-01  Nathaniel Bowditch  <nat@apn.org>


        * vc.texinfo: Fix expansion typos.


        * vc.el, vc-hooks.el: Don't call expand-file-name.
```

Normally, `C-x v a` separates log entries by a blank line, but you can mark several related log entries to be clumped together (without an intervening blank line) by starting the text of each related log entry with a label of the form '{*clumpname*} '. The label itself is not copied to 'ChangeLog'. For example, suppose the log entries are:

- For 'vc.texinfo': '{expand} Fix expansion typos.'
- For 'vc.el': '{expand} Don't call expand-file-name.'
- For 'vc-hooks.el': '{expand} Don't call expand-file-name.'

Then the text in 'ChangeLog' looks like this:

```
1999-04-01  Nathaniel Bowditch  <nat@apn.org>


        * vc.texinfo: Fix expansion typos.
        * vc.el, vc-hooks.el: Don't call expand-file-name.
```

A log entry whose text begins with '#' is not copied to 'ChangeLog'. For example, if you merely fix some misspellings in comments, you can log the change with an entry beginning with '#' to avoid putting such trivia into 'ChangeLog'.

14.7.8.2 Renaming VC Work Files and Master Files

When you rename a registered file, you must also rename its master file correspondingly to get proper results. Use `vc-rename-file` to rename the source file as you specify, and rename its master file accordingly. It also updates any snapshots (see Section 14.7.7 [Snapshots], page 131) that mention the file, so that they use the new name; despite this, the snapshot thus modified may not completely work (see Section 14.7.7.2 [Snapshot Caveats], page 132).

You cannot use `vc-rename-file` on a file that is locked by someone else.

14.7.8.3 Inserting Version Control Headers

Sometimes it is convenient to put version identification strings directly into working files. Certain special strings called *version headers* are replaced in each successive version by the number of that version.

If you are using RCS, and version headers are present in your working files, Emacs can use them to determine the current version and the locking state of the files. This is more reliable than referring to the master files, which is done when there are no version headers. Note that in a multi-branch environment, version headers are necessary to make VC behave correctly (see Section 14.7.6.4 [Multi-User Branching], page 131).

Searching for version headers is controlled by the variable **vc-consult-headers**. If it is non-**nil**, Emacs searches for headers to determine the version number you are editing. Setting it to **nil** disables this feature.

You can use the **C-x v h** command (**vc-insert-headers**) to insert a suitable header string.

C-x v h   Insert headers in a file for use with your version-control system.

The default header string is '**Id**' for RCS and '**%W%**' for SCCS. You can specify other headers to insert by setting the variable **vc-header-alist**. Its value is a list of elements of the form (*program . string*) where *program* is RCS or SCCS and *string* is the string to use.

Instead of a single string, you can specify a list of strings; then each string in the list is inserted as a separate header on a line of its own.

It is often necessary to use "superfluous" backslashes when writing the strings that you put in this variable. This is to prevent the string in the constant from being interpreted as a header itself if the Emacs Lisp file containing it is maintained with version control.

Each header is inserted surrounded by tabs, inside comment delimiters, on a new line at point. Normally the ordinary comment start and comment end strings of the current mode are used, but for certain modes, there are special comment delimiters for this purpose; the variable **vc-comment-alist** specifies them. Each element of this list has the form (*mode starter ender*).

The variable **vc-static-header-alist** specifies further strings to add based on the name of the buffer. Its value should be a list of elements of the form (*regexp . format*). Whenever *regexp* matches the buffer name, *format* is inserted as part of the header. A header line is inserted for each element that matches the buffer name, and for each string specified by **vc-header-alist**. The header line is made by processing the string from **vc-header-alist** with the format taken from the element. The default value for **vc-static-header-alist** is as follows:

```
(("\\.c$" .
  "\n#ifndef lint\nstatic char vcid[] = \"\%s\";\n\
#endif /* lint */\n"))
```

It specifies insertion of text of this form:

```
#ifndef lint
static char vcid[] = "string";
#endif /* lint */
```

Note that the text above starts with a blank line.

If you use more than one version header in a file, put them close together in the file. The mechanism in `revert-buffer` that preserves markers may not handle markers positioned between two version headers.

14.7.9 Customizing VC

There are many ways of customizing VC. The options you can set fall into four categories, described in the following sections.

14.7.9.1 Options for VC Backends

You can tell RCS and CVS whether to use locking for a file or not (see Section 14.7.1.2 [VC Concepts], page 121, for a description of locking). VC automatically recognizes what you have chosen, and behaves accordingly.

For RCS, the default is to use locking, but there is a mode called *non-strict locking* in which you can check-in changes without locking the file first. Use 'rcs -U' to switch to non-strict locking for a particular file, see the 'rcs' manpage for details.

Under CVS, the default is not to use locking; anyone can change a work file at any time. However, there are ways to restrict this, resulting in behavior that resembles locking.

For one thing, you can set the `CVSREAD` environment variable to an arbitrary value. If this variable is defined, CVS makes your work files read-only by default. In Emacs, you must type `C-x C-q` to make the file writeable, so that editing works in fact similar as if locking was used. Note however, that no actual locking is performed, so several users can make their files writeable at the same time. When setting `CVSREAD` for the first time, make sure to check out all your modules anew, so that the file protections are set correctly.

Another way to achieve something similar to locking is to use the *watch* feature of CVS. If a file is being watched, CVS makes it read-only by default, and you must also use `C-x C-q` in Emacs to make it writable. VC calls `cvs edit` to make the file writeable, and CVS takes care to notify other developers of the fact that you intend to change the file. See the CVS documentation for details on using the watch feature.

You can turn off use of VC for CVS-managed files by setting the variable `vc-handle-cvs` to `nil`. If you do this, Emacs treats these files as if they were not registered, and the VC commands are not available for them. You must do all CVS operations manually.

14.7.9.2 VC Workfile Handling

Emacs normally does not save backup files for source files that are maintained with version control. If you want to make backup files even for files that use version control, set the variable `vc-make-backup-files` to a non-`nil` value.

Normally the work file exists all the time, whether it is locked or not. If you set `vc-keep-workfiles` to `nil`, then checking in a new version with `C-x C-q` deletes the work file; but any attempt to visit the file with Emacs creates it again. (With CVS, work files are always kept.)

Editing a version-controlled file through a symbolic link can be dangerous. It bypasses the version control system—you can edit the file without locking it, and fail to check your changes in. Also, your changes might overwrite those of another user. To protect against this, VC checks each symbolic link that you visit, to see if it points to a file under version control.

The variable `vc-follow-symlinks` controls what to do when a symbolic link points to a version-controlled file. If it is `nil`, VC only displays a warning message. If it is `t`, VC automatically follows the link, and visits the real file instead, telling you about this in the echo area. If the value is `ask` (the default), VC asks you each time whether to follow the link.

14.7.9.3 VC Status Retrieval

When deducing the locked/unlocked state of a file, VC first looks for an RCS version header string in the file (see Section 14.7.8.3 [Version Headers], page 135). If there is no header string, or if you are using SCCS, VC normally looks at the file permissions of the work file; this is fast. But there might be situations when the file permissions cannot be trusted. In this case the master file has to be consulted, which is rather expensive. Also the master file can only tell you *if* there's any lock on the file, but not whether your work file really contains that locked version.

You can tell VC not to use version headers to determine lock status by setting `vc-consult-headers` to `nil`. VC then always uses the file permissions (if it can trust them), or else checks the master file.

You can specify the criterion for whether to trust the file permissions by setting the variable `vc-mistrust-permissions`. Its value can be `t` (always mistrust the file permissions and check the master file), `nil` (always trust the file permissions), or a function of one argument which makes the decision. The argument is the directory name of the 'RCS', 'CVS' or 'SCCS' subdirectory. A non-`nil` value from the function says to mistrust the file permissions. If you find that the file permissions of work files are changed erroneously, set `vc-mistrust-permissions` to `t`. Then VC always checks the master file to determine the file's status.

14.7.9.4 VC Command Execution

If `vc-suppress-confirm` is non-`nil`, then `C-x C-q` and `C-x v i` can save the current buffer without asking, and `C-x v u` also operates without asking for confirmation. (This variable does not affect `C-x v c`; that operation is so drastic that it should always ask for confirmation.)

VC mode does much of its work by running the shell commands for RCS, CVS and SCCS. If `vc-command-messages` is non-`nil`, VC displays messages to indicate which shell commands it runs, and additional messages when the commands finish.

You can specify additional directories to search for version control programs by setting the variable `vc-path`. These directories are searched before the usual search path. But the proper files are usually found automatically.

14.8 File Directories

The file system groups files into *directories*. A *directory listing* is a list of all the files in a directory. Emacs provides commands to create and delete directories, and to make directory listings in brief format (file names only) and verbose format (sizes, dates, and authors included). There is also a directory browser called Dired; see Chapter 28 [Dired], page 329.

`C-x C-d` *dir-or-pattern* (RET)
> Display a brief directory listing (`list-directory`).

`C-u C-x C-d` *dir-or-pattern* (RET)
> Display a verbose directory listing.

`M-x make-directory` (RET) *dirname* (RET)
> Create a new directory named *dirname*.

`M-x delete-directory` (RET) *dirname* (RET)
> Delete the directory named *dirname*. It must be empty, or you get an error.

The command to display a directory listing is `C-x C-d` (`list-directory`). It reads using the minibuffer a file name which is either a directory to be listed or a wildcard-containing pattern for the files to be listed. For example,

> `C-x C-d /u2/emacs/etc` (RET)

lists all the files in directory '`/u2/emacs/etc`'. Here is an example of specifying a file name pattern:

> `C-x C-d /u2/emacs/src/*.c` (RET)

Normally, `C-x C-d` prints a brief directory listing containing just file names. A numeric argument (regardless of value) tells it to make a verbose listing including sizes, dates, and authors (like '`ls -l`').

The text of a directory listing is obtained by running `ls` in an inferior process. Two Emacs variables control the switches passed to `ls`: `list-directory-brief-switches` is a string giving the switches to use in brief listings (`"-CF"` by default), and `list-directory-verbose-switches` is a string giving the switches to use in a verbose listing (`"-l"` by default).

14.9 Comparing Files

The command `M-x diff` compares two files, displaying the differences in an Emacs buffer named '`*Diff*`'. It works by running the `diff` program, using options taken from the variable `diff-switches`, whose value should be a string.

The buffer '`*Diff*`' has Compilation mode as its major mode, so you can use `C-x '` to visit successive changed locations in the two source files. You can also move to a particular hunk of changes and type (RET) or `C-c C-c`, or click `Mouse-2` on it, to move to the corresponding source location. You can also use the other special commands of Compilation mode: (SPC) and (DEL) for scrolling, and `M-p` and `M-n` for cursor motion. See Section 23.1 [Compilation], page 277.

The command `M-x diff-backup` compares a specified file with its most recent backup. If you specify the name of a backup file, `diff-backup` compares it with the source file that it is a backup of.

The command `M-x compare-windows` compares the text in the current window with that in the next window. Comparison starts at point in each window, and each starting position is pushed on the mark ring in its respective buffer. Then point moves forward in each window, a character at a time, until a mismatch between the two windows is reached. Then the command is finished. For more information about windows in Emacs, Chapter 16 [Windows], page 151.

With a numeric argument, `compare-windows` ignores changes in whitespace. If the variable `compare-ignore-case` is non-`nil`, it ignores differences in case as well.

See also Section 22.14 [Emerge], page 257, for convenient facilities for merging two similar files.

14.10 Miscellaneous File Operations

Emacs has commands for performing many other operations on files. All operate on one file; they do not accept wildcard file names.

`M-x view-file` allows you to scan or read a file by sequential screenfuls. It reads a file name argument using the minibuffer. After reading the file into an Emacs buffer, `view-file` displays the beginning. You can then type (SPC) to scroll forward one windowful, or (DEL) to scroll backward. Various other commands are provided for moving around in the file, but none for changing it; type **?** while viewing for a list of them. They are mostly the same as normal Emacs cursor motion commands. To exit from viewing, type **q**. The commands for viewing are defined by a special major mode called View mode.

A related command, `M-x view-buffer`, views a buffer already present in Emacs. See Section 15.3 [Misc Buffer], page 145.

`M-x insert-file` inserts a copy of the contents of the specified file into the current buffer at point, leaving point unchanged before the contents and the mark after them.

`M-x write-region` is the inverse of `M-x insert-file`; it copies the contents of the region into the specified file. `M-x append-to-file` adds the text of the region to the end of the specified file. See Section 9.3 [Accumulating Text], page 70.

`M-x delete-file` deletes the specified file, like the `rm` command in the shell. If you are deleting many files in one directory, it may be more convenient to use Dired (see Chapter 28 [Dired], page 329).

`M-x rename-file` reads two file names *old* and *new* using the minibuffer, then renames file *old* as *new*. If a file named *new* already exists, you must confirm with **yes** or renaming is not done; this is because renaming causes the old meaning of the name *new* to be lost. If *old* and *new* are on different file systems, the file *old* is copied and deleted.

The similar command `M-x add-name-to-file` is used to add an additional name to an existing file without removing its old name. The new name must belong on the same file system that the file is on.

`M-x copy-file` reads the file *old* and writes a new file named *new* with the same contents. Confirmation is required if a file named *new* already exists, because copying has the consequence of overwriting the old contents of the file *new*.

`M-x make-symbolic-link` reads two file names *target* and *linkname*, then creates a symbolic link named *linkname* and pointing at *target*. The effect is that future attempts to open file *linkname* will refer to whatever file is named *target* at the time the opening is done, or will get an error if the name *target* is not in use at that time. This command does not expand the argument *target*, so that it allows you to specify a relative name as the target of the link.

Confirmation is required when creating the link if *linkname* is in use. Note that not all systems support symbolic links.

14.11 Accessing Compressed Files

Emacs comes with a library that can automatically uncompress compressed files when you visit them, and automatically recompress them if you alter them and save them. To enable this feature, type the command `M-x auto-compression-mode`.

When automatic compression (which implies automatic uncompression as well) is enabled, Emacs recognizes compressed files by their file names. File names ending in '.gz' indicate a file compressed with gzip. Other endings indicate other compression programs.

Automatic uncompression and compression apply to all the operations in which Emacs uses the contents of a file. This includes visiting it, saving it, inserting its contents into a buffer, loading it, and byte compiling it.

14.12 Remote Files

You can refer to files on other machines using a special file name syntax:

/*host*:*filename*
/*user*@*host*:*filename*

When you do this, Emacs uses the FTP program to read and write files on the specified host. It logs in through FTP using your user name or the name *user*. It may ask you for a password from time to time; this is used for logging in on *host*.

Normally, if you do not specify a user name in a remote file name, that means to use your own user name. But if you set the variable ange-ftp-default-user to a string, that string is used instead. (The Emacs package that implements FTP file access is called ange-ftp.)

You can entirely turn off the FTP file name feature by setting the variable file-name-handler-alist to nil.

14.13 Quoted File Names

You can *quote* an absolute file name to prevent special characters and syntax in it from having their special effects. The way to do this is to add '/:' at the beginning.

For example, you can quote a local file name which appears remote, to prevent it from being treated as a remote file name. Thus, if you have a directory named '/foo:' and a file named 'bar' in it, you can refer to that file in Emacs as '/:/foo:/bar'.

'/:' can also prevent '~' from being treated as a special character for a user's home directory. For example, '/:/tmp/~hack' refers to a file whose name is '~hack' in directory '/tmp'.

Likewise, quoting with '/:' is one way to enter in the minibuffer a file name that contains '$'. However, the '/:' must be at the beginning of the buffer in order to quote '$'.

You can also quote wildcard characters with '/:', for visiting. For example, '/:/tmp/foo*bar' visits the file '/tmp/foo*bar'. However, in most cases you can simply type the wildcard characters for themselves. For example, if the only file name in '/tmp' that starts with 'foo' and ends with 'bar' is 'foo*bar', then specifying '/tmp/foo*bar' will visit just '/tmp/foo*bar'.

15 Using Multiple Buffers

The text you are editing in Emacs resides in an object called a *buffer*. Each time you visit a file, a buffer is created to hold the file's text. Each time you invoke Dired, a buffer is created to hold the directory listing. If you send a message with C-x m, a buffer named '*mail*' is used to hold the text of the message. When you ask for a command's documentation, that appears in a buffer called '*Help*'.

At any time, one and only one buffer is *selected*. It is also called the *current buffer*. Often we say that a command operates on "the buffer" as if there were only one; but really this means that the command operates on the selected buffer (most commands do).

When Emacs has multiple windows, each window has a chosen buffer which is displayed there, but at any time only one of the windows is selected and its chosen buffer is the selected buffer. Each window's mode line displays the name of the buffer that the window is displaying (see Chapter 16 [Windows], page 151).

Each buffer has a name, which can be of any length, and you can select any buffer by giving its name. Most buffers are made by visiting files, and their names are derived from the files' names. But you can also create an empty buffer with any name you want. A newly started Emacs has a buffer named '*scratch*' which can be used for evaluating Lisp expressions in Emacs. The distinction between upper and lower case matters in buffer names.

Each buffer records individually what file it is visiting, whether it is modified, and what major mode and minor modes are in effect in it (see Chapter 19 [Major Modes], page 191). Any Emacs variable can be made *local to* a particular buffer, meaning its value in that buffer can be different from the value in other buffers. See Section 31.2.4 [Locals], page 401.

15.1 Creating and Selecting Buffers

C-x b *buffer* (RET)
>   Select or create a buffer named *buffer* (**switch-to-buffer**).

C-x 4 b *buffer* (RET)
>   Similar, but select *buffer* in another window (**switch-to-buffer-other-window**).

C-x 5 b *buffer* (RET)
>   Similar, but select *buffer* in a separate frame (**switch-to-buffer-other-frame**).

To select the buffer named *bufname*, type C-x b *bufname* (RET). This runs the command **switch-to-buffer** with argument *bufname*. You can use completion on an abbreviation for the buffer name you want (see Section 5.3

[Completion], page 43). An empty argument to C-x b specifies the most recently selected buffer that is not displayed in any window.

Most buffers are created by visiting files, or by Emacs commands that want to display some text, but you can also create a buffer explicitly by typing C-x b *bufname* (RET). This makes a new, empty buffer that is not visiting any file, and selects it for editing. Such buffers are used for making notes to yourself. If you try to save one, you are asked for the file name to use. The new buffer's major mode is determined by the value of **default-major-mode** (see Chapter 19 [Major Modes], page 191).

Note that C-x C-f, and any other command for visiting a file, can also be used to switch to an existing file-visiting buffer. See Section 14.2 [Visiting], page 108.

Emacs uses buffer names that start with a space for internal purposes. It treats these buffers specially in minor ways—for example, by default they do not record undo information. It is best to avoid using such buffer names yourself.

15.2 Listing Existing Buffers

C-x C-b   List the existing buffers (`list-buffers`).

To display a list of all the buffers that exist, type C-x C-b. Each line in the list shows one buffer's name, major mode and visited file. The buffers are listed in the order that they were current; the buffers that were current most recently come first.

'*' at the beginning of a line indicates the buffer is "modified." If several buffers are modified, it may be time to save some with C-x s (see Section 14.3 [Saving], page 111). '%' indicates a read-only buffer. '.' marks the selected buffer. Here is an example of a buffer list:

```
 MR Buffer         Size   Mode            File
 -- ------         ----   ----            ----
 .* emacs.tex      383402 Texinfo         /u2/emacs/man/emacs.tex
    *Help*         1287   Fundamental
    files.el       23076  Emacs-Lisp      /u2/emacs/lisp/files.el
 %  RMAIL          64042  RMAIL           /u/rms/RMAIL
 *% man            747    Dired           /u2/emacs/man/
    net.emacs      343885 Fundamental     /u/rms/net.emacs
    fileio.c       27691  C               /u2/emacs/src/fileio.c
    NEWS           67340  Text            /u2/emacs/etc/NEWS
    *scratch*      0      Lisp Interaction
```

Note that the buffer '*Help*' was made by a help request; it is not visiting any file. The buffer **man** was made by Dired on the directory '/u2/emacs/man/'.

15.3 Miscellaneous Buffer Operations

C-x C-q   Toggle read-only status of buffer (`vc-toggle-read-only`).

M-x rename-buffer (RET) *name* (RET)
>   Change the name of the current buffer.

M-x rename-uniquely
>   Rename the current buffer by adding '<*number*>' to the end.

M-x view-buffer (RET) *buffer* (RET)
>   Scroll through buffer *buffer*.

A buffer can be *read-only*, which means that commands to change its contents are not allowed. The mode line indicates read-only buffers with '%%' or '%*' near the left margin. Read-only buffers are usually made by subsystems such as Dired and Rmail that have special commands to operate on the text; also by visiting a file whose access control says you cannot write it.

If you wish to make changes in a read-only buffer, use the command C-x C-q (`vc-toggle-read-only`). It makes a read-only buffer writable, and makes a writable buffer read-only. In most cases, this works by setting the variable `buffer-read-only`, which has a local value in each buffer and makes the buffer read-only if its value is non-`nil`. If the file is maintained with version control, C-x C-q works through the version control system to change the read-only status of the file as well as the buffer. See Section 14.7 [Version Control], page 120.

M-x rename-buffer changes the name of the current buffer. Specify the new name as a minibuffer argument. There is no default. If you specify a name that is in use for some other buffer, an error happens and no renaming is done.

M-x rename-uniquely renames the current buffer to a similar name with a numeric suffix added to make it both different and unique. This command does not need an argument. It is useful for creating multiple shell buffers: if you rename the '*Shell*' buffer, then do M-x shell again, it makes a new shell buffer named '*Shell*'; meanwhile, the old shell buffer continues to exist under its new name. This method is also good for mail buffers, compilation buffers, and most Emacs features that create special buffers with particular names.

M-x view-buffer is much like M-x view-file (see Section 14.10 [Misc File Ops], page 139) except that it examines an already existing Emacs buffer. View mode provides commands for scrolling through the buffer conveniently but not for changing it. When you exit View mode with q, that switches back to the buffer (and the position) which was previously displayed in the window. Alternatively, if you exit View mode with e, the buffer and the value of point that resulted from your perusal remain in effect.

The commands M-x append-to-buffer and M-x insert-buffer can be used to copy text from one buffer to another. See Section 9.3 [Accumulating Text], page 70.

15.4 Killing Buffers

If you continue an Emacs session for a while, you may accumulate a large number of buffers. You may then find it convenient to *kill* the buffers you no longer need. On most operating systems, killing a buffer releases its space back to the operating system so that other programs can use it. Here are some commands for killing buffers:

C-x k *bufname* (RET)
> Kill buffer *bufname* (kill-buffer).

M-x kill-some-buffers
> Offer to kill each buffer, one by one.

C-x k (kill-buffer) kills one buffer, whose name you specify in the minibuffer. The default, used if you type just (RET) in the minibuffer, is to kill the current buffer. If you kill the current buffer, another buffer is selected; one that has been selected recently but does not appear in any window now. If you ask to kill a file-visiting buffer that is modified (has unsaved editing), then you must confirm with yes before the buffer is killed.

The command M-x kill-some-buffers asks about each buffer, one by one. An answer of y means to kill the buffer. Killing the current buffer or a buffer containing unsaved changes selects a new buffer or asks for confirmation just like kill-buffer.

The buffer menu feature (see Section 15.5 [Several Buffers], page 147) is also convenient for killing various buffers.

If you want to do something special every time a buffer is killed, you can add hook functions to the hook kill-buffer-hook (see Section 31.2.3 [Hooks], page 400).

If you run one Emacs session for a period of days, as many people do, it can fill up with buffers that you used several days ago. The command M-x clean-buffer-list is a convenient way to purge them; it kills all the unmodified buffers that you have not used for a long time. An ordinary buffer is killed if it has not been displayed for three days; however, you can specify certain buffers that should never be killed automatically, and others that should be killed if they have been unused for a mere hour.

You can also have this buffer purging done for you, every day at midnight, by enabling Midnight mode. Midnight mode operates each day at midnight; at that time, it runs clean-buffer-list, or whichever functions you have placed in the normal hook midnight-hook (see Section 31.2.3 [Hooks], page 400).

To enable Midnight mode, use the Customization buffer to set the variable `midnight-mode` to `t`. See Section 31.2.2 [Easy Customization], page 394.

15.5 Operating on Several Buffers

The *buffer-menu* facility is like a "Dired for buffers"; it allows you to request operations on various Emacs buffers by editing an Emacs buffer containing a list of them. You can save buffers, kill them (here called *deleting* them, for consistency with Dired), or display them.

M-x buffer-menu
> Begin editing a buffer listing all Emacs buffers.

The command `buffer-menu` writes a list of all Emacs buffers into the buffer '`*Buffer List*`', and selects that buffer in Buffer Menu mode. The buffer is read-only, and can be changed only through the special commands described in this section. The usual Emacs cursor motion commands can be used in the '`*Buffer List*`' buffer. The following commands apply to the buffer described on the current line.

d
> Request to delete (kill) the buffer, then move down. The request shows as a 'D' on the line, before the buffer name. Requested deletions take place when you type the x command.

C-d
> Like d but move up afterwards instead of down.

s
> Request to save the buffer. The request shows as an 'S' on the line. Requested saves take place when you type the x command. You may request both saving and deletion for the same buffer.

x
> Perform previously requested deletions and saves.

u
> Remove any request made for the current line, and move down.

(DEL)
> Move to previous line and remove any request made for that line.

The d, C-d, s and u commands to add or remove flags also move down (or up) one line. They accept a numeric argument as a repeat count.

These commands operate immediately on the buffer listed on the current line:

~
> Mark the buffer "unmodified." The command ~ does this immediately when you type it.

%
> Toggle the buffer's read-only flag. The command % does this immediately when you type it.

t
> Visit the buffer as a tags table. See Section 22.13.3 [Select Tags Table], page 254.

There are also commands to select another buffer or buffers:

q   Quit the buffer menu—immediately display the most recent for-
                      merly visible buffer in its place.

(RET)
f   Immediately select this line's buffer in place of the '*Buffer
                      List*' buffer.

o   Immediately select this line's buffer in another window as if by
                      C-x 4 b, leaving '*Buffer List*' visible.

C-o   Immediately display this line's buffer in another window, but
                      don't select the window.

1   Immediately select this line's buffer in a full-screen window.

2   Immediately set up two windows, with this line's buffer in
                      one, and the previously selected buffer (aside from the buffer
                      '*Buffer List*') in the other.

b   Bury the buffer listed on this line.

m   Mark this line's buffer to be displayed in another window if you
                      exit with the v command. The request shows as a '>' at the
                      beginning of the line. (A single buffer may not have both a
                      delete request and a display request.)

v   Immediately select this line's buffer, and also display in other
                      windows any buffers previously marked with the m command. If
                      you have not marked any buffers, this command is equivalent to
                      1.

   All that buffer-menu does directly is create and switch to a suitable
buffer, and turn on Buffer Menu mode. Everything else described above is
implemented by the special commands provided in Buffer Menu mode. One
consequence of this is that you can switch from the '*Buffer List*' buffer
to another Emacs buffer, and edit there. You can reselect the '*Buffer
List*' buffer later, to perform the operations already requested, or you can
kill it, or pay no further attention to it.

   The only difference between buffer-menu and list-buffers is that
buffer-menu switches to the '*Buffer List*' buffer in the selected window;
list-buffers displays it in another window. If you run list-buffers (that
is, type C-x C-b) and select the buffer list manually, you can use all of the
commands described here.

   The buffer '*Buffer List*' is not updated automatically when buffers
are created and killed; its contents are just text. If you have created, deleted
or renamed buffers, the way to update '*Buffer List*' to show what you
have done is to type g (revert-buffer) or repeat the buffer-menu command.

15.6 Indirect Buffers

An *indirect buffer* shares the text of some other buffer, which is called the *base buffer* of the indirect buffer. In some ways it is the analogue, for buffers, of a symbolic link between files.

M-x make-indirect-buffer *base-buffer* (RET) *indirect-name* (RET)
> Create an indirect buffer named *indirect-name* whose base buffer is *base-buffer*.

The text of the indirect buffer is always identical to the text of its base buffer; changes made by editing either one are visible immediately in the other. But in all other respects, the indirect buffer and its base buffer are completely separate. They have different names, different values of point, different narrowing, different markers, different major modes, and different local variables.

An indirect buffer cannot visit a file, but its base buffer can. If you try to save the indirect buffer, that actually works by saving the base buffer. Killing the base buffer effectively kills the indirect buffer, but killing an indirect buffer has no effect on its base buffer.

One way to use indirect buffers is to display multiple views of an outline. See Section 21.8.4 [Outline Views], page 214.

16 Multiple Windows

Emacs can split a frame into two or many windows. Multiple windows can display parts of different buffers, or different parts of one buffer. Multiple frames always imply multiple windows, because each frame has its own set of windows. Each window belongs to one and only one frame.

16.1 Concepts of Emacs Windows

Each Emacs window displays one Emacs buffer at any time. A single buffer may appear in more than one window; if it does, any changes in its text are displayed in all the windows where it appears. But the windows showing the same buffer can show different parts of it, because each window has its own value of point.

At any time, one of the windows is the *selected window*; the buffer this window is displaying is the current buffer. The terminal's cursor shows the location of point in this window. Each other window has a location of point as well, but since the terminal has only one cursor there is no way to show where those locations are. When multiple frames are visible in X Windows, each frame has a cursor which appears in the frame's selected window. The cursor in the selected frame is solid; the cursor in other frames is a hollow box.

Commands to move point affect the value of point for the selected Emacs window only. They do not change the value of point in any other Emacs window, even one showing the same buffer. The same is true for commands such as C-x b to change the selected buffer in the selected window; they do not affect other windows at all. However, there are other commands such as C-x 4 b that select a different window and switch buffers in it. Also, all commands that display information in a window, including (for example) C-h f (describe-function) and C-x C-b (list-buffers), work by switching buffers in a nonselected window without affecting the selected window.

When multiple windows show the same buffer, they can have different regions, because they can have different values of point. However, they all have the same value for the mark, because each buffer has only one mark position.

Each window has its own mode line, which displays the buffer name, modification status and major and minor modes of the buffer that is displayed in the window. See Section 1.3 [Mode Line], page 17, for full details on the mode line.

16.2 Splitting Windows

C-x 2   Split the selected window into two windows, one above the other
(`split-window-vertically`).

C-x 3   Split the selected window into two windows positioned side by
side (`split-window-horizontally`).

C-Mouse-2

      In the mode line or scroll bar of a window, split that window.

The command `C-x 2` (`split-window-vertically`) breaks the selected
window into two windows, one above the other. Both windows start out
displaying the same buffer, with the same value of point. By default the two
windows each get half the height of the window that was split; a numeric
argument specifies how many lines to give to the top window.

`C-x 3` (`split-window-horizontally`) breaks the selected window into
two side-by-side windows. A numeric argument specifies how many columns
to give the one on the left. A line of vertical bars separates the two windows.
Windows that are not the full width of the screen have mode lines, but they
are truncated. On terminals where Emacs does not support highlighting,
truncated mode lines sometimes do not appear in inverse video.

You can split a window horizontally or vertically by clicking `C-Mouse-2`
in the mode line or the scroll bar. The line of splitting goes through the place
where you click: if you click on the mode line, the new scroll bar goes above
the spot; if you click in the scroll bar, the mode line of the split window is
side by side with your click.

When a window is less than the full width, text lines too long to fit
are frequent. Continuing all those lines might be confusing. The variable
`truncate-partial-width-windows` can be set non-`nil` to force truncation
in all windows less than the full width of the screen, independent of the
buffer being displayed and its value for `truncate-lines`. See Section 4.8
[Continuation Lines], page 35.

Horizontal scrolling is often used in side-by-side windows. See Chapter 11
[Display], page 79.

If `split-window-keep-point` is non-`nil`, the default, both of the windows resulting from `C-x 2` inherit the value of point from the window that
was split. This means that scrolling is inevitable. If this variable is `nil`, then
`C-x 2` tries to avoid shifting any text the screen, by putting point in each
window at a position already visible in the window. It also selects whichever
window contain the screen line that the cursor was previously on. Some
users prefer the latter mode on slow terminals.

16.3 Using Other Windows

C-x o   Select another window (`other-window`). That is o, not zero.

C-M-v   Scroll the next window (`scroll-other-window`).

M-x compare-windows

> Find next place where the text in the selected window does not match the text in the next window.

Mouse-1   Mouse-1, in a window's mode line, selects that window but does not move point in it (`mouse-select-window`).

To select a different window, click with `Mouse-1` on its mode line. With the keyboard, you can switch windows by typing `C-x o` (`other-window`). That is an `o`, for 'other', not a zero. When there are more than two windows, this command moves through all the windows in a cyclic order, generally top to bottom and left to right. After the rightmost and bottommost window, it goes back to the one at the upper left corner. A numeric argument means to move several steps in the cyclic order of windows. A negative argument moves around the cycle in the opposite order. When the minibuffer is active, the minibuffer is the last window in the cycle; you can switch from the minibuffer window to one of the other windows, and later switch back and finish supplying the minibuffer argument that is requested. See Section 5.2 [Minibuffer Edit], page 42.

The usual scrolling commands (see Chapter 11 [Display], page 79) apply to the selected window only, but there is one command to scroll the next window. `C-M-v` (`scroll-other-window`) scrolls the window that `C-x o` would select. It takes arguments, positive and negative, like `C-v`. (In the minibuffer, `C-M-v` scrolls the window that contains the minibuffer help display, if any, rather than the next window in the standard cyclic order.)

The command `M-x compare-windows` lets you compare two files or buffers visible in two windows, by moving through them to the next mismatch. See Section 14.9 [Comparing Files], page 139, for details.

16.4 Displaying in Another Window

`C-x 4` is a prefix key for commands that select another window (splitting the window if there is only one) and select a buffer in that window. Different `C-x 4` commands have different ways of finding the buffer to select.

C-x 4 b *bufname* (RET)

> Select buffer *bufname* in another window. This runs `switch-to-buffer-other-window`.

C-x 4 C-o *bufname* (RET)

> Display buffer *bufname* in another window, but don't select that buffer or that window. This runs `display-buffer`.

C-x 4 f *filename* (RET)

> Visit file *filename* and select its buffer in another window. This runs `find-file-other-window`. See Section 14.2 [Visiting], page 108.

C-x 4 d *directory* (RET)
>   Select a Dired buffer for directory *directory* in another win-
>   dow. This runs `dired-other-window`. See Chapter 28 [Dired],
>   page 329.

C-x 4 m   Start composing a mail message in another window. This runs
>   `mail-other-window`; its same-window analogue is C-x m (see
>   Chapter 26 [Sending Mail], page 301).

C-x 4 .   Find a tag in the current tags table, in another window. This
>   runs `find-tag-other-window`, the multiple-window variant of
>   M-. (see Section 22.13 [Tags], page 250).

C-x 4 r *filename* (RET)
>   Visit file *filename* read-only, and select its buffer in another win-
>   dow. This runs `find-file-read-only-other-window`. See Sec-
>   tion 14.2 [Visiting], page 108.

16.5 Forcing Display in the Same Window

Certain Emacs commands switch to a specific buffer with special contents. For example, M-x shell switches to a buffer named '*Shell*'. By
convention, all these commands are written to pop up the buffer in a separate window. But you can specify that certain of these buffers should appear
in the selected window.

If you add a buffer name to the list `same-window-buffer-names`, the
effect is that such commands display that particular buffer by switching to
it in the selected window. For example, if you add the element "*grep*"
to the list, the `grep` command will display its output buffer in the selected
window.

The default value of `same-window-buffer-names` is not `nil`: it specifies
buffer names '*info*', '*mail*' and '*shell*' (as well as others used by
more obscure Emacs packages). This is why M-x shell normally switches
to the '*shell*' buffer in the selected window. If you delete this element
from the value of `same-window-buffer-names`, the behavior of M-x shell
will change—it will pop up the buffer in another window instead.

You can specify these buffers more generally with the variable `same-
window-regexps`. Set it to a list of regular expressions; then any buffer whose
name matches one of those regular expressions is displayed by switching to
it in the selected window. (Once again, this applies only to buffers that
normally get displayed for you in a separate window.) The default value of
this variable specifies Telnet and rlogin buffers.

An analogous feature lets you specify buffers which should be displayed
in their own individual frames. See Section 17.9 [Special Buffer Frames],
page 163.

16.6 Deleting and Rearranging Windows

C-x 0   Delete the selected window (`delete-window`). The last charac-
            ter in this key sequence is a zero.

C-x 1   Delete all windows in the selected frame except the selected win-
            dow (`delete-other-windows`).

C-x 4 0   Delete the selected window and kill the buffer that was showing
            in it (`kill-buffer-and-window`). The last character in this key
            sequence is a zero.

C-x ^   Make selected window taller (`enlarge-window`).

C-x }   Make selected window wider (`enlarge-window-horizontally`).

C-x {   Make   selected   window   narrower   (`shrink-window-`
            `horizontally`).

C-x -   Shrink this window if its buffer doesn't need so many lines
            (`shrink-window-if-larger-than-buffer`).

C-x +   Make all windows the same height (`balance-windows`).

Drag-Mouse-1
            Dragging a window's mode line up or down with `Mouse-1`
            changes window heights.

Mouse-2   `Mouse-2` in a window's mode line deletes all other windows in
            the frame (`mouse-delete-other-windows`).

Mouse-3   `Mouse-3` in a window's mode line deletes that window (`mouse-`
            `delete-window`).

To delete a window, type C-x 0 (`delete-window`). (That is a zero.) The
space occupied by the deleted window is given to an adjacent window (but
not the minibuffer window, even if that is active at the time). Once a window
is deleted, its attributes are forgotten; only restoring a window configuration
can bring it back. Deleting the window has no effect on the buffer it used to
display; the buffer continues to exist, and you can select it in any window
with C-x b.

C-x 4 0 (`kill-buffer-and-window`) is a stronger command than C-x 0;
it kills the current buffer and then deletes the selected window.

C-x 1 (`delete-other-windows`) is more powerful in a different way; it
deletes all the windows except the selected one (and the minibuffer); the
selected window expands to use the whole frame except for the echo area.

You can also delete a window by clicking on its mode line with `Mouse-2`,
and delete all the windows in a frame except one window by clicking on that
window's mode line with `Mouse-3`.

The easiest way to adjust window heights is with a mouse. If you press
`Mouse-1` on a mode line, you can drag that mode line up or down, changing
the heights of the windows above and below it.

To readjust the division of space among vertically adjacent windows, use C-x ^ (enlarge-window). It makes the currently selected window get one line bigger, or as many lines as is specified with a numeric argument. With a negative argument, it makes the selected window smaller. C-x } (enlarge-window-horizontally) makes the selected window wider by the specified number of columns. C-x { (shrink-window-horizontally) makes the selected window narrower by the specified number of columns.

When you make a window bigger, the space comes from one of its neighbors. If this makes any window too small, it is deleted and its space is given to an adjacent window. The minimum size is specified by the variables window-min-height and window-min-width.

The command C-x - (shrink-window-if-larger-than-buffer) reduces the height of the selected window, if it is taller than necessary to show the whole text of the buffer it is displaying. It gives the extra lines to other windows in the frame.

You can also use C-x + (balance-windows) to even out the heights of all the windows in the selected frame.

See Section 5.2 [Minibuffer Edit], page 42, for information about the Resize-Minibuffer mode, which automatically changes the size of the mini-buffer window to fit the text in the minibuffer.

17 Frames and X Windows

When using the X Window System, you can create multiple windows at the X level in a single Emacs session. Each X window that belongs to Emacs displays a *frame* which can contain one or several Emacs windows. A frame initially contains a single general-purpose Emacs window which you can subdivide vertically or horizontally into smaller windows. A frame normally contains its own echo area and minibuffer, but you can make frames that don't have these—they use the echo area and minibuffer of another frame.

Editing you do in one frame also affects the other frames. For instance, if you put text in the kill ring in one frame, you can yank it in another frame. If you exit Emacs through `C-x C-c` in one frame, it terminates all the frames. To delete just one frame, use `C-x 5 0`.

To avoid confusion, we reserve the word "window" for the subdivisions that Emacs implements, and never use it to refer to a frame.

Emacs compiled for MS-DOS emulates some aspects of the window system so that you can use many of the features described in this chapter. See Section C.1 [MS-DOS Input], page 463, for more information.

17.1 Mouse Commands for Editing

The mouse commands for selecting and copying a region are mostly compatible with the `xterm` program. You can use the same mouse commands for copying between Emacs and other X client programs.

If you select a region with any of these mouse commands, and then immediately afterward type the (DELETE) function key, it deletes the region that you selected. The (BACKSPACE) function key and the ASCII character (DEL) do not do this; if you type any other key in between the mouse command and (DELETE), it does not do this.

Mouse-1   Move point to where you click (`mouse-set-point`). This is normally the left button.

Drag-Mouse-1

Set the region to the text you select by dragging, and copy it to the kill ring (`mouse-set-region`). You can specify both ends of the region with this single command.

If you move the mouse off the top or bottom of the window while dragging, the window scrolls at a steady rate until you move the mouse back into the window. This way, you can select regions that don't fit entirely on the screen. The number of lines scrolled per step depends on how far away from the window edge the mouse has gone; the variable `mouse-scroll-min-lines` specifies a minimum step size.

Mouse-2   Yank the last killed text, where you click (`mouse-yank-at-click`). This is normally the middle button.

Mouse-3   This command, `mouse-save-then-kill`, has several functions depending on where you click and the status of the region.

The most basic case is when you click `Mouse-1` in one place and then `Mouse-3` in another. This selects the text between those two positions as the region. It also copies the new region to the kill ring, so that you can copy it to someplace else.

If you click `Mouse-1` in the text, scroll with the scroll bar, and then click `Mouse-3`, it remembers where point was before scrolling (where you put it with `Mouse-1`), and uses that position as the other end of the region. This is so that you can select a region that doesn't fit entirely on the screen.

More generally, if you do not have a highlighted region, `Mouse-3` selects the text between point and the click position as the region. It does this by setting the mark where point was, and moving point to where you click.

If you have a highlighted region, or if the region was set just before by dragging button 1, `Mouse-3` adjusts the nearer end of the region by moving it to where you click. The adjusted region's text also replaces the old region's text in the kill ring.

If you originally specified the region using a double or triple `Mouse-1`, so that the region is defined to consist of entire words or lines, then adjusting the region with `Mouse-3` also proceeds by entire words or lines.

If you use `Mouse-3` a second time consecutively, at the same place, that kills the region already selected.

Double-Mouse-1

This key sets the region around the word which you click on. If you click on a character with "symbol" syntax (such as underscore, in C mode), it sets the region around the symbol surrounding that character.

If you click on a character with open-parenthesis or close-parenthesis syntax, it sets the region around the parenthetical grouping (sexp) which that character starts or ends. If you click on a character with string-delimiter syntax (such as a single-quote or doublequote in C), it sets the region around the string constant (using heuristics to figure out whether that character is the beginning or the end of it).

Double-Drag-Mouse-1

This key selects a region made up of the words you drag across.

Triple-Mouse-1

This key sets the region around the line you click on.

Triple-Drag-Mouse-1

This key selects a region made up of the lines you drag across.

The simplest way to kill text with the mouse is to press Mouse-1 at one end, then press Mouse-3 twice at the other end. See Section 9.1 [Killing], page 65. To copy the text into the kill ring without deleting it from the buffer, press Mouse-3 just once—or just drag across the text with Mouse-1. Then you can copy it elsewhere by yanking it.

To yank the killed or copied text somewhere else, move the mouse there and press Mouse-2. See Section 9.2 [Yanking], page 67. However, if mouse-yank-at-point is non-nil, Mouse-2 yanks at point. Then it does not matter where you click, or even which of the frame's windows you click on. The default value is nil. This variable also affects yanking the secondary selection.

To copy text to another X window, kill it or save it in the kill ring. Under X, this also sets the *primary selection*. Then use the "paste" or "yank" command of the program operating the other window to insert the text from the selection.

To copy text from another X window, use the "cut" or "copy" command of the program operating the other window, to select the text you want. Then yank it in Emacs with C-y or Mouse-2.

These cutting and pasting commands also work on MS-Windows.

When Emacs puts text into the kill ring, or rotates text to the front of the kill ring, it sets the *primary selection* in the X server. This is how other X clients can access the text. Emacs also stores the text in the cut buffer, but only if the text is short enough (x-cut-buffer-max specifies the maximum number of characters); putting long strings in the cut buffer can be slow.

The commands to yank the first entry in the kill ring actually check first for a primary selection in another program; after that, they check for text in the cut buffer. If neither of those sources provides text to yank, the kill ring contents are used.

17.2 Secondary Selection

The *secondary selection* is another way of selecting text using X. It does not use point or the mark, so you can use it to kill text without setting point or the mark.

M-Drag-Mouse-1

> Set the secondary selection, with one end at the place where you press down the button, and the other end at the place where you release it (mouse-set-secondary). The highlighting appears and changes as you drag.
>
> If you move the mouse off the top or bottom of the window while dragging, the window scrolls at a steady rate until you move the mouse back into the window. This way, you can mark regions that don't fit entirely on the screen.

M-Mouse-1

> Set one endpoint for the *secondary selection* (`mouse-start-secondary`).

M-Mouse-3

> Make a secondary selection, using the place specified with `M-Mouse-1` as the other end (`mouse-secondary-save-then-kill`). A second click at the same place kills the secondary selection just made.

M-Mouse-2

> Insert the secondary selection where you click (`mouse-yank-secondary`). This places point at the end of the yanked text.

Double or triple clicking of `M-Mouse-1` operates on words and lines, much like `Mouse-1`.

If `mouse-yank-at-point` is non-`nil`, `M-Mouse-2` yanks at point. Then it does not matter precisely where you click; all that matters is which window you click on. See Section 17.1 [Mouse Commands], page 157.

17.3 Following References with the Mouse

Some Emacs buffers display lists of various sorts. These include lists of files, of buffers, of possible completions, of matches for a pattern, and so on.

Since yanking text into these buffers is not very useful, most of them define `Mouse-2` specially, as a command to use or view the item you click on.

For example, if you click `Mouse-2` on a file name in a Dired buffer, you visit that file. If you click `Mouse-2` on an error message in the '`*Compilation*`' buffer, you go to the source code for that error message. If you click `Mouse-2` on a completion in the '`*Completions*`' buffer, you choose that completion.

You can usually tell when `Mouse-2` has this special sort of meaning because the sensitive text highlights when you move the mouse over it.

17.4 Mouse Clicks for Menus

Mouse clicks modified with the (CTRL) and (SHIFT) keys bring up menus.

C-Mouse-1

> This menu is for selecting a buffer.

C-Mouse-2

> This menu is for specifying faces and other text properties for editing formatted text. See Section 21.11 [Formatted Text], page 219.

C-Mouse-3

> This menu is mode-specific. For most modes, this menu has the same items as all the mode-specific menu-bar menus put

together. Some modes may specify a different menu for this button.[1]

S-mouse-1

This menu is for specifying the frame's principal font.

17.5 Mode Line Mouse Commands

You can use mouse clicks on window mode lines to select and manipulate windows.

Mouse-1   Mouse-1 on a mode line selects the window above. By dragging Mouse-1 on the mode line, you can move it, thus changing the height of the windows above and below.

Mouse-2   Mouse-2 on a mode line expands that window to fill its frame.

Mouse-3   Mouse-3 on a mode line deletes the window above.

C-Mouse-2

C-Mouse-2 on a mode line splits the window above horizontally, above the place in the mode line where you click.

C-Mouse-2 on a scroll bar splits the corresponding window vertically. See Section 16.2 [Split Window], page 152.

17.6 Creating Frames

The prefix key C-x 5 is analogous to C-x 4, with parallel subcommands. The difference is that C-x 5 commands create a new frame rather than just a new window in the selected frame (see Section 16.4 [Pop Up Window], page 153). If an existing visible or iconified frame already displays the requested material, these commands use the existing frame, after raising or deiconifying as necessary.

The various C-x 5 commands differ in how they find or create the buffer to select:

C-x 5 2   Create a new frame (make-frame-command).

C-x 5 b *bufname* (RET)
             Select buffer *bufname* in another frame. This runs switch-to-buffer-other-frame.

C-x 5 f *filename* (RET)
             Visit file *filename* and select its buffer in another frame. This runs find-file-other-frame. See Section 14.2 [Visiting], page 108.

---

[1] Some systems use Mouse-3 for a mode-specific menu. We took a survey of users, and found they preferred to keep Mouse-3 for selecting and killing regions. Hence the decision to use C-Mouse-3 for this menu.

C-x 5 d *directory* (RET)
>   Select a Dired buffer for directory *directory* in another frame. This runs `dired-other-frame`.   See   Chapter 28 [Dired], page 329.

C-x 5 m   Start composing a mail message in another frame. This runs `mail-other-frame`. It is the other-frame variant of C-x m. See Chapter 26 [Sending Mail], page 301.

C-x 5 .   Find a tag in the current tag table in another frame. This runs `find-tag-other-frame`, the multiple-frame variant of M-.. See Section 22.13 [Tags], page 250.

C-x 5 r *filename* (RET)
>   Visit file *filename* read-only, and select its buffer in another frame. This runs `find-file-read-only-other-frame`. See Section 14.2 [Visiting], page 108.

You can control the appearance of new frames you create by setting the frame parameters in `default-frame-alist`. You can use the variable `initial-frame-alist` to specify parameters that affect only the initial frame. See section "Initial Parameters" in *The Emacs Lisp Reference Manual*, for more information.

The easiest way to specify the principal font for all your Emacs frames is with an X resource (see Section A.7 [Font X], page 449), but you can also do it by modifying `default-frame-alist` to specify the `font` parameter, as shown here:

```
(add-to-list 'default-frame-alist '(font . "10x20"))
```

17.7 Making and Using a Speedbar Frame

An Emacs frame can have a *speedbar*, which is a vertical window that serves as a scrollable menu of files you could visit and tags within those files. To create a speedbar, type M-x `speedbar`; this creates a speedbar window for the selected frame. From then on, you can click on a file name in the speedbar to visit that file in the corresponding Emacs frame, or click on a tag name to jump to that tag in the Emacs frame.

Initially the speedbar lists the immediate contents of the current directory, one file per line. Each line also has a box, '[+]' or '<+>', that you can click on with Mouse-2 to "open up" the contents of that item. If the line names a directory, opening it adds the contents of that directory to the speedbar display, underneath the directory's own line. If the line lists an ordinary file, opening it up adds a list of the tags in that file to the speedbar display. When a file is opened up, the '[+]' changes to '[-]'; you can click on that box to "close up" that file (hide its contents).

Some major modes, including Rmail mode, Info, and GUD, have specialized ways of putting useful items into the speedbar for you to select. For example, in Rmail mode, the speedbar shows a list of Rmail files, and lets you move the current message to another Rmail file by clicking on its '<M>' box.

A speedbar belongs to one Emacs frame, and always operates on that frame. If you use multiple frames, you can make a speedbar for some or all of the frames; type `M-x speedbar` in any given frame to make a speedbar for it.

17.8 Multiple Displays

A single Emacs can talk to more than one X Windows display. Initially, Emacs uses just one display—the one specified with the `DISPLAY` environment variable or with the '`--display`' option (see Section A.2 [Initial Options], page 442). To connect to another display, use the command `make-frame-on-display`:

`M-x make-frame-on-display` (RET) *display* (RET)
> Create a new frame on display *display*.

A single X server can handle more than one screen. When you open frames on two screens belonging to one server, Emacs knows they share a single keyboard, and it treats all the commands arriving from these screens as a single stream of input.

When you open frames on different X servers, Emacs makes a separate input stream for each server. This way, two users can type simultaneously on the two displays, and Emacs will not garble their input. Each server also has its own selected frame. The commands you enter with a particular X server apply to that server's selected frame.

Despite these features, people using the same Emacs job from different displays can still interfere with each other if they are not careful. For example, if any one types `C-x C-c`, that exits the Emacs job for all of them!

17.9 Special Buffer Frames

You can make certain chosen buffers, for which Emacs normally creates a second window when you have just one window, appear in special frames of their own. To do this, set the variable `special-display-buffer-names` to a list of buffer names; any buffer whose name is in that list automatically gets a special frame, when an Emacs command wants to display it "in another window."

For example, if you set the variable this way,

```
(setq special-display-buffer-names
      '("*Completions*" "*grep*" "*tex-shell*"))
```

then completion lists, `grep` output and the TeX mode shell buffer get individual frames of their own. These frames, and the windows in them, are

never automatically split or reused for any other buffers. They continue
to show the buffers they were created for, unless you alter them by hand.
Killing the special buffer deletes its frame automatically.

More generally, you can set `special-display-regexps` to a list of regular
expressions; then a buffer gets its own frame if its name matches any of those
regular expressions. (Once again, this applies only to buffers that normally
get displayed for you in a separate window.)

The variable `special-display-frame-alist` specifies the frame parameters for these frames. It has a default value, so you don't need to set it.

For those who know Lisp, an element of `special-display-buffer-
names` or `special-display-regexps` can also be a list. Then the first ele-
ment is the buffer name or regular expression; the rest of the list specifies
how to create the frame. It can be an association list specifying frame parameter values; these values take precedence over parameter values specified
in `special-display-frame-alist`. Alternatively, it can have this form:

> (*function args*. . .)

where *function* is a symbol. Then the frame is constructed by calling *function*; its first argument is the buffer, and its remaining arguments are *args*.

An analogous feature lets you specify buffers which should be displayed
in the selected window. See Section 16.5 [Force Same Window], page 154.
The same-window feature takes precedence over the special-frame feature;
therefore, if you add a buffer name to `special-display-buffer-names` and
it has no effect, check to see whether that feature is also in use for the same
buffer name.

17.10 Setting Frame Parameters

This section describes commands for altering the display style and window management behavior of the selected frame.

M-x `set-foreground-color` (RET) *color* (RET)
> Specify color *color* for the foreground of the selected frame.

M-x `set-background-color` (RET) *color* (RET)
> Specify color *color* for the background of the selected frame.
> This changes the foreground color of the `modeline` face also, so
> that it remains in inverse video compared with the default.

M-x `set-cursor-color` (RET) *color* (RET)
> Specify color *color* for the cursor of the selected frame.

M-x `set-mouse-color` (RET) *color* (RET)
> Specify color *color* for the mouse cursor when it is over the
> selected frame.

M-x `set-border-color` (RET) *color* (RET)
> Specify color *color* for the border of the selected frame.

M-x list-colors-display

> Display the defined color names and show what the colors look like. This command is somewhat slow.

M-x auto-raise-mode

> Toggle whether or not the selected frame should auto-raise. Auto-raise means that every time you move the mouse onto the frame, it raises the frame.
>
> Note that this auto-raise feature is implemented by Emacs itself. Some window managers also implement auto-raise. If you enable auto-raise for Emacs frames in your X window manager, it should work, but it is beyond Emacs's control and therefore auto-raise-mode has no effect on it.

M-x auto-lower-mode

> Toggle whether or not the selected frame should auto-lower. Auto-lower means that every time you move the mouse off the frame, the frame moves to the bottom of the stack of X windows.
>
> The command auto-lower-mode has no effect on auto-lower implemented by the X window manager. To control that, you must use the appropriate window manager features.

M-x set-frame-font (RET) *font* (RET)

> Specify font *font* as the principal font for the selected frame. The principal font is used for all text displayed in the frame, except when a face (see Section 17.13 [Faces], page 166) specifies a different font to use for certain text. See Section A.7 [Font X], page 449, for ways to list the available fonts on your system.
>
> You can also set a frame's principal font through a pop-up menu. Press S-Mouse-1 to activate this menu.

In Emacs versions that use an X toolkit, the color-setting and font-setting functions don't affect menus and the menu bar, since they are displayed by their own widget classes. To change the appearance of the menus and menu bar, you must use X resources (see Section A.13 [Resources X], page 453). See Section A.8 [Colors X], page 450, regarding colors. See Section A.7 [Font X], page 449, regarding choice of font.

For information on frame parameters and customization, see section "Frame Parameters" in *The Emacs Lisp Reference Manual*.

17.11 Scroll Bars

When using X, Emacs normally makes a *scroll bar* at the left of each Emacs window. The scroll bar runs the height of the window, and shows a moving rectangular inner box which represents the portion of the buffer currently displayed. The entire height of the scroll bar represents the entire length of the buffer.

You can use `Mouse-2` (normally, the middle button) in the scroll bar to move or drag the inner box up and down. If you move it to the top of the scroll bar, you see the top of the buffer. If you move it to the bottom of the scroll bar, you see the bottom of the buffer

The left and right buttons in the scroll bar scroll by controlled increments. `Mouse-1` (normally, the left button) moves the line at the level where you click up to the top of the window. `Mouse-3` (normally, the right button) moves the line at the top of the window down to the level where you click. By clicking repeatedly in the same place, you can scroll by the same distance over and over.

Aside from scrolling, you can also click `C-Mouse-2` in the scroll bar to split a window vertically. The split occurs on the line where you click.

You can enable or disable Scroll Bar mode with the command `M-x scroll-bar-mode`. With no argument, it toggles the use of scroll bars. With an argument, it turns use of scroll bars on if and only if the argument is positive. This command applies to all frames, including frames yet to be created. You can use the X resource '`verticalScrollBars`' to control the initial setting of Scroll Bar mode. See Section A.13 [Resources X], page 453.

To enable or disable scroll bars for just the selected frame, use the `M-x toggle-scroll-bar` command.

17.12 Menu Bars

You can turn display of menu bars on or off with `M-x menu-bar-mode`. With no argument, this command toggles Menu Bar mode, a minor mode. With an argument, the command turns Menu Bar mode on if the argument is positive, off if the argument is not positive. You can use the X resource '`menuBarLines`' to control the initial setting of Menu Bar mode. See Section A.13 [Resources X], page 453. Expert users often turn off the menu bar, especially on text-only terminals, where this makes one additional line available for text.

See Section 1.4 [Menu Bar], page 19, for information on how to invoke commands with the menu bar.

17.13 Using Multiple Typefaces

When using Emacs with X, you can set up multiple styles of displaying characters. The aspects of style that you can control are the type font, the foreground color, the background color, and whether to underline. Emacs on MS-DOS supports faces partially by letting you control the foreground and background colors of each face (see Appendix C [MS-DOS], page 463).

The way you control display style is by defining named *faces*. Each face can specify a type font, a foreground color, a background color, and an underline flag; but it does not have to specify all of them. Then by specifying the face or faces to use for a given part of the text in the buffer, you control how that text appears.

The style of display used for a given character in the text is determined by combining several faces. Any aspect of the display style that isn't specified by overlays or text properties comes from the frame itself.

Enriched mode, the mode for editing formatted text, includes several commands and menus for specifying faces. See Section 21.11.4 [Format Faces], page 221, for how to specify the font for text in the buffer. See Section 21.11.5 [Format Colors], page 223, for how to specify the foreground and background color.

To alter the appearance of a face, use the customization buffer. See Section 31.2.2.3 [Face Customization], page 398. You can also use X resources to specify attributes of particular faces (see Section A.13 [Resources X], page 453).

To see what faces are currently defined, and what they look like, type `M-x list-faces-display`. It's possible for a given face to look different in different frames; this command shows the appearance in the frame in which you type it. Here's a list of the standardly defined faces:

default   This face is used for ordinary text that doesn't specify any other face.

modeline   This face is used for mode lines. By default, it's set up as the inverse of the default face. See Section 11.7 [Display Vars], page 83.

highlight
           This face is used for highlighting portions of text, in various modes.

region   This face is used for displaying a selected region (when Transient Mark mode is enabled—see below).

secondary-selection
           This face is used for displaying a secondary selection (see Section 17.2 [Secondary Selection], page 159).

bold   This face uses a bold variant of the default font, if it has one.

italic   This face uses an italic variant of the default font, if it has one.

bold-italic
           This face uses a bold italic variant of the default font, if it has one.

underline
           This face underlines text.

When Transient Mark mode is enabled, the text of the region is highlighted when the mark is active. This uses the face named `region`; you can control the style of highlighting by changing the style of this face (see Section 31.2.2.3 [Face Customization], page 398). See Section 8.2 [Transient Mark], page 60, for more information about Transient Mark mode and activation and deactivation of the mark.

One easy way to use faces is to turn on Font Lock mode. This minor mode, which is always local to a particular buffer, arranges to choose faces according to the syntax of the text you are editing. It can recognize comments and strings in most languages; in several languages, it can also recognize and properly highlight various other important constructs. See Section 17.14 [Font Lock], page 168, for more information about Font Lock mode and syntactic highlighting.

You can print out the buffer with the highlighting that appears on your screen using the command `ps-print-buffer-with-faces`. See Section 30.5 [Postscript], page 378.

17.14 Font Lock mode

Font Lock mode is a minor mode, always local to a particular buffer, which highlights (or "fontifies") using various faces according to the syntax of the text you are editing. It can recognize comments and strings in most languages; in several languages, it can also recognize and properly highlight various other important constructs—for example, names of functions being defined or reserved keywords.

The command `M-x font-lock-mode` turns Font Lock mode on or off according to the argument, and toggles the mode when it has no argument. The function `turn-on-font-lock` unconditionally enables Font Lock mode. This is useful in mode-hook functions. For example, to enable Font Lock mode whenever you edit a C file, you can do this:

```
(add-hook 'c-mode-hook 'turn-on-font-lock)
```

To turn on Font Lock mode automatically in all modes which support it, use the function `global-font-lock-mode`, like this:

```
(global-font-lock-mode 1)
```

In Font Lock mode, when you edit the text, the highlighting updates automatically in the line that you changed. Most changes don't affect the highlighting of subsequent lines, but occasionally they do. To rehighlight a range of lines, use the command `M-g M-g` (`font-lock-fontify-block`).

In certain major modes, `M-g M-g` refontifies the entire current function. (The variable `font-lock-mark-block-function` controls how to find the current function.) In other major modes, `M-g M-g` refontifies 16 lines above and below point.

With a prefix argument n, `M-g M-g` refontifies n lines above and below point, regardless of the mode.

To get the full benefit of Font Lock mode, you need to choose a default font which has bold, italic, and bold-italic variants; or else you need to have a color or gray-scale screen.

The variable `font-lock-maximum-decoration` specifies the preferred level of fontification, for modes that provide multiple levels. Level 1 is the least amount of fontification; some modes support levels as high as 3. The normal default is "as high as possible." You can specify an integer, which applies to all modes, or you can specify different numbers for particular major modes; for example, to use level 1 for C/C++ modes, and the default level otherwise, use this:

```
(setq font-lock-maximum-decoration
      '((c-mode . 1) (c++-mode . 1)))
```

Fontification can be too slow for large buffers, so you can suppress it. The variable `font-lock-maximum-size` specifies a buffer size, beyond which buffer fontification is suppressed.

Comment and string fontification (or "syntactic" fontification) relies on analysis of the syntactic structure of the buffer text. For the purposes of speed, some modes including C mode and Lisp mode rely on a special convention: an open-parenthesis in the leftmost column always defines the beginning of a defun, and is thus always outside any string or comment. (See Section 22.4 [Defuns], page 230.) If you don't follow this convention, then Font Lock mode can misfontify the text after an open-parenthesis in the leftmost column that is inside a string or comment.

The variable `font-lock-beginning-of-syntax-function` (always buffer-local) specifies how Font Lock mode can find a position guaranteed to be outside any comment or string. In modes which use the leftmost column parenthesis convention, the default value of the variable is `beginning-of-defun`—that tells Font Lock mode to use the convention. If you set this variable to `nil`, Font Lock no longer relies on the convention. This avoids incorrect results, but the price is that, in some cases, fontification for a changed text must rescan buffer text from the beginning of the buffer.

Font Lock highlighting patterns already exist for many modes, but you may want to fontify additional patterns. You can use the function `font-lock-add-keywords`, to add your own highlighting patterns for a particular mode. For example, to highlight 'FIXME:' words in C comments, use this:

```
(font-lock-add-keywords
 'c-mode
 '(("\\<\\(FIXME\\):" 1 font-lock-warning-face t)))
```

17.15 Font Lock Support Modes

Font Lock support modes make Font Lock mode faster for large buffers. There are two support modes: Fast Lock mode and Lazy Lock mode. They use two different methods of speeding up Font Lock mode.

17.15.1 Fast Lock Mode

To make Font Lock mode faster for buffers visiting large files, you can use Fast Lock mode. Fast Lock mode saves the font information for each file in a separate cache file; each time you visit the file, it rereads the font information from the cache file instead of refontifying the text from scratch.

The command M-x fast-lock-mode turns Fast Lock mode on or off, according to the argument (with no argument, it toggles). You can also arrange to enable Fast Lock mode whenever you use Font Lock mode, like this:

```
(setq font-lock-support-mode 'fast-lock-mode)
```

It is not worth writing a cache file for small buffers. Therefore, the variable fast-lock-minimum-size specifies a minimum file size for caching font information.

The variable fast-lock-cache-directories specifies where to put the cache files. Its value is a list of directories to try; "." means the same directory as the file being edited. The default value is ("." "~/.emacs-flc"), which means to use the same directory if possible, and otherwise the directory '~/.emacs-flc'.

The variable fast-lock-save-others specifies whether Fast Lock mode should save cache files for files that you do not own. A non-nil value means yes (and that is the default).

17.15.2 Lazy Lock Mode

To make Font Lock mode faster for large buffers, you can use Lazy Lock mode to reduce the amount of text that is fontified. In Lazy Lock mode, buffer fontification is demand-driven; it happens to portions of the buffer that are about to be displayed. And fontification of your changes is deferred; it happens only when Emacs has been idle for a certain short period of time.

The command M-x lazy-lock-mode turns Lazy Lock mode on or off, according to the argument (with no argument, it toggles). You can also arrange to enable Lazy Lock mode whenever you use Font Lock mode, like this:

```
(setq font-lock-support-mode 'lazy-lock-mode)
```

It is not worth avoiding buffer fontification for small buffers. Therefore, the variable lazy-lock-minimum-size specifies a minimum buffer size for demand-driven buffer fontification. Buffers smaller than that are fontified all at once, as in plain Font Lock mode.

When you alter the buffer, Lazy Lock mode defers fontification of the text you changed. The variable `lazy-lock-defer-time` specifies how many seconds Emacs must be idle before it starts fontifying your changes. If the value is 0, then changes are fontified immediately, as in plain Font Lock mode.

Lazy Lock mode normally fontifies newly visible portions of the buffer before they are first displayed. However, if the value of `lazy-lock-defer-on-scrolling` is non-`nil`, newly visible text is fontified only when Emacs is idle for `lazy-lock-defer-time` seconds.

In some modes, including C mode and Emacs Lisp mode, changes in one line's contents can alter the context for subsequent lines, and thus change how they ought to be fontified. Ordinarily, you must type `M-g M-g` to re-fontify the subsequent lines. However, if you set the variable `lazy-lock-defer-contextually` to non-`nil`, Lazy Lock mode does this automatically, after `lazy-lock-defer-time` seconds.

When Emacs is idle for a long time, Lazy Lock fontifies additional portions of the buffer, not yet displayed, in case you will display them later. This is called *stealth fontification*.

The variable `lazy-lock-stealth-time` specifies how many seconds Emacs has to be idle before stealth fontification starts. A value of `nil` means no stealth fontification. The variables `lazy-lock-stealth-lines` and `lazy-lock-stealth-verbose` specify the granularity and verbosity of stealth fontification.

17.15.3 Fast Lock or Lazy Lock?

Here is a simple guide to help you choose one of the Font Lock support modes.

- Fast Lock mode intervenes only during file visiting and buffer killing (and related events); therefore buffer editing and window scrolling are no faster or slower than in plain Font Lock mode.

- Fast Lock mode is slower at reading a cache file than Lazy Lock mode is at fontifying a window; therefore Fast Lock mode is slower at visiting a file than Lazy Lock mode.

- Lazy Lock mode intervenes during window scrolling to fontify text that scrolls onto the screen; therefore, scrolling is slower than in plain Font Lock mode.

- Lazy Lock mode doesn't fontify during buffer editing (it defers fontification of changes); therefore, editing is faster than in plain Font Lock mode.

- Fast Lock mode can be fooled by a file that is kept under version control software; therefore buffer fontification may occur even when a cache file exists for the file.

- Fast Lock mode only works with a buffer visiting a file; Lazy Lock mode works with any buffer.
- Fast Lock mode generates cache files; Lazy Lock mode does not.

The variable `font-lock-support-mode` specifies which of these support modes to use; for example, to specify that Fast Lock mode is used for C/C++ modes, and Lazy Lock mode otherwise, set the variable like this:

```
(setq font-lock-support-mode
      '((c-mode . fast-lock-mode) (c++-mode . fast-lock-mode)
      (t . lazy-lock-mode)))
```

17.16 Highlight Changes Mode

Use M-x `highlight-changes-mode` to enable a minor mode that uses faces (colors, typically) to indicate which parts of the buffer were changed most recently.

17.17 Miscellaneous X Window Features

The following commands let you create, delete and operate on frames:

C-z   Iconify the selected Emacs frame (`iconify-or-deiconify-frame`). The normal meaning of C-z, to suspend Emacs, is not useful under a window system, so it has a different binding in that case.

            If you type this command on an Emacs frame's icon, it deiconifies the frame.

C-x 5 0   Delete the selected frame (`delete-frame`). This is not allowed if there is only one frame.

C-x 5 o   Select another frame, raise it, and warp the mouse to it so that it stays selected. If you repeat this command, it cycles through all the frames on your terminal.

17.18 Non-Window Terminals

If your terminal does not have a window system that Emacs supports, then it can display only one Emacs frame at a time. However, you can still create multiple Emacs frames, and switch between them. Switching frames on these terminals is much like switching between different window configurations.

Use C-x 5 2 to create a new frame and switch to it; use C-x 5 o to cycle through the existing frames; use C-x 5 0 to delete the current frame.

Each frame has a number to distinguish it. If your terminal can display only one frame at a time, the selected frame's number n appears near the beginning of the mode line, in the form 'Fn'.

'F*n*' is actually the frame's name. You can also specify a different name if you wish, and you can select a frame by its name. Use the command M-x set-frame-name (RET) *name* (RET) to specify a new name for the selected frame, and use M-x select-frame-by-name (RET) *name* (RET) to select a frame according to its name. The name you specify appears in the mode line when the frame is selected.

18 International Character Set Support

Emacs supports a wide variety of international character sets, including European variants of the Latin alphabet, as well as Chinese, Devanagari (Hindi and Marathi), Ethiopian, Greek, IPA, Japanese, Korean, Lao, Russian, Thai, Tibetan, and Vietnamese scripts. These features have been merged from the modified version of Emacs known as MULE (for "MULtilingual Enhancement to GNU Emacs")

18.1 Introduction to International Character Sets

The users of these scripts have established many more-or-less standard coding systems for storing files. Emacs internally uses a single multibyte character encoding, so that it can intermix characters from all these scripts in a single buffer or string. This encoding represents each non-ASCII character as a sequence of bytes in the range 0200 through 0377. Emacs translates between the multibyte character encoding and various other coding systems when reading and writing files, when exchanging data with subprocesses, and (in some cases) in the `C-q` command (see Section 18.6 [Multibyte Conversion], page 179).

The command `C-h h` (`view-hello-file`) displays the file 'etc/HELLO', which shows how to say "hello" in many languages. This illustrates various scripts.

Keyboards, even in the countries where these character sets are used, generally don't have keys for all the characters in them. So Emacs supports various *input methods*, typically one for each script or language, to make it convenient to type them.

The prefix key `C-x` (RET) is used for commands that pertain to multibyte characters, coding systems, and input methods.

18.2 Enabling Multibyte Characters

You can enable or disable multibyte character support, either for Emacs as a whole, or for a single buffer. When multibyte characters are disabled in a buffer, then each byte in that buffer represents a character, even codes 0200 through 0377. The old features for supporting the European character sets, ISO Latin-1 and ISO Latin-2, work as they did in Emacs 19 and also work for the other ISO 8859 character sets.

However, there is no need to turn off multibyte character support to use ISO Latin; the Emacs multibyte character set includes all the characters in these character sets, and Emacs can translate automatically to and from the ISO codes.

To edit a particular file in unibyte representation, visit it using `find-file-literally`. See Section 14.2 [Visiting], page 108. To convert a buffer in multibyte representation into a single-byte representation of the same characters, the easiest way is to save the contents in a file, kill the buffer, and find the file again with `find-file-literally`. You can also use C-x (RET) c (`universal-coding-system-argument`) and specify 'raw-text' as the coding system with which to find or save a file. See Section 18.9 [Specify Coding], page 184. Finding a file as 'raw-text' doesn't disable format conversion, uncompression and auto mode selection as `find-file-literally` does.

To turn off multibyte character support by default, start Emacs with the '--unibyte' option (see Section A.2 [Initial Options], page 442), or set the environment variable 'EMACS_UNIBYTE'. You can also customize `enable-multibyte-characters` or, equivalently, directly set the variable `default-enable-multibyte-characters` in your init file to have basically the same effect as '--unibyte'.

Multibyte strings are not created during initialization from the values of environment variables, '/etc/passwd' entries etc. that contain non-ASCII 8-bit characters. However, the initialization file is normally read as multibyte—like Lisp files in general—even with '--unibyte'. To avoid multibyte strings being generated by non-ASCII characters in it, put '-*-unibyte: t;-*-' in a comment on the first line. Do the same for initialization files for packages like Gnus.

The mode line indicates whether multibyte character support is enabled in the current buffer. If it is, there are two or more characters (most often two dashes) before the colon near the beginning of the mode line. When multibyte characters are not enabled, just one dash precedes the colon.

18.3 Language Environments

All supported character sets are supported in Emacs buffers whenever multibyte characters are enabled; there is no need to select a particular language in order to display its characters in an Emacs buffer. However, it is important to select a *language environment* in order to set various defaults. The language environment really represents a choice of preferred script (more or less) rather than a choice of language.

The language environment controls which coding systems to recognize when reading text (see Section 18.8 [Recognize Coding], page 182). This applies to files, incoming mail, netnews, and any other text you read into Emacs. It may also specify the default coding system to use when you create a file. Each language environment also specifies a default input method.

The way to select a language environment is with the command M-x `set-language-environment`. It makes no difference which buffer is current when you use this command, because the effects apply globally to the Emacs session. The supported language environments include:

Chinese-BIG5, Chinese-CNS, Chinese-GB, Cyrillic-Alternativnyj, Cyrillic-ISO, Cyrillic-KOI8, Devanagari, English, Ethiopic, Greek, Hebrew, Japanese, Korean, Lao, Latin-1, Latin-2, Latin-3, Latin-4, Latin-5, Thai, Tibetan, and Vietnamese.

Some operating systems let you specify the language you are using by setting locale environment variables. Emacs handles one common special case of this: if your locale name for character types contains the string '8859-*n*', Emacs automatically selects the corresponding language environment.

To display information about the effects of a certain language environment *lang-env*, use the command C-h L *lang-env* (RET) (describe-language-environment). This tells you which languages this language environment is useful for, and lists the character sets, coding systems, and input methods that go with it. It also shows some sample text to illustrate scripts used in this language environment. By default, this command describes the chosen language environment.

You can customize any language environment with the normal hook set-language-environment-hook. The command set-language-environment runs that hook after setting up the new language environment. The hook functions can test for a specific language environment by checking the variable current-language-environment.

Before it starts to set up the new language environment, set-language-environment first runs the hook exit-language-environment-hook. This hook is useful for undoing customizations that were made with set-language-environment-hook. For instance, if you set up a special key binding in a specific language environment using set-language-environment-hook, you should set up exit-language-environment-hook to restore the normal binding for that key.

18.4 Input Methods

An *input method* is a kind of character conversion designed specifically for interactive input. In Emacs, typically each language has its own input method; sometimes several languages which use the same characters can share one input method. A few languages support several input methods.

The simplest kind of input method works by mapping ASCII letters into another alphabet. This is how the Greek and Russian input methods work.

A more powerful technique is composition: converting sequences of characters into one letter. Many European input methods use composition to produce a single non-ASCII letter from a sequence that consists of a letter followed by accent characters (or vice versa). For example, some methods convert the sequence a' into a single accented letter. These input methods have no special commands of their own; all they do is compose sequences of printing characters.

The input methods for syllabic scripts typically use mapping followed by composition. The input methods for Thai and Korean work this way. First, letters are mapped into symbols for particular sounds or tone marks; then, sequences of these which make up a whole syllable are mapped into one syllable sign.

Chinese and Japanese require more complex methods. In Chinese input methods, first you enter the phonetic spelling of a Chinese word (in input method `chinese-py`, among others), or a sequence of portions of the character (input methods `chinese-4corner` and `chinese-sw`, and others). Since one phonetic spelling typically corresponds to many different Chinese characters, you must select one of the alternatives using special Emacs commands. Keys such as `C-f`, `C-b`, `C-n`, `C-p`, and digits have special definitions in this situation, used for selecting among the alternatives. ⟨TAB⟩ displays a buffer showing all the possibilities.

In Japanese input methods, first you input a whole word using phonetic spelling; then, after the word is in the buffer, Emacs converts it into one or more characters using a large dictionary. One phonetic spelling corresponds to many differently written Japanese words, so you must select one of them; use `C-n` and `C-p` to cycle through the alternatives.

Sometimes it is useful to cut off input method processing so that the characters you have just entered will not combine with subsequent characters. For example, in input method `latin-1-postfix`, the sequence e ' combines to form an 'e' with an accent. What if you want to enter them as separate characters?

One way is to type the accent twice; that is a special feature for entering the separate letter and accent. For example, e ' ' gives you the two characters 'e''. Another way is to type another letter after the e—something that won't combine with that—and immediately delete it. For example, you could type e e ⟨DEL⟩ ' to get separate 'e' and '''.

Another method, more general but not quite as easy to type, is to use `C-\ C-\` between two characters to stop them from combining. This is the command `C-\` (`toggle-input-method`) used twice.

`C-\ C-\` is especially useful inside an incremental search, because it stops waiting for more characters to combine, and starts searching for what you have already entered.

The variables `input-method-highlight-flag` and `input-method-verbose-flag` control how input methods explain what is happening. If `input-method-highlight-flag` is non-`nil`, the partial sequence is highlighted in the buffer. If `input-method-verbose-flag` is non-`nil`, the list of possible characters to type next is displayed in the echo area (but not when you are in the minibuffer).

18.5 Selecting an Input Method

C-\   Enable or disable use of the selected input method.

C-x (RET) C-\ *method* (RET)
              Select a new input method for the current buffer.

C-h I *method* (RET)
C-h C-\ *method* (RET)
              Describe the input method *method* (`describe-input-method`).
              By default, it describes the current input method (if any). This
              description should give you the full details of how to use any
              particular input method.

M-x list-input-methods
              Display a list of all the supported input methods.

To choose an input method for the current buffer, use C-x (RET) C-\
(`set-input-method`). This command reads the input method name with the
minibuffer; the name normally starts with the language environment that
it is meant to be used with. The variable `current-input-method` records
which input method is selected.

Input methods use various sequences of ASCII characters to stand for
non-ASCII characters. Sometimes it is useful to turn off the input method
temporarily. To do this, type C-\ (`toggle-input-method`). To reenable the
input method, type C-\ again.

If you type C-\ and you have not yet selected an input method, it prompts
for you to specify one. This has the same effect as using C-x (RET) C-\ to
specify an input method.

Selecting a language environment specifies a default input method for use
in various buffers. When you have a default input method, you can select
it in the current buffer by typing C-\. The variable `default-input-method`
specifies the default input method (`nil` means there is none).

Some input methods for alphabetic scripts work by (in effect) remapping
the keyboard to emulate various keyboard layouts commonly used for those
scripts. How to do this remapping properly depends on your actual keyboard
layout. To specify which layout your keyboard has, use the command M-x
quail-set-keyboard-layout.

To display a list of all the supported input methods, type M-x
list-input-methods. The list gives information about each input method,
including the string that stands for it in the mode line.

18.6 Unibyte and Multibyte Non-ASCII characters

When multibyte characters are enabled, character codes 0240 (octal)
through 0377 (octal) are not really legitimate in the buffer. The valid non-
ASCII printing characters have codes that start from 0400.

If you type a self-inserting character in the invalid range 0240 through 0377, Emacs assumes you intended to use one of the ISO Latin-*n* character sets, and converts it to the Emacs code representing that Latin-*n* character. You select *which* ISO Latin character set to use through your choice of language environment (see above). If you do not specify a choice, the default is Latin-1.

The same thing happens when you use C-q to enter an octal code in this range.

18.7 Coding Systems

Users of various languages have established many more-or-less standard coding systems for representing them. Emacs does not use these coding systems internally; instead, it converts from various coding systems to its own system when reading data, and converts the internal coding system to other coding systems when writing data. Conversion is possible in reading or writing files, in sending or receiving from the terminal, and in exchanging data with subprocesses.

Emacs assigns a name to each coding system. Most coding systems are used for one language, and the name of the coding system starts with the language name. Some coding systems are used for several languages; their names usually start with 'iso'. There are also special coding systems no-conversion, raw-text and emacs-mule which do not convert printing characters at all.

In addition to converting various representations of non-ASCII characters, a coding system can perform end-of-line conversion. Emacs handles three different conventions for how to separate lines in a file: newline, carriage-return linefeed, and just carriage-return.

C-h C *coding* (RET)
> Describe coding system *coding*.

C-h C (RET)
> Describe the coding systems currently in use.

M-x list-coding-systems
> Display a list of all the supported coding systems.

The command C-h C (describe-coding-system) displays information about particular coding systems. You can specify a coding system name as argument; alternatively, with an empty argument, it describes the coding systems currently selected for various purposes, both in the current buffer and as the defaults, and the priority list for recognizing coding systems (see Section 18.8 [Recognize Coding], page 182).

To display a list of all the supported coding systems, type M-x list-coding-systems. The list gives information about each coding system, including the letter that stands for it in the mode line (see Section 1.3 [Mode Line], page 17).

Each of the coding systems that appear in this list—except for `no-conversion`, which means no conversion of any kind—specifies how and whether to convert printing characters, but leaves the choice of end-of-line conversion to be decided based on the contents of each file. For example, if the file appears to use the sequence carriage-return linefeed to separate lines, DOS end-of-line conversion will be used.

Each of the listed coding systems has three variants which specify exactly what to do for end-of-line conversion:

`...-unix`   Don't do any end-of-line conversion; assume the file uses newline to separate lines. (This is the convention normally used on Unix and GNU systems.)

`...-dos`   Assume the file uses carriage-return linefeed to separate lines, and do the appropriate conversion. (This is the convention normally used on Microsoft systems.[1])

`...-mac`   Assume the file uses carriage-return to separate lines, and do the appropriate conversion. (This is the convention normally used on the Macintosh system.)

These variant coding systems are omitted from the `list-coding-systems` display for brevity, since they are entirely predictable. For example, the coding system `iso-latin-1` has variants `iso-latin-1-unix`, `iso-latin-1-dos` and `iso-latin-1-mac`.

The coding system `raw-text` is good for a file which is mainly ASCII text, but may contain byte values above 127 which are not meant to encode non-ASCII characters. With `raw-text`, Emacs copies those byte values unchanged, and sets `enable-multibyte-characters` to `nil` in the current buffer so that they will be interpreted properly. `raw-text` handles end-of-line conversion in the usual way, based on the data encountered, and has the usual three variants to specify the kind of end-of-line conversion to use.

In contrast, the coding system `no-conversion` specifies no character code conversion at all—none for non-ASCII byte values and none for end of line. This is useful for reading or writing binary files, tar files, and other files that must be examined verbatim. It, too, sets `enable-multibyte-characters` to `nil`.

The easiest way to edit a file with no conversion of any kind is with the `M-x find-file-literally` command. This uses `no-conversion`, and also suppresses other Emacs features that might convert the file contents before you see them. See Section 14.2 [Visiting], page 108.

---

[1]   It is also specified for MIME 'text/*' bodies and in other network transport contexts. It is different from the SGML reference syntax record-start/record-end format which Emacs doesn't support directly.

The coding system `emacs-mule` means that the file contains non-ASCII characters stored with the internal Emacs encoding. It handles end-of-line conversion based on the data encountered, and has the usual three variants to specify the kind of end-of-line conversion.

18.8 Recognizing Coding Systems

Most of the time, Emacs can recognize which coding system to use for any given file—once you have specified your preferences.

Some coding systems can be recognized or distinguished by which byte sequences appear in the data. However, there are coding systems that cannot be distinguished, not even potentially. For example, there is no way to distinguish between Latin-1 and Latin-2; they use the same byte values with different meanings.

Emacs handles this situation by means of a priority list of coding systems. Whenever Emacs reads a file, if you do not specify the coding system to use, Emacs checks the data against each coding system, starting with the first in priority and working down the list, until it finds a coding system that fits the data. Then it converts the file contents assuming that they are represented in this coding system.

The priority list of coding systems depends on the selected language environment (see Section 18.3 [Language Environments], page 176). For example, if you use French, you probably want Emacs to prefer Latin-1 to Latin-2; if you use Czech, you probably want Latin-2 to be preferred. This is one of the reasons to specify a language environment.

However, you can alter the priority list in detail with the command M-x `prefer-coding-system`. This command reads the name of a coding system from the minibuffer, and adds it to the front of the priority list, so that it is preferred to all others. If you use this command several times, each use adds one element to the front of the priority list.

If you use a coding system that specifies the end-of-line conversion type, such as `iso-8859-1-dos`, what that means is that Emacs should attempt to recognize `iso-8859-1` with priority, and should use DOS end-of-line conversion in case it recognizes `iso-8859-1`.

Sometimes a file name indicates which coding system to use for the file. The variable `file-coding-system-alist` specifies this correspondence. There is a special function `modify-coding-system-alist` for adding elements to this list. For example, to read and write all '`.txt`' files using the coding system `china-iso-8bit`, you can execute this Lisp expression:

```
(modify-coding-system-alist 'file "\\.txt\\'" 'china-iso-8bit)
```

The first argument should be `file`, the second argument should be a regular expression that determines which files this applies to, and the third argument says which coding system to use for these files.

Emacs recognizes which kind of end-of-line conversion to use based on the contents of the file: if it sees only carriage-returns, or only carriage-return linefeed sequences, then it chooses the end-of-line conversion accordingly. You can inhibit the automatic use of end-of-line conversion by setting the variable `inhibit-eol-conversion` to non-`nil`.

You can specify the coding system for a particular file using the '-*-...-*-' construct at the beginning of a file, or a local variables list at the end (see Section 31.2.5 [File Variables], page 403). You do this by defining a value for the "variable" named `coding`. Emacs does not really have a variable `coding`; instead of setting a variable, it uses the specified coding system for the file. For example, '-*-mode: C; coding: latin-1;-*-' specifies use of the Latin-1 coding system, as well as C mode. If you specify the coding explicitly in the file, that overrides `file-coding-system-alist`.

The variable `auto-coding-alist` is the strongest way to specify the coding system for certain patterns of file names; this variable even overrides '-*-coding:-*-' tags in the file itself. Emacs uses this feature for tar and archive files, to prevent Emacs from being confused by a '-*-coding:-*-' tag in a member of the archive and thinking it applies to the archive file as a whole.

Once Emacs has chosen a coding system for a buffer, it stores that coding system in `buffer-file-coding-system` and uses that coding system, by default, for operations that write from this buffer into a file. This includes the commands `save-buffer` and `write-region`. If you want to write files from this buffer using a different coding system, you can specify a different coding system for the buffer using `set-buffer-file-coding-system` (see Section 18.9 [Specify Coding], page 184).

When you send a message with Mail mode (see Chapter 26 [Sending Mail], page 301), Emacs has four different ways to determine the coding system to use for encoding the message text. It tries the buffer's own value of `buffer-file-coding-system`, if that is non-`nil`. Otherwise, it uses the value of `sendmail-coding-system`, if that is non-`nil`. The third way is to use the default coding system for new files, which is controlled by your choice of language environment, if that is non-`nil`. If all of these three values are `nil`, Emacs encodes outgoing mail using the Latin-1 coding system.

When you get new mail in Rmail, each message is translated automatically from the coding system it is written in—as if it were a separate file. This uses the priority list of coding systems that you have specified. If a MIME message specifies a character set, Rmail obeys that specification, unless `rmail-decode-mime-charset` is `nil`.

For reading and saving Rmail files themselves, Emacs uses the coding system specified by the variable `rmail-file-coding-system`. The default value is `nil`, which means that Rmail files are not translated (they are read and written in the Emacs internal character code).

18.9 Specifying a Coding System

In cases where Emacs does not automatically choose the right coding system, you can use these commands to specify one:

C-x (RET) f *coding* (RET)
> Use coding system *coding* for the visited file in the current buffer.

C-x (RET) c *coding* (RET)
> Specify coding system *coding* for the immediately following command.

C-x (RET) k *coding* (RET)
> Use coding system *coding* for keyboard input.

C-x (RET) t *coding* (RET)
> Use coding system *coding* for terminal output.

C-x (RET) p *input-coding* (RET) *output-coding* (RET)
> Use coding systems *input-coding* and *output-coding* for subprocess input and output in the current buffer.

C-x (RET) x *coding* (RET)
> Use coding system *coding* for transferring selections to and from other programs through the window system.

C-x (RET) X *coding* (RET)
> Use coding system *coding* for transferring *one* selection—the next one—to or from the window system.

The command C-x (RET) f (set-buffer-file-coding-system) specifies the file coding system for the current buffer—in other words, which coding system to use when saving or rereading the visited file. You specify which coding system using the minibuffer. Since this command applies to a file you have already visited, it affects only the way the file is saved.

Another way to specify the coding system for a file is when you visit the file. First use the command C-x (RET) c (universal-coding-system-argument); this command uses the minibuffer to read a coding system name. After you exit the minibuffer, the specified coding system is used for *the immediately following command.*

So if the immediately following command is C-x C-f, for example, it reads the file using that coding system (and records the coding system for when the file is saved). Or if the immediately following command is C-x C-w, it writes the file using that coding system. Other file commands affected by a specified coding system include C-x C-i and C-x C-v, as well as the other-window variants of C-x C-f.

C-x (RET) c also affects commands that start subprocesses, including M-x shell (see Section 30.2 [Shell], page 367).

However, if the immediately following command does not use the coding system, then C-x (RET) c ultimately has no effect.

An easy way to visit a file with no conversion is with the M-x find-file-literally command. See Section 14.2 [Visiting], page 108.

The variable default-buffer-file-coding-system specifies the choice of coding system to use when you create a new file. It applies when you find a new file, and when you create a buffer and then save it in a file. Selecting a language environment typically sets this variable to a good choice of default coding system for that language environment.

The command C-x (RET) t (set-terminal-coding-system) specifies the coding system for terminal output. If you specify a character code for terminal output, all characters output to the terminal are translated into that coding system.

This feature is useful for certain character-only terminals built to support specific languages or character sets—for example, European terminals that support one of the ISO Latin character sets. You need to specify the terminal coding system when using multibyte text, so that Emacs knows which characters the terminal can actually handle.

By default, output to the terminal is not translated at all, unless Emacs can deduce the proper coding system from your terminal type.

The command C-x (RET) k (set-keyboard-coding-system) specifies the coding system for keyboard input. Character-code translation of keyboard input is useful for terminals with keys that send non-ASCII graphic characters—for example, some terminals designed for ISO Latin-1 or subsets of it.

By default, keyboard input is not translated at all.

There is a similarity between using a coding system translation for keyboard input, and using an input method: both define sequences of keyboard input that translate into single characters. However, input methods are designed to be convenient for interactive use by humans, and the sequences that are translated are typically sequences of ASCII printing characters. Coding systems typically translate sequences of non-graphic characters.

The command C-x (RET) x (set-selection-coding-system) specifies the coding system for sending selected text to the window system, and for receiving the text of selections made in other applications. This command applies to all subsequent selections, until you override it by using the command again. The command C-x (RET) X (set-next-selection-coding-system) specifies the coding system for the next selection made in Emacs or read by Emacs.

The command C-x (RET) p (set-buffer-process-coding-system) specifies the coding system for input and output to a subprocess. This command applies to the current buffer; normally, each subprocess has its own buffer, and thus you can use this command to specify translation to and from a particular subprocess by giving the command in the corresponding buffer.

By default, process input and output are not translated at all.

The variable `file-name-coding-system` specifies a coding system to use for encoding file names. If you set the variable to a coding system name (as a Lisp symbol or a string), Emacs encodes file names using that coding system for all file operations. This makes it possible to use non-ASCII characters in file names—or, at least, those non-ASCII characters which the specified coding system can encode.

If `file-name-coding-system` is `nil`, Emacs uses a default coding system determined by the selected language environment. In the default language environment, any non-ASCII characters in file names are not encoded specially; they appear in the file system using the internal Emacs representation.

Warning: if you change `file-name-coding-system` (or the language environment) in the middle of an Emacs session, problems can result if you have already visited files whose names were encoded using the earlier coding system and cannot be encoded (or are encoded differently) under the new coding system. If you try to save one of these buffers under the visited file name, saving may use the wrong file name, or it may get an error. If such a problem happens, use `C-x C-w` to specify a new file name for that buffer.

18.10 Fontsets

A font for X Windows typically defines shapes for one alphabet or script. Therefore, displaying the entire range of scripts that Emacs supports requires a collection of many fonts. In Emacs, such a collection is called a *fontset*. A fontset is defined by a list of fonts, each assigned to handle a range of character codes.

Each fontset has a name, like a font. The available X fonts are defined by the X server; fontsets, however, are defined within Emacs itself. Once you have defined a fontset, you can use it within Emacs by specifying its name, anywhere that you could use a single font. Of course, Emacs fontsets can use only the fonts that the X server supports; if certain characters appear on the screen as hollow boxes, this means that the fontset in use for them has no font for those characters.

Emacs creates two fontsets automatically: the *standard fontset* and the *startup fontset*. The standard fontset is most likely to have fonts for a wide variety of non-ASCII characters; however, this is not the default for Emacs to use. (By default, Emacs tries to find a font which has bold and italic variants.) You can specify use of the standard fontset with the '`-fn`' option, or with the '`Font`' X resource (see Section A.7 [Font X], page 449). For example,

```
emacs -fn fontset-standard
```

A fontset does not necessarily specify a font for every character code. If a fontset specifies no font for a certain character, or if it specifies a font that does not exist on your system, then it cannot display that character properly. It will display that character as an empty box instead.

The fontset height and width are determined by the ASCII characters (that is, by the font used for ASCII characters in that fontset). If another font in the fontset has a different height, or a different width, then characters assigned to that font are clipped to the fontset's size. If `highlight-wrong-size-font` is non-`nil`, a box is displayed around these wrong-size characters as well.

18.11 Defining fontsets

Emacs creates a standard fontset automatically according to the value of `standard-fontset-spec`. This fontset's name is

    -*-fixed-medium-r-normal-*-16-*-*-*-*-*-fontset-standard

or just '`fontset-standard`' for short.

Bold, italic, and bold-italic variants of the standard fontset are created automatically. Their names have '`bold`' instead of '`medium`', or '`i`' instead of '`r`', or both.

If you specify a default ASCII font with the '`Font`' resource or the '`-fn`' argument, Emacs generates a fontset from it automatically. This is the *startup fontset* and its name is `fontset-startup`. It does this by replacing the *foundry*, *family*, *add_style*, and *average_width* fields of the font name with '`*`', replacing *charset_registry* field with '`fontset`', and replacing *charset_encoding* field with '`startup`', then using the resulting string to specify a fontset.

For instance, if you start Emacs this way,

    emacs -fn "*courier-medium-r-normal--14-140-*-iso8859-1"

Emacs generates the following fontset and uses it for the initial X window frame:

    -*-*-medium-r-normal-*-14-140-*-*-*-*-fontset-startup

With the X resource '`Emacs.Font`', you can specify a fontset name just like an actual font name. But be careful not to specify a fontset name in a wildcard resource like '`Emacs*Font`'—that wildcard specification applies to various other purposes, such as menus, and menus cannot handle fontsets.

You can specify additional fontsets using X resources named '`Fontset-n`', where *n* is an integer starting from 0. The resource value should have this form:

    fontpattern, [*charsetname*:*fontname*]...

fontpattern should have the form of a standard X font name, except for the last two fields. They should have the form '`fontset-alias`'.

The fontset has two names, one long and one short. The long name is *fontpattern*. The short name is '`fontset-alias`'. You can refer to the fontset by either name.

The construct '*charset*:*font*' specifies which font to use (in this fontset) for one particular character set. Here, *charset* is the name of a character set, and *font* is the font to use for that character set. You can use this construct any number of times in defining one fontset.

For the other character sets, Emacs chooses a font based on *fontpattern*. It replaces '`fontset-`*alias*' with values that describe the character set. For the ASCII character font, '`fontset-`*alias*' is replaced with '`ISO8859-1`'.

In addition, when several consecutive fields are wildcards, Emacs collapses them into a single wildcard. This is to prevent use of auto-scaled fonts. Fonts made by scaling larger fonts are not usable for editing, and scaling a smaller font is not useful because it is better to use the smaller font in its own size, which Emacs does.

Thus if *fontpattern* is this,

```
-*-fixed-medium-r-normal-*-24-*-*-*-*-*-fontset-24
```

the font specification for ASCII characters would be this:

```
-*-fixed-medium-r-normal-*-24-*-ISO8859-1
```

and the font specification for Chinese GB2312 characters would be this:

```
-*-fixed-medium-r-normal-*-24-*-gb2312*-*
```

You may not have any Chinese font matching the above font specification. Most X distributions include only Chinese fonts that have '`song ti`' or '`fangsong ti`' in *family* field. In such a case, '`Fontset-`*n*' can be specified as below:

```
Emacs.Fontset-0: -*-fixed-medium-r-normal-*-24-*-*-*-*-*-fontset-24,\
        chinese-gb2312:-*-*-medium-r-normal-*-24-*-gb2312*-*
```

Then, the font specifications for all but Chinese GB2312 characters have '`fixed`' in the *family* field, and the font specification for Chinese GB2312 characters has a wild card '`*`' in the *family* field.

The function that processes the fontset resource value to create the fontset is called `create-fontset-from-fontset-spec`. You can also call this function explicitly to create a fontset.

See Section A.7 [Font X], page 449, for more information about font naming in X.

18.12 Single-byte European Character Support

The ISO 8859 Latin-*n* character sets define character codes in the range 160 to 255 to handle the accented letters and punctuation needed by various European languages. If you disable multibyte characters, Emacs can still handle *one* of these character codes at a time. To specify *which* of these codes to use, invoke `M-x set-language-environment` and specify a suitable language environment such as '`Latin-`*n*'.

For more information about unibyte operation, see Section 18.2 [Enabling Multibyte], page 175. Note particularly that you probably want to ensure that your initialization files are read as unibyte if they contain non-ASCII characters.

Emacs can also display those characters, provided the terminal or font in use supports them. This works automatically. Alternatively, if you are using a window system, Emacs can also display single-byte characters through fontsets, in effect by displaying the equivalent multibyte characters according to the current language environment. To request this, set the variable `unibyte-display-via-language-environment` to a non-`nil` value.

If your terminal does not support display of the Latin-1 character set, Emacs can display these characters as ASCII sequences which at least give you a clear idea of what the characters are. To do this, load the library `iso-ascii`. Similar libraries for other Latin-*n* character sets could be implemented, but we don't have them yet.

Normally non-ISO-8859 characters (between characters 128 and 159 inclusive) are displayed as octal escapes. You can change this for non-standard 'extended' versions of ISO-8859 character sets by using the function `standard-display-8bit` in the `disp-table` library.

There are three different ways you can input single-byte non-ASCII characters:

- If your keyboard can generate character codes 128 and up, representing non-ASCII characters, execute the following expression to enable Emacs to understand them:

  ```
  (set-input-mode (car (current-input-mode))
                  (nth 1 (current-input-mode))
                  0)
  ```

- You can use an input method for the selected language environment. See Section 18.4 [Input Methods], page 177. When you use an input method in a unibyte buffer, the non-ASCII character you specify with it is converted to unibyte.

- For Latin-1 only, you can use the key `C-x 8` as a "compose character" prefix for entry of non-ASCII Latin-1 printing characters. `C-x 8` is good for insertion (in the minibuffer as well as other buffers), for searching, and in any other context where a key sequence is allowed.

  `C-x 8` works by loading the `iso-transl` library. Once that library is loaded, the (ALT) modifier key, if you have one, serves the same purpose as `C-x 8`; use (ALT) together with an accent character to modify the following letter. In addition, if you have keys for the Latin-1 "dead accent characters", they too are defined to compose with the following character, once `iso-transl` is loaded.

19 Major Modes

Emacs provides many alternative *major modes*, each of which customizes Emacs for editing text of a particular sort. The major modes are mutually exclusive, and each buffer has one major mode at any time. The mode line normally shows the name of the current major mode, in parentheses (see Section 1.3 [Mode Line], page 17).

The least specialized major mode is called *Fundamental mode*. This mode has no mode-specific redefinitions or variable settings, so that each Emacs command behaves in its most general manner, and each option is in its default state. For editing text of a specific type that Emacs knows about, such as Lisp code or English text, you should switch to the appropriate major mode, such as Lisp mode or Text mode.

Selecting a major mode changes the meanings of a few keys to become more specifically adapted to the language being edited. The ones that are changed frequently are (TAB), (DEL), and C-j. The prefix key C-c normally contains mode-specific commands. In addition, the commands which handle comments use the mode to determine how comments are to be delimited. Many major modes redefine the syntactical properties of characters appearing in the buffer. See Section 31.6 [Syntax], page 419.

The major modes fall into three major groups. Lisp mode (which has several variants), C mode, Fortran mode and others are for specific programming languages. Text mode, Nroff mode, TEX mode and Outline mode are for editing English text. The remaining major modes are not intended for use on users' files; they are used in buffers created for specific purposes by Emacs, such as Dired mode for buffers made by Dired (see Chapter 28 [Dired], page 329), Mail mode for buffers made by C-x m (see Chapter 26 [Sending Mail], page 301), and Shell mode for buffers used for communicating with an inferior shell process (see Section 30.2.2 [Interactive Shell], page 368).

Most programming-language major modes specify that only blank lines separate paragraphs. This is to make the paragraph commands useful. (See Section 21.3 [Paragraphs], page 201.) They also cause Auto Fill mode to use the definition of (TAB) to indent the new lines it creates. This is because most lines in a program are usually indented. (See Chapter 20 [Indentation], page 195.)

19.1 How Major Modes are Chosen

You can select a major mode explicitly for the current buffer, but most of the time Emacs determines which mode to use based on the file name or on special text in the file.

Explicit selection of a new major mode is done with a M-x command. From the name of a major mode, add **-mode** to get the name of a com-

mand to select that mode. Thus, you can enter Lisp mode by executing M-x
lisp-mode.

When you visit a file, Emacs usually chooses the right major mode based
on the file's name. For example, files whose names end in '.c' are edited
in C mode. The correspondence between file names and major modes is
controlled by the variable auto-mode-alist. Its value is a list in which each
element has this form,

    (regexp . mode-function)

or this form,

    (regexp mode-function flag)

For example, one element normally found in the list has the form ("\\.c\\'"
. c-mode), and it is responsible for selecting C mode for files whose names
end in '.c'. (Note that '\\' is needed in Lisp syntax to include a '\' in the
string, which is needed to suppress the special meaning of '.' in regexps.) If
the element has the form (regexp mode-function flag) and flag is non-nil,
then after calling function, the suffix that matched regexp is discarded and
the list is searched again for another match.

You can specify which major mode should be used for editing a certain
file by a special sort of text in the first nonblank line of the file. The mode
name should appear in this line both preceded and followed by '-*-'. Other
text may appear on the line as well. For example,

    ;-*-Lisp-*-

tells Emacs to use Lisp mode. Such an explicit specification overrides any
defaulting based on the file name. Note how the semicolon is used to make
Lisp treat this line as a comment.

Another format of mode specification is

    -*- mode: modename;-*-

which allows you to specify local variables as well, like this:

    -*- mode: modename; var: value; ... -*-

See Section 31.2.5 [File Variables], page 403, for more information about
this.

When a file's contents begin with '#!', it can serve as an executable shell
command, which works by running an interpreter named on the file's first
line. The rest of the file is used as input to the interpreter.

When you visit such a file in Emacs, if the file's name does not specify a
major mode, Emacs uses the interpreter name on the first line to choose a
mode. If the first line is the name of a recognized interpreter program, such
as 'perl' or 'tcl', Emacs uses a mode appropriate for programs for that
interpreter. The variable interpreter-mode-alist specifies the correspondence between interpreter program names and major modes.

When the first line starts with '#!', you cannot (on many systems) use
the '-*-' feature on the first line, because the system would get confused

when running the interpreter. So Emacs looks for '-*-' on the second line in such files as well as on the first line.

When you visit a file that does not specify a major mode to use, or when you create a new buffer with C-x b, the variable default-major-mode specifies which major mode to use. Normally its value is the symbol fundamental-mode, which specifies Fundamental mode. If default-major-mode is nil, the major mode is taken from the previously selected buffer.

If you change the major mode of a buffer, you can go back to the major mode Emacs would choose automatically: use the command M-x normal-mode to do this. This is the same function that find-file calls to choose the major mode. It also processes the file's local variables list if any.

The commands C-x C-w and set-visited-file-name change to a new major mode if the new file name implies a mode (see Section 14.3 [Saving], page 111). However, this does not happen if the buffer contents specify a major mode, and certain "special" major modes do not allow the mode to change. You can turn off this mode-changing feature by setting change-major-mode-with-file-name to nil.

20 Indentation

This chapter describes the Emacs commands that add, remove, or adjust indentation.

(TAB)   Indent current line "appropriately" in a mode-dependent fashion.

C-j   Perform (RET) followed by (TAB) (newline-and-indent).

M-^   Merge two lines (delete-indentation). This would cancel out the effect of C-j.

C-M-o   Split line at point; text on the line after point becomes a new line indented to the same column that it now starts in (split-line).

M-m   Move (forward or back) to the first nonblank character on the current line (back-to-indentation).

C-M-\   Indent several lines to same column (indent-region).

C-x (TAB)   Shift block of lines rigidly right or left (indent-rigidly).

M-i   Indent from point to the next prespecified tab stop column (tab-to-tab-stop).

M-x indent-relative
             Indent from point to under an indentation point in the previous line.

Most programming languages have some indentation convention. For Lisp code, lines are indented according to their nesting in parentheses. The same general idea is used for C code, though many details are different.

Whatever the language, to indent a line, use the (TAB) command. Each major mode defines this command to perform the sort of indentation appropriate for the particular language. In Lisp mode, (TAB) aligns the line according to its depth in parentheses. No matter where in the line you are when you type (TAB), it aligns the line as a whole. In C mode, (TAB) implements a subtle and sophisticated indentation style that knows about many aspects of C syntax.

In Text mode, (TAB) runs the command tab-to-tab-stop, which indents to the next tab stop column. You can set the tab stops with M-x edit-tab-stops.

20.1 Indentation Commands and Techniques

To move over the indentation on a line, do M-m (back-to-indentation). This command, given anywhere on a line, positions point at the first non-blank character on the line.

To insert an indented line before the current line, do C-a C-o (TAB). To make an indented line after the current line, use C-e C-j.

If you just want to insert a tab character in the buffer, you can type `C-q` (TAB).

`C-M-o` (`split-line`) moves the text from point to the end of the line vertically down, so that the current line becomes two lines. `C-M-o` first moves point forward over any spaces and tabs. Then it inserts after point a newline and enough indentation to reach the same column point is on. Point remains before the inserted newline; in this regard, `C-M-o` resembles `C-o`.

To join two lines cleanly, use the `M-^` (`delete-indentation`) command. It deletes the indentation at the front of the current line, and the line boundary as well, replacing them with a single space. As a special case (useful for Lisp code) the single space is omitted if the characters to be joined are consecutive open parentheses or closing parentheses, or if the junction follows another newline. To delete just the indentation of a line, go to the beginning of the line and use `M-\` (`delete-horizontal-space`), which deletes all spaces and tabs around the cursor.

If you have a fill prefix, `M-^` deletes the fill prefix if it appears after the newline that is deleted. See Section 21.5.3 [Fill Prefix], page 206.

There are also commands for changing the indentation of several lines at once. `C-M-\` (`indent-region`) applies to all the lines that begin in the region; it indents each line in the "usual" way, as if you had typed (TAB) at the beginning of the line. A numeric argument specifies the column to indent to, and each line is shifted left or right so that its first nonblank character appears in that column. `C-x` (TAB) (`indent-rigidly`) moves all of the lines in the region right by its argument (left, for negative arguments). The whole group of lines moves rigidly sideways, which is how the command gets its name.

`M-x indent-relative` indents at point based on the previous line (actually, the last nonempty line). It inserts whitespace at point, moving point, until it is underneath an indentation point in the previous line. An indentation point is the end of a sequence of whitespace or the end of the line. If point is farther right than any indentation point in the previous line, the whitespace before point is deleted and the first indentation point then applicable is used. If no indentation point is applicable even then, `indent-relative` runs `tab-to-tab-stop` (see next section).

`indent-relative` is the definition of (TAB) in Indented Text mode. See Chapter 21 [Text], page 199.

See Section 21.11.6 [Format Indentation], page 223, for another way of specifying the indentation for part of your text.

20.2 Tab Stops

For typing in tables, you can use Text mode's definition of (TAB), `tab-to-tab-stop`. This command inserts indentation before point, enough to reach the next tab stop column. If you are not in Text mode, this command can be found on the key `M-i`.

You can specify the tab stops used by `M-i`. They are stored in a variable called `tab-stop-list`, as a list of column-numbers in increasing order.

The convenient way to set the tab stops is with `M-x edit-tab-stops`, which creates and selects a buffer containing a description of the tab stop settings. You can edit this buffer to specify different tab stops, and then type `C-c C-c` to make those new tab stops take effect. `edit-tab-stops` records which buffer was current when you invoked it, and stores the tab stops back in that buffer; normally all buffers share the same tab stops and changing them in one buffer affects all, but if you happen to make `tab-stop-list` local in one buffer then `edit-tab-stops` in that buffer will edit the local settings.

Here is what the text representing the tab stops looks like for ordinary tab stops every eight columns.

```
        :       :       :       :       :       :
0       1       2       3       4
0123456789012345678901234567890123456789012345678
To install changes, type C-c C-c
```

The first line contains a colon at each tab stop. The remaining lines are present just to help you see where the colons are and know what to do.

Note that the tab stops that control `tab-to-tab-stop` have nothing to do with displaying tab characters in the buffer. See Section 11.7 [Display Vars], page 83, for more information on that.

20.3 Tabs vs. Spaces

Emacs normally uses both tabs and spaces to indent lines. If you prefer, all indentation can be made from spaces only. To request this, set `indent-tabs-mode` to `nil`. This is a per-buffer variable; altering the variable affects only the current buffer, but there is a default value which you can change as well. See Section 31.2.4 [Locals], page 401.

There are also commands to convert tabs to spaces or vice versa, always preserving the columns of all nonblank text. `M-x tabify` scans the region for sequences of spaces, and converts sequences of at least three spaces to tabs if that can be done without changing indentation. `M-x untabify` changes all tabs in the region to appropriate numbers of spaces.

21 Commands for Human Languages

The term *text* has two widespread meanings in our area of the computer field. One is data that is a sequence of characters. Any file that you edit with Emacs is text, in this sense of the word. The other meaning is more restrictive: a sequence of characters in a human language for humans to read (possibly after processing by a text formatter), as opposed to a program or commands for a program.

Human languages have syntactic/stylistic conventions that can be supported or used to advantage by editor commands: conventions involving words, sentences, paragraphs, and capital letters. This chapter describes Emacs commands for all of these things. There are also commands for *filling*, which means rearranging the lines of a paragraph to be approximately equal in length. The commands for moving over and killing words, sentences and paragraphs, while intended primarily for editing text, are also often useful for editing programs.

Emacs has several major modes for editing human-language text. If the file contains text pure and simple, use Text mode, which customizes Emacs in small ways for the syntactic conventions of text. Outline mode provides special commands for operating on text with an outline structure. See Section 21.8 [Outline Mode], page 210.

For text which contains embedded commands for text formatters, Emacs has other major modes, each for a particular text formatter. Thus, for input to TeX, you would use TeX mode (see Section 21.9 [TeX Mode], page 214). For input to nroff, use Nroff mode.

Instead of using a text formatter, you can edit formatted text in WYSIWYG style ("what you see is what you get"), with Enriched mode. Then the formatting appears on the screen in Emacs while you edit. See Section 21.11 [Formatted Text], page 219.

21.1 Words

Emacs has commands for moving over or operating on words. By convention, the keys for them are all Meta characters.

M-f   Move forward over a word (`forward-word`).

M-b   Move backward over a word (`backward-word`).

M-d   Kill up to the end of a word (`kill-word`).

M-⟨DEL⟩   Kill back to the beginning of a word (`backward-kill-word`).

M-@   Mark the end of the next word (`mark-word`).

M-t   Transpose two words or drag a word across other words (`transpose-words`).

Notice how these keys form a series that parallels the character-based C-f, C-b, C-d, (DEL) and C-t. M-@ is cognate to C-@, which is an alias for C-(SPC).

The commands M-f (forward-word) and M-b (backward-word) move forward and backward over words. These Meta characters are thus analogous to the corresponding control characters, C-f and C-b, which move over single characters in the text. The analogy extends to numeric arguments, which serve as repeat counts. M-f with a negative argument moves backward, and M-b with a negative argument moves forward. Forward motion stops right after the last letter of the word, while backward motion stops right before the first letter.

M-d (kill-word) kills the word after point. To be precise, it kills everything from point to the place M-f would move to. Thus, if point is in the middle of a word, M-d kills just the part after point. If some punctuation comes between point and the next word, it is killed along with the word. (If you wish to kill only the next word but not the punctuation before it, simply do M-f to get the end, and kill the word backwards with M-(DEL).) M-d takes arguments just like M-f.

M-(DEL) (backward-kill-word) kills the word before point. It kills everything from point back to where M-b would move to. If point is after the space in 'FOO, BAR', then 'FOO, ' is killed. (If you wish to kill just 'FOO', and not the comma and the space, use M-b M-d instead of M-(DEL).)

M-t (transpose-words) exchanges the word before or containing point with the following word. The delimiter characters between the words do not move. For example, 'FOO, BAR' transposes into 'BAR, FOO' rather than 'BAR FOO, '. See Section 13.2 [Transpose], page 101, for more on transposition and on arguments to transposition commands.

To operate on the next n words with an operation which applies between point and mark, you can either set the mark at point and then move over the words, or you can use the command M-@ (mark-word) which does not move point, but sets the mark where M-f would move to. M-@ accepts a numeric argument that says how many words to scan for the place to put the mark. In Transient Mark mode, this command activates the mark.

The word commands' understanding of syntax is completely controlled by the syntax table. Any character can, for example, be declared to be a word delimiter. See Section 31.6 [Syntax], page 419.

21.2 Sentences

The Emacs commands for manipulating sentences and paragraphs are mostly on Meta keys, so as to be like the word-handling commands.

M-a   Move back to the beginning of the sentence (backward-sentence).

M-e   Move forward to the end of the sentence (forward-sentence).

M-k   Kill forward to the end of the sentence (`kill-sentence`).

C-x (DEL)   Kill back to the beginning of the sentence (`backward-kill-sentence`).

The commands M-a and M-e (`backward-sentence` and `forward-sentence`) move to the beginning and end of the current sentence, respectively. They were chosen to resemble C-a and C-e, which move to the beginning and end of a line. Unlike them, M-a and M-e if repeated or given numeric arguments move over successive sentences.

Moving backward over a sentence places point just before the first character of the sentence; moving forward places point right after the punctuation that ends the sentence. Neither one moves over the whitespace at the sentence boundary.

Just as C-a and C-e have a kill command, C-k, to go with them, so M-a and M-e have a corresponding kill command M-k (`kill-sentence`) which kills from point to the end of the sentence. With minus one as an argument it kills back to the beginning of the sentence. Larger arguments serve as a repeat count. There is also a command, C-x (DEL) (`backward-kill-sentence`), for killing back to the beginning of a sentence. This command is useful when you change your mind in the middle of composing text.

The sentence commands assume that you follow the American typist's convention of putting two spaces at the end of a sentence; they consider a sentence to end wherever there is a '.', '?' or '!' followed by the end of a line or two spaces, with any number of ')', ']', '’', or '"' characters allowed in between. A sentence also begins or ends wherever a paragraph begins or ends.

The variable **sentence-end** controls recognition of the end of a sentence. It is a regexp that matches the last few characters of a sentence, together with the whitespace following the sentence. Its normal value is

```
"[.?!][]\"')]*\\($\\|\t\\|  \\)[ \t\n]*"
```

This example is explained in the section on regexps. See Section 12.5 [Regexps], page 90.

If you want to use just one space between sentences, you should set **sentence-end** to this value:

```
"[.?!][]\"')]*\\($\\|\t\\|  \\)[ \t\n]*"
```

You should also set the variable **sentence-end-double-space** to `nil` so that the fill commands expect and leave just one space at the end of a sentence. Note that this makes it impossible to distinguish between periods that end sentences and those that indicate abbreviations.

21.3 Paragraphs

The Emacs commands for manipulating paragraphs are also Meta keys.

M-{   Move back to previous paragraph beginning (backward-paragraph).

M-}   Move forward to next paragraph end (forward-paragraph).

M-h   Put point and mark around this or next paragraph (mark-paragraph).

M-{ moves to the beginning of the current or previous paragraph, while M-} moves to the end of the current or next paragraph. Blank lines and text-formatter command lines separate paragraphs and are not considered part of any paragraph. In Fundamental mode, but not in Text mode, an indented line also starts a new paragraph. (If a paragraph is preceded by a blank line, these commands treat that blank line as the beginning of the paragraph.)

In major modes for programs, paragraphs begin and end only at blank lines. This makes the paragraph commands continue to be useful even though there are no paragraphs per se.

When there is a fill prefix, then paragraphs are delimited by all lines which don't start with the fill prefix. See Section 21.5 [Filling], page 203.

When you wish to operate on a paragraph, you can use the command M-h (mark-paragraph) to set the region around it. Thus, for example, M-h C-w kills the paragraph around or after point. The M-h command puts point at the beginning and mark at the end of the paragraph point was in. In Transient Mark mode, it activates the mark. If point is between paragraphs (in a run of blank lines, or at a boundary), the paragraph following point is surrounded by point and mark. If there are blank lines preceding the first line of the paragraph, one of these blank lines is included in the region.

The precise definition of a paragraph boundary is controlled by the variables paragraph-separate and paragraph-start. The value of paragraph-start is a regexp that should match any line that either starts or separates paragraphs. The value of paragraph-separate is another regexp that should match only lines that separate paragraphs without being part of any paragraph (for example, blank lines). Lines that start a new paragraph and are contained in it must match only paragraph-start, not paragraph-separate. For example, in Fundamental mode, paragraph-start is "[\t\n\f]" and paragraph-separate is "[\t\f]*$".

Normally it is desirable for page boundaries to separate paragraphs. The default values of these variables recognize the usual separator for pages.

21.4 Pages

Files are often thought of as divided into *pages* by the *formfeed* character (ASCII control-L, octal code 014). When you print hardcopy for a file, this character forces a page break; thus, each page of the file goes on a separate page on paper. Most Emacs commands treat the page-separator character just like any other character: you can insert it with C-q C-l, and delete it with (DEL). Thus, you are free to paginate your file or not. However, since pages are often meaningful divisions of the file, Emacs provides commands to move over them and operate on them.

C-x [Move point to previous page boundary (backward-page).

C-x]   Move point to next page boundary (forward-page).

C-x C-p Put point and mark around this page (or another page) (mark-page).

C-x l   Count the lines in this page (count-lines-page).

The C-x [(backward-page) command moves point to immediately after the previous page delimiter. If point is already right after a page delimiter, it skips that one and stops at the previous one. A numeric argument serves as a repeat count. The C-x] (forward-page) command moves forward past the next page delimiter.

The C-x C-p command (mark-page) puts point at the beginning of the current page and the mark at the end. The page delimiter at the end is included (the mark follows it). The page delimiter at the front is excluded (point follows it). C-x C-p C-w is a handy way to kill a page to move it elsewhere. If you move to another page delimiter with C-x [and C-x], then yank the killed page, all the pages will be properly delimited once again. The reason C-x C-p includes only the following page delimiter in the region is to ensure that.

A numeric argument to C-x C-p is used to specify which page to go to, relative to the current one. Zero means the current page. One means the next page, and −1 means the previous one.

The C-x l command (count-lines-page) is good for deciding where to break a page in two. It prints in the echo area the total number of lines in the current page, and then divides it up into those preceding the current line and those following, as in

    Page has 96 (72+25) lines

Notice that the sum is off by one; this is correct if point is not at the beginning of a line.

The variable page-delimiter controls where pages begin. Its value is a regexp that matches the beginning of a line that separates pages. The normal value of this variable is "^\f", which matches a formfeed character at the beginning of a line.

21.5 Filling Text

Filling text means breaking it up into lines that fit a specified width. Emacs does filling in two ways. In Auto Fill mode, inserting text with self-inserting characters also automatically fills it. There are also explicit fill commands that you can use when editing text leaves it unfilled. When you edit formatted text, you can specify a style of filling for each portion of the text (see Section 21.11 [Formatted Text], page 219).

21.5.1 Auto Fill Mode

Auto Fill mode is a minor mode in which lines are broken automatically when they become too wide. Breaking happens only when you type a (SPC) or (RET).

M-x auto-fill-mode
      Enable or disable Auto Fill mode.

(SPC)
(RET)   In Auto Fill mode, break lines when appropriate.

M-x auto-fill-mode turns Auto Fill mode on if it was off, or off if it was on. With a positive numeric argument it always turns Auto Fill mode on, and with a negative argument always turns it off. You can see when Auto Fill mode is in effect by the presence of the word 'Fill' in the mode line, inside the parentheses. Auto Fill mode is a minor mode which is enabled or disabled for each buffer individually. See Section 31.1 [Minor Modes], page 391.

In Auto Fill mode, lines are broken automatically at spaces when they get longer than the desired width. Line breaking and rearrangement takes place only when you type (SPC) or (RET). If you wish to insert a space or newline without permitting line-breaking, type C-q (SPC) or C-q C-j (recall that a newline is really a control-J). Also, C-o inserts a newline without line breaking.

Auto Fill mode works well with programming-language modes, because it indents new lines with (TAB). If a line ending in a comment gets too long, the text of the comment is split into two comment lines. Optionally, new comment delimiters are inserted at the end of the first line and the beginning of the second so that each line is a separate comment; the variable comment-multi-line controls the choice (see Section 22.7 [Comments], page 244).

Adaptive filling (see the following section) works for Auto Filling as well as for explicit fill commands. It takes a fill prefix automatically from the second or first line of a paragraph.

Auto Fill mode does not refill entire paragraphs; it can break lines but cannot merge lines. So editing in the middle of a paragraph can result in a paragraph that is not correctly filled. The easiest way to make the paragraph properly filled again is usually with the explicit fill commands.

Many users like Auto Fill mode and want to use it in all text files. The section on init files says how to arrange this permanently for yourself. See Section 31.7 [Init File], page 419.

21.5.2 Explicit Fill Commands

M-q   Fill current paragraph (`fill-paragraph`).

C-x f   Set the fill column (`set-fill-column`).

M-x fill-region
             Fill each paragraph in the region (`fill-region`).

M-x fill-region-as-paragraph
             Fill the region, considering it as one paragraph.

M-s   Center a line.

To refill a paragraph, use the command M-q (`fill-paragraph`). This operates on the paragraph that point is inside, or the one after point if point is between paragraphs. Refilling works by removing all the line-breaks, then inserting new ones where necessary.

To refill many paragraphs, use M-x `fill-region`, which divides the region into paragraphs and fills each of them.

M-q and `fill-region` use the same criteria as M-h for finding paragraph boundaries (see Section 21.3 [Paragraphs], page 201). For more control, you can use M-x `fill-region-as-paragraph`, which refills everything between point and mark. This command deletes any blank lines within the region, so separate blocks of text end up combined into one block.

A numeric argument to M-q causes it to *justify* the text as well as filling it. This means that extra spaces are inserted to make the right margin line up exactly at the fill column. To remove the extra spaces, use M-q with no argument. (Likewise for `fill-region`.) Another way to control justification, and choose other styles of filling, is with the `justification` text property; see Section 21.11.7 [Format Justification], page 224.

The command M-s (`center-line`) centers the current line within the current fill column. With an argument *n*, it centers *n* lines individually and moves past them.

The maximum line width for filling is in the variable `fill-column`. Altering the value of `fill-column` makes it local to the current buffer; until that time, the default value is in effect. The default is initially 70. See Section 31.2.4 [Locals], page 401. The easiest way to set `fill-column` is to use the command C-x f (`set-fill-column`). With a numeric argument, it uses that as the new fill column. With just C-u as argument, it sets `fill-column` to the current horizontal position of point.

Emacs commands normally consider a period followed by two spaces or by a newline as the end of a sentence; a period followed by just one space indicates an abbreviation and not the end of a sentence. To preserve the distinction between these two ways of using a period, the fill commands do not break a line after a period followed by just one space.

If the variable `sentence-end-double-space` is `nil`, the fill commands expect and leave just one space at the end of a sentence. Ordinarily this variable is `t`, so the fill commands insist on two spaces for the end of a sentence, as explained above. See Section 21.2 [Sentences], page 200.

If the variable `colon-double-space` is non-`nil`, the fill commands put two spaces after a colon.

21.5.3 The Fill Prefix

To fill a paragraph in which each line starts with a special marker (which might be a few spaces, giving an indented paragraph), you can use the *fill prefix* feature. The fill prefix is a string that Emacs expects every line to start with, and which is not included in filling. You can specify a fill prefix explicitly; Emacs can also deduce the fill prefix automatically (see Section 21.5.4 [Adaptive Fill], page 207).

C-x .   Set the fill prefix (`set-fill-prefix`).

M-q   Fill a paragraph using current fill prefix (`fill-paragraph`).

M-x fill-individual-paragraphs
              Fill the region, considering each change of indentation as starting a new paragraph.

M-x fill-nonuniform-paragraphs
              Fill the region, considering only paragraph-separator lines as starting a new paragraph.

To specify a fill prefix, move to a line that starts with the desired prefix, put point at the end of the prefix, and give the command `C-x .` (`set-fill-prefix`). That's a period after the `C-x`. To turn off the fill prefix, specify an empty prefix: type `C-x .` with point at the beginning of a line.

When a fill prefix is in effect, the fill commands remove the fill prefix from each line before filling and insert it on each line after filling. Auto Fill mode also inserts the fill prefix automatically when it makes a new line. The `C-o` command inserts the fill prefix on new lines it creates, when you use it at the beginning of a line (see Section 4.7 [Blank Lines], page 34). Conversely, the command `M-^` deletes the prefix (if it occurs) after the newline that it deletes (see Chapter 20 [Indentation], page 195).

For example, if `fill-column` is 40 and you set the fill prefix to '`;; `', then `M-q` in the following text

```
;; This is an
;; example of a paragraph
;; inside a Lisp-style comment.
```
produces this:
```
;; This is an example of a paragraph
;; inside a Lisp-style comment.
```
Lines that do not start with the fill prefix are considered to start paragraphs, both in `M-q` and the paragraph commands; this gives good results

for paragraphs with hanging indentation (every line indented except the first one). Lines which are blank or indented once the prefix is removed also separate or start paragraphs; this is what you want if you are writing multi-paragraph comments with a comment delimiter on each line.

You can use `M-x fill-individual-paragraphs` to set the fill prefix for each paragraph automatically. This command divides the region into paragraphs, treating every change in the amount of indentation as the start of a new paragraph, and fills each of these paragraphs. Thus, all the lines in one "paragraph" have the same amount of indentation. That indentation serves as the fill prefix for that paragraph.

`M-x fill-nonuniform-paragraphs` is a similar command that divides the region into paragraphs in a different way. It considers only paragraph-separating lines (as defined by `paragraph-separate`) as starting a new paragraph. Since this means that the lines of one paragraph may have different amounts of indentation, the fill prefix used is the smallest amount of indentation of any of the lines of the paragraph. This gives good results with styles that indent a paragraph's first line more or less that the rest of the paragraph.

The fill prefix is stored in the variable `fill-prefix`. Its value is a string, or `nil` when there is no fill prefix. This is a per-buffer variable; altering the variable affects only the current buffer, but there is a default value which you can change as well. See Section 31.2.4 [Locals], page 401.

The `indentation` text property provides another way to control the amount of indentation paragraphs receive. See Section 21.11.6 [Format Indentation], page 223.

21.5.4 Adaptive Filling

The fill commands can deduce the proper fill prefix for a paragraph automatically in certain cases: either whitespace or certain punctuation characters at the beginning of a line are propagated to all lines of the paragraph.

If the paragraph has two or more lines, the fill prefix is taken from the paragraph's second line, but only if it appears on the first line as well.

If a paragraph has just one line, fill commands *may* take a prefix from that line. The decision is complicated because there are three reasonable things to do in such a case:

- Use the first line's prefix on all the lines of the paragraph.
- Indent subsequent lines with whitespace, so that they line up under the text that follows the prefix on the first line, but don't actually copy the prefix from the first line.
- Don't do anything special with the second and following lines.

All three of these styles of formatting are commonly used. So the fill commands try to determine what you would like, based on the prefix that appears and on the major mode. Here is how.

If the prefix found on the first line matches `adaptive-fill-first-line-regexp`, or if it appears to be a comment-starting sequence (this depends on the major mode), then the prefix found is used for filling the paragraph, provided it would not act as a paragraph starter on subsequent lines.

Otherwise, the prefix found is converted to an equivalent number of spaces, and those spaces are used as the fill prefix for the rest of the lines, provided they would not act as a paragraph starter on subsequent lines.

In Text mode, and other modes where only blank lines and page delimiters separate paragraphs, the prefix chosen by adaptive filling never acts as a paragraph starter, so it can always be used for filling.

The variable `adaptive-fill-regexp` determines what kinds of line beginnings can serve as a fill prefix: any characters at the start of the line that match this regular expression are used. If you set the variable `adaptive-fill-mode` to `nil`, the fill prefix is never chosen automatically.

You can specify more complex ways of choosing a fill prefix automatically by setting the variable `adaptive-fill-function` to a function. This function is called with point after the left margin of a line, and it should return the appropriate fill prefix based on that line. If it returns `nil`, that means it sees no fill prefix in that line.

21.6 Case Conversion Commands

Emacs has commands for converting either a single word or any arbitrary range of text to upper case or to lower case.

M-l   Convert following word to lower case (`downcase-word`).

M-u   Convert following word to upper case (`upcase-word`).

M-c   Capitalize the following word (`capitalize-word`).

C-x C-l   Convert region to lower case (`downcase-region`).

C-x C-u   Convert region to upper case (`upcase-region`).

The word conversion commands are the most useful. M-l (`downcase-word`) converts the word after point to lower case, moving past it. Thus, repeating M-l converts successive words. M-u (`upcase-word`) converts to all capitals instead, while M-c (`capitalize-word`) puts the first letter of the word into upper case and the rest into lower case. All these commands convert several words at once if given an argument. They are especially convenient for converting a large amount of text from all upper case to mixed case, because you can move through the text using M-l, M-u or M-c on each word as appropriate, occasionally using M-f instead to skip a word.

When given a negative argument, the word case conversion commands apply to the appropriate number of words before point, but do not move point. This is convenient when you have just typed a word in the wrong case: you can give the case conversion command and continue typing.

If a word case conversion command is given in the middle of a word, it applies only to the part of the word which follows point. This is just like what M-d (kill-word) does. With a negative argument, case conversion applies only to the part of the word before point.

The other case conversion commands are C-x C-u (upcase-region) and C-x C-l (downcase-region), which convert everything between point and mark to the specified case. Point and mark do not move.

The region case conversion commands upcase-region and downcase-region are normally disabled. This means that they ask for confirmation if you try to use them. When you confirm, you may enable the command, which means it will not ask for confirmation again. See Section 31.4.11 [Disabling], page 418.

21.7 Text Mode

When you edit files of text in a human language, it's more convenient to use Text mode rather than Fundamental mode. To enter Text mode, type M-x text-mode.

In Text mode, only blank lines and page delimiters separate paragraphs. As a result, paragraphs can be indented, and adaptive filling determines what indentation to use when filling a paragraph. See Section 21.5.4 [Adaptive Fill], page 207.

Text mode defines (TAB) to run indent-relative (see Chapter 20 [Indentation], page 195), so that you can conveniently indent a line like the previous line. When the previous line is not indented, indent-relative runs tab-to-tab-stop, which uses Emacs tab stops that you can set (see Section 20.2 [Tab Stops], page 196).

Text mode turns off the features concerned with comments except when you explicitly invoke them. It changes the syntax table so that periods are not considered part of a word, while apostrophes, backspaces and underlines are considered part of words.

If you indent the first lines of paragraphs, then you should use Paragraph-Indent Text mode rather than Text mode. In this mode, you do not need to have blank lines between paragraphs, because the first-line indentation is sufficient to start a paragraph; however paragraphs in which every line is indented are not supported. Use M-x paragraph-indent-text-mode to enter this mode.

Text mode, and all the modes based on it, define M-(TAB) as the command ispell-complete-word, which performs completion of the partial word in the buffer before point, using the spelling dictionary as the space of possible words. See Section 13.4 [Spelling], page 103.

Entering Text mode runs the hook text-mode-hook. Other major modes related to Text mode also run this hook, followed by hooks of their own; this includes Paragraph-Indent Text mode, Nroff mode, TeX mode, Outline mode, and Mail mode. Hook functions on `text-mode-hook` can look at the value of `major-mode` to see which of these modes is actually being entered. See Section 31.2.3 [Hooks], page 400.

21.8 Outline Mode

Outline mode is a major mode much like Text mode but intended for editing outlines. It allows you to make parts of the text temporarily invisible so that you can see the outline structure. Type `M-x outline-mode` to switch to Outline mode as the major mode of the current buffer.

When Outline mode makes a line invisible, the line does not appear on the screen. The screen appears exactly as if the invisible line were deleted, except that an ellipsis (three periods in a row) appears at the end of the previous visible line (only one ellipsis no matter how many invisible lines follow).

Editing commands that operate on lines, such as `C-n` and `C-p`, treat the text of the invisible line as part of the previous visible line. Killing an entire visible line, including its terminating newline, really kills all the following invisible lines along with it.

Outline minor mode provides the same commands as the major mode, Outline mode, but you can use it in conjunction with other major modes. Type `M-x outline-minor-mode` to enable the Outline minor mode in the current buffer. You can also specify this in the text of a file, with a file local variable of the form 'mode: outline-minor' (see Section 31.2.5 [File Variables], page 403).

The major mode, Outline mode, provides special key bindings on the `C-c` prefix. Outline minor mode provides similar bindings with `C-c @` as the prefix; this is to reduce the conflicts with the major mode's special commands. (The variable `outline-minor-mode-prefix` controls the prefix used.)

Entering Outline mode runs the hook `text-mode-hook` followed by the hook `outline-mode-hook` (see Section 31.2.3 [Hooks], page 400).

21.8.1 Format of Outlines

Outline mode assumes that the lines in the buffer are of two types: *heading lines* and *body lines*. A heading line represents a topic in the outline. Heading lines start with one or more stars; the number of stars determines the depth of the heading in the outline structure. Thus, a heading line with one star is a major topic; all the heading lines with two stars between it and the next one-star heading are its subtopics; and so on. Any line that is not a heading line is a body line. Body lines belong with the preceding heading line. Here is an example:

```
* Food
```

```
This is the body,
which says something about the topic of food.

** Delicious Food
This is the body of the second-level header.

** Distasteful Food
This could have
a body too, with
several lines.

*** Dormitory Food

* Shelter
Another first-level topic with its header line.
```

A heading line together with all following body lines is called collectively an *entry*. A heading line together with all following deeper heading lines and their body lines is called a *subtree*.

You can customize the criterion for distinguishing heading lines by setting the variable `outline-regexp`. Any line whose beginning has a match for this regexp is considered a heading line. Matches that start within a line (not at the left margin) do not count. The length of the matching text determines the level of the heading; longer matches make a more deeply nested level. Thus, for example, if a text formatter has commands '`@chapter`', '`@section`' and '`@subsection`' to divide the document into chapters and sections, you could make those lines count as heading lines by setting `outline-regexp` to '`"@chap\\|@\\(sub\\)*section"`'. Note the trick: the two words '`chapter`' and '`section`' are equally long, but by defining the regexp to match only '`chap`' we ensure that the length of the text matched on a chapter heading is shorter, so that Outline mode will know that sections are contained in chapters. This works as long as no other command starts with '`@chap`'.

It is possible to change the rule for calculating the level of a heading line by setting the variable `outline-level`. The value of `outline-level` should be a function that takes no arguments and returns the level of the current heading. Some major modes such as C, Nroff, and Emacs Lisp mode set this variable in order to work with Outline minor mode.

21.8.2 Outline Motion Commands

Outline mode provides special motion commands that move backward and forward to heading lines.

C-c C-n   Move point to the next visible heading line (`outline-next-visible-heading`).

C-c C-p	Move point to the previous visible heading line (`outline-previous-visible-heading`).
C-c C-f	Move point to the next visible heading line at the same level as the one point is on (`outline-forward-same-level`).
C-c C-b	Move point to the previous visible heading line at the same level (`outline-backward-same-level`).
C-c C-u	Move point up to a lower-level (more inclusive) visible heading line (`outline-up-heading`).

C-c C-n (`outline-next-visible-heading`) moves down to the next heading line. C-c C-p (`outline-previous-visible-heading`) moves similarly backward. Both accept numeric arguments as repeat counts. The names emphasize that invisible headings are skipped, but this is not really a special feature. All editing commands that look for lines ignore the invisible lines automatically.

More powerful motion commands understand the level structure of headings. C-c C-f (`outline-forward-same-level`) and C-c C-b (`outline-backward-same-level`) move from one heading line to another visible heading at the same depth in the outline. C-c C-u (`outline-up-heading`) moves backward to another heading that is less deeply nested.

21.8.3 Outline Visibility Commands

The other special commands of outline mode are used to make lines visible or invisible. Their names all start with `hide` or `show`. Most of them fall into pairs of opposites. They are not undoable; instead, you can undo right past them. Making lines visible or invisible is simply not recorded by the undo mechanism.

C-c C-t	Make all body lines in the buffer invisible (`hide-body`).
C-c C-a	Make all lines in the buffer visible (`show-all`).
C-c C-d	Make everything under this heading invisible, not including this heading itself (`hide-subtree`).
C-c C-s	Make everything under this heading visible, including body, subheadings, and their bodies (`show-subtree`).
C-c C-l	Make the body of this heading line, and of all its subheadings, invisible (`hide-leaves`).
C-c C-k	Make all subheadings of this heading line, at all levels, visible (`show-branches`).
C-c C-i	Make immediate subheadings (one level down) of this heading line visible (`show-children`).
C-c C-c	Make this heading line's body invisible (`hide-entry`).

C-c C-e   Make this heading line's body visible (`show-entry`).

C-c C-q   Hide everything except the top *n* levels of heading lines (`hide-sublevels`).

C-c C-o   Hide everything except for the heading or body that point is in, plus the headings leading up from there to the top level of the outline (`hide-other`).

Two commands that are exact opposites are C-c C-c (`hide-entry`) and C-c C-e (`show-entry`). They are used with point on a heading line, and apply only to the body lines of that heading. Subheadings and their bodies are not affected.

Two more powerful opposites are C-c C-d (`hide-subtree`) and C-c C-s (`show-subtree`). Both expect to be used when point is on a heading line, and both apply to all the lines of that heading's *subtree*: its body, all its subheadings, both direct and indirect, and all of their bodies. In other words, the subtree contains everything following this heading line, up to and not including the next heading of the same or higher rank.

Intermediate between a visible subtree and an invisible one is having all the subheadings visible but none of the body. There are two commands for doing this, depending on whether you want to hide the bodies or make the subheadings visible. They are C-c C-l (`hide-leaves`) and C-c C-k (`show-branches`).

A little weaker than `show-branches` is C-c C-i (`show-children`). It makes just the direct subheadings visible—those one level down. Deeper subheadings remain invisible, if they were invisible.

Two commands have a blanket effect on the whole file. C-c C-t (`hide-body`) makes all body lines invisible, so that you see just the outline structure. C-c C-a (`show-all`) makes all lines visible. These commands can be thought of as a pair of opposites even though C-c C-a applies to more than just body lines.

The command C-c C-q (`hide-sublevels`) hides all but the top level headings. With a numeric argument *n*, it hides everything except the top *n* levels of heading lines.

The command C-c C-o (`hide-other`) hides everything except the heading or body text that point is in, plus its parents (the headers leading up from there to top level in the outline).

You can turn off the use of ellipses at the ends of visible lines by setting `selective-display-ellipses` to `nil`. Then there is no visible indication of the presence of invisible lines.

When incremental search finds text that is hidden by Outline mode, it makes that part of the buffer visible. If you exit the search at that position, the text remains visible.

21.8.4 Viewing One Outline in Multiple Views

You can display two views of a single outline at the same time, in different windows. To do this, you must create an indirect buffer using `M-x make-indirect-buffer`. The first argument of this command is the existing outline buffer name, and its second argument is the name to use for the new indirect buffer. See Section 15.6 [Indirect Buffers], page 149.

Once the indirect buffer exists, you can display it in a window in the normal fashion, with `C-x 4 b` or other Emacs commands. The Outline mode commands to show and hide parts of the text operate on each buffer independently; as a result, each buffer can have its own view. If you want more than two views on the same outline, create additional indirect buffers.

21.9 TeX Mode

TeX is a powerful text formatter written by Donald Knuth; it is also free, like GNU Emacs. LaTeX is a simplified input format for TeX, implemented by TeX macros; it comes with TeX. SliTeX is a special form of LaTeX.

Emacs has a special TeX mode for editing TeX input files. It provides facilities for checking the balance of delimiters and for invoking TeX on all or part of the file.

TeX mode has three variants, Plain TeX mode, LaTeX mode, and SliTeX mode (these three distinct major modes differ only slightly). They are designed for editing the three different formats. The command `M-x tex-mode` looks at the contents of the buffer to determine whether the contents appear to be either LaTeX input or SliTeX input; if so, it selects the appropriate mode. If the file contents do not appear to be LaTeX or SliTeX, it selects Plain TeX mode. If the contents are insufficient to determine this, the variable `tex-default-mode` controls which mode is used.

When `M-x tex-mode` does not guess right, you can use the commands `M-x plain-tex-mode`, `M-x latex-mode`, and `M-x slitex-mode` to select explicitly the particular variants of TeX mode.

21.9.1 TeX Editing Commands

Here are the special commands provided in TeX mode for editing the text of the file.

"   Insert, according to context, either " ' " or " " " or " ' ' " (`tex-insert-quote`).

`C-j`   Insert a paragraph break (two newlines) and check the previous paragraph for unbalanced braces or dollar signs (`tex-terminate-paragraph`).

`M-x tex-validate-region`
>   Check each paragraph in the region for unbalanced braces or dollar signs.

`C-c {`   Insert '{}' and position point between them (`tex-insert-braces`).

`C-c }`   Move forward past the next unmatched close brace (`up-list`).

In TEX, the character '"' is not normally used; we use ' " ' to start a quotation and ' " ' to end one. To make editing easier under this formatting convention, TEX mode overrides the normal meaning of the key " with a command that inserts a pair of single-quotes or backquotes (`tex-insert-quote`). To be precise, this command inserts ' " ' after whitespace or an open brace, '"' after a backslash, and ' " ' after any other character.

If you need the character '"' itself in unusual contexts, use `C-q` to insert it. Also, " with a numeric argument always inserts that number of '"' characters. You can turn off the feature of " expansion by eliminating that binding in the local map (see Section 31.4 [Key Bindings], page 408).

In TEX mode, '$' has a special syntax code which attempts to understand the way TEX math mode delimiters match. When you insert a '$' that is meant to exit math mode, the position of the matching '$' that entered math mode is displayed for a second. This is the same feature that displays the open brace that matches a close brace that is inserted. However, there is no way to tell whether a '$' enters math mode or leaves it; so when you insert a '$' that enters math mode, the previous '$' position is shown as if it were a match, even though they are actually unrelated.

TEX uses braces as delimiters that must match. Some users prefer to keep braces balanced at all times, rather than inserting them singly. Use `C-c {` (`tex-insert-braces`) to insert a pair of braces. It leaves point between the two braces so you can insert the text that belongs inside. Afterward, use the command `C-c }` (`up-list`) to move forward past the close brace.

There are two commands for checking the matching of braces. `C-j` (`tex-terminate-paragraph`) checks the paragraph before point, and inserts two newlines to start a new paragraph. It prints a message in the echo area if any mismatch is found. `M-x tex-validate-region` checks a region, paragraph by paragraph. The errors are listed in the '*Occur*' buffer, and you can use `C-c C-c` or `Mouse-2` in that buffer to go to a particular mismatch.

Note that Emacs commands count square brackets and parentheses in TEX mode, not just braces. This is not strictly correct for the purpose of checking TEX syntax. However, parentheses and square brackets are likely to be used in text as matching delimiters and it is useful for the various motion commands and automatic match display to work with them.

21.9.2 LaTeX Editing Commands

LaTeX mode, and its variant, SliTeX mode, provide a few extra features not applicable to plain TeX.

C-c C-o   Insert '\begin' and '\end' for LaTeX block and position point on a line between them (`tex-latex-block`).

C-c C-e   Close the innermost LaTeX block not yet closed (`tex-close-latex-block`).

In LaTeX input, '\begin' and '\end' commands are used to group blocks of text. To insert a '\begin' and a matching '\end' (on a new line following the '\begin'), use C-c C-o (`tex-latex-block`). A blank line is inserted between the two, and point is left there. You can use completion when you enter the block type; to specify additional block type names beyond the standard list, set the variable `latex-block-names`. For example, here's how to add 'theorem', 'corollary', and 'proof':

```
(setq latex-block-names '("theorem" "corollary" "proof"))
```

In LaTeX input, '\begin' and '\end' commands must balance. You can use C-c C-e (`tex-close-latex-block`) to insert automatically a matching '\end' to match the last unmatched '\begin'. It indents the '\end' to match the corresponding '\begin'. It inserts a newline after '\end' if point is at the beginning of a line.

21.9.3 TeX Printing Commands

You can invoke TeX as an inferior of Emacs on either the entire contents of the buffer or just a region at a time. Running TeX in this way on just one chapter is a good way to see what your changes look like without taking the time to format the entire file.

C-c C-r   Invoke TeX on the current region, together with the buffer's header (`tex-region`).

C-c C-b   Invoke TeX on the entire current buffer (`tex-buffer`).

C-c (TAB) Invoke BibTeX on the current file (`tex-bibtex-file`).

C-c C-f   Invoke TeX on the current file (`tex-file`).

C-c C-l   Recenter the window showing output from the inferior TeX so that the last line can be seen (`tex-recenter-output-buffer`).

C-c C-k   Kill the TeX subprocess (`tex-kill-job`).

C-c C-p   Print the output from the last C-c C-r, C-c C-b, or C-c C-f command (`tex-print`).

C-c C-v   Preview the output from the last C-c C-r, C-c C-b, or C-c C-f command (`tex-view`).

C-c C-q   Show the printer queue (`tex-show-print-queue`).

You can pass the current buffer through an inferior TeX by means of C-c C-b (`tex-buffer`). The formatted output appears in a temporary file; to print it, type C-c C-p (`tex-print`). Afterward, you can use C-c C q (`tex-show-print-queue`) to view the progress of your output towards being printed. If your terminal has the ability to display TeX output files, you can preview the output on the terminal with C-c C-v (`tex-view`).

You can specify the directory to use for running TeX by setting the variable `tex-directory`. `"."` is the default value. If your environment variable `TEXINPUTS` contains relative directory names, or if your files contains '\input' commands with relative file names, then `tex-directory` *must* be `"."` or you will get the wrong results. Otherwise, it is safe to specify some other directory, such as `"/tmp"`.

If you want to specify which shell commands are used in the inferior TeX, you can do so by setting the values of the variables `tex-run-command`, `latex-run-command`, `slitex-run-command`, `tex-dvi-print-command`, `tex-dvi-view-command`, and `tex-show-queue-command`. You *must* set the value of `tex-dvi-view-command` for your particular terminal; this variable has no default value. The other variables have default values that may (or may not) be appropriate for your system.

Normally, the file name given to these commands comes at the end of the command string; for example, '`latex` *filename*'. In some cases, however, the file name needs to be embedded in the command; an example is when you need to provide the file name as an argument to one command whose output is piped to another. You can specify where to put the file name with '*' in the command string. For example,

    (setq tex-dvi-print-command "dvips -f * | lpr")

The terminal output from TeX, including any error messages, appears in a buffer called '`*tex-shell*`'. If TeX gets an error, you can switch to this buffer and feed it input (this works as in Shell mode; see Section 30.2.2 [Interactive Shell], page 368). Without switching to this buffer you can scroll it so that its last line is visible by typing C-c C-l.

Type C-c C-k (`tex-kill-job`) to kill the TeX process if you see that its output is no longer useful. Using C-c C-b or C-c C-r also kills any TeX process still running.

You can also pass an arbitrary region through an inferior TeX by typing C-c C-r (`tex-region`). This is tricky, however, because most files of TeX input contain commands at the beginning to set parameters and define macros, without which no later part of the file will format correctly. To solve this problem, C-c C-r allows you to designate a part of the file as containing essential commands; it is included before the specified region as part of the input to TeX. The designated part of the file is called the *header*.

To indicate the bounds of the header in Plain TeX mode, you insert two special strings in the file. Insert '`%**start of header`' before the header, and '%**end of header' after it. Each string must appear entirely on one line, but there may be other text on the line before or after. The lines containing the two strings are included in the header. If '%**start of header' does not appear within the first 100 lines of the buffer, C-c C-r assumes that there is no header.

In LaTeX mode, the header begins with '\documentstyle' and ends with '\begin{document}'. These are commands that LaTeX requires you to use in any case, so nothing special needs to be done to identify the header.

The commands (tex-buffer) and (tex-region) do all of their work in a temporary directory, and do not have available any of the auxiliary files needed by TeX for cross-references; these commands are generally not suitable for running the final copy in which all of the cross-references need to be correct.

When you want the auxiliary files for cross references, use C-c C-f (tex-file) which runs TeX on the current buffer's file, in that file's directory. Before running TeX, it offers to save any modified buffers. Generally, you need to use (tex-file) twice to get the cross-references right.

The value of the variable tex-start-options-string specifies options for the TeX run. The default value causes TeX to run in nonstopmode. To run TeX interactively, set the variable to "".

Large TeX documents are often split into several files—one main file, plus subfiles. Running TeX on a subfile typically does not work; you have to run it on the main file. In order to make tex-file useful when you are editing a subfile, you can set the variable tex-main-file to the name of the main file. Then tex-file runs TeX on that file.

The most convenient way to use tex-main-file is to specify it in a local variable list in each of the subfiles. See Section 31.2.5 [File Variables], page 403.

For LaTeX files, you can use BibTeX to process the auxiliary file for the current buffer's file. BibTeX looks up bibliographic citations in a data base and prepares the cited references for the bibliography section. The command C-c TAB (tex-bibtex-file) runs the shell command (tex-bibtex-command) to produce a '.bbl' file for the current buffer's file. Generally, you need to do C-c C-f (tex-file) once to generate the '.aux' file, then do C-c TAB (tex-bibtex-file), and then repeat C-c C-f (tex-file) twice more to get the cross-references correct.

Entering any kind of TeX mode runs the hooks text-mode-hook and tex-mode-hook. Then it runs either plain-tex-mode-hook or latex-mode-hook, whichever is appropriate. For SliTeX files, it calls slitex-mode-hook. Starting the TeX shell runs the hook tex-shell-hook. See Section 31.2.3 [Hooks], page 400.

21.10 Nroff Mode

Nroff mode is a mode like Text mode but modified to handle nroff commands present in the text. Invoke `M-x nroff-mode` to enter this mode. It differs from Text mode in only a few ways. All nroff command lines are considered paragraph separators, so that filling will never garble the nroff commands. Pages are separated by '`.bp`' commands. Comments start with backslash-doublequote. Also, three special commands are provided that are not in Text mode:

`M-n`   Move to the beginning of the next line that isn't an nroff command (`forward-text-line`). An argument is a repeat count.

`M-p`   Like `M-n` but move up (`backward-text-line`).

`M-?`   Prints in the echo area the number of text lines (lines that are not nroff commands) in the region (`count-text-lines`).

The other feature of Nroff mode is that you can turn on Electric Nroff mode. This is a minor mode that you can turn on or off with `M-x electric-nroff-mode` (see Section 31.1 [Minor Modes], page 391). When the mode is on, each time you use (RET) to end a line that contains an nroff command that opens a kind of grouping, the matching nroff command to close that grouping is automatically inserted on the following line. For example, if you are at the beginning of a line and type `. ( b` (RET), this inserts the matching command '`.)b`' on a new line following point.

If you use Outline minor mode with Nroff mode (see Section 21.8 [Outline Mode], page 210), heading lines are lines of the form '`.H`' followed by a number (the header level).

Entering Nroff mode runs the hook `text-mode-hook`, followed by the hook `nroff-mode-hook` (see Section 31.2.3 [Hooks], page 400).

21.11 Editing Formatted Text

Enriched mode is a minor mode for editing files that contain formatted text in WYSIWYG fashion, as in a word processor. Currently, formatted text in Enriched mode can specify fonts, colors, underlining, margins, and types of filling and justification. In the future, we plan to implement other formatting features as well.

Enriched mode is a minor mode (see Section 31.1 [Minor Modes], page 391). Typically it is used in conjunction with Text mode (see Section 21.7 [Text Mode], page 209). However, you can also use it with other major modes such as Outline mode and Paragraph-Indent Text mode.

Potentially, Emacs can store formatted text files in various file formats. Currently, only one format is implemented: *text/enriched* format, which is defined by the MIME protocol. See section "Format Conversion" in *the*

Emacs Lisp Reference Manual, for details of how Emacs recognizes and converts file formats.

The Emacs distribution contains a formatted text file that can serve as an example. Its name is 'etc/enriched.doc'. It contains samples illustrating all the features described in this section. It also contains a list of ideas for future enhancements.

21.11.1 Requesting to Edit Formatted Text

Whenever you visit a file that Emacs saved in the text/enriched format, Emacs automatically converts the formatting information in the file into Emacs's own internal format (text properties), and turns on Enriched mode.

To create a new file of formatted text, first visit the nonexistent file, then type **M-x enriched-mode** before you start inserting text. This command turns on Enriched mode. Do this before you begin inserting text, to ensure that the text you insert is handled properly.

More generally, the command **enriched-mode** turns Enriched mode on if it was off, and off if it was on. With a prefix argument, this command turns Enriched mode on if the argument is positive, and turns the mode off otherwise.

When you save a buffer while Enriched mode is enabled in it, Emacs automatically converts the text to text/enriched format while writing it into the file. When you visit the file again, Emacs will automatically recognize the format, reconvert the text, and turn on Enriched mode again.

Normally, after visiting a file in text/enriched format, Emacs refills each paragraph to fit the specified right margin. You can turn off this refilling, to save time, by setting the variable **enriched-fill-after-visiting** to **nil** or to **ask**.

However, when visiting a file that was saved from Enriched mode, there is no need for refilling, because Emacs saves the right margin settings along with the text.

You can add annotations for saving additional text properties, which Emacs normally does not save, by adding to **enriched-translations**. Note that the text/enriched standard requires any non-standard annotations to have names starting with 'x-', as in 'x-read-only'. This ensures that they will not conflict with standard annotations that may be added later.

21.11.2 Hard and Soft Newlines

In formatted text, Emacs distinguishes between two different kinds of newlines, *hard* newlines and *soft* newlines.

Hard newlines are used to separate paragraphs, or items in a list, or anywhere that there should always be a line break regardless of the margins. The RET command (**newline**) and C-o (**open-line**) insert hard newlines.

Soft newlines are used to make text fit between the margins. All the fill commands, including Auto Fill, insert soft newlines—and they delete only soft newlines.

Although hard and soft newlines look the same, it is important to bear the difference in mind. Do not use (RET) to break lines in the middle of filled paragraphs, or else you will get hard newlines that are barriers to further filling. Instead, let Auto Fill mode break lines, so that if the text or the margins change, Emacs can refill the lines properly. See Section 21.5.1 [Auto Fill], page 204.

On the other hand, in tables and lists, where the lines should always remain as you type them, you can use (RET) to end lines. For these lines, you may also want to set the justification style to unfilled. See Section 21.11.7 [Format Justification], page 224.

21.11.3 Editing Format Information

There are two ways to alter the formatting information for a formatted text file: with keyboard commands, and with the mouse.

The easiest way to add properties to your document is by using the Text Properties menu. You can get to this menu in two ways: from the Edit menu in the menu bar, or with C-mouse-2 (hold the (CTRL) key and press the middle mouse button).

Most of the items in the Text Properties menu lead to other submenus. These are described in the sections that follow. Some items run commands directly:

Remove Properties
> Delete from the region all the text properties that the Text Properties menu works with (facemenu-remove-props).

Remove All
> Delete *all* text properties from the region (facemenu-remove-all).

List Properties
> List all the text properties of the character following point (list-text-properties-at).

Display Faces
> Display a list of all the defined faces.

Display Colors
> Display a list of all the defined colors.

21.11.4 Faces in Formatted Text

The Faces submenu lists various Emacs faces including bold, italic, and underline. Selecting one of these adds the chosen face to the region.

See Section 17.13 [Faces], page 166. You can also specify a face with these
keyboard commands:

M-g d   Set the region, or the next inserted character, to the default
             face (facemenu-set-default).

M-g b   Set the region, or the next inserted character, to the bold face
             (facemenu-set-bold).

M-g i   Set the region, or the next inserted character, to the italic face
             (facemenu-set-italic).

M-g l   Set the region, or the next inserted character, to the bold-
             italic face (facemenu-set-bold-italic).

M-g u   Set the region, or the next inserted character, to the underline
             face (facemenu-set-underline).

M-g o face (RET)
             Set the region, or the next inserted character, to the face face
             (facemenu-set-face).

If you use these commands with a prefix argument—or, in Transient Mark
mode, if the region is not active—then these commands specify a face to use
for your next self-inserting input. See Section 8.2 [Transient Mark], page 60.
This applies to both the keyboard commands and the menu commands.

Enriched mode defines two additional faces: excerpt and fixed. These
correspond to codes used in the text/enriched file format.

The excerpt face is intended for quotations. This face is the same as
italic unless you customize it (see Section 31.2.2.3 [Face Customization],
page 398).

The fixed face is meant to say, "Use a fixed-width font for this part
of the text." Emacs currently supports only fixed-width fonts; therefore,
the fixed annotation is not necessary now. However, we plan to support
variable width fonts in future Emacs versions, and other systems that display
text/enriched format may not use a fixed-width font as the default. So if
you specifically want a certain part of the text to use a fixed-width font, you
should specify the fixed face for that part.

The fixed face is normally defined to use a different font from the default.
However, different systems have different fonts installed, so you may need to
customize this.

If your terminal cannot display different faces, you will not be able to see
them, but you can still edit documents containing faces. You can even add
faces and colors to documents. They will be visible when the file is viewed
on a terminal that can display them.

21.11.5 Colors in Formatted Text

You can specify foreground and background colors for portions of the text. There is a menu for specifying the foreground color and a menu for specifying the background color. Each color menu lists all the colors that you have used in Enriched mode in the current Emacs session.

If you specify a color with a prefix argument—or, in Transient Mark mode, if the region is not active—then it applies to your next self-inserting input. See Section 8.2 [Transient Mark], page 60. Otherwise, the command applies to the region.

Each color menu contains one additional item: 'Other'. You can use this item to specify a color that is not listed in the menu; it reads the color name with the minibuffer. To display list of available colors and their names, use the 'Display Colors' menu item in the Text Properties menu (see Section 21.11.3 [Editing Format Info], page 221).

Any color that you specify in this way, or that is mentioned in a formatted text file that you read in, is added to both color menus for the duration of the Emacs session.

There are no key bindings for specifying colors, but you can do so with the extended commands M-x facemenu-set-foreground and M-x facemenu-set-background. Both of these commands read the name of the color with the minibuffer.

21.11.6 Indentation in Formatted Text

When editing formatted text, you can specify different amounts of indentation for the right or left margin of an entire paragraph or a part of a paragraph. The margins you specify automatically affect the Emacs fill commands (see Section 21.5 [Filling], page 203) and line-breaking commands.

The Indentation submenu provides a convenient interface for specifying these properties. The submenu contains four items:

Indent More
> Indent the region by 4 columns (increase-left-margin). In Enriched mode, this command is also available on C-x (TAB); if you supply a numeric argument, that says how many columns to add to the margin (a negative argument reduces the number of columns).

Indent Less
> Remove 4 columns of indentation from the region.

Indent Right More
> Make the text narrower by indenting 4 columns at the right margin.

Indent Right Less
> Remove 4 columns of indentation from the right margin.

You can use these commands repeatedly to increase or decrease the indentation.

The most common way to use these commands is to change the indentation of an entire paragraph. However, that is not the only use. You can change the margins at any point; the new values take effect at the end of the line (for right margins) or the beginning of the next line (for left margins).

This makes it possible to format paragraphs with *hanging indents*, which means that the first line is indented less than subsequent lines. To set up a hanging indent, increase the indentation of the region starting after the first word of the paragraph and running until the end of the paragraph.

Indenting the first line of a paragraph is easier. Set the margin for the whole paragraph where you want it to be for the body of the paragraph, then indent the first line by inserting extra spaces or tabs.

Sometimes, as a result of editing, the filling of a paragraph becomes messed up—parts of the paragraph may extend past the left or right margins. When this happens, use `M-q` (`fill-paragraph`) to refill the paragraph.

The variable `standard-indent` specifies how many columns these commands should add to or subtract from the indentation. The default value is 4. The overall default right margin for Enriched mode is controlled by the variable `fill-column`, as usual.

The fill prefix, if any, works in addition to the specified paragraph indentation: `C-x .` does not include the specified indentation's whitespace in the new value for the fill prefix, and the fill commands look for the fill prefix after the indentation on each line. See Section 21.5.3 [Fill Prefix], page 206.

21.11.7 Justification in Formatted Text

When editing formatted text, you can specify various styles of justification for a paragraph. The style you specify automatically affects the Emacs fill commands.

The Justification submenu provides a convenient interface for specifying the style. The submenu contains five items:

Flush Left
> This is the most common style of justification (at least for English). Lines are aligned at the left margin but left uneven at the right.

Flush Right
> This aligns each line with the right margin. Spaces and tabs are added on the left, if necessary, to make lines line up on the right.

Full
> This justifies the text, aligning both edges of each line. Justified text looks very nice in a printed book, where the spaces can all be adjusted equally, but it does not look as nice with a fixed-width font on the screen. Perhaps a future version of Emacs will

be able to adjust the width of spaces in a line to achieve elegant justification.

Center   This centers every line between the current margins.

None   This turns off filling entirely. Each line will remain as you wrote it; the fill and auto-fill functions will have no effect on text which has this setting. You can, however, still indent the left margin. In unfilled regions, all newlines are treated as hard newlines (see Section 21.11.2 [Hard and Soft Newlines], page 220) .

In Enriched mode, you can also specify justification from the keyboard using the `M-j` prefix character:

M-j l   Make the region left-filled (`set-justification-left`).

M-j r   Make the region right-filled (`set-justification-right`).

M-j f   Make the region fully-justified (`set-justification-full`).

M-j c
M-S   Make the region centered (`set-justification-center`).

M-j u   Make the region unfilled (`set-justification-none`).

Justification styles apply to entire paragraphs. All the justification-changing commands operate on the paragraph containing point, or, if the region is active, on all paragraphs which overlap the region.

The default justification style is specified by the variable `default-justification`. Its value should be one of the symbols `left`, `right`, `full`, `center`, or `none`.

21.11.8 Setting Other Text Properties

The Other Properties menu lets you add or remove three other useful text properties: `read-only`, `invisible` and `intangible`. The `intangible` property disallows moving point within the text, the `invisible` text property hides text from display, and the `read-only` property disallows alteration of the text.

Each of these special properties has a menu item to add it to the region. The last menu item, '`Remove Special`', removes all of these special properties from the text in the region.

Currently, the `invisible` and `intangible` properties are *not* saved in the text/enriched format. The `read-only` property is saved, but it is not a standard part of the text/enriched format, so other editors may not respect it.

21.11.9 Forcing Enriched Mode

Normally, Emacs knows when you are editing formatted text because it recognizes the special annotations used in the file that you visited. However, there are situations in which you must take special actions to convert file contents or turn on Enriched mode:

- When you visit a file that was created with some other editor, Emacs may not recognize the file as being in the text/enriched format. In this case, when you visit the file you will see the formatting commands rather than the formatted text. Type `M-x format-decode-buffer` to translate it.

- When you *insert* a file into a buffer, rather than visiting it. Emacs does the necessary conversions on the text which you insert, but it does not enable Enriched mode. If you wish to do that, type `M-x enriched-mode`.

The command `format-decode-buffer` translates text in various formats into Emacs's internal format. It asks you to specify the format to translate from; however, normally you can type just $\boxed{\text{RET}}$, which tells Emacs to guess the format.

If you wish to look at text/enriched file in its raw form, as a sequence of characters rather than as formatted text, use the `M-x find-file-literally` command. This visits a file, like `find-file`, but does not do format conversion. It also inhibits character code conversion (see Section 18.7 [Coding Systems], page 180) and automatic uncompression (see Section 14.11 [Compressed Files], page 140). To disable format conversion but allow character code conversion and/or automatic uncompression if appropriate, use `format-find-file` with suitable arguments.

22 Editing Programs

Emacs has many commands designed to understand the syntax of programming languages such as Lisp and C. These commands can

- Move over or kill balanced expressions or *sexps* (see Section 22.2 [Lists], page 228).

- Move over or mark top-level expressions—*defuns*, in Lisp; functions, in C (see Section 22.4 [Defuns], page 230).

- Show how parentheses balance (see Section 22.6 [Matching], page 243).

- Insert, kill or align comments (see Section 22.7 [Comments], page 244).

- Follow the usual indentation conventions of the language (see Section 22.5 [Program Indent], page 231).

The commands for words, sentences and paragraphs are very useful in editing code even though their canonical application is for editing human language text. Most symbols contain words (see Section 21.1 [Words], page 199); sentences can be found in strings and comments (see Section 21.2 [Sentences], page 200). Paragraphs per se don't exist in code, but the paragraph commands are useful anyway, because programming language major modes define paragraphs to begin and end at blank lines (see Section 21.3 [Paragraphs], page 201). Judicious use of blank lines to make the program clearer will also provide useful chunks of text for the paragraph commands to work on.

The selective display feature is useful for looking at the overall structure of a function (see Section 11.4 [Selective Display], page 81). This feature causes only the lines that are indented less than a specified amount to appear on the screen.

22.1 Major Modes for Programming Languages

Emacs also has major modes for the programming languages Lisp, Scheme (a variant of Lisp), Awk, C, C++, Fortran, Icon, Java, Objective-C, Pascal, Perl, Pike, CORBA IDL, and Tcl. There is also a major mode for makefiles, called Makefile mode. An second alternative mode for Perl is called CPerl mode.

Ideally, a major mode should be implemented for each programming language that you might want to edit with Emacs; but often the mode for one language can serve for other syntactically similar languages. The language modes that exist are those that someone decided to take the trouble to write.

There are several forms of Lisp mode, which differ in the way they interface to Lisp execution. See Section 23.6 [Executing Lisp], page 284.

Each of the programming language major modes defines the (TAB) key to run an indentation function that knows the indentation conventions of that language and updates the current line's indentation accordingly. For example, in C mode ⟨TAB⟩ is bound to `c-indent-line`. C-j is normally defined to do ⟨RET⟩ followed by ⟨TAB⟩; thus, it too indents in a mode-specific fashion.

In most programming languages, indentation is likely to vary from line to line. So the major modes for those languages rebind ⟨DEL⟩ to treat a tab as if it were the equivalent number of spaces (using the command `backward-delete-char-untabify`). This makes it possible to rub out indentation one column at a time without worrying whether it is made up of spaces or tabs. Use C-b C-d to delete a tab character before point, in these modes.

Programming language modes define paragraphs to be separated only by blank lines, so that the paragraph commands remain useful. Auto Fill mode, if enabled in a programming language major mode, indents the new lines which it creates.

Turning on a major mode runs a normal hook called the *mode hook*, which is the value of a Lisp variable. Each major mode has a mode hook, and the hook's name is always made from the mode command's name by adding '`-hook`'. For example, turning on C mode runs the hook `c-mode-hook`, while turning on Lisp mode runs the hook `lisp-mode-hook`. See Section 31.2.3 [Hooks], page 400.

22.2 Lists and Sexps

By convention, Emacs keys for dealing with balanced expressions are usually Control-Meta characters. They tend to be analogous in function to their Control and Meta equivalents. These commands are usually thought of as pertaining to expressions in programming languages, but can be useful with any language in which some sort of parentheses exist (including human languages).

These commands fall into two classes. Some deal only with *lists* (parenthetical groupings). They see nothing except parentheses, brackets, braces (whichever ones must balance in the language you are working with), and escape characters that might be used to quote those.

The other commands deal with expressions or *sexps*. The word 'sexp' is derived from *s-expression*, the ancient term for an expression in Lisp. But in Emacs, the notion of 'sexp' is not limited to Lisp. It refers to an expression in whatever language your program is written in. Each programming language has its own major mode, which customizes the syntax tables so that expressions in that language count as sexps.

Sexps typically include symbols, numbers, and string constants, as well as anything contained in parentheses, brackets or braces.

In languages that use prefix and infix operators, such as C, it is not possible for all expressions to be sexps. For example, C mode does not recognize '`foo + bar`' as a sexp, even though it *is* a C expression; it recognizes '`foo`' as one sexp and '`bar`' as another, with the '`+`' as punctuation between them. This is a fundamental ambiguity: both '`foo + bar`' and '`foo`' are legitimate choices for the sexp to move over if point is at the '`f`'. Note that '`(foo + bar)`' is a single sexp in C mode.

Some languages have obscure forms of expression syntax that nobody has bothered to make Emacs understand properly.

22.3 List And Sexp Commands

`C-M-f`   Move forward over a sexp (`forward-sexp`).

`C-M-b`   Move backward over a sexp (`backward-sexp`).

`C-M-k`   Kill sexp forward (`kill-sexp`).

`C-M-`⟨DEL⟩   Kill sexp backward (`backward-kill-sexp`).

`C-M-u`   Move up and backward in list structure (`backward-up-list`).

`C-M-d`   Move down and forward in list structure (`down-list`).

`C-M-n`   Move forward over a list (`forward-list`).

`C-M-p`   Move backward over a list (`backward-list`).

`C-M-t`   Transpose expressions (`transpose-sexps`).

`C-M-@`   Put mark after following expression (`mark-sexp`).

To move forward over a sexp, use `C-M-f` (`forward-sexp`). If the first significant character after point is an opening delimiter ('`(`' in Lisp; '`(`', '`[`' or '`{`' in C), `C-M-f` moves past the matching closing delimiter. If the character begins a symbol, string, or number, `C-M-f` moves over that.

The command `C-M-b` (`backward-sexp`) moves backward over a sexp. The detailed rules are like those above for `C-M-f`, but with directions reversed. If there are any prefix characters (single-quote, backquote and comma, in Lisp) preceding the sexp, `C-M-b` moves back over them as well. The sexp commands move across comments as if they were whitespace in most modes.

`C-M-f` or `C-M-b` with an argument repeats that operation the specified number of times; with a negative argument, it moves in the opposite direction.

Killing a whole sexp can be done with `C-M-k` (`kill-sexp`) or `C-M-`⟨DEL⟩ (`backward-kill-sexp`). `C-M-k` kills the characters that `C-M-f` would move over, and `C-M-`⟨DEL⟩ kills the characters that `C-M-b` would move over.

The *list commands* move over lists, as the sexp commands do, but skip blithely over any number of other kinds of sexps (symbols, strings, etc.). They are `C-M-n` (`forward-list`) and `C-M-p` (`backward-list`). The main reason they are useful is that they usually ignore comments (since the comments usually do not contain any lists).

`C-M-n` and `C-M-p` stay at the same level in parentheses, when that's possible. To move *up* one (or *n*) levels, use `C-M-u` (`backward-up-list`). `C-M-u` moves backward up past one unmatched opening delimiter. A positive argument serves as a repeat count; a negative argument reverses direction of motion and also requests repetition, so it moves forward and up one or more levels.

To move *down* in list structure, use C-M-d (down-list). In Lisp mode, where '(' is the only opening delimiter, this is nearly the same as searching for a '('. An argument specifies the number of levels of parentheses to go down.

A somewhat random-sounding command which is nevertheless handy is C-M-t (transpose-sexps), which drags the previous sexp across the next one. An argument serves as a repeat count, and a negative argument drags backwards (thus canceling out the effect of C-M-t with a positive argument). An argument of zero, rather than doing nothing, transposes the sexps ending after point and the mark.

To set the region around the next sexp in the buffer, use C-M-@ (mark-sexp), which sets mark at the same place that C-M-f would move to. C-M-@ takes arguments like C-M-f. In particular, a negative argument is useful for putting the mark at the beginning of the previous sexp.

The list and sexp commands' understanding of syntax is completely controlled by the syntax table. Any character can, for example, be declared to be an opening delimiter and act like an open parenthesis. See Section 31.6 [Syntax], page 419.

22.4 Defuns

In Emacs, a parenthetical grouping at the top level in the buffer is called a *defun*. The name derives from the fact that most top-level lists in a Lisp file are instances of the special form defun, but any top-level parenthetical grouping counts as a defun in Emacs parlance regardless of what its contents are, and regardless of the programming language in use. For example, in C, the body of a function definition is a defun.

C-M-a   Move to beginning of current or preceding defun (beginning-of-defun).

C-M-e   Move to end of current or following defun (end-of-defun).

C-M-h   Put region around whole current or following defun (mark-defun).

The commands to move to the beginning and end of the current defun are C-M-a (beginning-of-defun) and C-M-e (end-of-defun).

If you wish to operate on the current defun, use C-M-h (mark-defun) which puts point at the beginning and mark at the end of the current or next defun. For example, this is the easiest way to get ready to move the defun to a different place in the text. In C mode, C-M-h runs the function c-mark-function, which is almost the same as mark-defun; the difference is that it backs up over the argument declarations, function name and returned data type so that the entire C function is inside the region. See Section 8.4 [Marking Objects], page 62.

Emacs assumes that any open-parenthesis found in the leftmost column is the start of a defun. Therefore, **never put an open-parenthesis at the left margin in a Lisp file unless it is the start of a top-level list. Never put an open-brace or other opening delimiter at the beginning of a line of C code unless it starts the body of a function.** The most likely problem case is when you want an opening delimiter at the start of a line inside a string. To avoid trouble, put an escape character ('\', in C and Emacs Lisp, '/' in some other Lisp dialects) before the opening delimiter. It will not affect the contents of the string.

In the remotest past, the original Emacs found defuns by moving upward a level of parentheses until there were no more levels to go up. This always required scanning all the way back to the beginning of the buffer, even for a small function. To speed up the operation, Emacs was changed to assume that any '(' (or other character assigned the syntactic class of opening-delimiter) at the left margin is the start of a defun. This heuristic is nearly always right and avoids the costly scan; however, it mandates the convention described above.

22.5 Indentation for Programs

The best way to keep a program properly indented is to use Emacs to reindent it as you change it. Emacs has commands to indent properly either a single line, a specified number of lines, or all of the lines inside a single parenthetical grouping.

Emacs also provides a Lisp pretty-printer in the library **pp**. This program reformats a Lisp object with indentation chosen to look nice.

22.5.1 Basic Program Indentation Commands

⟨TAB⟩   Adjust indentation of current line.

C-j   Equivalent to ⟨RET⟩ followed by ⟨TAB⟩ (`newline-and-indent`).

The basic indentation command is ⟨TAB⟩, which gives the current line the correct indentation as determined from the previous lines. The function that ⟨TAB⟩ runs depends on the major mode; it is `lisp-indent-line` in Lisp mode, `c-indent-line` in C mode, etc. These functions understand different syntaxes for different languages, but they all do about the same thing. ⟨TAB⟩ in any programming-language major mode inserts or deletes whitespace at the beginning of the current line, independent of where point is in the line. If point is inside the whitespace at the beginning of the line, ⟨TAB⟩ leaves it at the end of that whitespace; otherwise, ⟨TAB⟩ leaves point fixed with respect to the characters around it.

Use C-q (TAB) to insert a tab at point.

When entering lines of new code, use C-j (newline-and-indent), which is equivalent to a (RET) followed by a (TAB). C-j creates a blank line and then gives it the appropriate indentation.

(TAB) indents the second and following lines of the body of a parenthetical grouping each under the preceding one; therefore, if you alter one line's indentation to be nonstandard, the lines below will tend to follow it. This behavior is convenient in cases where you have overridden the standard result of (TAB) because you find it unaesthetic for a particular line.

Remember that an open-parenthesis, open-brace or other opening delimiter at the left margin is assumed by Emacs (including the indentation routines) to be the start of a function. Therefore, you must never have an opening delimiter in column zero that is not the beginning of a function, not even inside a string. This restriction is vital for making the indentation commands fast; you must simply accept it. See Section 22.4 [Defuns], page 230, for more information on this.

22.5.2 Indenting Several Lines

When you wish to reindent several lines of code which have been altered or moved to a different level in the list structure, you have several commands available.

C-M-q   Reindent all the lines within one list (indent-sexp).

C-u (TAB)   Shift an entire list rigidly sideways so that its first line is properly indented.

C-M-\   Reindent all lines in the region (indent-region).

You can reindent the contents of a single list by positioning point before the beginning of it and typing C-M-q (indent-sexp in Lisp mode, c-indent-exp in C mode; also bound to other suitable commands in other modes). The indentation of the line the sexp starts on is not changed; therefore, only the relative indentation within the list, and not its position, is changed. To correct the position as well, type a (TAB) before the C-M-q.

If the relative indentation within a list is correct but the indentation of its first line is not, go to that line and type C-u (TAB). (TAB) with a numeric argument reindents the current line as usual, then reindents by the same amount all the lines in the grouping starting on the current line. In other words, it reindents the whole grouping rigidly as a unit. It is clever, though, and does not alter lines that start inside strings, or C preprocessor lines when in C mode.

Another way to specify the range to be reindented is with the region. The command C-M-\ (indent-region) applies (TAB) to every line whose first character is between point and mark.

22.5.3 Customizing Lisp Indentation

The indentation pattern for a Lisp expression can depend on the function called by the expression. For each Lisp function, you can choose among several predefined patterns of indentation, or define an arbitrary one with a Lisp program.

The standard pattern of indentation is as follows: the second line of the expression is indented under the first argument, if that is on the same line as the beginning of the expression; otherwise, the second line is indented underneath the function name. Each following line is indented under the previous line whose nesting depth is the same.

If the variable `lisp-indent-offset` is non-`nil`, it overrides the usual indentation pattern for the second line of an expression, so that such lines are always indented `lisp-indent-offset` more columns than the containing list.

The standard pattern is overridden for certain functions. Functions whose names start with `def` always indent the second line by `lisp-body-indent` extra columns beyond the open-parenthesis starting the expression.

The standard pattern can be overridden in various ways for individual functions, according to the `lisp-indent-function` property of the function name. There are four possibilities for this property:

`nil`   This is the same as no property; the standard indentation pattern is used.

`defun`   The pattern used for function names that start with `def` is used for this function also.

a number, *number*

The first *number* arguments of the function are *distinguished* arguments; the rest are considered the *body* of the expression. A line in the expression is indented according to whether the first argument on it is distinguished or not. If the argument is part of the body, the line is indented `lisp-body-indent` more columns than the open-parenthesis starting the containing expression. If the argument is distinguished and is either the first or second argument, it is indented *twice* that many extra columns. If the argument is distinguished and not the first or second argument, the standard pattern is followed for that line.

a symbol, *symbol*

symbol should be a function name; that function is called to calculate the indentation of a line within this expression. The function receives two arguments:

  state   The value returned by `parse-partial-sexp` (a Lisp primitive for indentation and nesting computation) when it parses up to the beginning of this line.

pos   The position at which the line being indented begins.

It should return either a number, which is the number of columns of indentation for that line, or a list whose car is such a number. The difference between returning a number and returning a list is that a number says that all following lines at the same nesting level should be indented just like this one; a list says that following lines might call for different indentations. This makes a difference when the indentation is being computed by C-M-q; if the value is a number, C-M-q need not recalculate indentation for the following lines until the end of the list.

22.5.4 Commands for C Indentation

Here are the commands for indentation in C mode and related modes:

C-c C-q   Reindent the current top-level function definition or aggregate type declaration (`c-indent-defun`).

C-M-q   Reindent each line in the balanced expression that follows point (`c-indent-exp`). A prefix argument inhibits error checking and warning messages about invalid syntax.

(TAB)   Reindent the current line, and/or in some cases insert a tab character (`c-indent-command`).

            If `c-tab-always-indent` is `t`, this command always reindents the current line and does nothing else. This is the default.

            If that variable is `nil`, this command reindents the current line only if point is at the left margin or in the line's indentation; otherwise, it inserts a tab (or the equivalent number of spaces, if `indent-tabs-mode` is `nil`).

            Any other value (not `nil` or `t`) means always reindent the line, and also insert a tab if within a comment, a string, or a preprocessor directive.

C-u (TAB)   Reindent the current line according to its syntax; also rigidly reindent any other lines of the expression that starts on the current line. See Section 22.5.2 [Multi-line Indent], page 232.

To reindent the whole current buffer, type C-x h C-M-\. This first selects the whole buffer as the region, then reindents that region.

To reindent the current block, use C-M-u C-M-q. This moves to the front of the block and then reindents it all.

22.5.5 Customizing C Indentation

C mode and related modes use a simple yet flexible mechanism for customizing indentation. The mechanism works in two steps: first it classifies the line syntactically according to its contents and context; second, it associates each kind of syntactic construct with an indentation offset which you can customize.

22.5.5.1 Step 1—Syntactic Analysis

In the first step, the C indentation mechanism looks at the line before the one you are currently indenting and determines the syntactic components of the construct on that line. It builds a list of these syntactic components, each of which contains a *syntactic symbol* and sometimes also a buffer position. Some syntactic symbols describe grammatical elements, for example `statement` and `substatement`; others describe locations amidst grammatical elements, for example `class-open` and `knr-argdecl`.

Conceptually, a line of C code is always indented relative to the indentation of some line higher up in the buffer. This is represented by the buffer positions in the syntactic component list.

Here is an example. Suppose we have the following code in a C++ mode buffer (the line numbers don't actually appear in the buffer):

```
1: void swap (int& a, int& b)
2: {
3:   int tmp = a;
4:   a = b;
5:   b = tmp;
6: }
```

If you type C-c C-s (which runs the command c-show-syntactic-information) on line 4, it shows the result of the indentation mechanism for that line:

```
((statement . 32))
```

This indicates that the line is a statement and it is indented relative to buffer position 32, which happens to be the 'i' in `int` on line 3. If you move the cursor to line 3 and type C-c C-s, it displays this:

```
((defun-block-intro . 28))
```

This indicates that the `int` line is the first statement in a block, and is indented relative to buffer position 28, which is the brace just after the function header.

Here is another example:

```
1: int add (int val, int incr, int doit)
2: {
3:   if (doit)
4:     {
5:       return (val + incr);
6:     }
7:   return (val);
```

```
8: }
```
Typing C-c C-s on line 4 displays this:
```
((substatement-open . 43))
```
This says that the brace *opens* a substatement block. By the way, a *substatement* indicates the line after an if, else, while, do, switch, for, try, catch, finally, or synchronized statement.

Within the C indentation commands, after a line has been analyzed syntactically for indentation, the variable c-syntactic-context contains a list that describes the results. Each element in this list is a *syntactic component*: a cons cell containing a syntactic symbol and (optionally) its corresponding buffer position. There may be several elements in a component list; typically only one element has a buffer position.

22.5.5.2 Step 2—Indentation Calculation

The C indentation mechanism calculates the indentation for the current line using the list of syntactic components, c-syntactic-context, derived from syntactic analysis. Each component is a cons cell that contains a syntactic symbol and may also contain a buffer position.

Each component contributes to the final total indentation of the line in two ways. First, the syntactic symbol identifies an element of c-offsets-alist, which is an association list mapping syntactic symbols into indentation offsets. Each syntactic symbol's offset adds to the total indentation. Second, if the component includes a buffer position, the column number of that position adds to the indentation. All these offsets and column numbers, added together, give the total indentation.

The following examples demonstrate the workings of the C indentation mechanism:
```
1: void swap (int& a, int& b)
2: {
3:   int tmp = a;
4:   a = b;
5:   b = tmp;
6: }
```
Suppose that point is on line 3 and you type (TAB) to reindent the line. As explained above (see Section 22.5.5.1 [Syntactic Analysis], page 235), the syntactic component list for that line is:
```
((defun-block-intro . 28))
```
In this case, the indentation calculation first looks up defun-block-intro in the c-offsets-alist alist. Suppose that it finds the integer 2; it adds this to the running total (initialized to zero), yielding a updated total indentation of 2 spaces.

The next step is to find the column number of buffer position 28. Since the brace at buffer position 28 is in column zero, this adds 0 to the running total. Since this line has only one syntactic component, the total indentation for the line is 2 spaces.

```
1: int add (int val, int incr, int doit)
2: {
3:   if (doit)
4:     {
5:       return(val + incr);
6:     }
7:   return(val);
8: }
```

If you type (TAB) on line 4, the same process is performed, but with different data. The syntactic component list for this line is:

```
((substatement-open . 43))
```

Here, the indentation calculation's first job is to look up the symbol `substatement-open` in `c-offsets-alist`. Let's assume that the offset for this symbol is 2. At this point the running total is 2 $(0 + 2 = 2)$. Then it adds the column number of buffer position 43, which is the 'i' in `if` on line 3. This character is in column 2 on that line. Adding this yields a total indentation of 4 spaces.

If a syntactic symbol in the analysis of a line does not appear in `c-offsets-alist`, it is ignored; if in addition the variable `c-strict-syntax-p` is non-`nil`, it is an error.

22.5.5.3 Changing Indentation Style

There are two ways to customize the indentation style for the C-like modes. First, you can select one of several predefined styles, each of which specifies offsets for all the syntactic symbols. For more flexibility, you can customize the handling of individual syntactic symbols. See Section 22.5.5.4 [Syntactic Symbols], page 238, for a list of all defined syntactic symbols.

M-x c-set-style (RET) *style* (RET)

> Select predefined indentation style *style*. Type ? when entering *style* to see a list of supported styles; to find out what a style looks like, select it and reindent some C code.

C-c C-o *symbol* (RET) *offset* (RET)

> Set the indentation offset for syntactic symbol *symbol* (`c-set-offset`). The second argument *offset* specifies the new indentation offset.

The `c-offsets-alist` variable controls the amount of indentation to give to each syntactic symbol. Its value is an association list, and each element of the list has the form (*syntactic-symbol* . *offset*). By changing the offsets for various syntactic symbols, you can customize indentation in fine detail. To change this alist, use `c-set-offset` (see below).

Each offset value in `c-offsets-alist` can be an integer, a function or variable name, a list, or one of the following symbols: +, -, ++, --, *, or /, indicating positive or negative multiples of the variable `c-basic-offset`. Thus, if you want to change the levels of indentation to be 3 spaces instead of 2 spaces, set `c-basic-offset` to 3.

Using a function as the offset value provides the ultimate flexibility in customizing indentation. The function is called with a single argument containing the `cons` of the syntactic symbol and the buffer position, if any. The function should return an integer offset.

If the offset value is a list, its elements are processed according to the rules above until a non-`nil` value is found. That value is then added to the total indentation in the normal manner. The primary use for this is to combine the results of several functions.

The command C-c C-o (`c-set-offset`) is the easiest way to set offsets, both interactively or in your '~/.emacs' file. First specify the syntactic symbol, then the offset you want. See Section 22.5.5.4 [Syntactic Symbols], page 238, for a list of valid syntactic symbols and their meanings.

22.5.5.4 Syntactic Symbols

Here is a table of valid syntactic symbols for indentation in C and related modes, with their syntactic meanings. Normally, most of these symbols are assigned offsets in `c-offsets-alist`.

`string`   Inside a multi-line string.

`c`   Inside a multi-line C style block comment.

`defun-open`
            On a brace that opens a function definition.

`defun-close`
            On a brace that closes a function definition.

`defun-block-intro`
            In the first line in a top-level defun.

`class-open`
            On a brace that opens a class definition.

`class-close`
            On a brace that closes a class definition.

`inline-open`
            On a brace that opens an in-class inline method.

`inline-close`
            On a brace that closes an in-class inline method.

`extern-lang-open`
            On a brace that opens an external language block.

`extern-lang-close`

> On a brace that closes an external language block.

`func-decl-cont`

> The region between a function definition's argument list and the defun opening brace (excluding K&R function definitions). In C, you cannot put anything but whitespace and comments between them; in C++ and Java, **throws** declarations and other things can appear in this context.

`knr-argdecl-intro`

> On the first line of a K&R C argument declaration.

`knr-argdecl`

> In one of the subsequent lines in a K&R C argument declaration.

`topmost-intro`

> On the first line in a topmost construct definition.

`topmost-intro-cont`

> On the topmost definition continuation lines.

`member-init-intro`

> On the first line in a member initialization list.

`member-init-cont`

> On one of the subsequent member initialization list lines.

`inher-intro`

> On the first line of a multiple inheritance list.

`inher-cont`

> On one of the subsequent multiple inheritance lines.

`block-open`

> On a statement block open brace.

`block-close`

> On a statement block close brace.

`brace-list-open`

> On the opening brace of an **enum** or **static** array list.

`brace-list-close`

> On the closing brace of an **enum** or **static** array list.

`brace-list-intro`

> On the first line in an **enum** or **static** array list.

`brace-list-entry`

> On one of the subsequent lines in an **enum** or **static** array list.

`brace-entry-open`

> On one of the subsequent lines in an **enum** or **static** array list, when the line begins with an open brace.

statement
> On an ordinary statement.

statement-cont
> On a continuation line of a statement.

statement-block-intro
> On the first line in a new statement block.

statement-case-intro
> On the first line in a case "block."

statement-case-open
> On the first line in a case block starting with brace.

inexpr-statement
> On a statement block inside an expression. This is used for a GNU extension to the C language, and for Pike special functions that take a statement block as an argument.

inexpr-class
> On a class definition inside an expression. This is used for anonymous classes and anonymous array initializers in Java.

substatement
> On the first line after an if, while, for, do, or else.

substatement-open
> On the brace that opens a substatement block.

case-label
> On a case or default label.

access-label
> On a C++ private, protected, or public access label.

label   On any ordinary label.

do-while-closure
> On the while that ends a do-while construct.

else-clause
> On the else of an if-else construct.

catch-clause
> On the catch and finally lines in try...catch constructs in C++ and Java.

comment-intro
> On a line containing only a comment introduction.

arglist-intro
> On the first line in an argument list.

arglist-cont
> On one of the subsequent argument list lines when no arguments follow on the same line as the arglist opening parenthesis.

arglist-cont-nonempty
> On one of the subsequent argument list lines when at least one argument follows on the same line as the arglist opening parenthesis.

arglist-close
> On the closing parenthesis of an argument list.

stream-op
> On one of the lines continuing a stream operator construct.

inclass   On a construct that is nested inside a class definition. The indentation is relative to the open brace of the class definition.

inextern-lang
> On a construct that is nested inside an external language block.

inexpr-statement
> On the first line of statement block inside an expression. This is used for the GCC extension to C that uses the syntax ({ ... }). It is also used for the special functions that takes a statement block as an argument in Pike.

inexpr-class
> On the first line of a class definition inside an expression. This is used for anonymous classes and anonymous array initializers in Java.

cpp-macro
> On the start of a cpp macro.

friend   On a C++ **friend** declaration.

objc-method-intro
> On the first line of an Objective-C method definition.

objc-method-args-cont
> On one of the lines continuing an Objective-C method definition.

objc-method-call-cont
> On one of the lines continuing an Objective-C method call.

inlambda   Like **inclass**, but used inside lambda (i.e. anonymous) functions. Only used in Pike.

lambda-intro-cont
> On a line continuing the header of a lambda function, between the **lambda** keyword and the function body. Only used in Pike.

22.5.5.5 Variables for C Indentation

This section describes additional variables which control the indentation behavior of C mode and related mode.

c-offsets-alist

Association list of syntactic symbols and their indentation offsets. You should not set this directly, only with c-set-offset. See Section 22.5.5.3 [Changing Indent Style], page 237, for details.

c-style-alist

Variable for defining indentation styles; see below.

c-basic-offset

Amount of basic offset used by + and − symbols in c-offsets-alist.

c-special-indent-hook

Hook for user-defined special indentation adjustments. This hook is called after a line is indented by C mode and related modes.

The variable c-style-alist specifies the predefined indentation styles. Each element has form (name variable-setting...), where name is the name of the style. Each variable-setting has the form (variable . value); variable is one of the customization variables used by C mode, and value is the value for that variable when using the selected style.

When variable is c-offsets-alist, that is a special case: value is appended to the front of the value of c-offsets-alist instead of replacing that value outright. Therefore, it is not necessary for value to specify each and every syntactic symbol—only those for which the style differs from the default.

The indentation of lines containing only comments is also affected by the variable c-comment-only-line-offset (see Section 22.15.5 [Comments in C], page 267).

22.5.5.6 C Indentation Styles

A C style is a collection of indentation style customizations. Emacs comes with several predefined indentation styles for C and related modes, including gnu, k&r, bsd, stroustrup, linux, python, java, whitesmith, ellemtel, and cc-mode. The default style is gnu.

To choose the style you want, use the command M-x c-set-style. Specify a style name as an argument (case is not significant in C style names). The chosen style only affects newly visited buffers, not those you are already editing. You can also set the variable c-default-style to specify the style for various major modes. Its value should be an alist, in which each element specifies one major mode and which indentation style to use for it. For example,

```
(setq c-default-style
      '((java-mode . "java") (other . "gnu")))
```

specifies an explicit choice for Java mode, and the default 'gnu' style for the other C-like modes.

To define a new C indentation style, call the function `c-add-style`:

```
(c-add-style name values use-now)
```

Here *name* is the name of the new style (a string), and *values* is an alist whose elements have the form (*variable . value*). The variables you specify should be among those documented in Section 22.5.5.5 [Variables for C Indent], page 242.

If *use-now* is non-`nil`, `c-add-style` switches to the new style after defining it.

22.6 Automatic Display Of Matching Parentheses

The Emacs parenthesis-matching feature is designed to show automatically how parentheses match in the text. Whenever you type a self-inserting character that is a closing delimiter, the cursor moves momentarily to the location of the matching opening delimiter, provided that is on the screen. If it is not on the screen, some text near it is displayed in the echo area. Either way, you can tell what grouping is being closed off.

In Lisp, automatic matching applies only to parentheses. In C, it applies to braces and brackets too. Emacs knows which characters to regard as matching delimiters based on the syntax table, which is set by the major mode. See Section 31.6 [Syntax], page 419.

If the opening delimiter and closing delimiter are mismatched—such as in '[x)'—a warning message is displayed in the echo area. The correct matches are specified in the syntax table.

Three variables control parenthesis match display. `blink-matching-paren` turns the feature on or off; `nil` turns it off, but the default is `t` to turn match display on. `blink-matching-delay` says how many seconds to wait; the default is 1, but on some systems it is useful to specify a fraction of a second. `blink-matching-paren-distance` specifies how many characters back to search to find the matching opening delimiter. If the match is not found in that far, scanning stops, and nothing is displayed. This is to prevent scanning for the matching delimiter from wasting lots of time when there is no match. The default is 12,000.

When using X Windows, you can request a more powerful alternative kind of automatic parenthesis matching by enabling Show Paren mode. This mode turns off the usual kind of matching parenthesis display and instead uses highlighting to show what matches. Whenever point is after a close parenthesis, the close parenthesis and its matching open parenthesis are both highlighted; otherwise, if point is before an open parenthesis, the matching close parenthesis is highlighted. (There is no need to highlight the open parenthesis after point because the cursor appears on top of that character.) Use the command M-x show-paren-mode to enable or disable this mode.

22.7 Manipulating Comments

Because comments are such an important part of programming, Emacs provides special commands for editing and inserting comments.

22.7.1 Comment Commands

The comment commands insert, kill and align comments.

M-;   Insert or align comment (indent-for-comment).

C-x ;   Set comment column (set-comment-column).

C-u - C-x ;
             Kill comment on current line (kill-comment).

C-M-j   Like (RET) followed by inserting and aligning a comment
             (indent-new-comment-line).

M-x comment-region
             Add or remove comment delimiters on all the lines in the region.

The command that creates a comment is M-; (indent-for-comment). If there is no comment already on the line, a new comment is created, aligned at a specific column called the *comment column*. The comment is created by inserting the string Emacs thinks comments should start with (the value of comment-start; see below). Point is left after that string. If the text of the line extends past the comment column, then the indentation is done to a suitable boundary (usually, at least one space is inserted). If the major mode has specified a string to terminate comments, that is inserted after point, to keep the syntax valid.

M-; can also be used to align an existing comment. If a line already contains the string that starts comments, then M-; just moves point after it and reindents it to the conventional place. Exception: comments starting in column 0 are not moved.

Some major modes have special rules for indenting certain kinds of comments in certain contexts. For example, in Lisp code, comments which start with two semicolons are indented as if they were lines of code, instead of at the comment column. Comments which start with three semicolons are supposed to start at the left margin. Emacs understands these conventions by indenting a double-semicolon comment using (TAB), and by not changing the indentation of a triple-semicolon comment at all.

```
;; This function is just an example
;;; Here either two or three semicolons are appropriate.
(defun foo (x)
;;; And now, the first part of the function:
  ;; The following line adds one.
  (1+ x))              ; This line adds one.
```

In C code, a comment preceded on its line by nothing but whitespace is indented like a line of code.

Even when an existing comment is properly aligned, M-; is still useful for moving directly to the start of the comment.

C-u - C-x ; (kill-comment) kills the comment on the current line, if there is one. The indentation before the start of the comment is killed as well. If there does not appear to be a comment in the line, nothing is done. To reinsert the comment on another line, move to the end of that line, do C-y, and then do M-; to realign it. Note that C-u - C-x ; is not a distinct key; it is C-x ; (set-comment-column) with a negative argument. That command is programmed so that when it receives a negative argument it calls kill-comment. However, kill-comment is a valid command which you could bind directly to a key if you wanted to.

22.7.2 Multiple Lines of Comments

If you are typing a comment and wish to continue it on another line, you can use the command C-M-j (indent-new-comment-line). This terminates the comment you are typing, creates a new blank line afterward, and begins a new comment indented under the old one. When Auto Fill mode is on, going past the fill column while typing a comment causes the comment to be continued in just this fashion. If point is not at the end of the line when C-M-j is typed, the text on the rest of the line becomes part of the new comment line.

To turn existing lines into comment lines, use the M-x comment-region command. It adds comment delimiters to the lines that start in the region, thus commenting them out. With a negative argument, it does the opposite—it deletes comment delimiters from the lines in the region.

With a positive argument, comment-region duplicates the last character of the comment start sequence it adds; the argument specifies how many copies of the character to insert. Thus, in Lisp mode, C-u 2 M-x comment-region adds ';;' to each line. Duplicating the comment delimiter is a way of calling attention to the comment. It can also affect how the comment is indented. In Lisp, for proper indentation, you should use an argument of two, if between defuns, and three, if within a defun.

The variable comment-padding specifies how many spaces comment-region should insert on each line between the comment delimiter and the line's original text. The default is 1.

22.7.3 Options Controlling Comments

The comment column is stored in the variable `comment-column`. You can set it to a number explicitly. Alternatively, the command C-x ; (`set-comment-column`) sets the comment column to the column point is at. C-u C-x ; sets the comment column to match the last comment before point in the buffer, and then does a M-; to align the current line's comment under the previous one. Note that C-u - C-x ; runs the function `kill-comment` as described above.

The variable `comment-column` is per-buffer: setting the variable in the normal fashion affects only the current buffer, but there is a default value which you can change with `setq-default`. See Section 31.2.4 [Locals], page 401. Many major modes initialize this variable for the current buffer.

The comment commands recognize comments based on the regular expression that is the value of the variable `comment-start-skip`. Make sure this regexp does not match the null string. It may match more than the comment starting delimiter in the strictest sense of the word; for example, in C mode the value of the variable is "/*+ *", which matches extra stars and spaces after the '/*' itself. (Note that '\\' is needed in Lisp syntax to include a '\' in the string, which is needed to deny the first star its special meaning in regexp syntax. See Section 12.5 [Regexps], page 90.)

When a comment command makes a new comment, it inserts the value of `comment-start` to begin it. The value of `comment-end` is inserted after point, so that it will follow the text that you will insert into the comment. In C mode, `comment-start` has the value "/* " and `comment-end` has the value " */".

The variable `comment-multi-line` controls how C-M-j (`indent-new-comment-line`) behaves when used inside a comment. If `comment-multi-line` is `nil`, as it normally is, then the comment on the starting line is terminated and a new comment is started on the new following line. If `comment-multi-line` is not `nil`, then the new following line is set up as part of the same comment that was found on the starting line. This is done by not inserting a terminator on the old line, and not inserting a starter on the new line. In languages where multi-line comments work, the choice of value for this variable is a matter of taste.

The variable `comment-indent-function` should contain a function that will be called to compute the indentation for a newly inserted comment or for aligning an existing comment. It is set differently by various major modes. The function is called with no arguments, but with point at the beginning of the comment, or at the end of a line if a new comment is to be inserted. It should return the column in which the comment ought to start. For example, in Lisp mode, the indent hook function bases its decision on how many semicolons begin an existing comment, and on the code in the preceding lines.

22.8 Editing Without Unbalanced Parentheses

M-(Put parentheses around next sexp(s) (insert-parentheses).

M-)   Move past next close parenthesis and reindent (move-past-close-and-reindent).

The commands M-((insert-parentheses) and M-) (move-past-close-and-reindent) are designed to facilitate a style of editing which keeps parentheses balanced at all times. M-(inserts a pair of parentheses, either together as in '()', or, if given an argument, around the next several sexps. It leaves point after the open parenthesis. The command M-) moves past the close parenthesis, deleting any indentation preceding it, and indenting with C-j after it.

For example, instead of typing (F O O), you can type M-(F O O, which has the same effect except for leaving the cursor before the close parenthesis.

M-(may insert a space before the open parenthesis, depending on the syntax class of the preceding character. Set parens-require-spaces to nil value if you wish to inhibit this.

22.9 Completion for Symbol Names

Usually completion happens in the minibuffer. But one kind of completion is available in all buffers: completion for symbol names.

The character M-⟨TAB⟩ runs a command to complete the partial symbol before point against the set of meaningful symbol names. Any additional characters determined by the partial name are inserted at point.

If the partial name in the buffer has more than one possible completion and they have no additional characters in common, a list of all possible completions is displayed in another window.

In most programming language major modes, M-⟨TAB⟩ runs the command complete-symbol, which provides two kinds of completion. Normally it does completion based on a tags table (see Section 22.13 [Tags], page 250); with a numeric argument (regardless of the value), it does completion based on the names listed in the Info file indexes for your language. Thus, to complete the name of a symbol defined in your own program, use M-⟨TAB⟩ with no argument; to complete the name of a standard library function, use C-u M-⟨TAB⟩. Of course, Info-based completion works only if there is an Info file for the standard library functions of your language, and only if it is installed at your site.

In Emacs-Lisp mode, the name space for completion normally consists of nontrivial symbols present in Emacs—those that have function definitions, values or properties. However, if there is an open-parenthesis immediately before the beginning of the partial symbol, only symbols with function definitions are considered as completions. The command which implements this is lisp-complete-symbol.

In Text mode and related modes, M-⟨TAB⟩ completes words based on the spell-checker's dictionary. See Section 13.4 [Spelling], page 103.

22.10 Which Function Mode

Which Function mode is a minor mode that displays the current function name in the mode line, as you move around in a buffer.

To enable (or disable) Which Function mode, use the command M-x which-function-mode. This command is global; it applies to all buffers, both existing ones and those yet to be created. However, this only affects certain major modes, those listed in the value of which-func-modes. (If the value is t, then Which Function mode applies to all major modes that know how to support it—which are the major modes that support Imenu.)

22.11 Documentation Commands

As you edit Lisp code to be run in Emacs, the commands C-h f (describe-function) and C-h v (describe-variable) can be used to print documentation of functions and variables that you want to call. These commands use the minibuffer to read the name of a function or variable to document, and display the documentation in a window.

For extra convenience, these commands provide default arguments based on the code in the neighborhood of point. C-h f sets the default to the function called in the innermost list containing point. C-h v uses the symbol name around or adjacent to point as its default.

For Emacs Lisp code, you can also use Eldoc mode. This minor mode constantly displays in the echo area the argument list for the function being called at point. (In other words, it finds the function call that point is contained in, and displays the argument list of that function.) Eldoc mode applies in Emacs Lisp and Lisp Interaction modes only. Use the command M-x eldoc-mode to enable or disable this feature.

For C, Lisp, and other languages, you can use C-h C-i (info-lookup-symbol) to view the Info documentation for a symbol. You specify the symbol with the minibuffer; by default, it uses the symbol that appears in the buffer at point. The major mode determines where to look for documentation for the symbol—which Info files and which indices. You can also use M-x info-lookup-file to look for documentation for a file name.

You can read the "man page" for an operating system command, library function, or system call, with the M-x manual-entry command. It runs the man program to format the man page, and runs it asynchronously if your system permits, so that you can keep on editing while the page is being formatted. (MS-DOS and MS-Windows 3 do not permit asynchronous subprocesses, so on these systems you cannot edit while Emacs waits for man to exit.) The result goes in a buffer named '*Man topic*'. These buffers use a special major mode, Man mode, that facilitates scrolling and examining other manual pages. For details, type `C-h m` while in a man page buffer.

For a long man page, setting the faces properly can take substantial time. By default, Emacs uses faces in man pages if Emacs can display different fonts or colors. You can turn off use of faces in man pages by setting the variable `Man-fontify-manpage-flag` to `nil`.

If you insert the text of a man page into an Emacs buffer in some other fashion, you can use the command `M-x Man-fontify-manpage` to perform the same conversions that `M-x manual-entry` does.

Eventually the GNU project hopes to replace most man pages with better-organized manuals that you can browse with Info. See Section 7.7 [Misc Help], page 57. Since this process is only partially completed, it is still useful to read manual pages.

22.12 Change Logs

The Emacs command `C-x 4 a` adds a new entry to the change log file for the file you are editing (`add-change-log-entry-other-window`).

A change log file contains a chronological record of when and why you have changed a program, consisting of a sequence of entries describing individual changes. Normally it is kept in a file called 'ChangeLog' in the same directory as the file you are editing, or one of its parent directories. A single 'ChangeLog' file can record changes for all the files in its directory and all its subdirectories.

A change log entry starts with a header line that contains your name, your email address (taken from the variable `user-mail-address`), and the current date and time. Aside from these header lines, every line in the change log starts with a space or a tab. The bulk of the entry consists of *items*, each of which starts with a line starting with whitespace and a star. Here are two entries, both dated in May 1993, each with two items:

```
1993-05-25  Richard Stallman  <rms@gnu.org>

        * man.el: Rename symbols 'man-*' to 'Man-*'.
        (manual-entry): Make prompt string clearer.

        * simple.el (blink-matching-paren-distance):
        Change default to 12,000.

1993-05-24  Richard Stallman  <rms@gnu.org>

        * vc.el (minor-mode-map-alist): Don't use it if it's void.
        (vc-cancel-version): Doc fix.
```

(Previous Emacs versions used a different format for the date.)

One entry can describe several changes; each change should have its own item. Normally there should be a blank line between items. When items are related (parts of the same change, in different places), group them by leaving no blank line between them. The second entry above contains two items grouped in this way.

C-x 4 a visits the change log file and creates a new entry unless the most recent entry is for today's date and your name. It also creates a new item for the current file. For many languages, it can even guess the name of the function or other object that was changed.

The change log file is visited in Change Log mode. In this major mode, each bunch of grouped items counts as one paragraph, and each entry is considered a page. This facilitates editing the entries. C-j and auto-fill indent each new line like the previous line; this is convenient for entering the contents of an entry.

Version control systems are another way to keep track of changes in your program and keep a change log. See Section 14.7.3.3 [Log Buffer], page 124.

22.13 Tags Tables

A *tags table* is a description of how a multi-file program is broken up into files. It lists the names of the component files and the names and positions of the functions (or other named subunits) in each file. Grouping the related files makes it possible to search or replace through all the files with one command. Recording the function names and positions makes possible the M-. command which finds the definition of a function by looking up which of the files it is in.

Tags tables are stored in files called *tags table files*. The conventional name for a tags table file is 'TAGS'.

Each entry in the tags table records the name of one tag, the name of the file that the tag is defined in (implicitly), and the position in that file of the tag's definition.

Just what names from the described files are recorded in the tags table depends on the programming language of the described file. They normally include all functions and subroutines, and may also include global variables, data types, and anything else convenient. Each name recorded is called a *tag*.

22.13.1 Source File Tag Syntax

Here is how tag syntax is defined for the most popular languages:

- In C code, any C function or typedef is a tag, and so are definitions of **struct**, **union** and **enum**. **#define** macro definitions and **enum** constants are also tags, unless you specify '--no-defines' when making the tags table. Similarly, global variables are tags, unless you specify

'--no-globals'. Use of '--no-globals' and '--no-defines' can make the tags table file much smaller.

- In C++ code, in addition to all the tag constructs of C code, member functions are also recognized, and optionally member variables if you use the '--members' option. Tags for variables and functions in classes are named '*class*::*variable*' and '*class*::*function*'.

- In Java code, tags include all the constructs recognized in C++, plus the **extends** and **implements** constructs. Tags for variables and functions in classes are named '*class.variable*' and '*class.function*'.

- In LaTeX text, the argument of any of the commands \chapter, \section, \subsection, \subsubsection, \eqno, \label, \ref, \cite, \bibitem, \part, \appendix, \entry, or \index, is a tag.

  Other commands can make tags as well, if you specify them in the environment variable TEXTAGS before invoking **etags**. The value of this environment variable should be a colon-separated list of command names. For example,

  ```
  TEXTAGS="def:newcommand:newenvironment"
  export TEXTAGS
  ```

  specifies (using Bourne shell syntax) that the commands '\def', '\newcommand' and '\newenvironment' also define tags.

- In Lisp code, any function defined with **defun**, any variable defined with **defvar** or **defconst**, and in general the first argument of any expression that starts with '(def' in column zero, is a tag.

- In Scheme code, tags include anything defined with **def** or with a construct whose name starts with '**def**'. They also include variables set with **set!** at top level in the file.

Several other languages are also supported:

- In assembler code, labels appearing at the beginning of a line, followed by a colon, are tags.

- In Bison or Yacc input files, each rule defines as a tag the nonterminal it constructs. The portions of the file that contain C code are parsed as C code.

- In Cobol code, tags are paragraph names; that is, any word starting in column 8 and followed by a period.

- In Erlang code, the tags are the functions, records, and macros defined in the file.

- In Fortran code, functions, subroutines and blockdata are tags.

- In Objective C code, tags include Objective C definitions for classes, class categories, methods, and protocols.

- In Pascal code, the tags are the functions and procedures defined in the file.

- In Perl code, the tags are the procedures defined by the **sub** keyword.

- In Postscript code, the tags are the functions.
- In Prolog code, a tag name appears at the left margin.

You can also generate tags based on regexp matching (see Section 22.13.2 [Create Tags Table], page 252) to handle other formats and languages.

22.13.2 Creating Tags Tables

The `etags` program is used to create a tags table file. It knows the syntax of several languages, as described in the previous section. Here is how to run `etags`:

    etags inputfiles...

The `etags` program reads the specified files, and writes a tags table named 'TAGS' in the current working directory. `etags` recognizes the language used in an input file based on its file name and contents. You can specify the language with the '--language=name' option, described below.

If the tags table data become outdated due to changes in the files described in the table, the way to update the tags table is the same way it was made in the first place. It is not necessary to do this often.

If the tags table fails to record a tag, or records it for the wrong file, then Emacs cannot possibly find its definition. However, if the position recorded in the tags table becomes a little bit wrong (due to some editing in the file that the tag definition is in), the only consequence is a slight delay in finding the tag. Even if the stored position is very wrong, Emacs will still find the tag, but it must search the entire file for it.

So you should update a tags table when you define new tags that you want to have listed, or when you move tag definitions from one file to another, or when changes become substantial. Normally there is no need to update the tags table after each edit, or even every day.

One tags table can effectively include another. Specify the included tags file name with the '--include=file' option when creating the file that is to include it. The latter file then acts as if it contained all the files specified in the included file, as well as the files it directly contains.

If you specify the source files with relative file names when you run `etags`, the tags file will contain file names relative to the directory where the tags file was initially written. This way, you can move an entire directory tree containing both the tags file and the source files, and the tags file will still refer correctly to the source files.

If you specify absolute file names as arguments to `etags`, then the tags file will contain absolute file names. This way, the tags file will still refer to the same files even if you move it, as long as the source files remain in the same place. Absolute file names start with '/', or with 'device:/' on MS-DOS and MS-Windows.

When you want to make a tags table from a great number of files, you may have problems listing them on the command line, because some systems have a limit on its length. The simplest way to circumvent this limit is to tell `etags` to read the file names from its standard input, by typing a dash in place of the file names, like this:

```
find . -name "*.[chCH]" -print | etags -
```

Use the option '`--language=`*name*' to specify the language explicitly. You can intermix these options with file names; each one applies to the file names that follow it. Specify '`--language=auto`' to tell `etags` to resume guessing the language from the file names and file contents. Specify '`--language=none`' to turn off language-specific processing entirely; then `etags` recognizes tags by regexp matching alone. '`etags --help`' prints the list of the languages `etags` knows, and the file name rules for guessing the language.

The '`--regex`' option provides a general way of recognizing tags based on regexp matching. You can freely intermix it with file names. Each '`--regex`' option adds to the preceding ones, and applies only to the following files. The syntax is:

```
--regex=/tagregexp[/nameregexp]/
```

where *tagregexp* is used to match the lines to tag. It is always anchored, that is, it behaves as if preceded by '`^`'. If you want to account for indentation, just match any initial number of blanks by beginning your regular expression with '`[ \t]*`'. In the regular expressions, '`\`' quotes the next character, and '`\t`' stands for the tab character. Note that `etags` does not handle the other C escape sequences for special characters.

The syntax of regular expressions in `etags` is the same as in Emacs, augmented with the *interval operator*, which works as in `grep` and `ed`. The syntax of an interval operator is '`\{m,n\}`', and its meaning is to match the preceding expression at least *m* times and up to *n* times.

You should not match more characters with *tagregexp* than that needed to recognize what you want to tag. If the match is such that more characters than needed are unavoidably matched by *tagregexp*, you may find useful to add a *nameregexp*, in order to narrow the tag scope. You can find some examples below.

The '`-R`' option deletes all the regexps defined with '`--regex`' options. It applies to the file names following it, as you can see from the following example:

```
etags --regex=/reg1/ voo.doo --regex=/reg2/ \
      bar.ber -R --lang=lisp los.er
```

Here `etags` chooses the parsing language for '`voo.doo`' and '`bar.ber`' according to their contents. `etags` also uses *reg1* to recognize additional tags in '`voo.doo`', and both *reg1* and *reg2* to recognize additional tags in '`bar.ber`'. `etags` uses the Lisp tags rules, and no regexp matching, to recognize tags in '`los.er`'.

Here are some more examples. The regexps are quoted to protect them from shell interpretation.

- Tag the `DEFVAR` macros in the emacs source files:

  ```
  --regex='/[ \t]*DEFVAR_[A-Z_ \t(]+"\([^"]+\)"/'
  ```

- Tag VHDL files (this example is a single long line, broken here for formatting reasons):

  ```
  --language=none
  --regex='/[ \t]*\(ARCHITECTURE\|CONFIGURATION\) +[^ ]* +OF/'
  --regex='/[ \t]*\(ATTRIBUTE\|ENTITY\|FUNCTION\|PACKAGE\
  \( BODY\)?\|PROCEDURE\|PROCESS\|TYPE\)[ \t]+\([^ \t(]+\)/\3/'
  ```

- Tag Tcl files (this last example shows the usage of a *nameregexp*):

  ```
  --lang=none --regex='/proc[ \t]+\([^ \t]+\)/\1/'
  ```

For a list of the other available `etags` options, execute `etags --help`.

22.13.3 Selecting a Tags Table

Emacs has at any time one *selected* tags table, and all the commands for working with tags tables use the selected one. To select a tags table, type `M-x visit-tags-table`, which reads the tags table file name as an argument. The name 'TAGS' in the default directory is used as the default file name.

All this command does is store the file name in the variable `tags-file-name`. Emacs does not actually read in the tags table contents until you try to use them. Setting this variable yourself is just as good as using `visit-tags-table`. The variable's initial value is `nil`; that value tells all the commands for working with tags tables that they must ask for a tags table file name to use.

Using `visit-tags-table` when a tags table is already loaded gives you a choice: you can add the new tags table to the current list of tags tables, or start a new list. The tags commands use all the tags tables in the current list. If you start a new list, the new tags table is used *instead* of others. If you add the new table to the current list, it is used *as well as* the others. When the tags commands scan the list of tags tables, they don't always start at the beginning of the list; they start with the first tags table (if any) that describes the current file, proceed from there to the end of the list, and then scan from the beginning of the list until they have covered all the tables in the list.

You can specify a precise list of tags tables by setting the variable `tags-table-list` to a list of strings, like this:

```
(setq tags-table-list
      '("~/emacs" "/usr/local/lib/emacs/src"))
```

This tells the tags commands to look at the 'TAGS' files in your '~/emacs' directory and in the '/usr/local/lib/emacs/src' directory. The order depends on which file you are in and which tags table mentions that file, as explained above.

Do not set both `tags-file-name` and `tags-table-list`.

22.13.4 Finding a Tag

The most important thing that a tags table enables you to do is to find the definition of a specific tag.

M-. *tag* (RET)
> Find first definition of *tag* (**find-tag**).

C-u M-.   Find next alternate definition of last tag specified.

C-u - M-.   Go back to previous tag found.

C-M-. *pattern* (RET)
> Find a tag whose name matches *pattern* (**find-tag-regexp**).

C-u C-M-.   Find the next tag whose name matches the last pattern used.

C-x 4 . *tag* (RET)
> Find first definition of *tag*, but display it in another window (**find-tag-other-window**).

C-x 5 . *tag* (RET)
> Find first definition of *tag*, and create a new frame to select the buffer (**find-tag-other-frame**).

M-*   Pop back to where you previously invoked M-. and friends.

M-. (**find-tag**) is the command to find the definition of a specified tag. It searches through the tags table for that tag, as a string, and then uses the tags table info to determine the file that the definition is in and the approximate character position in the file of the definition. Then **find-tag** visits that file, moves point to the approximate character position, and searches ever-increasing distances away to find the tag definition.

If an empty argument is given (just type (RET)), the sexp in the buffer before or around point is used as the *tag* argument. See Section 22.2 [Lists], page 228, for info on sexps.

You don't need to give M-. the full name of the tag; a part will do. This is because M-. finds tags in the table which contain *tag* as a substring. However, it prefers an exact match to a substring match. To find other tags that match the same substring, give **find-tag** a numeric argument, as in C-u M-.; this does not read a tag name, but continues searching the tags table's text for another tag containing the same substring last used. If you have a real (META) key, M-0 M-. is an easier alternative to C-u M-..

Like most commands that can switch buffers, **find-tag** has a variant that displays the new buffer in another window, and one that makes a new frame for it. The former is C-x 4 ., which invokes the command **find-tag-other-window**. The latter is C-x 5 ., which invokes **find-tag-other-frame**.

To move back to places you've found tags recently, use C-u - M-.; more generally, M-. with a negative numeric argument. This command can take

you to another buffer. C-x 4 . with a negative argument finds the previous
tag location in another window.

As well as going back to places you've found tags recently, you can go
back to places *from where* you found them. Use M-*, which invokes the
command **pop-tag-mark**, for this. Typically you would find and study the
definition of something with M-. and then return to where you were with
M-*.

Both C-u - M-. and M-* allow you to retrace your steps to a depth determined by the variable **find-tag-marker-ring-length**.

The command C-M-. (**find-tag-regexp**) visits the tags that match a
specified regular expression. It is just like M-. except that it does regexp
matching instead of substring matching.

22.13.5 Searching and Replacing with Tags Tables

The commands in this section visit and search all the files listed in the
selected tags table, one by one. For these commands, the tags table serves
only to specify a sequence of files to search.

M-x **tags-search** (RET) *regexp* (RET)
> Search for *regexp* through the files in the selected tags table.

M-x **tags-query-replace** (RET) *regexp* (RET) *replacement* (RET)
> Perform a **query-replace-regexp** on each file in the selected
> tags table.

M-,
> Restart one of the commands above, from the current location
> of point (**tags-loop-continue**).

M-x **tags-search** reads a regexp using the minibuffer, then searches for
matches in all the files in the selected tags table, one file at a time. It displays
the name of the file being searched so you can follow its progress. As soon
as it finds an occurrence, **tags-search** returns.

Having found one match, you probably want to find all the rest. To
find one more match, type M-, (**tags-loop-continue**) to resume the **tags-
search**. This searches the rest of the current buffer, followed by the remaining files of the tags table.

M-x **tags-query-replace** performs a single **query-replace-regexp**
through all the files in the tags table. It reads a regexp to search for and
a string to replace with, just like ordinary M-x **query-replace-regexp**. It
searches much like M-x **tags-search**, but repeatedly, processing matches
according to your input. See Section 12.7 [Replace], page 95, for more
information on query replace.

It is possible to get through all the files in the tags table with a single
invocation of M-x **tags-query-replace**. But often it is useful to exit temporarily, which you can do with any input event that has no special query
replace meaning. You can resume the query replace subsequently by typing

M-,; this command resumes the last tags search or replace command that you did.

The commands in this section carry out much broader searches than the `find-tag` family. The `find-tag` commands search only for definitions of tags that match your substring or regexp. The commands `tags-search` and `tags-query-replace` find every occurrence of the regexp, as ordinary search commands and replace commands do in the current buffer.

These commands create buffers only temporarily for the files that they have to search (those which are not already visited in Emacs buffers). Buffers in which no match is found are quickly killed; the others continue to exist.

It may have struck you that `tags-search` is a lot like `grep`. You can also run `grep` itself as an inferior of Emacs and have Emacs show you the matching lines one by one. This works much like running a compilation; finding the source locations of the `grep` matches works like finding the compilation errors. See Section 23.1 [Compilation], page 277.

22.13.6 Tags Table Inquiries

M-x `list-tags` (RET) *file* (RET)
> Display a list of the tags defined in the program file *file*.

M-x `tags-apropos` (RET) *regexp* (RET)
> Display a list of all tags matching *regexp*.

M-x `list-tags` reads the name of one of the files described by the selected tags table, and displays a list of all the tags defined in that file. The "file name" argument is really just a string to compare against the file names recorded in the tags table; it is read as a string rather than as a file name. Therefore, completion and defaulting are not available, and you must enter the file name the same way it appears in the tags table. Do not include a directory as part of the file name unless the file name recorded in the tags table includes a directory.

M-x `tags-apropos` is like `apropos` for tags (see Section 7.3 [Apropos], page 54). It reads a regexp, then finds all the tags in the selected tags table whose entries match that regexp, and displays the tag names found.

You can also perform completion in the buffer on the name space of tag names in the current tags tables. See Section 22.9 [Symbol Completion], page 247.

22.14 Merging Files with Emerge

It's not unusual for programmers to get their signals crossed and modify the same program in two different directions. To recover from this confusion, you need to merge the two versions. Emerge makes this easier. See also Section 14.9 [Comparing Files], page 139, for commands to compare in a more manual fashion, and section "Emerge" in *The Ediff Manual*.

22.14.1 Overview of Emerge

To start Emerge, run one of these four commands:

M-x emerge-files
> Merge two specified files.

M-x emerge-files-with-ancestor
> Merge two specified files, with reference to a common ancestor.

M-x emerge-buffers
> Merge two buffers.

M-x emerge-buffers-with-ancestor
> Merge two buffers with reference to a common ancestor in a third buffer.

The Emerge commands compare two files or buffers, and display the comparison in three buffers: one for each input text (the *A buffer* and the *B buffer*), and one (the *merge buffer*) where merging takes place. The merge buffer shows the full merged text, not just the differences. Wherever the two input texts differ, you can choose which one of them to include in the merge buffer.

The Emerge commands that take input from existing buffers use only the accessible portions of those buffers, if they are narrowed (see Section 30.8 [Narrowing], page 382).

If a common ancestor version is available, from which the two texts to be merged were both derived, Emerge can use it to guess which alternative is right. Wherever one current version agrees with the ancestor, Emerge presumes that the other current version is a deliberate change which should be kept in the merged version. Use the 'with-ancestor' commands if you want to specify a common ancestor text. These commands read three file or buffer names—variant A, variant B, and the common ancestor.

After the comparison is done and the buffers are prepared, the interactive merging starts. You control the merging by typing special *merge commands* in the merge buffer. The merge buffer shows you a full merged text, not just differences. For each run of differences between the input texts, you can choose which one of them to keep, or edit them both together.

The merge buffer uses a special major mode, Emerge mode, with commands for making these choices. But you can also edit the buffer with ordinary Emacs commands.

At any given time, the attention of Emerge is focused on one particular difference, called the *selected* difference. This difference is marked off in the three buffers like this:

```
vvvvvvvvvvvvvvvvvvvvvv
text that differs
^^^^^^^^^^^^^^^^^^^^^^
```

Emerge numbers all the differences sequentially and the mode line always shows the number of the selected difference.

Normally, the merge buffer starts out with the A version of the text. But when the A version of a difference agrees with the common ancestor, then the B version is initially preferred for that difference.

Emerge leaves the merged text in the merge buffer when you exit. At that point, you can save it in a file with C-x C-w. If you give a numeric argument to emerge-files or emerge-files-with-ancestor, it reads the name of the output file using the minibuffer. (This is the last file name those commands read.) Then exiting from Emerge saves the merged text in the output file.

Normally, Emerge commands save the output buffer in its file when you exit. If you abort Emerge with C-], the Emerge command does not save the output buffer, but you can save it yourself if you wish.

22.14.2 Submodes of Emerge

You can choose between two modes for giving merge commands: Fast mode and Edit mode. In Fast mode, basic merge commands are single characters, but ordinary Emacs commands are disabled. This is convenient if you use only merge commands. In Edit mode, all merge commands start with the prefix key C-c C-c, and the normal Emacs commands are also available. This allows editing the merge buffer, but slows down Emerge operations.

Use e to switch to Edit mode, and C-c C-c f to switch to Fast mode. The mode line indicates Edit and Fast modes with 'E' and 'F'.

Emerge has two additional submodes that affect how particular merge commands work: Auto Advance mode and Skip Prefers mode.

If Auto Advance mode is in effect, the a and b commands advance to the next difference. This lets you go through the merge faster as long as you simply choose one of the alternatives from the input. The mode line indicates Auto Advance mode with 'A'.

If Skip Prefers mode is in effect, the n and p commands skip over differences in states prefer-A and prefer-B (see Section 22.14.3 [State of Difference], page 260). Thus you see only differences for which neither version is presumed "correct." The mode line indicates Skip Prefers mode with 'S'.

Use the command s a (emerge-auto-advance-mode) to set or clear Auto Advance mode. Use s s (emerge-skip-prefers-mode) to set or clear Skip Prefers mode. These commands turn on the mode with a positive argument, turns it off with a negative or zero argument, and toggle the mode with no argument.

22.14.3 State of a Difference

In the merge buffer, a difference is marked with lines of 'v' and '˄' characters. Each difference has one of these seven states:

A   The difference is showing the A version. The **a** command always produces this state; the mode line indicates it with 'A'.

B   The difference is showing the B version. The **b** command always produces this state; the mode line indicates it with 'B'.

default-A
default-B   The difference is showing the A or the B state by default, because you haven't made a choice. All differences start in the default-A state (and thus the merge buffer is a copy of the A buffer), except those for which one alternative is "preferred" (see below).

When you select a difference, its state changes from default-A or default-B to plain A or B. Thus, the selected difference never has state default-A or default-B, and these states are never displayed in the mode line.

The command **d a** chooses default-A as the default state, and **d b** chooses default-B. This chosen default applies to all differences which you haven't ever selected and for which no alternative is preferred. If you are moving through the merge sequentially, the differences you haven't selected are those following the selected one. Thus, while moving sequentially, you can effectively make the A version the default for some sections of the merge buffer and the B version the default for others by using **d a** and **d b** between sections.

prefer-A
prefer-B   The difference is showing the A or B state because it is *preferred*. This means that you haven't made an explicit choice, but one alternative seems likely to be right because the other alternative agrees with the common ancestor. Thus, where the A buffer agrees with the common ancestor, the B version is preferred, because chances are it is the one that was actually changed.

These two states are displayed in the mode line as 'A*' and 'B*'.

combined   The difference is showing a combination of the A and B states, as a result of the **x c** or **x C** commands.

Once a difference is in this state, the **a** and **b** commands don't do anything to it unless you give them a numeric argument.

The mode line displays this state as 'comb'.

22.14.4 Merge Commands

Here are the Merge commands for Fast mode; in Edit mode, precede them with C-c C-c:

p	Select the previous difference.
n	Select the next difference.
a	Choose the A version of this difference.
b	Choose the B version of this difference.
C-u *n* j	Select difference number *n*.
.	Select the difference containing point. You can use this command in the merge buffer or in the A or B buffer.
q	Quit—finish the merge.
C-]	Abort—exit merging and do not save the output.
f	Go into Fast mode. (In Edit mode, this is actually C-c C-c f.)
e	Go into Edit mode.
l	Recenter (like C-l) all three windows.
-	Specify part of a prefix numeric argument.
digit	Also specify part of a prefix numeric argument.
d a	Choose the A version as the default from here down in the merge buffer.
d b	Choose the B version as the default from here down in the merge buffer.
c a	Copy the A version of this difference into the kill ring.
c b	Copy the B version of this difference into the kill ring.
i a	Insert the A version of this difference at point.
i b	Insert the B version of this difference at point.
m	Put point and mark around the difference.
^	Scroll all three windows down (like M-v).
v	Scroll all three windows up (like C-v).
<	Scroll all three windows left (like C-x <).
>	Scroll all three windows right (like C-x >).
|	Reset horizontal scroll on all three windows.
x 1	Shrink the merge window to one line. (Use C-u l to restore it to full size.)
x c	Combine the two versions of this difference (see Section 22.14.6 [Combining in Emerge], page 262).

x f   Show the names of the files/buffers Emerge is operating on, in
              a Help window. (Use C-u l to restore windows.)

x j   Join this difference with the following one. (C-u x j joins this
              difference with the previous one.)

x s   Split this difference into two differences. Before you use this
              command, position point in each of the three buffers at the place
              where you want to split the difference.

x t   Trim identical lines off the top and bottom of the difference.
              Such lines occur when the A and B versions are identical but
              differ from the ancestor version.

22.14.5 Exiting Emerge

The q command (emerge-quit) finishes the merge, storing the results
into the output file if you specified one. It restores the A and B buffers to
their proper contents, or kills them if they were created by Emerge and you
haven't changed them. It also disables the Emerge commands in the merge
buffer, since executing them later could damage the contents of the various
buffers.

C-] aborts the merge. This means exiting without writing the output file.
If you didn't specify an output file, then there is no real difference between
aborting and finishing the merge.

If the Emerge command was called from another Lisp program, then its
return value is t for successful completion, or nil if you abort.

22.14.6 Combining the Two Versions

Sometimes you want to keep *both* alternatives for a particular difference.
To do this, use x c, which edits the merge buffer like this:

```
#ifdef NEW
version from A buffer
#else /* not NEW */
version from B buffer
#endif /* not NEW */
```

While this example shows C preprocessor conditionals delimiting the two
alternative versions, you can specify the strings to use by setting the variable
emerge-combine-versions-template to a string of your choice. In the
string, '%a' says where to put version A, and '%b' says where to put version
B. The default setting, which produces the results shown above, looks like
this:

```
"#ifdef NEW\n%a#else /* not NEW */\n%b#endif /* not NEW */\n"
```

22.14.7 Fine Points of Emerge

During the merge, you mustn't try to edit the A and B buffers yourself. Emerge modifies them temporarily, but ultimately puts them back the way they were.

You can have any number of merges going at once—just don't use any one buffer as input to more than one merge at once, since the temporary changes made in these buffers would get in each other's way.

Starting Emerge can take a long time because it needs to compare the files fully. Emacs can't do anything else until `diff` finishes. Perhaps in the future someone will change Emerge to do the comparison in the background when the input files are large—then you could keep on doing other things with Emacs until Emerge is ready to accept commands.

After setting up the merge, Emerge runs the hook `emerge-startup-hook` (see Section 31.2.3 [Hooks], page 400).

22.15 C and Related Modes

This section describes special features available in C, C++, Objective-C, Java, CORBA IDL, and Pike modes. When we say "C mode and related modes," those are the modes we mean.

22.15.1 C Mode Motion Commands

This section describes commands for moving point, in C mode and related modes.

C-c C-u   Move point back to the containing preprocessor conditional, leaving the mark behind. A prefix argument acts as a repeat count. With a negative argument, move point forward to the end of the containing preprocessor conditional. When going backwards, `#elif` is treated like `#else` followed by `#if`. When going forwards, `#elif` is ignored.

C-c C-p   Move point back over a preprocessor conditional, leaving the mark behind. A prefix argument acts as a repeat count. With a negative argument, move forward.

C-c C-n   Move point forward across a preprocessor conditional, leaving the mark behind. A prefix argument acts as a repeat count. With a negative argument, move backward.

M-a   Move point to the beginning of the innermost C statement (`c-beginning-of-statement`). If point is already at the beginning of a statement, move to the beginning of the preceding statement. With prefix argument n, move back $n - 1$ statements.

If point is within a string or comment, or next to a comment (only whitespace between them), this command moves by sentences instead of statements.

When called from a program, this function takes three optional arguments: the numeric prefix argument, a buffer position limit (don't move back before that place), and a flag that controls whether to do sentence motion when inside of a comment.

M-e   Move point to the end of the innermost C statement; like M-a except that it moves in the other direction (`c-end-of-statement`).

M-x c-backward-into-nomenclature
           Move point backward to beginning of a C++ nomenclature section or word. With prefix argument *n*, move *n* times. If *n* is negative, move forward. C++ nomenclature means a symbol name in the style of NamingSymbolsWithMixedCaseAndNoUnderlines; each capital letter begins a section or word.

           In the GNU project, we recommend using underscores to separate words within an identifier in C or C++, rather than using case distinctions.

M-x c-forward-into-nomenclature
           Move point forward to end of a C++ nomenclature section or word. With prefix argument *n*, move *n* times.

22.15.2 Electric C Characters

In C mode and related modes, certain printing characters are "electric"—in addition to inserting themselves, they also reindent the current line and may insert newlines. This feature is controlled by the variable `c-auto-newline`. The "electric" characters are {, }, :, #, ;, ,, <, >, /, *, (, and).

Electric characters insert newlines only when the *auto-newline* feature is enabled (indicated by '/a' in the mode line after the mode name). This feature is controlled by the variable `c-auto-newline`. You can turn this feature on or off with the command C-c C-a:

C-c C-a   Toggle the auto-newline feature (`c-toggle-auto-state`). With a prefix argument, this command turns the auto-newline feature on if the argument is positive, and off if it is negative.

The colon character is electric because that is appropriate for a single colon. But when you want to insert a double colon in C++, the electric behavior of colon is inconvenient. You can insert a double colon with no reindentation or newlines by typing C-c ::

C-c :   Insert a double colon scope operator at point, without reindenting the line or adding any newlines (`c-scope-operator`).

The electric **#** key reindents the line if it appears to be the beginning of a preprocessor directive. This happens when the value of `c-electric-pound-behavior` is (`alignleft`). You can turn this feature off by setting `c-electric-pound-behavior` to `nil`.

The variable `c-hanging-braces-alist` controls the insertion of newlines before and after inserted braces. It is an association list with elements of the following form: (*syntactic-symbol* . *nl-list*). Most of the syntactic symbols that appear in `c-offsets-alist` are meaningful here as well.

The list *nl-list* may contain either of the symbols **before** or **after**, or both; or it may be `nil`. When a brace is inserted, the syntactic context it defines is looked up in `c-hanging-braces-alist`; if it is found, the *nl-list* is used to determine where newlines are inserted: either before the brace, after, or both. If not found, the default is to insert a newline both before and after braces.

The variable `c-hanging-colons-alist` controls the insertion of newlines before and after inserted colons. It is an association list with elements of the following form: (*syntactic-symbol* . *nl-list*). The list *nl-list* may contain either of the symbols **before** or **after**, or both; or it may be `nil`.

When a colon is inserted, the syntactic symbol it defines is looked up in this list, and if found, the *nl-list* is used to determine where newlines are inserted: either before the brace, after, or both. If the syntactic symbol is not found in this list, no newlines are inserted.

Electric characters can also delete newlines automatically when the auto-newline feature is enabled. This feature makes auto-newline more acceptable, by deleting the newlines in the most common cases where you do not want them. Emacs can recognize several cases in which deleting a newline might be desirable; by setting the variable `c-cleanup-list`, you can specify *which* of these cases that should happen. The variable's value is a list of symbols, each describing one case for possible deletion of a newline. Here are the meaningful symbols, and their meanings:

`brace-catch-brace`
> Clean up '**}** `catch` (*condition*) **{**' constructs by placing the entire construct on a single line. The clean-up occurs when you type the '**{**', if there is nothing between the braces aside from `catch` and *condition*.

`brace-else-brace`
> Clean up '**}** `else` **{**' constructs by placing the entire construct on a single line. The clean-up occurs when you type the '**{**' after the `else`, but only if there is nothing but white space between the braces and the `else`.

`brace-elseif-brace`
> Clean up '**}** `else if` (...) **{**' constructs by placing the entire construct on a single line. The clean-up occurs when you type

the '{', if there is nothing but white space between the '}' and '{' aside from the keywords and the `if`-condition.

empty-defun-braces
Clean up empty defun braces by placing the braces on the same line. Clean-up occurs when you type the closing brace.

defun-close-semi
Clean up the semicolon after a `struct` or similar type declaration, by placing the semicolon on the same line as the closing brace. Clean-up occurs when you type the semicolon.

list-close-comma
Clean up commas following braces in array and aggregate initializers. Clean-up occurs when you type the comma.

scope-operator
Clean up double colons which may designate a C++ scope operator, by placing the colons together. Clean-up occurs when you type the second colon, but only when the two colons are separated by nothing but whitespace.

22.15.3 Hungry Delete Feature in C

When the *hungry-delete* feature is enabled (indicated by '/h' or '/ah' in the mode line after the mode name), a single (DEL) command deletes all preceding whitespace, not just one space. To turn this feature on or off, use C-c C-d:

C-c C-d   Toggle the hungry-delete feature (`c-toggle-hungry-state`). With a prefix argument, this command turns the hungry-delete feature on if the argument is positive, and off if it is negative.

C-c C-t   Toggle the auto-newline and hungry-delete features, both at once (`c-toggle-auto-hungry-state`).

The variable `c-hungry-delete-key` controls whether the hungry-delete feature is enabled.

22.15.4 Other Commands for C Mode

C-M-h   Put mark at the end of a function definition, and put point at the beginning (`c-mark-function`).

M-q   Fill a paragraph, handling C and C++ comments (`c-fill-paragraph`). If any part of the current line is a comment or within a comment, this command fills the comment or the paragraph of it that point is in, preserving the comment indentation and comment delimiters.

C-c C-e   Run the C preprocessor on the text in the region, and show
           the result, which includes the expansion of all the macro calls
           (c-macro-expand). The buffer text before the region is also
           included in preprocessing, for the sake of macros defined there,
           but the output from this part isn't shown.

           When you are debugging C code that uses macros, sometimes
           it is hard to figure out precisely how the macros expand. With
           this command, you don't have to figure it out; you can see the
           expansions.

C-c C-\   Insert or align '\' characters at the ends of the lines of the region
           (c-backslash-region). This is useful after writing or editing a
           C macro definition.

           If a line already ends in '\', this command adjusts the amount of
           whitespace before it. Otherwise, it inserts a new '\'. However,
           the last line in the region is treated specially; no '\' is inserted
           on that line, and any '\' there is deleted.

M-x cpp-highlight-buffer
           Highlight parts of the text according to its preprocessor con-
           ditionals. This command displays another buffer named '*CPP
           Edit*', which serves as a graphic menu for selecting how to dis-
           play particular kinds of conditionals and their contents. After
           changing various settings, click on '[A]pply these settings'
           (or go to that buffer and type a) to rehighlight the C mode
           buffer accordingly.

C-c C-s   Display the syntactic information about the current source line
           (c-show-syntactic-information). This is the information
           that directs how the line is indented.

22.15.5 Comments in C Modes

C mode and related modes use a number of variables for controlling comment format.

c-comment-only-line-offset
           Extra offset for line which contains only the start of a com-
           ment. It can be either an integer or a cons cell of the form
           (non-anchored-offset . anchored-offset), where non-anchored-
           offset is the amount of offset given to non-column-zero anchored
           comment-only lines, and anchored-offset is the amount of off-
           set to give column-zero anchored comment-only lines. Just an
           integer as value is equivalent to (val . 0).

c-comment-start-regexp
           This buffer-local variable specifies how to recognize the start of
           a comment.

`c-hanging-comment-ender-p`

> If this variable is `nil`, `c-fill-paragraph` leaves the comment
> terminator of a block comment on a line by itself. The default
> value is `t`, which puts the comment-end delimiter '`*/`' at the end
> of the last line of the comment text.

`c-hanging-comment-starter-p`

> If this variable is `nil`, `c-fill-paragraph` leaves the starting
> delimiter of a block comment on a line by itself. The default
> value is `t`, which puts the comment-start delimiter '`/*`' at the
> beginning of the first line of the comment text.

22.16 Fortran Mode

Fortran mode provides special motion commands for Fortran statements
and subprograms, and indentation commands that understand Fortran conventions of nesting, line numbers and continuation statements. Fortran mode
has its own Auto Fill mode that breaks long lines into proper Fortran continuation lines.

Special commands for comments are provided because Fortran comments
are unlike those of other languages. Built-in abbrevs optionally save typing
when you insert Fortran keywords.

Use `M-x fortran-mode` to switch to this major mode. This command
runs the hook `fortran-mode-hook` (see Section 31.2.3 [Hooks], page 400).

22.16.1 Motion Commands

Fortran mode provides special commands to move by subprograms (functions and subroutines) and by statements. There is also a command to put
the region around one subprogram, convenient for killing it or moving it.

`C-M-a`   Move to beginning of subprogram (`beginning-of-fortran-subprogram`).

`C-M-e`   Move to end of subprogram (`end-of-fortran-subprogram`).

`C-M-h`   Put point at beginning of subprogram and mark at end (`mark-fortran-subprogram`).

`C-c C-n` Move to beginning of current or next statement (`fortran-next-statement`).

`C-c C-p` Move to beginning of current or previous statement (`fortran-previous-statement`).

22.16.2 Fortran Indentation

Special commands and features are needed for indenting Fortran code
in order to make sure various syntactic entities (line numbers, comment

line indicators and continuation line flags) appear in the columns that are required for standard Fortran.

22.16.2.1 Fortran Indentation Commands

(TAB)   Indent the current line (`fortran-indent-line`).

C-j   Indent the current and start a new indented line (`fortran-indent-new-line`).

C-M-j   Break the current line and set up a continuation line.

M-^   Join this line to the previous line.

C-M-q   Indent all the lines of the subprogram point is in (`fortran-indent-subprogram`).

Fortran mode redefines (TAB) to reindent the current line for Fortran (`fortran-indent-line`). This command indents line numbers and continuation markers to their required columns, and independently indents the body of the statement based on its nesting in the program.

The key C-j runs the command `fortran-indent-new-line`, which reindents the current line then makes and indents a new line. This command is useful to reindent the closing statement of 'do' loops and other blocks before starting a new line.

The key C-M-q runs `fortran-indent-subprogram`, a command to reindent all the lines of the Fortran subprogram (function or subroutine) containing point.

The key C-M-j runs `fortran-split-line`, which splits a line in the appropriate fashion for Fortran. In a non-comment line, the second half becomes a continuation line and is indented accordingly. In a comment line, both halves become separate comment lines.

M-^ runs the command `fortran-join-line`, which is more or less the inverse of `fortran-split-line`. It joins the current line to the previous line in a suitable way for Fortran code.

22.16.2.2 Continuation Lines

Most modern Fortran compilers allow two ways of writing continuation lines. If the first non-space character on a line is in column 5, then that line is a continuation of the previous line. We call this *fixed format*. (In GNU Emacs we always count columns from 0.) The variable `fortran-continuation-string` specifies what character to put on column 5. A line that starts with a tab character followed by any digit except '0' is also a continuation line. We call this style of continuation *tab format*.

Fortran mode can make either style of continuation line, but you must specify which one you prefer. The value of the variable `indent-tabs-mode` controls the choice: `nil` for fixed format, and non-`nil` for tab format. You can tell which style is presently in effect by the presence or absence of the string 'Tab' in the mode line.

If the text on a line starts with the conventional Fortran continuation marker '$', or if it begins with any non-whitespace character in column 5, Fortran mode treats it as a continuation line. When you indent a continuation line with (TAB), it converts the line to the current continuation style. When you split a Fortran statement with C-M-j, the continuation marker on the newline is created according to the continuation style.

The setting of continuation style affects several other aspects of editing in Fortran mode. In fixed format mode, the minimum column number for the body of a statement is 6. Lines inside of Fortran blocks that are indented to larger column numbers always use only the space character for whitespace. In tab format mode, the minimum column number for the statement body is 8, and the whitespace before column 8 must always consist of one tab character.

When you enter Fortran mode for an existing file, it tries to deduce the proper continuation style automatically from the file contents. The first line that begins with either a tab character or six spaces determines the choice. The variable `fortran-analyze-depth` specifies how many lines to consider (at the beginning of the file); if none of those lines indicates a style, then the variable `fortran-tab-mode-default` specifies the style. If it is `nil`, that specifies fixed format, and non-`nil` specifies tab format.

22.16.2.3 Line Numbers

If a number is the first non-whitespace in the line, Fortran indentation assumes it is a line number and moves it to columns 0 through 4. (Columns always count from 0 in GNU Emacs.)

Line numbers of four digits or less are normally indented one space. The variable `fortran-line-number-indent` controls this; it specifies the maximum indentation a line number can have. Line numbers are indented to right-justify them to end in column 4 unless that would require more than this maximum indentation. The default value of the variable is 1.

Simply inserting a line number is enough to indent it according to these rules. As each digit is inserted, the indentation is recomputed. To turn off this feature, set the variable `fortran-electric-line-number` to `nil`. Then inserting line numbers is like inserting anything else.

22.16.2.4 Syntactic Conventions

Fortran mode assumes that you follow certain conventions that simplify the task of understanding a Fortran program well enough to indent it properly:

- Two nested 'do' loops never share a 'continue' statement.

- Fortran keywords such as 'if', 'else', 'then', 'do' and others are written without embedded whitespace or line breaks.

  Fortran compilers generally ignore whitespace outside of string constants, but Fortran mode does not recognize these keywords if they are not contiguous. Constructs such as 'else if' or 'end do' are acceptable, but the second word should be on the same line as the first and not on a continuation line.

If you fail to follow these conventions, the indentation commands may indent some lines unaesthetically. However, a correct Fortran program retains its meaning when reindented even if the conventions are not followed.

22.16.2.5 Variables for Fortran Indentation

Several additional variables control how Fortran indentation works:

fortran-do-indent
> Extra indentation within each level of 'do' statement (default 3).

fortran-if-indent
> Extra indentation within each level of 'if' statement (default 3). This value is also used for extra indentation within each level of the Fortran 90 'where' statement.

fortran-structure-indent
> Extra indentation within each level of 'structure', 'union', or 'map' statements (default 3).

fortran-continuation-indent
> Extra indentation for bodies of continuation lines (default 5).

fortran-check-all-num-for-matching-do
> If this is nil, indentation assumes that each 'do' statement ends on a 'continue' statement. Therefore, when computing indentation for a statement other than 'continue', it can save time by not checking for a 'do' statement ending there. If this is non-nil, indenting any numbered statement must check for a 'do' that ends there. The default is nil.

fortran-blink-matching-if
> If this is t, indenting an 'endif' statement moves the cursor momentarily to the matching 'if' statement to show where it is. The default is nil.

fortran-minimum-statement-indent-fixed
> Minimum indentation for fortran statements when using fixed format continuation line style. Statement bodies are never indented less than this much. The default is 6.

```
fortran-minimum-statement-indent-tab
```
> Minimum indentation for fortran statements for tab format continuation line style. Statement bodies are never indented less than this much. The default is 8.

22.16.3 Fortran Comments

The usual Emacs comment commands assume that a comment can follow a line of code. In Fortran, the standard comment syntax requires an entire line to be just a comment. Therefore, Fortran mode replaces the standard Emacs comment commands and defines some new variables.

Fortran mode can also handle a nonstandard comment syntax where comments start with '!' and can follow other text. Because only some Fortran compilers accept this syntax, Fortran mode will not insert such comments unless you have said in advance to do so. To do this, set the variable `comment-start` to '"!"' (see Section 31.2 [Variables], page 393).

M-;   Align comment or insert new comment (`fortran-comment-indent`).

C-x ;   Applies to nonstandard '!' comments only.

C-c ;   Turn all lines of the region into comments, or (with argument) turn them back into real code (`fortran-comment-region`).

M-; in Fortran mode is redefined as the command `fortran-comment-indent`. Like the usual M-; command, this recognizes any kind of existing comment and aligns its text appropriately; if there is no existing comment, a comment is inserted and aligned. But inserting and aligning comments are not the same in Fortran mode as in other modes.

When a new comment must be inserted, if the current line is blank, a full-line comment is inserted. On a non-blank line, a nonstandard '!' comment is inserted if you have said you want to use them. Otherwise a full-line comment is inserted on a new line before the current line.

Nonstandard '!' comments are aligned like comments in other languages, but full-line comments are different. In a standard full-line comment, the comment delimiter itself must always appear in column zero. What can be aligned is the text within the comment. You can choose from three styles of alignment by setting the variable `fortran-comment-indent-style` to one of these values:

fixed   Align the text at a fixed column, which is the sum of `fortran-comment-line-extra-indent` and the minimum statement indentation. This is the default.

               The minimum statement indentation is `fortran-minimum-statement-indent-fixed` for fixed format continuation line style and `fortran-minimum-statement-indent-tab` for tab format style.

`relative`   Align the text as if it were a line of code, but with an additional `fortran-comment-line-extra-indent` columns of indentation.

`nil`   Don't move text in full-line comments automatically at all.

In addition, you can specify the character to be used to indent within full-line comments by setting the variable `fortran-comment-indent-char` to the single-character string you want to use.

Fortran mode introduces two variables `comment-line-start` and `comment-line-start-skip`, which play for full-line comments the same roles played by `comment-start` and `comment-start-skip` for ordinary text-following comments. Normally these are set properly by Fortran mode, so you do not need to change them.

The normal Emacs comment command `C-x ;` has not been redefined. If you use '!' comments, this command can be used with them. Otherwise it is useless in Fortran mode.

The command `C-c ;` (`fortran-comment-region`) turns all the lines of the region into comments by inserting the string 'C$$$' at the front of each one. With a numeric argument, it turns the region back into live code by deleting 'C$$$' from the front of each line in it. The string used for these comments can be controlled by setting the variable `fortran-comment-region`. Note that here we have an example of a command and a variable with the same name; these two uses of the name never conflict because in Lisp and in Emacs it is always clear from the context which one is meant.

22.16.4 Fortran Auto Fill Mode

Fortran Auto Fill mode is a minor mode which automatically splits Fortran statements as you insert them when they become too wide. Splitting a statement involves making continuation lines using `fortran-continuation-string` (see Section 22.16.2.2 [ForIndent Cont], page 269). This splitting happens when you type (SPC), (RET), or (TAB), and also in the Fortran indentation commands.

`M-x fortran-auto-fill-mode` turns Fortran Auto Fill mode on if it was off, or off if it was on. This command works the same as `M-x auto-fill-mode` does for normal Auto Fill mode (see Section 21.5 [Filling], page 203). A positive numeric argument turns Fortran Auto Fill mode on, and a negative argument turns it off. You can see when Fortran Auto Fill mode is in effect by the presence of the word 'Fill' in the mode line, inside the parentheses. Fortran Auto Fill mode is a minor mode, turned on or off for each buffer individually. See Section 31.1 [Minor Modes], page 391.

Fortran Auto Fill mode breaks lines at spaces or delimiters when the lines get longer than the desired width (the value of `fill-column`). The delimiters that Fortran Auto Fill mode may break at are ',', ''', '+', '-', '/', '*', '=', and ')'. The line break comes after the delimiter if the variable `fortran-break-before-delimiters` is `nil`. Otherwise (and by default), the break comes before the delimiter.

By default, Fortran Auto Fill mode is not enabled. If you want this feature turned on permanently, add a hook function to `fortran-mode-hook` to execute (`fortran-auto-fill-mode 1`). See Section 31.2.3 [Hooks], page 400.

22.16.5 Checking Columns in Fortran

`C-c C-r`   Display a "column ruler" momentarily above the current line (`fortran-column-ruler`).

`C-c C-w`   Split the current window horizontally temporarily so that it is 72 columns wide. This may help you avoid making lines longer than the 72-character limit that some Fortran compilers impose (`fortran-window-create-momentarily`).

The command `C-c C-r` (`fortran-column-ruler`) shows a column ruler momentarily above the current line. The comment ruler is two lines of text that show you the locations of columns with special significance in Fortran programs. Square brackets show the limits of the columns for line numbers, and curly brackets show the limits of the columns for the statement body. Column numbers appear above them.

Note that the column numbers count from zero, as always in GNU Emacs. As a result, the numbers may be one less than those you are familiar with; but the positions they indicate in the line are standard for Fortran.

The text used to display the column ruler depends on the value of the variable `indent-tabs-mode`. If `indent-tabs-mode` is `nil`, then the value of the variable `fortran-column-ruler-fixed` is used as the column ruler. Otherwise, the variable `fortran-column-ruler-tab` is displayed. By changing these variables, you can change the column ruler display.

For even more help, use `C-c C-w` (`fortran-window-create`), a command which splits the current window horizontally, making a window 72 columns wide. By editing in this window you can immediately see when you make a line too wide to be correct Fortran.

22.16.6 Fortran Keyword Abbrevs

Fortran mode provides many built-in abbrevs for common keywords and declarations. These are the same sort of abbrev that you can define yourself. To use them, you must turn on Abbrev mode. See Chapter 24 [Abbrevs], page 289.

The built-in abbrevs are unusual in one way: they all start with a semicolon. You cannot normally use semicolon in an abbrev, but Fortran mode makes this possible by changing the syntax of semicolon to "word constituent."

For example, one built-in Fortran abbrev is ';c' for 'continue'. If you insert ';c' and then insert a punctuation character such as a space or a newline, the ';c' expands automatically to 'continue', provided Abbrev mode is enabled.

Type ';?' or ';C-h' to display a list of all the built-in Fortran abbrevs and what they stand for.

22.16.7 Other Fortran Mode Commands

C-x n d   Narrow to the current Fortran subprogram.

Fortran mode redefines the key C-x n d to run the command fortran-narrow-to-subprogram, which is the Fortran analogue of the key's usual definition. It narrows the buffer to the subprogram containing point.

22.17 Asm Mode

Asm mode is a major mode for editing files of assembler code. It defines these commands:

(TAB)   tab-to-tab-stop.

C-j   Insert a newline and then indent using tab-to-tab-stop.

:   Insert a colon and then remove the indentation from before the label preceding colon. Then do tab-to-tab-stop.

;   Insert or align a comment.

The variable asm-comment-char specifies which character starts comments in assembler syntax.

23 Compiling and Testing Programs

The previous chapter discusses the Emacs commands that are useful for making changes in programs. This chapter deals with commands that assist in the larger process of developing and maintaining programs.

23.1 Running Compilations under Emacs

Emacs can run compilers for noninteractive languages such as C and Fortran as inferior processes, feeding the error log into an Emacs buffer. It can also parse the error messages and show you the source lines where compilation errors occurred.

M-x compile
> Run a compiler asynchronously under Emacs, with error messages to '*compilation*' buffer.

M-x grep   Run grep asynchronously under Emacs, with matching lines listed in the buffer named '*grep*'.

M-x grep-find
> Run grep via find, with user-specified arguments, and collect output in the buffer named '*grep*'.

M-x kill-compilation
M-x kill-grep
> Kill the running compilation or grep subprocess.

To run make or another compilation command, do M-x compile. This command reads a shell command line using the minibuffer, and then executes the command in an inferior shell, putting output in the buffer named '*compilation*'. The current buffer's default directory is used as the working directory for the execution of the command; normally, therefore, the compilation happens in this directory.

When the shell command line is read, the minibuffer appears containing a default command line, which is the command you used the last time you did M-x compile. If you type just (RET), the same command line is used again. For the first M-x compile, the default is 'make -k'. The default compilation command comes from the variable compile-command; if the appropriate compilation command for a file is something other than 'make -k', it can be useful for the file to specify a local value for compile-command (see Section 31.2.5 [File Variables], page 403).

Starting a compilation displays the buffer '*compilation*' in another window but does not select it. The buffer's mode line tells you whether compilation is finished, with the word 'run' or 'exit' inside the parentheses. You do not have to keep this buffer visible; compilation continues in any case. While a compilation is going on, the string 'Compiling' appears in the mode lines of all windows. When this string disappears, the compilation is finished.

If you want to watch the compilation transcript as it appears, switch to the '*compilation*' buffer and move point to the end of the buffer. When point is at the end, new compilation output is inserted above point, which remains at the end. If point is not at the end of the buffer, it remains fixed while more compilation output is added at the end of the buffer.

If you set the variable `compilation-scroll-output` to a non-`nil` value, then the compilation buffer always scrolls to follow output as it comes in.

To kill the compilation process, do M-x kill-compilation. When the compiler process terminates, the mode line of the '*compilation*' buffer changes to say 'signal' instead of 'run'. Starting a new compilation also kills any running compilation, as only one can exist at any time. However, M-x compile asks for confirmation before actually killing a compilation that is running.

23.2 Searching with Grep under Emacs

Just as you can run a compiler from Emacs and then visit the lines where there were compilation errors, you can also run grep and then visit the lines on which matches were found. This works by treating the matches reported by grep as if they were "errors."

To do this, type M-x grep, then enter a command line that specifies how to run grep. Use the same arguments you would give grep when running it normally: a grep-style regexp (usually in single-quotes to quote the shell's special characters) followed by file names, which may use wildcards. The output from grep goes in the '*grep*' buffer. You can find the corresponding lines in the original files using C-x ' and (RET), as with compilation errors.

If you specify a prefix argument for M-x grep, it figures out the tag (see Section 22.13 [Tags], page 250) around point, and puts that into the default grep command.

The command M-x grep-find is similar to M-x grep, but it supplies a different initial default for the command—one that runs both find and grep, so as to search every file in a directory tree. See also the find-grep-dired command, in Section 28.15 [Dired and Find], page 340.

23.3 Compilation Mode

The '*compilation*' buffer uses a special major mode, Compilation mode, whose main feature is to provide a convenient way to look at the source line where the error happened.

C-x '   Visit the locus of the next compiler error message or **grep** match.

(RET)   Visit the locus of the error message that point is on. This command is used in the compilation buffer.

`Mouse-2`   Visit the locus of the error message that you click on.

You can visit the source for any particular error message by moving point in '`*compilation*`' to that error message and typing (RET) (`compile-goto-error`). Or click `Mouse-2` on the error message; you need not switch to the '`*compilation*`' buffer first.

To parse the compiler error messages sequentially, type `C-x` ' (`next-error`). The character following the `C-x` is the backquote or "grave accent," not the single-quote. This command is available in all buffers, not just in '`*compilation*`'; it displays the next error message at the top of one window and source location of the error in another window.

The first time `C-x` ' is used after the start of a compilation, it moves to the first error's location. Subsequent uses of `C-x` ' advance down to subsequent errors. If you visit a specific error message with (RET) or `Mouse-2`, subsequent `C-x` ' commands advance from there. When `C-x` ' gets to the end of the buffer and finds no more error messages to visit, it fails and signals an Emacs error.

`C-u C-x` ' starts scanning from the beginning of the compilation buffer. This is one way to process the same set of errors again.

Compilation mode also redefines the keys (SPC) and (DEL) to scroll by screenfuls, and `M-n` and `M-p` to move to the next or previous error message. You can also use `M-{` and `M-}` to move up or down to an error message for a different source file.

The features of Compilation mode are also available in a minor mode called Compilation Minor mode. This lets you parse error messages in any buffer, not just a normal compilation output buffer. Type `M-x compilation-minor-mode` to enable the minor mode. This defines the keys (RET) and `Mouse-2`, as in the Compilation major mode.

Compilation minor mode works in any buffer, as long as the contents are in a format that it understands. In an Rlogin buffer (see Section 30.2.6 [Remote Host], page 375), Compilation minor mode automatically accesses remote source files by FTP (see Section 14.1 [File Names], page 107).

23.4 Subshells for Compilation

Emacs uses a shell to run the compilation command, but specifies the option for a noninteractive shell. This means, in particular, that the shell should start with no prompt. If you find your usual shell prompt making an unsightly appearance in the '`*compilation*`' buffer, it means you have made a mistake in your shell's init file by setting the prompt unconditionally. (This init file's name may be '`.bashrc`', '`.profile`', '`.cshrc`', '`.shrc`', or various other things, depending on the shell you use.) The shell init file should set the prompt only if there already is a prompt. In csh, here is how to do it:

```
if ($?prompt) set prompt = ...
```

And here's how to do it in bash:

```
if [ "${PS1+set}" = set ]
then PS1=...
fi
```

There may well be other things that your shell's init file ought to do only for an interactive shell. You can use the same method to conditionalize them.

The MS-DOS "operating system" does not support asynchronous subprocesses; to work around this lack, M-x compile runs the compilation command synchronously on MS-DOS. As a consequence, you must wait until the command finishes before you can do anything else in Emacs. See Appendix C [MS-DOS], page 463.

23.5 Running Debuggers Under Emacs

The GUD (Grand Unified Debugger) library provides an interface to various symbolic debuggers from within Emacs. We recommend the debugger GDB, which is free software, but you can also run DBX, SDB or XDB if you have them. GUD can also serve as an interface to the Perl's debugging mode, the Python debugger PDB, and to JDB, the Java Debugger.

23.5.1 Starting GUD

There are several commands for starting a debugger, each corresponding to a particular debugger program.

M-x gdb (RET) *file* (RET)
> Run GDB as a subprocess of Emacs. This command creates a buffer for input and output to GDB, and switches to it. If a GDB buffer already exists, it just switches to that buffer.

M-x dbx (RET) *file* (RET)
> Similar, but run DBX instead of GDB.

M-x xdb (RET) *file* (RET)
> Similar, but run XDB instead of GDB. Use the variable gud-xdb-directories to specify directories to search for source files.

M-x sdb (RET) *file* (RET)
> Similar, but run SDB instead of GDB.
>
> Some versions of SDB do not mention source file names in their messages. When you use them, you need to have a valid tags table (see Section 22.13 [Tags], page 250) in order for GUD to find functions in the source code. If you have not visited a tags table or the tags table doesn't list one of the functions, you get a message saying 'The sdb support requires a valid tags

`table to work`'. If this happens, generate a valid tags table in the working directory and try again.

M-x perldb `(RET)` *file* `(RET)`
> Run the Perl interpreter in debug mode to debug *file*, a Perl program.

M-x jdb `(RET)` *file* `(RET)`
> Run the Java debugger to debug *file*.

M-x pdb `(RET)` *file* `(RET)`
> Run the Python debugger to debug *file*.

Each of these commands takes one argument: a command line to invoke the debugger. In the simplest case, specify just the name of the executable file you want to debug. You may also use options that the debugger supports. However, shell wildcards and variables are not allowed. GUD assumes that the first argument not starting with a '-' is the executable file name.

Emacs can only run one debugger process at a time.

23.5.2 Debugger Operation

When you run a debugger with GUD, the debugger uses an Emacs buffer for its ordinary input and output. This is called the GUD buffer. The debugger displays the source files of the program by visiting them in Emacs buffers. An arrow ('=>') in one of these buffers indicates the current execution line. Moving point in this buffer does not move the arrow.

You can start editing these source files at any time in the buffers that were made to display them. The arrow is not part of the file's text; it appears only on the screen. If you do modify a source file, keep in mind that inserting or deleting lines will throw off the arrow's positioning; GUD has no way of figuring out which line corresponded before your changes to the line number in a debugger message. Also, you'll typically have to recompile and restart the program for your changes to be reflected in the debugger's tables.

If you wish, you can control your debugger process entirely through the debugger buffer, which uses a variant of Shell mode. All the usual commands for your debugger are available, and you can use the Shell mode history commands to repeat them. See Section 30.2.3 [Shell Mode], page 370.

23.5.3 Commands of GUD

The GUD interaction buffer uses a variant of Shell mode, so the commands of Shell mode are available (see Section 30.2.3 [Shell Mode], page 370). GUD mode also provides commands for setting and clearing breakpoints, for selecting stack frames, and for stepping through the program. These commands are available both in the GUD buffer and globally, but with different key bindings.

The breakpoint commands are usually used in source file buffers, because that is the way to specify where to set or clear the breakpoint. Here's the global command to set a breakpoint:

C-x (SPC)   Set a breakpoint on the source line that point is on.

Here are the other special commands provided by GUD. The keys starting with C-c are available only in the GUD interaction buffer. The key bindings that start with C-x C-a are available in the GUD interaction buffer and also in source files.

C-c C-l
C-x C-a C-l
>   Display in another window the last line referred to in the GUD
            buffer (that is, the line indicated in the last location message).
            This runs the command **gud-refresh**.

C-c C-s
C-x C-a C-s
>   Execute a single line of code (**gud-step**). If the line contains a
            function call, execution stops after entering the called function.

C-c C-n
C-x C-a C-n
>   Execute a single line of code, stepping across entire function calls
            at full speed (**gud-next**).

C-c C-i
C-x C-a C-i
>   Execute a single machine instruction (**gud-stepi**).

C-c C-r
C-x C-a C-r
>   Continue execution without specifying any stopping point. The
            program will run until it hits a breakpoint, terminates, or gets
            a signal that the debugger is checking for (**gud-cont**).

C-c C-d
C-x C-a C-d
>   Delete the breakpoint(s) on the current source line, if any (**gud-
            remove**). If you use this command in the GUD interaction buffer,
            it applies to the line where the program last stopped.

C-c C-t
C-x C-a C-t
>   Set a temporary breakpoint on the current source line, if any. If
            you use this command in the GUD interaction buffer, it applies
            to the line where the program last stopped.

The above commands are common to all supported debuggers. If you are using GDB or (some versions of) DBX, these additional commands are available:

```
C-c <
C-x C-a <   Select the next enclosing stack frame (gud-up). This is equiva-
            lent to the 'up' command.

C-c >
C-x C-a >   Select the next inner stack frame (gud-down). This is equivalent
            to the 'down' command.
```

If you are using GDB, these additional key bindings are available:

(TAB)   With GDB, complete a symbol name (gud-gdb-complete-command). This key is available only in the GUD interaction buffer, and requires GDB versions 4.13 and later.

```
C-c C-f
C-x C-a C-f
            Run the program until the selected stack frame returns (or until
            it stops for some other reason).
```

These commands interpret a numeric argument as a repeat count, when that makes sense.

Because (TAB) serves as a completion command, you can't use it to enter a tab as input to the program you are debugging with GDB. Instead, type C-q (TAB) to enter a tab.

23.5.4 GUD Customization

On startup, GUD runs one of the following hooks: gdb-mode-hook, if you are using GDB; dbx-mode-hook, if you are using DBX; sdb-mode-hook, if you are using SDB; xdb-mode-hook, if you are using XDB; perldb-mode-hook, for Perl debugging mode; jdb-mode-hook, for PDB; jdb-mode-hook, for JDB. You can use these hooks to define custom key bindings for the debugger interaction buffer. See Section 31.2.3 [Hooks], page 400.

Here is a convenient way to define a command that sends a particular command string to the debugger, and set up a key binding for it in the debugger interaction buffer:

(gud-def *function cmdstring binding docstring*)

This defines a command named *function* which sends *cmdstring* to the debugger process, and gives it the documentation string *docstring*. You can use the command thus defined in any buffer. If *binding* is non-nil, gud-def also binds the command to C-c *binding* in the GUD buffer's mode and to C-x C-a *binding* generally.

The command string *cmdstring* may contain certain '%'-sequences that stand for data to be filled in at the time *function* is called:

'%f'   The name of the current source file. If the current buffer is the GUD buffer, then the "current source file" is the file that the program stopped in.

'%l'   The number of the current source line. If the current buffer is
            the GUD buffer, then the "current source line" is the line that
            the program stopped in.

'%e'   The text of the C lvalue or function-call expression at or adjacent
            to point.

'%a'   The text of the hexadecimal address at or adjacent to point.

'%p'   The numeric argument of the called function, as a decimal num-
            ber. If the command is used without a numeric argument, '%p'
            stands for the empty string.

            If you don't use '%p' in the command string, the command you
            define ignores any numeric argument.

23.6 Executing Lisp Expressions

Emacs has several different major modes for Lisp and Scheme. They
are the same in terms of editing commands, but differ in the commands for
executing Lisp expressions. Each mode has its own purpose.

Emacs-Lisp mode
            The mode for editing source files of programs to run in Emacs
            Lisp. This mode defines C-M-x to evaluate the current defun.
            See Section 23.7 [Lisp Libraries], page 285.

Lisp Interaction mode
            The mode for an interactive session with Emacs Lisp. It defines
            C-j to evaluate the sexp before point and insert its value in the
            buffer. See Section 23.9 [Lisp Interaction], page 287.

Lisp mode   The mode for editing source files of programs that run in Lisps
            other than Emacs Lisp. This mode defines C-M-x to send the
            current defun to an inferior Lisp process. See Section 23.10
            [External Lisp], page 287.

Inferior Lisp mode
            The mode for an interactive session with an inferior Lisp process.
            This mode combines the special features of Lisp mode and Shell
            mode (see Section 30.2.3 [Shell Mode], page 370).

Scheme mode
            Like Lisp mode but for Scheme programs.

Inferior Scheme mode
            The mode for an interactive session with an inferior Scheme
            process.

Most editing commands for working with Lisp programs are in fact available globally. See Chapter 22 [Programs], page 227.

23.7 Libraries of Lisp Code for Emacs

Lisp code for Emacs editing commands is stored in files whose names conventionally end in '.el'. This ending tells Emacs to edit them in Emacs-Lisp mode (see Section 23.6 [Executing Lisp], page 284).

To execute a file of Emacs Lisp code, use M-x load-file. This command reads a file name using the minibuffer and then executes the contents of that file as Lisp code. It is not necessary to visit the file first; in any case, this command reads the file as found on disk, not text in an Emacs buffer.

Once a file of Lisp code is installed in the Emacs Lisp library directories, users can load it using M-x load-library. Programs can load it by calling load-library, or with load, a more primitive function that is similar but accepts some additional arguments.

M-x load-library differs from M-x load-file in that it searches a sequence of directories and tries three file names in each directory. Suppose your argument is *lib*; the three names are '*lib*.elc', '*lib*.el', and lastly just '*lib*'. If '*lib*.elc' exists, it is by convention the result of compiling '*lib*.el'; it is better to load the compiled file, since it will load and run faster.

If load-library finds that '*lib*.el' is newer than '*lib*.elc' file, it prints a warning, because it's likely that somebody made changes to the '.el' file and forgot to recompile it.

Because the argument to load-library is usually not in itself a valid file name, file name completion is not available. Indeed, when using this command, you usually do not know exactly what file name will be used.

The sequence of directories searched by M-x load-library is specified by the variable load-path, a list of strings that are directory names. The default value of the list contains the directory where the Lisp code for Emacs itself is stored. If you have libraries of your own, put them in a single directory and add that directory to load-path. nil in this list stands for the current default directory, but it is probably not a good idea to put nil in the list. If you find yourself wishing that nil were in the list, most likely what you really want to do is use M-x load-file this once.

Often you do not have to give any command to load a library, because the commands defined in the library are set up to *autoload* that library. Trying to run any of those commands calls load to load the library; this replaces the autoload definitions with the real ones from the library.

Emacs Lisp code can be compiled into byte-code which loads faster, takes up less space when loaded, and executes faster. See section "Byte Compilation" in *the Emacs Lisp Reference Manual*. By convention, the compiled code for a library goes in a separate file whose name consists of the library source file with 'c' appended. Thus, the compiled code for 'foo.el' goes in 'foo.elc'. That's why load-library searches for '.elc' files first.

23.8 Evaluating Emacs-Lisp Expressions

Lisp programs intended to be run in Emacs should be edited in Emacs-Lisp mode; this happens automatically for file names ending in '.el'. By contrast, Lisp mode itself is used for editing Lisp programs intended for other Lisp systems. To switch to Emacs-Lisp mode explicitly, use the command M-x emacs-lisp-mode.

For testing of Lisp programs to run in Emacs, it is often useful to evaluate part of the program as it is found in the Emacs buffer. For example, after changing the text of a Lisp function definition, evaluating the definition installs the change for future calls to the function. Evaluation of Lisp expressions is also useful in any kind of editing, for invoking noninteractive functions (functions that are not commands).

M-:   Read a single Lisp expression in the minibuffer, evaluate it, and print the value in the echo area (eval-expression).

C-x C-e   Evaluate the Lisp expression before point, and print the value in the echo area (eval-last-sexp).

C-M-x   Evaluate the defun containing or after point, and print the value in the echo area (eval-defun).

M-x eval-region
           Evaluate all the Lisp expressions in the region.

M-x eval-current-buffer
           Evaluate all the Lisp expressions in the buffer.

M-: (eval-expression) is the most basic command for evaluating a Lisp expression interactively. It reads the expression using the minibuffer, so you can execute any expression on a buffer regardless of what the buffer contains. When the expression is evaluated, the current buffer is once again the buffer that was current when M-: was typed.

In Emacs-Lisp mode, the key C-M-x is bound to the command eval-defun, which parses the defun containing or following point as a Lisp expression and evaluates it. The value is printed in the echo area. This command is convenient for installing in the Lisp environment changes that you have just made in the text of a function definition.

C-M-x treats defvar expressions specially. Normally, evaluating a defvar expression does nothing if the variable it defines already has a value. But C-M-x unconditionally resets the variable to the initial value specified in the defvar expression. This special feature is convenient for debugging Lisp programs.

The command C-x C-e (eval-last-sexp) evaluates the Lisp expression preceding point in the buffer, and displays the value in the echo area. It is available in all major modes, not just Emacs-Lisp mode. It does not treat defvar specially.

If C-M-x, C-x C-e, or M-: is given a numeric argument, it inserts the value into the current buffer at point, rather than displaying it in the echo area. The argument's value does not matter.

The most general command for evaluating Lisp expressions from a buffer is eval-region. M-x eval-region parses the text of the region as one or more Lisp expressions, evaluating them one by one. M-x eval-current-buffer is similar but evaluates the entire buffer. This is a reasonable way to install the contents of a file of Lisp code that you are just ready to test. Later, as you find bugs and change individual functions, use C-M-x on each function that you change. This keeps the Lisp world in step with the source file.

23.9 Lisp Interaction Buffers

The buffer '*scratch*' which is selected when Emacs starts up is provided for evaluating Lisp expressions interactively inside Emacs.

The simplest way to use the '*scratch*' buffer is to insert Lisp expressions and type C-j after each expression. This command reads the Lisp expression before point, evaluates it, and inserts the value in printed representation before point. The result is a complete typescript of the expressions you have evaluated and their values.

The '*scratch*' buffer's major mode is Lisp Interaction mode, which is the same as Emacs-Lisp mode except for the binding of C-j.

The rationale for this feature is that Emacs must have a buffer when it starts up, but that buffer is not useful for editing files since a new buffer is made for every file that you visit. The Lisp interpreter typescript is the most useful thing I can think of for the initial buffer to do. Type M-x lisp-interaction-mode to put the current buffer in Lisp Interaction mode.

An alternative way of evaluating Emacs Lisp expressions interactively is to use Inferior Emacs-Lisp mode, which provides an interface rather like Shell mode (see Section 30.2.3 [Shell Mode], page 370) for evaluating Emacs Lisp expressions. Type M-x ielm to create an '*ielm*' buffer which uses this mode.

23.10 Running an External Lisp

Emacs has facilities for running programs in other Lisp systems. You can run a Lisp process as an inferior of Emacs, and pass expressions to it to be evaluated. You can also pass changed function definitions directly from the Emacs buffers in which you edit the Lisp programs to the inferior Lisp process.

To run an inferior Lisp process, type M-x run-lisp. This runs the program named lisp, the same program you would run by typing lisp as a shell command, with both input and output going through an Emacs buffer named '`*lisp*`'. That is to say, any "terminal output" from Lisp will go into the buffer, advancing point, and any "terminal input" for Lisp comes from text in the buffer. (You can change the name of the Lisp executable file by setting the variable `inferior-lisp-program`.)

To give input to Lisp, go to the end of the buffer and type the input, terminated by (RET). The '`*lisp*`' buffer is in Inferior Lisp mode, which combines the special characteristics of Lisp mode with most of the features of Shell mode (see Section 30.2.3 [Shell Mode], page 370). The definition of (RET) to send a line to a subprocess is one of the features of Shell mode.

For the source files of programs to run in external Lisps, use Lisp mode. This mode can be selected with `M-x lisp-mode`, and is used automatically for files whose names end in '`.l`', '`.lsp`', or '`.lisp`', as most Lisp systems usually expect.

When you edit a function in a Lisp program you are running, the easiest way to send the changed definition to the inferior Lisp process is the key `C-M-x`. In Lisp mode, this runs the function `lisp-eval-defun`, which finds the defun around or following point and sends it as input to the Lisp process. (Emacs can send input to any inferior process regardless of what buffer is current.)

Contrast the meanings of `C-M-x` in Lisp mode (for editing programs to be run in another Lisp system) and Emacs-Lisp mode (for editing Lisp programs to be run in Emacs): in both modes it has the effect of installing the function definition that point is in, but the way of doing so is different according to where the relevant Lisp environment is found. See Section 23.6 [Executing Lisp], page 284.

24 Abbrevs

A defined *abbrev* is a word which *expands*, if you insert it, into some different text. Abbrevs are defined by the user to expand in specific ways. For example, you might define 'foo' as an abbrev expanding to 'find outer otter'. Then you would be able to insert 'find outer otter ' into the buffer by typing f o o (SPC).

A second kind of abbreviation facility is called *dynamic abbrev expansion*. You use dynamic abbrev expansion with an explicit command to expand the letters in the buffer before point by looking for other words in the buffer that start with those letters. See Section 24.6 [Dynamic Abbrevs], page 293.

24.1 Abbrev Concepts

An *abbrev* is a word which has been defined to *expand* into a specified *expansion*. When you insert a word-separator character following the abbrev, that expands the abbrev—replacing the abbrev with its expansion. For example, if 'foo' is defined as an abbrev expanding to 'find outer otter', then you can insert 'find outer otter.' into the buffer by typing f o o ..

Abbrevs expand only when Abbrev mode (a minor mode) is enabled. Disabling Abbrev mode does not cause abbrev definitions to be forgotten, but they do not expand until Abbrev mode is enabled again. The command M-x abbrev-mode toggles Abbrev mode; with a numeric argument, it turns Abbrev mode on if the argument is positive, off otherwise. See Section 31.1 [Minor Modes], page 391. abbrev-mode is also a variable; Abbrev mode is on when the variable is non-nil. The variable abbrev-mode automatically becomes local to the current buffer when it is set.

Abbrev definitions can be *mode-specific*—active only in one major mode. Abbrevs can also have *global* definitions that are active in all major modes. The same abbrev can have a global definition and various mode-specific definitions for different major modes. A mode-specific definition for the current major mode overrides a global definition.

Abbrevs can be defined interactively during the editing session. Lists of abbrev definitions can also be saved in files and reloaded in later sessions. Some users keep extensive lists of abbrevs that they load in every session.

24.2 Defining Abbrevs

C-x a g   Define an abbrev, using one or more words before point as its expansion (add-global-abbrev).

C-x a l   Similar, but define an abbrev specific to the current major mode (add-mode-abbrev).

C-x a i g   Define a word in the buffer as an abbrev (inverse-add-global-abbrev).

C-x a i l   Define a word in the buffer as a mode-specific abbrev (`inverse-add-mode-abbrev`).

M-x kill-all-abbrevs

This command discards all abbrev definitions currently in effect, leaving a blank slate.

The usual way to define an abbrev is to enter the text you want the abbrev to expand to, position point after it, and type `C-x a g` (`add-global-abbrev`). This reads the abbrev itself using the minibuffer, and then defines it as an abbrev for one or more words before point. Use a numeric argument to say how many words before point should be taken as the expansion. For example, to define the abbrev 'foo' as mentioned above, insert the text 'find outer otter' and then type `C-u 3 C-x a g f o o` ⟨RET⟩.

An argument of zero to `C-x a g` means to use the contents of the region as the expansion of the abbrev being defined.

The command `C-x a l` (`add-mode-abbrev`) is similar, but defines a mode-specific abbrev. Mode-specific abbrevs are active only in a particular major mode. `C-x a l` defines an abbrev for the major mode in effect at the time `C-x a l` is typed. The arguments work the same as for `C-x a g`.

If the text already in the buffer is the abbrev, rather than its expansion, use command `C-x a i g` (`inverse-add-global-abbrev`) instead of `C-x a g`, or use `C-x a i l` (`inverse-add-mode-abbrev`) instead of `C-x a l`. These commands are called "inverse" because they invert the meaning of the two text strings they use (one from the buffer and one read with the minibuffer).

To change the definition of an abbrev, just define a new definition. When the abbrev has a prior definition, the abbrev definition commands ask for confirmation for replacing it.

To remove an abbrev definition, give a negative argument to the abbrev definition command: `C-u - C-x a g` or `C-u - C-x a l`. The former removes a global definition, while the latter removes a mode-specific definition.

`M-x kill-all-abbrevs` removes all the abbrev definitions there are, both global and local.

24.3 Controlling Abbrev Expansion

An abbrev expands whenever it is present in the buffer just before point and you type a self-inserting whitespace or punctuation character (⟨SPC⟩, comma, etc.). More precisely, any character that is not a word constituent expands an abbrev, and any word-constituent character can be part of an abbrev. The most common way to use an abbrev is to insert it and then insert a punctuation character to expand it.

Abbrev expansion preserves case; thus, 'foo' expands into 'find outer otter'; 'Foo' into 'Find outer otter', and 'FOO' into 'FIND OUTER OTTER' or 'Find Outer Otter' according to the variable `abbrev-all-caps` (a non-nil value chooses the first of the two expansions).

These commands are used to control abbrev expansion:

M-'   Separate a prefix from a following abbrev to be expanded
           (`abbrev-prefix-mark`).

C-x a e   Expand the abbrev before point (`expand-abbrev`). This is ef-
           fective even when Abbrev mode is not enabled.

M-x expand-region-abbrevs
           Expand some or all abbrevs found in the region.

You may wish to expand an abbrev with a prefix attached; for example,
if 'cnst' expands into '`construction`', you might want to use it to enter
'`reconstruction`'. It does not work to type **recnst**, because that is not
necessarily a defined abbrev. What you can do is use the command M-'
(`abbrev-prefix-mark`) in between the prefix 're' and the abbrev 'cnst'.
First, insert 're'. Then type M-'; this inserts a hyphen in the buffer to indicate that it has done its work. Then insert the abbrev 'cnst'; the buffer now
contains 're-cnst'. Now insert a non-word character to expand the abbrev
'cnst' into '`construction`'. This expansion step also deletes the hyphen that
indicated M-' had been used. The result is the desired '`reconstruction`'.

If you actually want the text of the abbrev in the buffer, rather than its
expansion, you can accomplish this by inserting the following punctuation
with C-q. Thus, **foo** C-q **,** leaves '`foo,`' in the buffer.

If you expand an abbrev by mistake, you can undo the expansion and
bring back the abbrev itself by typing C-_ to undo (see Section 4.4 [Undo],
page 32). This also undoes the insertion of the non-word character that expanded the abbrev. If the result you want is the terminating non-word
character plus the unexpanded abbrev, you must reinsert the terminating character, quoting it with C-q. You can also use the command M-x
unexpand-abbrev to cancel the last expansion without deleting the terminating character.

M-x **expand-region-abbrevs** searches through the region for defined abbrevs, and for each one found offers to replace it with its expansion. This
command is useful if you have typed in text using abbrevs but forgot to
turn on Abbrev mode first. It may also be useful together with a special set
of abbrev definitions for making several global replacements at once. This
command is effective even if Abbrev mode is not enabled.

Expanding an abbrev runs the hook **pre-abbrev-expand-hook** (see Section 31.2.3 [Hooks], page 400).

24.4 Examining and Editing Abbrevs

`M-x list-abbrevs`
> Display a list of all abbrev definitions.

`M-x edit-abbrevs`
> Edit a list of abbrevs; you can add, alter or remove definitions.

The output from `M-x list-abbrevs` looks like this:

```
(lisp-mode-abbrev-table)
"dk"        0    "define-key"
(global-abbrev-table)
"dfn"       0    "definition"
```

(Some blank lines of no semantic significance, and some other abbrev tables, have been omitted.)

A line containing a name in parentheses is the header for abbrevs in a particular abbrev table; `global-abbrev-table` contains all the global abbrevs, and the other abbrev tables that are named after major modes contain the mode-specific abbrevs.

Within each abbrev table, each nonblank line defines one abbrev. The word at the beginning of the line is the abbrev. The number that follows is the number of times the abbrev has been expanded. Emacs keeps track of this to help you see which abbrevs you actually use, so that you can eliminate those that you don't use often. The string at the end of the line is the expansion.

`M-x edit-abbrevs` allows you to add, change or kill abbrev definitions by editing a list of them in an Emacs buffer. The list has the same format described above. The buffer of abbrevs is called '`*Abbrevs*`', and is in Edit-Abbrevs mode. Type `C-c C-c` in this buffer to install the abbrev definitions as specified in the buffer—and delete any abbrev definitions not listed.

The command `edit-abbrevs` is actually the same as `list-abbrevs` except that it selects the buffer '`*Abbrevs*`' whereas `list-abbrevs` merely displays it in another window.

24.5 Saving Abbrevs

These commands allow you to keep abbrev definitions between editing sessions.

`M-x write-abbrev-file` (RET) *file* (RET)
> Write a file *file* describing all defined abbrevs.

`M-x read-abbrev-file` (RET) *file* (RET)
> Read the file *file* and define abbrevs as specified therein.

M-x quietly-read-abbrev-file (RET) *file* (RET)
> Similar but do not display a message about what is going on.

M-x define-abbrevs
> Define abbrevs from definitions in current buffer.

M-x insert-abbrevs
> Insert all abbrevs and their expansions into current buffer.

M-x write-abbrev-file reads a file name using the minibuffer and then writes a description of all current abbrev definitions into that file. This is used to save abbrev definitions for use in a later session. The text stored in the file is a series of Lisp expressions that, when executed, define the same abbrevs that you currently have.

M-x read-abbrev-file reads a file name using the minibuffer and then reads the file, defining abbrevs according to the contents of the file. M-x quietly-read-abbrev-file is the same except that it does not display a message in the echo area saying that it is doing its work; it is actually useful primarily in the '.emacs' file. If an empty argument is given to either of these functions, they use the file name specified in the variable abbrev-file-name, which is by default "~/.abbrev_defs".

Emacs will offer to save abbrevs automatically if you have changed any of them, whenever it offers to save all files (for C-x s or C-x C-c). This feature can be inhibited by setting the variable save-abbrevs to nil.

The commands M-x insert-abbrevs and M-x define-abbrevs are similar to the previous commands but work on text in an Emacs buffer. M-x insert-abbrevs inserts text into the current buffer before point, describing all current abbrev definitions; M-x define-abbrevs parses the entire current buffer and defines abbrevs accordingly.

24.6 Dynamic Abbrev Expansion

The abbrev facility described above operates automatically as you insert text, but all abbrevs must be defined explicitly. By contrast, *dynamic abbrevs* allow the meanings of abbrevs to be determined automatically from the contents of the buffer, but dynamic abbrev expansion happens only when you request it explicitly.

M-/
> Expand the word in the buffer before point as a *dynamic abbrev*, by searching in the buffer for words starting with that abbreviation (dabbrev-expand).

C-M-/
> Complete the word before point as a dynamic abbrev (dabbrev-completion).

For example, if the buffer contains 'does this follow ' and you type f o M-/, the effect is to insert 'follow' because that is the last word in the buffer that starts with 'fo'. A numeric argument to M-/ says to take the

second, third, etc. distinct expansion found looking backward from point.
Repeating M-/ searches for an alternative expansion by looking farther back.
After scanning all the text before point, it searches the text after point. The
variable dabbrev-limit, if non-nil, specifies how far in the buffer to search
for an expansion.

After scanning the current buffer, M-/ normally searches other buffers,
unless you have set dabbrev-check-all-buffers to nil.

A negative argument to M-/, as in C-u - M-/, says to search first for
expansions after point, and second for expansions before point. If you repeat
the M-/ to look for another expansion, do not specify an argument. This
tries all the expansions after point and then the expansions before point.

After you have expanded a dynamic abbrev, you can copy additional
words that follow the expansion in its original context. Simply type (SPC)
M-/ for each word you want to copy. The spacing and punctuation between
words is copied along with the words.

The command C-M-/ (dabbrev-completion) performs completion of a
dynamic abbreviation. Instead of trying the possible expansions one by one,
it finds all of them, then inserts the text that they have in common. If they
have nothing in common, C-M-/ displays a list of completions, from which
you can select a choice in the usual manner. See Section 5.3 [Completion],
page 43.

Dynamic abbrev expansion is completely independent of Abbrev mode;
the expansion of a word with M-/ is completely independent of whether it
has a definition as an ordinary abbrev.

24.7 Customizing Dynamic Abbreviation

Normally, dynamic abbrev expansion ignores case when searching for
expansions. That is, the expansion need not agree in case with the word you
are expanding.

This feature is controlled by the variable dabbrev-case-fold-search.
If it is t, case is ignored in this search; if nil, the word and the expansion
must match in case. If the value of dabbrev-case-fold-search is case-
fold-search, which is true by default, then the variable case-fold-search
controls whether to ignore case while searching for expansions.

Normally, dynamic abbrev expansion preserves the case pattern *of the
abbrev you have typed*, by converting the expansion to that case pattern.

The variable dabbrev-case-replace controls whether to preserve the
case pattern of the abbrev. If it is t, the abbrev's case pattern is preserved
in most cases; if nil, the expansion is always copied verbatim. If the value of
dabbrev-case-replace is case-replace, which is true by default, then the
variable case-replace controls whether to copy the expansion verbatim.

However, if the expansion contains a complex mixed case pattern, and
the abbrev matches this pattern as far as it goes, then the expansion is

always copied verbatim, regardless of those variables. Thus, for example, if the buffer contains `variableWithSillyCasePattern`, and you type `v a M-/`, it copies the expansion verbatim including its case pattern.

The variable `dabbrev-abbrev-char-regexp`, if non-`nil`, controls which characters are considered part of a word, for dynamic expansion purposes. The regular expression must match just one character, never two or more. The same regular expression also determines which characters are part of an expansion. The value `nil` has a special meaning: abbreviations are made of word characters, but expansions are made of word and symbol characters.

In shell scripts and makefiles, a variable name is sometimes prefixed with '`$`' and sometimes not. Major modes for this kind of text can customize dynamic abbreviation to handle optional prefixes by setting the variable `dabbrev-abbrev-skip-leading-regexp`. Its value should be a regular expression that matches the optional prefix that dynamic abbreviation should ignore.

25 Editing Pictures

To edit a picture made out of text characters (for example, a picture of the division of a register into fields, as a comment in a program), use the command M-x edit-picture to enter Picture mode.

In Picture mode, editing is based on the *quarter-plane* model of text, according to which the text characters lie studded on an area that stretches infinitely far to the right and downward. The concept of the end of a line does not exist in this model; the most you can say is where the last nonblank character on the line is found.

Of course, Emacs really always considers text as a sequence of characters, and lines really do have ends. But Picture mode replaces the most frequently-used commands with variants that simulate the quarter-plane model of text. They do this by inserting spaces or by converting tabs to spaces.

Most of the basic editing commands of Emacs are redefined by Picture mode to do essentially the same thing but in a quarter-plane way. In addition, Picture mode defines various keys starting with the C-c prefix to run special picture editing commands.

One of these keys, C-c C-c, is pretty important. Often a picture is part of a larger file that is usually edited in some other major mode. M-x edit-picture records the name of the previous major mode so you can use the C-c C-c command (picture-mode-exit) later to go back to that mode. C-c C-c also deletes spaces from the ends of lines, unless given a numeric argument.

The special commands of Picture mode all work in other modes (provided the 'picture' library is loaded), but are not bound to keys except in Picture mode. The descriptions below talk of moving "one column" and so on, but all the picture mode commands handle numeric arguments as their normal equivalents do.

Turning on Picture mode runs the hook picture-mode-hook (see Section 31.2.3 [Hooks], page 400).

25.1 Basic Editing in Picture Mode

Most keys do the same thing in Picture mode that they usually do, but do it in a quarter-plane style. For example, C-f is rebound to run picture-forward-column, a command which moves point one column to the right, inserting a space if necessary so that the actual end of the line makes no difference. C-b is rebound to run picture-backward-column, which always moves point left one column, converting a tab to multiple spaces if necessary. C-n and C-p are rebound to run picture-move-down and picture-move-up, which can either insert spaces or convert tabs as necessary to make sure that point stays in exactly the same column. C-e runs picture-end-of-line, which moves to after the last nonblank character on the line. There is no need to change C-a, as the choice of screen model does not affect beginnings of lines.

Insertion of text is adapted to the quarter-plane screen model through the use of Overwrite mode (see Section 31.1 [Minor Modes], page 391). Self-inserting characters replace existing text, column by column, rather than pushing existing text to the right. (RET) runs `picture-newline`, which just moves to the beginning of the following line so that new text will replace that line.

Picture mode provides erasure instead of deletion and killing of text. (DEL) (`picture-backward-clear-column`) replaces the preceding character with a space rather than removing it; this moves point backwards. C-d (`picture-clear-column`) replaces the next character or characters with spaces, but does not move point. (If you want to clear characters to spaces and move forward over them, use (SPC).) C-k (`picture-clear-line`) really kills the contents of lines, but does not delete the newlines from the buffer.

To do actual insertion, you must use special commands. C-o (`picture-open-line`) creates a blank line after the current line; it never splits a line. C-M-o (`split-line`) makes sense in Picture mode, so it is not changed. C-j (`picture-duplicate-line`) inserts below the current line another line with the same contents.

To do actual deletion in Picture mode, use C-w, C-c C-d (which is defined as `delete-char`, as C-d is in other modes), or one of the picture rectangle commands (see Section 25.4 [Rectangles in Picture], page 299).

25.2 Controlling Motion after Insert

Since "self-inserting" characters in Picture mode overwrite and move point, there is no essential restriction on how point should be moved. Normally point moves right, but you can specify any of the eight orthogonal or diagonal directions for motion after a "self-inserting" character. This is useful for drawing lines in the buffer.

C-c <   Move left after insertion (`picture-movement-left`).

C-c >   Move right after insertion (`picture-movement-right`).

C-c ^   Move up after insertion (`picture-movement-up`).

C-c .   Move down after insertion (`picture-movement-down`).

C-c '   Move up and left ("northwest") after insertion (`picture-movement-nw`).

C-c '   Move up and right ("northeast") after insertion (`picture-movement-ne`).

C-c /   Move down and left ("southwest") after insertion (`picture-movement-sw`).

C-c \   Move down and right ("southeast") after insertion
             (picture-movement-se).

Two motion commands move based on the current Picture insertion direction. The command C-c C-f (picture-motion) moves in the same direction as motion after "insertion" currently does, while C-c C-b (picture-motion-reverse) moves in the opposite direction.

25.3 Picture Mode Tabs

Two kinds of tab-like action are provided in Picture mode. Use M-⟨TAB⟩ (picture-tab-search) for context-based tabbing. With no argument, it moves to a point underneath the next "interesting" character that follows whitespace in the previous nonblank line. "Next" here means "appearing at a horizontal position greater than the one point starts out at." With an argument, as in C-u M-⟨TAB⟩, this command moves to the next such interesting character in the current line. M-⟨TAB⟩ does not change the text; it only moves point. "Interesting" characters are defined by the variable picture-tab-chars, which should define a set of characters. The syntax for this variable is like the syntax used inside of '[...]' in a regular expression—but without the '[' and the ']'. Its default value is "!-~".

⟨TAB⟩ itself runs picture-tab, which operates based on the current tab stop settings; it is the Picture mode equivalent of tab-to-tab-stop. Normally it just moves point, but with a numeric argument it clears the text that it moves over.

The context-based and tab-stop-based forms of tabbing are brought together by the command C-c ⟨TAB⟩ (picture-set-tab-stops). This command sets the tab stops to the positions which M-⟨TAB⟩ would consider significant in the current line. The use of this command, together with ⟨TAB⟩, can get the effect of context-based tabbing. But M-⟨TAB⟩ is more convenient in the cases where it is sufficient.

It may be convenient to prevent use of actual tab characters in pictures. For example, this prevents C-x ⟨TAB⟩ from messing up the picture. You can do this by setting the variable indent-tabs-mode to nil. See Section 20.3 [Just Spaces], page 197.

25.4 Picture Mode Rectangle Commands

Picture mode defines commands for working on rectangular pieces of the text in ways that fit with the quarter-plane model. The standard rectangle commands may also be useful (see Section 9.4 [Rectangles], page 71).

C-c C-k   Clear out the region-rectangle with spaces (picture-clear-rectangle). With argument, delete the text.

C-c C-w r   Similar but save rectangle contents in register r first (picture-clear-rectangle-to-register).

C-c C-y   Copy last killed rectangle into the buffer by overwriting, with upper left corner at point (`picture-yank-rectangle`). With argument, insert instead.

C-c C-x r   Similar, but use the rectangle in register r (`picture-yank-rectangle-from-register`).

The picture rectangle commands C-c C-k (`picture-clear-rectangle`) and C-c C-w (`picture-clear-rectangle-to-register`) differ from the standard rectangle commands in that they normally clear the rectangle instead of deleting it; this is analogous with the way C-d is changed in Picture mode.

However, deletion of rectangles can be useful in Picture mode, so these commands delete the rectangle if given a numeric argument. C-c C-k either with or without a numeric argument saves the rectangle for C-c C-y.

The Picture mode commands for yanking rectangles differ from the standard ones in overwriting instead of inserting. This is the same way that Picture mode insertion of other text differs from other modes. C-c C-y (`picture-yank-rectangle`) inserts (by overwriting) the rectangle that was most recently killed, while C-c C-x (`picture-yank-rectangle-from-register`) does likewise for the rectangle found in a specified register.

26 Sending Mail

To send a message in Emacs, you start by typing a command (C-x m) to select and initialize the '*mail*' buffer. Then you edit the text and headers of the message in this buffer, and type another command (C-c C-s or C-c C-c) to send the message.

C-x m   Begin composing a message to send (compose-mail).

C-x 4 m   Likewise, but display the message in another window (compose-mail-other-window).

C-x 5 m   Likewise, but make a new frame (compose-mail-other-frame).

C-c C-s   In Mail mode, send the message (mail-send).

C-c C-c   Send the message and bury the mail buffer (mail-send-and-exit).

The command C-x m (compose-mail) selects a buffer named '*mail*' and initializes it with the skeleton of an outgoing message. C-x 4 m (compose-mail-other-window) selects the '*mail*' buffer in a different window, leaving the previous current buffer visible. C-x 5 m (compose-mail-other-frame) creates a new frame to select the '*mail*' buffer.

Because the mail-composition buffer is an ordinary Emacs buffer, you can switch to other buffers while in the middle of composing mail, and switch back later (or never). If you use the C-x m command again when you have been composing another message but have not sent it, you are asked to confirm before the old message is erased. If you answer n, the '*mail*' buffer is left selected with its old contents, so you can finish the old message and send it. C-u C-x m is another way to do this. Sending the message marks the '*mail*' buffer "unmodified," which avoids the need for confirmation when C-x m is next used.

If you are composing a message in the '*mail*' buffer and want to send another message before finishing the first, rename the '*mail*' buffer using M-x rename-uniquely (see Section 15.3 [Misc Buffer], page 145). Then you can use C-x m or its variants described above to make a new '*mail*' buffer. Once you've done that, you can work with each mail buffer independently.

26.1 The Format of the Mail Buffer

In addition to the *text* or *body*, a message has *header fields* which say who sent it, when, to whom, why, and so on. Some header fields, such as 'Date' and 'Sender', are created automatically when you send the message. Others, such as the recipient names, must be specified by you in order to send the message properly.

Mail mode provides a few commands to help you edit some header fields, and some are preinitialized in the buffer automatically at times. You can insert and edit header fields using ordinary editing commands.

The line in the buffer that says

```
--text follows this line--
```

is a special delimiter that separates the headers you have specified from the text. Whatever follows this line is the text of the message; the headers precede it. The delimiter line itself does not appear in the message actually sent. The text used for the delimiter line is controlled by the variable `mail-header-separator`.

Here is an example of what the headers and text in the mail buffer might look like.

```
To: gnu@gnu.org
CC: lungfish@spam.org, byob@spam.org
Subject: The Emacs Manual
--Text follows this line--
Please ignore this message.
```

26.2 Mail Header Fields

A header field in the mail buffer starts with a field name at the beginning of a line, terminated by a colon. Upper and lower case are equivalent in field names (and in mailing addresses also). After the colon and optional whitespace comes the contents of the field.

You can use any name you like for a header field, but normally people use only standard field names with accepted meanings. Here is a table of fields commonly used in outgoing messages.

'To'   This field contains the mailing addresses to which the message is addressed. If you list more than one address, use commas, not spaces, to separate them.

'Subject'   The contents of the 'Subject' field should be a piece of text that says what the message is about. The reason 'Subject' fields are useful is that most mail-reading programs can provide a summary of messages, listing the subject of each message but not its text.

'CC'   This field contains additional mailing addresses to send the message to, like 'To' except that these readers should not regard the message as directed at them.

'BCC'   This field contains additional mailing addresses to send the message to, which should not appear in the header of the message actually sent. Copies sent this way are called *blind carbon copies*.

              To send a blind carbon copy of every outgoing message to yourself, set the variable `mail-self-blind` to `t`.

'FCC'   This field contains the name of one file and directs Emacs to append a copy of the message to that file when you send the message. If the file is in Rmail format, Emacs writes the message in Rmail format; otherwise, Emacs writes the message in system mail file format.

To put a fixed file name in the 'FCC' field each time you start editing an outgoing message, set the variable `mail-archive-file-name` to that file name. Unless you remove the 'FCC' field before sending, the message will be written into that file when it is sent.

'From'   Use the 'From' field to say who you are, when the account you are using to send the mail is not your own. The contents of the 'From' field should be a valid mailing address, since replies will normally go there. If you don't specify the 'From' field yourself, Emacs uses the value of `user-mail-address` as the default.

'Reply-to'

Use this field to direct replies to a different address. Most mail-reading programs (including Rmail) automatically send replies to the 'Reply-to' address in preference to the 'From' address. By adding a 'Reply-to' field to your header, you can work around any problems your 'From' address may cause for replies.

To put a fixed 'Reply-to' address into every outgoing message, set the variable `mail-default-reply-to` to that address (as a string). Then `mail` initializes the message with a 'Reply-to' field as specified. You can delete or alter that header field before you send the message, if you wish. When Emacs starts up, if the environment variable `REPLYTO` is set, `mail-default-reply-to` is initialized from that environment variable.

'In-reply-to'

This field contains a piece of text describing a message you are replying to. Some mail systems can use this information to correlate related pieces of mail. Normally this field is filled in by Rmail when you reply to a message in Rmail, and you never need to think about it (see Chapter 27 [Rmail], page 311).

'References'

This field lists the message IDs of related previous messages. Rmail sets up this field automatically when you reply to a message.

The 'To', 'CC', 'BCC' and 'FCC' header fields can appear any number of times, and each such header field can contain multiple addresses, separated by commas. This way, you can specify any number of places to send the message. A 'To', 'CC', or 'BCC' field can also have continuation lines: one or more lines starting with whitespace, following the starting line of the field, are considered part of the field. Here's an example of a 'To' field with a continuation line:

```
To: foo@here.net, this@there.net,
   me@gnu.cambridge.mass.usa.earth.spiral3281
```

When you send the message, if you didn't write a 'From' field yourself, Emacs puts in one for you. The variable `mail-from-style` controls the format:

nil   Use just the email address, as in 'king@grassland.com'.

parens   Use both email address and full name, as in 'king@grassland.com (Elvis Parsley)'.

angles   Use both email address and full name, as in 'Elvis Parsley <king@grassland.com>'.

system-default
            Allow the system to insert the 'From' field.

26.3 Mail Aliases

You can define *mail aliases* in a file named '~/.mailrc'. These are short mnemonic names which stand for mail addresses or groups of mail addresses. Like many other mail programs, Emacs expands aliases when they occur in the 'To', 'From', 'CC', 'BCC', and 'Reply-to' fields, plus their 'Resent-' variants.

To define an alias in '~/.mailrc', write a line in the following format:

   alias *shortaddress fulladdresses*

Here *fulladdresses* stands for one or more mail addresses for *shortaddress* to expand into. Separate multiple addresses with spaces; if an address contains a space, quote the whole address with a pair of double-quotes.

For instance, to make `maingnu` stand for `gnu@gnu.org` plus a local address of your own, put in this line:

   alias maingnu gnu@gnu.org local-gnu

Emacs also recognizes include commands in '.mailrc' files. They look like this:

   source *filename*

The file '~/.mailrc' is used primarily by other mail-reading programs; it can contain various other commands. Emacs ignores everything in it except for alias definitions and include commands.

Another way to define a mail alias, within Emacs alone, is with the `define-mail-alias` command. It prompts for the alias and then the full address. You can use it to define aliases in your '.emacs' file, like this:

   (define-mail-alias "maingnu" "gnu@gnu.org")

`define-mail-alias` records aliases by adding them to a variable named `mail-aliases`. If you are comfortable with manipulating Lisp lists, you can set `mail-aliases` directly. The initial value of `mail-aliases` is t, which means that Emacs should read '.mailrc' to get the proper value.

You can specify a different file name to use instead of '~/.mailrc' by setting the variable `mail-personal-alias-file`.

Normally, Emacs expands aliases when you send the message. You do not need to expand mail aliases before sending the message, but you can expand them if you want to see where the mail will actually go. To do this, use the command `M-x expand-mail-aliases`; it expands all mail aliases currently present in the mail headers that hold addresses.

If you like, you can have mail aliases expand as abbrevs, as soon as you type them in (see Chapter 24 [Abbrevs], page 289). To enable this feature, execute the following:

```
(add-hook 'mail-setup-hook 'mail-abbrevs-setup)
```

This can go in your '.emacs' file. See Section 31.2.3 [Hooks], page 400. If you use this feature, you must use `define-mail-abbrev` instead of `define-mail-alias`; the latter does not work with this package. Note that the mail abbreviation package uses the variable `mail-abbrevs` instead of `mail-aliases`, and that all alias names are converted to lower case.

The mail abbreviation package also provides the `C-c C-a` (`mail-interactive-insert-alias`) command, which reads an alias name (with completion) and inserts its definition at point. This is useful when editing the message text itself or a header field such as 'Subject' in which Emacs does not normally expand aliases.

Note that abbrevs expand only if you insert a word-separator character afterward. However, you can rebind `C-n` and `M->` to cause expansion as well. Here's how to do that:

```
(add-hook 'mail-setup-hook
          '(lambda ()
             (substitute-key-definition
               'next-line 'mail-abbrev-next-line
               mail-mode-map global-map)
             (substitute-key-definition
               'end-of-buffer 'mail-abbrev-end-of-buffer
               mail-mode-map global-map)))
```

26.4 Mail Mode

The major mode used in the mail buffer is Mail mode, which is much like Text mode except that various special commands are provided on the `C-c` prefix. These commands all have to do specifically with editing or sending the message. In addition, Mail mode defines the character '%' as a word separator; this is helpful for using the word commands to edit mail addresses.

Mail mode is normally used in buffers set up automatically by the `mail` command and related commands. However, you can also switch to Mail mode in a file-visiting buffer. That is a useful thing to do if you have saved draft message text in a file.

26.4.1 Mail Sending

Mail mode has two commands for sending the message you have been editing:

C-c C-s   Send the message, and leave the mail buffer selected (mail-
           send).

C-c C-c   Send the message, and select some other buffer (mail-send-
           and-exit).

C-c C-s (mail-send) sends the message and marks the mail buffer un-modified, but leaves that buffer selected so that you can modify the message (perhaps with new recipients) and send it again. C-c C-c (mail-send-and-exit) sends and then deletes the window or switches to another buffer. It puts the mail buffer at the lowest priority for reselection by default, since you are finished with using it. This is the usual way to send the message.

In a file-visiting buffer, sending the message does not clear the modified flag, because only saving the file should do that. As a result, you don't get a warning if you try to send the same message twice.

When you send a message that contains non-ASCII characters, they need to be encoded with a coding system (see Section 18.7 [Coding Systems], page 180). Usually the coding system is specified automatically by your chosen language environment (see Section 18.3 [Language Environments], page 176). You can explicitly specify the coding system for outgoing mail by setting the variable sendmail-coding-system.

If the coding system thus determined does not handle the characters in a particular message, Emacs asks you to select the coding system to use, showing a list of possible coding systems.

26.4.2 Mail Header Editing

Mail mode provides special commands to move to particular header fields and to complete addresses in headers.

C-c C-f C-t
           Move to the 'To' header field, creating one if there is none (mail-
           to).

C-c C-f C-s
           Move to the 'Subject' header field, creating one if there is none
           (mail-subject).

C-c C-f C-c
           Move to the 'CC' header field, creating one if there is none (mail-
           cc).

C-c C-f C-b
           Move to the 'BCC' header field, creating one if there is none
           (mail-bcc).

C-c C-f C-f
> Move to the 'FCC' header field, creating one if there is none (`mail-fcc`).

M-⟨TAB⟩   Complete a mailing address (`mail-complete`).

There are five commands to move point to particular header fields, all based on the prefix C-c C-f ('C-f' is for "field"). They are listed in the table above. If the field in question does not exist, these commands create one. We provide special motion commands for these particular fields because they are the fields users most often want to edit.

While editing a header field that contains mailing addresses, such as 'To:', 'CC:' and 'BCC:', you can complete a mailing address by typing M-⟨TAB⟩ (`mail-complete`). It inserts the full name corresponding to the address, if it can determine the full name. The variable `mail-complete-style` controls whether to insert the full name, and what style to use, as in `mail-from-style` (see Section 26.2 [Mail Headers], page 302).

For completion purposes, the valid mailing addresses are taken to be the local users' names plus your personal mail aliases. You can specify additional sources of valid addresses; use the customization buffer to see the options for this.

If you type M-⟨TAB⟩ in the body of the message, it invokes `ispell-complete-word`, as in Text mode.

26.4.3 Citing Mail

Mail mode also has commands for yanking or *citing* all or part of a message that you are replying to. These commands are active only when you started sending a message using an Rmail command.

C-c C-y   Yank the selected message from Rmail (`mail-yank-original`).

C-c C-r   Yank the region from the Rmail buffer (`mail-yank-region`).

C-c C-q   Fill each paragraph cited from another message (`mail-fill-yanked-message`).

When mail sending is invoked from the Rmail mail reader using an Rmail command, C-c C-y can be used inside the mail buffer to insert the text of the message you are replying to. Normally it indents each line of that message three spaces and eliminates most header fields. A numeric argument specifies the number of spaces to indent. An argument of just C-u says not to indent at all and not to eliminate anything. C-c C-y always uses the current message from the Rmail buffer, so you can insert several old messages by selecting one in Rmail, switching to '*mail*' and yanking it, then switching back to Rmail to select another.

You can specify the text for C-c C-y to insert at the beginning of each line: set `mail-yank-prefix` to the desired string. (A value of `nil` means to use indentation; this is the default.) However, C-u C-c C-y never adds anything at the beginning of the inserted lines, regardless of the value of mail-yank-prefix.

To yank just a part of an incoming message, set the region in Rmail to the part you want; then go to the '*Mail*' message and type C-c C-r (mail-yank-region). Each line that is copied is indented or prefixed according to mail-yank-prefix.

After using C-c C-y or C-c C-r, you can type C-c C-q (mail-fill-yanked-message) to fill the paragraphs of the yanked old message or messages. One use of C-c C-q fills all such paragraphs, each one individually. To fill a single paragraph of the quoted message, use M-q. If filling does not automatically handle the type of citation prefix you use, try setting the fill prefix explicitly. See Section 21.5 [Filling], page 203.

26.4.4 Mail Mode Miscellany

C-c C-t   Move to the beginning of the message body text (mail-text).

C-c C-w   Insert the file '~/.signature' at the end of the message text (mail-signature).

C-c C-i file (RET)
           Insert the contents of file at the end of the outgoing message (mail-attach-file).

M-x ispell-message
           Do spelling correction on the message text, but not on citations from other messages.

C-c C-t (mail-text) moves point to just after the header separator line—that is, to the beginning of the message body text.

C-c C-w (mail-signature) adds a standard piece of text at the end of the message to say more about who you are. The text comes from the file '~/.signature' in your home directory. To insert your signature automatically, set the variable mail-signature to t; then starting a mail message automatically inserts the contents of your '~/.signature' file. If you want to omit your signature from a particular message, delete it from the buffer before you send the message.

You can also set mail-signature to a string; then that string is inserted automatically as your signature when you start editing a message to send. If you set it to some other Lisp expression, the expression is evaluated each time, and its value (which should be a string) specifies the signature.

You can do spelling correction on the message text you have written with the command M-x ispell-message. If you have yanked an incoming message into the outgoing draft, this command skips what was yanked, but it checks the text that you yourself inserted. (It looks for indentation or mail-yank-prefix to distinguish the cited lines from your input.) See Section 13.4 [Spelling], page 103.

To include a file in the outgoing message, you can use C-x i, the usual command to insert a file in the current buffer. But it is often more convenient to use a special command, C-c C-i (mail-attach-file). This command inserts the file contents at the end of the buffer, after your signature if any, with a delimiter line that includes the file name.

Turning on Mail mode (which C-x m does automatically) runs the normal hooks text-mode-hook and mail-mode-hook. Initializing a new outgoing message runs the normal hook mail-setup-hook; if you want to add special fields to your mail header or make other changes to the appearance of the mail buffer, use that hook. See Section 31.2.3 [Hooks], page 400.

The main difference between these hooks is just when they are invoked. Whenever you type M-x mail, mail-mode-hook runs as soon as the '*mail*' buffer is created. Then the mail-setup function puts in the default contents of the buffer. After these default contents are inserted, mail-setup-hook runs.

26.5 Distracting the NSA

M-x spook adds a line of randomly chosen keywords to an outgoing mail message. The keywords are chosen from a list of words that suggest you are discussing something subversive.

The idea behind this feature is the suspicion that the NSA snoops on all electronic mail messages that contain keywords suggesting they might find them interesting. (The NSA says they don't, but that's what they *would* say.) The idea is that if lots of people add suspicious words to their messages, the NSA will get so busy with spurious input that they will have to give up reading it all.

Here's how to insert spook keywords automatically whenever you start entering an outgoing message:

```
(add-hook 'mail-setup-hook 'spook)
```

Whether or not this confuses the NSA, it at least amuses people.

26.6 Mail-Composition Methods

This chapter describes the usual Emacs mode for editing and sending mail—Mail mode. Emacs has alternative facilities for editing and sending mail, including MH-E and Message mode, not documented in this manual. You can choose any of them as your preferred method. The commands C-x m, C-x 4 m and C-x 5 m use whichever agent you have specified. So do various other Emacs commands and facilities that send mail.

To specify your mail-composition method, set the variable `mail-user-agent`. Currently legitimate values include `sendmail-user-agent`, `mh-e-user-agent`, and `message-user-agent`.

If you select a different mail-composition method, the information in this chapter about the '`*mail*`' buffer and Mail mode does not apply; other methods may use completely different commands with a different format in a differently named buffer.

27 Reading Mail with Rmail

Rmail is an Emacs subsystem for reading and disposing of mail that you receive. Rmail stores mail messages in files called Rmail files. Reading the message in an Rmail file is done in a special major mode, Rmail mode, which redefines most letters to run commands for managing mail. The command `rmail-mode` is used to switch into Rmail mode, and it runs the hook `rmail-mode-hook` as usual, but don't run this command by hand; it can't do a reasonable job unless the buffer is visiting a proper Rmail file.

27.1 Basic Concepts of Rmail

Using Rmail in the simplest fashion, you have one Rmail file '`~/RMAIL`' in which all of your mail is saved. It is called your *primary Rmail file*. The command `M-x rmail` reads your primary Rmail file, merges new mail in from your inboxes, displays the first message you haven't read yet, and lets you begin reading. The variable `rmail-file-name` specifies the name of the primary Rmail file.

Rmail uses narrowing to hide all but one message in the Rmail file. The message that is shown is called the *current message*. Rmail mode's special commands can do such things as delete the current message, copy it into another file, send a reply, or move to another message. You can also create multiple Rmail files and use Rmail to move messages between them.

Within the Rmail file, messages are normally arranged sequentially in order of receipt; you can specify other ways to sort them. Messages are assigned consecutive integers as their *message numbers*. The number of the current message is displayed in Rmail's mode line, followed by the total number of messages in the file. You can move to a message by specifying its message number with the j key (see Section 27.3 [Rmail Motion], page 312).

Following the usual conventions of Emacs, changes in an Rmail file become permanent only when the file is saved. You can save it with s (`rmail-save`), which also expunges deleted messages from the file first (see Section 27.4 [Rmail Deletion], page 313). To save the file without expunging, use `C-x C-s`. Rmail also saves the Rmail file after merging new mail from an inbox file (see Section 27.5 [Rmail Inbox], page 314).

You can exit Rmail with q (`rmail-quit`); this expunges and saves the Rmail file and then switches to another buffer. But there is no need to 'exit' formally. If you switch from Rmail to editing in other buffers, and never happen to switch back, you have exited. (The Rmail command b, `rmail-bury`, does this for you.) Just make sure to save the Rmail file eventually (like any other file you have changed). `C-x s` is a good enough way to do this (see Section 14.3 [Saving], page 111).

27.2 Scrolling Within a Message

When Rmail displays a message that does not fit on the screen, you must scroll through it to read the rest. You could do this with C-v, M-v and M-<, but in Rmail scrolling is so frequent that it deserves to be easier to type.

(SPC)   Scroll forward (`scroll-up`).

(DEL)   Scroll backward (`scroll-down`).

.   Scroll to start of message (`rmail-beginning-of-message`).

Since the most common thing to do while reading a message is to scroll through it by screenfuls, Rmail makes (SPC) and (DEL) synonyms of C-v (`scroll-up`) and M-v (`scroll-down`)

The command . (`rmail-beginning-of-message`) scrolls back to the beginning of the selected message. This is not quite the same as M-<: for one thing, it does not set the mark; for another, it resets the buffer boundaries to the current message if you have changed them.

27.3 Moving Among Messages

The most basic thing to do with a message is to read it. The way to do this in Rmail is to make the message current. The usual practice is to move sequentially through the file, since this is the order of receipt of messages. When you enter Rmail, you are positioned at the first message that you have not yet made current (that is, the first one that has the 'unseen' attribute; see Section 27.9 [Rmail Attributes], page 319). Move forward to see the other new messages; move backward to reexamine old messages.

n   Move to the next nondeleted message, skipping any intervening deleted messages (`rmail-next-undeleted-message`).

p   Move to the previous nondeleted message (`rmail-previous-undeleted-message`).

M-n   Move to the next message, including deleted messages (`rmail-next-message`).

M-p   Move to the previous message, including deleted messages (`rmail-previous-message`).

j   Move to the first message. With argument n, move to message number n (`rmail-show-message`).

>   Move to the last message (`rmail-last-message`).

<   Move to the first message (`rmail-first-message`).

M-s regexp (RET)
            Move to the next message containing a match for regexp (`rmail-search`).

- M-s *regexp* (RET)

  Move to the previous message containing a match for *regexp*.

  n and p are the usual way of moving among messages in Rmail. They move through the messages sequentially, but skip over deleted messages, which is usually what you want to do. Their command definitions are named `rmail-next-undeleted-message` and `rmail-previous-undeleted-message`. If you do not want to skip deleted messages—for example, if you want to move to a message to undelete it—use the variants M-n and M-p (`rmail-next-message` and `rmail-previous-message`). A numeric argument to any of these commands serves as a repeat count.

  In Rmail, you can specify a numeric argument by typing just the digits. You don't need to type C-u first.

  The M-s (`rmail-search`) command is Rmail's version of search. The usual incremental search command C-s works in Rmail, but it searches only within the current message. The purpose of M-s is to search for another message. It reads a regular expression (see Section 12.5 [Regexps], page 90) nonincrementally, then searches starting at the beginning of the following message for a match. It then selects that message. If *regexp* is empty, M-s reuses the regexp used the previous time.

  To search backward in the file for another message, give M-s a negative argument. In Rmail you can do this with - M-s.

  It is also possible to search for a message based on labels. See Section 27.8 [Rmail Labels], page 318.

  To move to a message specified by absolute message number, use j (`rmail-show-message`) with the message number as argument. With no argument, j selects the first message. < (`rmail-first-message`) also selects the first message. > (`rmail-last-message`) selects the last message.

27.4 Deleting Messages

  When you no longer need to keep a message, you can *delete* it. This flags it as ignorable, and some Rmail commands pretend it is no longer present; but it still has its place in the Rmail file, and still has its message number.

  Expunging the Rmail file actually removes the deleted messages. The remaining messages are renumbered consecutively. Expunging is the only action that changes the message number of any message, except for undigestifying (see Section 27.15 [Rmail Digest], page 326).

d   Delete the current message, and move to the next nondeleted
     message (`rmail-delete-forward`).

C-d   Delete the current message, and move to the previous nondeleted
     message (`rmail-delete-backward`).

u   Undelete the current message, or move back to a deleted message
     and undelete it (`rmail-undelete-previous-message`).

x   Expunge the Rmail file (`rmail-expunge`).

There are two Rmail commands for deleting messages. Both delete the current message and select another message. d (`rmail-delete-forward`) moves to the following message, skipping messages already deleted, while C-d (`rmail-delete-backward`) moves to the previous nondeleted message. If there is no nondeleted message to move to in the specified direction, the message that was just deleted remains current. A numeric argument to either command reverses the direction of motion after deletion.

Whenever Rmail deletes a message, it invokes the function(s) listed in `rmail-delete-message-hook`. When the hook functions are invoked, the message has been marked deleted, but it is still the current message in the Rmail buffer.

To make all the deleted messages finally vanish from the Rmail file, type x (`rmail-expunge`). Until you do this, you can still *undelete* the deleted messages. The undeletion command, u (`rmail-undelete-previous-message`), is designed to cancel the effect of a d command in most cases. It undeletes the current message if the current message is deleted. Otherwise it moves backward to previous messages until a deleted message is found, and undeletes that message.

You can usually undo a d with a u because the u moves back to and undeletes the message that the d deleted. But this does not work when the d skips a few already-deleted messages that follow the message being deleted; then the u command undeletes the last of the messages that were skipped. There is no clean way to avoid this problem. However, by repeating the u command, you can eventually get back to the message that you intend to undelete. You can also select a particular deleted message with the M-p command, then type u to undelete it.

A deleted message has the '`deleted`' attribute, and as a result '`deleted`' appears in the mode line when the current message is deleted. In fact, deleting or undeleting a message is nothing more than adding or removing this attribute. See Section 27.9 [Rmail Attributes], page 319.

27.5 Rmail Files and Inboxes

The operating system places incoming mail for you in a file that we call your *inbox*. When you start up Rmail, it runs a C program called `movemail` to copy the new messages from your inbox into your primary Rmail file, which also contains other messages saved from previous Rmail sessions. It is in this file that you actually read the mail with Rmail. This operation is called *getting new mail*. You can get new mail at any time in Rmail by typing g.

The variable `rmail-primary-inbox-list` contains a list of the files which are inboxes for your primary Rmail file. If you don't set this variable explicitly, it is initialized from the `MAIL` environment variable, or, as a last resort, set to `nil`, which means to use the default inbox. The default inbox is '`/var/mail/`*username*', '`/usr/spool/mail/`*username*', or '`/usr/mail/`*username*', depending on your operating system.

To see what the default is on your system, use `C-h v rmail-primary-inbox` (RET). You can specify the inbox file(s) for any Rmail file with the command `set-rmail-inbox-list`; see Section 27.6 [Rmail Files], page 315.

There are two reasons for having separate Rmail files and inboxes.

1. The inbox file format varies between operating systems and according to the other mail software in use. Only one part of Rmail needs to know about the alternatives, and it need only understand how to convert all of them to Rmail's own format.

2. It is very cumbersome to access an inbox file without danger of losing mail, because it is necessary to interlock with mail delivery. Moreover, different operating systems use different interlocking techniques. The strategy of moving mail out of the inbox once and for all into a separate Rmail file avoids the need for interlocking in all the rest of Rmail, since only Rmail operates on the Rmail file.

Rmail was written to use Babyl format as its internal format. Since then, we have recognized that the usual inbox format on Unix and GNU systems is adequate for the job, and we plan to change Rmail to use that as its internal format. However, the Rmail file will still be separate from the inbox file, even on systems where their format is the same.

27.6 Multiple Rmail Files

Rmail operates by default on your *primary Rmail file*, which is named '`~/RMAIL`' and receives your incoming mail from your system inbox file. But you can also have other Rmail files and edit them with Rmail. These files can receive mail through their own inboxes, or you can move messages into them with explicit Rmail commands (see Section 27.7 [Rmail Output], page 316).

`i` *file* (RET)
> Read *file* into Emacs and run Rmail on it (`rmail-input`).

`M-x set-rmail-inbox-list` (RET) *files* (RET)
> Specify inbox file names for current Rmail file to get mail from.

`g`
> Merge new mail from current Rmail file's inboxes (`rmail-get-new-mail`).

`C-u g` *file* (RET)
> Merge new mail from inbox file *file*.

To run Rmail on a file other than your primary Rmail file, you may use the `i` (`rmail-input`) command in Rmail. This visits the file in Rmail mode. You can use `M-x rmail-input` even when not in Rmail.

The file you read with i should normally be a valid Rmail file. If it is not, Rmail tries to decompose it into a stream of messages in various known formats. If it succeeds, it converts the whole file to an Rmail file. If you specify a file name that doesn't exist, i initializes a new buffer for creating a new Rmail file.

You can also select an Rmail file from a menu. Choose first the menu bar Classify item, then from the Classify menu choose the Input Rmail File item; then choose the Rmail file you want. The variables `rmail-secondary-file-directory` and `rmail-secondary-file-regexp` specify which files to offer in the menu: the first variable says which directory to find them in; the second says which files in that directory to offer (all those that match the regular expression). These variables also apply to choosing a file for output (see Section 27.7 [Rmail Output], page 316).

Each Rmail file can contain a list of inbox file names; you can specify this list with `M-x set-rmail-inbox-list` (RET) *files* (RET). The argument can contain any number of file names, separated by commas. It can also be empty, which specifies that this file should have no inboxes. Once a list of inboxes is specified, the Rmail file remembers it permanently until you specify a different list.

As a special exception, if your primary Rmail file does not specify any inbox files, it uses your standard system inbox.

The g command (`rmail-get-new-mail`) merges mail into the current Rmail file from its specified inboxes. If the Rmail file has no inboxes, g does nothing. The command `M-x rmail` also merges new mail into your primary Rmail file.

To merge mail from a file that is not the usual inbox, give the g key a numeric argument, as in `C-u g`. Then it reads a file name and merges mail from that file. The inbox file is not deleted or changed in any way when g with an argument is used. This is, therefore, a general way of merging one file of messages into another.

27.7 Copying Messages Out to Files

These commands copy messages from an Rmail file into another file.

o *file* (RET)
> Append a copy of the current message to the file *file*, using Rmail file format by default (`rmail-output-to-rmail-file`).

C-o *file* (RET)
> Append a copy of the current message to the file *file*, using system inbox file format by default (`rmail-output`).

w *file* (RET)
> Output just the message body to the file *file*, taking the default file name from the message 'Subject' header.

The commands o and C-o copy the current message into a specified file. This file may be an Rmail file or it may be in system inbox format; the output commands ascertain the file's format and write the copied message in that format.

When copying a message to a file in Unix mail file format, these commands include whichever header fields are currently visible. Use the t command first, if you wish, to specify which headers to show (and copy).

The o and C-o commands differ in two ways: each has its own separate default file name, and each specifies a choice of format to use when the file does not already exist. The o command uses Rmail format when it creates a new file, while C-o uses system inbox format for a new file. The default file name for o is the file name used last with o, and the default file name for C-o is the file name used last with C-o.

If the output file is an Rmail file currently visited in an Emacs buffer, the output commands copy the message into that buffer. It is up to you to save the buffer eventually in its file.

Sometimes you may receive a message whose body holds the contents of a file. You can save the body to a file (excluding the message header) with the w command (`rmail-output-body-to-file`). Often these messages contain the intended file name in the 'Subject' field, so the w command uses the 'Subject' field as the default for the output file name. However, the file name is read using the minibuffer, so you can specify a different name if you wish.

You can also output a message to an Rmail file chosen with a menu. Choose first the menu bar Classify item, then from the Classify menu choose the Output Rmail File menu item; then choose the Rmail file you want. This outputs the current message to that file, like the o command. The variables `rmail-secondary-file-directory` and `rmail-secondary-file-regexp` specify which files to offer in the menu: the first variable says which directory to find them in; the second says which files in that directory to offer (all those that match the regular expression).

Copying a message gives the original copy of the message the 'filed' attribute, so that 'filed' appears in the mode line when such a message is current. If you like to keep just a single copy of every mail message, set the variable `rmail-delete-after-output` to t; then the o and C-o commands delete the original message after copying it. (You can undelete the original afterward if you wish.)

Copying messages into files in system inbox format uses the header fields that are displayed in Rmail at the time. Thus, if you use the t command to view the entire header and then copy the message, the entire header is copied. See Section 27.13 [Rmail Display], page 324.

The variable `rmail-output-file-alist` lets you specify intelligent defaults for the output file, based on the contents of the current message. The value should be a list whose elements have this form:

(*regexp* . *name-exp*)

If there's a match for *regexp* in the current message, then the default file name for output is *name-exp*. If multiple elements match the message, the first matching element decides the default file name. The subexpression *name-exp* may be a string constant giving the file name to use, or more generally it may be any Lisp expression that returns a file name as a string. `rmail-output-file-alist` applies to both o and C-o.

27.8 Labels

Each message can have various *labels* assigned to it as a means of classification. Each label has a name; different names are different labels. Any given label is either present or absent on a particular message. A few label names have standard meanings and are given to messages automatically by Rmail when appropriate; these special labels are called *attributes*. All other labels are assigned only by users.

a *label* (RET)
> Assign the label *label* to the current message (**rmail-add-label**).

k *label* (RET)
> Remove the label *label* from the current message (**rmail-kill-label**).

C-M-n *labels* (RET)
> Move to the next message that has one of the labels *labels* (**rmail-next-labeled-message**).

C-M-p *labels* (RET)
> Move to the previous message that has one of the labels *labels* (**rmail-previous-labeled-message**).

C-M-l *labels* (RET)
> Make a summary of all messages containing any of the labels *labels* (**rmail-summary-by-labels**).

The a (**rmail-add-label**) and k (**rmail-kill-label**) commands allow you to assign or remove any label on the current message. If the *label* argument is empty, it means to assign or remove the same label most recently assigned or removed.

Once you have given messages labels to classify them as you wish, there are two ways to use the labels: in moving and in summaries.

The command C-M-n *labels* (RET) (**rmail-next-labeled-message**) moves to the next message that has one of the labels *labels*. The argument *labels* specifies one or more label names, separated by commas. C-M-p (**rmail-previous-labeled-message**) is similar, but moves backwards to previous messages. A numeric argument to either command serves as a repeat count.

The command C-M-l *labels* (RET) (`rmail-summary-by-labels`) displays a summary containing only the messages that have at least one of a specified set of labels. The argument *labels* is one or more label names, separated by commas. See Section 27.11 [Rmail Summary], page 322, for information on summaries.

If the *labels* argument to C-M-n, C-M-p or C-M-l is empty, it means to use the last set of labels specified for any of these commands.

27.9 Rmail Attributes

Some labels such as '`deleted`' and '`filed`' have built-in meanings and are assigned to or removed from messages automatically at appropriate times; these labels are called *attributes*. Here is a list of Rmail attributes:

'`unseen`'   Means the message has never been current. Assigned to messages when they come from an inbox file, and removed when a message is made current. When you start Rmail, it initially shows the first message that has this attribute.

'`deleted`'   Means the message is deleted. Assigned by deletion commands and removed by undeletion commands (see Section 27.4 [Rmail Deletion], page 313).

'`filed`'   Means the message has been copied to some other file. Assigned by the file output commands (see Section 27.6 [Rmail Files], page 315).

'`answered`'
         Means you have mailed an answer to the message. Assigned by the `r` command (`rmail-reply`). See Section 27.10 [Rmail Reply], page 320.

'`forwarded`'
         Means you have forwarded the message. Assigned by the `f` command (`rmail-forward`). See Section 27.10 [Rmail Reply], page 320.

'`edited`'   Means you have edited the text of the message within Rmail. See Section 27.14 [Rmail Editing], page 325.

'`resent`'   Means you have resent the message. Assigned by the command `M-x rmail-resend`. See Section 27.10 [Rmail Reply], page 320.

All other labels are assigned or removed only by the user, and have no standard meaning.

27.10 Sending Replies

Rmail has several commands that use Mail mode to send outgoing mail. See Chapter 26 [Sending Mail], page 301, for information on using Mail mode, including certain features meant to work with Rmail. What this section documents are the special commands of Rmail for entering Mail mode. Note that the usual keys for sending mail—C-x m, C-x 4 m, and C-x 5 m—are available in Rmail mode and work just as they usually do.

m   Send a message (`rmail-mail`).

c   Continue editing the already started outgoing message (`rmail-continue`).

r   Send a reply to the current Rmail message (`rmail-reply`).

f   Forward the current message to other users (`rmail-forward`).

C-u f   Resend the current message to other users (`rmail-resend`).

M-m   Try sending a bounced message a second time (`rmail-retry-failure`).

The most common reason to send a message while in Rmail is to reply to the message you are reading. To do this, type r (`rmail-reply`). This displays the '*mail*' buffer in another window, much like C-x 4 m, but preinitializes the 'Subject', 'To', 'CC' and 'In-reply-to' header fields based on the message you are replying to. The 'To' field starts out as the address of the person who sent the message you received, and the 'CC' field starts out with all the other recipients of that message.

You can exclude certain recipients from being placed automatically in the 'CC', using the variable `rmail-dont-reply-to-names`. Its value should be a regular expression (as a string); any recipient that the regular expression matches, is excluded from the 'CC' field. The default value matches your own name, and any name starting with 'info-'. (Those names are excluded because there is a convention of using them for large mailing lists to broadcast announcements.)

To omit the 'CC' field completely for a particular reply, enter the reply command with a numeric argument: C-u r or 1 r.

Once the '*mail*' buffer has been initialized, editing and sending the mail goes as usual (see Chapter 26 [Sending Mail], page 301). You can edit the presupplied header fields if they are not right for you. You can also use the commands of Mail mode (see Section 26.4 [Mail Mode], page 305), including C-c C-y which yanks in the message that you are replying to. You can switch to the Rmail buffer, select a different message there, switch back, and yank the new current message.

Sometimes a message does not reach its destination. Mailers usually send the failed message back to you, enclosed in a *failure message*. The Rmail command M-m (`rmail-retry-failure`) prepares to send the same message a second time: it sets up a '*mail*' buffer with the same text and header fields as before. If you type C-c C-c right away, you send the message again exactly the same as the first time. Alternatively, you can edit the text or headers and then send it. The variable `rmail-retry-ignored-headers`, in the same format as `rmail-ignored-headers` (see Section 27.13 [Rmail Display], page 324), controls which headers are stripped from the failed message when retrying it; it defaults to `nil`.

Another frequent reason to send mail in Rmail is to *forward* the current message to other users. f (`rmail-forward`) makes this easy by preinitializing the '*mail*' buffer with the current message as the text, and a subject designating a forwarded message. All you have to do is fill in the recipients and send. When you forward a message, recipients get a message which is "from" you, and which has the original message in its contents.

Forwarding a message encloses it between two delimiter lines. It also modifies every line that starts with a dash, by inserting '- ' at the start of the line. When you receive a forwarded message, if it contains something besides ordinary text—for example, program source code—you might find it useful to undo that transformation. You can do this by selecting the forwarded message and typing M-x unforward-rmail-message. This command extracts the original forwarded message, deleting the inserted '- ' strings, and inserts it into the Rmail file as a separate message immediately following the current one.

Resending is an alternative similar to forwarding; the difference is that re-sending sends a message that is "from" the original sender, just as it reached you—with a few added header fields 'Resent-from' and 'Resent-to' to in-dicate that it came via you. To resend a message in Rmail, use C-u f. (f runs `rmail-forward`, which is programmed to invoke `rmail-resend` if you provide a numeric argument.)

The m (`rmail-mail`) command is used to start editing an outgoing mes-sage that is not a reply. It leaves the header fields empty. Its only difference from C-x 4 m is that it makes the Rmail buffer accessible for C-c C-y, just as r does. Thus, m can be used to reply to or forward a message; it can do anything r or f can do.

The c (`rmail-continue`) command resumes editing the '*mail*' buffer, to finish editing an outgoing message you were already composing, or to alter a message you have sent.

If you set the variable `rmail-mail-new-frame` to a non-nil value, then all the Rmail commands to start sending a message create a new frame to edit it in. This frame is deleted when you send the message, or when you use the 'Don't Send' item in the 'Mail' menu.

All the Rmail commands to send a message use the mail-composition method that you have chosen (see Section 26.6 [Mail Methods], page 309).

27.11 Summaries

A *summary* is a buffer containing one line per message to give you an overview of the mail in an Rmail file. Each line shows the message number, the sender, the labels, and the subject. Almost all Rmail commands are valid in the summary buffer also; these apply to the message described by the current line of the summary. Moving point in the summary buffer selects messages as you move to their summary lines.

A summary buffer applies to a single Rmail file only; if you are editing multiple Rmail files, each one can have its own summary buffer. The summary buffer name is made by appending '-summary' to the Rmail buffer's name. Normally only one summary buffer is displayed at a time.

27.11.1 Making Summaries

Here are the commands to create a summary for the current Rmail file. Once the Rmail file has a summary buffer, changes in the Rmail file (such as deleting or expunging messages, and getting new mail) automatically update the summary.

h
C-M-h   Summarize all messages (`rmail-summary`).

l *labels* (RET)
C-M-l *labels* (RET)
            Summarize messages that have one or more of the specified labels
            (`rmail-summary-by-labels`).

C-M-r *rcpts* (RET)
            Summarize messages that have one or more of the specified re-
            cipients (`rmail-summary-by-recipients`).

C-M-t *topic* (RET)
            Summarize messages that have a match for the specified regexp
            topic in their subjects (`rmail-summary-by-topic`).

The `h` or `C-M-h` (`rmail-summary`) command fills the summary buffer for the current Rmail file with a summary of all the messages in the file. It then displays and selects the summary buffer in another window.

`C-M-l` *labels* (RET) (`rmail-summary-by-labels`) makes a partial summary mentioning only the messages that have one or more of the labels *labels*. *labels* should contain label names separated by commas.

`C-M-r` *rcpts* (RET) (`rmail-summary-by-recipients`) makes a partial summary mentioning only the messages that have one or more of the recipients *rcpts*. *rcpts* should contain mailing addresses separated by commas.

`C-M-t` *topic* (RET) (`rmail-summary-by-topic`) makes a partial summary mentioning only the messages whose subjects have a match for the regular expression *topic*.

Note that there is only one summary buffer for any Rmail file; making one kind of summary discards any previously made summary.

The variable `rmail-summary-window-size` says how many lines to use for the summary window. The variable `rmail-summary-line-count-flag` controls whether the summary line for a message should include the line count of the message.

27.11.2 Editing in Summaries

You can use the Rmail summary buffer to do almost anything you can do in the Rmail buffer itself. In fact, once you have a summary buffer, there's no need to switch back to the Rmail buffer.

You can select and display various messages in the Rmail buffer, from the summary buffer, just by moving point in the summary buffer to different lines. It doesn't matter what Emacs command you use to move point; whichever line point is on at the end of the command, that message is selected in the Rmail buffer.

Almost all Rmail commands work in the summary buffer as well as in the Rmail buffer. Thus, d in the summary buffer deletes the current message, u undeletes, and x expunges. o and C-o output the current message to a file; r starts a reply to it. You can scroll the current message while remaining in the summary buffer using (SPC) and (DEL).

The Rmail commands to move between messages also work in the summary buffer, but with a twist: they move through the set of messages included in the summary. They also ensure the Rmail buffer appears on the screen (unlike cursor motion commands, which update the contents of the Rmail buffer but don't display it in a window unless it already appears). Here is a list of these commands:

n   Move to next line, skipping lines saying 'deleted', and select its
            message.

p   Move to previous line, skipping lines saying 'deleted', and select
            its message.

M-n   Move to next line and select its message.

M-p   Move to previous line and select its message.

>   Move to the last line, and select its message.

<   Move to the first line, and select its message.

M-s *pattern* (RET)
            Search through messages for *pattern* starting with the current
            message; select the message found, and move point in the sum-
            mary buffer to that message's line.

Deletion, undeletion, and getting new mail, and even selection of a different message all update the summary buffer when you do them in the Rmail

buffer. If the variable `rmail-redisplay-summary` is non-`nil`, these actions also bring the summary buffer back onto the screen.

When you are finished using the summary, type Q (`rmail-summary-wipe`) to delete the summary buffer's window. You can also exit Rmail while in the summary: q (`rmail-summary-quit`) deletes the summary window, then exits from Rmail by saving the Rmail file and switching to another buffer.

27.12 Sorting the Rmail File

`M-x rmail-sort-by-date`
> Sort messages of current Rmail file by date.

`M-x rmail-sort-by-subject`
> Sort messages of current Rmail file by subject.

`M-x rmail-sort-by-author`
> Sort messages of current Rmail file by author's name.

`M-x rmail-sort-by-recipient`
> Sort messages of current Rmail file by recipient's names.

`M-x rmail-sort-by-correspondent`
> Sort messages of current Rmail file by the name of the other correspondent.

`M-x rmail-sort-by-lines`
> Sort messages of current Rmail file by size (number of lines).

`M-x rmail-sort-by-keywords` (RET) *labels* (RET)
> Sort messages of current Rmail file by labels. The argument *labels* should be a comma-separated list of labels. The order of these labels specifies the order of messages; messages with the first label come first, messages with the second label come second, and so on. Messages which have none of these labels come last.

The Rmail sort commands perform a *stable sort*: if there is no reason to prefer either one of two messages, their order remains unchanged. You can use this to sort by more than one criterion. For example, if you use `rmail-sort-by-date` and then `rmail-sort-by-author`, messages from the same author appear in order by date.

With a numeric argument, all these commands reverse the order of comparison. This means they sort messages from newest to oldest, from biggest to smallest, or in reverse alphabetical order.

27.13 Display of Messages

Rmail reformats the header of each message before displaying it for the first time. Reformatting hides uninteresting header fields to reduce clutter.

You can use the t command to show the entire header or to repeat the header reformatting operation.

t   Toggle display of complete header (`rmail-toggle-header`).

Reformatting the header involves deleting most header fields, on the grounds that they are not interesting. The variable `rmail-ignored-headers` holds a regular expression that specifies which header fields to hide in this way—if it matches the beginning of a header field, that whole field is hidden.

Rmail saves the complete original header before reformatting; to see it, use the t command (`rmail-toggle-header`). This discards the reformatted headers of the current message and displays it with the original header. Repeating t reformats the message again. Selecting the message again also reformats.

One consequence of this is that if you edit the reformatted header (using e; see Section 27.14 [Rmail Editing], page 325), subsequent use of t will discard your edits. On the other hand, if you use e after t, to edit the original (unreformatted) header, those changes are permanent.

When the t command has a prefix argument, a positive argument means to show the reformatted header, and a zero or negative argument means to show the full header.

When used with a window system that supports multiple fonts, Rmail highlights certain header fields that are especially interesting—by default, the 'From' and 'Subject' fields. The variable `rmail-highlighted-headers` holds a regular expression that specifies the header fields to highlight; if it matches the beginning of a header field, that whole field is highlighted.

If you specify unusual colors for your text foreground and background, the colors used for highlighting may not go well with them. If so, specify different colors for the `highlight` face. That is worth doing because the `highlight` face is used for other kinds of highlighting as well. See Section 17.13 [Faces], page 166, for how to do this.

To turn off highlighting entirely in Rmail, set `rmail-highlighted-headers` to `nil`.

27.14 Editing Within a Message

Most of the usual Emacs commands are available in Rmail mode, though a few, such as `C-M-n` and `C-M-h`, are redefined by Rmail for other purposes. However, the Rmail buffer is normally read only, and most of the letters are redefined as Rmail commands. If you want to edit the text of a message, you must use the Rmail command e.

e   Edit the current message as ordinary text.

The e command (`rmail-edit-current-message`) switches from Rmail mode into Rmail Edit mode, another major mode which is nearly the same as Text mode. The mode line indicates this change.

In Rmail Edit mode, letters insert themselves as usual and the Rmail commands are not available. When you are finished editing the message and are ready to go back to Rmail, type C-c C-c, which switches back to Rmail mode. Alternatively, you can return to Rmail mode but cancel all the editing that you have done, by typing C-c C-].

Entering Rmail Edit mode runs the hook `text-mode-hook`; then it runs the hook `rmail-edit-mode-hook` (see Section 31.2.3 [Hooks], page 400). It adds the attribute 'edited' to the message. It also displays the full headers of the message, so that you can edit the headers as well as the body of the message, and your changes in the the headers will be permanent.

27.15 Digest Messages

A *digest message* is a message which exists to contain and carry several other messages. Digests are used on some moderated mailing lists; all the messages that arrive for the list during a period of time such as one day are put inside a single digest which is then sent to the subscribers. Transmitting the single digest uses much less computer time than transmitting the individual messages even though the total size is the same, because the per-message overhead in network mail transmission is considerable.

When you receive a digest message, the most convenient way to read it is to *undigestify* it: to turn it back into many individual messages. Then you can read and delete the individual messages as it suits you.

To do this, select the digest message and type the command M-x `undigestify-rmail-message`. This extracts the submessages as separate Rmail messages, and inserts them following the digest. The digest message itself is flagged as deleted.

27.16 Converting an Rmail File to Inbox Format

The command M-x `unrmail` converts a file in Rmail format to inbox format (also known as the system mailbox format), so that you can use it with other mail-editing tools. You must specify two arguments, the name of the Rmail file and the name to use for the converted file. M-x `unrmail` does not alter the Rmail file itself.

27.17 Reading Rot13 Messages

Mailing list messages that might offend some readers are sometimes encoded in a simple code called *rot13*—so named because it rotates the alphabet by 13 letters. This code is not for secrecy, as it provides none; rather, it enables those who might be offended to avoid ever seeing the real text of the message.

To view a buffer using the rot13 code, use the command M-x
rot13-other-window. This displays the current buffer in another window
which applies the code when displaying the text.

27.18 movemail and POP

When getting new mail, Rmail first copies the new mail from the inbox
file to the Rmail file; then it saves the Rmail file; then it truncates the inbox
file. This way, a system crash may cause duplication of mail between the
inbox and the Rmail file, but cannot lose mail. If rmail-preserve-inbox is
non-nil, then Rmail will copy new mail from the inbox file to the Rmail file
without truncating the inbox file. You may wish to set this, for example, on
a portable computer you use to check your mail via POP while traveling, so
that your mail will remain on the server and you can save it later on your
workstation.

In some cases, Rmail copies the new mail from the inbox file indirectly.
First it runs the movemail program to move the mail from the inbox to
an intermediate file called '~/.newmail-*inboxname*'. Then Rmail merges
the new mail from that file, saves the Rmail file, and only then deletes the
intermediate file. If there is a crash at the wrong time, this file continues to
exist, and Rmail will use it again the next time it gets new mail from that
inbox.

If Rmail is unable to convert the data in '~/.newmail-*inboxname*' into
Babyl format, it renames the file to '~/RMAILOSE.*n*' (*n* is an integer chosen
to make the name unique) so that Rmail will not have trouble with the
data again. You should look at the file, find whatever message confuses
Rmail (probably one that includes the control-underscore character, octal
code 037), and delete it. Then you can use 1 g to get new mail from the
corrected file.

Some sites use a method called POP for accessing users' inbox data instead of storing the data in inbox files. movemail can work with POP if you
compile it with the macro MAIL_USE_POP defined. (You can achieve that by
specifying '--with-pop' when you run configure during the installation of
Emacs.) movemail only works with POP3, not with older versions of POP.

Assuming you have compiled and installed movemail appropriately, you
can specify a POP inbox by using a "file name" of the form 'po:*username*', in
the inbox list of an Rmail file. movemail handles such a name by opening a
connection to the POP server. The MAILHOST environment variable specifies
the machine to look for the server on.

Accessing mail via POP may require a password. If the variable rmail-
pop-password is non-nil, it specifies the password to use for POP. Alternatively, if rmail-pop-password-required is non-nil, then Rmail asks you
for the password to use.

If you need to pass additional command-line flags to movemail, set the
variable rmail-movemail-flags a list of the flags you wish to use. Do not

use this variable to pass the '-p' flag to preserve your inbox contents; use `rmail-preserve-inbox` instead.

The `movemail` program installed at your site may support Kerberos authentication. If it is supported, it is used by default whenever you attempt to retrieve POP mail when `rmail-pop-password` and `rmail-pop-password-required` are unset.

Some POP servers store messages in reverse order. If your server does this, and you would rather read your mail in the order in which it was received, you can tell `movemail` to reverse the order of downloaded messages by adding the '-r' flag to `rmail-movemail-flags`.

28 Dired, the Directory Editor

Dired makes an Emacs buffer containing a listing of a directory, and optionally some of its subdirectories as well. You can use the normal Emacs commands to move around in this buffer, and special Dired commands to operate on the files listed.

28.1 Entering Dired

To invoke Dired, do C-x d or M-x dired. The command reads a directory name or wildcard file name pattern as a minibuffer argument to specify which files to list. Where dired differs from list-directory is in putting the buffer into Dired mode so that the special commands of Dired are available.

The variable dired-listing-switches specifies the options to give to ls for listing directory; this string *must* contain '-l'. If you use a numeric prefix argument with the dired command, you can specify the ls switches with the minibuffer before you enter the directory specification.

To display the Dired buffer in another window rather than in the selected window, use C-x 4 d (dired-other-window) instead of C-x d. C-x 5 d (dired-other-frame) uses a separate frame to display the Dired buffer.

28.2 Commands in the Dired Buffer

The Dired buffer is "read-only," and inserting text in it is not useful, so ordinary printing characters such as d and x are used for special Dired commands. Some Dired commands *mark* or *flag* the *current file* (that is, the file on the current line); other commands operate on the marked files or on the flagged files.

All the usual Emacs cursor motion commands are available in Dired buffers. Some special-purpose cursor motion commands are also provided. The keys C-n and C-p are redefined to put the cursor at the beginning of the file name on the line, rather than at the beginning of the line.

For extra convenience, (SPC) and n in Dired are equivalent to C-n. p is equivalent to C-p. (Moving by lines is so common in Dired that it deserves to be easy to type.) (DEL) (move up and unflag) is often useful simply for moving up.

28.3 Deleting Files with Dired

The primary use of Dired is to *flag* files for deletion and then delete the files previously flagged.

d   Flag this file for deletion.

u   Remove deletion flag on this line.

⟨DEL⟩   Move point to previous line and remove the deletion flag on that
               line.

x   Delete the files that are flagged for deletion.

     You can flag a file for deletion by moving to the line describing the file
and typing d (`dired-flag-file-deletion`). The deletion flag is visible as
a 'D' at the beginning of the line. This command moves point to the next
line, so that repeated d commands flag successive files. A numeric argument
serves as a repeat count.

     The files are flagged for deletion rather than deleted immediately to re-
duce the danger of deleting a file accidentally. Until you direct Dired to
expunge the flagged files, you can remove deletion flags using the commands
u and ⟨DEL⟩. u (`dired-unmark`) works just like d, but removes flags rather
than making flags. ⟨DEL⟩ (`dired-unmark-backward`) moves upward, removing flags; it is like u with argument −1.

     To delete the flagged files, type x (`dired-expunge`). This command first
displays a list of all the file names flagged for deletion, and requests confirmation with **yes**. If you confirm, Dired deletes the flagged files, then deletes
their lines from the text of the Dired buffer. The shortened Dired buffer
remains selected.

     If you answer **no** or quit with C-g when asked to confirm, you return
immediately to Dired, with the deletion flags still present in the buffer, and
no files actually deleted.

28.4 Flagging Many Files at Once

Flag all auto-save files (files whose names start and end with '#')
               for deletion (see Section 14.5 [Auto Save], page 117).

~   Flag all backup files (files whose names end with '~') for deletion
               (see Section 14.3.1 [Backup], page 113).

&   Flag for deletion all files with certain kinds of names, names that
               suggest you could easily create the files again.

. (Period)   Flag excess numeric backup files for deletion. The oldest and
               newest few backup files of any one file are exempt; the middle
               ones are flagged.

% d *regexp* ⟨RET⟩
               Flag for deletion all files whose names match the regular expres-
               sion *regexp*.

     The #, ~, &, and . commands flag many files for deletion, based on their
file names. These commands are useful precisely because they do not themselves delete any files; you can remove the deletion flags from any flagged
files that you really wish to keep.

& (`dired-flag-garbage-files`) flags files whose names match the regular expression specified by the variable `dired-garbage-files-regexp`. By default, this matches certain files produced by TEX, and the '.orig' and '.rej' files produced by `patch`.

(`dired-flag-auto-save-files`) flags for deletion all files whose names look like auto-save files (see Section 14.5 [Auto Save], page 117)—that is, files whose names begin and end with '#'. ~ (`dired-flag-backup-files`) flags for deletion all files whose names say they are backup files (see Section 14.3.1 [Backup], page 113)—that is, whose names end in '~'.

. (period, `dired-clean-directory`) flags just some of the backup files for deletion: all but the oldest few and newest few backups of any one file. Normally `dired-kept-versions` (**not** `kept-new-versions`; that applies only when saving) specifies the number of newest versions of each file to keep, and `kept-old-versions` specifies the number of oldest versions to keep.

Period with a positive numeric argument, as in C-u 3 ., specifies the number of newest versions to keep, overriding `dired-kept-versions`. A negative numeric argument overrides `kept-old-versions`, using minus the value of the argument to specify the number of oldest versions of each file to keep.

The % d command flags all files whose names match a specified regular expression (`dired-flag-files-regexp`). Only the non-directory part of the file name is used in matching. You can use '^' and '$' to anchor matches. You can exclude subdirectories by hiding them (see Section 28.13 [Hiding Subdirectories], page 339).

28.5 Visiting Files in Dired

There are several Dired commands for visiting or examining the files listed in the Dired buffer. All of them apply to the current line's file; if that file is really a directory, these commands invoke Dired on that subdirectory (making a separate Dired buffer).

f   Visit the file described on the current line, like typing C-x C-f and supplying that file name (`dired-find-file`). See Section 14.2 [Visiting], page 108.

(RET)   Equivalent to f.

o   Like f, but uses another window to display the file's buffer (`dired-find-file-other-window`). The Dired buffer remains visible in the first window. This is like using C-x 4 C-f to visit the file. See Chapter 16 [Windows], page 151.

C-o   Visit the file described on the current line, and display the buffer in another window, but do not select that window (`dired-display-file`).

Mouse-2	Visit the file named by the line you click on (`dired-mouse-find-file-other-window`). This uses another window to display the file, like the o command.
v	View the file described on the current line, using M x view-file (`dired-view-file`).
	Viewing a file is like visiting it, but is slanted toward moving around in the file conveniently and does not allow changing the file. See Section 14.10 [Misc File Ops], page 139.

28.6 Dired Marks vs. Flags

Instead of flagging a file with 'D', you can *mark* the file with some other character (usually '*'). Most Dired commands to operate on files, aside from "expunge" (x), look for files marked with '*'.

Here are some commands for marking with '*', or for unmarking or operating on marks. (See Section 28.3 [Dired Deletion], page 329, for commands to flag and unflag files.)

m	
* m	Mark the current file with '*' (`dired-mark`). With a numeric argument *n*, mark the next *n* files starting with the current file. (If *n* is negative, mark the previous −*n* files.)
* *	Mark all executable files with '*' (`dired-mark-executables`). With a numeric argument, unmark all those files.
* @	Mark all symbolic links with '*' (`dired-mark-symlinks`). With a numeric argument, unmark all those files.
* /	Mark with '*' all files which are actually directories, except for '.' and '..' (`dired-mark-directories`). With a numeric argument, unmark all those files.
* s	Mark all the files in the current subdirectory, aside from '.' and '..' (`dired-mark-subdir-files`).
u	
* u	Remove any mark on this line (`dired-unmark`).
(DEL)	
* (DEL)	Move point to previous line and remove any mark on that line (`dired-unmark-backward`).
* !	Remove all marks from all the files in this Dired buffer (`dired-unmark-all-files-no-query`).
* ? *markchar*	Remove all marks that use the character *markchar* (`dired-unmark-all-files`). The argument is a single character—do not use (RET) to terminate it.

With a numeric argument, this command queries about each marked file, asking whether to remove its mark. You can answer y meaning yes, n meaning no, or ! to remove the marks from the remaining files without asking about them.

* C-n   Move down to the next marked file (`dired-next-marked-file`) A file is "marked" if it has any kind of mark.

* C-p   Move up to the previous marked file (`dired-prev-marked-file`)

* t   Toggle all marks (`dired-do-toggle`): files marked with '*' become unmarked, and unmarked files are marked with '*'. Files marked in any other way are not affected.

* c *old* *new*

Replace all marks that use the character *old* with marks that use the character *new* (`dired-change-marks`). This command is the primary way to create or use marks other than '*' or 'D'. The arguments are single characters—do not use (RET) to terminate them.

You can use almost any character as a mark character by means of this command, to distinguish various classes of files. If *old* is a space (' '), then the command operates on all unmarked files; if *new* is a space, then the command unmarks the files it acts on.

To illustrate the power of this command, here is how to put 'D' flags on all the files that have no marks, while unflagging all those that already have 'D' flags:

         * c D t   * c SPC D   * c t SPC

This assumes that no files are marked with 't'.

% m *regexp* (RET)
* % *regexp* (RET)

Mark (with '*') all files whose names match the regular expression *regexp* (`dired-mark-files-regexp`). This command is like % d, except that it marks files with '*' instead of flagging with 'D'. See Section 28.4 [Flagging Many Files], page 330.

Only the non-directory part of the file name is used in matching. Use '^' and '$' to anchor matches. Exclude subdirectories by hiding them (see Section 28.13 [Hiding Subdirectories], page 339).

% g *regexp* (RET)

Mark (with '*') all files whose *contents* contain a match for the regular expression *regexp* (`dired-mark-files-containing-regexp`). This command is like % m, except that it searches the file contents instead of the file name.

C-_   Undo changes in the Dired buffer, such as adding or removing
             marks (`dired-undo`).

28.7 Operating on Files

This section describes the basic Dired commands to operate on one file
or several files. All of these commands are capital letters; all of them use the
minibuffer, either to read an argument or to ask for confirmation, before they
act. All of them give you several ways to specify which files to manipulate:

- If you give the command a numeric prefix argument n, it operates on
  the next n files, starting with the current file. (If n is negative, the
  command operates on the $-n$ files preceding the current line.)

- Otherwise, if some files are marked with '*', the command operates on
  all those files.

- Otherwise, the command operates on the current file only.

Here are the file-manipulating commands that operate on files in this
way. (Some other Dired commands, such as ! and the '%' commands, also
use these conventions to decide which files to work on.)

C *new* (RET)
             Copy the specified files (`dired-do-copy`). The argument *new* is
             the directory to copy into, or (if copying a single file) the new
             name.

             If `dired-copy-preserve-time` is non-`nil`, then copying with
             this command sets the modification time of the new file to be
             the same as that of the old file.

D   Delete the specified files (`dired-do-delete`). Like the other
             commands in this section, this command operates on the *marked*
             files, or the next n files. By contrast, **x** (`dired-expunge`) deletes
             all *flagged* files.

R *new* (RET)
             Rename the specified files (`dired-do-rename`). The argument
             new is the directory to rename into, or (if renaming a single file)
             the new name.

             Dired automatically changes the visited file name of buffers as-
             sociated with renamed files so that they refer to the new names.

H *new* (RET)
             Make hard links to the specified files (`dired-do-hardlink`). The
             argument *new* is the directory to make the links in, or (if making
             just one link) the name to give the link.

S *new* (RET)
>Make symbolic links to the specified files (`dired-do-symlink`). The argument *new* is the directory to make the links in, or (if making just one link) the name to give the link.

M *modespec* (RET)
>Change the mode (also called "permission bits") of the specified files (`dired-do-chmod`). This uses the `chmod` program, so *modespec* can be any argument that `chmod` can handle.

G *newgroup* (RET)
>Change the group of the specified files to *newgroup* (`dired-do-chgrp`).

O *newowner* (RET)
>Change the owner of the specified files to *newowner* (`dired-do-chown`). (On most systems, only the superuser can do this.)
>
>The variable `dired-chown-program` specifies the name of the program to use to do the work (different systems put `chown` in different places).

P *command* (RET)
>Print the specified files (`dired-do-print`). You must specify the command to print them with, but the minibuffer starts out with a suitable guess made using the variables `lpr-command` and `lpr-switches` (the same variables that `lpr-buffer` uses; see Section 30.4 [Hardcopy], page 377).

Z
>Compress the specified files (`dired-do-compress`). If the file appears to be a compressed file already, it is uncompressed instead.

L
>Load the specified Emacs Lisp files (`dired-do-load`). See Section 23.7 [Lisp Libraries], page 285.

B
>Byte compile the specified Emacs Lisp files (`dired-do-byte-compile`). See section "Byte Compilation" in *The Emacs Lisp Reference Manual*.

A *regexp* (RET)
>Search all the specified files for the regular expression *regexp* (`dired-do-search`).
>
>This command is a variant of `tags-search`. The search stops at the first match it finds; use M-, to resume the search and find the next match. See Section 22.13.5 [Tags Search], page 256.

Q *from* (RET) *to* (RET)
>Perform `query-replace-regexp` on each of the specified files, replacing matches for *from* (a regular expression) with the string *to* (`dired-do-query-replace`).

This command is a variant of `tags-query-replace`. If you exit the query replace loop, you can use M-, to resume the scan and replace more matches. See Section 22.13.5 [Tags Search], page 256.

One special file-operation command is + (`dired-create-directory`). This command reads a directory name and creates the directory if it does not already exist.

28.8 Shell Commands in Dired

The dired command ! (`dired-do-shell-command`) reads a shell command string in the minibuffer and runs that shell command on all the specified files. You can specify the files to operate on in the usual ways for Dired commands (see Section 28.7 [Operating on Files], page 334). There are two ways of applying a shell command to multiple files:

- If you use '*' in the shell command, then it runs just once, with the list of file names substituted for the '*'. The order of file names is the order of appearance in the Dired buffer.

  Thus, ! `tar cf foo.tar *` (RET) runs `tar` on the entire list of file names, putting them into one tar file 'foo.tar'.

- If the command string doesn't contain '*', then it runs once *for each file*, with the file name added at the end.

  For example, ! `uudecode` (RET) runs `uudecode` on each file.

What if you want to run the shell command once for each file but with the file name inserted in the middle? Or if you want to use the file names in a more complicated fashion? Use a shell loop. For example, this shell command would run **uuencode** on each of the specified files, writing the output into a corresponding '.uu' file:

```
for file in *; do uuencode $file $file >$file.uu; done
```

The working directory for the shell command is the top-level directory of the Dired buffer.

The ! command does not attempt to update the Dired buffer to show new or modified files, because it doesn't really understand shell commands, and does not know what files the shell command changed. Use the **g** command to update the Dired buffer (see Section 28.14 [Dired Updating], page 339).

28.9 Transforming File Names in Dired

Here are commands that alter file names in a systematic way:

% u   Rename each of the selected files to an upper-case name (**dired-upcase**). If the old file names are 'Foo' and 'bar', the new names are 'FOO' and 'BAR'.

% l   Rename each of the selected files to a lower-case name (**dired-
               downcase**). If the old file names are 'Foo' and 'bar', the new
               names are 'foo' and 'bar'.

% R *from* ⟨RET⟩ *to* ⟨RET⟩
% C *from* ⟨RET⟩ *to* ⟨RET⟩
% H *from* ⟨RET⟩ *to* ⟨RET⟩
% S *from* ⟨RET⟩ *to* ⟨RET⟩
               These four commands rename, copy, make hard links and make
               soft links, in each case computing the new name by regular-
               expression substitution from the name of the old file.

The four regular-expression substitution commands effectively perform a
search-and-replace on the selected file names in the Dired buffer. They read
two arguments: a regular expression *from*, and a substitution pattern *to*.

The commands match each "old" file name against the regular expression
from, and then replace the matching part with *to*. You can use '\&' and
'*digit*' in *to* to refer to all or part of what the pattern matched in the
old file name, as in **replace-regexp** (see Section 12.7.2 [Regexp Replace],
page 96). If the regular expression matches more than once in a file name,
only the first match is replaced.

For example, % R ^.*$ ⟨RET⟩ x-\& ⟨RET⟩ renames each selected file by
prepending 'x-' to its name. The inverse of this, removing 'x-' from the
front of each file name, is also possible: one method is % R ^x-\(.*\)$ ⟨RET⟩
\1 ⟨RET⟩; another is % R ^x- ⟨RET⟩ ⟨RET⟩. (Use '^' and '$' to anchor matches
that should span the whole filename.)

Normally, the replacement process does not consider the files' directory
names; it operates on the file name within the directory. If you specify a
numeric argument of zero, then replacement affects the entire absolute file
name including directory name.

Often you will want to select the set of files to operate on using the same
regexp that you will use to operate on them. To do this, mark those files
with % m *regexp* ⟨RET⟩, then use the same regular expression in the command
to operate on the files. To make this easier, the % commands to operate on
files use the last regular expression specified in any % command as a default.

28.10 File Comparison with Dired

Here are two Dired commands that compare specified files using **diff**.

=   Compare the current file (the file at point) with another file (the
               file at the mark) using the **diff** program (**dired-diff**). The file
               at the mark is the first argument of **diff**, and the file at point
               is the second argument.

M-=   Compare the current file with its latest backup file (**dired-
               backup-diff**). If the current file is itself a backup, compare

it with the file it is a backup of; this way, you can compare a file with any backup version of your choice.

The backup file is the first file given to `diff`.

28.11 Subdirectories in Dired

A Dired buffer displays just one directory in the normal case; but you can optionally include its subdirectories as well.

The simplest way to include multiple directories in one Dired buffer is to specify the options '`-lR`' for running `ls`. (If you give a numeric argument when you run Dired, then you can specify these options in the minibuffer.) That produces a recursive directory listing showing all subdirectories at all levels.

But usually all the subdirectories are too many; usually you will prefer to include specific subdirectories only. You can do this with the `i` command:

i   Insert the contents of a subdirectory later in the buffer.

Use the `i` (`dired-maybe-insert-subdir`) command on a line that describes a file which is a directory. It inserts the contents of that directory into the same Dired buffer, and moves there. Inserted subdirectory contents follow the top-level directory of the Dired buffer, just as they do in '`ls -lR`' output.

If the subdirectory's contents are already present in the buffer, the `i` command just moves to it.

In either case, `i` sets the Emacs mark before moving, so `C-u C-`(SPC) takes you back to the old position in the buffer (the line describing that subdirectory).

Use the `l` command (`dired-do-redisplay`) to update the subdirectory's contents. Use `k` to delete the subdirectory. See Section 28.14 [Dired Updating], page 339.

28.12 Moving Over Subdirectories

When a Dired buffer lists subdirectories, you can use the page motion commands `C-x [` and `C-x ]` to move by entire directories.

The following commands move across, up and down in the tree of directories within one Dired buffer. They move to *directory header lines*, which are the lines that give a directory's name, at the beginning of the directory's contents.

C-M-n   Go to next subdirectory header line, regardless of level (`dired-next-subdir`).

C-M-p   Go to previous subdirectory header line, regardless of level (`dired-prev-subdir`).

C-M-u   Go up to the parent directory's header line (`dired-tree-up`).

C-M-d   Go down in the directory tree, to the first subdirectory's header line (`dired-tree-down`).

<   Move up to the previous directory-file line (`dired-prev-dirline`). These lines are the ones that describe a directory as a file in its parent directory.

>   Move down to the next directory-file line (`dired-prev-dirline`).

28.13 Hiding Subdirectories

Hiding a subdirectory means to make it invisible, except for its header line, via selective display (see Section 11.4 [Selective Display], page 81).

$ Hide or reveal the subdirectory that point is in, and move point to the next subdirectory (`dired-hide-subdir`). A numeric argument serves as a repeat count.

M-$ Hide all subdirectories in this Dired buffer, leaving only their header lines (`dired-hide-all`). Or, if any subdirectory is currently hidden, make all subdirectories visible again. You can use this command to get an overview in very deep directory trees or to move quickly to subdirectories far away.

Ordinary Dired commands never consider files inside a hidden subdirectory. For example, the commands to operate on marked files ignore files in hidden directories even if they are marked. Thus you can use hiding to temporarily exclude subdirectories from operations without having to remove the markers.

The subdirectory hiding commands toggle; that is, they hide what was visible, and show what was hidden.

28.14 Updating the Dired Buffer

This section describes commands to update the Dired buffer to reflect outside (non-Dired) changes in the directories and files, and to delete part of the Dired buffer.

g   Update the entire contents of the Dired buffer (`revert-buffer`).

l   Update the specified files (`dired-do-redisplay`).

k   Delete the specified *file lines*—not the files, just the lines (`dired-do-kill-lines`).

s   Toggle between alphabetical order and date/time order (`dired-sort-toggle-or-edit`).

C-u s *switches* (RET)
> Refresh the Dired buffer using *switches* as `dired-listing-switches`.

Type `g` (`revert-buffer`) to update the contents of the Dired buffer, based on changes in the files and directories listed. This preserves all marks except for those on files that have vanished. Hidden subdirectories are updated but remain hidden.

To update only some of the files, type `l` (`dired-do-redisplay`). This command applies to the next *n* files, or to the marked files if any, or to the current file. Updating them means reading their current status from the file system and changing the buffer to reflect it properly.

If you use `l` on a subdirectory header line, it updates the contents of the corresponding subdirectory.

To delete the specified *file lines*—not the files, just the lines—type `k` (`dired-do-kill-lines`). With a numeric argument *n*, this command applies to the next *n* files; otherwise, it applies to the marked files.

If you kill the line for a file that is a directory, the directory's contents are also deleted from the buffer. Typing `C-u k` on the header line for a subdirectory is another way to delete a subdirectory from the Dired buffer.

The `g` command brings back any individual lines that you have killed in this way, but not subdirectories—you must use `i` to reinsert each subdirectory.

The files in a Dired buffers are normally listed in alphabetical order by file names. Alternatively Dired can sort them by date/time. The Dired command `s` (`dired-sort-toggle-or-edit`) switches between these two sorting modes. The mode line in a Dired buffer indicates which way it is currently sorted—by name, or by date.

C-u s *switches* (RET) lets you specify a new value for `dired-listing-switches`.

28.15 Dired and `find`

You can select a set of files for display in a Dired buffer more flexibly by using the `find` utility to choose the files.

To search for files with names matching a wildcard pattern use `M-x find-name-dired`. It reads arguments *directory* and *pattern*, and chooses all the files in *directory* or its subdirectories whose individual names match *pattern*.

The files thus chosen are displayed in a Dired buffer in which the ordinary Dired commands are available.

If you want to test the contents of files, rather than their names, use `M-x find-grep-dired`. This command reads two minibuffer arguments, *directory* and *regexp*; it chooses all the files in *directory* or its subdirectories that contain a match for *regexp*. It works by running the programs `find` and `grep`. See also M-x `grep-find`, in Section 23.1 [Compilation], page 277. Remember to write the regular expression for `grep`, not for Emacs.

The most general command in this series is M-x `find-dired`, which lets you specify any condition that `find` can test. It takes two minibuffer arguments, *directory* and *find-args*; it runs `find` in *directory*, passing *find-args* to tell `find` what condition to test. To use this command, you need to know how to use `find`.

The format of listing produced by these commands is controlled by the variable `find-ls-option`, whose default value specifies using options '-ld' for `ls`. If your listings are corrupted, you may need to change the value of this variable.

29 The Calendar and the Diary

Emacs provides the functions of a desk calendar, with a diary of planned or past events. To enter the calendar, type M-x calendar; this displays a three-month calendar centered on the current month, with point on the current date. With a numeric argument, as in C-u M-x calendar, it prompts you for the month and year to be the center of the three-month calendar. The calendar uses its own buffer, whose major mode is Calendar mode.

Mouse-2 in the calendar brings up a menu of operations on a particular date; C-Mouse-3 brings up a menu of commonly used calendar features that are independent of any particular date. To exit the calendar, type q. See section "Calendar" in *The Emacs Lisp Reference Manual*, for customization information about the calendar and diary.

29.1 Movement in the Calendar

Calendar mode lets you move through the calendar in logical units of time such as days, weeks, months, and years. If you move outside the three months originally displayed, the calendar display "scrolls" automatically through time to make the selected date visible. Moving to a date lets you view its holidays or diary entries, or convert it to other calendars; moving longer time periods is also useful simply to scroll the calendar.

29.1.1 Motion by Standard Lengths of Time

The commands for movement in the calendar buffer parallel the commands for movement in text. You can move forward and backward by days, weeks, months, and years.

C-f   Move point one day forward (calendar-forward-day).

C-b   Move point one day backward (calendar-backward-day).

C-n   Move point one week forward (calendar-forward-week).

C-p   Move point one week backward (calendar-backward-week).

M-}   Move point one month forward (calendar-forward-month).

M-{   Move point one month backward (calendar-backward-month).

C-x]   Move point one year forward (calendar-forward-year).

C-x [Move point one year backward (calendar-backward-year).

The day and week commands are natural analogues of the usual Emacs commands for moving by characters and by lines. Just as C-n usually moves to the same column in the following line, in Calendar mode it moves to the same day in the following week. And C-p moves to the same day in the previous week.

The arrow keys are equivalent to `C-f`, `C-b`, `C-n` and `C-p`, just as they normally are in other modes.

The commands for motion by months and years work like those for weeks, but move a larger distance. The month commands `M-}` and `M-{` move forward or backward by an entire month's time. The year commands `C-x ]` and `C-x [` move forward or backward a whole year.

The easiest way to remember these commands is to consider months and years analogous to paragraphs and pages of text, respectively. But the commands themselves are not quite analogous. The ordinary Emacs paragraph commands move to the beginning or end of a paragraph, whereas these month and year commands move by an entire month or an entire year, which usually involves skipping across the end of a month or year.

All these commands accept a numeric argument as a repeat count. For convenience, the digit keys and the minus sign specify numeric arguments in Calendar mode even without the Meta modifier. For example, `100 C-f` moves point 100 days forward from its present location.

29.1.2 Beginning or End of Week, Month or Year

A week (or month, or year) is not just a quantity of days; we think of weeks (months, years) as starting on particular dates. So Calendar mode provides commands to move to the beginning or end of a week, month or year:

C-a   Move point to start of week (`calendar-beginning-of-week`).

C-e   Move point to end of week (`calendar-end-of-week`).

M-a   Move point to start of month (`calendar-beginning-of-month`).

M-e   Move point to end of month (`calendar-end-of-month`).

M-<   Move point to start of year (`calendar-beginning-of-year`).

M->   Move point to end of year (`calendar-end-of-year`).

These commands also take numeric arguments as repeat counts, with the repeat count indicating how many weeks, months, or years to move backward or forward.

By default, weeks begin on Sunday. To make them begin on Monday instead, set the variable `calendar-week-start-day` to 1.

29.1.3 Specified Dates

Calendar mode provides commands for moving to a particular date specified in various ways.

g d   Move point to specified date (`calendar-goto-date`).

o   Center calendar around specified month (`calendar-other-month`).

.   Move point to today's date (`calendar-goto-today`).

`g d` (`calendar-goto-date`) prompts for a year, a month, and a day of the month, and then moves to that date. Because the calendar includes all dates from the beginning of the current era, you must type the year in its entirety; that is, type '1990', not '90'.

`o` (`calendar-other-month`) prompts for a month and year, then centers the three-month calendar around that month.

You can return to today's date with `.` (`calendar-goto-today`).

29.2 Scrolling in the Calendar

The calendar display scrolls automatically through time when you move out of the visible portion. You can also scroll it manually. Imagine that the calendar window contains a long strip of paper with the months on it. Scrolling it means moving the strip so that new months become visible in the window.

`C-x <`   Scroll calendar one month forward (`scroll-calendar-left`).

`C-x >`   Scroll calendar one month backward (`scroll-calendar-right`).

`C-v`
(NEXT)   Scroll calendar three months forward (`scroll-calendar-left-three-months`).

`M-v`
(PRIOR)   Scroll calendar three months backward (`scroll-calendar-right-three-months`).

The most basic calendar scroll commands scroll by one month at a time. This means that there are two months of overlap between the display before the command and the display after. `C-x <` scrolls the calendar contents one month to the left; that is, it moves the display forward in time. `C-x >` scrolls the contents to the right, which moves backwards in time.

The commands `C-v` and `M-v` scroll the calendar by an entire "screenful"— three months—in analogy with the usual meaning of these commands. `C-v` makes later dates visible and `M-v` makes earlier dates visible. These commands take a numeric argument as a repeat count; in particular, since `C-u` multiplies the next command by four, typing `C-u C-v` scrolls the calendar forward by a year and typing `C-u M-v` scrolls the calendar backward by a year.

The function keys (NEXT) and (PRIOR) are equivalent to `C-v` and `M-v`, just as they are in other modes.

29.3 Counting Days

M-=   Display the number of days in the current region (`calendar-count-days-region`).

To determine the number of days in the region, type M-= (`calendar-count-days-region`). The numbers of days printed is *inclusive*; that is, it includes the days specified by mark and point.

29.4 Miscellaneous Calendar Commands

p d   Display day-in-year (`calendar-print-day-of-year`).

C-c C-l   Regenerate the calendar window (`redraw-calendar`).

SPC   Scroll the next window (`scroll-other-window`).

q   Exit from calendar (`exit-calendar`).

To print the number of days elapsed since the start of the year, or the number of days remaining in the year, type the p d command (`calendar-print-day-of-year`). This displays both of those numbers in the echo area. The number of days elapsed includes the selected date. The number of days remaining does not include that date.

If the calendar window text gets corrupted, type C-c C-l (`redraw-calendar`) to redraw it. (This can only happen if you use non-Calendar-mode editing commands.)

In Calendar mode, you can use SPC (`scroll-other-window`) to scroll the other window. This is handy when you display a list of holidays or diary entries in another window.

To exit from the calendar, type q (`exit-calendar`). This buries all buffers related to the calendar, selecting other buffers. (If a frame contains a dedicated calendar window, exiting from the calendar iconifies that frame.)

29.5 LaTeX Calendar

The Calendar LaTeX commands produce a buffer of LaTeX code that prints as a calendar. Depending on the command you use, the printed calendar covers the day, week, month or year that point is in.

t m   Generate a one-month calendar (`cal-tex-cursor-month`).

t M   Generate a sideways-printing one-month calendar (`cal-tex-cursor-month-landscape`).

t d   Generate a one-day calendar (`cal-tex-cursor-day`).

t w 1   Generate a one-page calendar for one week (`cal-tex-cursor-week`).

t w 2   Generate a two-page calendar for one week (`cal-tex-cursor-week2`).

t w 3   Generate an ISO-style calendar for one week (`cal-tex-cursor-week-iso`).

t w 4   Generate a calendar for one Monday-starting week (`cal-tex-cursor-week-monday`).

t f w   Generate a Filofax-style two-weeks-at-a-glance calendar (`cal-tex-cursor-filofax-2week`).

t f W   Generate a Filofax-style one-week-at-a-glance calendar (`cal-tex-cursor-filofax-week`).

t y   Generate a calendar for one year (`cal-tex-cursor-year`).

t Y   Generate a sideways-printing calendar for one year (`cal-tex-cursor-year-landscape`).

t f y   Generate a Filofax-style calendar for one year (`cal-tex-cursor-filofax-year`).

Some of these commands print the calendar sideways (in "landscape mode"), so it can be wider than it is long. Some of them use Filofax paper size (3.75in x 6.75in). All of these commands accept a prefix argument which specifies how many days, weeks, months or years to print (starting always with the selected one).

If the variable `cal-tex-holidays` is non-`nil` (the default), then the printed calendars show the holidays in `calendar-holidays`. If the variable `cal-tex-diary` is non-`nil` (the default is `nil`), diary entries are included also (in weekly and monthly calendars only).

29.6 Holidays

The Emacs calendar knows about all major and many minor holidays, and can display them.

h   Display holidays for the selected date (`calendar-cursor-holidays`).

Mouse-2 Holidays
             Display any holidays for the date you click on.

x   Mark holidays in the calendar window (`mark-calendar-holidays`).

u   Unmark calendar window (`calendar-unmark`).

a   List all holidays for the displayed three months in another window (`list-calendar-holidays`).

`M-x holidays`
             List all holidays for three months around today's date in another window.

`M-x list-holidays`
             List holidays in another window for a specified range of years.

To see if any holidays fall on a given date, position point on that date in the calendar window and use the `h` command. Alternatively, click on that date with `Mouse-2` and then choose `Holidays` from the menu that appears. Either way, this displays the holidays for that date, in the echo area if they fit there, otherwise in a separate window.

To view the distribution of holidays for all the dates shown in the calendar, use the `x` command. This displays the dates that are holidays in a different face (or places a '`*`' after these dates, if display with multiple faces is not available). The command applies both to the currently visible months and to other months that subsequently become visible by scrolling. To turn marking off and erase the current marks, type `u`, which also erases any diary marks (see Section 29.10 [Diary], page 355).

To get even more detailed information, use the `a` command, which displays a separate buffer containing a list of all holidays in the current three-month range. You can use (SPC) in the calendar window to scroll that list.

The command `M-x holidays` displays the list of holidays for the current month and the preceding and succeeding months; this works even if you don't have a calendar window. If you want the list of holidays centered around a different month, use `C-u M-x holidays`, which prompts for the month and year.

The holidays known to Emacs include United States holidays and the major Christian, Jewish, and Islamic holidays; also the solstices and equinoxes.

The command `M-x list-holidays` displays the list of holidays for a range of years. This function asks you for the starting and stopping years, and allows you to choose all the holidays or one of several categories of holidays. You can use this command even if you don't have a calendar window.

The dates used by Emacs for holidays are based on *current practice*, not historical fact. Historically, for instance, the start of daylight savings time and even its existence have varied from year to year, but present United States law mandates that daylight savings time begins on the first Sunday in April. When the daylight savings rules are set up for the United States, Emacs always uses the present definition, even though it is wrong for some prior years.

29.7 Times of Sunrise and Sunset

Special calendar commands can tell you, to within a minute or two, the times of sunrise and sunset for any date.

S   Display times of sunrise and sunset for the selected date (`calendar-sunrise-sunset`).

`Mouse-2 Sunrise/Sunset`
Display times of sunrise and sunset for the date you click on.

`M-x sunrise-sunset`
Display times of sunrise and sunset for today's date.

`C-u M-x sunrise-sunset`
Display times of sunrise and sunset for a specified date.

Within the calendar, to display the *local times* of sunrise and sunset in the echo area, move point to the date you want, and type S. Alternatively, click `Mouse-2` on the date, then choose `Sunrise/Sunset` from the menu that appears. The command `M-x sunrise-sunset` is available outside the calendar to display this information for today's date or a specified date. To specify a date other than today, use `C-u M-x sunrise-sunset`, which prompts for the year, month, and day.

You can display the times of sunrise and sunset for any location and any date with `C-u C-u M-x sunrise-sunset`. This asks you for a longitude, latitude, number of minutes difference from Coordinated Universal Time, and date, and then tells you the times of sunrise and sunset for that location on that date.

Because the times of sunrise and sunset depend on the location on earth, you need to tell Emacs your latitude, longitude, and location name before using these commands. Here is an example of what to set:

```
(setq calendar-latitude 40.1)
(setq calendar-longitude -88.2)
(setq calendar-location-name "Urbana, IL")
```

Use one decimal place in the values of `calendar-latitude` and `calendar-longitude`.

Your time zone also affects the local time of sunrise and sunset. Emacs usually gets time zone information from the operating system, but if these values are not what you want (or if the operating system does not supply them), you must set them yourself. Here is an example:

```
(setq calendar-time-zone -360)
(setq calendar-standard-time-zone-name "CST")
(setq calendar-daylight-time-zone-name "CDT")
```

The value of `calendar-time-zone` is the number of minutes difference between your local standard time and Coordinated Universal Time (Greenwich time). The values of `calendar-standard-time-zone-name` and `calendar-daylight-time-zone-name` are the abbreviations used in your time zone. Emacs displays the times of sunrise and sunset *corrected for daylight savings time*. See Section 29.12 [Daylight Savings], page 362, for how daylight savings time is determined.

As a user, you might find it convenient to set the calendar location variables for your usual physical location in your '.emacs' file. And when you install Emacs on a machine, you can create a 'default.el' file which sets them properly for the typical location of most users of that machine. See Section 31.7 [Init File], page 419.

29.8 Phases of the Moon

These calendar commands display the dates and times of the phases of the moon (new moon, first quarter, full moon, last quarter). This feature is useful for debugging problems that "depend on the phase of the moon."

M   Display the dates and times for all the quarters of the moon for the three-month period shown (`calendar-phases-of-moon`).

M-x phases-of-moon
                   Display dates and times of the quarters of the moon for three months around today's date.

Within the calendar, use the M command to display a separate buffer of the phases of the moon for the current three-month range. The dates and times listed are accurate to within a few minutes.

Outside the calendar, use the command `M-x phases-of-moon` to display the list of the phases of the moon for the current month and the preceding and succeeding months. For information about a different month, use `C-u M-x phases-of-moon`, which prompts for the month and year.

The dates and times given for the phases of the moon are given in local time (corrected for daylight savings, when appropriate); but if the variable `calendar-time-zone` is void, Coordinated Universal Time (the Greenwich time zone) is used. See Section 29.12 [Daylight Savings], page 362.

29.9 Conversion To and From Other Calendars

The Emacs calendar displayed is *always* the Gregorian calendar, sometimes called the "new style" calendar, which is used in most of the world today. However, this calendar did not exist before the sixteenth century and was not widely used before the eighteenth century; it did not fully displace the Julian calendar and gain universal acceptance until the early twentieth century. The Emacs calendar can display any month since January, year 1 of the current era, but the calendar displayed is the Gregorian, even for a date at which the Gregorian calendar did not exist.

While Emacs cannot display other calendars, it can convert dates to and from several other calendars.

29.9.1 Supported Calendar Systems

The ISO commercial calendar is used largely in Europe.

The Julian calendar, named after Julius Caesar, was the one used in Europe throughout medieval times, and in many countries up until the nineteenth century.

Astronomers use a simple counting of days elapsed since noon, Monday, January 1, 4713 B.C. on the Julian calendar. The number of days elapsed is called the *Julian day number* or the *Astronomical day number*.

The Hebrew calendar is used by tradition in the Jewish religion. The Emacs calendar program uses the Hebrew calendar to determine the dates of Jewish holidays. Hebrew calendar dates begin and end at sunset.

The Islamic calendar is used in many predominantly Islamic countries. Emacs uses it to determine the dates of Islamic holidays. There is no universal agreement in the Islamic world about the calendar; Emacs uses a widely accepted version, but the precise dates of Islamic holidays often depend on proclamation by religious authorities, not on calculations. As a consequence, the actual dates of observance can vary slightly from the dates computed by Emacs. Islamic calendar dates begin and end at sunset.

The French Revolutionary calendar was created by the Jacobins after the 1789 revolution, to represent a more secular and nature-based view of the annual cycle, and to install a 10-day week in a rationalization measure similar to the metric system. The French government officially abandoned this calendar at the end of 1805.

The Maya of Central America used three separate, overlapping calendar systems, the *long count*, the *tzolkin*, and the *haab*. Emacs knows about all three of these calendars. Experts dispute the exact correlation between the Mayan calendar and our calendar; Emacs uses the Goodman-Martinez-Thompson correlation in its calculations.

The Copts use a calendar based on the ancient Egyptian solar calendar. Their calendar consists of twelve 30-day months followed by an extra five-day period. Once every fourth year they add a leap day to this extra period to make it six days. The Ethiopic calendar is identical in structure, but has different year numbers and month names.

The Persians use a solar calendar based on a design of Omar Khayyam. Their calendar consists of twelve months of which the first six have 31 days, the next five have 30 days, and the last has 29 in ordinary years and 30 in leap years. Leap years occur in a complicated pattern every four or five years.

The Chinese calendar is a complicated system of lunar months arranged into solar years. The years go in cycles of sixty, each year containing either

twelve months in an ordinary year or thirteen months in a leap year; each
month has either 29 or 30 days. Years, ordinary months, and days are named
by combining one of ten "celestial stems" with one of twelve "terrestrial
branches" for a total of sixty names that are repeated in a cycle of sixty.

29.9.2 Converting To Other Calendars

The following commands describe the selected date (the date at point)
in various other calendar systems:

Mouse-2 Other Calendars
> Display the date that you click on, expressed in various other
> calendars.

p c
> Display ISO commercial calendar equivalent for selected day
> (`calendar-print-iso-date`).

p j
> Display Julian date for selected day (`calendar-print-julian-
> date`).

p a
> Display astronomical (Julian) day number for selected day
> (`calendar-print-astro-day-number`).

p h
> Display Hebrew date for selected day (`calendar-print-
> hebrew-date`).

p i
> Display Islamic date for selected day (`calendar-print-
> islamic-date`).

p f
> Display French Revolutionary date for selected day (`calendar-
> print-french-date`).

p C
> Display Chinese date for selected day (`calendar-print-
> chinese-date`).

p k
> Display Coptic date for selected day (`calendar-print-coptic-
> date`).

p e
> Display Ethiopic date for selected day (`calendar-print-
> ethiopic-date`).

p p
> Display Persian date for selected day (`calendar-print-
> persian-date`).

p m
> Display Mayan date for selected day (`calendar-print-mayan-
> date`).

If you are using X, the easiest way to translate a date into other calendars is to click on it with **Mouse-2**, then choose **Other Calendars** from
the menu that appears. This displays the equivalent forms of the date in
all the calendars Emacs understands, in the form of a menu. (Choosing an
alternative from this menu doesn't actually do anything—the menu is used
only for display.)

Put point on the desired date of the Gregorian calendar, then type the appropriate keys. The p is a mnemonic for "print" since Emacs "prints" the equivalent date in the echo area.

29.9.3 Converting From Other Calendars

You can use the other supported calendars to specify a date to move to. This section describes the commands for doing this using calendars other than Mayan; for the Mayan calendar, see the following section.

g c   Move to a date specified in the ISO commercial calendar (`calendar-goto-iso-date`).

g j   Move to a date specified in the Julian calendar (`calendar-goto-julian-date`).

g a   Move to a date specified in astronomical (Julian) day number (`calendar-goto-astro-day-number`).

g h   Move to a date specified in the Hebrew calendar (`calendar-goto-hebrew-date`).

g i   Move to a date specified in the Islamic calendar (`calendar-goto-islamic-date`).

g f   Move to a date specified in the French Revolutionary calendar (`calendar-goto-french-date`).

g C   Move to a date specified in the Chinese calendar (`calendar-goto-chinese-date`).

g p   Move to a date specified in the Persian calendar (`calendar-goto-persian-date`).

g k   Move to a date specified in the Coptic calendar (`calendar-goto-coptic-date`).

g e   Move to a date specified in the Ethiopic calendar (`calendar-goto-ethiopic-date`).

These commands ask you for a date on the other calendar, move point to the Gregorian calendar date equivalent to that date, and display the other calendar's date in the echo area. Emacs uses strict completion (see Section 5.3 [Completion], page 43) whenever it asks you to type a month name, so you don't have to worry about the spelling of Hebrew, Islamic, or French names.

One common question concerning the Hebrew calendar is the computation of the anniversary of a date of death, called a "yahrzeit." The Emacs calendar includes a facility for such calculations. If you are in the calendar, the command M-x list-yahrzeit-dates asks you for a range of years and then displays a list of the yahrzeit dates for those years for the date given by point. If you are not in the calendar, this command first asks you for the date of death and the range of years, and then displays the list of yahrzeit dates.

29.9.4 Converting from the Mayan Calendar

Here are the commands to select dates based on the Mayan calendar:

g m l   Move to a date specified by the long count calendar (`calendar-goto-mayan-long-count-date`).

g m n t   Move to the next occurrence of a place in the tzolkin calendar (`calendar-next-tzolkin-date`).

g m p t   Move to the previous occurrence of a place in the tzolkin calendar (`calendar-previous-tzolkin-date`).

g m n h   Move to the next occurrence of a place in the haab calendar (`calendar-next-haab-date`).

g m p h   Move to the previous occurrence of a place in the haab calendar (`calendar-previous-haab-date`).

g m n c   Move to the next occurrence of a place in the calendar round (`calendar-next-calendar-round-date`).

g m p c   Move to the previous occurrence of a place in the calendar round (`calendar-previous-calendar-round-date`).

To understand these commands, you need to understand the Mayan calendars. The *long count* is a counting of days with these units:

1 kin = 1 day   1 uinal = 20 kin   1 tun = 18 uinal
1 katun = 20 tun   1 baktun = 20 katun

Thus, the long count date 12.16.11.16.6 means 12 baktun, 16 katun, 11 tun, 16 uinal, and 6 kin. The Emacs calendar can handle Mayan long count dates as early as 7.17.18.13.1, but no earlier. When you use the **g m l** command, type the Mayan long count date with the baktun, katun, tun, uinal, and kin separated by periods.

The Mayan tzolkin calendar is a cycle of 260 days formed by a pair of independent cycles of 13 and 20 days. Since this cycle repeats endlessly, Emacs provides commands to move backward and forward to the previous or next point in the cycle. Type **g m p t** to go to the previous tzolkin date; Emacs asks you for a tzolkin date and moves point to the previous occurrence of that date. Similarly, type **g m n t** to go to the next occurrence of a tzolkin date.

The Mayan haab calendar is a cycle of 365 days arranged as 18 months of 20 days each, followed a 5-day monthless period. Like the tzolkin cycle, this cycle repeats endlessly, and there are commands to move backward and forward to the previous or next point in the cycle. Type **g m p h** to go to the previous haab date; Emacs asks you for a haab date and moves point to the previous occurrence of that date. Similarly, type **g m n h** to go to the next occurrence of a haab date.

The Maya also used the combination of the tzolkin date and the haab date. This combination is a cycle of about 52 years called a *calendar round*. If you type **g m p c**, Emacs asks you for both a haab and a tzolkin date and then moves point to the previous occurrence of that combination. Use **g m n c** to move point to the next occurrence of a combination. These commands signal an error if the haab/tzolkin date combination you have typed is impossible.

Emacs uses strict completion (see Section 5.3.3 [Strict Completion], page 45) whenever it asks you to type a Mayan name, so you don't have to worry about spelling.

29.10 The Diary

The Emacs diary keeps track of appointments or other events on a daily basis, in conjunction with the calendar. To use the diary feature, you must first create a *diary file* containing a list of events and their dates. Then Emacs can automatically pick out and display the events for today, for the immediate future, or for any specified date.

By default, Emacs uses '~/diary' as the diary file. This is the same file that the `calendar` utility uses. A sample '~/diary' file is:

```
12/22/1988   Twentieth wedding anniversary!!
&1/1.        Happy New Year!
10/22        Ruth's birthday.
* 21, *:     Payday
Tuesday--weekly meeting with grad students at 10am
        Supowit, Shen, Bitner, and Kapoor to attend.
1/13/89      Friday the thirteenth!!
&thu 4pm     squash game with Lloyd.
mar 16       Dad's birthday
April 15, 1989 Income tax due.
&* 15        time cards due.
```

This example uses extra spaces to align the event descriptions of most of the entries. Such formatting is purely a matter of taste.

Although you probably will start by creating a diary manually, Emacs provides a number of commands to let you view, add, and change diary entries.

29.10.1 Commands Displaying Diary Entries

Once you have created a '~/diary' file, you can use the calendar to view it. You can also view today's events outside of Calendar mode.

d   Display all diary entries for the selected date (`view-diary-entries`).

Mouse-2 Diary
>   Display all diary entries for the date you click on.

s   Display the entire diary file (`show-all-diary-entries`).

m   Mark all visible dates that have diary entries (`mark-diary-entries`).

u   Unmark the calendar window (`calendar-unmark`).

M-x print-diary-entries
>   Print hard copy of the diary display as it appears.

M-x diary Display all diary entries for today's date.

M-x diary-mail-entries
>   Mail yourself email reminders about upcoming diary entries.

Displaying the diary entries with **d** shows in a separate window the diary entries for the selected date in the calendar. The mode line of the new window shows the date of the diary entries and any holidays that fall on that date. If you specify a numeric argument with **d**, it shows all the diary entries for that many successive days. Thus, **2 d** displays all the entries for the selected date and for the following day.

Another way to display the diary entries for a date is to click **Mouse-2** on the date, and then choose **Diary** from the menu that appears.

To get a broader view of which days are mentioned in the diary, use the **m** command. This displays the dates that have diary entries in a different face (or places a '+' after these dates, if display with multiple faces is not available). The command applies both to the currently visible months and to other months that subsequently become visible by scrolling. To turn marking off and erase the current marks, type **u**, which also turns off holiday marks (see Section 29.6 [Holidays], page 347).

To see the full diary file, rather than just some of the entries, use the **s** command.

Display of selected diary entries uses the selective display feature to hide entries that don't apply.

The diary buffer as you see it is an illusion, so simply printing the buffer does not print what you see on your screen. There is a special command to print hard copy of the diary buffer *as it appears*; this command is **M-x print-diary-entries**. It sends the data directly to the printer. You can customize it like `lpr-region` (see Section 30.4 [Hardcopy], page 377).

The command **M-x diary** displays the diary entries for the current date, independently of the calendar display, and optionally for the next few days as well; the variable `number-of-diary-entries` specifies how many days to include. See section "Calendar" in *The Emacs Lisp Reference Manual*.

If you put **(diary)** in your '.emacs' file, this automatically displays a window with the day's diary entries, when you enter Emacs. The mode line of the displayed window shows the date and any holidays that fall on that date.

Many users like to receive notice of events in their diary as email. To send such mail to yourself, use the command M-x diary-mail-entries. A prefix argument specifies how many days (starting with today) to check; otherwise, the variable diary-mail-days says how many days.

29.10.2 The Diary File

Your *diary file* is a file that records events associated with particular dates. The name of the diary file is specified by the variable diary-file; '~/diary' is the default. The calendar utility program supports a subset of the format allowed by the Emacs diary facilities, so you can use that utility to view the diary file, with reasonable results aside from the entries it cannot understand.

Each entry in the diary file describes one event and consists of one or more lines. An entry always begins with a date specification at the left margin. The rest of the entry is simply text to describe the event. If the entry has more than one line, then the lines after the first must begin with whitespace to indicate they continue a previous entry. Lines that do not begin with valid dates and do not continue a preceding entry are ignored.

You can inhibit the marking of certain diary entries in the calendar window; to do this, insert an ampersand ('&') at the beginning of the entry, before the date. This has no effect on display of the entry in the diary window; it affects only marks on dates in the calendar window. Nonmarking entries are especially useful for generic entries that would otherwise mark many different dates.

If the first line of a diary entry consists only of the date or day name with no following blanks or punctuation, then the diary window display doesn't include that line; only the continuation lines appear. For example, this entry:

```
02/11/1989
        Bill B. visits Princeton today
        2pm Cognitive Studies Committee meeting
        2:30-5:30 Liz at Lawrenceville
        4:00pm Dentist appt
        7:30pm Dinner at George's
        8:00-10:00pm concert
```

appears in the diary window without the date line at the beginning. This style of entry looks neater when you display just a single day's entries, but can cause confusion if you ask for more than one day's entries.

You can edit the diary entries as they appear in the window, but it is important to remember that the buffer displayed contains the *entire* diary file, with portions of it concealed from view. This means, for instance, that the C-f (forward-char) command can put point at what appears to be the end of the line, but what is in reality the middle of some concealed line.

Be careful when editing the diary entries! Inserting additional lines or adding/deleting characters in the middle of a visible line cannot cause problems, but editing at the end of a line may not do what you expect. Deleting a line may delete other invisible entries that follow it. Before editing the diary, it is best to display the entire file with s (show-all-diary-entries).

29.10.3 Date Formats

Here are some sample diary entries, illustrating different ways of formatting a date. The examples all show dates in American order (month, day, year), but Calendar mode supports European order (day, month, year) as an option.

```
4/20/93  Switch-over to new tabulation system
apr. 25  Start tabulating annual results
4/30  Results for April are due
*/25  Monthly cycle finishes
Friday  Don't leave without backing up files
```

The first entry appears only once, on April 20, 1993. The second and third appear every year on the specified dates, and the fourth uses a wildcard (asterisk) for the month, so it appears on the 25th of every month. The final entry appears every week on Friday.

You can use just numbers to express a date, as in '*month/day*' or '*month/day/year*'. This must be followed by a nondigit. In the date itself, *month* and *day* are numbers of one or two digits. The optional *year* is also a number, and may be abbreviated to the last two digits; that is, you can use '11/12/1989' or '11/12/89'.

Dates can also have the form '*monthname day*' or '*monthname day, year*', where the month's name can be spelled in full or abbreviated to three characters (with or without a period). Case is not significant.

A date may be *generic*; that is, partially unspecified. Then the entry applies to all dates that match the specification. If the date does not contain a year, it is generic and applies to any year. Alternatively, *month*, *day*, or *year* can be a '*'; this matches any month, day, or year, respectively. Thus, a diary entry '3/*/*' matches any day in March of any year; so does 'march *'.

If you prefer the European style of writing dates—in which the day comes before the month—type M-x european-calendar while in the calendar, or set the variable european-calendar-style to t *before* using any calendar or diary command. This mode interprets all dates in the diary in the European manner, and also uses European style for displaying diary dates. (Note that there is no comma after the *monthname* in the European style.) To go back to the (default) American style of writing dates, type M-x american-calendar.

You can use the name of a day of the week as a generic date which applies to any date falling on that day of the week. You can abbreviate the day of the week to three letters (with or without a period) or spell it in full; case is not significant.

29.10.4 Commands to Add to the Diary

While in the calendar, there are several commands to create diary entries:

i d   Add a diary entry for the selected date (insert-diary-entry).

i w   Add a diary entry for the selected day of the week (insert-weekly-diary-entry).

i m   Add a diary entry for the selected day of the month (insert-monthly-diary-entry).

i y   Add a diary entry for the selected day of the year (insert-yearly-diary-entry).

You can make a diary entry for a specific date by selecting that date in the calendar window and typing the i d command. This command displays the end of your diary file in another window and inserts the date; you can then type the rest of the diary entry.

If you want to make a diary entry that applies to a specific day of the week, select that day of the week (any occurrence will do) and type i w. This inserts the day-of-week as a generic date; you can then type the rest of the diary entry. You can make a monthly diary entry in the same fashion. Select the day of the month, use the i m command, and type rest of the entry. Similarly, you can insert a yearly diary entry with the i y command.

All of the above commands make marking diary entries by default. To make a nonmarking diary entry, give a numeric argument to the command. For example, C-u i w makes a nonmarking weekly diary entry.

When you modify the diary file, be sure to save the file before exiting Emacs.

29.10.5 Special Diary Entries

In addition to entries based on calendar dates, the diary file can contain *sexp entries* for regular events such as anniversaries. These entries are based on Lisp expressions (sexps) that Emacs evaluates as it scans the diary file. Instead of a date, a sexp entry contains '%%' followed by a Lisp expression which must begin and end with parentheses. The Lisp expression determines which dates the entry applies to.

Calendar mode provides commands to insert certain commonly used sexp entries:

i a   Add an anniversary diary entry for the selected date (insert-anniversary-diary-entry).

i b   Add a block diary entry for the current region (insert-block-diary-entry).

i c   Add a cyclic diary entry starting at the date (insert-cyclic-diary-entry).

If you want to make a diary entry that applies to the anniversary of a specific date, move point to that date and use the i a command. This displays the end of your diary file in another window and inserts the anniversary description; you can then type the rest of the diary entry. The entry looks like this:

    %%(diary-anniversary 10 31 1948) Arthur's birthday

This entry applies to October 31 in any year after 1948; '10 31 1948' specifies the date. (If you are using the European calendar style, the month and day are interchanged.) The reason this expression requires a beginning year is that advanced diary functions can use it to calculate the number of elapsed years.

A *block* diary entry applies to a specified range of consecutive dates. Here is a block diary entry that applies to all dates from June 24, 1990 through July 10, 1990:

    %%(diary-block 6 24 1990 7 10 1990) Vacation

The '6 24 1990' indicates the starting date and the '7 10 1990' indicates the stopping date. (Again, if you are using the European calendar style, the month and day are interchanged.)

To insert a block entry, place point and the mark on the two dates that begin and end the range, and type i b. This command displays the end of your diary file in another window and inserts the block description; you can then type the diary entry.

Cyclic diary entries repeat after a fixed interval of days. To create one, select the starting date and use the i c command. The command prompts for the length of interval, then inserts the entry, which looks like this:

    %%(diary-cyclic 50 3 1 1990) Renew medication

This entry applies to March 1, 1990 and every 50th day following; '3 1 1990' specifies the starting date. (If you are using the European calendar style, the month and day are interchanged.)

All three of these commands make marking diary entries. To insert a nonmarking entry, give a numeric argument to the command. For example, C-u i a makes a nonmarking anniversary diary entry.

Marking sexp diary entries in the calendar is *extremely* time-consuming, since every date visible in the calendar window must be individually checked. So it's a good idea to make sexp diary entries nonmarking (with '&') when possible.

Another sophisticated kind of sexp entry, a *floating* diary entry, specifies a regularly occurring event by offsets specified in days, weeks, and months. It is comparable to a crontab entry interpreted by the **cron** utility. Here is a nonmarking, floating diary entry that applies to the last Thursday in November:

```
&%%(diary-float 11 4 -1) American Thanksgiving
```

The 11 specifies November (the eleventh month), the 4 specifies Thursday (the fourth day of the week, where Sunday is numbered zero), and the -1 specifies "last" (1 would mean "first," 2 would mean "second," -2 would mean "second-to-last," and so on). The month can be a single month or a list of months. Thus you could change the 11 above to ''(1 2 3)' and have the entry apply to the last Thursday of January, February, and March. If the month is **t**, the entry applies to all months of the year.

Most generally, sexp diary entries can perform arbitrary computations to determine when they apply. See section "Sexp Diary Entries" in *The Emacs Lisp Reference Manual*.

29.11 Appointments

If you have a diary entry for an appointment, and that diary entry begins with a recognizable time of day, Emacs can warn you, several minutes beforehand, that that appointment is pending. Emacs alerts you to the appointment by displaying a message in the mode line.

To enable appointment notification, you must enable the time display feature of Emacs, M-x display-time (see Section 1.3 [Mode Line], page 17). You must also add the function **appt-make-list** to the **diary-hook**, like this:

```
(add-hook 'diary-hook 'appt-make-list)
```

Adding this text to your '.emacs' file does the whole job:

```
(display-time)
(add-hook 'diary-hook 'appt-make-list)
(diary 0)
```

With these preparations done, when you display the diary (either with the **d** command in the calendar window or with the M-x **diary** command), it sets up an appointment list of all the diary entries found with recognizable times of day, and reminds you just before each of them.

For example, suppose the diary file contains these lines:

```
Monday
   9:30am Coffee break
  12:00pm Lunch
```

Then on Mondays, after you have displayed the diary, you will be reminded at 9:20am about your coffee break and at 11:50am about lunch.

You can write times in am/pm style (with '12:00am' standing for midnight and '12:00pm' standing for noon), or 24-hour European/military style. You need not be consistent; your diary file can have a mixture of the two styles.

Emacs updates the appointments list automatically just after midnight. This also displays the next day's diary entries in the diary buffer, unless you set `appt-display-diary` to `nil`.

You can also use the appointment notification facility like an alarm clock. The command `M-x appt-add` adds entries to the appointment list without affecting your diary file. You delete entries from the appointment list with `M-x appt-delete`.

You can turn off the appointment notification feature at any time by setting `appt-issue-message` to `nil`.

29.12 Daylight Savings Time

Emacs understands the difference between standard time and daylight savings time—the times given for sunrise, sunset, solstices, equinoxes, and the phases of the moon take that into account. The rules for daylight savings time vary from place to place and have also varied historically from year to year. To do the job properly, Emacs needs to know which rules to use.

Some operating systems keep track of the rules that apply to the place where you are; on these systems, Emacs gets the information it needs from the system automatically. If some or all of this information is missing, Emacs fills in the gaps with the rules currently used in Cambridge, Massachusetts. If the resulting rules are not what you want, you can tell Emacs the rules to use by setting certain variables: `calendar-daylight-savings-starts` and `calendar-daylight-savings-ends`.

These values should be Lisp expressions that refer to the variable `year`, and evaluate to the Gregorian date on which daylight savings time starts or (respectively) ends, in the form of a list (*month day year*). The values should be `nil` if your area does not use daylight savings time.

Emacs uses these expressions to determine the starting date of daylight savings time for the holiday list and for correcting times of day in the solar and lunar calculations.

The values for Cambridge, Massachusetts are as follows:

```
(calendar-nth-named-day 1 0 4 year)
(calendar-nth-named-day -1 0 10 year)
```

That is, the first 0th day (Sunday) of the fourth month (April) in the year specified by `year`, and the last Sunday of the tenth month (October) of that year. If daylight savings time were changed to start on October 1, you would set `calendar-daylight-savings-starts` to this:

```
(list 10 1 year)
```

If there is no daylight savings time at your location, or if you want all times in standard time, set `calendar-daylight-savings-starts` and `calendar-daylight-savings-ends` to `nil`.

The variable `calendar-daylight-time-offset` specifies the difference between daylight savings time and standard time, measured in minutes. The value for Cambridge, Massachusetts is 60.

The two variables `calendar-daylight-savings-starts-time` and `calendar-daylight-savings-ends-time` specify the number of minutes after midnight local time when the transition to and from daylight savings time should occur. For Cambridge, Massachusetts both variables' values are 120.

30 Miscellaneous Commands

This chapter contains several brief topics that do not fit anywhere else: reading netnews, running shell commands and shell subprocesses, using a single shared Emacs for utilities that expect to run an editor as a subprocess, printing hardcopy, sorting text, narrowing display to part of the buffer, editing double-column files and binary files, saving an Emacs session for later resumption, emulating other editors, and various diversions and amusements.

30.1 Gnus

Gnus is an Emacs package primarily designed for reading and posting Usenet news. It can also be used to read and respond to messages from a number of other sources—mail, remote directories, digests, and so on.

Here we introduce Gnus and describe several basic features. For full details on Gnus, type `M-x info` and then select the Gnus manual.

To start Gnus, type `M-x gnus` (RET).

30.1.1 Gnus Buffers

As opposed to most normal Emacs packages, Gnus uses a number of different buffers to display information and to receive commands. The three buffers users spend most of their time in are the *group buffer*, the *summary buffer* and the *article buffer*.

The *group buffer* contains a list of groups. This is the first buffer Gnus displays when it starts up. It normally displays only the groups to which you subscribe and that contain unread articles. Use this buffer to select a specific group.

The *summary buffer* lists one line for each article in a single group. By default, the author, the subject and the line number are displayed for each article, but this is customizable, like most aspects of Gnus display. The summary buffer is created when you select a group in the group buffer, and is killed when you exit the group. Use this buffer to select an article.

The *article buffer* displays the article. In normal Gnus usage, you don't select this buffer—all useful article-oriented commands work in the summary buffer. But you can select the article buffer, and execute all Gnus commands from that buffer, if you want to.

30.1.2 When Gnus Starts Up

At startup, Gnus reads your '`.newsrc`' news initialization file and attempts to communicate with the local news server, which is a repository of news articles. The news server need not be the same computer you are logged in on.

If you start Gnus and connect to the server, but do not see any newsgroups listed in the group buffer, type L or A k to get a listing of all the groups. Then type u to toggle subscription to groups.

The first time you start Gnus, Gnus subscribes you to a few selected groups. All other groups start out as *killed groups* for you; you can list them with A k. All new groups that subsequently come to exist at the news server become *zombie groups* for you; type A z to list them. You can subscribe to a group shown in these lists using the u command.

When you quit Gnus with q, it automatically records in your '.newsrc' and '.newsrc.eld' initialization files the subscribed or unsubscribed status of all groups. You should normally not edit these files manually, but you may if you know how.

30.1.3 Summary of Gnus Commands

Reading news is a two step process:
1. Choose a group in the group buffer.
2. Select articles from the summary buffer. Each article selected is displayed in the article buffer in a large window, below the summary buffer in its small window.

Each Gnus buffer has its own special commands; however, the meanings of any given key in the various Gnus buffers are usually analogous, even if not identical. Here are commands for the group and summary buffers:

q   In the group buffer, update your '.newsrc' initialization file and quit Gnus.

            In the summary buffer, exit the current group and return to the group buffer. Thus, typing q twice quits Gnus.

L   In the group buffer, list all the groups available on your news server (except those you have killed). This may be a long list!

l   In the group buffer, list only the groups to which you subscribe and which contain unread articles.

u   In the group buffer, unsubscribe from (or subscribe to) the group listed in the line that point is on. When you quit Gnus by typing q, Gnus lists in your '.newsrc' file which groups you have subscribed to. The next time you start Gnus, you won't see this group, because Gnus normally displays only subscribed-to groups.

C-k   In the group buffer, "kill" the current line's group—don't even list it in '.newsrc' from now on. This affects future Gnus sessions as well as the present session.

            When you quit Gnus by typing q, Gnus writes information in the file '.newsrc' describing all newsgroups except those you have "killed."

SPC In the group buffer, select the group on the line under the cursor and display the first unread article in that group.

In the summary buffer,

- Select the article on the line under the cursor if none is selected.
- Scroll the text of the selected article (if there is one).
- Select the next unread article if at the end of the current article.

Thus, you can move through all the articles by repeatedly typing SPC.

DEL In the group buffer, move point to the previous group containing unread articles.

In the summary buffer, scroll the text of the article backwards.

n Move point to the next unread group, or select the next unread article.

p Move point to the previous unread group, or select the previous unread article.

C-n
C-p Move point to the next or previous item, even if it is marked as read. This does not select the article or group on that line.

s In the summary buffer, do an incremental search of the current text in the article buffer, just as if you switched to the article buffer and typed C-s.

M-s regexp RET

In the summary buffer, search forward for articles containing a match for regexp.

30.2 Running Shell Commands from Emacs

Emacs has commands for passing single command lines to inferior shell processes; it can also run a shell interactively with input and output to an Emacs buffer named '*shell*'.

M-! cmd RET

Run the shell command line cmd and display the output (shell-command).

M-| cmd RET

Run the shell command line cmd with region contents as input; optionally replace the region with the output (shell-command-on-region).

M-x shell Run a subshell with input and output through an Emacs buffer. You can then give commands interactively.

30.2.1 Single Shell Commands

M-! (shell-command) reads a line of text using the minibuffer and executes it as a shell command in a subshell made just for that command. Standard input for the command comes from the null device. If the shell command produces any output, the output goes into an Emacs buffer named '*Shell Command Output*', which is displayed in another window but not selected. A numeric argument, as in M-1 M-!, directs this command to insert any output into the current buffer. In that case, point is left before the output and the mark is set after the output.

If the shell command line ends in '&', it runs asynchronously. For a synchronous shell command, shell-command returns the command's exit status (0 means success), when it is called from a Lisp program.

M-| (shell-command-on-region) is like M-! but passes the contents of the region as the standard input to the shell command, instead of no input. If a numeric argument is used, meaning insert the output in the current buffer, then the old region is deleted first and the output replaces it as the contents of the region. It returns the command's exit status when it is called from a Lisp program.

Both M-! and M-| use shell-file-name to specify the shell to use. This variable is initialized based on your SHELL environment variable when Emacs is started. If the file name does not specify a directory, the directories in the list exec-path are searched; this list is initialized based on the environment variable PATH when Emacs is started. Your '.emacs' file can override either or both of these default initializations.

Both M-! and M-| wait for the shell command to complete. To stop waiting, type C-g to quit; that terminates the shell command with the signal SIGINT—the same signal that C-c normally generates in the shell. Emacs waits until the command actually terminates. If the shell command doesn't stop (because it ignores the SIGINT signal), type C-g again; this sends the command a SIGKILL signal which is impossible to ignore.

To specify a coding system for M-! or M-|, use the command C-x (RET) c immediately beforehand. See Section 18.9 [Specify Coding], page 184.

Error output from the command is normally intermixed with the regular output. If you set the variable shell-command-default-error-buffer to a string, which is a buffer name, error output is inserted before point in the buffer of that name.

30.2.2 Interactive Inferior Shell

To run a subshell interactively, putting its typescript in an Emacs buffer, use M-x shell. This creates (or reuses) a buffer named '*shell*' and runs a subshell with input coming from and output going to that buffer. That is to say, any "terminal output" from the subshell goes into the buffer, advancing point, and any "terminal input" for the subshell comes from text in the buffer. To give input to the subshell, go to the end of the buffer and type the input, terminated by (RET).

Emacs does not wait for the subshell to do anything. You can switch windows or buffers and edit them while the shell is waiting, or while it is running a command. Output from the subshell waits until Emacs has time to process it; this happens whenever Emacs is waiting for keyboard input or for time to elapse.

To make multiple subshells, rename the buffer '*shell*' to something different using M-x rename-uniquely. Then type M-x shell again to create a new buffer '*shell*' with its own subshell. If you rename this buffer as well, you can create a third one, and so on. All the subshells run independently and in parallel.

The file name used to load the subshell is the value of the variable explicit-shell-file-name, if that is non-nil. Otherwise, the environment variable ESHELL is used, or the environment variable SHELL if there is no ESHELL. If the file name specified is relative, the directories in the list exec-path are searched; this list is initialized based on the environment variable PATH when Emacs is started. Your '.emacs' file can override either or both of these default initializations.

To specify a coding system for the shell, you can use the command C-x (RET) c immediately before M-x shell. You can also specify a coding system after starting the shell by using C-x (RET) p in the shell buffer. See Section 18.9 [Specify Coding], page 184.

As soon as the subshell is started, it is sent as input the contents of the file '~/.emacs_*shellname*', if that file exists, where *shellname* is the name of the file that the shell was loaded from. For example, if you use bash, the file sent to it is '~/.emacs_bash'.

cd, pushd and popd commands given to the inferior shell are watched by Emacs so it can keep the '*shell*' buffer's default directory the same as the shell's working directory. These commands are recognized syntactically by examining lines of input that are sent. If you use aliases for these commands, you can tell Emacs to recognize them also. For example, if the value of the variable shell-pushd-regexp matches the beginning of a shell command line, that line is regarded as a pushd command. Change this variable when you add aliases for 'pushd'. Likewise, shell-popd-regexp and shell-cd-regexp are used to recognize commands with the meaning of 'popd' and 'cd'. These commands are recognized only at the beginning of a shell command line.

If Emacs gets an error while trying to handle what it believes is a 'cd', 'pushd' or 'popd' command, it runs the hook shell-set-directory-error-hook (see Section 31.2.3 [Hooks], page 400).

If Emacs does not properly track changes in the current directory of the subshell, use the command M-x dirs to ask the shell what its current directory is. This command works for shells that support the most common command syntax; it may not work for unusual shells.

You can also use M-x dirtrack-mode to enable (or disable) an alternative and more aggressive method of tracking changes in the current directory.

Emacs defines the environment variable EMACS in the subshell, with value t. A shell script can check this variable to determine whether it has been run from an Emacs subshell.

30.2.3 Shell Mode

Shell buffers use Shell mode, which defines several special keys attached to the C-c prefix. They are chosen to resemble the usual editing and job control characters present in shells that are not under Emacs, except that you must type C-c first. Here is a complete list of the special key bindings of Shell mode:

RET   At end of buffer send line as input; otherwise, copy current line
            to end of buffer and send it (comint-send-input). When a line
            is copied, any text at the beginning of the line that matches the
            variable shell-prompt-pattern is left out; this variable's value
            should be a regexp string that matches the prompts that your
            shell uses.

TAB   Complete the command name or file name before point in the
            shell buffer (comint-dynamic-complete). TAB also completes
            history references (see Section 30.2.4.3 [History References],
            page 374) and environment variable names.

            The variable shell-completion-fignore specifies a list of file
            name extensions to ignore in Shell mode completion. The default
            setting ignores file names ending in '~', '#' or '%'. Other related
            Comint modes use the variable comint-completion-fignore
            instead.

M-?   Display temporarily a list of the possible completions of the file
            name before point in the shell buffer (comint-dynamic-list-
            filename-completions).

C-d   Either delete a character or send EOF (comint-delchar-or-
            maybe-eof). Typed at the end of the shell buffer, C-d sends
            EOF to the subshell. Typed at any other position in the buffer,
            C-d deletes a character as usual.

C-c C-a   Move to the beginning of the line, but after the prompt if any
            (comint-bol). If you repeat this command twice in a row, the
            second time it moves back to the process mark, which is the
            beginning of the input that you have not yet sent to the subshell.
            (Normally that is the same place—the end of the prompt on this
            line—but after C-c SPC the process mark may be in a previous
            line.)

C-c (SPC)   Accumulate multiple lines of input, then send them together. This command inserts a newline before point, but does not send the preceding text as input to the subshell—at least, not yet. Both lines, the one before this newline and the one after, will be sent together (along with the newline that separates them), when you type (RET).

C-c C-u   Kill all text pending at end of buffer to be sent as input (**comint-kill-input**).

C-c C-w   Kill a word before point (**backward-kill-word**).

C-c C-c   Interrupt the shell or its current subjob if any (**comint-interrupt-subjob**). This command also kills any shell input pending in the shell buffer and not yet sent.

C-c C-z   Stop the shell or its current subjob if any (**comint-stop-subjob**). This command also kills any shell input pending in the shell buffer and not yet sent.

C-c C-\   Send quit signal to the shell or its current subjob if any (**comint-quit-subjob**). This command also kills any shell input pending in the shell buffer and not yet sent.

C-c C-o   Kill the last batch of output from a shell command (**comint-kill-output**). This is useful if a shell command spews out lots of output that just gets in the way.

C-c C-r
C-M-l   Scroll to display the beginning of the last batch of output at the top of the window; also move the cursor there (**comint-show-output**).

C-c C-e   Scroll to put the end of the buffer at the bottom of the window (**comint-show-maximum-output**).

C-c C-f   Move forward across one shell command, but not beyond the current line (**shell-forward-command**). The variable **shell-command-regexp** specifies how to recognize the end of a command.

C-c C-b   Move backward across one shell command, but not beyond the current line (**shell-backward-command**).

C-c C-l   Display the buffer's history of shell commands in another window (**comint-dynamic-list-input-ring**).

M-x dirs   Ask the shell what its current directory is, so that Emacs can agree with the shell.

M-x send-invisible (RET) *text* (RET)

       Send *text* as input to the shell, after reading it without echoing. This is useful when a shell command runs a program that asks for a password.

Alternatively, you can arrange for Emacs to notice password prompts and turn off echoing for them, as follows:

```
(add-hook 'comint-output-filter-functions
          'comint-watch-for-password-prompt)
```

M-x comint-continue-subjob

Continue the shell process. This is useful if you accidentally suspend the shell process.[1]

M-x comint-strip-ctrl-m

Discard all control-M characters from the current group of shell output. The most convenient way to use this command is to make it run automatically when you get output from the subshell. To do that, evaluate this Lisp expression:

```
(add-hook 'comint-output-filter-functions
          'comint-strip-ctrl-m)
```

M-x comint-truncate-buffer

This command truncates the shell buffer to a certain maximum number of lines, specified by the variable comint-buffer-maximum-size. Here's how to do this automatically each time you get output from the subshell:

```
(add-hook 'comint-output-filter-functions
          'comint-truncate-buffer)
```

Shell mode also customizes the paragraph commands so that only shell prompts start new paragraphs. Thus, a paragraph consists of an input command plus the output that follows it in the buffer.

Shell mode is a derivative of Comint mode, a general-purpose mode for communicating with interactive subprocesses. Most of the features of Shell mode actually come from Comint mode, as you can see from the command names listed above. The special features of Shell mode in particular include the choice of regular expression for detecting prompts, the directory tracking feature, and a few user commands.

Other Emacs features that use variants of Comint mode include GUD (see Section 23.5 [Debuggers], page 280) and M-x run-lisp (see Section 23.10 [External Lisp], page 287).

You can use M-x comint-run to execute any program of your choice in a subprocess using unmodified Comint mode—without the specializations of Shell mode.

---

[1] You should not suspend the shell process. Suspending a subjob of the shell is a completely different matter—that is normal practice, but you must use the shell to continue the subjob; this command won't do it.

30.2.4 Shell Command History

Shell buffers support three ways of repeating earlier commands. You can use the same keys used in the minibuffer; these work much as they do in the minibuffer, inserting text from prior commands while point remains always at the end of the buffer. You can move through the buffer to previous inputs in their original place, then resubmit them or copy them to the end. Or you can use a '!'-style history reference.

30.2.4.1 Shell History Ring

M-p   Fetch the next earlier old shell command.

M-n   Fetch the next later old shell command.

M-r *regexp* (RET)
M-s *regexp* (RET)
             Search backwards or forwards for old shell commands that match *regexp*.

C-c C-x (Shell mode)
             Fetch the next subsequent command from the history.

Shell buffers provide a history of previously entered shell commands. To reuse shell commands from the history, use the editing commands M-p, M-n, M-r and M-s. These work just like the minibuffer history commands except that they operate on the text at the end of the shell buffer, where you would normally insert text to send to the shell.

M-p fetches an earlier shell command to the end of the shell buffer. Successive use of M-p fetches successively earlier shell commands, each replacing any text that was already present as potential shell input. M-n does likewise except that it finds successively more recent shell commands from the buffer.

The history search commands M-r and M-s read a regular expression and search through the history for a matching command. Aside from the choice of which command to fetch, they work just like M-p and M-r. If you enter an empty regexp, these commands reuse the same regexp used last time.

When you find the previous input you want, you can resubmit it by typing (RET), or you can edit it first and then resubmit it if you wish.

Often it is useful to reexecute several successive shell commands that were previously executed in sequence. To do this, first find and reexecute the first command of the sequence. Then type C-c C-x; that will fetch the following command—the one that follows the command you just repeated. Then type (RET) to reexecute this command. You can reexecute several successive commands by typing C-c C-x (RET) over and over.

These commands get the text of previous shell commands from a special history list, not from the shell buffer itself. Thus, editing the shell buffer, or even killing large parts of it, does not affect the history that these commands access.

Some shells store their command histories in files so that you can refer to previous commands from previous shell sessions. Emacs reads the command history file for your chosen shell, to initialize its own command history. The file name is '`~/.bash_history`' for bash, '`~/.sh_history`' for ksh, and '`~/.history`' for other shells.

30.2.4.2 Shell History Copying

C-c C-p   Move point to the previous prompt (`comint-previous-prompt`).

C-c C-n   Move point to the following prompt (`comint-next-prompt`).

C-c (RET)   Copy the input command which point is in, inserting the copy at the end of the buffer (`comint-copy-old-input`). This is useful if you move point back to a previous command. After you copy the command, you can submit the copy as input with (RET). If you wish, you can edit the copy before resubmitting it.

Moving to a previous input and then copying it with `C-c` (RET) produces the same results—the same buffer contents—that you would get by using `M-p` enough times to fetch that previous input from the history list. However, `C-c` (RET) copies the text from the buffer, which can be different from what is in the history list if you edit the input text in the buffer after it has been sent.

30.2.4.3 Shell History References

Various shells including csh and bash support *history references* that begin with '!' and '^'. Shell mode can understand these constructs and perform the history substitution for you. If you insert a history reference and type (TAB), this searches the input history for a matching command, performs substitution if necessary, and places the result in the buffer in place of the history reference. For example, you can fetch the most recent command beginning with 'mv' with ! m v (TAB). You can edit the command if you wish, and then resubmit the command to the shell by typing (RET).

History references take effect only following a shell prompt. The variable `shell-prompt-pattern` specifies how to recognize a shell prompt. Comint modes in general use the variable `comint-prompt-regexp` to specify how to find a prompt; Shell mode uses `shell-prompt-pattern` to set up the local value of `comint-prompt-regexp`.

Shell mode can optionally expand history references in the buffer when you send them to the shell. To request this, set the variable `comint-input-autoexpand` to `input`.

You can make (SPC) perform history expansion by binding (SPC) to the command `comint-magic-space`.

30.2.5 Shell Mode Options

If the variable `comint-scroll-to-bottom-on-input` is non-`nil`, insertion and yank commands scroll the selected window to the bottom before inserting.

If `comint-scroll-show-maximum-output` is non-`nil`, then scrolling due to arrival of output tries to place the last line of text at the bottom line of the window, so as to show as much useful text as possible. (This mimics the scrolling behavior of many terminals.) The default is `nil`.

By setting `comint-scroll-to-bottom-on-output`, you can opt for having point jump to the end of the buffer whenever output arrives—no matter where in the buffer point was before. If the value is `this`, point jumps in the selected window. If the value is `all`, point jumps in each window that shows the comint buffer. If the value is `other`, point jumps in all nonselected windows that show the current buffer. The default value is `nil`, which means point does not jump to the end.

The variable `comint-input-ignoredups` controls whether successive identical inputs are stored in the input history. A non-`nil` value means to omit an input that is the same as the previous input. The default is `nil`, which means to store each input even if it is equal to the previous input.

Three variables customize file name completion. The variable `comint-completion-addsuffix` controls whether completion inserts a space or a slash to indicate a fully completed file or directory name (non-`nil` means do insert a space or slash). `comint-completion-recexact`, if non-`nil`, directs (TAB) to choose the shortest possible completion if the usual Emacs completion algorithm cannot add even a single character. `comint-completion-autolist`, if non-`nil`, says to list all the possible completions whenever completion is not exact.

The command `comint-dynamic-complete-variable` does variable-name completion using the environment variables as set within Emacs. The variables controlling file name completion apply to variable-name completion too. This command is normally available through the menu bar.

Command completion normally considers only executable files. If you set `shell-command-execonly` to `nil`, it considers nonexecutable files as well.

You can configure the behavior of 'pushd'. Variables control whether 'pushd' behaves like 'cd' if no argument is given (`shell-pushd-tohome`), pop rather than rotate with a numeric argument (`shell-pushd-dextract`), and only add directories to the directory stack if they are not already on it (`shell-pushd-dunique`). The values you choose should match the underlying shell, of course.

30.2.6 Remote Host Shell

Emacs provides two commands for logging in to another computer and communicating with it through an Emacs buffer.

M-x telnet (RET) *hostname* (RET)
> Set up a Telnet connection to the computer named *hostname*.

M-x rlogin (RET) *hostname* (RET)
> Set up an Rlogin connection to the computer named *hostname*.

Use M-x telnet to set up a Telnet connection to another computer. (Telnet is the standard Internet protocol for remote login.) It reads the host name of the other computer as an argument with the minibuffer. Once the connection is established, talking to the other computer works like talking to a subshell: you can edit input with the usual Emacs commands, and send it a line at a time by typing (RET). The output is inserted in the Telnet buffer interspersed with the input.

Use M-x rlogin to set up an Rlogin connection. Rlogin is another remote login communication protocol, essentially much like the Telnet protocol but incompatible with it, and supported only by certain systems. Rlogin's advantages are that you can arrange not to have to give your user name and password when communicating between two machines you frequently use, and that you can make an 8-bit-clean connection. (To do that in Emacs, set rlogin-explicit-args to ("-8") before you run Rlogin.)

M-x rlogin sets up the default file directory of the Emacs buffer to access the remote host via FTP (see Section 14.1 [File Names], page 107), and it tracks the shell commands that change the current directory, just like Shell mode.

There are two ways of doing directory tracking in an Rlogin buffer—either with remote directory names '/host:dir/' or with local names (that works if the "remote" machine shares file systems with your machine of origin). You can use the command rlogin-directory-tracking-mode to switch modes. No argument means use remote directory names, a positive argument means use local names, and a negative argument means turn off directory tracking.

30.3 Using Emacs as a Server

Various programs such as mail can invoke your choice of editor to edit a particular piece of text, such as a message that you are sending. By convention, most of these programs use the environment variable EDITOR to specify which editor to run. If you set EDITOR to 'emacs', they invoke Emacs—but in an inconvenient fashion, by starting a new, separate Emacs process. This is inconvenient because it takes time and because the new Emacs process doesn't share the buffers in the existing Emacs process.

You can arrange to use your existing Emacs process as the editor for programs like mail by using the Emacs client and Emacs server programs. Here is how.

First, the preparation. Within Emacs, call the function server-start. (Your '.emacs' file can do this automatically if you add the expression (server-start) to it.) Then, outside Emacs, set the EDITOR environment variable to 'emacsclient'. (Note that some programs use a different environment variable; for example, to make TEX use 'emacsclient', you should set the TEXEDIT environment variable to 'emacsclient +%d %s'.)

Then, whenever any program invokes your specified EDITOR program, the effect is to send a message to your principal Emacs telling it to visit a file. (That's what the program emacsclient does.) Emacs displays the buffer immediately and you can immediately begin editing it.

When you've finished editing that buffer, type C-x # (server-edit). This saves the file and sends a message back to the emacsclient program telling it to exit. The programs that use EDITOR wait for the "editor" (actually, emacsclient) to exit. C-x # also checks for other pending external requests to edit various files, and selects the next such file.

You can switch to a server buffer manually if you wish; you don't have to arrive at it with C-x #. But C-x # is the only way to say that you are "finished" with one.

If you set the variable server-window to a window or a frame, C-x # displays the server buffer in that window or in that frame.

While mail or another application is waiting for emacsclient to finish, emacsclient does not read terminal input. So the terminal that mail was using is effectively blocked for the duration. In order to edit with your principal Emacs, you need to be able to use it without using that terminal. There are two ways to do this:

- Using a window system, run mail and the principal Emacs in two separate windows. While mail is waiting for emacsclient, the window where it was running is blocked, but you can use Emacs by switching windows.

- Use Shell mode in Emacs to run the other program such as mail; then, emacsclient blocks only the subshell under Emacs, and you can still use Emacs to edit the file.

Some programs write temporary files for you to edit. After you edit the temporary file, the program reads it back and deletes it. If the Emacs server is later asked to edit the same file name, it should assume this has nothing to do with the previous occasion for that file name. The server accomplishes this by killing the temporary file's buffer when you finish with the file. Use the variable server-temp-file-regexp to specify which files are temporary in this sense; its value should be a regular expression that matches file names that are temporary.

If you run emacsclient with the option '--no-wait', it returns immediately without waiting for you to "finish" the buffer in Emacs.

30.4 Hardcopy Output

The Emacs commands for making hardcopy let you print either an entire buffer or just part of one, either with or without page headers. See also the

hardcopy commands of Dired (see Section 14.10 [Misc File Ops], page 139)
and the diary (see Section 29.10.1 [Diary Commands], page 355).

M-x print-buffer
              Print hardcopy of current buffer with page headings containing
              the file name and page number.

M-x lpr-buffer
              Print hardcopy of current buffer without page headings.

M-x print-region
              Like print-buffer but print only the current region.

M-x lpr-region
              Like lpr-buffer but print only the current region.

The hardcopy commands (aside from the Postscript commands) pass extra switches to the lpr program based on the value of the variable lpr-
switches. Its value should be a list of strings, each string an option starting
with '-'. For example, to specify a line width of 80 columns for all the
printing you do in Emacs, set lpr-switches like this:

      (setq lpr-switches '("-w80"))

You can specify the printer to use by setting the variable printer-name.

The variable lpr-command specifies the name of the printer program to
run; the default value depends on your operating system type. On most systems, the default is "lpr". The variable lpr-headers-switches similarly
specifies the extra switches to use to make page headers. The variable lpr-
add-switches controls whether to supply '-T' and '-J' options (suitable for
lpr) to the printer program: nil means don't add them. lpr-add-switches
should be nil if your printer program is not compatible with lpr.

30.5 Postscript Hardcopy

These commands convert buffer contents to Postscript, either printing it
or leaving it in another Emacs buffer.

M-x ps-print-buffer
              Print hardcopy of the current buffer in Postscript form.

M-x ps-print-region
              Print hardcopy of the current region in Postscript form.

M-x ps-print-buffer-with-faces
              Print hardcopy of the current buffer in Postscript form, showing
              the faces used in the text by means of Postscript features.

M-x ps-print-region-with-faces
              Print hardcopy of the current region in Postscript form, showing
              the faces used in the text.

`M-x ps-spool-buffer`
> Generate Postscript for the current buffer text.

`M-x ps-spool-region`
> Generate Postscript for the current region.

`M-x ps-spool-buffer-with-faces`
> Generate Postscript for the current buffer, showing the faces used.

`M-x ps-spool-region-with-faces`
> Generate Postscript for the current region, showing the faces used.

The Postscript commands, `ps-print-buffer` and `ps-print-region`, print buffer contents in Postscript form. One command prints the entire buffer; the other, just the region. The corresponding '-with-faces' commands, `ps-print-buffer-with-faces` and `ps-print-region-with-faces`, use Postscript features to show the faces (fonts and colors) in the text properties of the text being printed.

If you are using a color display, you can print a buffer of program code with color highlighting by turning on Font-Lock mode in that buffer, and using `ps-print-buffer-with-faces`.

The commands whose names have 'spool' instead of 'print' generate the Postscript output in an Emacs buffer instead of sending it to the printer.

30.6 Variables for Postscript Hardcopy

All the Postscript hardcopy commands use the variables `ps-lpr-command` and `ps-lpr-switches` to specify how to print the output. `ps-lpr-command` specifies the command name to run, `ps-lpr-switches` specifies command line options to use, and `ps-printer-name` specifies the printer. If you don't set the first two variables yourself, they take their initial values from `lpr-command` and `lpr-switches`. If `ps-printer-name` is `nil`, `printer-name` is used.

The variable `ps-print-header` controls whether these commands add header lines to each page—set it to `nil` to turn headers off. You can turn off color processing by setting `ps-print-color-p` to `nil`.

The variable `ps-paper-type` specifies which size of paper to format for; legitimate values include `a4`, `a3`, `a4small`, `b4`, `b5`, `executive`, `ledger`, `legal`, `letter`, `letter-small`, `statement`, `tabloid`. The default is `letter`. You can define additional paper sizes by changing the variable `ps-page-dimensions-database`.

The variable `ps-landscape-mode` specifies the orientation of printing on the page. The default is `nil`, which stands for "portrait" mode. Any non-`nil` value specifies "landscape" mode.

The variable `ps-number-of-columns` specifies the number of columns; it takes effect in both landscape and portrait mode. The default is 1.

The variable `ps-font-family` specifies which font family to use for printing ordinary text. Legitimate values include `Courier`, `Helvetica`, `NewCenturySchlbk`, `Palatino` and `Times`. The variable `ps-font-size` specifies the size of the font for ordinary text. It defaults to 8.5 points.

Many other customization variables for these commands are defined and described in the Lisp file 'ps-print.el'.

30.7 Sorting Text

Emacs provides several commands for sorting text in the buffer. All operate on the contents of the region (the text between point and the mark). They divide the text of the region into many *sort records*, identify a *sort key* for each record, and then reorder the records into the order determined by the sort keys. The records are ordered so that their keys are in alphabetical order, or, for numeric sorting, in numeric order. In alphabetic sorting, all upper-case letters 'A' through 'Z' come before lower-case 'a', in accord with the ASCII character sequence.

The various sort commands differ in how they divide the text into sort records and in which part of each record is used as the sort key. Most of the commands make each line a separate sort record, but some commands use paragraphs or pages as sort records. Most of the sort commands use each entire sort record as its own sort key, but some use only a portion of the record as the sort key.

`M-x sort-lines`
> Divide the region into lines, and sort by comparing the entire text of a line. A numeric argument means sort into descending order.

`M-x sort-paragraphs`
> Divide the region into paragraphs, and sort by comparing the entire text of a paragraph (except for leading blank lines). A numeric argument means sort into descending order.

`M-x sort-pages`
> Divide the region into pages, and sort by comparing the entire text of a page (except for leading blank lines). A numeric argument means sort into descending order.

`M-x sort-fields`
> Divide the region into lines, and sort by comparing the contents of one field in each line. Fields are defined as separated by whitespace, so the first run of consecutive non-whitespace characters in a line constitutes field 1, the second such run constitutes field 2, etc.

Specify which field to sort by with a numeric argument: 1 to sort by field 1, etc. A negative argument means count fields from the right instead of from the left; thus, minus 1 means sort by the last field. If several lines have identical contents in the field being sorted, they keep same relative order that they had in the original buffer.

M-x sort-numeric-fields

Like M-x **sort-fields** except the specified field is converted to an integer for each line, and the numbers are compared. '10' comes before '2' when considered as text, but after it when considered as a number.

M-x sort-columns

Like M-x **sort-fields** except that the text within each line used for comparison comes from a fixed range of columns. See below for an explanation.

M-x reverse-region

Reverse the order of the lines in the region. This is useful for sorting into descending order by fields or columns, since those sort commands do not have a feature for doing that.

For example, if the buffer contains this:

```
On systems where clash detection (locking of files being edited) is
implemented, Emacs also checks the first time you modify a buffer
whether the file has changed on disk since it was last visited or
saved.  If it has, you are asked to confirm that you want to change
the buffer.
```

applying M-x **sort-lines** to the entire buffer produces this:

```
On systems where clash detection (locking of files being edited) is
implemented, Emacs also checks the first time you modify a buffer
saved.  If it has, you are asked to confirm that you want to change
the buffer.
whether the file has changed on disk since it was last visited or
```

where the upper-case 'O' sorts before all lower-case letters. If you use C-u 2 M-x sort-fields instead, you get this:

```
implemented, Emacs also checks the first time you modify a buffer
saved.  If it has, you are asked to confirm that you want to change
the buffer.
On systems where clash detection (locking of files being edited) is
whether the file has changed on disk since it was last visited or
```

where the sort keys were 'Emacs', 'If', 'buffer', 'systems' and 'the'.

M-x sort-columns requires more explanation. You specify the columns by putting point at one of the columns and the mark at the other column. Because this means you cannot put point or the mark at the beginning of the first line of the text you want to sort, this command uses an unusual definition of 'region': all of the line point is in is considered part of the region, and so is all of the line the mark is in, as well as all the lines in between.

For example, to sort a table by information found in columns 10 to 15, you could put the mark on column 10 in the first line of the table, and point on column 15 in the last line of the table, and then run `sort-columns`. Equivalently, you could run it with the mark on column 15 in the first line and point on column 10 in the last line.

This can be thought of as sorting the rectangle specified by point and the mark, except that the text on each line to the left or right of the rectangle moves along with the text inside the rectangle. See Section 9.4 [Rectangles], page 71.

Many of the sort commands ignore case differences when comparing, if `sort-fold-case` is non-`nil`.

30.8 Narrowing

Narrowing means focusing in on some portion of the buffer, making the rest temporarily inaccessible. The portion which you can still get to is called the *accessible portion*. Canceling the narrowing, which makes the entire buffer once again accessible, is called *widening*. The amount of narrowing in effect in a buffer at any time is called the buffer's *restriction*.

Narrowing can make it easier to concentrate on a single subroutine or paragraph by eliminating clutter. It can also be used to restrict the range of operation of a replace command or repeating keyboard macro.

C-x n n   Narrow down to between point and mark (`narrow-to-region`).

C-x n w   Widen to make the entire buffer accessible again (`widen`).

C-x n p   Narrow down to the current page (`narrow-to-page`).

C-x n d   Narrow down to the current defun (`narrow-to-defun`).

When you have narrowed down to a part of the buffer, that part appears to be all there is. You can't see the rest, you can't move into it (motion commands won't go outside the accessible part), you can't change it in any way. However, it is not gone, and if you save the file all the inaccessible text will be saved. The word '`Narrow`' appears in the mode line whenever narrowing is in effect.

The primary narrowing command is C-x n n (`narrow-to-region`). It sets the current buffer's restrictions so that the text in the current region remains accessible but all text before the region or after the region is inaccessible. Point and mark do not change.

Alternatively, use C-x n p (`narrow-to-page`) to narrow down to the current page. See Section 21.4 [Pages], page 202, for the definition of a page. C-x n d (`narrow-to-defun`) narrows down to the defun containing point (see Section 22.4 [Defuns], page 230).

The way to cancel narrowing is to widen with `C-x n w` (**widen**). This makes all text in the buffer accessible again.

You can get information on what part of the buffer you are narrowed down to using the `C-x =` command. See Section 4.9 [Position Info], page 35.

Because narrowing can easily confuse users who do not understand it, **narrow-to-region** is normally a disabled command. Attempting to use this command asks for confirmation and gives you the option of enabling it; if you enable the command, confirmation will no longer be required for it. See Section 31.4.11 [Disabling], page 418.

30.9 Two-Column Editing

Two-column mode lets you conveniently edit two side-by-side columns of text. It uses two side-by-side windows, each showing its own buffer.

There are three ways to enter two-column mode:

F2 **2** or `C-x 6 2`

> Enter two-column mode with the current buffer on the left, and on the right, a buffer whose name is based on the current buffer's name (**2C-two-columns**). If the right-hand buffer doesn't already exist, it starts out empty; the current buffer's contents are not changed.
>
> This command is appropriate when the current buffer is empty or contains just one column and you want to add another column.

F2 **s** or `C-x 6 s`

> Split the current buffer, which contains two-column text, into two buffers, and display them side by side (**2C-split**). The current buffer becomes the left-hand buffer, but the text in the right-hand column is moved into the right-hand buffer. The current column specifies the split point. Splitting starts with the current line and continues to the end of the buffer.
>
> This command is appropriate when you have a buffer that already contains two-column text, and you wish to separate the columns temporarily.

F2 **b** *buffer* RET
`C-x 6 b` *buffer* RET

> Enter two-column mode using the current buffer as the left-hand buffer, and using buffer *buffer* as the right-hand buffer (**2C-associate-buffer**).

F2 **s** or `C-x 6 s` looks for a column separator, which is a string that appears on each line between the two columns. You can specify the width of the separator with a numeric argument to F2 **s**; that many characters, before point, constitute the separator string. By default, the width is 1, so the column separator is the character before point.

When a line has the separator at the proper place, (F2) s puts the text after the separator into the right-hand buffer, and deletes the separator. Lines that don't have the column separator at the proper place remain unsplit; they stay in the left-hand buffer, and the right-hand buffer gets an empty line to correspond. (This is the way to write a line that "spans both columns while in two-column mode": write it in the left-hand buffer, and put an empty line in the right-hand buffer.)

The command C-x 6 (RET) or (F2) (RET) (2C-newline) inserts a newline in each of the two buffers at corresponding positions. This is the easiest way to add a new line to the two-column text while editing it in split buffers.

When you have edited both buffers as you wish, merge them with (F2) 1 or C-x 6 1 (2C-merge). This copies the text from the right-hand buffer as a second column in the other buffer. To go back to two-column editing, use (F2) s.

Use (F2) d or C-x 6 d to dissociate the two buffers, leaving each as it stands (2C-dissociate). If the other buffer, the one not current when you type (F2) d, is empty, (F2) d kills it.

30.10 Editing Binary Files

There is a special major mode for editing binary files: Hexl mode. To use it, use M-x hexl-find-file instead of C-x C-f to visit the file. This command converts the file's contents to hexadecimal and lets you edit the translation. When you save the file, it is converted automatically back to binary.

You can also use M-x hexl-mode to translate an existing buffer into hex. This is useful if you visit a file normally and then discover it is a binary file.

Ordinary text characters overwrite in Hexl mode. This is to reduce the risk of accidentally spoiling the alignment of data in the file. There are special commands for insertion. Here is a list of the commands of Hexl mode:

C-M-d	Insert a byte with a code typed in decimal.
C-M-o	Insert a byte with a code typed in octal.
C-M-x	Insert a byte with a code typed in hex.
C-x [	Move to the beginning of a 1k-byte "page."
C-x]	Move to the end of a 1k-byte "page."
M-g	Move to an address specified in hex.
M-j	Move to an address specified in decimal.
C-c C-c	Leave Hexl mode, going back to the major mode this buffer had before you invoked hexl-mode.

30.11 Saving Emacs Sessions

You can use the Desktop library to save the state of Emacs from one session to another. Saving the state means that Emacs starts up with the same set of buffers, major modes, buffer positions, and so on that the previous Emacs session had.

To use Desktop, you should use the Customization buffer (see Section 31.2.2 [Easy Customization], page 394) to set `desktop-enable` to a non-`nil` value, or add these lines at the end of your '`.emacs`' file:

```
(desktop-load-default)
(desktop-read)
```

The first time you save the state of the Emacs session, you must do it manually, with the command M-x `desktop-save`. Once you have done that, exiting Emacs will save the state again—not only the present Emacs session, but also subsequent sessions. You can also save the state at any time, without exiting Emacs, by typing M-x `desktop-save` again.

In order for Emacs to recover the state from a previous session, you must start it with the same current directory as you used when you started the previous session. This is because `desktop-read` looks in the current directory for the file to read. This means that you can have separate saved sessions in different directories; the directory in which you start Emacs will control which saved session to use.

The variable `desktop-files-not-to-save` controls which files are excluded from state saving. Its value is a regular expression that matches the files to exclude. By default, remote (ftp-accessed) files are excluded; this is because visiting them again in the subsequent session would be slow. If you want to include these files in state saving, set `desktop-files-not-to-save` to "`^$`". See Section 14.12 [Remote Files], page 141.

30.12 Recursive Editing Levels

A *recursive edit* is a situation in which you are using Emacs commands to perform arbitrary editing while in the middle of another Emacs command. For example, when you type C-r inside of a `query-replace`, you enter a recursive edit in which you can change the current buffer. On exiting from the recursive edit, you go back to the `query-replace`.

Exiting the recursive edit means returning to the unfinished command, which continues execution. The command to exit is C-M-c (`exit-recursive-edit`).

You can also *abort* the recursive edit. This is like exiting, but also quits the unfinished command immediately. Use the command C-] (`abort-recursive-edit`) to do this. See Section 32.1 [Quitting], page 425.

The mode line shows you when you are in a recursive edit by displaying square brackets around the parentheses that always surround the major and minor mode names. Every window's mode line shows this, in the same way, since being in a recursive edit is true of Emacs as a whole rather than any particular window or buffer.

It is possible to be in recursive edits within recursive edits. For example, after typing C-r in a query-replace, you may type a command that enters the debugger. This begins a recursive editing level for the debugger, within the recursive editing level for C-r. Mode lines display a pair of square brackets for each recursive editing level currently in progress.

Exiting the inner recursive edit (such as, with the debugger c command) resumes the command running in the next level up. When that command finishes, you can then use C-M-c to exit another recursive editing level, and so on. Exiting applies to the innermost level only. Aborting also gets out of only one level of recursive edit; it returns immediately to the command level of the previous recursive edit. If you wish, you can then abort the next recursive editing level.

Alternatively, the command M-x top-level aborts all levels of recursive edits, returning immediately to the top-level command reader.

The text being edited inside the recursive edit need not be the same text that you were editing at top level. It depends on what the recursive edit is for. If the command that invokes the recursive edit selects a different buffer first, that is the buffer you will edit recursively. In any case, you can switch buffers within the recursive edit in the normal manner (as long as the buffer-switching keys have not been rebound). You could probably do all the rest of your editing inside the recursive edit, visiting files and all. But this could have surprising effects (such as stack overflow) from time to time. So remember to exit or abort the recursive edit when you no longer need it.

In general, we try to minimize the use of recursive editing levels in GNU Emacs. This is because they constrain you to "go back" in a particular order—from the innermost level toward the top level. When possible, we present different activities in separate buffers so that you can switch between them as you please. Some commands switch to a new major mode which provides a command to switch back. These approaches give you more flexibility to go back to unfinished tasks in the order you choose.

30.13 Emulation

GNU Emacs can be programmed to emulate (more or less) most other editors. Standard facilities can emulate these:

EDT (DEC VMS editor)

> Turn on EDT emulation with M-x edt-emulation-on. M-x edt-emulation-off restores normal Emacs command bindings.

> Most of the EDT emulation commands are keypad keys, and most standard Emacs key bindings are still available. The EDT emulation rebindings are done in the global keymap, so there

is no problem switching buffers or major modes while in EDT emulation.

vi (Berkeley editor)

Viper is the newest emulator for vi. It implements several levels of emulation; level 1 is closest to vi itself, while level 5 departs somewhat from strict emulation to take advantage of the capabilities of Emacs. To invoke Viper, type `M-x viper-mode`; it will guide you the rest of the way and ask for the emulation level. See Info file 'viper', node 'Top'.

vi (another emulator)

`M-x vi-mode` enters a major mode that replaces the previously established major mode. All of the vi commands that, in real vi, enter "input" mode are programmed instead to return to the previous major mode. Thus, ordinary Emacs serves as vi's "input" mode.

Because vi emulation works through major modes, it does not work to switch buffers during emulation. Return to normal Emacs first.

If you plan to use vi emulation much, you probably want to bind a key to the `vi-mode` command.

vi (alternate emulator)

`M-x vip-mode` invokes another vi emulator, said to resemble real vi more thoroughly than `M-x vi-mode`. "Input" mode in this emulator is changed from ordinary Emacs so you can use (ESC) to go back to emulated vi command mode. To get from emulated vi command mode back to ordinary Emacs, type `C-z`.

This emulation does not work through major modes, and it is possible to switch buffers in various ways within the emulator. It is not so necessary to assign a key to the command `vip-mode` as it is with `vi-mode` because terminating insert mode does not use it.

See Info file 'vip', node 'Top', for full information.

30.14 Dissociated Press

`M-x dissociated-press` is a command for scrambling a file of text either word by word or character by character. Starting from a buffer of straight English, it produces extremely amusing output. The input comes from the current Emacs buffer. Dissociated Press writes its output in a buffer named '*Dissociation*', and redisplays that buffer after every couple of lines (approximately) so you can read the output as it comes out.

Dissociated Press asks every so often whether to continue generating output. Answer n to stop it. You can also stop at any time by typing C-g. The dissociation output remains in the '*Dissociation*' buffer for you to copy elsewhere if you wish.

Dissociated Press operates by jumping at random from one point in the buffer to another. In order to produce plausible output rather than gibberish, it insists on a certain amount of overlap between the end of one run of consecutive words or characters and the start of the next. That is, if it has just printed out 'president' and then decides to jump to a different point in the file, it might spot the 'ent' in 'pentagon' and continue from there, producing 'presidentagon'.[2] Long sample texts produce the best results.

A positive argument to M-x dissociated-press tells it to operate character by character, and specifies the number of overlap characters. A negative argument tells it to operate word by word and specifies the number of overlap words. In this mode, whole words are treated as the elements to be permuted, rather than characters. No argument is equivalent to an argument of two. For your againformation, the output goes only into the buffer '*Dissociation*'. The buffer you start with is not changed.

Dissociated Press produces nearly the same results as a Markov chain based on a frequency table constructed from the sample text. It is, however, an independent, ignoriginal invention. Dissociated Press techniquitously copies several consecutive characters from the sample between random choices, whereas a Markov chain would choose randomly for each word or character. This makes for more plausible sounding results, and runs faster.

It is a mustatement that too much use of Dissociated Press can be a developediment to your real work. Sometimes to the point of outragedy. And keep dissociwords out of your documentation, if you want it to be well userenced and properbose. Have fun. Your buggestions are welcome.

30.15 Other Amusements

If you are a little bit bored, you can try M-x hanoi. If you are considerably bored, give it a numeric argument. If you are very very bored, try an argument of 9. Sit back and watch.

If you want a little more personal involvement, try M-x gomoku, which plays the game Go Moku with you.

M-x blackbox and M-x mpuz are two kinds of puzzles. blackbox challenges you to determine the location of objects inside a box by tomography. mpuz displays a multiplication puzzle with letters standing for digits in a code that you must guess—to guess a value, type a letter and then the digit you think it stands for.

M-x dunnet runs an adventure-style exploration game, which is a bigger sort of puzzle.

---

[2] This dissociword actually appeared during the Vietnam War, when it was very appropriate.

When you are frustrated, try the famous Eliza program. Just do `M-x` `doctor`. End each input by typing (RET) twice.

When you are feeling strange, type `M-x` `yow`.

31 Customization

This chapter talks about various topics relevant to adapting the behavior of Emacs in minor ways. See *The Emacs Lisp Reference Manual* for how to make more far-reaching changes.

All kinds of customization affect only the particular Emacs session that you do them in. They are completely lost when you kill the Emacs session, and have no effect on other Emacs sessions you may run at the same time or later. The only way an Emacs session can affect anything outside of it is by writing a file; in particular, the only way to make a customization "permanent" is to put something in your '.emacs' file or other appropriate file to do the customization in each session. See Section 31.7 [Init File], page 419.

31.1 Minor Modes

Minor modes are optional features which you can turn on or off. For example, Auto Fill mode is a minor mode in which (SPC) breaks lines between words as you type. All the minor modes are independent of each other and of the selected major mode. Most minor modes say in the mode line when they are on; for example, 'Fill' in the mode line means that Auto Fill mode is on.

Append -mode to the name of a minor mode to get the name of a command function that turns the mode on or off. Thus, the command to enable or disable Auto Fill mode is called M-x auto-fill-mode. These commands are usually invoked with M-x, but you can bind keys to them if you wish. With no argument, the function turns the mode on if it was off and off if it was on. This is known as *toggling*. A positive argument always turns the mode on, and an explicit zero argument or a negative argument always turns it off.

Enabling or disabling some minor modes applies only to the current buffer; each buffer is independent of the other buffers. Therefore, you can enable the mode in particular buffers and disable it in others. The per-buffer minor modes include Abbrev mode, Auto Fill mode, Auto Save mode, Font-Lock mode, Hscroll mode, ISO Accents mode, Outline minor mode, Overwrite mode, and Binary Overwrite mode.

Abbrev mode allows you to define abbreviations that automatically expand as you type them. For example, 'amd' might expand to 'abbrev mode'. See Chapter 24 [Abbrevs], page 289, for full information.

Auto Fill mode allows you to enter filled text without breaking lines explicitly. Emacs inserts newlines as necessary to prevent lines from becoming too long. See Section 21.5 [Filling], page 203.

Auto Save mode causes the contents of a buffer to be saved periodically to reduce the amount of work you can lose in case of a system crash. See Section 14.5 [Auto Save], page 117.

Enriched mode enables editing and saving of formatted text. See Section 21.11 [Formatted Text], page 219.

Flyspell mode automatically highlights misspelled words. See Section 13.4 [Spelling], page 103.

Font-Lock mode automatically highlights certain textual units found in programs, such as comments, strings, and function names being defined. This requires a window system that can display multiple fonts. See Section 17.13 [Faces], page 166.

Hscroll mode performs horizontal scrolling automatically to keep point on the screen. See Section 11.2 [Horizontal Scrolling], page 80.

ISO Accents mode makes the characters ' ' ', ' ' ', ' " ', ' ^ ', ' / ' and ' ~ ' combine with the following letter, to produce an accented letter in the ISO Latin-1 character set. See Section 18.12 [Single-Byte European Support], page 188.

Outline minor mode provides the same facilities as the major mode called Outline mode; but since it is a minor mode instead, you can combine it with any major mode. See Section 21.8 [Outline Mode], page 210.

Overwrite mode causes ordinary printing characters to replace existing text instead of shoving it to the right. For example, if point is in front of the 'B' in 'FOOBAR', then in Overwrite mode typing a G changes it to 'FOOGAR', instead of producing 'FOOGBAR' as usual. In Overwrite mode, the command C-q inserts the next character whatever it may be, even if it is a digit— this gives you a way to insert a character instead of replacing an existing character.

Binary Overwrite mode is a variant of Overwrite mode for editing binary files; it treats newlines and tabs like other characters, so that they overwrite other characters and can be overwritten by them.

The following minor modes normally apply to all buffers at once. Since each is enabled or disabled by the value of a variable, you *can* set them differently for particular buffers, by explicitly making the corresponding variables local in those buffers. See Section 31.2.4 [Locals], page 401.

Icomplete mode displays an indication of available completions when you are in the minibuffer and completion is active. See Section 5.3.4 [Completion Options], page 45.

Line Number mode enables continuous display in the mode line of the line number of point. See Section 1.3 [Mode Line], page 17.

Resize-Minibuffer mode makes the minibuffer expand as necessary to hold the text that you put in it. See Section 5.2 [Minibuffer Edit], page 42.

Scroll Bar mode gives each window a scroll bar (see Section 17.11 [Scroll Bars], page 165). Menu Bar mode gives each frame a menu bar (see Section 17.12 [Menu Bars], page 166). Both of these modes are enabled by default when you use the X Window System.

In Transient Mark mode, every change in the buffer contents "deactivates" the mark, so that commands that operate on the region will get an error. This means you must either set the mark, or explicitly "reactivate" it, before each command that uses the region. The advantage of Transient Mark mode is that Emacs can display the region highlighted (currently only when using X). See Section 8.1 [Setting Mark], page 59.

For most minor modes, the command name is also the name of a variable which directly controls the mode. The mode is enabled whenever this variable's value is non-`nil`, and the minor-mode command works by setting the variable. For example, the command `outline-minor-mode` works by setting the value of `outline-minor-mode` as a variable; it is this variable that directly turns Outline minor mode on and off. To check whether a given minor mode works this way, use `C-h v` to ask for documentation on the variable name.

These minor-mode variables provide a good way for Lisp programs to turn minor modes on and off; they are also useful in a file's local variables list. But please think twice before setting minor modes with a local variables list, because most minor modes are matter of user preference—other users editing the same file might not want the same minor modes you prefer.

31.2 Variables

A *variable* is a Lisp symbol which has a value. The symbol's name is also called the name of the variable. A variable name can contain any characters that can appear in a file, but conventionally variable names consist of words separated by hyphens. A variable can have a documentation string which describes what kind of value it should have and how the value will be used.

Lisp allows any variable to have any kind of value, but most variables that Emacs uses require a value of a certain type. Often the value should always be a string, or should always be a number. Sometimes we say that a certain feature is turned on if a variable is "non-`nil`," meaning that if the variable's value is `nil`, the feature is off, but the feature is on for *any* other value. The conventional value to use to turn on the feature—since you have to pick one particular value when you set the variable—is `t`.

Emacs uses many Lisp variables for internal record keeping, as any Lisp program must, but the most interesting variables for you are the ones that exist for the sake of customization. Emacs does not (usually) change the values of these variables; instead, you set the values, and thereby alter and control the behavior of certain Emacs commands. These variables are called *user options*. Most user options are documented in this manual, and appear in the Variable Index (see [Variable Index], page 527).

One example of a variable which is a user option is `fill-column`, which specifies the position of the right margin (as a number of characters from the left margin) to be used by the fill commands (see Section 21.5 [Filling], page 203).

31.2.1 Examining and Setting Variables

C-h v *var* (RET)

> Display the value and documentation of variable *var* (describe-variable).

M-x set-variable (RET) *var* (RET) *value* (RET)

> Change the value of variable *var* to *value*.

To examine the value of a single variable, use C-h v (describe-variable), which reads a variable name using the minibuffer, with completion. It displays both the value and the documentation of the variable. For example,

> C-h v fill-column (RET)

displays something like this:

```
fill-column's value is 75


Documentation:
*Column beyond which automatic line-wrapping should happen.
Automatically becomes buffer-local when set in any fashion.
```

The star at the beginning of the documentation indicates that this variable is a user option. C-h v is not restricted to user options; it allows any variable name.

The most convenient way to set a specific user option is with M-x set-variable. This reads the variable name with the minibuffer (with completion), and then reads a Lisp expression for the new value using the minibuffer a second time. For example,

> M-x set-variable (RET) fill-column (RET) 75 (RET)

sets fill-column to 75.

M-x set-variable is limited to user option variables, but you can set any variable with a Lisp expression, using the function setq. Here is a setq expression to set fill-column:

> (setq fill-column 75)

To execute an expression like this one, go to the '*scratch*' buffer, type in the expression, and then type C-j. See Section 23.9 [Lisp Interaction], page 287.

Setting variables, like all means of customizing Emacs except where otherwise stated, affects only the current Emacs session.

31.2.2 Easy Customization Interface

A convenient way to find the user option variables that you want to change, and then change them, is with M-x customize. This command creates a *customization buffer* with which you can browse through the Emacs user options in a logically organized structure, then edit and set their values.

You can also use the customization buffer to save settings permanently. (Not all Emacs user options are included in this structure as of yet, but we are adding the rest.)

31.2.2.1 Customization Groups

For customization purposes, user options are organized into *groups* to help you find them. Groups are collected into bigger groups, all the way up to a master group called `Emacs`.

`M-x customize` creates a customization buffer that shows the top-level `Emacs` group and the second-level groups immediately under it. It looks like this, in part:

```
/- Emacs group: -------------------------------------------------\
      [State]: visible group members are all at standard settings.
   Customization of the One True Editor.
   See also [Manual].


   Editing group: [Go to Group]
   Basic text editing facilities.


   External group: [Go to Group]
   Interfacing to external utilities.


   more second-level groups


   \- Emacs group end ------------------------------------------------/
```

This says that the buffer displays the contents of the `Emacs` group. The other groups are listed because they are its contents. But they are listed differently, without indentation and dashes, because *their* contents are not included. Each group has a single-line documentation string; the `Emacs` group also has a '`[State]`' line.

Most of the text in the customization buffer is read-only, but it typically includes some *editable fields* that you can edit. There are also *active fields*; this means a field that does something when you *invoke* it. To invoke an active field, either click on it with `Mouse-1`, or move point to it and type ⟨RET⟩.

For example, the phrase '`[Go to Group]`' that appears in a second-level group is an active field. Invoking the '`[Go to Group]`' field for a group creates a new customization buffer, which shows that group and its contents. This field is a kind of hypertext link to another group.

The `Emacs` group does not include any user options itself, but other groups do. By examining various groups, you will eventually find the options and faces that belong to the feature you are interested in customizing. Then you can use the customization buffer to set them.

You can view the structure of customization groups on a larger scale with M-x customize-browse. This command creates a special kind of customization buffer which shows only the names of the groups (and options and faces), and their structure.

In this buffer, you can show the contents of a group by invoking '[+]'. When the group contents are visible, this button changes to '[-]'; invoking that hides the group contents.

Each group, option or face name in this buffer has an active field which says '[Group]', '[Option]' or '[Face]'. Invoking that active field creates an ordinary customization buffer showing just that group and its contents, just that option, or just that face. This is the way to set values in it.

31.2.2.2 Changing an Option

Here is an example of what a user option looks like in the customization buffer:

```
Kill Ring Max: [Hide] 30
    [State]: this option is unchanged from its standard setting.
Maximum length of kill ring before oldest elements are thrown away.
```

The text following '[Hide]', '30' in this case, indicates the current value of the option. If you see '[Show]' instead of '[Hide]', it means that the value is hidden; the customization buffer initially hides values that take up several lines. Invoke '[Show]' to show the value.

The line after the option name indicates the *customization state* of the option: in the example above, it says you have not changed the option yet. The word '[State]' at the beginning of this line is active; you can get a menu of various operations by invoking it with Mouse-1 or (RET). These operations are essential for customizing the variable.

The line after the '[State]' line displays the beginning of the option's documentation string. If there are more lines of documentation, this line ends with '[More]'; invoke this to show the full documentation string.

To enter a new value for 'Kill Ring Max', move point to the value and edit it textually. For example, you can type M-d, then insert another number.

When you begin to alter the text, you will see the '[State]' line change to say that you have edited the value:

```
[State]: you have edited the value as text, but not set the option.
```

Editing the value does not actually set the option variable. To do that, you must *set* the option. To do this, invoke the word '[State]' and choose 'Set for Current Session'.

The state of the option changes visibly when you set it:

```
[State]: you have set this option, but not saved it for future sessions.
```

You don't have to worry about specifying a value that is not valid; setting the option checks for validity and will not really install an unacceptable value.

While editing a value or field that is a file name, directory name, command name, or anything else for which completion is defined, you can type M-⟨TAB⟩ (`widget-complete`) to do completion.

Some options have a small fixed set of possible legitimate values. These options don't let you edit the value textually. Instead, an active field '[Value Menu]' appears before the value; invoke this field to edit the value. For a boolean "on or off" value, the active field says '[Toggle]', and it changes to the other value. '[Value Menu]' and '[Toggle]' edit the buffer; the changes take effect when you use the 'Set for Current Session' operation.

Some options have values with complex structure. For example, the value of `load-path` is a list of directories. Here is how it appears in the customization buffer:

```
Load Path:
[INS] [DEL] [Current dir?]: /usr/local/share/emacs/20.3/site-lisp
[INS] [DEL] [Current dir?]: /usr/local/share/emacs/site-lisp
[INS] [DEL] [Current dir?]: /usr/local/share/emacs/20.3/leim
[INS] [DEL] [Current dir?]: /usr/local/share/emacs/20.3/lisp
[INS] [DEL] [Current dir?]: /build/emacs/e20/lisp
[INS] [DEL] [Current dir?]: /build/emacs/e20/lisp/gnus
[INS]
    [State]: this item has been changed outside the customization buffer.
  List of directories to search for files to load....
```

Each directory in the list appears on a separate line, and each line has several editable or active fields.

You can edit any of the directory names. To delete a directory from the list, invoke '[DEL]' on that line. To insert a new directory in the list, invoke '[INS]' at the point where you want to insert it.

You can also invoke '[Current dir?]' to switch between including a specific named directory in the path, and including `nil` in the path. (`nil` in a search path means "try the current directory.")

Two special commands, ⟨TAB⟩ and S-⟨TAB⟩, are useful for moving through the customization buffer. ⟨TAB⟩ (`widget-forward`) moves forward to the next active or editable field; S-⟨TAB⟩ (`widget-backward`) moves backward to the previous active or editable field.

Typing ⟨RET⟩ on an editable field also moves forward, just like ⟨TAB⟩. The reason for this is that people have a tendency to type ⟨RET⟩ when they are finished editing a field. If you have occasion to insert a newline in an editable field, use C-o or C-q C-j.

Setting the option changes its value in the current Emacs session; *saving* the value changes it for future sessions as well. This works by writing code into your '~/.emacs' file so as to set the option variable again each time you start Emacs. To save the option, invoke '[State]' and select the 'Save for Future Sessions' operation.

You can also restore the option to its standard value by invoking '[State]' and selecting the 'Reset to Standard Settings' operation. There are actually three reset operations:

'Reset'   If you have made some modifications and not yet set the option, this restores the text in the customization buffer to match the actual value.

'Reset to Saved'
               This restores the value of the option to the last saved value, and updates the text accordingly.

'Reset to Standard Settings'
               This sets the option to its standard value, and updates the text accordingly. This also eliminates any saved value for the option, so that you will get the standard value in future Emacs sessions.

The state of a group indicates whether anything in that group has been edited, set or saved. You can select 'Set for Current Session', 'Save for Future Sessions' and the various kinds of 'Reset' operation for the group; these operations on the group apply to all options in the group and its subgroups.

Near the top of the customization buffer there are two lines containing several active fields:

```
[Set for Current Session] [Save for Future Sessions]

[Reset] [Reset to Saved] [Reset to Standard]   [Bury Buffer]
```

Invoking '[Bury Buffer]' buries this customization buffer. Each of the other fields performs an operation—set, save or reset—on each of the items in the buffer that could meaningfully be set, saved or reset.

31.2.2.3 Customizing Faces

In addition to user options, some customization groups also include faces. When you show the contents of a group, both the user options and the faces in the group appear in the customization buffer. Here is an example of how a face looks:

```
Custom Changed Face: (sample)
    [State]: this face is unchanged from its standard setting.
Face used when the customize item has been changed.
Attributes: [ ] Bold: [toggle] off
            [X] Italic: [toggle] on
            [ ] Underline: [toggle] off
            [ ] Inverse-Video: [toggle] on
            [ ] Foreground: black (sample)
            [ ] Background: white (sample)
```

[ ] `Stipple:`

Each face attribute has its own line. The '`[x]`' field before the attribute name indicates whether the attribute is *enabled*; '`X`' means that it is. You can enable or disable the attribute by invoking that field. When the attribute is enabled, you can change the attribute value in the usual ways.

On a black-and-white display, the colors you can use for the background are '`black`', '`white`', '`gray`', '`gray1`', and '`gray3`'. Emacs supports these shades of gray by using background stipple patterns instead of a color.

Setting, saving and resetting a face work like the same operations for options (see Section 31.2.2.2 [Changing an Option], page 396).

A face can specify different appearances for different types of display. For example, a face can make text red on a color display, but use a bold font on a monochrome display. To specify multiple appearances for a face, select '`Show Display Types`' in the menu you get from invoking '`[State]`'.

Another more basic way to set the attributes of a specific face is with `M-x modify-face`. This command reads the name of a face, then reads the attributes one by one. For the color and stipple attributes, the attribute's current value is the default—type just ⟨RET⟩ if you don't want to change that attribute. Type '`none`' if you want to clear out the attribute.

31.2.2.4 Customizing Specific Items

Instead of finding the options you want to change by moving down through the structure of groups, you can specify the particular option, face or group that you want to customize.

`M-x customize-option` ⟨RET⟩ *option* ⟨RET⟩
> Set up a customization buffer with just one option, *option*.

`M-x customize-face` ⟨RET⟩ *face* ⟨RET⟩
> Set up a customization buffer with just one face, *face*.

`M-x customize-group` ⟨RET⟩ *group* ⟨RET⟩
> Set up a customization buffer with just one group, *group*.

`M-x customize-apropos` ⟨RET⟩ *regexp* ⟨RET⟩
> Set up a customization buffer with all the options, faces and groups that match *regexp*.

`M-x customize-changed-options` ⟨RET⟩ *version* ⟨RET⟩
> Set up a customization buffer with all the options, faces and groups whose meaning has changed since Emacs version *version*.

`M-x customize-saved`
> Set up a customization buffer containing all options and faces that you have saved with customization buffers.

`M-x customize-customized`
> Set up a customization buffer containing all options and faces that you have customized but not saved.

If you want to alter a particular user option variable with the customization buffer, and you know its name, you can use the command M-x customize-option and specify the option name. This sets up the customization buffer with just one option—the one that you asked for. Editing, setting and saving the value work as described above, but only for the specified option.

Likewise, you can modify a specific face, chosen by name, using M-x customize-face.

You can also set up the customization buffer with a specific group, using M-x customize-group. The immediate contents of the chosen group, including option variables, faces, and other groups, all appear as well. However, these subgroups' own contents start out hidden. You can show their contents in the usual way, by invoking '[Show]'.

To control more precisely what to customize, you can use M-x customize-apropos. You specify a regular expression as argument; then all options, faces and groups whose names match this regular expression are set up in the customization buffer. If you specify an empty regular expression, this includes *all* groups, options and faces in the customization buffer (but that takes a long time).

When you upgrade to a new Emacs version, you might want to customize new options and options whose meanings or default values have changed. To do this, use M-x customize-changed-options and specify a previous Emacs version number using the minibuffer. It creates a customization buffer which shows all the options (and groups) whose definitions have been changed since the specified version.

If you change option values and then decide the change was a mistake, you can use two special commands to revisit your previous changes. Use customize-saved to look at the options and faces that you have saved. Use M-x customize-customized to look at the options and faces that you have set but not saved.

31.2.3 Hooks

A *hook* is a variable where you can store a function or functions to be called on a particular occasion by an existing program. Emacs provides a number of hooks for the sake of customization.

Most of the hooks in Emacs are *normal hooks*. These variables contain lists of functions to be called with no arguments. The reason most hooks are normal hooks is so that you can use them in a uniform way. Every variable in Emacs whose name ends in '-hook' is a normal hook.

Most major modes run hooks as the last step of initialization. This makes it easy for a user to customize the behavior of the mode, by overriding the local variable assignments already made by the mode. But hooks may also be used in other contexts. For example, the hook suspend-hook runs just before Emacs suspends itself (see Section 3.1 [Exiting], page 25).

The recommended way to add a hook function to a normal hook is by calling **add-hook**. You can use any valid Lisp function as the hook function. For example, here's how to set up a hook to turn on Auto Fill mode when entering Text mode and other modes based on Text mode:

```
(add-hook 'text-mode-hook 'turn-on-auto-fill)
```

The next example shows how to use a hook to customize the indentation of C code. (People often have strong personal preferences for one format compared to another.) Here the hook function is an anonymous lambda expression.

```
(setq my-c-style
  '((c-comment-only-line-offset . 4)
    (c-cleanup-list . (scope-operator
        empty-defun-braces
        defun-close-semi))
    (c-offsets-alist . ((arglist-close . c-lineup-arglist)
(substatement-open . 0)))))

(add-hook 'c-mode-common-hook
  (function (lambda ()
    (c-add-style "my-style" my-c-style t))))
```

It is best to design your hook functions so that the order in which they are executed does not matter. Any dependence on the order is "asking for trouble." However, the order is predictable: the most recently added hook functions are executed first.

31.2.4 Local Variables

M-x make-local-variable (RET) *var* (RET)
> Make variable *var* have a local value in the current buffer.

M-x kill-local-variable (RET) *var* (RET)
> Make variable *var* use its global value in the current buffer.

M-x make-variable-buffer-local (RET) *var* (RET)
> Mark variable *var* so that setting it will make it local to the buffer that is current at that time.

Almost any variable can be made *local* to a specific Emacs buffer. This means that its value in that buffer is independent of its value in other buffers. A few variables are always local in every buffer. Every other Emacs variable has a *global* value which is in effect in all buffers that have not made the variable local.

M-x make-local-variable reads the name of a variable and makes it local to the current buffer. Further changes in this buffer will not affect others, and further changes in the global value will not affect this buffer.

`M-x make-variable-buffer-local` reads the name of a variable and changes the future behavior of the variable so that it will become local automatically when it is set. More precisely, once a variable has been marked in this way, the usual ways of setting the variable automatically do `make-local-variable` first. We call such variables *per-buffer* variables.

Major modes (see Chapter 19 [Major Modes], page 191) always make variables local to the buffer before setting the variables. This is why changing major modes in one buffer has no effect on other buffers. Minor modes also work by setting variables—normally, each minor mode has one controlling variable which is non-`nil` when the mode is enabled (see Section 31.1 [Minor Modes], page 391). For most minor modes, the controlling variable is per buffer.

Emacs contains a number of variables that are always per-buffer. These include `abbrev-mode`, `auto-fill-function`, `case-fold-search`, `comment-column`, `ctl-arrow`, `fill-column`, `fill-prefix`, `indent-tabs-mode`, `left-margin`, `mode-line-format`, `overwrite-mode`, `selective-display-ellipses`, `selective-display`, `tab-width`, and `truncate-lines`. Some other variables are always local in every buffer, but they are used for internal purposes.

A few variables cannot be local to a buffer because they are always local to each display instead (see Section 17.8 [Multiple Displays], page 163). If you try to make one of these variables buffer-local, you'll get an error message.

`M-x kill-local-variable` reads the name of a variable and makes it cease to be local to the current buffer. The global value of the variable henceforth is in effect in this buffer. Setting the major mode kills all the local variables of the buffer except for a few variables specially marked as *permanent locals*.

To set the global value of a variable, regardless of whether the variable has a local value in the current buffer, you can use the Lisp construct `setq-default`. This construct is used just like `setq`, but it sets variables' global values instead of their local values (if any). When the current buffer does have a local value, the new global value may not be visible until you switch to another buffer. Here is an example:

```
(setq-default fill-column 75)
```

`setq-default` is the only way to set the global value of a variable that has been marked with `make-variable-buffer-local`.

Lisp programs can use `default-value` to look at a variable's default value. This function takes a symbol as argument and returns its default value. The argument is evaluated; usually you must quote it explicitly. For example, here's how to obtain the default value of `fill-column`:

```
(default-value 'fill-column)
```

31.2.5 Local Variables in Files

A file can specify local variable values for use when you edit the file with Emacs. Visiting the file checks for local variable specifications; it automatically makes these variables local to the buffer, and sets them to the values specified in the file.

There are two ways to specify local variable values: in the first line, or with a local variables list. Here's how to specify them in the first line:

```
-*- mode: modename; var: value; ... -*-
```

You can specify any number of variables/value pairs in this way, each pair with a colon and semicolon as shown above. `mode:` *modename*; specifies the major mode; this should come first in the line. The *values* are not evaluated; they are used literally. Here is an example that specifies Lisp mode and sets two variables with numeric values:

```
;; -*-mode: Lisp; fill-column: 75; comment-column: 50; -*-
```

You can also specify the coding system for a file in this way: just specify a value for the "variable" named `coding`. The "value" must be a coding system name that Emacs recognizes. See Section 18.7 [Coding Systems], page 180.

A *local variables list* goes near the end of the file, in the last page. (It is often best to put it on a page by itself.) The local variables list starts with a line containing the string '`Local Variables:`', and ends with a line containing the string '`End:`'. In between come the variable names and values, one set per line, as '*variable*: *value*'. The *values* are not evaluated; they are used literally. If a file has both a local variables list and a '-*-' line, Emacs processes *everything* in the '-*-' line first, and *everything* in the local variables list afterward.

Here is an example of a local variables list:

```
;;; Local Variables: ***
;;; mode:lisp ***
;;; comment-column:0 ***
;;; comment-start: ";;; "  ***
;;; comment-end:"***" ***
;;; End: ***
```

As you see, each line starts with the prefix ';;; ' and each line ends with the suffix ' ***'. Emacs recognizes these as the prefix and suffix based on the first line of the list, by finding them surrounding the magic string '`Local Variables:`'; then it automatically discards them from the other lines of the list.

The usual reason for using a prefix and/or suffix is to embed the local variables list in a comment, so it won't confuse other programs that the file is intended as input for. The example above is for a language where comment lines start with ';;; ' and end with '***'; the local values for `comment-start` and `comment-end` customize the rest of Emacs for this unusual syntax. Don't use a prefix (or a suffix) if you don't need one.

Two "variable names" have special meanings in a local variables list: a value for the variable `mode` really sets the major mode, and a value for the variable `eval` is simply evaluated as an expression and the value is ignored. `mode` and `eval` are not real variables; setting variables named `mode` and `eval` in any other context has no special meaning. If `mode` is used to set a major mode, it should be the first "variable" in the list.

You can use the `mode` "variable" to set minor modes as well as major modes; in fact, you can use it more than once, first to set the major mode and then to set minor modes which are specific to particular buffers. But most minor modes should not be specified in the file in any fashion, because they represent user preferences.

For example, you may be tempted to try to turn on Auto Fill mode with a local variable list. That is a mistake. The choice of Auto Fill mode or not is a matter of individual taste, not a matter of the contents of particular files. If you want to use Auto Fill, set up major mode hooks with your '.emacs' file to turn it on (when appropriate) for you alone (see Section 31.7 [Init File], page 419). Don't use a local variable list to impose your taste on everyone.

The start of the local variables list must be no more than 3000 characters from the end of the file, and must be in the last page if the file is divided into pages. Otherwise, Emacs will not notice it is there. The purpose of this rule is so that a stray 'Local Variables:' not in the last page does not confuse Emacs, and so that visiting a long file that is all one page and has no local variables list need not take the time to search the whole file.

Use the command `normal-mode` to reset the local variables and major mode of a buffer according to the file name and contents, including the local variables list if any. See Section 19.1 [Choosing Modes], page 191.

The variable `enable-local-variables` controls whether to process local variables in files, and thus gives you a chance to override them. Its default value is `t`, which means do process local variables in files. If you set the value to `nil`, Emacs simply ignores local variables in files. Any other value says to query you about each file that has local variables, showing you the local variable specifications so you can judge.

The `eval` "variable," and certain actual variables, create a special risk; when you visit someone else's file, local variable specifications for these could affect your Emacs in arbitrary ways. Therefore, the option `enable-local-eval` controls whether Emacs processes `eval` variables, as well variables with names that end in '-hook', '-hooks', '-function' or '-functions', and certain other variables. The three possibilities for the option's value are `t`, `nil`, and anything else, just as for `enable-local-variables`. The default is `maybe`, which is neither `t` nor `nil`, so normally Emacs does ask for confirmation about file settings for these variables.

31.3 Keyboard Macros

A *keyboard macro* is a command defined by the user to stand for another sequence of keys. For example, if you discover that you are about to type C-n C-d forty times, you can speed your work by defining a keyboard macro to do C-n C-d and calling it with a repeat count of forty.

C-x (Start defining a keyboard macro (**start-kbd-macro**).

C-x)   End the definition of a keyboard macro (**end-kbd-macro**).

C-x e   Execute the most recent keyboard macro (**call-last-kbd-macro**).

C-u C-x (Re-execute last keyboard macro, then add more keys to its definition.

C-x q   When this point is reached during macro execution, ask for confirmation (**kbd-macro-query**).

M-x name-last-kbd-macro
             Give a command name (for the duration of the session) to the most recently defined keyboard macro.

M-x insert-kbd-macro
             Insert in the buffer a keyboard macro's definition, as Lisp code.

C-x C-k   Edit a previously defined keyboard macro (**edit-kbd-macro**).

M-x apply-macro-to-region-lines
             Run the last keyboard macro on each complete line in the region.

Keyboard macros differ from ordinary Emacs commands in that they are written in the Emacs command language rather than in Lisp. This makes it easier for the novice to write them, and makes them more convenient as temporary hacks. However, the Emacs command language is not powerful enough as a programming language to be useful for writing anything intelligent or general. For such things, Lisp must be used.

You define a keyboard macro while executing the commands which are the definition. Put differently, as you define a keyboard macro, the definition is being executed for the first time. This way, you can see what the effects of your commands are, so that you don't have to figure them out in your head. When you are finished, the keyboard macro is defined and also has been, in effect, executed once. You can then do the whole thing over again by invoking the macro.

31.3.1 Basic Use

To start defining a keyboard macro, type the C-x (command (**start-kbd-macro**). From then on, your keys continue to be executed, but also become part of the definition of the macro. 'Def' appears in the mode line to

remind you of what is going on. When you are finished, the C-x) command
(end-kbd-macro) terminates the definition (without becoming part of it!).
For example,

>   C-x (M-f foo C-x)

defines a macro to move forward a word and then insert 'foo'.

The macro thus defined can be invoked again with the C-x e command
(call-last-kbd-macro), which may be given a repeat count as a numeric
argument to execute the macro many times. C-x) can also be given a repeat
count as an argument, in which case it repeats the macro that many times
right after defining it, but defining the macro counts as the first repetition
(since it is executed as you define it). Therefore, giving C-x) an argument
of 4 executes the macro immediately 3 additional times. An argument of
zero to C-x e or C-x) means repeat the macro indefinitely (until it gets an
error or you type C-g or, on MS-DOS, C-BREAK).

If you wish to repeat an operation at regularly spaced places in the text,
define a macro and include as part of the macro the commands to move to
the next place you want to use it. For example, if you want to change each
line, you should position point at the start of a line, and define a macro to
change that line and leave point at the start of the next line. Then repeating
the macro will operate on successive lines.

After you have terminated the definition of a keyboard macro, you can
add to the end of its definition by typing C-u C-x (. This is equivalent to
plain C-x (followed by retyping the whole definition so far. As a consequence
it re-executes the macro as previously defined.

You can use function keys in a keyboard macro, just like keyboard keys.
You can even use mouse events, but be careful about that: when the macro
replays the mouse event, it uses the original mouse position of that event,
the position that the mouse had while you were defining the macro. The
effect of this may be hard to predict. (Using the current mouse position
would be even less predictable.)

One thing that doesn't always work well in a keyboard macro is the command C-M-c (exit-recursive-edit). When this command exits a recursive
edit that started within the macro, it works as you'd expect. But if it exits
a recursive edit that started before you invoked the keyboard macro, it also
necessarily exits the keyboard macro as part of the process.

You can edit a keyboard macro already defined by typing C-x C-k (edit-
kbd-macro). Follow that with the keyboard input that you would use to
invoke the macro—C-x e or M-x *name* or some other key sequence. This
formats the macro definition in a buffer and enters a specialized major mode
for editing it. Type C-h m once in that buffer to display details of how to
edit the macro. When you are finished editing, type C-c C-c.

The command M-x apply-macro-to-region-lines repeats the last defined keyboard macro on each complete line within the current region. It

does this line by line, by moving point to the beginning of the line and then executing the macro.

31.3.2 Naming and Saving Keyboard Macros

If you wish to save a keyboard macro for longer than until you define the next one, you must give it a name using M-x name-last-kbd-macro. This reads a name as an argument using the minibuffer and defines that name to execute the macro. The macro name is a Lisp symbol, and defining it in this way makes it a valid command name for calling with M-x or for binding a key to with global-set-key (see Section 31.4.1 [Keymaps], page 408). If you specify a name that has a prior definition other than another keyboard macro, an error message is printed and nothing is changed.

Once a macro has a command name, you can save its definition in a file. Then it can be used in another editing session. First, visit the file you want to save the definition in. Then use this command:

> M-x insert-kbd-macro (RET) macroname (RET)

This inserts some Lisp code that, when executed later, will define the same macro with the same definition it has now. (You need not understand Lisp code to do this, because insert-kbd-macro writes the Lisp code for you.) Then save the file. You can load the file later with load-file (see Section 23.7 [Lisp Libraries], page 285). If the file you save in is your init file '~/.emacs' (see Section 31.7 [Init File], page 419) then the macro will be defined each time you run Emacs.

If you give insert-kbd-macro a numeric argument, it makes additional Lisp code to record the keys (if any) that you have bound to the keyboard macro, so that the macro will be reassigned the same keys when you load the file.

31.3.3 Executing Macros with Variations

Using C-x q (kbd-macro-query), you can get an effect similar to that of query-replace, where the macro asks you each time around whether to make a change. While defining the macro, type C-x q at the point where you want the query to occur. During macro definition, the C-x q does nothing, but when you run the macro later, C-x q asks you interactively whether to continue.

The valid responses when C-x q asks are (SPC) (or y), (DEL) (or n), (RET) (or q), C-l and C-r. The answers are the same as in query-replace, though not all of the query-replace options are meaningful.

These responses include (SPC) to continue, and (DEL) to skip the remainder of this repetition of the macro and start right away with the next repetition. (RET) means to skip the remainder of this repetition and cancel further repetitions. C-l redraws the screen and asks you again for a character to say what to do.

C-r enters a recursive editing level, in which you can perform editing which is not part of the macro. When you exit the recursive edit using C-M-c, you are asked again how to continue with the keyboard macro. If you type a (SPC) at this time, the rest of the macro definition is executed. It is up to you to leave point and the text in a state such that the rest of the macro will do what you want.

C-u C-x q, which is C-x q with a numeric argument, performs a completely different function. It enters a recursive edit reading input from the keyboard, both when you type it during the definition of the macro, and when it is executed from the macro. During definition, the editing you do inside the recursive edit does not become part of the macro. During macro execution, the recursive edit gives you a chance to do some particularized editing on each repetition. See Section 30.12 [Recursive Edit], page 385.

31.4 Customizing Key Bindings

This section describes *key bindings*, which map keys to commands, and *keymaps*, which record key bindings. It also explains how to customize key bindings.

Recall that a command is a Lisp function whose definition provides for interactive use. Like every Lisp function, a command has a function name which usually consists of lower-case letters and hyphens.

31.4.1 Keymaps

The bindings between key sequences and command functions are recorded in data structures called *keymaps*. Emacs has many of these, each used on particular occasions.

Recall that a *key sequence* (*key*, for short) is a sequence of *input events* that have a meaning as a unit. Input events include characters, function keys and mouse buttons—all the inputs that you can send to the computer with your terminal. A key sequence gets its meaning from its *binding*, which says what command it runs. The function of keymaps is to record these bindings.

The *global* keymap is the most important keymap because it is always in effect. The global keymap defines keys for Fundamental mode; most of these definitions are common to most or all major modes. Each major or minor mode can have its own keymap which overrides the global definitions of some keys.

For example, a self-inserting character such as g is self-inserting because the global keymap binds it to the command **self-insert-command**. The standard Emacs editing characters such as C-a also get their standard meanings from the global keymap. Commands to rebind keys, such as M-x **global-set-key**, actually work by storing the new binding in the proper place in the global map. See Section 31.4.5 [Rebinding], page 411.

Meta characters work differently; Emacs translates each Meta character into a pair of characters starting with ⟨ESC⟩. When you type the character M-a in a key sequence, Emacs replaces it with ⟨ESC⟩ a. A meta key comes in as a single input event, but becomes two events for purposes of key bindings. The reason for this is historical, and we might change it someday.

Most modern keyboards have function keys as well as character keys. Function keys send input events just as character keys do, and keymaps can have bindings for them.

On many terminals, typing a function key actually sends the computer a sequence of characters; the precise details of the sequence depends on which function key and on the model of terminal you are using. (Often the sequence starts with ⟨ESC⟩ [.) If Emacs understands your terminal type properly, it recognizes the character sequences forming function keys wherever they occur in a key sequence (not just at the beginning). Thus, for most purposes, you can pretend the function keys reach Emacs directly and ignore their encoding as character sequences.

Mouse buttons also produce input events. These events come with other data—the window and position where you pressed or released the button, and a time stamp. But only the choice of button matters for key bindings; the other data matters only if a command looks at it. (Commands designed for mouse invocation usually do look at the other data.)

A keymap records definitions for single events. Interpreting a key sequence of multiple events involves a chain of keymaps. The first keymap gives a definition for the first event; this definition is another keymap, which is used to look up the second event in the sequence, and so on.

Key sequences can mix function keys and characters. For example, C-x ⟨SELECT⟩ is meaningful. If you make ⟨SELECT⟩ a prefix key, then ⟨SELECT⟩ C-n makes sense. You can even mix mouse events with keyboard events, but we recommend against it, because such sequences are inconvenient to type in.

As a user, you can redefine any key; but it might be best to stick to key sequences that consist of C-c followed by a letter. These keys are "reserved for users," so they won't conflict with any properly designed Emacs extension. The function keys ⟨F5⟩ through ⟨F9⟩ are also reserved for users. If you redefine some other key, your definition may be overridden by certain extensions or major modes which redefine the same key.

31.4.2 Prefix Keymaps

A prefix key such as C-x or ⟨ESC⟩ has its own keymap, which holds the definition for the event that immediately follows that prefix.

The definition of a prefix key is usually the keymap to use for looking up the following event. The definition can also be a Lisp symbol whose function definition is the following keymap; the effect is the same, but it provides a command name for the prefix key that can be used as a description of what the prefix key is for. Thus, the binding of C-x is the symbol Ctl-X-Prefix, whose function definition is the keymap for C-x commands. The definitions of C-c, C-x, C-h and (ESC) as prefix keys appear in the global map, so these prefix keys are always available.

Aside from ordinary prefix keys, there is a fictitious "prefix key" which represents the menu bar; see section "Menu Bar" in *The Emacs Lisp Reference Manual*, for special information about menu bar key bindings. Mouse button events that invoke pop-up menus are also prefix keys; see section "Menu Keymaps" in *The Emacs Lisp Reference Manual*, for more details.

Some prefix keymaps are stored in variables with names:

- **ctl-x-map** is the variable name for the map used for characters that follow C-x.

- **help-map** is for characters that follow C-h.

- **esc-map** is for characters that follow (ESC). Thus, all Meta characters are actually defined by this map.

- **ctl-x-4-map** is for characters that follow C-x 4.

- **mode-specific-map** is for characters that follow C-c.

31.4.3 Local Keymaps

So far we have explained the ins and outs of the global map. Major modes customize Emacs by providing their own key bindings in *local keymaps*. For example, C mode overrides (TAB) to make it indent the current line for C code. Portions of text in the buffer can specify their own keymaps to substitute for the keymap of the buffer's major mode.

Minor modes can also have local keymaps. Whenever a minor mode is in effect, the definitions in its keymap override both the major mode's local keymap and the global keymap.

The local keymaps for Lisp mode and several other major modes always exist even when not in use. These are kept in variables named **lisp-mode-map** and so on. For major modes less often used, the local keymap is normally constructed only when the mode is used for the first time in a session. This is to save space. If you wish to change one of these keymaps, you must use the major mode's *mode hook*—see below.

All minor mode keymaps are created in advance. There is no way to defer their creation until the first time the minor mode is enabled.

A local keymap can locally redefine a key as a prefix key by defining it as a prefix keymap. If the key is also defined globally as a prefix, then its local and global definitions (both keymaps) effectively combine: both of them are used to look up the event that follows the prefix key. Thus, if the mode's local keymap defines C-c as another keymap, and that keymap defines C-z as a command, this provides a local meaning for C-c C-z. This does not affect other sequences that start with C-c; if those sequences don't have their own local bindings, their global bindings remain in effect.

Another way to think of this is that Emacs handles a multi-event key sequence by looking in several keymaps, one by one, for a binding of the whole key sequence. First it checks the minor mode keymaps for minor modes that are enabled, then it checks the major mode's keymap, and then it checks the global keymap. This is not precisely how key lookup works, but it's good enough for understanding ordinary circumstances.

To change the local bindings of a major mode, you must change the mode's local keymap. Normally you must wait until the first time the mode is used, because most major modes don't create their keymaps until then. If you want to specify something in your '~/.emacs' file to change a major mode's bindings, you must use the mode's mode hook to delay the change until the mode is first used.

For example, the command `texinfo-mode` to select Texinfo mode runs the hook `texinfo-mode-hook`. Here's how you can use the hook to add local bindings (not very useful, we admit) for C-c n and C-c p in Texinfo mode:

```
(add-hook 'texinfo-mode-hook
          '(lambda ()
             (define-key texinfo-mode-map
                         "\C-cp"
                         'backward-paragraph)
             (define-key texinfo-mode-map
                         "\C-cn"
                         'forward-paragraph)
             ))
```
See Section 31.2.3 [Hooks], page 400.

31.4.4 Minibuffer Keymaps

The minibuffer has its own set of local keymaps; they contain various completion and exit commands.

- `minibuffer-local-map` is used for ordinary input (no completion).
- `minibuffer-local-ns-map` is similar, except that (SPC) exits just like (RET). This is used mainly for Mocklisp compatibility.
- `minibuffer-local-completion-map` is for permissive completion.
- `minibuffer-local-must-match-map` is for strict completion and for cautious completion.

31.4.5 Changing Key Bindings Interactively

The way to redefine an Emacs key is to change its entry in a keymap. You can change the global keymap, in which case the change is effective in all major modes (except those that have their own overriding local definitions for the same key). Or you can change the current buffer's local map, which affects all buffers using the same major mode.

`M-x global-set-key` (RET) *key cmd* (RET)
> Define *key* globally to run *cmd*.

`M-x local-set-key` (RET) *key cmd* (RET)
> Define *key* locally (in the major mode now in effect) to run *cmd*.

`M-x global-unset-key` (RET) *key*
> Make *key* undefined in the global map.

`M-x local-unset-key` (RET) *key*
> Make *key* undefined locally (in the major mode now in effect).

For example, suppose you like to execute commands in a subshell within an Emacs buffer, instead of suspending Emacs and executing commands in your login shell. Normally, `C-z` is bound to the function `suspend-emacs` (when not using the X Window System), but you can change `C-z` to invoke an interactive subshell within Emacs, by binding it to `shell` as follows:

> `M-x global-set-key` (RET) `C-z shell` (RET)

`global-set-key` reads the command name after the key. After you press the key, a message like this appears so that you can confirm that you are binding the key you want:

> `Set key C-z to command:`

You can redefine function keys and mouse events in the same way; just type the function key or click the mouse when it's time to specify the key to rebind.

You can rebind a key that contains more than one event in the same way. Emacs keeps reading the key to rebind until it is a complete key (that is, not a prefix key). Thus, if you type `C-f` for *key*, that's the end; the minibuffer is entered immediately to read *cmd*. But if you type `C-x`, another character is read; if that is `4`, another character is read, and so on. For example,

> `M-x global-set-key` (RET) `C-x 4 $ spell-other-window` (RET)

redefines `C-x 4 $` to run the (fictitious) command `spell-other-window`.

The two-character keys consisting of `C-c` followed by a letter are reserved for user customizations. Lisp programs are not supposed to define these keys, so the bindings you make for them will be available in all major modes and will never get in the way of anything.

You can remove the global definition of a key with `global-unset-key`. This makes the key *undefined*; if you type it, Emacs will just beep. Similarly, `local-unset-key` makes a key undefined in the current major mode keymap, which makes the global definition (or lack of one) come back into effect in that major mode.

If you have redefined (or undefined) a key and you subsequently wish to retract the change, undefining the key will not do the job—you need to redefine the key with its standard definition. To find the name of the standard definition of a key, go to a Fundamental mode buffer and use `C-h c`. The documentation of keys in this manual also lists their command names.

If you want to prevent yourself from invoking a command by mistake, it is better to disable the command than to undefine the key. A disabled command is less work to invoke when you really want to. See Section 31.4.11 [Disabling], page 418.

31.4.6 Rebinding Keys in Your Init File

If you have a set of key bindings that you like to use all the time, you can specify them in your '.emacs' file by using their Lisp syntax.

The simplest method for doing this works for ASCII characters and Meta-modified ASCII characters only. This method uses a string to represent the key sequence you want to rebind. For example, here's how to bind C-z to shell:

```
(global-set-key "\C-z" 'shell)
```

This example uses a string constant containing one character, C-z. The single-quote before the command name, shell, marks it as a constant symbol rather than a variable. If you omit the quote, Emacs would try to evaluate shell immediately as a variable. This probably causes an error; it certainly isn't what you want.

Here is another example that binds a key sequence two characters long:

```
(global-set-key "\C-xl" 'make-symbolic-link)
```

When the key sequence includes function keys or mouse button events, or non-ASCII characters such as C-= or H-a, you must use the more general method of rebinding, which uses a vector to specify the key sequence.

The way to write a vector in Emacs Lisp is with square brackets around the vector elements. Use spaces to separate the elements. If an element is a symbol, simply write the symbol's name—no other delimiters or punctuation are needed. If a vector element is a character, write it as a Lisp character constant: '?' followed by the character as it would appear in a string.

Here are examples of using vectors to rebind C-= (a control character outside of ASCII), H-a (a Hyper character; ASCII doesn't have Hyper at all), F7 (a function key), and C-Mouse-1 (a keyboard-modified mouse button):

```
(global-set-key [?\C-=] 'make-symbolic-link)
(global-set-key [?\H-a] 'make-symbolic-link)
(global-set-key [f7] 'make-symbolic-link)
(global-set-key [C-mouse-1] 'make-symbolic-link)
```

You can use a vector for the simple cases too. Here's how to rewrite the first two examples, above, to use vectors:

```
(global-set-key [?\C-z] 'shell)

(global-set-key [?\C-x ?l] 'make-symbolic-link)
```

31.4.7 Rebinding Function Keys

Key sequences can contain function keys as well as ordinary characters. Just as Lisp characters (actually integers) represent keyboard characters, Lisp symbols represent function keys. If the function key has a word as its label, then that word is also the name of the corresponding Lisp symbol. Here are the conventional Lisp names for common function keys:

`left`, `up`, `right`, `down`
> Cursor arrow keys.

`begin`, `end`, `home`, `next`, `prior`
> Other cursor repositioning keys.

`select`, `print`, `execute`, `backtab`
`insert`, `undo`, `redo`, `clearline`
`insertline`, `deleteline`, `insertchar`, `deletechar`,
> Miscellaneous function keys.

`f1`, `f2`, ... `f35`
> Numbered function keys (across the top of the keyboard).

`kp-add`, `kp-subtract`, `kp-multiply`, `kp-divide`
`kp-backtab`, `kp-space`, `kp-tab`, `kp-enter`
`kp-separator`, `kp-decimal`, `kp-equal`
> Keypad keys (to the right of the regular keyboard), with names or punctuation.

`kp-0`, `kp-1`, ... `kp-9`
> Keypad keys with digits.

`kp-f1`, `kp-f2`, `kp-f3`, `kp-f4`
> Keypad PF keys.

These names are conventional, but some systems (especially when using X windows) may use different names. To make certain what symbol is used for a given function key on your terminal, type `C-h c` followed by that key.

A key sequence which contains function key symbols (or anything but ASCII characters) must be a vector rather than a string. The vector syntax uses spaces between the elements, and square brackets around the whole vector. Thus, to bind function key 'f1' to the command `rmail`, write the following:

```
(global-set-key [f1] 'rmail)
```

To bind the right-arrow key to the command `forward-char`, you can use this expression:

```
(global-set-key [right] 'forward-char)
```

This uses the Lisp syntax for a vector containing the symbol `right`. (This binding is present in Emacs by default.)

See Section 31.4.6 [Init Rebinding], page 413, for more information about using vectors for rebinding.

You can mix function keys and characters in a key sequence. This example binds C-x (NEXT) to the command forward-page.

    (global-set-key [?\C-x next] 'forward-page)

where ?\C-x is the Lisp character constant for the character C-x. The vector element next is a symbol and therefore does not take a question mark.

You can use the modifier keys (CTRL), (META), (HYPER), (SUPER), (ALT) and (SHIFT) with function keys. To represent these modifiers, add the strings 'C-', 'M-', 'H-', 's-', 'A-' and 'S-' at the front of the symbol name. Thus, here is how to make Hyper-Meta-(RIGHT) move forward a word:

    (global-set-key [H-M-right] 'forward-word)

31.4.8 Named ASCII Control Characters

(TAB), (RET), (BS), (LFD), (ESC) and (DEL) started out as names for certain ASCII control characters, used so often that they have special keys of their own. Later, users found it convenient to distinguish in Emacs between these keys and the "same" control characters typed with the (CTRL) key.

Emacs distinguishes these two kinds of input, when used with the X Window System. It treats the "special" keys as function keys named tab, return, backspace, linefeed, escape, and delete. These function keys translate automatically into the corresponding ASCII characters *if* they have no bindings of their own. As a result, neither users nor Lisp programs need to pay attention to the distinction unless they care to.

If you do not want to distinguish between (for example) (TAB) and C-i, make just one binding, for the ASCII character (TAB) (octal code 011). If you do want to distinguish, make one binding for this ASCII character, and another for the "function key" tab.

With an ordinary ASCII terminal, there is no way to distinguish between (TAB) and C-i (and likewise for other such pairs), because the terminal sends the same character in both cases.

31.4.9 Non-ASCII Characters on the Keyboard

If your keyboard has keys that send non-ASCII characters, such as accented letters, rebinding these keys is a bit tricky. There are two solutions you can use. One is to specify a keyboard coding system, using set-keyboard-coding-system (see Section 18.9 [Specify Coding], page 184). Then you can bind these keys in the usual way, but writing

    (global-set-key [?char] 'some-function)

and typing the key you want to bind to insert *char*.

If you don't specify the keyboard coding system, that approach won't work. Instead, you need to find out the actual code that the terminal sends. The easiest way to do this in Emacs is to create an empty buffer with C-x b temp (RET), make it unibyte with M-x `toggle-enable-multibyte-characters` (RET), then type the key to insert the character into this buffer.

Move point before the character, then type `C-b C-x =`. This displays a message in the minibuffer, showing the character code in three ways, octal, decimal and hexadecimal, all within a set of parentheses. Use the second of the three numbers, the decimal one, inside the vector to bind:

```
(global-set-key [decimal-code] 'some-function)
```

31.4.10 Rebinding Mouse Buttons

Emacs uses Lisp symbols to designate mouse buttons, too. The ordinary mouse events in Emacs are *click* events; these happen when you press a button and release it without moving the mouse. You can also get *drag* events, when you move the mouse while holding the button down. Drag events happen when you finally let go of the button.

The symbols for basic click events are `mouse-1` for the leftmost button, `mouse-2` for the next, and so on. Here is how you can redefine the second mouse button to split the current window:

```
(global-set-key [mouse-2] 'split-window-vertically)
```

The symbols for drag events are similar, but have the prefix 'drag-' before the word 'mouse'. For example, dragging the first button generates a `drag-mouse-1` event.

You can also define bindings for events that occur when a mouse button is pressed down. These events start with 'down-' instead of 'drag-'. Such events are generated only if they have key bindings. When you get a button-down event, a corresponding click or drag event will always follow.

If you wish, you can distinguish single, double, and triple clicks. A double click means clicking a mouse button twice in approximately the same place. The first click generates an ordinary click event. The second click, if it comes soon enough, generates a double-click event instead. The event type for a double-click event starts with 'double-': for example, `double-mouse-3`.

This means that you can give a special meaning to the second click at the same place, but it must act on the assumption that the ordinary single click definition has run when the first click was received.

This constrains what you can do with double clicks, but user interface designers say that this constraint ought to be followed in any case. A double click should do something similar to the single click, only "more so." The command for the double-click event should perform the extra work for the double click.

If a double-click event has no binding, it changes to the corresponding single-click event. Thus, if you don't define a particular double click specially, it executes the single-click command twice.

Emacs also supports triple-click events whose names start with 'triple-'. Emacs does not distinguish quadruple clicks as event types; clicks beyond the third generate additional triple-click events. However, the full number of clicks is recorded in the event list, so you can distinguish if you really want to. We don't recommend distinct meanings for more than three clicks, but sometimes it is useful for subsequent clicks to cycle through the same set of three meanings, so that four clicks are equivalent to one click, five are equivalent to two, and six are equivalent to three.

Emacs also records multiple presses in drag and button-down events. For example, when you press a button twice, then move the mouse while holding the button, Emacs gets a 'double-drag-' event. And at the moment when you press it down for the second time, Emacs gets a 'double-down-' event (which is ignored, like all button-down events, if it has no binding).

The variable double-click-time specifies how long may elapse between clicks that are recognized as a pair. Its value is measured in milliseconds. If the value is nil, double clicks are not detected at all. If the value is t, then there is no time limit.

The symbols for mouse events also indicate the status of the modifier keys, with the usual prefixes 'C-', 'M-', 'H-', 's-', 'A-' and 'S-'. These always precede 'double-' or 'triple-', which always precede 'drag-' or 'down-'.

A frame includes areas that don't show text from the buffer, such as the mode line and the scroll bar. You can tell whether a mouse button comes from a special area of the screen by means of dummy "prefix keys." For example, if you click the mouse in the mode line, you get the prefix key mode-line before the ordinary mouse-button symbol. Thus, here is how to define the command for clicking the first button in a mode line to run scroll-up:

```
(global-set-key [mode-line mouse-1] 'scroll-up)
```

Here is the complete list of these dummy prefix keys and their meanings:

mode-line
>   The mouse was in the mode line of a window.

vertical-line
>   The mouse was in the vertical line separating side-by-side windows. (If you use scroll bars, they appear in place of these vertical lines.)

vertical-scroll-bar
>   The mouse was in a vertical scroll bar. (This is the only kind of scroll bar Emacs currently supports.)

You can put more than one mouse button in a key sequence, but it isn't usual to do so.

31.4.11 Disabling Commands

Disabling a command marks the command as requiring confirmation before it can be executed. The purpose of disabling a command is to prevent beginning users from executing it by accident and being confused.

An attempt to invoke a disabled command interactively in Emacs displays a window containing the command's name, its documentation, and some instructions on what to do immediately; then Emacs asks for input saying whether to execute the command as requested, enable it and execute it, or cancel. If you decide to enable the command, you are asked whether to do this permanently or just for the current session. Enabling permanently works by automatically editing your '.emacs' file.

The direct mechanism for disabling a command is to put a non-**nil** **disabled** property on the Lisp symbol for the command. Here is the Lisp program to do this:

```
(put 'delete-region 'disabled t)
```

If the value of the **disabled** property is a string, that string is included in the message printed when the command is used:

```
(put 'delete-region 'disabled
     "It's better to use `kill-region' instead.\n")
```

You can make a command disabled either by editing the '.emacs' file directly or with the command M-x disable-command, which edits the '.emacs' file for you. Likewise, M-x enable-command edits '.emacs' to enable a command permanently. See Section 31.7 [Init File], page 419.

Whether a command is disabled is independent of what key is used to invoke it; disabling also applies if the command is invoked using M-x. Disabling a command has no effect on calling it as a function from Lisp programs.

31.5 Keyboard Translations

Some keyboards do not make it convenient to send all the special characters that Emacs uses. The most common problem case is the (DEL) character. Some keyboards provide no convenient way to type this very important character—usually because they were designed to expect the character C-h to be used for deletion. On these keyboards, if you press the key normally used for deletion, Emacs handles the C-h as a prefix character and offers you a list of help options, which is not what you want.

You can work around this problem within Emacs by setting up keyboard translations to turn C-h into (DEL) and (DEL) into C-h, as follows:

```
;; Translate C-h to (DEL).
(keyboard-translate ?\C-h ?\C-?)
```

```
;; Translate (DEL) to C-h.
(keyboard-translate ?\C-? ?\C-h)
```

Keyboard translations are not the same as key bindings in keymaps (see Section 31.4.1 [Keymaps], page 408). Emacs contains numerous keymaps that apply in different situations, but there is only one set of keyboard translations, and it applies to every character that Emacs reads from the terminal. Keyboard translations take place at the lowest level of input processing; the keys that are looked up in keymaps contain the characters that result from keyboard translation.

Under X, the keyboard key named (DELETE) is a function key and is distinct from the ASCII character named (DEL). See Section 31.4.8 [Named ASCII Chars], page 415. Keyboard translations affect only ASCII character input, not function keys; thus, the above example used under X does not affect the (DELETE) key. However, the translation above isn't necessary under X, because Emacs can also distinguish between the (BACKSPACE) key and C-h; and it normally treats (BACKSPACE) as (DEL).

For full information about how to use keyboard translations, see section "Translating Input" in *The Emacs Lisp Reference Manual*.

31.6 The Syntax Table

All the Emacs commands which parse words or balance parentheses are controlled by the *syntax table*. The syntax table says which characters are opening delimiters, which are parts of words, which are string quotes, and so on. Each major mode has its own syntax table (though sometimes related major modes use the same one) which it installs in each buffer that uses that major mode. The syntax table installed in the current buffer is the one that all commands use, so we call it "the" syntax table. A syntax table is a Lisp object, a char-table, whose elements are numbers.

To display a description of the contents of the current syntax table, type C-h s (describe-syntax). The description of each character includes both the string you would have to give to modify-syntax-entry to set up that character's current syntax, and some English to explain that string if necessary.

For full information on the syntax table, see section "Syntax Tables" in *The Emacs Lisp Reference Manual*.

31.7 The Init File, '~/.emacs'

When Emacs is started, it normally loads a Lisp program from the file '.emacs' or '.emacs.el' in your home directory. We call this file your *init file* because it specifies how to initialize Emacs for you. You can use the command line switch '-q' to prevent loading your init file, and '-u' (or '--user') to specify a different user's init file (see Chapter 3 [Entering Emacs], page 25).

There can also be a *default init file*, which is the library named
'`default.el`', found via the standard search path for libraries. The Emacs
distribution contains no such library; your site may create one for local customizations. If this library exists, it is loaded whenever you start Emacs
(except when you specify '`-q`'). But your init file, if any, is loaded first; if it
sets `inhibit-default-init` non-nil, then '`default`' is not loaded.

Your site may also have a *site startup file*; this is named '`site-start.el`',
if it exists. Emacs loads this library before it loads your init file. To inhibit
loading of this library, use the option '`-no-site-file`'.

If you have a large amount of code in your '`.emacs`' file, you should
rename it to '`~/.emacs.el`', and byte-compile it. See section "Byte Compilation" in *the Emacs Lisp Reference Manual*, for more information about
compiling Emacs Lisp programs.

If you are going to write actual Emacs Lisp programs that go beyond
minor customization, you should read the *Emacs Lisp Reference Manual*.

31.7.1 Init File Syntax

The '`.emacs`' file contains one or more Lisp function call expressions.
Each of these consists of a function name followed by arguments, all surrounded by parentheses. For example, (`setq fill-column 60`) calls the
function `setq` to set the variable `fill-column` (see Section 21.5 [Filling],
page 203) to 60.

The second argument to `setq` is an expression for the new value of the
variable. This can be a constant, a variable, or a function call expression.
In '`.emacs`', constants are used most of the time. They can be:

Numbers: Numbers are written in decimal, with an optional initial minus
             sign.

Strings: Lisp string syntax is the same as C string syntax with a few
             extra features. Use a double-quote character to begin and end
             a string constant.

             In a string, you can include newlines and special characters liter-
             ally. But often it is cleaner to use backslash sequences for them:
             '`\n`' for newline, '`\b`' for backspace, '`\r`' for carriage return, '`\t`'
             for tab, '`\f`' for formfeed (control-L), '`\e`' for escape, '`\\`' for a
             backslash, '`\"`' for a double-quote, or '`\ooo`' for the character
             whose octal code is *ooo*. Backslash and double-quote are the
             only characters for which backslash sequences are mandatory.

             '`\C-`' can be used as a prefix for a control character, as in
             '`\C-s`' for ASCII control-S, and '`\M-`' can be used as a prefix
             for a Meta character, as in '`\M-a`' for `Meta-A` or '`\M-\C-a`' for
             `Control-Meta-A`.

Characters:

Lisp character constant syntax consists of a '?' followed by either a character or an escape sequence starting with '\'. Examples: `?x, ?\n, ?\", ?\)`. Note that strings and characters are not interchangeable in Lisp; some contexts require one and some contexts require the other.

True: `t` stands for 'true'.

False: `nil` stands for 'false'.

Other Lisp objects:

Write a single-quote (') followed by the Lisp object you want.

31.7.2 Init File Examples

Here are some examples of doing certain commonly desired things with Lisp expressions:

- Make (TAB) in C mode just insert a tab if point is in the middle of a line.

  ```
  (setq c-tab-always-indent nil)
  ```

  Here we have a variable whose value is normally `t` for 'true' and the alternative is `nil` for 'false'.

- Make searches case sensitive by default (in all buffers that do not override this).

  ```
  (setq-default case-fold-search nil)
  ```

  This sets the default value, which is effective in all buffers that do not have local values for the variable. Setting `case-fold-search` with `setq` affects only the current buffer's local value, which is not what you probably want to do in an init file.

- Specify your own email address, if Emacs can't figure it out correctly.

  ```
  (setq user-mail-address "coon@yoyodyne.com")
  ```

  Various Emacs packages that need your own email address use the value of `user-mail-address`.

- Make Text mode the default mode for new buffers.

  ```
  (setq default-major-mode 'text-mode)
  ```

  Note that `text-mode` is used because it is the command for entering Text mode. The single-quote before it makes the symbol a constant; otherwise, `text-mode` would be treated as a variable name.

- Set up defaults for the Latin-1 character set which supports most of the languages of Western Europe.

  ```
  (set-language-environment "Latin-1")
  ```

- Turn on Auto Fill mode automatically in Text mode and related modes.

  ```
  (add-hook 'text-mode-hook
     '(lambda () (auto-fill-mode 1)))
  ```

  This shows how to add a hook function to a normal hook variable (see Section 31.2.3 [Hooks], page 400). The function we supply is a list starting with `lambda`, with a single-quote in front of it to make it a list constant rather than an expression.

  It's beyond the scope of this manual to explain Lisp functions, but for this example it is enough to know that the effect is to execute `(auto-fill-mode 1)` when Text mode is entered. You can replace that with any other expression that you like, or with several expressions in a row.

  Emacs comes with a function named `turn-on-auto-fill` whose definition is `(lambda () (auto-fill-mode 1))`. Thus, a simpler way to write the above example is as follows:

  ```
  (add-hook 'text-mode-hook 'turn-on-auto-fill)
  ```

- Load the installed Lisp library named 'foo' (actually a file 'foo.elc' or 'foo.el' in a standard Emacs directory).

  ```
  (load "foo")
  ```

  When the argument to `load` is a relative file name, not starting with '/' or '~', `load` searches the directories in `load-path` (see Section 23.7 [Lisp Libraries], page 285).

- Load the compiled Lisp file 'foo.elc' from your home directory.

  ```
  (load "~/foo.elc")
  ```

  Here an absolute file name is used, so no searching is done.

- Rebind the key C-x l to run the function `make-symbolic-link`.

  ```
  (global-set-key "\C-xl" 'make-symbolic-link)
  ```

  or

  ```
  (define-key global-map "\C-xl" 'make-symbolic-link)
  ```

  Note once again the single-quote used to refer to the symbol `make-symbolic-link` instead of its value as a variable.

- Do the same thing for Lisp mode only.

  ```
  (define-key lisp-mode-map "\C-xl" 'make-symbolic-link)
  ```

- Redefine all keys which now run `next-line` in Fundamental mode so that they run `forward-line` instead.

  ```
  (substitute-key-definition 'next-line 'forward-line
                             global-map)
  ```

- Make C-x C-v undefined.

```
(global-unset-key "\C-x\C-v")
```

One reason to undefine a key is so that you can make it a prefix. Simply defining C-x C-v *anything* will make C-x C-v a prefix, but C-x C-v must first be freed of its usual non-prefix definition.

- Make '$' have the syntax of punctuation in Text mode. Note the use of a character constant for '$'.

```
(modify-syntax-entry ?\$ "." text-mode-syntax-table)
```

- Enable the use of the command narrow-to-region without confirmation.

```
(put 'narrow-to-region 'disabled nil)
```

31.7.3 Terminal-specific Initialization

Each terminal type can have a Lisp library to be loaded into Emacs when it is run on that type of terminal. For a terminal type named *termtype*, the library is called 'term/*termtype*' and it is found by searching the directories load-path as usual and trying the suffixes '.elc' and '.el'. Normally it appears in the subdirectory 'term' of the directory where most Emacs libraries are kept.

The usual purpose of the terminal-specific library is to map the escape sequences used by the terminal's function keys onto more meaningful names, using function-key-map. See the file 'term/lk201.el' for an example of how this is done. Many function keys are mapped automatically according to the information in the Termcap data base; the terminal-specific library needs to map only the function keys that Termcap does not specify.

When the terminal type contains a hyphen, only the part of the name before the first hyphen is significant in choosing the library name. Thus, terminal types 'aaa-48' and 'aaa-30-rv' both use the library 'term/aaa'. The code in the library can use (getenv "TERM") to find the full terminal type name.

The library's name is constructed by concatenating the value of the variable term-file-prefix and the terminal type. Your '.emacs' file can prevent the loading of the terminal-specific library by setting term-file-prefix to nil.

Emacs runs the hook term-setup-hook at the end of initialization, after both your '.emacs' file and any terminal-specific library have been read in. Add hook functions to this hook if you wish to override part of any of the terminal-specific libraries and to define initializations for terminals that do not have a library. See Section 31.2.3 [Hooks], page 400.

31.7.4 How Emacs Finds Your Init File

Normally Emacs uses the environment variable HOME to find '.emacs'; that's what '~' means in a file name. But if you have done su, Emacs tries to find your own '.emacs', not that of the user you are currently pretending to be. The idea is that you should get your own editor customizations even if you arc running as the super user.

More precisely, Emacs first determines which user's init file to use. It gets the user name from the environment variables LOGNAME and USER; if neither of those exists, it uses effective user-ID. If that user name matches the real user-ID, then Emacs uses HOME; otherwise, it looks up the home directory corresponding to that user name in the system's data base of users.

32 Dealing with Common Problems

If you type an Emacs command you did not intend, the results are often mysterious. This chapter tells what you can do to cancel your mistake or recover from a mysterious situation. Emacs bugs and system crashes are also considered.

32.1 Quitting and Aborting

`C-g`
`C-`(BREAK) (MS-DOS)

>   Quit. Cancel running or partially typed command.

`C-]`   Abort innermost recursive editing level and cancel the command which invoked it (`abort-recursive-edit`).

(ESC) (ESC) (ESC)

>   Either quit or abort, whichever makes sense (`keyboard-escape-quit`).

`M-x top-level`

>   Abort all recursive editing levels that are currently executing.

`C-x u`   Cancel a previously made change in the buffer contents (`undo`).

There are two ways of canceling commands which are not finished executing: *quitting* with `C-g`, and *aborting* with `C-]` or `M-x top-level`. Quitting cancels a partially typed command or one which is already running. Aborting exits a recursive editing level and cancels the command that invoked the recursive edit. (See Section 30.12 [Recursive Edit], page 385.)

Quitting with `C-g` is used for getting rid of a partially typed command, or a numeric argument that you don't want. It also stops a running command in the middle in a relatively safe way, so you can use it if you accidentally give a command which takes a long time. In particular, it is safe to quit out of killing; either your text will *all* still be in the buffer, or it will *all* be in the kill ring (or maybe both). Quitting an incremental search does special things documented under searching; in general, it may take two successive `C-g` characters to get out of a search (see Section 12.1 [Incremental Search], page 85).

On MS-DOS, the character `C-`(BREAK) serves as a quit character like `C-g`. The reason is that it is not feasible, on MS-DOS, to recognize `C-g` while a command is running, between interactions with the user. By contrast, it *is* feasible to recognize `C-`(BREAK) at all times. See Section C.1 [MS-DOS Input], page 463.

`C-g` works by setting the variable `quit-flag` to `t` the instant `C-g` is typed; Emacs Lisp checks this variable frequently and quits if it is non-`nil`. `C-g` is only actually executed as a command if you type it while Emacs is waiting for input.

If you quit with C-g a second time before the first C-g is recognized, you activate the "emergency escape" feature and return to the shell. See Section 32.2.8 [Emergency Escape], page 429.

There may be times when you cannot quit. When Emacs is waiting for the operating system to do something, quitting is impossible unless special pains are taken for the particular system call within Emacs where the waiting occurs. We have done this for the system calls that users are likely to want to quit from, but it's possible you will find another. In one very common case—waiting for file input or output using NFS—Emacs itself knows how to quit, but most NFS implementations simply do not allow user programs to stop waiting for NFS when the NFS server is hung.

Aborting with C-] (abort-recursive-edit) is used to get out of a recursive editing level and cancel the command which invoked it. Quitting with C-g does not do this, and could not do this, because it is used to cancel a partially typed command *within* the recursive editing level. Both operations are useful. For example, if you are in a recursive edit and type C-u 8 to enter a numeric argument, you can cancel that argument with C-g and remain in the recursive edit.

The command (ESC) (ESC) (ESC) (keyboard-escape-quit) can either quit or abort. This key was defined because (ESC) is used to "get out" in many PC programs. It can cancel a prefix argument, clear a selected region, or get out of a Query Replace, like C-g. It can get out of the minibuffer or a recursive edit, like C-]. It can also get out of splitting the frame into multiple windows, like C-x 1. One thing it cannot do, however, is stop a command that is running. That's because it executes as an ordinary command, and Emacs doesn't notice it until it is ready for a command.

The command M-x top-level is equivalent to "enough" C-] commands to get you out of all the levels of recursive edits that you are in. C-] gets you out one level at a time, but M-x top-level goes out all levels at once. Both C-] and M-x top-level are like all other commands, and unlike C-g, in that they take effect only when Emacs is ready for a command. C-] is an ordinary key and has its meaning only because of its binding in the keymap. See Section 30.12 [Recursive Edit], page 385.

C-x u (undo) is not strictly speaking a way of canceling a command, but you can think of it as canceling a command that already finished executing. See Section 4.4 [Undo], page 32.

32.2 Dealing with Emacs Trouble

This section describes various conditions in which Emacs fails to work normally, and how to recognize them and correct them.

32.2.1 If (DEL) Fails to Delete

If you find that (DEL) enters Help like `Control-h` instead of deleting a character, your terminal is sending the wrong code for (DEL). You can work around this problem by changing the keyboard translation table (see Section 31.5 [Keyboard Translations], page 418).

32.2.2 Recursive Editing Levels

Recursive editing levels are important and useful features of Emacs, but they can seem like malfunctions to the user who does not understand them.

If the mode line has square brackets '[...]' around the parentheses that contain the names of the major and minor modes, you have entered a recursive editing level. If you did not do this on purpose, or if you don't understand what that means, you should just get out of the recursive editing level. To do so, type `M-x top-level`. This is called getting back to top level. See Section 30.12 [Recursive Edit], page 385.

32.2.3 Garbage on the Screen

If the data on the screen looks wrong, the first thing to do is see whether the text is really wrong. Type `C-l`, to redisplay the entire screen. If the screen appears correct after this, the problem was entirely in the previous screen update. (Otherwise, see Section 32.2.4 [Text Garbled], page 427.)

Display updating problems often result from an incorrect termcap entry for the terminal you are using. The file 'etc/TERMS' in the Emacs distribution gives the fixes for known problems of this sort. 'INSTALL' contains general advice for these problems in one of its sections. Very likely there is simply insufficient padding for certain display operations. To investigate the possibility that you have this sort of problem, try Emacs on another terminal made by a different manufacturer. If problems happen frequently on one kind of terminal but not another kind, it is likely to be a bad termcap entry, though it could also be due to a bug in Emacs that appears for terminals that have or that lack specific features.

32.2.4 Garbage in the Text

If `C-l` shows that the text is wrong, try undoing the changes to it using `C-x u` until it gets back to a state you consider correct. Also try `C-h l` to find out what command you typed to produce the observed results.

If a large portion of text appears to be missing at the beginning or end of the buffer, check for the word 'Narrow' in the mode line. If it appears, the text you don't see is probably still present, but temporarily off-limits. To make it accessible again, type `C-x n w`. See Section 30.8 [Narrowing], page 382.

32.2.5 Spontaneous Entry to Incremental Search

If Emacs spontaneously displays 'I-search:' at the bottom of the screen, it means that the terminal is sending C-s and C-q according to the poorly designed xon/xoff "flow control" protocol.

If this happens to you, your best recourse is to put the terminal in a mode where it will not use flow control, or give it so much padding that it will never send a C-s. (One way to increase the amount of padding is to set the variable **baud-rate** to a larger value. Its value is the terminal output speed, measured in the conventional units of baud.)

If you don't succeed in turning off flow control, the next best thing is to tell Emacs to cope with it. To do this, call the function **enable-flow-control**.

Typically there are particular terminal types with which you must use flow control. You can conveniently ask for flow control on those terminal types only, using **enable-flow-control-on**. For example, if you find you must use flow control on VT-100 and H19 terminals, put the following in your '.emacs' file:

```
(enable-flow-control-on "vt100" "h19")
```

When flow control is enabled, you must type C-\ to get the effect of a C-s, and type C-^ to get the effect of a C-q. (These aliases work by means of keyboard translations; see Section 31.5 [Keyboard Translations], page 418.)

32.2.6 Running out of Memory

If you get the error message 'Virtual memory exceeded', save your modified buffers with C-x s. This method of saving them has the smallest need for additional memory. Emacs keeps a reserve of memory which it makes available when this error happens; that should be enough to enable C-x s to complete its work.

Once you have saved your modified buffers, you can exit this Emacs job and start another, or you can use M-x kill-some-buffers to free space in the current Emacs job. If you kill buffers containing a substantial amount of text, you can safely go on editing. Emacs refills its memory reserve automatically when it sees sufficient free space available, in case you run out of memory another time.

Do not use M-x buffer-menu to save or kill buffers when you run out of memory, because the buffer menu needs a fair amount memory itself, and the reserve supply may not be enough.

32.2.7 Recovery After a Crash

If Emacs or the computer crashes, you can recover the files you were editing at the time of the crash from their auto-save files. To do this, start Emacs again and type the command M-x recover-session.

This command initially displays a buffer which lists interrupted session files, each with its date. You must choose which session to recover from. Typically the one you want is the most recent one. Move point to the one you choose, and type C-c C-c.

Then `recover-session` asks about each of the files that you were editing during that session; it asks whether to recover that file. If you answer y for a file, it shows the dates of that file and its auto-save file, then asks once again whether to recover that file. For the second question, you must confirm with yes. If you do, Emacs visits the file but gets the text from the auto-save file.

When `recover-session` is done, the files you've chosen to recover are present in Emacs buffers. You should then save them. Only this—saving them—updates the files themselves.

32.2.8 Emergency Escape

Because at times there have been bugs causing Emacs to loop without checking `quit-flag`, a special feature causes Emacs to be suspended immediately if you type a second C-g while the flag is already set, so you can always get out of GNU Emacs. Normally Emacs recognizes and clears `quit-flag` (and quits!) quickly enough to prevent this from happening. (On MS-DOS and compatible systems, type C-⟨BREAK⟩ twice.)

When you resume Emacs after a suspension caused by multiple C-g, it asks two questions before going back to what it had been doing:

```
Auto-save? (y or n)
Abort (and dump core)? (y or n)
```

Answer each one with y or n followed by ⟨RET⟩.

Saying y to 'Auto-save?' causes immediate auto-saving of all modified buffers in which auto-saving is enabled.

Saying y to 'Abort (and dump core)?' causes an illegal instruction to be executed, dumping core. This is to enable a wizard to figure out why Emacs was failing to quit in the first place. Execution does not continue after a core dump. If you answer n, execution does continue. With luck, GNU Emacs will ultimately check `quit-flag` and quit normally. If not, and you type another C-g, it is suspended again.

If Emacs is not really hung, just slow, you may invoke the double C-g feature without really meaning to. Then just resume and answer n to both questions, and you will arrive at your former state. Presumably the quit you requested will happen soon.

The double-C-g feature is turned off when Emacs is running under the X Window System, since you can use the window manager to kill Emacs or to create another window and run another program.

On MS-DOS and compatible systems, the emergency escape feature is sometimes unavailable, even if you press C-⟨BREAK⟩ twice, when some system call (MS-DOS or BIOS) hangs, or when Emacs is stuck in a very tight endless loop (in C code, **not** in Lisp code).

32.2.9 Help for Total Frustration

If using Emacs (or something else) becomes terribly frustrating and none of the techniques described above solve the problem, Emacs can still help you.

First, if the Emacs you are using is not responding to commands, type C-g C-g to get out of it and then start a new one.

Second, type M-x doctor (RET).

The doctor will help you feel better. Each time you say something to the doctor, you must end it by typing (RET) (RET). This lets the doctor know you are finished.

32.3 Reporting Bugs

Sometimes you will encounter a bug in Emacs. Although we cannot promise we can or will fix the bug, and we might not even agree that it is a bug, we want to hear about problems you encounter. Often we agree they are bugs and want to fix them.

To make it possible for us to fix a bug, you must report it. In order to do so effectively, you must know when and how to do it.

32.3.1 When Is There a Bug

If Emacs executes an illegal instruction, or dies with an operating system error message that indicates a problem in the program (as opposed to something like "disk full"), then it is certainly a bug.

If Emacs updates the display in a way that does not correspond to what is in the buffer, then it is certainly a bug. If a command seems to do the wrong thing but the problem corrects itself if you type C-l, it is a case of incorrect display updating.

Taking forever to complete a command can be a bug, but you must make certain that it was really Emacs's fault. Some commands simply take a long time. Type C-g (C-(BREAK) on MS-DOS) and then C-h l to see whether the input Emacs received was what you intended to type; if the input was such that you *know* it should have been processed quickly, report a bug. If you don't know whether the command should take a long time, find out by looking in the manual or by asking for assistance.

If a command you are familiar with causes an Emacs error message in a case where its usual definition ought to be reasonable, it is probably a bug.

If a command does the wrong thing, that is a bug. But be sure you know for certain what it ought to have done. If you aren't familiar with the command, or don't know for certain how the command is supposed to work, then it might actually be working right. Rather than jumping to conclusions, show the problem to someone who knows for certain.

Finally, a command's intended definition may not be best for editing with. This is a very important sort of problem, but it is also a matter of judgment. Also, it is easy to come to such a conclusion out of ignorance of some of the existing features. It is probably best not to complain about such a problem until you have checked the documentation in the usual ways, feel confident that you understand it, and know for certain that what you want is not available. If you are not sure what the command is supposed to do after a careful reading of the manual, check the index and glossary for any terms that may be unclear.

If after careful rereading of the manual you still do not understand what the command should do, that indicates a bug in the manual, which you should report. The manual's job is to make everything clear to people who are not Emacs experts—including you. It is just as important to report documentation bugs as program bugs.

If the on-line documentation string of a function or variable disagrees with the manual, one of them must be wrong; that is a bug.

32.3.2 Understanding Bug Reporting

When you decide that there is a bug, it is important to report it and to report it in a way which is useful. What is most useful is an exact description of what commands you type, starting with the shell command to run Emacs, until the problem happens.

The most important principle in reporting a bug is to report *facts*. Hypotheses and verbal descriptions are no substitute for the detailed raw data. Reporting the facts is straightforward, but many people strain to posit explanations and report them instead of the facts. If the explanations are based on guesses about how Emacs is implemented, they will be useless; meanwhile, lacking the facts, we will have no real information about the bug.

For example, suppose that you type `C-x C-f /glorp/baz.ugh` (RET), visiting a file which (you know) happens to be rather large, and Emacs displayed 'I feel pretty today'. The best way to report the bug is with a sentence like the preceding one, because it gives all the facts.

A bad way would be to assume that the problem is due to the size of the file and say, "I visited a large file, and Emacs displayed 'I feel pretty today'." This is what we mean by "guessing explanations." The problem is just as likely to be due to the fact that there is a 'z' in the file name. If this is so, then when we got your report, we would try out the problem with some "large file," probably with no 'z' in its name, and not see any problem. There is no way in the world that we could guess that we should try visiting a file with a 'z' in its name.

Alternatively, the problem might be due to the fact that the file starts with exactly 25 spaces. For this reason, you should make sure that you inform us of the exact contents of any file that is needed to reproduce the bug. What if the problem only occurs when you have typed the C-x C-a command previously? This is why we ask you to give the exact sequence of characters you typed since starting the Emacs session.

You should not even say "visit a file" instead of C-x C-f unless you *know* that it makes no difference which visiting command is used. Similarly, rather than saying "if I have three characters on the line," say "after I type (RET) A B C (RET) C-p," if that is the way you entered the text.

So please don't guess any explanations when you report a bug. If you want to actually *debug* the problem, and report explanations that are more than guesses, that is useful—but please include the facts as well.

32.3.3 Checklist for Bug Reports

The best way to send a bug report is to mail it electronically to the Emacs maintainers at 'bug-gnu-emacs@gnu.org'. (If you want to suggest a change as an improvement, use the same address.)

If you'd like to read the bug reports, you can find them on the newsgroup 'gnu.emacs.bug'; keep in mind, however, that as a spectator you should not criticize anything about what you see there. The purpose of bug reports is to give information to the Emacs maintainers. Spectators are welcome only as long as they do not interfere with this. In particular, some bug reports contain large amounts of data; spectators should not complain about this.

Please do not post bug reports using netnews; mail is more reliable than netnews about reporting your correct address, which we may need in order to ask you for more information.

If you can't send electronic mail, then mail the bug report on paper or machine-readable media to this address:

GNU Emacs Bugs
Free Software Foundation
59 Temple Place, Suite 330
Boston, MA 02111-1307 USA

We do not promise to fix the bug; but if the bug is serious, or ugly, or easy to fix, chances are we will want to.

A convenient way to send a bug report for Emacs is to use the command M-x report-emacs-bug. This sets up a mail buffer (see Chapter 26 [Sending Mail], page 301) and automatically inserts *some* of the essential information. However, it cannot supply all the necessary information; you should still read and follow the guidelines below, so you can enter the other crucial information by hand before you send the message.

To enable maintainers to investigate a bug, your report should include all these things:

- The version number of Emacs. Without this, we won't know whether there is any point in looking for the bug in the current version of GNU Emacs.

  You can get the version number by typing `M-x emacs-version` (RET). If that command does not work, you probably have something other than GNU Emacs, so you will have to report the bug somewhere else.

- The type of machine you are using, and the operating system name and version number. `M-x emacs-version` (RET) provides this information too. Copy its output from the '*Messages*' buffer, so that you get it all and get it accurately.

- The operands given to the **configure** command when Emacs was installed.

- A complete list of any modifications you have made to the Emacs source. (We may not have time to investigate the bug unless it happens in an unmodified Emacs. But if you've made modifications and you don't tell us, you are sending us on a wild goose chase.)

  Be precise about these changes. A description in English is not enough— send a context diff for them.

  Adding files of your own, or porting to another machine, is a modification of the source.

- Details of any other deviations from the standard procedure for installing GNU Emacs.

- The complete text of any files needed to reproduce the bug.

  If you can tell us a way to cause the problem without visiting any files, please do so. This makes it much easier to debug. If you do need files, make sure you arrange for us to see their exact contents. For example, it can often matter whether there are spaces at the ends of lines, or a newline after the last line in the buffer (nothing ought to care whether the last line is terminated, but try telling the bugs that).

- The precise commands we need to type to reproduce the bug.

  The easy way to record the input to Emacs precisely is to write a dribble file. To start the file, execute the Lisp expression

      (open-dribble-file "~/dribble")

  using `M-:` or from the '*scratch*' buffer just after starting Emacs. From then on, Emacs copies all your input to the specified dribble file until the Emacs process is killed.

- For possible display bugs, the terminal type (the value of environment variable `TERM`), the complete termcap entry for the terminal from '/etc/termcap' (since that file is not identical on all machines), and the output that Emacs actually sent to the terminal.

  The way to collect the terminal output is to execute the Lisp expression

      (open-termscript "~/termscript")

using M-: or from the '*scratch*' buffer just after starting Emacs. From then on, Emacs copies all terminal output to the specified termscript file as well, until the Emacs process is killed. If the problem happens when Emacs starts up, put this expression into your '.emacs' file so that the termscript file will be open when Emacs displays the screen for the first time.

Be warned: it is often difficult, and sometimes impossible, to fix a terminal-dependent bug without access to a terminal of the type that stimulates the bug.

- A description of what behavior you observe that you believe is incorrect. For example, "The Emacs process gets a fatal signal," or, "The resulting text is as follows, which I think is wrong."

  Of course, if the bug is that Emacs gets a fatal signal, then one can't miss it. But if the bug is incorrect text, the maintainer might fail to notice what is wrong. Why leave it to chance?

  Even if the problem you experience is a fatal signal, you should still say so explicitly. Suppose something strange is going on, such as, your copy of the source is out of sync, or you have encountered a bug in the C library on your system. (This has happened!) Your copy might crash and the copy here might not. If you *said* to expect a crash, then when Emacs here fails to crash, we would know that the bug was not happening. If you don't say to expect a crash, then we would not know whether the bug was happening—we would not be able to draw any conclusion from our observations.

- If the manifestation of the bug is an Emacs error message, it is important to report the precise text of the error message, and a backtrace showing how the Lisp program in Emacs arrived at the error.

  To get the error message text accurately, copy it from the '*Messages*' buffer into the bug report. Copy all of it, not just part.

  To make a backtrace for the error, evaluate the Lisp expression (setq debug-on-error t) before the error happens (that is to say, you must execute that expression and then make the bug happen). This causes the error to run the Lisp debugger, which shows you a backtrace. Copy the text of the debugger's backtrace into the bug report.

  This use of the debugger is possible only if you know how to make the bug happen again. If you can't make it happen again, at least copy the whole error message.

- Check whether any programs you have loaded into the Lisp world, including your '.emacs' file, set any variables that may affect the functioning of Emacs. Also, see whether the problem happens in a freshly started Emacs without loading your '.emacs' file (start Emacs with the -q switch to prevent loading the init file). If the problem does *not* occur then, you must report the precise contents of any programs that you must load into the Lisp world in order to cause the problem to occur.

- If the problem does depend on an init file or other Lisp programs that are not part of the standard Emacs system, then you should make sure it is not a bug in those programs by complaining to their maintainers first. After they verify that they are using Emacs in a way that is supposed to work, they should report the bug.

- If you wish to mention something in the GNU Emacs source, show the line of code with a few lines of context. Don't just give a line number.

  The line numbers in the development sources don't match those in your sources. It would take extra work for the maintainers to determine what code is in your version at a given line number, and we could not be certain.

- Additional information from a C debugger such as GDB might enable someone to find a problem on a machine which he does not have available. If you don't know how to use GDB, please read the GDB manual— it is not very long, and using GDB is easy. You can find the GDB distribution, including the GDB manual in online form, in most of the same places you can find the Emacs distribution. To run Emacs under GDB, you should switch to the 'src' subdirectory in which Emacs was compiled, then do 'gdb emacs'. It is important for the directory 'src' to be current so that GDB will read the '.gdbinit' file in this directory.

  However, you need to think when you collect the additional information if you want it to show what causes the bug.

  For example, many people send just a backtrace, but that is not very useful by itself. A simple backtrace with arguments often conveys little about what is happening inside GNU Emacs, because most of the arguments listed in the backtrace are pointers to Lisp objects. The numeric values of these pointers have no significance whatever; all that matters is the contents of the objects they point to (and most of the contents are themselves pointers).

  To provide useful information, you need to show the values of Lisp objects in Lisp notation. Do this for each variable which is a Lisp object, in several stack frames near the bottom of the stack. Look at the source to see which variables are Lisp objects, because the debugger thinks of them as integers.

  To show a variable's value in Lisp syntax, first print its value, then use the user-defined GDB command **pr** to print the Lisp object in Lisp syntax. (If you must use another debugger, call the function **debug‐ print** with the object as an argument.) The **pr** command is defined by the file '.gdbinit', and it works only if you are debugging a running process (not with a core dump).

  To make Lisp errors stop Emacs and return to GDB, put a breakpoint at **Fsignal**.

  For a short listing of Lisp functions running, type the GDB command **xbacktrace**.

If you want to examine Lisp function arguments, move up the stack, and each time you get to a frame for the function **Ffuncall**, type these GDB commands:

```
p *args
pr
```

To print the first argument that the function received, use these commands:

```
p args[1]
pr
```

You can print the other arguments likewise. The argument **nargs** of **Ffuncall** says how many arguments **Ffuncall** received; these include the Lisp function itself and the arguments for that function.

The file '**.gdbinit**' defines several other commands that are useful for examining the data types and contents of Lisp objects. Their names begin with '**x**'. These commands work at a lower level than **pr**, and are less convenient, but they may work even when **pr** does not, such as when debugging a core dump or when Emacs has had a fatal signal.

- If the symptom of the bug is that Emacs fails to respond, don't assume Emacs is "hung"—it may instead be in an infinite loop. To find out which, make the problem happen under GDB and stop Emacs once it is not responding. (If Emacs is using X Windows directly, you can stop Emacs by typing **C-z** at the GDB job.) Then try stepping with '**step**'. If Emacs is hung, the '**step**' command won't return. If it is looping, '**step**' will return.

  If this shows Emacs is hung in a system call, stop it again and examine the arguments of the call. In your bug report, state exactly where in the source the system call is, and what the arguments are.

  If Emacs is in an infinite loop, please determine where the loop starts and ends. The easiest way to do this is to use the GDB command '**finish**'. Each time you use it, Emacs resumes execution until it exits one stack frame. Keep typing '**finish**' until it doesn't return—that means the infinite loop is in the stack frame which you just tried to finish.

  Stop Emacs again, and use '**finish**' repeatedly again until you get *back to* that frame. Then use '**next**' to step through that frame. By stepping, you will see where the loop starts and ends. Also please examine the data being used in the loop and try to determine why the loop does not exit when it should. Include all of this information in your bug report.

Here are some things that are not necessary in a bug report:

- A description of the envelope of the bug—this is not necessary for a reproducible bug.

Often people who encounter a bug spend a lot of time investigating which changes to the input file will make the bug go away and which changes will not affect it.

This is often time-consuming and not very useful, because the way we will find the bug is by running a single example under the debugger with breakpoints, not by pure deduction from a series of examples. You might as well save time by not searching for additional examples.

Of course, if you can find a simpler example to report *instead* of the original one, that is a convenience. Errors in the output will be easier to spot, running under the debugger will take less time, etc.

However, simplification is not vital; if you can't do this or don't have time to try, please report the bug with your original test case.

- A system-call trace of Emacs execution.

System-call traces are very useful for certain special kinds of debugging, but in most cases they give little useful information. It is therefore strange that many people seem to think that *the* way to report information about a crash is to send a system-call trace. Perhaps this is a habit formed from experience debugging programs that don't have source code or debugging symbols.

In most programs, a backtrace is normally far, far more informative than a system-call trace. Even in Emacs, a simple backtrace is generally more informative, though to give full information you should supplement the backtrace by displaying variable values and printing them as Lisp objects with `pr` (see above).

- A patch for the bug.

A patch for the bug is useful if it is a good one. But don't omit the other information that a bug report needs, such as the test case, on the assumption that a patch is sufficient. We might see problems with your patch and decide to fix the problem another way, or we might not understand it at all. And if we can't understand what bug you are trying to fix, or why your patch should be an improvement, we mustn't install it.

- A guess about what the bug is or what it depends on.

Such guesses are usually wrong. Even experts can't guess right about such things without first using the debugger to find the facts.

32.3.4 Sending Patches for GNU Emacs

If you would like to write bug fixes or improvements for GNU Emacs, that is very helpful. When you send your changes, please follow these guidelines to make it easy for the maintainers to use them. If you don't follow these guidelines, your information might still be useful, but using it will take extra work. Maintaining GNU Emacs is a lot of work in the best of circumstances, and we can't keep up unless you do your best to help.

- Send an explanation with your changes of what problem they fix or what improvement they bring about. For a bug fix, just include a copy of the bug report, and explain why the change fixes the bug.

  (Referring to a bug report is not as good as including it, because then we will have to look it up, and we have probably already deleted it if we've already fixed the bug.)

- Always include a proper bug report for the problem you think you have fixed. We need to convince ourselves that the change is right before installing it. Even if it is correct, we might have trouble understanding it if we don't have a way to reproduce the problem.

- Include all the comments that are appropriate to help people reading the source in the future understand why this change was needed.

- Don't mix together changes made for different reasons. Send them *individually*.

  If you make two changes for separate reasons, then we might not want to install them both. We might want to install just one. If you send them all jumbled together in a single set of diffs, we have to do extra work to disentangle them—to figure out which parts of the change serve which purpose. If we don't have time for this, we might have to ignore your changes entirely.

  If you send each change as soon as you have written it, with its own explanation, then two changes never get tangled up, and we can consider each one properly without any extra work to disentangle them.

- Send each change as soon as that change is finished. Sometimes people think they are helping us by accumulating many changes to send them all together. As explained above, this is absolutely the worst thing you could do.

  Since you should send each change separately, you might as well send it right away. That gives us the option of installing it immediately if it is important.

- Use 'diff -c' to make your diffs. Diffs without context are hard to install reliably. More than that, they are hard to study; we must always study a patch to decide whether we want to install it. Unidiff format is better than contextless diffs, but not as easy to read as '-c' format.

  If you have GNU diff, use 'diff -c -F'^[_a-zA-Z0-9$]+ *('' when making diffs of C code. This shows the name of the function that each change occurs in.

- Avoid any ambiguity as to which is the old version and which is the new. Please make the old version the first argument to diff, and the new version the second argument. And please give one version or the other a name that indicates whether it is the old version or your new changed one.

- Write the change log entries for your changes. This is both to save us the extra work of writing them, and to help explain your changes so we can understand them.

  The purpose of the change log is to show people where to find what was changed. So you need to be specific about what functions you changed; in large functions, it's often helpful to indicate where within the function the change was.

  On the other hand, once you have shown people where to find the change, you need not explain its purpose in the change log. Thus, if you add a new function, all you need to say about it is that it is new. If you feel that the purpose needs explaining, it probably does—but put the explanation in comments in the code. It will be more useful there.

  Please read the 'ChangeLog' files in the 'src' and 'lisp' directories to see what sorts of information to put in, and to learn the style that we use. If you would like your name to appear in the header line, showing who made the change, send us the header line. See Section 22.12 [Change Log], page 249.

- When you write the fix, keep in mind that we can't install a change that would break other systems. Please think about what effect your change will have if compiled on another type of system.

  Sometimes people send fixes that *might* be an improvement in general— but it is hard to be sure of this. It's hard to install such changes because we have to study them very carefully. Of course, a good explanation of the reasoning by which you concluded the change was correct can help convince us.

  The safest changes are changes to the configuration files for a particular machine. These are safe because they can't create new bugs on other machines.

  Please help us keep up with the workload by designing the patch in a form that is clearly safe to install.

32.4 Contributing to Emacs Development

If you would like to help pretest Emacs releases to assure they work well, or if you would like to work on improving Emacs, please contact the maintainers at **bug-gnu-emacs@gnu.org**. A pretester should be prepared to investigate bugs as well as report them. If you'd like to work on improving Emacs, please ask for suggested projects or suggest your own ideas.

If you have already written an improvement, please tell us about it. If you have not yet started work, it is useful to contact **bug-gnu-emacs@gnu.org** before you start; it might be possible to suggest ways to make your extension fit in better with the rest of Emacs.

32.5 How To Get Help with GNU Emacs

If you need help installing, using or changing GNU Emacs, there are two ways to find it:

- Send a message to the mailing list `help-gnu-emacs@gnu.org`, or post your request on newsgroup `gnu.emacs.help`. (This mailing list and newsgroup interconnect, so it does not matter which one you use.)

- Look in the service directory for someone who might help you for a fee. The service directory is found in the file named '`etc/SERVICE`' in the Emacs distribution.

Appendix A Command Line Arguments

GNU Emacs supports command line arguments to request various actions when invoking Emacs. These are for compatibility with other editors and for sophisticated activities. We don't recommend using them for ordinary editing.

Arguments starting with '-' are *options*. Other arguments specify files to visit. Emacs visits the specified files while it starts up. The last file name on your command line becomes the current buffer; the other files are also present in other buffers. As usual, the special argument '--' says that all subsequent arguments are file names, not options, even if they start with '-'.

Emacs command options can specify many things, such as the size and position of the X window Emacs uses, its colors, and so on. A few options support advanced usage, such as running Lisp functions on files in batch mode. The sections of this chapter describe the available options, arranged according to their purpose.

There are two ways of writing options: the short forms that start with a single '-', and the long forms that start with '--'. For example, '-d' is a short form and '--display' is the corresponding long form.

The long forms with '--' are easier to remember, but longer to type. However, you don't have to spell out the whole option name; any unambiguous abbreviation is enough. When a long option takes an argument, you can use either a space or an equal sign to separate the option name and the argument. Thus, you can write either '--display sugar-bombs:0.0' or '--display=sugar-bombs:0.0'. We recommend an equal sign because it makes the relationship clearer, and the tables below always show an equal sign.

Most options specify how to initialize Emacs, or set parameters for the Emacs session. We call them *initial options*. A few options specify things to do: for example, load libraries, call functions, or exit Emacs. These are called *action options*. These and file names together are called *action arguments*. Emacs processes all the action arguments in the order they are written.

A.1 Action Arguments

Here is a table of the action arguments and options:

'*file*'   Visit *file* using `find-file`. See Section 14.2 [Visiting], page 108.

'+*linenum file*'
                  Visit *file* using `find-file`, then go to line number *linenum* in it.

'-l *file*'
'--load=*file*'
> Load a Lisp library named *file* with the function `load`. See Section 23.7 [Lisp Libraries], page 285. The library can be found either in the current directory, or in the Emacs library search path as specified with `EMACSLOADPATH` (see Section A.5.1 [General Variables], page 445).

'-f *function*'
'--funcall=*function*'
> Call Lisp function *function* with no arguments.

'--eval *expression*'
> Evaluate Lisp expression *expression*.

'--insert=*file*'
> Insert the contents of *file* into the current buffer. This is like what `M-x insert-file` does. See Section 14.10 [Misc File Ops], page 139.

'--kill' Exit from Emacs without asking for confirmation.

The init file can access the values of the action arguments as the elements of a list in the variable `command-line-args`. The init file can override the normal processing of the action arguments, or define new ones, by reading and setting this variable.

A.2 Initial Options

The initial options specify parameters for the Emacs session. This section describes the more general initial options; some other options specifically related to X Windows appear in the following sections.

Some initial options affect the loading of init files. The normal actions of Emacs are to first load 'site-start.el' if it exists, then your own init file '~/.emacs' if it exists, and finally 'default.el' if it exists; certain options prevent loading of some of these files or substitute other files for them.

'-t *device*'
'--terminal=*device*'
> Use *device* as the device for terminal input and output.

'-d *display*'
'--display=*display*'
> Use the X Window System and use the display named *display* to open the initial Emacs frame.

'-nw'
'--no-windows'
> Don't communicate directly with X, disregarding the `DISPLAY` environment variable even if it is set.

'-batch'
'--batch'   Run Emacs in *batch mode*, which means that the text being
              edited is not displayed and the standard terminal interrupt char-
              acters such as C-z and C-c continue to have their normal effect.
              Emacs in batch mode outputs to stderr only what would nor-
              mally be printed in the echo area under program control.

              Batch mode is used for running programs written in Emacs Lisp
              from shell scripts, makefiles, and so on. Normally the '-l' option
              or '-f' option will be used as well, to invoke a Lisp program to
              do the batch processing.

              '-batch' implies '-q' (do not load an init file). It also causes
              Emacs to kill itself after all command options have been pro-
              cessed. In addition, auto-saving is not done except in buffers for
              which it has been explicitly requested.

'-q'
'--no-init-file'
              Do not load your Emacs init file '~/.emacs', or 'default.el'
              either.

'--no-site-file'
              Do not load 'site-start.el'. The options '-q', '-u' and
              '-batch' have no effect on the loading of this file—this is the
              only option that blocks it.

'-u *user*'
'--user=*user*'
              Load *user*'s Emacs init file '~*user*/.emacs' instead of your own.

'--debug-init'
              Enable the Emacs Lisp debugger for errors in the init file.

'--unibyte'
              Set up to do almost everything with single-byte buffers and
              strings. All buffers and strings are unibyte unless you (or a Lisp
              program) explicitly ask for a multibyte buffer or string. Setting
              the environment variable EMACS_UNIBYTE has the same effect.

'--multibyte'
              Inhibit the effect of EMACS_UNIBYTE, so that Emacs uses multi-
              byte characters by default, as usual.

A.3 Command Argument Example

Here is an example of using Emacs with arguments and options. It assumes you have a Lisp program file called 'hack-c.el' which, when loaded,
performs some useful operation on the current buffer, expected to be a C
program.

```
emacs -batch foo.c -l hack-c -f save-buffer >& log
```

This says to visit 'foo.c', load 'hack-c.el' (which makes changes in the visited file), save 'foo.c' (note that save-buffer is the function that C-x C-s is bound to), and then exit back to the shell (because of '-batch'). '-batch' also guarantees there will be no problem redirecting output to 'log', because Emacs will not assume that it has a display terminal to work with.

A.4 Resuming Emacs with Arguments

You can specify action arguments for Emacs when you resume it after a suspension. To prepare for this, put the following code in your '.emacs' file (see Section 31.2.3 [Hooks], page 400):

```
(add-hook 'suspend-hook 'resume-suspend-hook)
(add-hook 'suspend-resume-hook 'resume-process-args)
```

As further preparation, you must execute the shell script 'emacs.csh' (if you use csh as your shell) or 'emacs.bash' (if you use bash as your shell). These scripts define an alias named edit, which will resume Emacs giving it new command line arguments such as files to visit.

Only action arguments work properly when you resume Emacs. Initial arguments are not recognized—it's too late to execute them anyway.

Note that resuming Emacs (with or without arguments) must be done from within the shell that is the parent of the Emacs job. This is why edit is an alias rather than a program or a shell script. It is not possible to implement a resumption command that could be run from other subjobs of the shell; no way to define a command that could be made the value of EDITOR, for example. Therefore, this feature does not take the place of the Emacs Server feature (see Section 30.3 [Emacs Server], page 376).

The aliases use the Emacs Server feature if you appear to have a server Emacs running. However, they cannot determine this with complete accuracy. They may think that a server is still running when in actuality you have killed that Emacs, because the file '/tmp/.esrv...' still exists. If this happens, find that file and delete it.

A.5 Environment Variables

This appendix describes how Emacs uses environment variables. An environment variable is a string passed from the operating system to Emacs, and the collection of environment variables is known as the environment. Environment variable names are case sensitive and it is conventional to use upper case letters only.

Because environment variables come from the operating system there is no general way to set them; it depends on the operating system and especially the shell that you are using. For example, here's how to set the environment variable ORGANIZATION to 'not very much' using bash:

```
export ORGANIZATION="not very much"
```
and here's how to do it in csh or tcsh:
```
setenv ORGANIZATION "not very much"
```
When Emacs is set-up to use the X windowing system, it inherits the use of a large number of environment variables from the X library. See the X documentation for more information.

A.5.1 General Variables

AUTHORCOPY
> The name of a file used to archive news articles posted with the GNUS package.

CDPATH
> Used by the **cd** command to search for the directory you specify, when you specify a relative directory name.

DOMAINNAME
> The name of the Internet domain that the machine running Emacs is located in. Used by the GNUS package.

EMACS_UNIBYTE
> Defining this environment variable directs Emacs to do almost everything with single-byte buffers and strings. It is equivalent to using the '**--unibyte**' command-line option on each invocation. See Section A.2 [Initial Options], page 442.

EMACSDATA
> Used to initialize the variable **data-directory** used to locate the architecture-independent files that come with Emacs. Setting this variable overrides the setting in '**paths.h**' when Emacs was built.

EMACSLOADPATH
> A colon-separated list of directories from which to load Emacs Lisp files. Setting this variable overrides the setting in '**paths.h**' when Emacs was built.

EMACSLOCKDIR
> The directory that Emacs places lock files—files used to protect users from editing the same files simultaneously. Setting this variable overrides the setting in '**paths.h**' when Emacs was built.

EMACSPATH
> The location of Emacs-specific binaries. Setting this variable overrides the setting in '**paths.h**' when Emacs was built.

ESHELL
> Used for shell-mode to override the **SHELL** environment variable.

HISTFILE   The name of the file that shell commands are saved in between
            logins. This variable defaults to '~/.history' if you use (t)csh as
            shell, to '~/.bash_history' if you use bash, to '~/.sh_history'
            if you use ksh, and to '~/.history' otherwise.

HOME   The location of the user's files in the directory tree; used for
            expansion of file names starting with a tilde ('~'). On MS-DOS,
            it defaults to the directory from which Emacs was started, with
            '/bin' removed from the end if it was present.

HOSTNAME   The name of the machine that Emacs is running on.

INCPATH   A colon-separated list of directories. Used by the **complete**
            package to search for files.

INFOPATH   A colon-separated list of directories holding info files. Setting
            this variable overrides the setting in 'paths.el' when Emacs
            was built.

LANG
LC_ALL
LC_CTYPE   The user's preferred locale. A locale name which contains
            '8859-n', '8859_n' or '8859n', where n is between 1 and 4, au-
            tomatically specifies the 'Latin-n' language environment when
            Emacs starts up. If n is 9, that specifies 'Latin-5'.

LOGNAME   The user's login name. See also USER.

MAIL   The name of the user's system mail inbox.

MAILRC   Name of file containing mail aliases. This defaults to
            '~/.mailrc'.

MH   Name of setup file for the mh system. This defaults to
            '~/.mh_profile'.

NAME   The real-world name of the user.

NNTPSERVER
            The name of the news server. Used by the mh and GNUS pack-
            ages.

ORGANIZATION
            The name of the organization to which you belong. Used for
            setting the 'Organization:' header in your posts from the GNUS
            package.

PATH   A colon-separated list of directories in which executables reside.
            (On MS-DOS, it is semicolon-separated instead.) This variable
            is used to set the Emacs Lisp variable **exec-path** which you
            should consider to use instead.

PWD   If set, this should be the default directory when Emacs was
            started.

REPLYTO   If set, this specifies an initial value for the variable `mail-default-reply-to`. See Section 26.2 [Mail Headers], page 302.

SAVEDIR   The name of a directory in which news articles are saved by default. Used by the GNUS package.

SHELL   The name of an interpreter used to parse and execute programs run from inside Emacs.

TERM   The name of the terminal that Emacs is running on. The variable must be set unless Emacs is run in batch mode. On MS-DOS, it defaults to '`internal`', which specifies a built-in terminal emulation that handles the machine's own display.

TERMCAP   The name of the termcap library file describing how to program the terminal specified by the `TERM` variable. This defaults to '`/etc/termcap`'.

TMPDIR   Used by the Emerge package as a prefix for temporary files.

TZ   This specifies the current time zone and possibly also daylight savings information. On MS-DOS, the default is based on country code; see the file '`msdos.c`' for details.

USER   The user's login name. See also `LOGNAME`. On MS-DOS, this defaults to '`root`'.

VERSION_CONTROL
            Used to initialize the `version-control` variable (see Section 14.3.1.1 [Backup Names], page 114).

A.5.2 Miscellaneous Variables

These variables are used only on particular configurations:

COMSPEC   On MS-DOS, the name of the command interpreter to use. This is used to make a default value for the `SHELL` environment variable.

NAME   On MS-DOS, this variable defaults to the value of the `USER` variable.

TEMP
TMP   On MS-DOS, these specify the name of the directory for storing temporary files in.

EMACSTEST
            On MS-DOS, this specifies a file to use to log the operation of the internal terminal emulator. This feature is useful for submitting bug reports.

EMACSCOLORS
            Used on MS-DOS systems to set screen colors early, so that the screen won't momentarily flash the default colors when Emacs

starts up. The value of this variable should be two-character encoding of the foreground (the first character) and the background (the second character) colors of the default face. Each character should be the hexadecimal code for the desired color on a standard PC text-mode display.

The PC display usually supports only eight background colors. However, Emacs switches the DOS display to a mode where all 16 colors can be used for the background, so all four bits of the background color are actually used.

`WINDOW_GFX`

Used when initializing the Sun windows system.

A.6 Specifying the Display Name

The environment variable `DISPLAY` tells all X clients, including Emacs, where to display their windows. Its value is set up by default in ordinary circumstances, when you start an X server and run jobs locally. Occasionally you may need to specify the display yourself; for example, if you do a remote login and want to run a client program remotely, displaying on your local screen.

With Emacs, the main reason people change the default display is to let them log into another system, run Emacs on that system, but have the window displayed at their local terminal. You might need to use login to another system because the files you want to edit are there, or because the Emacs executable file you want to run is there.

The syntax of the `DISPLAY` environment variable is '*host*:*display*.*screen*', where *host* is the host name of the X Window System server machine, *display* is an arbitrarily-assigned number that distinguishes your server (X terminal) from other servers on the same machine, and *screen* is a rarely-used field that allows an X server to control multiple terminal screens. The period and the *screen* field are optional. If included, *screen* is usually zero.

For example, if your host is named '`glasperle`' and your server is the first (or perhaps the only) server listed in the configuration, your `DISPLAY` is '`glasperle:0.0`'.

You can specify the display name explicitly when you run Emacs, either by changing the `DISPLAY` variable, or with the option '`-d` *display*' or '`--display=`*display*'. Here is an example:

```
emacs --display=glasperle:0 &
```

You can inhibit the direct use of X with the '`-nw`' option. This is also an initial option. It tells Emacs to display using ordinary ASCII on its controlling terminal.

Sometimes, security arrangements prevent a program on a remote system from displaying on your local system. In this case, trying to run Emacs produces messages like this:

```
Xlib:  connection to "glasperle:0.0" refused by server
```
You might be able to overcome this problem by using the **xhost** command on the local system to give permission for access from your remote machine.

A.7 Font Specification Options

By default, Emacs displays text in the font named '**9x15**', which makes each character nine pixels wide and fifteen pixels high. You can specify a different font on your command line through the option '**-fn** *name*'.

'**-fn** *name*'
> Use font *name* as the default font.

'**--font=***name*'
> '**--font**' is an alias for '**-fn**'.

Under X, each font has a long name which consists of eleven words or numbers, separated by dashes. Some fonts also have shorter nicknames— '**9x15**' is such a nickname. You can use either kind of name. You can use wildcard patterns for the font name; then Emacs lets X choose one of the fonts that match the pattern. Here is an example, which happens to specify the font whose nickname is '**6x13**':

```
emacs -fn "-misc-fixed-medium-r-semicondensed--13-*-*-*-c-60-iso8859-1" &
```
You can also specify the font in your '**.Xdefaults**' file:

```
emacs.font: -misc-fixed-medium-r-semicondensed--13-*-*-*-c-60-iso8859-1
```
A long font name has the following form:

> *-maker-family-weight-slant-widthtype-style...*
> *...-pixels-height-horiz-vert-spacing-width-charset*

family
> This is the name of the font family—for example, '**courier**'.

weight
> This is normally '**bold**', '**medium**' or '**light**'. Other words may appear here in some font names.

slant
> This is '**r**' (roman), '**i**' (italic), '**o**' (oblique), '**ri**' (reverse italic), or '**ot**' (other).

widthtype
> This is normally '**condensed**', '**extended**', '**semicondensed**' or '**normal**'. Other words may appear here in some font names.

style
> This is an optional additional style name. Usually it is empty— most long font names have two hyphens in a row at this point.

pixels
> This is the font height, in pixels.

height
> This is the font height on the screen, measured in tenths of a printer's point—approximately 1/720 of an inch. In other words, it is the point size of the font, times ten. For a given vertical resolution, *height* and *pixels* are proportional; therefore, it is common to specify just one of them and use '*****' for the other.

horiz   This is the horizontal resolution, in pixels per inch, of the screen
              for which the font is intended.

vert   This is the vertical resolution, in dots per inch, of the screen for
              which the font is intended. Normally the resolution of the fonts
              on your system is the right value for your screen; therefore, you
              normally specify '*' for this and *horiz*.

spacing   This is 'm' (monospace), 'p' (proportional) or 'c' (character cell).
              Emacs can use 'm' and 'c' fonts.

width   This is the average character width, in pixels, multiplied by ten.

charset   This is the character set that the font depicts. Normally you
              should use 'iso8859-1'.

Use only fixed-width fonts—that is, fonts in which all characters have
the same width; Emacs cannot yet handle display properly for variable-
width fonts. Any font with 'm' or 'c' in the *spacing* field of the long name is
a fixed-width font. Here's how to use the xlsfonts program to list all the
fixed-width fonts available on your system:

```
xlsfonts -fn '*x*' | egrep "^[0-9]+x[0-9]+"
xlsfonts -fn '*-*-*-*-*-*-*-*-*-*-*-m*'
xlsfonts -fn '*-*-*-*-*-*-*-*-*-*-*-c*'
```

To see what a particular font looks like, use the xfd command. For example:

```
xfd -fn 6x13
```

displays the entire font '6x13'.

While running Emacs, you can set the font of the current frame (see
Section 17.10 [Frame Parameters], page 164) or for a specific kind of text
(see Section 17.13 [Faces], page 166).

A.8 Window Color Options

On a color display, you can specify which color to use for various parts
of the Emacs display. To find out what colors are available on your system,
look at the '/usr/lib/X11/rgb.txt' file. If you do not specify colors, the
default for the background is white and the default for all other colors is
black. On a monochrome display, the foreground is black, the background
is white, and the border is gray if the display supports that.

Here is a list of the options for specifying colors:

'-fg *color*'
'--foreground-color=*color*'
          Specify the foreground color.

'-bg *color*'
'--background-color=*color*'
          Specify the background color.

'-bd *color*'
'--border-color=*color*'

> Specify the color of the border of the X window.

'-cr *color*'
'--cursor-color=*color*'

> Specify the color of the Emacs cursor which indicates where point is.

'-ms *color*'
'--mouse-color=*color*'

> Specify the color for the mouse cursor when the mouse is in the Emacs window.

'-r'
'--reverse-video'

> Reverse video—swap the foreground and background colors.

For example, to use a coral mouse cursor and a slate blue text cursor, enter:

```
emacs -ms coral -cr 'slate blue' &
```

You can reverse the foreground and background colors through the '-r' option or with the X resource 'reverseVideo'.

A.9 Options for Window Geometry

The '-geometry' option controls the size and position of the initial Emacs frame. Here is the format for specifying the window geometry:

'-g *width*x*height*{+-}*xoffset*{+-}*yoffset*'

> Specify window size *width* and *height* (measured in character columns and lines), and positions *xoffset* and *yoffset* (measured in pixels).

'--geometry=*width*x*height*{+-}*xoffset*{+-}*yoffset*'

> This is another way of writing the same thing.

{+-} means either a plus sign or a minus sign. A plus sign before *xoffset* means it is the distance from the left side of the screen; a minus sign means it counts from the right side. A plus sign before *yoffset* means it is the distance from the top of the screen, and a minus sign there indicates the distance from the bottom. The values *xoffset* and *yoffset* may themselves be positive or negative, but that doesn't change their meaning, only their direction.

Emacs uses the same units as xterm does to interpret the geometry. The *width* and *height* are measured in characters, so a large font creates a larger frame than a small font. The *xoffset* and *yoffset* are measured in pixels.

Since the mode line and the echo area occupy the last 2 lines of the frame, the height of the initial text window is 2 less than the height specified in

your geometry. In non-X-toolkit versions of Emacs, the menu bar also takes
one line of the specified number.

You do not have to specify all of the fields in the geometry specification.

If you omit both *xoffset* and *yoffset*, the window manager decides where
to put the Emacs frame, possibly by letting you place it with the mouse.
For example, '**164x55**' specifies a window 164 columns wide, enough for two
ordinary width windows side by side, and 55 lines tall.

The default width for Emacs is 80 characters and the default height is
40 lines. You can omit either the width or the height or both. If you start
the geometry with an integer, Emacs interprets it as the width. If you start
with an '**x**' followed by an integer, Emacs interprets it as the height. Thus,
'**81**' specifies just the width; '**x45**' specifies just the height.

If you start with '**+**' or '**-**', that introduces an offset, which means both
sizes are omitted. Thus, '**-3**' specifies the *xoffset* only. (If you give just one
offset, it is always *xoffset*.) '**+3-3**' specifies both the *xoffset* and the *yoffset*,
placing the frame near the bottom left of the screen.

You can specify a default for any or all of the fields in '**.Xdefaults**' file,
and then override selected fields with a '**--geometry**' option.

A.10 Internal and External Borders

An Emacs frame has an internal border and an external border. The
internal border is an extra strip of the background color around all four
edges of the frame. Emacs itself adds the internal border. The external
border is added by the window manager outside the internal border; it may
contain various boxes you can click on to move or iconify the window.

'**-ib** *width*'
'**--internal-border=***width*'
> Specify *width* as the width of the internal border.

'**-bw** *width*'
'**--border-width=***width*'
> Specify *width* as the width of the main border.

When you specify the size of the frame, that does not count the borders. The frame's position is measured from the outside edge of the external
border.

Use the '**-ib** *n*' option to specify an internal border *n* pixels wide. The
default is 1. Use '**-bw** *n*' to specify the width of the external border (though
the window manager may not pay attention to what you specify). The
default width of the external border is 2.

A.11 Frame Titles

An Emacs frame may or may not have a specified title. The frame title, if specified, appears in window decorations and icons as the name of the frame. If an Emacs frame has no specified title, the default title is the name of the executable program (if there is only one frame) or the selected window's buffer name (if there is more than one frame).

You can specify a title for the initial Emacs frame with a command line option:

'`-title` *title*'
'`--title=`*title*'
'`-T` *title*'   Specify *title* as the title for the initial Emacs frame.

The '`--name`' option (see Section A.13 [Resources X], page 453) also specifies the title for the initial Emacs frame.

A.12 Icons

Most window managers allow the user to "iconify" a frame, removing it from sight, and leaving a small, distinctive "icon" window in its place. Clicking on the icon window makes the frame itself appear again. If you have many clients running at once, you can avoid cluttering up the screen by iconifying most of the clients.

'`-i`'
'`--icon-type`'
            Use a picture of a gnu as the Emacs icon.

'`-iconic`'
'`--iconic`'
            Start Emacs in iconified state.

The '`-i`' or '`--icon-type`' option tells Emacs to use an icon window containing a picture of the GNU gnu. If omitted, Emacs lets the window manager choose what sort of icon to use—usually just a small rectangle containing the frame's title.

The '`-iconic`' option tells Emacs to begin running as an icon, rather than opening a frame right away. In this situation, the icon window provides only indication that Emacs has started; the usual text frame doesn't appear until you deiconify it.

A.13 X Resources

Programs running under the X Window System organize their user options under a hierarchy of classes and resources. You can specify default values for these options in your X resources file, usually named '`~/.Xdefaults`'.

Each line in the file specifies a value for one option or for a collection of related options, for one program or for several programs (optionally even for all programs).

Programs define named resources with particular meanings. They also define how to group resources into named classes. For instance, in Emacs, the 'internalBorder' resource controls the width of the internal border, and the 'borderWidth' resource controls the width of the external border. Both of these resources are part of the 'BorderWidth' class. Case distinctions are significant in these names.

In '~/.Xdefaults', you can specify a value for a single resource on one line, like this:

    emacs.borderWidth: 2

Or you can use a class name to specify the same value for all resources in that class. Here's an example:

    emacs.BorderWidth: 2

If you specify a value for a class, it becomes the default for all resources in that class. You can specify values for individual resources as well; these override the class value, for those particular resources. Thus, this example specifies 2 as the default width for all borders, but overrides this value with 4 for the external border:

    emacs.Borderwidth: 2
    emacs.borderwidth: 4

The order in which the lines appear in the file does not matter. Also, command-line options always override the X resources file.

The string 'emacs' in the examples above is also a resource name. It actually represents the name of the executable file that you invoke to run Emacs. If Emacs is installed under a different name, it looks for resources under that name instead of 'emacs'.

'-name name'
'--name=name'

> Use name as the resource name (and the title) for the initial Emacs frame. This option does not affect subsequent frames, but Lisp programs can specify frame names when they create frames.
>
> If you don't specify this option, the default is to use the Emacs executable's name as the resource name.

'-xrm resource-values'
'--xrm=resource-values'

> Specify X resource values for this Emacs job (see below).

For consistency, '-name' also specifies the name to use for other resource values that do not belong to any particular frame.

The resources that name Emacs invocations also belong to a class; its name is 'Emacs'. If you write 'Emacs' instead of 'emacs', the resource applies to all frames in all Emacs jobs, regardless of frame titles and regardless of the name of the executable file. Here is an example:

```
Emacs.BorderWidth: 2
Emacs.borderWidth: 4
```

You can specify a string of additional resource values for Emacs to use with the command line option '-xrm *resources*'. The text *resources* should have the same format that you would use inside a file of X resources. To include multiple resource specifications in *data*, put a newline between them, just as you would in a file. You can also use '#include "*filename*"' to include a file full of resource specifications. Resource values specified with '-xrm' take precedence over all other resource specifications.

The following table lists the resource names that designate options for Emacs, each with the class that it belongs to:

background (class Background)
> Background color name.

bitmapIcon (class BitmapIcon)
> Use a bitmap icon (a picture of a gnu) if 'on', let the window manager choose an icon if 'off'.

borderColor (class BorderColor)
> Color name for the external border.

borderWidth (class BorderWidth)
> Width in pixels of the external border.

cursorColor (class Foreground)
> Color name for text cursor (point).

font (class Font)
> Font name for text (or fontset name, see Section 18.10 [Fontsets], page 186).

foreground (class Foreground)
> Color name for text.

geometry (class Geometry)
> Window size and position. Be careful not to specify this resource as 'emacs*geometry', because that may affect individual menus as well as the Emacs frame itself.
>
> If this resource specifies a position, that position applies only to the initial Emacs frame (or, in the case of a resource for a specific frame name, only that frame). However, the size if specified here applies to all frames.

iconName (class Title)
> Name to display in the icon.

internalBorder (class BorderWidth)
> Width in pixels of the internal border.

menuBar (class **MenuBar**)

Give frames menu bars if 'on'; don't have menu bars if 'off'.

minibuffer (class **Minibuffer**)

If 'none', don't make a minibuffer in this frame. It will use a separate minibuffer frame instead.

paneFont (class **Font**)

Font name for menu pane titles, in non-toolkit versions of Emacs.

pointerColor (class **Foreground**)

Color of the mouse cursor.

reverseVideo (class **ReverseVideo**)

Switch foreground and background default colors if 'on', use colors as specified if 'off'.

verticalScrollBars (class **ScrollBars**)

Give frames scroll bars if 'on'; don't have scroll bars if 'off'.

selectionFont (class **Font**)

Font name for pop-up menu items, in non-toolkit versions of Emacs. (For toolkit versions, see Section A.14 [Lucid Resources], page 456, also see Section A.15 [Motif Resources], page 457.)

title (class **Title**)

Name to display in the title bar of the initial Emacs frame.

Here are resources for controlling the appearance of particular faces (see Section 17.13 [Faces], page 166):

face.**attributeFont**

Font for face *face*.

face.**attributeForeground**

Foreground color for face *face*.

face.**attributeBackground**

Background color for face *face*.

face.**attributeUnderline**

Underline flag for face *face*. Use 'on' or 'true' for yes.

A.14 Lucid Menu X Resources

If the Emacs installed at your site was built to use the X toolkit with the Lucid menu widgets, then the menu bar is a separate widget and has its own resources. The resource names contain 'pane.menubar' (following, as always, the name of the Emacs invocation or 'Emacs' which stands for all Emacs invocations). Specify them like this:

    Emacs.pane.menubar.*resource*:   *value*

For example, to specify the font '8x16' for the menu-bar items, write this:

    Emacs.pane.menubar.font: 8x16

Resources for *non-menubar* toolkit pop-up menus have '`menu*`', in like fashion. For example, to specify the font '`8x16`' for the pop-up menu items, write this:

    Emacs.menu*.font: 8x16

For dialog boxes, use '`dialog`' instead of '`menu`':

    Emacs.dialog*.font: 8x16

Experience shows that on some systems you may need to add '`shell.`' before the '`pane.menubar`' or '`menu*`'. On some other systems, you must not add '`shell.`'.

Here is a list of the specific resources for menu bars and pop-up menus:

font   Font for menu item text.

foreground
            Color of the foreground.

background
            Color of the background.

buttonForeground
            In the menu bar, the color of the foreground for a selected item.

horizontalSpacing
            Horizontal spacing in pixels between items. Default is 3.

verticalSpacing
            Vertical spacing in pixels between items. Default is 1.

arrowSpacing
            Horizontal spacing between the arrow (which indicates a submenu) and the associated text. Default is 10.

shadowThickness
            Thickness of shadow line around the widget.

A.15 Motif Menu X Resources

If the Emacs installed at your site was built to use the X toolkit with the Motif widgets, then the menu bar is a separate widget and has its own resources. The resource names contain '`pane.menubar`' (following, as always, the name of the Emacs invocation or '`Emacs`' which stands for all Emacs invocations). Specify them like this:

    Emacs.pane.menubar.*subwidget*.*resource*:   *value*

Each individual string in the menu bar is a subwidget; the subwidget's name is the same as the menu item string. For example, the word '`Files`' in the menu bar is part of a subwidget named '`emacs.pane.menubar.Files`'. Most likely, you want to specify the same resources for the whole menu bar.

To do this, use '*' instead of a specific subwidget name. For example, to specify the font '8x16' for the menu-bar items, write this:

        Emacs.pane.menubar.*.fontList: 8x16

This also specifies the resource value for submenus.

Each item in a submenu in the menu bar also has its own name for X resources; for example, the 'Files' submenu has an item named 'Save Buffer'. A resource specification for a submenu item looks like this:

        Emacs.pane.menubar.popup_*.*menu*.*item*.*resource*: *value*

For example, here's how to specify the font for the 'Save Buffer' item:

        Emacs.pane.menubar.popup_*.Files.Save Buffer.fontList: 8x16

For an item in a second-level submenu, such as 'Check Message' under 'Spell' under 'Edit', the resource fits this template:

        Emacs.pane.menubar.popup_*.popup_*.*menu*.*resource*: *value*

For example,

        Emacs.pane.menubar.popup_*.popup_*.Spell.Check Message: *value*

It's impossible to specify a resource for all the menu-bar items without also specifying it for the submenus as well. So if you want the submenu items to look different from the menu bar itself, you must ask for that in two steps. First, specify the resource for all of them; then, override the value for submenus alone. Here is an example:

        Emacs.pane.menubar.*.fontList: 8x16
        Emacs.pane.menubar.popup_*.fontList: 8x16

For toolkit pop-up menus, use 'menu*' instead of 'pane.menubar'. For example, to specify the font '8x16' for the pop-up menu items, write this:

        Emacs.menu*.fontList: 8x16

Here is a list of the specific resources for menu bars and pop-up menus:

armColor   The color to show in an armed button.

fontList   The font to use.

marginBottom
marginHeight
marginLeft
marginRight
marginTop
marginWidth
            Amount of space to leave around the item, within the border.

borderWidth
            The width of border around the menu item, on all sides.

shadowThickness
            The width of the border shadow.

`bottomShadowColor`
>   The color for the border shadow, on the bottom and the right.

`topShadowColor`
>   The color for the border shadow, on the top and the left.

Appendix B Emacs 19 Antinews

For those users who live backwards in time, here is information about downgrading to Emacs version 19. We hope you will enjoy the greater simplicity that results from the absence of certain Emacs 20 features.

- The multibyte character and end-of-line conversion support have been eliminated entirely. (Some users consider this a tremendous improvement.) Character codes are limited to the range 0 through 255 and files imported onto Unix-like systems may have a ^M at the end of each line to remind you to control MS-DOG type files.

- Fontsets, coding systems and input methods have been eliminated as well.

- The mode line normally displays the string 'Emacs', in case you forget what editor you are using.

- Scroll bars always appear on the right-hand side of the window. This clearly separates them from the text in the window.

- The M-x customize feature has been replaced with a very simple feature, M-x edit-options. This shows you *all* the user options right from the start, so you don't have to hunt for the ones you want. It also provides a few commands, such as s and x, to set a user option.

- The (DELETE) key does nothing special in Emacs 19 when you use it after selecting a region with the mouse. It does exactly the same thing in that situation as it does at all other times: delete one character backwards.

- C-x C-w no longer changes the major mode according to the new file name. If you want to change the mode, use M-x normal-mode.

- In Transient Mark mode, each window displays highlighting for the region as it exists in that window.

- Outline mode doesn't use overlay properties; instead, it hides a line by converting the preceding newline into code 015. Magically, however, if you save the file, the 015 character appears in the file as a newline.

- There is now a clever way you can activate the minibuffer recursively even if enable-recursive-minibuffers is nil. All you have to do is *switch windows* to a non-minibuffer window, and then use a minibuffer command. You can pile up any number of minibuffer levels this way, but M-x top-level will get you out of all of them.

- We have removed the limit on the length of minibuffer history lists; they now contain all the minibuffer arguments you have used since the beginning of the session.

- Dynamic abbrev expansion now handles case conversion in a very simple and straightforward way. If you have requested preserving case, it always converts the entire expansion to the case pattern of the abbrev that you have typed in.

- The `compose-mail` command does not exist; `C-x m` now runs `mail` directly.

- There is no way to quote a file name with special characters in it. What you see is what you get: if the name looks remote, it is remote.

- `M-x grep-find` has been eliminated, because `grep` has never been lost.

- Some Dired commands have been rearranged: two-character sequences have been replaced with quick single-character commands:

  - For `dired-mark-executables`, type *.
  - For `dired-mark-directories`, type /.
  - For `dired-mark-symlinks`, type @.
  - For `dired-change-marks`, type c.
  - For `dired-unmark-all-files`, type C-M-?.
  - For `dired-unmark-all-marks`, type C-M-? (RET).

  But if you want to use `dired-flag-garbage-files`, &, you'll just have to stop living in the past.

- In C mode, you can now specify your preferred style for block comments. If you want to use the style

  ```
  /*
  blah
  blah
  */
  ```

  then you should set the variable `c-block-comments-indent-p` to `t`.

- To customize faces used by Font Lock mode, use the variable `font-lock-face-attributes`. See its documentation string for details.

- For efficiency, Font Lock mode now uses by default the minimum supported level of decoration for the selected major mode.

- If you kill a buffer, any registers holding saved positions in that buffer are changed to point into limbo.

- The function `set-frame-font` has been renamed to `set-default-font`.

- The variable `tex-main-file` doesn't exist. Of course, you can create the variable by setting it, but that won't do anything special.

- The `scroll-preserve-screen-position` variable has been eliminated; and so has the feature that it controls.

- We have eliminated the functions `add-untranslated-filesystem` and `remove-untranslated-filesystem`, and replaced them with a simpler function, `using-unix-filesystems`.

- To keep up with decreasing computer memory capacity, many other functions and files have been eliminated in Emacs 19. There's no need to mention them all here. If you try to use one of them, you'll get an error message to tell you that it is undefined or unbound.

Appendix C Emacs and MS-DOS

This section briefly describes the peculiarities of using Emacs under the MS-DOS "operating system" (also known as "MS-DOG"). If you build Emacs for MS-DOS, the binary will also run on Windows 3.X, Windows NT, Windows 9X, or OS/2 as a DOS application; the information in this chapter applies for all of those systems, if you use an Emacs that was built for MS-DOS.

Note that it is possible to build Emacs specifically for Windows NT or Windows 9X. If you do that, most of this chapter does not apply; instead, you get behavior much closer to what is documented in the rest of the manual, including support for long file names, multiple frames, scroll bars, mouse menus, and subprocesses. However, the section on text files and binary files does still apply. There are also two sections at the end of this chapter which apply specifically for Windows NT and 9X.

C.1 Keyboard and Mouse on MS-DOS

The PC keyboard maps use the left (ALT) key as the (META) key. You have two choices for emulating the (SUPER) and (HYPER) keys: choose either the right (CTRL) key or the right (ALT) key by setting the variables dos-hyper-key and dos-super-key to 1 or 2 respectively. If neither dos-super-key nor dos-hyper-key is 1, then by default the right (ALT) key is also mapped to the (META) key. However, if the MS-DOS international keyboard support program 'KEYB.COM' is installed, Emacs will *not* map the right (ALT) to (META), since it is used for accessing characters like ~ and @ on non-US keyboard layouts; in this case, you may only use the left (ALT) as (META) key.

The variable dos-keypad-mode is a flag variable that controls what key codes are returned by keys in the numeric keypad. You can also define the keypad (ENTER) key to act like C-j, by putting the following line into your '_emacs' file:

```
;; Make the Enter key from the Numeric keypad act as C-j.
(define-key function-key-map [kp-enter] [?\C-j])
```

The key that is called (DEL) in Emacs (because that's how it is designated on most workstations) is known as (BS) (backspace) on a PC. That is why the PC-specific terminal initialization remaps the (BS) key to act as (DEL); the (DEL) key is remapped to act as C-d for the same reasons.

Emacs built for MS-DOS recognizes C-(BREAK) as a quit character, just like C-g. This is because Emacs cannot detect that you have typed C-g until it is ready for more input. As a consequence, you cannot use C-g to stop a running command (see Section 32.1 [Quitting], page 425). By contrast, C-(BREAK) *is* detected as soon as you type it (as C-g is on other systems), so it can be used to stop a running command and for emergency escape (see Section 32.2.8 [Emergency Escape], page 429).

Emacs on MS-DOS supports a mouse (on the default terminal only). The mouse commands work as documented, including those that use menus and the menu bar (see Section 1.4 [Menu Bar], page 19). Scroll bars don't work in MS-DOS Emacs. PC mice usually have only two buttons; these act as `Mouse-1` and `Mouse-2`, but if you press both of them together, that has the effect of `Mouse-3`.

Emacs built for MS-DOS supports clipboard operations when it runs on Windows. Commands that put text on the kill ring, or yank text from the ring, check the Windows clipboard first, just as Emacs does on X Windows (see Section 17.1 [Mouse Commands], page 157). Only the primary selection and the cut buffer are supported by MS-DOS Emacs on Windows; the secondary selection always appears as empty.

Due to the way clipboard access is implemented by Windows, the length of text you can put into the clipboard is limited by the amount of free DOS memory that is available to Emacs. Usually, up to 620KB of text can be put into the clipboard, but this limit depends on the system configuration and is lower if you run Emacs as a subprocess of another program. If the killed text does not fit, Emacs prints a message saying so, and does not put the text into the clipboard.

Null characters also cannot be put into the Windows clipboard. If the killed text includes null characters, Emacs does not put such text into the clipboard, and prints in the echo area a message to that effect.

The variable `dos-display-scancodes`, when non-`nil`, directs Emacs to display the ASCII value and the keyboard scan code of each keystroke; this feature serves as a complement to the `view-lossage` command, for debugging.

C.2 Display on MS-DOS

Display on MS-DOS cannot use font variants, like bold or italic, but it does support multiple faces, each of which can specify a foreground and a background color. Therefore, you can get the full functionality of Emacs packages that use fonts (such as `font-lock`, Enriched Text mode, and others) by defining the relevant faces to use different colors. Use the `list-colors-display` command (see Section 17.10 [Frame Parameters], page 164) and the `list-faces-display` command (see Section 17.13 [Faces], page 166) to see what colors and faces are available and what they look like.

The section Section C.6 [MS-DOS and MULE], page 470, later in this chapter, describes how Emacs displays glyphs and characters which aren't supported by the native font built into the DOS display.

Multiple frames (see Chapter 17 [Frames], page 157) are supported on MS-DOS, but they all overlap, so you only see a single frame at any given moment. That single visible frame occupies the entire screen. When you run Emacs from MS-Windows DOS box, you can make the visible frame smaller than the full screen, but Emacs still cannot display more than a single frame at a time.

The `mode4350` command switches the display to 43 or 50 lines, depending on your hardware; the `mode25` command switches to the default 80x25 screen size.

By default, Emacs only knows how to set screen sizes of 80 columns by 25, 28, 35, 40, 43 or 50 rows. However, if your video adapter has special video modes that will switch the display to other sizes, you can have Emacs support those too. When you ask Emacs to switch the frame to n rows by m columns dimensions, it checks if there is a variable called `screen-dimensions-`nxm, and if so, uses its value (which must be an integer) as the video mode to switch to. (Emacs switches to that video mode by calling the BIOS `Set Video Mode` function with the value of `screen-dimensions-`nxm in the `AL` register.) For example, suppose your adapter will switch to 66x80 dimensions when put into video mode 85. Then you can make Emacs support this screen size by putting the following into your '`_emacs`' file:

```
(setq screen-dimensions-66x80 85)
```

Since Emacs on MS-DOS can only set the frame size to specific supported dimensions, it cannot honor every possible frame resizing request. When an unsupported size is requested, Emacs chooses the next larger supported size beyond the specified size. For example, if you ask for 36x80 frame, you will get 40x80 instead.

The variables `screen-dimensions-`nxm are used only when they exactly match the specified size; the search for the next larger supported size ignores them. In the above example, even if your VGA supports 38x80 dimensions and you define a variable `screen-dimensions-38x80` with a suitable value, you will still get 40x80 screen when you ask for a 36x80 frame. If you want to get the 38x80 size in this case, you can do it by setting the variable named `screen-dimensions-36x80` with the same video mode value as `screen-dimensions-38x80`.

Changing frame dimensions on MS-DOS has the effect of changing all the other frames to the new dimensions.

C.3 File Names on MS-DOS

MS-DOS normally uses a backslash, '`\`', to separate name units within a file name, instead of the slash used on other systems. Emacs on MS-DOS permits use of either slash or backslash, and also knows about drive letters in file names.

On MS-DOS, file names are case-insensitive and limited to eight characters, plus optionally a period and three more characters. Emacs knows enough about these limitations to handle file names that were meant for other operating systems. For instance, leading dots '`.`' in file names are invalid in MS-DOS, so Emacs transparently converts them to underscores '_'; thus your default init file (see Section 31.7 [Init File], page 419) is called '_emacs' on MS-DOS. Excess characters before or after the period are generally ignored by MS-DOS itself; thus, if you visit the file 'LongFileName.EvenLongerExtension', you will silently get 'longfile.eve', but Emacs will still display the long file name on the mode line. Other than that, it's up to you to specify file names which are valid under MS-DOS; the transparent conversion as described above only works on file names built into Emacs.

The above restrictions on the file names on MS-DOS make it almost impossible to construct the name of a backup file (see Section 14.3.1.1 [Backup Names], page 114) without losing some of the original file name characters. For example, the name of a backup file for 'docs.txt' is 'docs.tx~' even if single backup is used.

If you run Emacs as a DOS application under Windows 9X, you can turn on support for long file names. If you do that, Emacs doesn't truncate file names or convert them to lower case; instead, it uses the file names that you specify, verbatim. To enable long file name support, set the environment variable LFN to 'y' before starting Emacs. Unfortunately, Windows NT doesn't allow DOS programs to access long file names, so Emacs built for MS-DOS will only see their short 8+3 aliases.

MS-DOS has no notion of home directory, so Emacs on MS-DOS pretends that the directory where it is installed is the value of HOME environment variable. That is, if your Emacs binary, 'emacs.exe', is in the directory 'c:/utils/emacs/bin', then Emacs acts as if HOME were set to 'c:/utils/emacs'. In particular, that is where Emacs looks for the init file '_emacs'. With this in mind, you can use '~' in file names as an alias for the home directory, as you would in Unix. You can also set HOME variable in the environment before starting Emacs; its value will then override the above default behavior.

Emacs on MS-DOS handles the directory name '/dev' specially, because of a feature in the emulator libraries of DJGPP that pretends I/O devices have names in that directory. We recommend that you avoid using an actual directory named '/dev' on any disk.

C.4 Text Files and Binary Files

GNU Emacs uses newline characters to separate text lines. This is the convention used on Unix, on which GNU Emacs was developed, and on GNU systems since they are modeled on Unix.

MS-DOS and MS-Windows normally use carriage-return linefeed, a two-character sequence, to separate text lines. (Linefeed is the same character as newline.) Therefore, convenient editing of typical files with Emacs requires conversion of these end-of-line (EOL) sequences. And that is what Emacs normally does: it converts carriage-return linefeed into newline when reading files, and converts newline into carriage-return linefeed when writing files. The same mechanism that handles conversion of international character codes does this conversion also (see Section 18.7 [Coding Systems], page 180).

One consequence of this special format-conversion of most files is that character positions as reported by Emacs (see Section 4.9 [Position Info], page 35) do not agree with the file size information known to the operating system.

Some kinds of files should not be converted, because their contents are not really text. Therefore, Emacs on MS-DOS distinguishes certain files as *binary files*, and reads and writes them verbatim. (This distinction is not part of MS-DOS; it is made by Emacs only.) These include executable programs, compressed archives, etc. Emacs uses the file name to decide whether to treat a file as binary: the variable `file-name-buffer-file-type-alist` defines the file-name patterns that indicate binary files. Note that if a file name matches one of the patterns for binary files in `file-name-buffer-file-type-alist`, Emacs uses the `no-conversion` coding system (see Section 18.7 [Coding Systems], page 180) which turns off *all* coding-system conversions, not only the EOL conversion.

In addition, if Emacs recognizes from a file's contents that it uses newline rather than carriage-return linefeed as its line separator, it does not perform conversion when reading or writing that file. Thus, you can read and edit files from Unix or GNU systems on MS-DOS with no special effort, and they will be left with their Unix-style EOLs.

You can visit a file and specify whether to treat a file as text or binary using the commands `find-file-text` and `find-file-binary`. End-of-line conversion is part of the general coding system conversion mechanism, so another way to control whether to treat a file as text or binary is with the commands for specifying a coding system (see Section 18.9 [Specify Coding], page 184). For example, `C-x` (RET) `c undecided-unix` (RET) `C-x C-f foobar.txt` visits the file 'foobar.txt' without converting the EOLs.

The mode line indicates whether end-of-line translation was used for the current buffer. Normally a colon appears after the coding system letter near the beginning of the mode line. If MS-DOS end-of-line translation is in use for the buffer, this character changes to a backslash.

When you use NFS or Samba to access file systems that reside on computers using Unix or GNU systems, Emacs should not perform end-of-line translation on any files in these file systems–not even when you create a new file. To request this, designate these file systems as *untranslated* file systems by calling the function `add-untranslated-filesystem`. It takes one argument: the file system name, including a drive letter and optionally a directory. For example,

```
(add-untranslated-filesystem "Z:")
```

designates drive Z as an untranslated file system, and

```
(add-untranslated-filesystem "Z:\\foo")
```

designates directory '\foo' on drive Z as an untranslated file system.

Most often you would use add-untranslated-filesystem in your '_emacs' file, or in 'site-start.el' so that all the users at your site get the benefit of it.

To countermand the effect of add-untranslated-filesystem, use the function remove-untranslated-filesystem. This function takes one argument, which should be a string just like the one that was used previously with add-untranslated-filesystem.

C.5 Printing and MS-DOS

Printing commands, such as lpr-buffer (see Section 30.4 [Hardcopy], page 377) and ps-print-buffer (see Section 30.5 [Postscript], page 378) can work in MS-DOS and MS-Windows by sending the output to one of the printer ports, if a Unix-style lpr program is unavailable. This behaviour is controlled by the same variables that control printing with lpr on Unix (see Section 30.4 [Hardcopy], page 377, see Section 30.6 [Postscript Variables], page 379), but the defaults for these variables on MS-DOS and MS-Windows are not the same as the defaults on Unix.

If you want to use your local printer, printing on it in the usual DOS manner, then set the Lisp variable lpr-command to "" (its default value) and printer-name to the name of the printer port—for example, "PRN", the usual local printer port (that's the default), or "LPT2", or "COM1" for a serial printer. You can also set printer-name to a file name, in which case "printed" output is actually appended to that file. If you set printer-name to "NUL", printed output is silently discarded (sent to the system null device).

On MS-Windows, when the Windows network software is installed, you can also use a printer shared by another machine by setting printer-name to the UNC share name for that printer–for example, "//joes_pc/hp4si". (It doesn't matter whether you use forward slashes or backslashes here.) To find out the names of shared printers, run the command 'net view' at a DOS command prompt to obtain a list of servers, and 'net view server-name' to see the names of printers (and directories) shared by that server.

If you set printer-name to a file name, it's best to use an absolute file name. Emacs changes the working directory according to the default directory of the current buffer, so if the file name in printer-name is relative, you will end up with several such files, each one in the directory of the buffer from which the printing was done.

The commands print-buffer and print-region call the pr program, or use special switches to the lpr program, to produce headers on each printed page. MS-DOS and MS-Windows don't normally have these programs, so by default, the variable lpr-headers-switches is set so that the requests to print page headers are silently ignored. Thus, print-buffer and `print-region` produce the same output as `lpr-buffer` and `lpr-region`, respectively. If you do have a suitable `pr` program (for example, from GNU Textutils), set `lpr-headers-switches` to `nil`; Emacs will then call `pr` to produce the page headers, and print the resulting output as specified by `printer-name`.

Finally, if you do have an `lpr` work-alike, you can set the variable `lpr-command` to `"lpr"`. Then Emacs will use `lpr` for printing, as on other systems. (If the name of the program isn't `lpr`, set `lpr-command` to specify where to find it.) The variable `lpr-switches` has its standard meaning when `lpr-command` is not `""`. If the variable `printer-name` has a string value, it is used as the value for the `-P` option to `lpr`, as on Unix.

A parallel set of variables, `ps-lpr-command`, `ps-lpr-switches`, and `ps-printer-name` (see Section 30.6 [Postscript Variables], page 379), defines how PostScript files should be printed. These variables are used in the same way as the corresponding variables described above for non-PostScript printing. Thus, the value of `ps-printer-name` is used as the name of the device (or file) to which PostScript output is sent, just as `printer-name` is used for non-PostScript printing. (There are two distinct sets of variables in case you have two printers attached to two different ports, and only one of them is a PostScript printer.)

The default value of the variable `ps-lpr-command` is `""`, which causes PostScript output to be sent to the printer port specified by `ps-printer-name`, but `ps-lpr-command` can also be set to the name of a program which will accept PostScript files. Thus, if you have a non-PostScript printer, you can set this variable to the name of a PostScript interpreter program (such as Ghostscript). Any switches that need to be passed to the interpreter program are specified using `ps-lpr-switches`. (If the value of `ps-printer-name` is a string, it will be added to the list of switches as the value for the `-P` option. This is probably only useful if you are using `lpr`, so when using an interpreter typically you would set `ps-printer-name` to something other than a string so it is ignored.)

For example, to use Ghostscript for printing on an Epson printer connected to the 'LPT2' port, put this in your '_emacs' file:

```
(setq ps-printer-name t)   ; Ghostscript doesn't understand -P
(setq ps-lpr-command "c:/gs/gs386")
(setq ps-lpr-switches '("-q" "-dNOPAUSE"
"-sDEVICE=epson"
"-r240x72"
"-sOutputFile=LPT2"
"-Ic:/gs"))
```

(This assumes that Ghostscript is installed in the '"c:/gs"' directory.)

For backwards compatibility, the value of `dos-printer` (`dos-ps-printer`), if it has a value, overrides the value of `printer-name` (`ps-printer-name`), on MS-DOS and MS-Windows only.

C.6 International Support on MS-DOS

Emacs on MS-DOS supports the same international character sets as it does on Unix and other platforms (see Chapter 18 [International], page 175), including coding systems for converting between the different character sets. However, due to incompatibilities between MS-DOS/MS-Windows and Unix, there are several DOS-specific aspects of this support that users should be aware of. This section describes these aspects.

M-x dos-codepage-setup
>   Set up Emacs display and coding systems as appropriate for the current DOS codepage.

M-x codepage-setup
>   Create a coding system for a certain DOS codepage.

MS-DOS is designed to support one character set of 256 characters at any given time, but gives you a variety of character sets to choose from. The alternative character sets are known as *DOS codepages*. Each codepage includes all 128 ASCII characters, but the other 128 characters (codes 128 through 255) vary from one codepage to another. Each DOS codepage is identified by a 3-digit number, such as 850, 862, etc.

In contrast to X Windows, which lets you use several fonts at the same time, MS-DOS doesn't allow use of several codepages in a single session. Instead, MS-DOS loads a single codepage at system startup, and you must reboot MS-DOS to change it[1]. Much the same limitation applies when you run DOS executables on other systems such as MS-Windows.

If you invoke Emacs on MS-DOS with the '--unibyte' option (see Section A.2 [Initial Options], page 442), Emacs does not perform any conversion of non-ASCII characters. Instead, it reads and writes any non-ASCII characters verbatim, and sends their 8-bit codes to the display verbatim. Thus, unibyte Emacs on MS-DOS supports the current codepage, whatever it may be, but cannot even represent any other characters.

For multibyte operation on MS-DOS, Emacs needs to know which characters the chosen DOS codepage can display. So it queries the system shortly after startup to get the chosen codepage number, and stores the number in the variable dos-codepage. Some systems return the default value 437 for the current codepage, even though the actual codepage is different. (This typically happens when you use the codepage built into the display hardware.) You can specify a different codepage for Emacs to use by setting the variable dos-codepage in your init file.

Multibyte Emacs supports only certain DOS codepages: those which can display Far-Eastern scripts, like the Japanese codepage 932, and those that encode a single ISO 8859 character set.

---

[1] Normally, one particular codepage is burnt into the display memory, while other codepages can be installed by modifying system configuration files, such as 'CONFIG.SYS', and rebooting.

The Far-Eastern codepages can directly display one of the MULE character sets for these countries, so Emacs simply sets up to use the appropriate terminal coding system that is supported by the codepage. The special features described in the rest of this section mostly pertain to codepages that encode ISO 8859 character sets.

For the codepages which correspond to one of the ISO character sets, Emacs knows the character set name based on the codepage number. Emacs automatically creates a coding system to support reading and writing files that use the current codepage, and uses this coding system by default. The name of this coding system is cp*nnn*, where *nnn* is the codepage number.[2]

All the cp*nnn* coding systems use the letter 'D' (for "DOS") as their mode-line mnemonic. Since both the terminal coding system and the default coding system for file I/O are set to the proper cp*nnn* coding system at startup, it is normal for the mode line on MS-DOS to begin with '-DD\-'. See Section 1.3 [Mode Line], page 17. Far-Eastern DOS terminals do not use the cp*nnn* coding systems, and thus their initial mode line looks like on Unix.

Since the codepage number also indicates which script you are using, Emacs automatically runs **set-language-environment** to select the language environment for that script (see Section 18.3 [Language Environments], page 176).

If a buffer contains a character belonging to some other ISO 8859 character set, not the one that the chosen DOS codepage supports, Emacs displays it using a sequence of ASCII characters. For example, if the current codepage doesn't have a glyph for the letter 'ò' (small 'o' with a grave accent), it is displayed as '{`o}', where the braces serve as a visual indication that this is a single character. (This may look awkward for some non-Latin characters, such as those from Greek or Hebrew alphabets, but it is still readable by a person who knows the language.) Even though the character may occupy several columns on the screen, it is really still just a single character, and all Emacs commands treat it as one.

Not all characters in DOS codepages correspond to ISO 8859 characters— some are used for other purposes, such as box-drawing characters and other graphics. Emacs cannot represent these characters internally, so when you read a file that uses these characters, they are converted into a particular character code, specified by the variable **dos-unsupported-character-glyph**.

Emacs supports many other characters sets aside from ISO 8859, but it cannot display them on MS-DOS. So if one of these multibyte characters appears in a buffer, Emacs on MS-DOS displays them as specified by the

---

[2] The standard Emacs coding systems for ISO 8859 are not quite right for the purpose, because typically the DOS codepage does not match the standard ISO character codes. For example, the letter 'ç' ('c' with cedilla) has code 231 in the standard Latin-1 character set, but the corresponding DOS codepage 850 uses code 135 for this glyph.

dos-unsupported-character-glyph variable; by default, this glyph is an empty triangle. Use the C-u C-x = command to display the actual code and character set of such characters. See Section 4.9 [Position Info], page 35.

By default, Emacs defines a coding system to support the current codepage. To define a coding system for some other codepage (e.g., to visit a file written on a DOS machine in another country), use the M-x codepage-setup command. It prompts for the 3-digit code of the codepage, with completion, then creates the coding system for the specified codepage. You can then use the new coding system to read and write files, but you must specify it explicitly for the file command when you want to use it (see Section 18.9 [Specify Coding], page 184).

These coding systems are also useful for visiting a file encoded using a DOS codepage, using Emacs running on some other operating system.

C.7 Subprocesses on MS-DOS

Because MS-DOS is a single-process "operating system," asynchronous subprocesses are not available. In particular, Shell mode and its variants do not work. Most Emacs features that use asynchronous subprocesses also don't work on MS-DOS, including spelling correction and GUD. When in doubt, try and see; commands that don't work print an error message saying that asynchronous processes aren't supported.

Compilation under Emacs with M-x compile, searching files with M-x grep and displaying differences between files with M-x diff do work, by running the inferior processes synchronously. This means you cannot do any more editing until the inferior process finishes.

By contrast, Emacs compiled as native Windows application **does** support asynchronous subprocesses. See Section C.8 [Windows Processes], page 473.

Printing commands, such as lpr-buffer (see Section 30.4 [Hardcopy], page 377) and ps-print-buffer (see Section 30.5 [Postscript], page 378), work in MS-DOS by sending the output to one of the printer ports. See Section C.5 [MS-DOS Printing], page 468.

When you run a subprocess synchronously on MS-DOS, make sure the program terminates and does not try to read keyboard input. If the program does not terminate on its own, you will be unable to terminate it, because MS-DOS provides no general way to terminate a process. Pressing C-c or C-(BREAK) might sometimes help in these cases.

Accessing files on other machines is not supported on MS-DOS. Other network-oriented commands such as sending mail, Web browsing, remote login, etc., don't work either, unless network access is built into MS-DOS with some network redirector.

Dired on MS-DOS uses the ls-lisp package where other platforms use the system ls command. Therefore, Dired on MS-DOS supports only some of the possible options you can mention in the dired-listing-switches variable. The options that work are '-A', '-a', '-c', '-i', '-r', '-S', '-s', '-t', and '-u'.

C.8 Subprocesses on Windows 95 and NT

Emacs compiled as a native Windows application (as opposed to the DOS version) includes full support for asynchronous subprocesses. In the Windows version, synchronous and asynchronous subprocesses work fine on both Windows 95 and Windows NT as long as you run only 32-bit Windows applications. However, when you run a DOS application in a subprocess, you may encounter problems or be unable to run the application at all; and if you run two DOS applications at the same time in two subprocesses, you may have to reboot your system.

Since the standard command interpreter (and most command line utilities) on Windows 95 are DOS applications, these problems are significant when using that system. But there's nothing we can do about them; only Microsoft can fix them.

If you run just one DOS application subprocess, the subprocess should work as expected as long as it is "well-behaved" and does not perform direct screen access or other unusual actions. If you have a CPU monitor application, your machine will appear to be 100% busy even when the DOS application is idle, but this is only an artifact of the way CPU monitors measure processor load.

You must terminate the DOS application before you start any other DOS application in a different subprocess. Emacs is unable to interrupt or terminate a DOS subprocess. The only way you can terminate such a subprocess is by giving it a command that tells its program to exit.

If you attempt to run two DOS applications at the same time in separate subprocesses, the second one that is started will be suspended until the first one finishes, even if either or both of them are asynchronous.

If you can go to the first subprocess, and tell it to exit, the second subprocess should continue normally. However, if the second subprocess is synchronous, Emacs itself will be hung until the first subprocess finishes. If it will not finish without user input, then you have no choice but to reboot if you are running on Windows 95. If you are running on Windows NT, you can use a process viewer application to kill the appropriate instance of ntvdm instead (this will terminate both DOS subprocesses).

If you have to reboot Windows 95 in this situation, do not use the **Shutdown** command on the **Start** menu; that usually hangs the system. Instead, type **CTL-ALT-**$\overline{\text{DEL}}$ and then choose **Shutdown**. That usually works, although it may take a few minutes to do its job.

C.9 Using the System Menu on Windows

Emacs compiled as a native Windows application normally turns off the Windows feature that tapping the (ALT) key invokes the Windows menu. The reason is that the (ALT) also serves as (META) in Emacs. When using Emacs, users often press the (META) key temporarily and then change their minds; if this has the effect of bringing up the Windows menu, it alters the meaning of subsequent commands. Many users find this frustrating.

You can reenable Windows's default handling of tapping the (ALT) key by setting `w32-pass-alt-to-system` to a non-`nil` value.

The GNU Manifesto

The GNU Manifesto which appears below was written by Richard Stallman at the beginning of the GNU project, to ask for participation and support. For the first few years, it was updated in minor ways to account for developments, but now it seems best to leave it unchanged as most people have seen it.

Since that time, we have learned about certain common misunderstandings that different wording could help avoid. Footnotes added in 1993 help clarify these points.

For up-to-date information about the available GNU software, please see the latest issue of the GNU's Bulletin. The list is much too long to include here.

What's GNU? Gnu's Not Unix!

GNU, which stands for Gnu's Not Unix, is the name for the complete Unix-compatible software system which I am writing so that I can give it away free to everyone who can use it.[1] Several other volunteers are helping me. Contributions of time, money, programs and equipment are greatly needed.

So far we have an Emacs text editor with Lisp for writing editor commands, a source level debugger, a yacc-compatible parser generator, a linker, and around 35 utilities. A shell (command interpreter) is nearly completed. A new portable optimizing C compiler has compiled itself and may be released this year. An initial kernel exists but many more features are needed to emulate Unix. When the kernel and compiler are finished, it will be possible to distribute a GNU system suitable for program development. We will use TₑX as our text formatter, but an nroff is being worked on. We will use the free, portable X window system as well. After this we will add a portable Common Lisp, an Empire game, a spreadsheet, and hundreds of other things, plus on-line documentation. We hope to supply, eventually, everything useful that normally comes with a Unix system, and more.

---

[1] The wording here was careless. The intention was that nobody would have to pay for *permission* to use the GNU system. But the words don't make this clear, and people often interpret them as saying that copies of GNU should always be distributed at little or no charge. That was never the intent; later on, the manifesto mentions the possibility of companies providing the service of distribution for a profit. Subsequently I have learned to distinguish carefully between "free" in the sense of freedom and "free" in the sense of price. Free software is software that users have the freedom to distribute and change. Some users may obtain copies at no charge, while others pay to obtain copies—and if the funds help support improving the software, so much the better. The important thing is that everyone who has a copy has the freedom to cooperate with others in using it.

GNU will be able to run Unix programs, but will not be identical to Unix. We will make all improvements that are convenient, based on our experience with other operating systems. In particular, we plan to have longer file names, file version numbers, a crashproof file system, file name completion perhaps, terminal-independent display support, and perhaps eventually a Lisp-based window system through which several Lisp programs and ordinary Unix programs can share a screen. Both C and Lisp will be available as system programming languages. We will try to support UUCP, MIT Chaosnet, and Internet protocols for communication.

GNU is aimed initially at machines in the 68000/16000 class with virtual memory, because they are the easiest machines to make it run on. The extra effort to make it run on smaller machines will be left to someone who wants to use it on them.

To avoid horrible confusion, please pronounce the 'G' in the word 'GNU' when it is the name of this project.

Why I Must Write GNU

I consider that the golden rule requires that if I like a program I must share it with other people who like it. Software sellers want to divide the users and conquer them, making each user agree not to share with others. I refuse to break solidarity with other users in this way. I cannot in good conscience sign a nondisclosure agreement or a software license agreement. For years I worked within the Artificial Intelligence Lab to resist such tendencies and other inhospitalities, but eventually they had gone too far: I could not remain in an institution where such things are done for me against my will.

So that I can continue to use computers without dishonor, I have decided to put together a sufficient body of free software so that I will be able to get along without any software that is not free. I have resigned from the AI lab to deny MIT any legal excuse to prevent me from giving GNU away.

Why GNU Will Be Compatible with Unix

Unix is not my ideal system, but it is not too bad. The essential features of Unix seem to be good ones, and I think I can fill in what Unix lacks without spoiling them. And a system compatible with Unix would be convenient for many other people to adopt.

How GNU Will Be Available

GNU is not in the public domain. Everyone will be permitted to modify and redistribute GNU, but no distributor will be allowed to restrict its further redistribution. That is to say, proprietary modifications will not be allowed. I want to make sure that all versions of GNU remain free.

Why Many Other Programmers Want to Help

I have found many other programmers who are excited about GNU and want to help.

Many programmers are unhappy about the commercialization of system software. It may enable them to make more money, but it requires them to feel in conflict with other programmers in general rather than feel as comrades. The fundamental act of friendship among programmers is the sharing of programs; marketing arrangements now typically used essentially forbid programmers to treat others as friends. The purchaser of software must choose between friendship and obeying the law. Naturally, many decide that friendship is more important. But those who believe in law often do not feel at ease with either choice. They become cynical and think that programming is just a way of making money.

By working on and using GNU rather than proprietary programs, we can be hospitable to everyone and obey the law. In addition, GNU serves as an example to inspire and a banner to rally others to join us in sharing. This can give us a feeling of harmony which is impossible if we use software that is not free. For about half the programmers I talk to, this is an important happiness that money cannot replace.

How You Can Contribute

I am asking computer manufacturers for donations of machines and money. I'm asking individuals for donations of programs and work.

One consequence you can expect if you donate machines is that GNU will run on them at an early date. The machines should be complete, ready to use systems, approved for use in a residential area, and not in need of sophisticated cooling or power.

I have found very many programmers eager to contribute part-time work for GNU. For most projects, such part-time distributed work would be very hard to coordinate; the independently-written parts would not work together. But for the particular task of replacing Unix, this problem is absent. A complete Unix system contains hundreds of utility programs, each of which is documented separately. Most interface specifications are fixed by Unix compatibility. If each contributor can write a compatible replacement for a single Unix utility, and make it work properly in place of the original on a Unix system, then these utilities will work right when put together. Even allowing for Murphy to create a few unexpected problems, assembling these components will be a feasible task. (The kernel will require closer communication and will be worked on by a small, tight group.)

If I get donations of money, I may be able to hire a few people full or part time. The salary won't be high by programmers' standards, but I'm looking for people for whom building community spirit is as important as making money. I view this as a way of enabling dedicated people to devote their full energies to working on GNU by sparing them the need to make a living in another way.

Why All Computer Users Will Benefit

Once GNU is written, everyone will be able to obtain good system software free, just like air.[2]

This means much more than just saving everyone the price of a Unix license. It means that much wasteful duplication of system programming effort will be avoided. This effort can go instead into advancing the state of the art.

Complete system sources will be available to everyone. As a result, a user who needs changes in the system will always be free to make them himself, or hire any available programmer or company to make them for him. Users will no longer be at the mercy of one programmer or company which owns the sources and is in sole position to make changes.

Schools will be able to provide a much more educational environment by encouraging all students to study and improve the system code. Harvard's computer lab used to have the policy that no program could be installed on the system if its sources were not on public display, and upheld it by actually refusing to install certain programs. I was very much inspired by this.

Finally, the overhead of considering who owns the system software and what one is or is not entitled to do with it will be lifted.

Arrangements to make people pay for using a program, including licensing of copies, always incur a tremendous cost to society through the cumbersome mechanisms necessary to figure out how much (that is, which programs) a person must pay for. And only a police state can force everyone to obey them. Consider a space station where air must be manufactured at great cost: charging each breather per liter of air may be fair, but wearing the metered gas mask all day and all night is intolerable even if everyone can afford to pay the air bill. And the TV cameras everywhere to see if you ever take the mask off are outrageous. It's better to support the air plant with a head tax and chuck the masks.

Copying all or parts of a program is as natural to a programmer as breathing, and as productive. It ought to be as free.

Some Easily Rebutted Objections to GNU's Goals

> "Nobody will use it if it is free, because that means they can't rely on any support."

---

[2] This is another place I failed to distinguish carefully between the two different meanings of "free". The statement as it stands is not false—you can get copies of GNU software at no charge, from your friends or over the net. But it does suggest the wrong idea.

"You have to charge for the program to pay for providing the support."

If people would rather pay for GNU plus service than get GNU free without service, a company to provide just service to people who have obtained GNU free ought to be profitable.[3]

We must distinguish between support in the form of real programming work and mere handholding. The former is something one cannot rely on from a software vendor. If your problem is not shared by enough people, the vendor will tell you to get lost.

If your business needs to be able to rely on support, the only way is to have all the necessary sources and tools. Then you can hire any available person to fix your problem; you are not at the mercy of any individual. With Unix, the price of sources puts this out of consideration for most businesses. With GNU this will be easy. It is still possible for there to be no available competent person, but this problem cannot be blamed on distribution arrangements. GNU does not eliminate all the world's problems, only some of them.

Meanwhile, the users who know nothing about computers need handholding: doing things for them which they could easily do themselves but don't know how.

Such services could be provided by companies that sell just hand-holding and repair service. If it is true that users would rather spend money and get a product with service, they will also be willing to buy the service having got the product free. The service companies will compete in quality and price; users will not be tied to any particular one. Meanwhile, those of us who don't need the service should be able to use the program without paying for the service.

"You cannot reach many people without advertising, and you must charge for the program to support that."

"It's no use advertising a program people can get free."

There are various forms of free or very cheap publicity that can be used to inform numbers of computer users about something like GNU. But it may be true that one can reach more microcomputer users with advertising. If this is really so, a business which advertises the service of copying and mailing GNU for a fee ought to be successful enough to pay for its advertising and more. This way, only the users who benefit from the advertising pay for it.

On the other hand, if many people get GNU from their friends, and such companies don't succeed, this will show that advertising was not really necessary to spread GNU. Why is it that free market advocates don't want to let the free market decide this?[4]

---

[3] Several such companies now exist.

[4] The Free Software Foundation raises most of its funds from a distribution service, although it is a charity rather than a company. If *no one* chooses to obtain copies by ordering from the FSF, it will be unable to do its work. But this does not mean that proprietary restrictions are justified to force every user to pay. If a small fraction of

"My company needs a proprietary operating system to get a competitive edge."

GNU will remove operating system software from the realm of competition. You will not be able to get an edge in this area, but neither will your competitors be able to get an edge over you. You and they will compete in other areas, while benefiting mutually in this one. If your business is selling an operating system, you will not like GNU, but that's tough on you. If your business is something else, GNU can save you from being pushed into the expensive business of selling operating systems.

I would like to see GNU development supported by gifts from many manufacturers and users, reducing the cost to each.[5]

"Don't programmers deserve a reward for their creativity?"

If anything deserves a reward, it is social contribution. Creativity can be a social contribution, but only in so far as society is free to use the results. If programmers deserve to be rewarded for creating innovative programs, by the same token they deserve to be punished if they restrict the use of these programs.

"Shouldn't a programmer be able to ask for a reward for his creativity?"

There is nothing wrong with wanting pay for work, or seeking to maximize one's income, as long as one does not use means that are destructive. But the means customary in the field of software today are based on destruction.

Extracting money from users of a program by restricting their use of it is destructive because the restrictions reduce the amount and the ways that the program can be used. This reduces the amount of wealth that humanity derives from the program. When there is a deliberate choice to restrict, the harmful consequences are deliberate destruction.

The reason a good citizen does not use such destructive means to become wealthier is that, if everyone did so, we would all become poorer from the mutual destructiveness. This is Kantian ethics; or, the Golden Rule. Since I do not like the consequences that result if everyone hoards information, I am required to consider it wrong for one to do so. Specifically, the desire to be rewarded for one's creativity does not justify depriving the world in general of all or part of that creativity.

"Won't programmers starve?"

I could answer that nobody is forced to be a programmer. Most of us cannot manage to get any money for standing on the street and making faces. But we are not, as a result, condemned to spend our lives standing on the street making faces, and starving. We do something else.

---

all the users order copies from the FSF, that is sufficient to keep the FSF afloat. So we ask users to choose to support us in this way. Have you done your part?

[5] A group of computer companies recently pooled funds to support maintenance of the GNU C Compiler.

But that is the wrong answer because it accepts the questioner's implicit assumption: that without ownership of software, programmers cannot possibly be paid a cent. Supposedly it is all or nothing.

The real reason programmers will not starve is that it will still be possible for them to get paid for programming; just not paid as much as now.

Restricting copying is not the only basis for business in software. It is the most common basis because it brings in the most money. If it were prohibited, or rejected by the customer, software business would move to other bases of organization which are now used less often. There are always numerous ways to organize any kind of business.

Probably programming will not be as lucrative on the new basis as it is now. But that is not an argument against the change. It is not considered an injustice that sales clerks make the salaries that they now do. If programmers made the same, that would not be an injustice either. (In practice they would still make considerably more than that.)

"Don't people have a right to control how their creativity is used?"

"Control over the use of one's ideas" really constitutes control over other people's lives; and it is usually used to make their lives more difficult.

People who have studied the issue of intellectual property rights carefully (such as lawyers) say that there is no intrinsic right to intellectual property. The kinds of supposed intellectual property rights that the government recognizes were created by specific acts of legislation for specific purposes.

For example, the patent system was established to encourage inventors to disclose the details of their inventions. Its purpose was to help society rather than to help inventors. At the time, the life span of 17 years for a patent was short compared with the rate of advance of the state of the art. Since patents are an issue only among manufacturers, for whom the cost and effort of a license agreement are small compared with setting up production, the patents often do not do much harm. They do not obstruct most individuals who use patented products.

The idea of copyright did not exist in ancient times, when authors frequently copied other authors at length in works of non-fiction. This practice was useful, and is the only way many authors' works have survived even in part. The copyright system was created expressly for the purpose of encouraging authorship. In the domain for which it was invented—books, which could be copied economically only on a printing press—it did little harm, and did not obstruct most of the individuals who read the books.

All intellectual property rights are just licenses granted by society because it was thought, rightly or wrongly, that society as a whole would benefit by granting them. But in any particular situation, we have to ask: are we really better off granting such license? What kind of act are we licensing a person to do?

The case of programs today is very different from that of books a hundred years ago. The fact that the easiest way to copy a program is from one neighbor to another, the fact that a program has both source code and object code which are distinct, and the fact that a program is used rather than read and enjoyed, combine to create a situation in which a person who enforces a copyright is harming society as a whole both materially and spiritually; in which a person should not do so regardless of whether the law enables him to.

"Competition makes things get done better."

The paradigm of competition is a race: by rewarding the winner, we encourage everyone to run faster. When capitalism really works this way, it does a good job; but its defenders are wrong in assuming it always works this way. If the runners forget why the reward is offered and become intent on winning, no matter how, they may find other strategies—such as, attacking other runners. If the runners get into a fist fight, they will all finish late.

Proprietary and secret software is the moral equivalent of runners in a fist fight. Sad to say, the only referee we've got does not seem to object to fights; he just regulates them ("For every ten yards you run, you can fire one shot"). He really ought to break them up, and penalize runners for even trying to fight.

"Won't everyone stop programming without a monetary incentive?"

Actually, many people will program with absolutely no monetary incentive. Programming has an irresistible fascination for some people, usually the people who are best at it. There is no shortage of professional musicians who keep at it even though they have no hope of making a living that way.

But really this question, though commonly asked, is not appropriate to the situation. Pay for programmers will not disappear, only become less. So the right question is, will anyone program with a reduced monetary incentive? My experience shows that they will.

For more than ten years, many of the world's best programmers worked at the Artificial Intelligence Lab for far less money than they could have had anywhere else. They got many kinds of non-monetary rewards: fame and appreciation, for example. And creativity is also fun, a reward in itself.

Then most of them left when offered a chance to do the same interesting work for a lot of money.

What the facts show is that people will program for reasons other than riches; but if given a chance to make a lot of money as well, they will come to expect and demand it. Low-paying organizations do poorly in competition with high-paying ones, but they do not have to do badly if the high-paying ones are banned.

"We need the programmers desperately. If they demand that we stop helping our neighbors, we have to obey."

You're never so desperate that you have to obey this sort of demand. Remember: millions for defense, but not a cent for tribute!

"Programmers need to make a living somehow."

In the short run, this is true. However, there are plenty of ways that programmers could make a living without selling the right to use a program. This way is customary now because it brings programmers and businessmen the most money, not because it is the only way to make a living. It is easy to find other ways if you want to find them. Here are a number of examples.

A manufacturer introducing a new computer will pay for the porting of operating systems onto the new hardware.

The sale of teaching, hand-holding and maintenance services could also employ programmers.

People with new ideas could distribute programs as freeware, asking for donations from satisfied users, or selling hand-holding services. I have met people who are already working this way successfully.

Users with related needs can form users' groups, and pay dues. A group would contract with programming companies to write programs that the group's members would like to use.

All sorts of development can be funded with a Software Tax:

Suppose everyone who buys a computer has to pay x percent of the price as a software tax. The government gives this to an agency like the NSF to spend on software development.

But if the computer buyer makes a donation to software development himself, he can take a credit against the tax. He can donate to the project of his own choosing—often, chosen because he hopes to use the results when it is done. He can take a credit for any amount of donation up to the total tax he had to pay.

The total tax rate could be decided by a vote of the payers of the tax, weighted according to the amount they will be taxed on.

The consequences:

- The computer-using community supports software development.

- This community decides what level of support is needed.

- Users who care which projects their share is spent on can choose this for themselves.

In the long run, making programs free is a step toward the post-scarcity world, where nobody will have to work very hard just to make a living. People will be free to devote themselves to activities that are fun, such as programming, after spending the necessary ten hours a week on required tasks such as legislation, family counseling, robot repair and asteroid prospecting. There will be no need to be able to make a living from programming.

We have already greatly reduced the amount of work that the whole society must do for its actual productivity, but only a little of this has translated itself into leisure for workers because much nonproductive activity is required to accompany productive activity. The main causes of this are bureaucracy and isometric struggles against competition. Free software will greatly reduce these drains in the area of software production. We must do this, in order for technical gains in productivity to translate into less work for us.

Glossary

Abbrev   An abbrev is a text string which expands into a different text string when present in the buffer. For example, you might define a few letters as an abbrev for a long phrase that you want to insert frequently. See Chapter 24 [Abbrevs], page 289.

Aborting   Aborting means getting out of a recursive edit (q.v.). The commands C-] and M-x top-level are used for this. See Section 32.1 [Quitting], page 425.

Alt   Alt is the name of a modifier bit which a keyboard input character may have. To make a character Alt, type it while holding down the (ALT) key. Such characters are given names that start with Alt- (usually written A- for short). (Note that many terminals have a key labeled (ALT) which is really a (META) key.) See Section 2.1 [User Input], page 21.

ASCII character
             An ASCII character is either an ASCII control character or an ASCII printing character. See Section 2.1 [User Input], page 21.

ASCII control character
             An ASCII control character is the Control version of an upper-case letter, or the Control version of one of the characters '@[\]^_?'.

ASCII printing character
             ASCII printing characters include letters, digits, space, and these punctuation characters: '!@#$%^& *()_-+=|\~' {}[]:;"' <>,.?/'.

Auto Fill Mode
             Auto Fill mode is a minor mode in which text that you insert is automatically broken into lines of fixed width. See Section 21.5 [Filling], page 203.

Auto Saving
             Auto saving is the practice of saving the contents of an Emacs buffer in a specially-named file, so that the information will not be lost if the buffer is lost due to a system error or user error. See Section 14.5 [Auto Save], page 117.

Backup File
             A backup file records the contents that a file had before the current editing session. Emacs makes backup files automatically to help you track down or cancel changes you later regret making. See Section 14.3.1 [Backup], page 113.

Balance Parentheses

>Emacs can balance parentheses manually or automatically. Manual balancing is done by the commands to move over balanced expressions (see Section 22.2 [Lists], page 228). Automatic balancing is done by blinking or highlighting the parenthesis that matches one just inserted (see Section 22.6 [Matching Parens], page 243).

Bind

>To bind a key sequence means to give it a binding (q.v.). See Section 31.4.5 [Rebinding], page 411.

Binding

>A key sequence gets its meaning in Emacs by having a binding, which is a command (q.v.), a Lisp function that is run when the user types that sequence. See Section 2.3 [Commands], page 23. Customization often involves rebinding a character to a different command function. The bindings of all key sequences are recorded in the keymaps (q.v.). See Section 31.4.1 [Keymaps], page 408.

Blank Lines

>Blank lines are lines that contain only whitespace. Emacs has several commands for operating on the blank lines in the buffer.

Buffer

>The buffer is the basic editing unit; one buffer corresponds to one text being edited. You can have several buffers, but at any time you are editing only one, the 'selected' buffer, though several can be visible when you are using multiple windows (q.v.). Most buffers are visiting (q.v.) some file. See Chapter 15 [Buffers], page 143.

Buffer Selection History

>Emacs keeps a buffer selection history which records how recently each Emacs buffer has been selected. This is used for choosing a buffer to select. See Chapter 15 [Buffers], page 143.

Button Down Event

>A button down event is the kind of input event generated right away when you press a mouse button. See Section 31.4.10 [Mouse Buttons], page 416.

C-

>C- in the name of a character is an abbreviation for Control. See Section 2.1 [User Input], page 21.

C-M-

>C-M- in the name of a character is an abbreviation for Control-Meta. See Section 2.1 [User Input], page 21.

Case Conversion

>Case conversion means changing text from upper case to lower case or vice versa. See Section 21.6 [Case], page 208, for the commands for case conversion.

Character   Characters form the contents of an Emacs buffer; see Section 2.4 [Text Characters], page 24. Also, key sequences (q.v.) are usually made up of characters (though they may include other input events as well). See Section 2.1 [User Input], page 21.

Character Set
             Emacs supports a number of character sets, each of which represents a particular alphabet or script. See Chapter 18 [International], page 175.

Click Event
             A click event is the kind of input event generated when you press a mouse button and release it without moving the mouse. See Section 31.4.10 [Mouse Buttons], page 416.

Coding System
             A coding system is an encoding for representing text characters in a file or in a stream of information. Emacs has the ability to convert text to or from a variety of coding systems when reading or writing it. See Section 18.7 [Coding Systems], page 180.

Command   A command is a Lisp function specially defined to be able to serve as a key binding in Emacs. When you type a key sequence (q.v.), its binding (q.v.) is looked up in the relevant keymaps (q.v.) to find the command to run. See Section 2.3 [Commands], page 23.

Command Name
             A command name is the name of a Lisp symbol which is a command (see Section 2.3 [Commands], page 23). You can invoke any command by its name using M-x (see Chapter 6 [M-x], page 49).

Comment   A comment is text in a program which is intended only for humans reading the program, and which is marked specially so that it will be ignored when the program is loaded or compiled. Emacs offers special commands for creating, aligning and killing comments. See Section 22.7 [Comments], page 244.

Compilation
             Compilation is the process of creating an executable program from source code. Emacs has commands for compiling files of Emacs Lisp code (see section "Byte Compilation" in *the Emacs Lisp Reference Manual*) and programs in C and other languages (see Section 23.1 [Compilation], page 277).

Complete Key
             A complete key is a key sequence which fully specifies one action to be performed by Emacs. For example, X and C-f and C-x m are complete keys. Complete keys derive their meanings from

being bound (q.v.) to commands (q.v.). Thus, X is conventionally bound to a command to insert 'X' in the buffer; C-x m is
conventionally bound to a command to begin composing a mail
message. See Section 2.2 [Keys], page 22.

Completion
    Completion is what Emacs does when it automatically fills out
    an abbreviation for a name into the entire name. Completion
    is done for minibuffer (q.v.) arguments when the set of possible
    valid inputs is known; for example, on command names, buffer
    names, and file names. Completion occurs when (TAB), (SPC) or
    (RET) is typed. See Section 5.3 [Completion], page 43.

Continuation Line
    When a line of text is longer than the width of the window, it
    takes up more than one screen line when displayed. We say that
    the text line is continued, and all screen lines used for it after the
    first are called continuation lines. See Chapter 4 [Basic Editing],
    page 29.

Control Character
    A control character is a character that you type by holding down
    the (CTRL) key. Some control characters also have their own keys,
    so that you can type them without using (CTRL). For example,
    (RET), (TAB), (ESC) and (DEL) are all control characters. See Sec-
    tion 2.1 [User Input], page 21.

Copyleft   A copyleft is a notice giving the public legal permission to re-
    distribute a program or other work of art. Copylefts are used
    by left-wing programmers to promote freedom and cooperation,
    just as copyrights are used by right-wing programmers to gain
    power over other people.

    The particular form of copyleft used by the GNU project is called
    the GNU General Public License. See [Copying], page 5.

Current Buffer
    The current buffer in Emacs is the Emacs buffer on which most
    editing commands operate. You can select any Emacs buffer as
    the current one. See Chapter 15 [Buffers], page 143.

Current Line
    The line point is on (see Section 1.1 [Point], page 15).

Current Paragraph
    The paragraph that point is in. If point is between paragraphs,
    the current paragraph is the one that follows point. See Sec-
    tion 21.3 [Paragraphs], page 201.

Current Defun

> The defun (q.v.) that point is in. If point is between defuns, the current defun is the one that follows point. See Section 22.4 [Defuns], page 230.

Cursor

> The cursor is the rectangle on the screen which indicates the position called point (q.v.) at which insertion and deletion takes place. The cursor is on or under the character that follows point. Often people speak of 'the cursor' when, strictly speaking, they mean 'point'. See Chapter 4 [Basic Editing], page 29.

Customization

> Customization is making minor changes in the way Emacs works. It is often done by setting variables (see Section 31.2 [Variables], page 393) or by rebinding key sequences (see Section 31.4.1 [Keymaps], page 408).

Default Argument

> The default for an argument is the value that will be assumed if you do not specify one. When the minibuffer is used to read an argument, the default argument is used if you just type (RET). See Chapter 5 [Minibuffer], page 41.

Default Directory

> When you specify a file name that does not start with '/' or '~', it is interpreted relative to the current buffer's default directory. See Section 5.1 [Minibuffer File], page 41.

Defun

> A defun is a list at the top level of parenthesis or bracket structure in a program. It is so named because most such lists in Lisp programs are calls to the Lisp function `defun`. See Section 22.4 [Defuns], page 230.

(DEL)

> (DEL) is a character that runs the command to delete one character of text. See Chapter 4 [Basic Editing], page 29.

Deletion

> Deletion means erasing text without copying it into the kill ring (q.v.). The alternative is killing (q.v.). See Section 9.1 [Killing], page 65.

Deletion of Files

> Deleting a file means erasing it from the file system. See Section 14.10 [Misc File Ops], page 139.

Deletion of Messages

> Deleting a message means flagging it to be eliminated from your mail file. Until you expunge (q.v.) the Rmail file, you can still undelete the messages you have deleted. See Section 27.4 [Rmail Deletion], page 313.

Deletion of Windows

> Deleting a window means eliminating it from the screen. Other windows expand to use up the space. The deleted window can never come back, but no actual text is thereby lost. See Chapter 16 [Windows], page 151.

Directory

> File directories are named collections in the file system, within which you can place individual files or subdirectories. See Section 14.8 [Directories], page 138.

Dired

> Dired is the Emacs facility that displays the contents of a file directory and allows you to "edit the directory," performing operations on the files in the directory. See Chapter 28 [Dired], page 329.

Disabled Command

> A disabled command is one that you may not run without special confirmation. The usual reason for disabling a command is that it is confusing for beginning users. See Section 31.4.11 [Disabling], page 418.

Down Event

> Short for 'button down event'.

Drag Event

> A drag event is the kind of input event generated when you press a mouse button, move the mouse, and then release the button. See Section 31.4.10 [Mouse Buttons], page 416.

Dribble File

> A file into which Emacs writes all the characters that the user types on the keyboard. Dribble files are used to make a record for debugging Emacs bugs. Emacs does not make a dribble file unless you tell it to. See Section 32.3 [Bugs], page 430.

Echo Area

> The echo area is the bottom line of the screen, used for echoing the arguments to commands, for asking questions, and printing brief messages (including error messages). The messages are stored in the buffer '*Messages*' so you can review them later. See Section 1.2 [Echo Area], page 16.

Echoing

> Echoing is acknowledging the receipt of commands by displaying them (in the echo area). Emacs never echoes single-character key sequences; longer key sequences echo only if you pause while typing them.

Electric

> We say that a character is electric if it is normally self-inserting (q.v.), but the current major mode (q.v.) redefines it to do something else as well. For example, some programming language major modes define particular delimiter characters to reindent the line or insert one or more newlines in addition to self-insertion.

Error   An error occurs when an Emacs command cannot execute in the
                 current circumstances. When an error occurs, execution of the
                 command stops (unless the command has been programmed to
                 do otherwise) and Emacs reports the error by printing an error
                 message (q.v.). Type-ahead is discarded. Then Emacs is ready
                 to read another editing command.

Error Message
                 An error message is a single line of output displayed by Emacs
                 when the user asks for something impossible to do (such as,
                 killing text forward when point is at the end of the buffer).
                 They appear in the echo area, accompanied by a beep.

(ESC)   (ESC) is a character used as a prefix for typing Meta charac-
                 ters on keyboards lacking a (META) key. Unlike the (META) key
                 (which, like the (SHIFT) key, is held down while another character
                 is typed), you press the (ESC) key as you would press a letter key,
                 and it applies to the next character you type.

Expunging
                 Expunging an Rmail file or Dired buffer is an operation that
                 truly discards the messages or files you have previously flagged
                 for deletion.

File Locking
                 Emacs used file locking to notice when two different users start to
                 edit one file at the same time. See Section 14.3.2 [Interlocking],
                 page 115.

File Name   A file name is a name that refers to a file. File names may be
                 relative or absolute; the meaning of a relative file name depends
                 on the current directory, but an absolute file name refers to the
                 same file regardless of which directory is current. On GNU and
                 Unix systems, an absolute file name starts with a slash (the root
                 directory) or with '~/' or '~user/' (a home directory).

                 Some people use the term "pathname" for file names, but we
                 do not; we use the word "path" only in the term "search path"
                 (q.v.).

File-Name Component
                 A file-name component names a file directly within a particular
                 directory. On GNU and Unix systems, a file name is a sequence
                 of file-name components, separated by slashes. For example,
                 'foo/bar' is a file name containing two components, 'foo' and
                 'bar'; it refers to the file named 'bar' in the directory named
                 'foo' in the current directory.

Fill Prefix   The fill prefix is a string that should be expected at the beginning
                 of each line when filling is done. It is not regarded as part of the
                 text to be filled. See Section 21.5 [Filling], page 203.

Filling   Filling text means shifting text between consecutive lines so that
                 all the lines are approximately the same length. See Section 21.5
                 [Filling], page 203.

Formatted Text
                 Formatted text is text that displays with formatting informa-
                 tion while you edit. Formatting information includes fonts, col-
                 ors, and specified margins. See Section 21.11 [Formatted Text],
                 page 219.

Frame   A frame is a rectangular cluster of Emacs windows. Emacs starts
                 out with one frame, but you can create more. You can subdivide
                 each frame into Emacs windows (q.v.). When you are using X
                 windows, all the frames can be visible at the same time. See
                 Chapter 17 [Frames], page 157.

Function Key
                 A function key is a key on the keyboard that sends input but does
                 not correspond to any character. See Section 31.4.7 [Function
                 Keys], page 414.

Global   Global means 'independent of the current environment; in effect
                 throughout Emacs'. It is the opposite of local (q.v.). Particular
                 examples of the use of 'global' appear below.

Global Abbrev
                 A global definition of an abbrev (q.v.) is effective in all major
                 modes that do not have local (q.v.) definitions for the same
                 abbrev. See Chapter 24 [Abbrevs], page 289.

Global Keymap
                 The global keymap (q.v.) contains key bindings that are in effect
                 except when overridden by local key bindings in a major mode's
                 local keymap (q.v.). See Section 31.4.1 [Keymaps], page 408.

Global Mark Ring
                 The global mark ring records the series of buffers you have re-
                 cently set a mark in. In many cases you can use this to backtrack
                 through buffers you have been editing in, or in which you have
                 found tags. See Section 8.6 [Global Mark Ring], page 63.

Global Substitution
                 Global substitution means replacing each occurrence of one
                 string by another string through a large amount of text. See
                 Section 12.7 [Replace], page 95.

Global Variable
                 The global value of a variable (q.v.) takes effect in all buffers
                 that do not have their own local (q.v.) values for the variable.
                 See Section 31.2 [Variables], page 393.

Graphic Character

Graphic characters are those assigned pictorial images rather than just names. All the non-Meta (q.v.) characters except for the Control (q.v.) characters are graphic characters. These include letters, digits, punctuation, and spaces; they do not include (RET) or (ESC). In Emacs, typing a graphic character inserts that character (in ordinary editing modes). See Chapter 4 [Basic Editing], page 29.

Highlighting

Highlighting text means displaying it with a different foreground and/or background color to make it stand out from the rest of the text in the buffer.

Hardcopy   Hardcopy means printed output. Emacs has commands for making printed listings of text in Emacs buffers. See Section 30.4 [Hardcopy], page 377.

(HELP)   (HELP) is the Emacs name for C-h or (F1). You can type (HELP) at any time to ask what options you have, or to ask what any command does. See Chapter 7 [Help], page 51.

Hyper   Hyper is the name of a modifier bit which a keyboard input character may have. To make a character Hyper, type it while holding down the (HYPER) key. Such characters are given names that start with Hyper- (usually written H- for short). See Section 2.1 [User Input], page 21.

Inbox   An inbox is a file in which mail is delivered by the operating system. Rmail transfers mail from inboxes to Rmail files (q.v.) in which the mail is then stored permanently or until explicitly deleted. See Section 27.5 [Rmail Inbox], page 314.

Indentation

Indentation means blank space at the beginning of a line. Most programming languages have conventions for using indentation to illuminate the structure of the program, and Emacs has special commands to adjust indentation. See Chapter 20 [Indentation], page 195.

Indirect Buffer

An indirect buffer is a buffer that shares the text of another buffer, called its base buffer. See Section 15.6 [Indirect Buffers], page 149.

Input Event

An input event represents, within Emacs, one action taken by the user on the terminal. Input events include typing characters, typing function keys, pressing or releasing mouse buttons, and switching between Emacs frames. See Section 2.1 [User Input], page 21.

Input Method
          An input method is a system for entering non-ASCII text char-
          acters by typing sequences of ASCII characters (q.v.). See Sec-
          tion 18.4 [Input Methods], page 177.

Insertion   Insertion means copying text into the buffer, either from the
          keyboard or from some other place in Emacs.

Interlocking
          Interlocking is a feature for warning when you start to alter
          a file that someone else is already editing. See Section 14.3.2
          [Simultaneous Editing], page 115.

Justification
          Justification means adding extra spaces to lines of text to make
          them come exactly to a specified width. See Section 21.5 [Fill-
          ing], page 203.

Keyboard Macro
          Keyboard macros are a way of defining new Emacs commands
          from sequences of existing ones, with no need to write a Lisp
          program. See Section 31.3 [Keyboard Macros], page 405.

Key Sequence
          A key sequence (key, for short) is a sequence of input events
          (q.v.) that are meaningful as a single unit. If the key sequence
          is enough to specify one action, it is a complete key (q.v.); if it
          is not enough, it is a prefix key (q.v.). See Section 2.2 [Keys],
          page 22.

Keymap   The keymap is the data structure that records the bindings (q.v.)
          of key sequences to the commands that they run. For exam-
          ple, the global keymap binds the character C-n to the command
          function next-line. See Section 31.4.1 [Keymaps], page 408.

Keyboard Translation Table
          The keyboard translation table is an array that translates the
          character codes that come from the terminal into the character
          codes that make up key sequences. See Section 31.5 [Keyboard
          Translations], page 418.

Kill Ring   The kill ring is where all text you have killed recently is saved.
          You can reinsert any of the killed text still in the ring; this is
          called yanking (q.v.). See Section 9.2 [Yanking], page 67.

Killing   Killing means erasing text and saving it on the kill ring so it can
          be yanked (q.v.) later. Some other systems call this "cutting."
          Most Emacs commands to erase text do killing, as opposed to
          deletion (q.v.). See Section 9.1 [Killing], page 65.

Killing Jobs

>Killing a job (such as, an invocation of Emacs) means making it cease to exist. Any data within it, if not saved in a file, is lost. See Section 3.1 [Exiting], page 25.

Language Environment

>Your choice of language environment specifies defaults for the input method (q.v.) and coding system (q.v.). See Section 18.3 [Language Environments], page 176. These defaults are relevant if you edit non-ASCII text (see Chapter 18 [International], page 175).

List

>A list is, approximately, a text string beginning with an open parenthesis and ending with the matching close parenthesis. In C mode and other non-Lisp modes, groupings surrounded by other kinds of matched delimiters appropriate to the language, such as braces, are also considered lists. Emacs has special commands for many operations on lists. See Section 22.2 [Lists], page 228.

Local

>Local means 'in effect only in a particular context'; the relevant kind of context is a particular function execution, a particular buffer, or a particular major mode. It is the opposite of 'global' (q.v.). Specific uses of 'local' in Emacs terminology appear below.

Local Abbrev

>A local abbrev definition is effective only if a particular major mode is selected. In that major mode, it overrides any global definition for the same abbrev. See Chapter 24 [Abbrevs], page 289.

Local Keymap

>A local keymap is used in a particular major mode; the key bindings (q.v.) in the current local keymap override global bindings of the same key sequences. See Section 31.4.1 [Keymaps], page 408.

Local Variable

>A local value of a variable (q.v.) applies to only one buffer. See Section 31.2.4 [Locals], page 401.

M-

>M- in the name of a character is an abbreviation for (META), one of the modifier keys that can accompany any character. See Section 2.1 [User Input], page 21.

M-C-

>M-C- in the name of a character is an abbreviation for Control-Meta; it means the same thing as C-M-. If your terminal lacks a real (META) key, you type a Control-Meta character by typing (ESC) and then typing the corresponding Control character. See Section 2.1 [User Input], page 21.

M-x   M-x is the key sequence which is used to call an Emacs command
             by name. This is how you run commands that are not bound to
             key sequences See Chapter 6 [M-x], page 49.

Mail   Mail means messages sent from one user to another through
             the computer system, to be read at the recipient's convenience.
             Emacs has commands for composing and sending mail, and for
             reading and editing the mail you have received. See Chapter 26
             [Sending Mail], page 301. See Chapter 27 [Rmail], page 311, for
             how to read mail.

Mail Composition Method
             A mail composition method is a program runnable within Emacs
             for editing and sending a mail message. Emacs lets you select
             from several alternative mail composition methods. See Sec-
             tion 26.6 [Mail Methods], page 309.

Major Mode
             The Emacs major modes are a mutually exclusive set of options,
             each of which configures Emacs for editing a certain sort of text.
             Ideally, each programming language has its own major mode.
             See Chapter 19 [Major Modes], page 191.

Mark   The mark points to a position in the text. It specifies one end
             of the region (q.v.), point being the other end. Many commands
             operate on all the text from point to the mark. Each buffer has
             its own mark. See Chapter 8 [Mark], page 59.

Mark Ring
             The mark ring is used to hold several recent previous locations
             of the mark, just in case you want to move back to them. Each
             buffer has its own mark ring; in addition, there is a single global
             mark ring (q.v.). See Section 8.5 [Mark Ring], page 63.

Menu Bar   The menu bar is the line at the top of an Emacs frame. It
             contains words you can click on with the mouse to bring up
             menus. The menu bar feature is supported only with X. See
             Section 17.12 [Menu Bars], page 166.

Message   See 'mail'.

Meta   Meta is the name of a modifier bit which a command charac-
             ter may have. It is present in a character if the character is
             typed with the (META) key held down. Such characters are given
             names that start with Meta- (usually written M- for short). For
             example, M-< is typed by holding down (META) and at the same
             time typing < (which itself is done, on most terminals, by hold-
             ing down (SHIFT) and typing ,). See Section 2.1 [User Input],
             page 21.

Meta Character

A Meta character is one whose character code includes the Meta bit.

Minibuffer   The minibuffer is the window that appears when necessary inside the echo area (q.v.), used for reading arguments to commands. See Chapter 5 [Minibuffer], page 41.

Minibuffer History

The minibuffer history records the text you have specified in the past for minibuffer arguments, so you can conveniently use the same text again. See Section 5.4 [Minibuffer History], page 46.

Minor Mode

A minor mode is an optional feature of Emacs which can be switched on or off independently of all other features. Each minor mode has a command to turn it on or off. See Section 31.1 [Minor Modes], page 391.

Minor Mode Keymap

A keymap that belongs to a minor mode and is active when that mode is enabled. Minor mode keymaps take precedence over the buffer's local keymap, just as the local keymap takes precedence over the global keymap. See Section 31.4.1 [Keymaps], page 408.

Mode Line

The mode line is the line at the bottom of each window (q.v.), giving status information on the buffer displayed in that window. See Section 1.3 [Mode Line], page 17.

Modified Buffer

A buffer (q.v.) is modified if its text has been changed since the last time the buffer was saved (or since when it was created, if it has never been saved). See Section 14.3 [Saving], page 111.

Moving Text

Moving text means erasing it from one place and inserting it in another. The usual way to move text by killing (q.v.) and then yanking (q.v.). See Section 9.1 [Killing], page 65.

MULE   MULE refers to the Emacs features for editing non-ASCII text using multibyte characters (q.v.). See Chapter 18 [International], page 175.

Multibyte Character

A multibyte character is a character that takes up several buffer positions. Emacs uses multibyte characters to represent non-ASCII text, since the number of non-ASCII characters is much more than 256. See Section 18.1 [International Intro], page 175.

Named Mark
> A named mark is a register (q.v.) in its role of recording a location in text so that you can move point to that location. See Chapter 10 [Registers], page 75.

Narrowing   Narrowing means creating a restriction (q.v.) that limits editing in the current buffer to only a part of the text in the buffer. Text outside that part is inaccessible to the user until the boundaries are widened again, but it is still there, and saving the file saves it all. See Section 30.8 [Narrowing], page 382.

Newline   Control-J characters in the buffer terminate lines of text and are therefore also called newlines. See Section 2.4 [Text Characters], page 24.

Numeric Argument
> A numeric argument is a number, specified before a command, to change the effect of the command. Often the numeric argument serves as a repeat count. See Section 4.10 [Arguments], page 37.

Overwrite Mode
> Overwrite mode is a minor mode. When it is enabled, ordinary text characters replace the existing text after point rather than pushing it to the right. See Section 31.1 [Minor Modes], page 391.

Page   A page is a unit of text, delimited by formfeed characters (ASCII control-L, code 014) coming at the beginning of a line. Some Emacs commands are provided for moving over and operating on pages. See Section 21.4 [Pages], page 202.

Paragraph   Paragraphs are the medium-size unit of English text. There are special Emacs commands for moving over and operating on paragraphs. See Section 21.3 [Paragraphs], page 201.

Parsing   We say that certain Emacs commands parse words or expressions in the text being edited. Really, all they know how to do is find the other end of a word or expression. See Section 31.6 [Syntax], page 419.

Point   Point is the place in the buffer at which insertion and deletion occur. Point is considered to be between two characters, not at one character. The terminal's cursor (q.v.) indicates the location of point. See Chapter 4 [Basic], page 29.

Prefix Argument
> See 'numeric argument'.

Prefix Key
> A prefix key is a key sequence (q.v.) whose sole function is to introduce a set of longer key sequences. C-x is an example of prefix

key; any two-character sequence starting with C-x is therefore a legitimate key sequence. See Section 2.2 [Keys], page 22.

Primary Rmail File

Your primary Rmail file is the file named 'RMAIL' in your home directory. That's where Rmail stores your incoming mail, unless you specify a different file name. See Chapter 27 [Rmail], page 311.

Primary Selection

The primary selection is one particular X selection (q.v.); it is the selection that most X applications use for transferring text to and from other applications.

The Emacs kill commands set the primary selection and the yank command uses the primary selection when appropriate. See Section 9.1 [Killing], page 65.

Prompt   A prompt is text printed to ask the user for input. Displaying a prompt is called prompting. Emacs prompts always appear in the echo area (q.v.). One kind of prompting happens when the minibuffer is used to read an argument (see Chapter 5 [Minibuffer], page 41); the echoing which happens when you pause in the middle of typing a multi-character key sequence is also a kind of prompting (see Section 1.2 [Echo Area], page 16).

Quitting   Quitting means canceling a partially typed command or a running command, using C-g (or C-⟨BREAK⟩ on MS-DOS). See Section 32.1 [Quitting], page 425.

Quoting   Quoting means depriving a character of its usual special significance. The most common kind of quoting in Emacs is with C-q. What constitutes special significance depends on the context and on convention. For example, an "ordinary" character as an Emacs command inserts itself; so in this context, a special character is any character that does not normally insert itself (such as ⟨DEL⟩, for example), and quoting it makes it insert itself as if it were not special. Not all contexts allow quoting. See Chapter 4 [Basic Editing], page 29.

Quoting File Names

Quoting a file name turns off the special significance of constructs such as '$', '~' and ':'. See Section 14.13 [Quoted File Names], page 141.

Read-Only Buffer

A read-only buffer is one whose text you are not allowed to change. Normally Emacs makes buffers read-only when they contain text which has a special significance to Emacs; for example, Dired buffers. Visiting a file that is write-protected also makes a read-only buffer. See Chapter 15 [Buffers], page 143.

Rectangle   A rectangle consists of the text in a given range of columns on a given range of lines. Normally you specify a rectangle by putting point at one corner and putting the mark at the opposite corner. See Section 9.4 [Rectangles], page 71.

Recursive Editing Level

A recursive editing level is a state in which part of the execution of a command involves asking the user to edit some text. This text may or may not be the same as the text to which the command was applied. The mode line indicates recursive editing levels with square brackets ('[' and ']'). See Section 30.12 [Recursive Edit], page 385.

Redisplay   Redisplay is the process of correcting the image on the screen to correspond to changes that have been made in the text being edited. See Chapter 1 [Screen], page 15.

Regexp   See 'regular expression'.

Region   The region is the text between point (q.v.) and the mark (q.v.). Many commands operate on the text of the region. See Chapter 8 [Mark], page 59.

Registers   Registers are named slots in which text or buffer positions or rectangles can be saved for later use. See Chapter 10 [Registers], page 75.

Regular Expression

A regular expression is a pattern that can match various text strings; for example, '1[0-9]+' matches '1' followed by one or more digits. See Section 12.5 [Regexps], page 90.

Repeat Count

See 'numeric argument'.

Replacement

See 'global substitution'.

Restriction

A buffer's restriction is the amount of text, at the beginning or the end of the buffer, that is temporarily inaccessible. Giving a buffer a nonzero amount of restriction is called narrowing (q.v.). See Section 30.8 [Narrowing], page 382.

⟨RET⟩   ⟨RET⟩ is a character that in Emacs runs the command to insert a newline into the text. It is also used to terminate most arguments read in the minibuffer (q.v.). See Section 2.1 [User Input], page 21.

Rmail File An Rmail file is a file containing text in a special format used by Rmail for storing mail. See Chapter 27 [Rmail], page 311.

Saving   Saving a buffer means copying its text into the file that was
              visited (q.v.) in that buffer. This is the way text in files actually
              gets changed by your Emacs editing. See Section 14.3 [Saving],
              page 111.

Scroll Bar   A scroll bar is a tall thin hollow box that appears at the side
              of a window. You can use mouse commands in the scroll bar to
              scroll the window. The scroll bar feature is supported only with
              X. See Section 17.11 [Scroll Bars], page 165.

Scrolling   Scrolling means shifting the text in the Emacs window so as
              to see a different part of the buffer. See Chapter 11 [Display],
              page 79.

Searching   Searching means moving point to the next occurrence of a spec-
              ified string or the next match for a specified regular expression.
              See Chapter 12 [Search], page 85.

Search Path
              A search path is a list of directory names, to be used for searching
              for files for certain purposes. For example, the variable load-
              path holds a search path for finding Lisp library files. See Sec-
              tion 23.7 [Lisp Libraries], page 285.

Secondary Selection
              The secondary selection is one particular X selection; some X
              applications can use it for transferring text to and from other ap-
              plications. Emacs has special mouse commands for transferring
              text using the secondary selection. See Section 17.2 [Secondary
              Selection], page 159.

Selecting   Selecting a buffer means making it the current (q.v.) buffer. See
              Chapter 15 [Buffers], page 143.

Selection   The X window system allows an application program to specify
              named selections whose values are text. A program can also
              read the selections that other programs have set up. This is the
              principal way of transferring text between window applications.
              Emacs has commands to work with the primary (q.v.) selection
              and the secondary (q.v.) selection.

Self-Documentation
              Self-documentation is the feature of Emacs which can tell you
              what any command does, or give you a list of all commands
              related to a topic you specify. You ask for self-documentation
              with the help character, C-h. See Chapter 7 [Help], page 51.

Self-Inserting Character
              A character is self-inserting if typing that character inserts that
              character in the buffer. Ordinary printing and whitespace char-
              acters are self-inserting in Emacs, except in certain special major
              modes.

Sentences   Emacs has commands for moving by or killing by sentences. See
             Section 21.2 [Sentences], page 200.

Sexp   A sexp (short for 's-expression') is the basic syntactic unit of
             Lisp in its textual form: either a list, or Lisp atom. Many Emacs
             commands operate on sexps. The term 'sexp' is generalized to
             languages other than Lisp, to mean a syntactically recognizable
             expression. See Section 22.2 [Lists], page 228.

Simultaneous Editing
             Simultaneous editing means two users modifying the same file
             at once. Simultaneous editing if not detected can cause one user
             to lose his work. Emacs detects all cases of simultaneous editing
             and warns one of the users to investigate. See Section 14.3.2
             [Simultaneous Editing], page 115.

String   A string is a kind of Lisp data object which contains a sequence
             of characters. Many Emacs variables are intended to have strings
             as values. The Lisp syntax for a string consists of the characters
             in the string with a '"' before and another '"' after. A '"' that
             is part of the string must be written as '\"' and a '\' that is
             part of the string must be written as '\\'. All other characters,
             including newline, can be included just by writing them inside
             the string; however, backslash sequences as in C, such as '\n' for
             newline or '\241' using an octal character code, are allowed as
             well.

String Substitution
             See 'global substitution'.

Syntax Table
             The syntax table tells Emacs which characters are part of a
             word, which characters balance each other like parentheses, etc.
             See Section 31.6 [Syntax], page 419.

Super   Super is the name of a modifier bit which a keyboard input
             character may have. To make a character Super, type it while
             holding down the (SUPER) key. Such characters are given names
             that start with **Super-** (usually written **s-** for short). See Sec-
             tion 2.1 [User Input], page 21.

Tags Table
             A tags table is a file that serves as an index to the function
             definitions in one or more other files. See Section 22.13 [Tags],
             page 250.

Termscript File
             A termscript file contains a record of all characters sent by
             Emacs to the terminal. It is used for tracking down bugs in
             Emacs redisplay. Emacs does not make a termscript file unless
             you tell it to. See Section 32.3 [Bugs], page 430.

Text   Two meanings (see Chapter 21 [Text], page 199):

- Data consisting of a sequence of characters, as opposed to binary numbers, images, graphics commands, executable programs, and the like. The contents of an Emacs buffer are always text in this sense.

- Data consisting of written human language, as opposed to programs, or following the stylistic conventions of human language.

Top Level   Top level is the normal state of Emacs, in which you are editing the text of the file you have visited. You are at top level whenever you are not in a recursive editing level (q.v.) or the minibuffer (q.v.), and not in the middle of a command. You can get back to top level by aborting (q.v.) and quitting (q.v.). See Section 32.1 [Quitting], page 425.

Transposition
                    Transposing two units of text means putting each one into the place formerly occupied by the other. There are Emacs commands to transpose two adjacent characters, words, sexps (q.v.) or lines (see Section 13.2 [Transpose], page 101).

Truncation
                    Truncating text lines in the display means leaving out any text on a line that does not fit within the right margin of the window displaying it. See also 'continuation line'. See Chapter 4 [Basic Editing], page 29.

Undoing   Undoing means making your previous editing go in reverse, bringing back the text that existed earlier in the editing session. See Section 4.4 [Undo], page 32.

User Option
                    A user option is a variable (q.v.) that exists so that you can customize Emacs by setting it to a new value. See Section 31.2 [Variables], page 393.

Variable   A variable is an object in Lisp that can store an arbitrary value. Emacs uses some variables for internal purposes, and has others (known as 'user options' (q.v.)) just so that you can set their values to control the behavior of Emacs. The variables used in Emacs that you are likely to be interested in are listed in the Variables Index in this manual. See Section 31.2 [Variables], page 393, for information on variables.

Version Control
                    Version control systems keep track of multiple versions of a source file. They provide a more powerful alternative to keeping backup files (q.v.). See Section 14.7 [Version Control], page 120.

Visiting   Visiting a file means loading its contents into a buffer (q.v.)
                  where they can be edited. See Section 14.2 [Visiting], page 108.

Whitespace
                  Whitespace is any run of consecutive formatting characters
                  (space, tab, newline, and backspace).

Widening   Widening is removing any restriction (q.v.) on the current buffer;
                  it is the opposite of narrowing (q.v.). See Section 30.8 [Narrow-
                  ing], page 382.

Window   Emacs divides a frame (q.v.) into one or more windows, each of
                  which can display the contents of one buffer (q.v.) at any time.
                  See Chapter 1 [Screen], page 15, for basic information on how
                  Emacs uses the screen. See Chapter 16 [Windows], page 151, for
                  commands to control the use of windows.

Word Abbrev
                  Synonymous with 'abbrev'.

Word Search
                  Word search is searching for a sequence of words, considering
                  the punctuation between them as insignificant. See Section 12.3
                  [Word Search], page 88.

WYSIWYG
                  WYSIWYG stands for 'What you see is what you get.' Emacs
                  generally provides WYSIWYG editing for files of characters; in
                  Enriched mode (see Section 21.11 [Formatted Text], page 219),
                  it provides WYSIWYG editing for files that include text format-
                  ting information.

Yanking   Yanking means reinserting text previously killed. It can be used
                  to undo a mistaken kill, or for copying or moving text. Some
                  other systems call this "pasting." See Section 9.2 [Yanking],
                  page 67.

Key (Character) Index

!

! (Dired) 336

#

(Dired) 331

$

$ (Dired) 339

%

% C (Dired) 337
% d (Dired) 331
% H (Dired) 337
% l (Dired) 337
% m (Dired) 333
% R (Dired) 337
% S (Dired) 337
% u (Dired) 336

&

& (Dired) 330

*

* ! (Dired) 332
* % (Dired) 333
* * (Dired) 332
* / (Dired) 332
* ? (Dired) 332
* @ (Dired) 332
* c (Dired) 333
* C-n (Dired) 333
* C-p (Dired) 333
* DEL (Dired) 332
* m (Dired) 332
* s (Dired) 332
* t (Dired) 333
* u (Dired) 332

.

. (Calendar mode) 345
. (Dired) 331
. (Rmail) 312

=

= (Dired) 337

~

~ (Dired) 331

"

" (TEX mode) 215

+

+ (Dired) 336

>

> (Dired) 339
> (Rmail) 313

<

< (Dired) 339
< (Rmail) 313

A

a (Calendar mode) 348
A (Dired) 335
a (Rmail) 318

B

B (Dired) 335
b (Rmail) 311
BS (MS-DOS) 463

C

C (Dired) 334
c (Rmail) 321
C-@ 60
C-] 426
C-_ 32
C-_ (Dired) 334
C-\ 179
C-a 30
C-a (Calendar mode) 344
C-b 30
C-b (Calendar mode) 343
C-BREAK (MS-DOS) 463
C-c ' (Picture mode) 298
C-c . (Picture mode) 298
C-c / (Picture mode) 298
C-c : (C mode) 264
C-c ; (Fortran mode) 273
C-c @ (Outline minor mode) 210
C-c ' (Picture mode) 298
C-c { (TeX mode) 215
C-c } (TeX mode) 215
C-c > (GUD) 283
C-c > (Picture mode) 298
C-c ^ (Picture mode) 298
C-c \ (Picture mode) 298
C-c < (GUD) 283
C-c < (Picture mode) 298
C-c C-\ (C mode) 267
C-c C-\ (Shell mode) 371
C-c C-a (C mode) 264
C-c C-a (Mail mode) 305
C-c C-a (Outline mode) 213
C-c C-a (Shell mode) 370
C-c C-b (Outline mode) 212
C-c C-b (Picture mode) 299
C-c C-b (Shell mode) 371
C-c C-b (TeX mode) 217
C-c C-c (Edit Abbrevs) 292
C-c C-c (Edit Tab Stops) 197
C-c C-c (Mail mode) 306
C-c C-c (Outline mode) 213
C-c C-c (Shell mode) 371
C-c C-d (C mode) 266
C-c C-d (GUD) 282
C-c C-d (Outline mode) 213

C-c C-d (Picture mode) 298
C-c C-e (C mode) 267
C-c C-e (LaTeX mode) 216
C-c C-e (Outline mode) 213
C-c C-e (Shell mode) 371
C-c C-f (GUD) 283
C-c C-f (Outline mode) 212
C-c C-f (Picture mode) 299
C-c C-f (Shell mode) 371
C-c C-f (TeX mode) 218
C-c C-f C-b (Mail mode) 307
C-c C-f C-c (Mail mode) 307
C-c C-f C-f (Mail mode) 307
C-c C-f C-s (Mail mode) 307
C-c C-f C-t (Mail mode) 307
C-c C-i (GUD) 282
C-c C-i (Mail mode) 309
C-c C-i (Outline mode) 213
C-c C-k (Outline mode) 213
C-c C-k (Picture mode) 300
C-c C-k (TeX mode) 217
C-c C-l (Calendar mode) 346
C-c C-l (GUD) 282
C-c C-l (Outline mode) 213
C-c C-l (Shell mode) 371
C-c C-l (TeX mode) 217
C-c C-n (C mode) 263
C-c C-n (Fortran mode) 268
C-c C-n (GUD) 282
C-c C-n (Outline mode) 212
C-c C-n (Shell mode) 374
C-c C-o (C mode) 238
C-c C-o (LaTeX mode) 216
C-c C-o (Outline mode) 213
C-c C-o (Shell mode) 371
C-c C-p (C mode) 263
C-c C-p (Fortran mode) 268
C-c C-p (Outline mode) 212
C-c C-p (Shell mode) 374
C-c C-p (TeX mode) 217
C-c C-q (C mode) 234
C-c C-q (Mail mode) 308
C-c C-q (Outline mode) 213
C-c C-q (TeX mode) 217
C-c C-r (Fortran mode) 274
C-c C-r (GUD) 282

C-c C-r (Mail mode) 308
C-c C-r (Shell mode) 371
C-c C-r (TEX mode) 217
C-c C-s (C mode) 267
C-c C-s (GUD) 282
C-c C-s (Mail mode) 306
C-c C-s (Outline mode) 213
C-c C-t (C mode) 266
C-c C-t (GUD) 282
C-c C-t (Mail mode) 308
C-c C-t (Outline mode) 213
C-c C-u (C mode) 263
C-c C-u (Outline mode) 212
C-c C-u (Shell mode) 371
C-c C-v (TEX mode) 217
C-c C-w (Fortran mode) 274
C-c C-w (Mail mode) 308
C-c C-w (Picture mode) 300
C-c C-w (Shell mode) 371
C-c C-x (Picture mode) 300
C-c C-y (Mail mode) 307
C-c C-y (Picture mode) 300
C-c C-z (Shell mode) 371
C-c RET (Shell mode) 374
C-c TAB (Picture mode) 299
C-c TAB (TEX mode) 218
C-d 65
C-d (Rmail) 314
C-d (Shell mode) 370
C-e 30
C-e (Calendar mode) 344
C-f 30
C-f (Calendar mode) 343
C-g 425
C-g (MS-DOS) 463
C-h 51
C-h a 54
C-h b 57
C-h c 53
C-h C 180
C-h C-\ 179
C-h C-c 57
C-h C-d 57
C-h C-f 57
C-h C-h 51
C-h C-i 248

C-h C-k 57
C-h C-p 57
C-h C-w 57
C-h f 53
C-h F 57
C-h h 175
C-h i 57
C-h I 179
C-h k 53
C-h l 57
C-h L 177
C-h m 57
C-h n 57
C-h p 55
C-h s 419
C-h t 29
C-h w 53
C-j 232
C-j (and major modes) 191
C-j (Fortran mode) 269
C-j (MS-DOS) 463
C-j (TEX mode) 215
C-k 66
C-k (Gnus) 366
C-l 79
C-M-% 97
C-M-. 256
C-M-/ 293
C-M-@ 230
C-M-\ 196
C-M-a 230
C-M-a (Fortran mode) 268
C-M-b 229
C-M-c 385
C-M-d 229
C-M-d (Dired) 339
C-M-DEL 229
C-M-e 230
C-M-e (Fortran mode) 268
C-M-f 229
C-M-h 230
C-M-h (C mode) 266
C-M-h (Fortran mode) 268
C-M-j 245
C-M-j (Fortran mode) 269
C-M-k 229

C-M-l 80
C-M-l (Rmail) 322
C-M-l (Shell mode) 371
C-M-n 229
C-M-n (Dired) 338
C-M-n (Rmail) 318
C-M-o 196
C-M-p 229
C-M-p (Dired) 338
C-M-p (Rmail) 318
C-M-q 232
C-M-q (C mode) 234
C-M-q (Fortran mode) 269
C-M-r 89
C-M-r (Rmail) 322
C-M-s 89
C-M-t 102, 230
C-M-t (Rmail) 322
C-M-u 229
C-M-u (Dired) 338
C-M-v 153
C-M-w 68
C-M-x (Emacs-Lisp mode) 286
C-M-x (Lisp mode) 288
C-Mouse-2 (scroll bar) 152
C-Mouse-3 160
C-n 30
C-n (Calendar mode) 343
C-n (Dired) 329
C-n (Gnus Group mode) 367
C-n (Gnus Summary mode) 367
C-o 34
C-o (Dired) 331
C-o (Rmail) 317
C-p 30
C-p (Calendar mode) 343
C-p (Dired) 329
C-p (Gnus Group mode) 367
C-p (Gnus Summary mode) 367
C-q 29
C-r 87
C-s 85
C-SPC 59
C-t 102
C-u 38
C-u - C-x ; 245

C-u C-@ 63
C-u C-SPC 63
C-u C-x u 32
C-u TAB 232
C-v 79
C-v (Calendar mode) 345
C-w 67
C-x # 377
C-x $ 81
C-x (............................ 405
C-x) 405
C-x - 156
C-x 206
C-x ; 246
C-x = ... 36
C-x [............................ 203
C-x [(Calendar mode) 344
C-x] 203
C-x] (Calendar mode) 344
C-x ' 279
C-x } 155
C-x + ... 156
C-x > 81
C-x > (Calendar mode) 345
C-x ^ 155
C-x < 81
C-x < (Calendar mode) 345
C-x 0 155
C-x 1 155
C-x 2 152
C-x 3 152
C-x 4 153
C-x 4 255
C-x 4 0 155
C-x 4 a 249
C-x 4 b 143
C-x 4 d 329
C-x 4 f 110
C-x 4 m 301
C-x 5 161
C-x 5 255
C-x 5 0 172
C-x 5 2 161
C-x 5 b 143
C-x 5 d 329
C-x 5 f 110

C-x 5 m 301
C-x 5 o 172
C-x 5 r 162
C-x 6 1 384
C-x 6 2 383
C-x 6 b 383
C-x 6 d 384
C-x 6 RET 384
C-x 6 s 383
C-x 8 189
C-x a g 290
C-x a i g 290
C-x a i l 290
C-x a l 290
C-x b 143
C-x C-a (GUD) 282
C-x C-b 144
C-x C-c 26
C-x C-d 138
C-x C-e 286
C-x C-f 109
C-x C-k 406
C-x C-l 209
C-x C-n 31
C-x C-o 34
C-x C-p 203
C-x C-q 145
C-x C-q (Version Control) 122
C-x C-r 110
C-x C-s 111
C-x C-SPC 64
C-x C-t 102
C-x C-u 209
C-x C-v 110
C-x C-w 112
C-x C-x 60
C-x C-z 287
C-x d 329
C-x DEL 201
C-x e 405
C-x ESC ESC 48
C-x f 205
C-x h 62
C-x k 146
C-x l 203
C-x m 301

C-x n d 382
C-x n d (Fortran mode) 275
C-x n n 382
C-x n p 382
C-x n w 382
C-x o 153
C-x q 407
C-x r + ... 77
C-x r b 77
C-x r d 72
C-x r f 76
C-x r i 76
C-x r j 75
C-x r k 72
C-x r l 78
C-x r m 77
C-x r n 76
C-x r o 72
C-x r r 76
C-x r s 76
C-x r SPC 75
C-x r t 72
C-x r w 76
C-x r y 72
C-x RET 175
C-x RET c 184
C-x RET C-\ 179
C-x RET f 184
C-x RET k 185
C-x RET p 185
C-x RET t 185
C-x RET x 185
C-x RET X 185
C-x s 111
C-x SPC 282
C-x TAB 196
C-x TAB (Enriched mode) 223
C-x u 32
C-x v = ... 125
C-x v ~ 124
C-x v a 133
C-x v c 126
C-x v d 127
C-x v g 125
C-x v h 135
C-x v i 125

`C-x v l` 126
`C-x v m` 130
`C-x v r` 132
`C-x v s` 131
`C-x v u` 126
`C-x v v` 122
`C-x z` 39
`C-y` 68
`C-z` 26
`C-z` (X windows) 172

D

`d` (Calendar mode) 356
`d` (Dired) 330
`D` (Dired) 334
`d` (Rmail) 314
`DEL` 65
`DEL` (and major modes) 191
`DEL` (Dired) 330
`DEL` (Gnus) 367
`DEL` (MS-DOS) 463
`DEL` (programming modes) 228
`DEL` (Rmail) 312
`DELETE` 157
`DOWN` 30

E

`e` (Rmail) 325
`ESC a` 263
`ESC e` 264
`ESC ESC ESC` 426

F

`f` (Dired) 331
`f` (Rmail) 321
`F1` 51
`F10` 19
`F2 1` 384
`F2 2` 383
`F2 b` 383
`F2 d` 384
`F2 RET` 384
`F2 s` 383

G

`g` (Dired) 340
`G` (Dired) 335
`g` (Rmail) 316
`g` *char* (Calendar mode) 353
`g d` (Calendar mode) 345
`g m` (Calendar mode) 354

H

`h` (Calendar mode) 348
`H` (Dired) 334
`h` (Rmail) 322
`Help` 51

I

`i` (Dired) 338
`i` (Rmail) 315
`i a` (Calendar mode) 360
`i b` (Calendar mode) 360
`i c` (Calendar mode) 360
`i d` (Calendar mode) 359
`i m` (Calendar mode) 359
`i w` (Calendar mode) 359
`i y` (Calendar mode) 359

J

`j` (Rmail) 313

K

`k` (Dired) 340
`k` (Rmail) 318

L

`l` (Dired) 340
`L` (Dired) 335
`l` (Gnus Group mode) 366
`L` (Gnus Group mode) 366
`l` (Rmail) 322
`LEFT` 30

M

m (Calendar mode) 356
M (Calendar mode) 350
m (Dired) 332
M (Dired) 335
m (Rmail) 321
M-! 368
M-$ 103
M-$ (Dired) 339
M-% 97
M-' 291
M-(. . . . 247
M-) 247
M-* 256
M-, ... 256
M-- 37
M-- M-c 102
M-- M-l 102
M-- M-u 102
M-. 255
M-/ 293
M-: 286
M-; 244
M-= 36
M-= (Calendar mode) 346
M-= (Dired) 337
M-? (Nroff mode) 219
M-? (Shell mode) 370
M-@ 200
M-' 19
M-{ 201
M-{ (Calendar mode) 344
M-| 368
M-} 201
M-} (Calendar mode) 344
M-~ 112
M-> 30
M-> (Calendar mode) 344
M-^ 196
M-^ (Fortran mode) 269
M-\ 66
M-< 30
M-< (Calendar mode) 344
M-1 37
M-a 201
M-a (Calendar mode) 344

M-b 200
M-c 208
M-d 200
M-DEL 200
M-Drag-Mouse-1 159
M-e 201
M-e (Calendar mode) 344
M-f 200
M-g b (Enriched mode) 222
M-g d (Enriched mode) 222
M-g i (Enriched mode) 222
M-g l (Enriched mode) 222
M-g M-g 168
M-g o (Enriched mode) 222
M-g u (Enriched mode) 222
M-h 202
M-i 196
M-j c (Enriched mode) 225
M-j f (Enriched mode) 225
M-j l (Enriched mode) 225
M-j r (Enriched mode) 225
M-j u (Enriched mode) 225
M-k 201
M-l 208
M-m 195
M-m (Rmail) 320
M-Mouse-1 159
M-Mouse-2 160
M-Mouse-3 160
M-n (minibuffer history) 46
M-n (Nroff mode) 219
M-n (Rmail) 313
M-n (Shell mode) 373
M-p (minibuffer history) 46
M-p (Nroff mode) 219
M-p (Rmail) 313
M-p (Shell mode) 373
M-q 205
M-q (C mode) 266
M-r 30
M-r (minibuffer history) 47
M-r (Shell mode) 373
M-S (Enriched mode) 225
M-s (Gnus Summary mode) 367
M-s (minibuffer history) 47
M-s (Rmail) 313

M-s (Shell mode) 373
M-s (Text mode).................... 205
M-SPC................................ 66
M-t........................... 102, 200
M-TAB............................... 247
M-TAB (customization buffer)........ 397
M-TAB (Mail mode)................... 307
M-TAB (Picture mode) 299
M-TAB (Text mode)................. 209
M-u............................... 208
M-v 79
M-v (Calendar mode)............... 345
M-w................................ 68
M-x............................... 49
M-y............................... 69
M-z............................... 67
Mouse-1........................... 157
Mouse-2........................... 157
Mouse-2 (selection) 160
Mouse-3........................... 157

N

n (Gnus) 367
n (Rmail) 313
NEXT 79

O

o (Calendar mode)................. 345
o (Dired)......................... 331
O (Dired)......................... 335
o (Rmail) 317

P

p (Calendar mode)................. 352
P (Dired)......................... 335
p (Gnus) 367
p (Rmail) 313
p d (Calendar mode) 346
PRIOR............................. 79

Q

q (Calendar mode)................. 346
Q (Dired)......................... 335
q (Gnus Group mode)............... 366
q (Rmail summary) 324
Q (Rmail summary) 324
q (Rmail) 311

R

R (Dired)......................... 334
r (Rmail) 320
RET 29
RET (Dired) 331
RET (Occur mode) 98
RET (Shell mode) 370
RIGHT 30

S

s (Calendar mode)................. 356
S (Calendar mode)................. 349
s (Dired)......................... 340
S (Dired)......................... 334
s (Gnus Summary mode)............. 367
s (Rmail) 311
S-Mouse-1 165
S-TAB (customization buffer)........ 397
S-TAB (Help mode) 56
SPC 44
SPC (Calendar mode)............... 346
SPC (Dired) 329
SPC (Gnus)........................ 366
SPC (Rmail) 312

T

t (Calendar mode)................. 346
t (Rmail) 325
TAB 195
TAB (and major modes)............. 191
TAB (completion).................. 43
TAB (customization buffer)........ 397
TAB (GUD)......................... 283
TAB (Help mode) 56

TAB (programming modes) 231
TAB (Shell mode) 370
TAB (Text mode) 209

U

u (Calendar mode) 348
u (Dired deletion) 330
u (Dired) 332
u (Gnus Group mode) 366
u (Rmail) 314
UP 30

V

v (Dired) 332

W

w (Rmail) 317

X

x (Calendar mode) 348
x (Dired) 330
x (Rmail) 314

Z

z (Dired) 335

Command and Function Index

2

2C-associate-buffer............... 383
2C-dissociate.................... 384
2C-merge......................... 384
2C-newline....................... 384
2C-split......................... 383
2C-two-columns................... 383

A

abbrev-mode...................... 289
abbrev-prefix-mark............... 291
abort-recursive-edit............. 426
add-change-log-entry-other-window
.... 249
add-global-abbrev................ 290
add-mode-abbrev.................. 290
add-name-to-file................. 140
add-untranslated-filesystem...... 467
american-calendar................ 358
append-next-kill................. 68
append-to-buffer................. 70
append-to-file................... 70
apply-macro-to-region-lines...... 406
appt-add......................... 362
appt-delete...................... 362
appt-make-list................... 361
apropos.......................... 54
apropos-command.................. 54
apropos-documentation............ 54
apropos-value.................... 55
apropos-variable................. 54
ask-user-about-lock.............. 116
auto-compression-mode............ 140
auto-fill-mode................... 204
auto-lower-mode.................. 164
auto-raise-mode.................. 164
auto-save-mode................... 118

B

back-to-indentation.............. 195
backward-char.................... 30
backward-delete-char-untabify.... 228
backward-kill-sentence........... 201
backward-kill-sexp............... 229

backward-kill-word............... 200
backward-list.................... 229
backward-page.................... 203
backward-paragraph............... 201
backward-sentence................ 201
backward-sexp.................... 229
backward-text-line............... 219
backward-up-list................. 229
backward-word.................... 200
balance-windows.................. 156
beginning-of-buffer.............. 30
beginning-of-defun............... 230
beginning-of-fortran-subprogram.. 268
beginning-of-line................ 30
binary-overwrite-mode............ 392
blackbox......................... 388
bookmark-delete.................. 78
bookmark-insert.................. 78
bookmark-insert-location......... 78
bookmark-jump.................... 77
bookmark-load.................... 78
bookmark-save.................... 77
bookmark-set..................... 77
bookmark-write................... 78
buffer-menu...................... 147

C

c-add-style...................... 243
c-backslash-region............... 267
c-backward-conditional........... 263
c-backward-into-nomenclature..... 264
c-beginning-of-statement......... 263
c-end-of-statement............... 264
c-fill-paragraph................. 266
c-forward-conditional............ 263
c-forward-into-nomenclature...... 264
c-indent-command................. 234
c-indent-defun................... 234
c-indent-exp..................... 234
c-indent-line.................... 231
c-macro-expand................... 267
c-mark-function.............. 230, 266
c-scope-operator................. 264
c-set-offset..................... 238
c-set-style...................... 242

c-show-syntactic-information 267
c-toggle-auto-hungry-state 266
c-toggle-auto-state 264
c-toggle-hungry-state 266
c-up-conditional 263
calendar 343
calendar-backward-day 343
calendar-backward-month 344
calendar-backward-week 343
calendar-beginning-of-month 344
calendar-beginning-of-week 344
calendar-beginning-of-year 344
calendar-count-days-region 346
calendar-cursor-holidays 348
calendar-end-of-month 344
calendar-end-of-week 344
calendar-end-of-year 344
calendar-forward-day 343
calendar-forward-month 344
calendar-forward-week 343
calendar-forward-year 344
calendar-goto-astro-day-number ... 353
calendar-goto-chinese-date 353
calendar-goto-coptic-date 353
calendar-goto-date 345
calendar-goto-ethiopic-date 353
calendar-goto-french-date 353
calendar-goto-hebrew-date 353
calendar-goto-islamic-date 353
calendar-goto-iso-date 353
calendar-goto-julian-date 353
calendar-goto-mayan-long-count-date
    354
calendar-goto-persian-date 353
calendar-goto-today 345
calendar-next-calendar-round-date
    355
calendar-next-haab-date 354
calendar-next-tzolkin-date 354
calendar-other-month 345
calendar-phases-of-moon 350
calendar-previous-haab-date 354
calendar-previous-tzolkin-date ... 354
calendar-print-astro-day-number .. 352
calendar-print-chinese-date 352
calendar-print-coptic-date 352

calendar-print-day-of-year 346
calendar-print-ethiopic-date 352
calendar-print french-date 352
calendar-print-hebrew-date 352
calendar-print-islamic-date 352
calendar-print-iso-date 352
calendar-print-julian-date 352
calendar-print-mayan-date 352
calendar-print-persian-date 352
calendar-sunrise-sunset 349
calendar-unmark 348
call-last-kbd-macro 405
capitalize-word 208
cd 107
center-line 205
change-log-mode 250
choose-completion 45
clean-buffer-list 146
clear-rectangle 72
codepage-setup 472
column-number-mode 82
comint-bol 370
comint-continue-subjob 372
comint-copy-old-input 374
comint-delchar-or-maybe-eof 370
comint-dynamic-complete 370
comint-dynamic-complete-variable
    375
comint-dynamic-list-filename 370
comint-dynamic-list-input-ring ... 371
comint-get-next-from-history 373
comint-interrupt-subjob 371
comint-kill-input 371
comint-kill-output 371
comint-magic-space 374
comint-next-input 373
comint-next-matching-input 373
comint-next-prompt 374
comint-previous-input 373
comint-previous-matching-input ... 373
comint-previous-prompt 374
comint-quit-subjob 371
comint-run 372
comint-send-input 370
comint-show-maximum-output 371
comint-show-output 371

comint-stop-subjob................ 371
comint-strip-ctrl-m............... 372
comint-truncate-buffer 372
comment-region 245
compare-windows 139
compile........................... 277
compile (MS-DOS) 472
compile-goto-error................ 278
complete-symbol 247
compose-mail 301
compose-mail-other-frame 301
compose-mail-other-window 301
copy-file 140
copy-rectangle-to-register 76
copy-to-buffer 70
copy-to-register 76
count-lines-page.................. 203
count-lines-region................ 36
count-matches 98
count-text-lines.................. 219
cpp-highlight-buffer.............. 267
create-fontset-from-fontset-spec

.... 188
customize 394
customize-apropos................. 400
customize-browse.................. 396
customize-changed-options 400
customize-customized.............. 400
customize-face 400
customize-group................... 400
customize-option.................. 400
customize-saved................... 400

D

dabbrev-completion................ 293
dabbrev-expand.................... 293
dbx............................... 280
debug_print 435
default-value..................... 402
define-abbrevs 293
define-key 413
define-mail-abbrev................ 305
define-mail-alias................. 304
delete-backward-char.............. 65
delete-blank-lines................ 34

delete-char 65
delete-file 140
delete-frame 172
delete-horizontal-space 66
delete-indontation 196
delete-matching-lines............. 98
delete-non-matching-lines 98
delete-other-windows.............. 155
delete-rectangle 72
delete-whitespace-rectangle 72
delete-window 155
describe-bindings................. 57
describe-coding-system 180
describe-copying.................. 57
describe-distribution............. 57
describe-function................. 53
describe-input-method............. 179
describe-key 53
describe-key-briefly.............. 53
describe-language-environment 177
describe-mode 57
describe-no-warranty.............. 57
describe-project.................. 57
describe-syntax................... 419
desktop-save 385
diary............................. 356
diary-anniversary................. 360
diary-block 360
diary-cyclic 360
diary-float 361
diary-mail-entries................ 357
diff.............................. 139
diff-backup 139
digit-argument 37
dired............................. 329
dired-backup-diff................. 337
dired-change-marks................ 333
dired-clean-directory............. 331
dired-create-directory 336
dired-diff 337
dired-display-file................ 331
dired-do-byte-compile............. 335
dired-do-chgrp 335
dired-do-chmod 335
dired-do-chown 335
dired-do-compress................. 335

dired-do-copy 334
dired-do-copy-regexp 337
dired-do-delete 334
dired-do-hardlink 334
dired-do-hardlink-regexp 337
dired-do-kill-lines 340
dired-do-load 335
dired-do-print 335
dired-do-query-replace 335
dired-do-redisplay 340
dired-do-rename 334
dired-do-rename-regexp 337
dired-do-search 335
dired-do-shell-command 336
dired-do-symlink 334
dired-do-symlink-regexp 337
dired-do-toggle 333
dired-downcase 337
dired-expunge 330
dired-find-file 331
dired-find-file-other-window 331
dired-flag-auto-save-files 331
dired-flag-backup-files 331
dired-flag-file-deletion 330
dired-flag-files-regexp 331
dired-flag-garbage-files 330
dired-hide-all 339
dired-hide-subdir 339
dired-mark 332
dired-mark-directories 332
dired-mark-executables 332
dired-mark-files-containing-regexp
. . . . 333
dired-mark-files-regexp 333
dired-mark-subdir-files 332
dired-mark-symlinks 332
dired-maybe-insert-subdir 338
dired-mouse-find-file-other-window
. . . . 332
dired-next-dirline 339
dired-next-marked-file 333
dired-next-subdir 338
dired-other-frame 329
dired-other-window 329
dired-prev-dirline 339
dired-prev-marked-file 333

dired-prev-subdir 338
dired-sort-toggle-or-edit 340
dired-tree-down 339
dired-tree-up 338
dired-undo 334
dired-unmark 332
dired-unmark-all-files 332
dired-unmark-all-files-no-query . . 332
dired-unmark-backward 332
dired-upcase 336
dired-view-file 332
dirs 369
dirtrack-mode 370
disable-command 418
display-time 82
dissociated-press 387
do-auto-save 119
doctor 430
down-list 229
downcase-region 209
downcase-word 208
dunnet 388

E

edit-abbrevs 292
edit-kbd-macro 406
edit-picture 297
edit-tab-stops 197
edit-tab-stops-note-changes 197
edt-emulation-off 386
edt-emulation-on 386
eldoc-mode 248
electric-nroff-mode 219
emacs-lisp-mode 286
emacs-version 431
emerge-auto-advance-mode 259
emerge-buffers 258
emerge-buffers-with-ancestor 258
emerge-files 258
emerge-files-with-ancestor 258
emerge-skip-prefers-mode 259
enable-command 418
enable-flow-control 428
enable-flow-control-on 428
enable-local-eval 404

enable-local-variables 404
end-kbd-macro 405
end-of-buffer 30
end-of-defun 230
end-of-fortran-subprogram 268
end-of-line 30
enlarge-window 155
enlarge-window-horizontally 155
enriched-mode 220
european-calendar 358
eval-current-buffer 287
eval-defun 286
eval-expression 286
eval-last-sexp 286
eval-region 287
exchange-point-and-mark 60
execute-extended-command 49
exit-calendar 346
exit-recursive-edit 385
expand-abbrev 291
expand-mail-aliases 305
expand-region-abbrevs 291

F

facemenu-remove-all 221
facemenu-remove-props 221
facemenu-set-background 223
facemenu-set-bold 222
facemenu-set-bold-italic 222
facemenu-set-default 222
facemenu-set-face 222
facemenu-set-foreground 223
facemenu-set-italic 222
facemenu-set-underline 222
fast-lock-mode 170
fill-individual-paragraphs 207
fill-nonuniform-paragraphs 207
fill-paragraph 205
fill-region 205
fill-region-as-paragraph 205
find-alternate-file 110
find-dired 341
find-file 109
find-file-binary 467
find-file-literally 110

find-file-other-frame 110
find-file-other-window 110
find-file-read-only 110
find-file-read-only-other-frame .. 162
find-file-text 467
find-grep-dired 340
find-name-dired 340
find-tag 255
find-tag-other-frame 255
find-tag-other-window 255
find-tag-regexp 256
finder-by-keyword 55
flush-lines 98
flyspell-mode 103
font-lock-add-keywords 169
font-lock-fontify-block 168
font-lock-mode 168
format-find-file 226
fortran-auto-fill-mode 273
fortran-column-ruler 274
fortran-comment-region 273
fortran-indent-line 269
fortran-indent-new-line 269
fortran-indent-subprogram 269
fortran-join-line 269
fortran-mode 268
fortran-narrow-to-subprogram 275
fortran-next-statement 268
fortran-previous-statement 268
fortran-split-line 269
fortran-window-create 274
forward-char 30
forward-list 229
forward-page 203
forward-paragraph 201
forward-sentence 201
forward-sexp 229
forward-text-line 219
forward-word 200
frame-configuration-to-register ... 76

G

gdb 280
global-font-lock-mode 168
global-set-key 411
global-unset-key 411
gnus 365
gnus-group-exit 366
gnus-group-kill-group 366
gnus-group-list-all-groups 366
gnus-group-list-groups 366
gnus-group-next-group 367
gnus-group-next-unread-group 367
gnus-group-prev-group 367
gnus-group-prev-unread-group 367
gnus-group-read-group 366
gnus-group-unsubscribe-current-group
.... 366
gnus-summary-isearch-article 367
gnus-summary-next-subject 367
gnus-summary-next-unread-article
.... 367
gnus-summary-prev-page 367
gnus-summary-prev-subject 367
gnus-summary-prev-unread-article
.... 367
gnus-summary-search-article-forward
.... 367
gomoku 388
goto-char 30
goto-line 30
grep 278
grep (MS-DOS) 472
grep-find 278
gud-cont 282
gud-def 283
gud-down 283
gud-finish 283
gud-gdb-complete-command 283
gud-next 282
gud-refresh 282
gud-remove 282
gud-step 282
gud-stepi 282
gud-tbreak 282
gud-up 283

H

hanoi 388
help-command 51
help-for-help 51
help-next-ref 56
help-previous-ref 56
help-with-tutorial 29
hide-body 213
hide-entry 213
hide-leaves 213
hide-other 213
hide-sublevels 213
hide-subtree 213
highlight-changes-mode 172
holidays 348
hscroll-mode 81

I

iconify-or-deiconify-frame 172
ielm 287
increase-left-margin 223
increment-register 77
indent-for-comment 244
indent-new-comment-line 245
indent-region 196
indent-relative 196
indent-rigidly 196
indent-sexp 232
info 57
Info-goto-emacs-command-node 57
Info-goto-emacs-key-command-node .. 57
info-lookup-file 248
info-lookup-symbol 248
insert-abbrevs 293
insert-anniversary-diary-entry ... 360
insert-block-diary-entry 360
insert-cyclic-diary-entry 360
insert-diary-entry 359
insert-file 140
insert-kbd-macro 407
insert-monthly-diary-entry 359
insert-parentheses 247
insert-register 76
insert-weekly-diary-entry 359
insert-yearly-diary-entry 359

inverse-add-global-abbrev 290

inverse-add-mode-abbrev 290

isearch-backward 87

isearch-backward-regexp 89

isearch-forward 85

isearch-forward-regexp 89

ispell-buffer 103

ispell-complete-word 105

ispell-kill-ispell 105

ispell-message 308

ispell-region 103

ispell-word 103

J

jdb 281

jump-to-register 75

just-one-space 66

K

kbd-macro-query 407

keep-lines 98

keyboard-escape-quit 426

keyboard-translate 418

kill-all-abbrevs 290

kill-buffer 146

kill-buffer-and-window 155

kill-comment 245

kill-compilation 278

kill-line 66

kill-local-variable 402

kill-rectangle 72

kill-region 67

kill-ring-save 68

kill-sentence 201

kill-sexp 229

kill-some-buffers 146

kill-word 200

L

latex-mode 214

lazy-lock-mode 170

line-number-mode 82

lisp-complete-symbol 247

lisp-eval-defun 288

lisp-indent-line 231

lisp-interaction-mode 287

lisp-mode 288

list-abbrevs 292

list-bookmarks 77

list-buffers 144

list-calendar-holidays 348

list-coding-systems 180

list-command-history 47

list-directory 138

list-faces-display 167

list-holidays 348

list-input-methods 179

list-matching-lines 98

list-tags 257

list-text-properties-at 221

list-yahrzeit-dates 353

load 285

load-file 285

load-library 285

local-set-key 411

local-unset-key 411

lpr-buffer 378

lpr-region 378

M

mail-attach-file 309

mail-bcc 307

mail-cc 307

mail-complete 307

mail-fcc 307

mail-fill-yanked-message 308

mail-interactive-insert-alias 305

mail-send 306

mail-send-and-exit 306

mail-signature 308

mail-subject 307

mail-text 308

mail-to 307

mail-yank-original 307

mail-yank-region 308

make-frame-command 161

make-frame-on-display 163

make-indirect-buffer 149

make-local-variable 401
make-symbolic-link 140
make-variable-buffer-local 401
Man-fontify-manpage 249
manual-entry 248
mark-calendar-holidays 348
mark-defun 230
mark-diary-entries 356
mark-fortran-subprogram 268
mark-page 203
mark-paragraph 202
mark-sexp 230
mark-whole-buffer 62
mark-word 200
minibuffer-complete 43
minibuffer-complete-word 44
mode25 465
mode4350 465
modify-face 399
mouse-choose-completion 44
mouse-save-then-click 157
mouse-secondary-save-then-kill . . . 160
mouse-set-point 157
mouse-set-region 157
mouse-set-secondary 159
mouse-start-secondary 159
mouse-yank-at-click 157
mouse-yank-secondary 160
move-past-close-and-reindent 247
move-to-window-line 30
mpuz 388

N

name-last-kbd-macro 407
narrow-to-defun 382
narrow-to-page 382
narrow-to-region 382
negative-argument 37
newline 30
newline-and-indent 232
next-completion 45
next-error 279
next-history-element 46
next-line 30
next-matching-history-element 47

normal-mode 193
not-modified 112
nroff-mode 219
number-to-register 76

O

occur 98
open-dribble-file 433
open-line 34
open-rectangle 72
open-termscript 433
other-frame 172
other-window 153
outline-backward-same-level 212
outline-forward-same-level 212
outline-minor-mode 210
outline-mode 210
outline-next-visible-heading 212
outline-previous-visible-heading
 212
outline-up-heading 212
overwrite-mode 392

P

paragraph-indent-text-mode 209
pdb 281
perldb 281
phases-of-moon 350
picture-backward-clear-column 298
picture-backward-column 297
picture-clear-column 298
picture-clear-line 298
picture-clear-rectangle 300
picture-clear-rectangle-to-register
 300
picture-forward-column 297
picture-motion 299
picture-motion-reverse 299
picture-move-down 297
picture-move-up 297
picture-movement-down 298
picture-movement-left 298
picture-movement-ne 298
picture-movement-nw 298

picture-movement-right 298
picture-movement-se.............. 298
picture-movement-sw.............. 298
picture-movement-up.............. 298
picture-newline.................. 298
picture-open-line................ 298
picture-set-tab-stops............ 299
picture-tab 299
picture-tab-search............... 299
picture-yank-rectangle 300
picture-yank-rectangle-from-register
.... 300
plain-tex-mode................... 214
point-to-register................ 75
pop-global-mark.................. 64
pop-tag-mark 256
prefer-coding-system............. 182
prepend-to-buffer................ 70
previous-completion.............. 45
previous-history-element 46
previous-line 30
previous-matching-history-element
.... 47
print-buffer 378
print-buffer (MS-DOS)............ 468
print-region 378
print-region (MS-DOS)............ 468
ps-print-buffer 379
ps-print-buffer (MS-DOS) 469
ps-print-buffer-with-faces 379
ps-print-region 379
ps-print-region-with-faces 379
ps-spool-buffer 379
ps-spool-buffer (MS-DOS) 469
ps-spool-buffer-with-faces 379
ps-spool-region 379
ps-spool-region-with-faces 379
pwd.............................. 107

Q

quail-set-keyboard-layout 179
query-replace 97
query-replace-regexp............. 97
quietly-read-abbrev-file 293
quoted-insert 29

R

re-search-backward................ 89
re-search-forward................. 89
read-abbrev-file.................. 293
recenter.......................... 79
recover-file 119
recover-session 119
redraw-calendar 346
remove-untranslated-filesystem... 468
rename-buffer 145
rename-file 140
repeat............................ 39
repeat-complex-command............ 48
replace-regexp 95
replace-string 95
report-emacs-bug.................. 432
reposition-window................. 80
resize-minibuffer-mode............ 42
revert-buffer 117
revert-buffer (Dired)............. 340
rlogin............................ 376
rlogin-directory-tracking-mode... 376
rmail............................. 311
rmail-add-label 318
rmail-beginning-of-message 312
rmail-bury 311
rmail-continue 321
rmail-delete-backward............. 314
rmail-delete-forward.............. 314
rmail-edit-current-message 325
rmail-expunge 314
rmail-first-message.............. 313
rmail-forward 321
rmail-get-new-mail................ 316
rmail-input 315
rmail-kill-label.................. 318
rmail-last-message................ 313
rmail-mail 321
rmail-mode 311
rmail-next-labeled-message 318
rmail-next-message................ 313
rmail-next-undeleted-message 313
rmail-output 317
rmail-output-body-to-file 317
rmail-output-to-rmail-file 317

rmail-previous-labeled-message ... 318
rmail-previous-message 313
rmail-previous-undeleted-message
    313
rmail-quit 311
rmail-reply 320
rmail-resend 321
rmail-retry-failure 320
rmail-save 311
rmail-search 313
rmail-show-message 313
rmail-summary 322
rmail-summary-by-labels 322
rmail-summary-by-recipients 322
rmail-summary-by-topic 322
rmail-summary-quit 324
rmail-summary-wipe 324
rmail-toggle-header 325
rmail-undelete-previous-message .. 314
rot13-other-window 326
run-lisp 287

S

save-buffer 111
save-buffers-kill-emacs 26
save-some-buffers 111
scroll-bar-mode 166
scroll-calendar-left 345
scroll-calendar-left-three-months
    345
scroll-calendar-right 345
scroll-calendar-right-three-months
    345
scroll-down 79
scroll-left 81
scroll-other-window 153
scroll-right 81
scroll-up 79
sdb 280
search-backward 88
search-forward 88
select-frame-by-name 172
self-insert 30
send-invisible 371
server-edit 377

set-background-color 164
set-border-color 164
set-buffer-file-coding-system 184
set-buffer-process-coding-system
    185
set-comment-column 246
set-cursor-color 164
set-fill-column 205
set-fill-prefix 206
set-foreground-color 164
set-frame-font 165
set-frame-name 172
set-goal-column 31
set-input-method 179
set-justification-center 225
set-justification-full 225
set-justification-left 225
set-justification-none 225
set-justification-right 225
set-keyboard-coding-system 185
set-language-environment 176
set-mark-command 59
set-mouse-color 164
set-next-selection-coding-system
    185
set-rmail-inbox-list 316
set-selection-coding-system 185
set-selective-display 81
set-terminal-coding-system 185
set-variable 394
set-visited-file-name 112
setq-default 402
shell 368
shell-backward-command 371
shell-command 368
shell-command-on-region 368
shell-forward-command 371
shell-pushd-dextract 375
shell-pushd-dunique 375
shell-pushd-tohome 375
show-all 213
show-all-diary-entries 356
show-branches 213
show-children 213
show-entry 213
show-paren-mode 243

show-subtree 213
shrink-window-if-larger-than-buffer
        156
slitex-mode 214
sort-columns 381
sort-fields 380
sort-lines 380
sort-numeric-fields 380
sort-pages 380
sort-paragraphs 380
split-line 196
split-window-horizontally 152
split-window-vertically 152
spook 309
standard-display-8bit 189
start-kbd-macro 405
string-rectangle 72
substitute-in-file-name 108
substitute-key-definition 413
sunrise-sunset 349
suspend-emacs 26
switch-to-buffer 143
switch-to-buffer-other-frame 143
switch-to-buffer-other-window 143
switch-to-completions 44

T

tab-to-tab-stop 196
tabify 197
tags-apropos 257
tags-loop-continue 256
tags-query-replace 256
tags-search 256
telnet 376
tex-bibtex-file 218
tex-buffer 217
tex-close-latex-block 216
tex-file 218
tex-insert-braces 215
tex-insert-quote 215
tex-kill-job 217
tex-latex-block 216
tex-mode 214
tex-print 217
tex-recenter-output-buffer 217

tex-region 217
tex-show-print-queue 217
tex-terminate-paragraph 215
tex-validate-region 215
tex-view 217
text-mode 209
tmm-menubar 19
toggle-input-method 179
toggle-scroll-bar 166
top-level 426
transient-mark-mode 60
transpose-chars 102
transpose-lines 102
transpose-sexps 102, 230
transpose-words 102, 200
turn-on-font-lock 168

U

undigestify-rmail-message 326
undo 32
unexpand-abbrev 291
unforward-rmail-message 321
universal-argument 38
universal-coding-system-argument
        184
unrmail 326
untabify 197
up-list 215
upcase-region 209
upcase-word 208

V

vc-annotate 125
vc-cancel-version 126
vc-create-snapshot 131
vc-diff 125
vc-directory 127
vc-dired-mark-locked 128
vc-dired-toggle-terse-mode 128
vc-insert-headers 135
vc-merge 130
vc-next-action 122
vc-print-log 126
vc-register 125

vc-rename-file 134
vc-retrieve-snapshot 132
vc-revert-buffer 126
vc-toggle-read-only 122, 145
vc-update-change-log 133
vc-version-other-window 124
vi-mode 387
view-buffer 145
view-diary-entries 356
view-emacs-FAQ 57
view-emacs-news 57
view-file 139
view-hello-file 175
view-lossage 57
view-register 75
vip-mode 387
viper-mode 387
visit-tags-table 254

W

what-cursor-position 36
what-line 36
what-page 36
where-is 53
which-function-mode 248

widen 382
widget-backward 397
widget-complete 397
widget-forward 397
window-configuration-to-register . . 76
word-search-backward 89
word-search-forward 89
write-abbrev-file 293
write-file 112
write-region 140

X

xdb 280

Y

yank 68
yank-pop 69
yank-rectangle 72
yow 388

Z

zap-to-char 67

Variable Index

A

abbrev-all-caps 290
abbrev-file-name 293
abbrev-mode 289
adaptive-fill-first-line-regexp . . 207
adaptive-fill-function 208
adaptive-fill-mode 208
adaptive-fill-regexp 208
ange-ftp-default-user 141
appt-display-diary 362
appt-issue-message 362
apropos-do-all 55
auto-coding-alist 183
auto-mode-alist 192
auto-save-default 118
auto-save-interval 119
auto-save-list-file-prefix 120
auto-save-timeout 119
auto-save-visited-file-name 118

B

backup-by-copying 115
backup-by-copying-when-linked 115
backup-by-copying-when-mismatch .. 115
backup-enable-predicate 113
baud-rate 84
blink-matching-delay 243
blink-matching-paren 243
blink-matching-paren-distance 243
bookmark-save-flag 78
bookmark-search-size 78
buffer-file-coding-system 183
buffer-read-only 145

C

c-basic-offset 242
c-comment-only-line-offset 267
c-comment-start-regexp 267
c-default-style 242
c-hanging-comment-ender-p 268
c-hanging-comment-starter-p 268
c-hungry-delete-key 266
c-mode-hook 228
c-mode-map 410

c-offsets-alist 242
c-special-indent-hook 242
c-strict-syntax-p 237
c-style-alist 242
c-syntactic-context 236
calendar-daylight-savings-ends ... 362
calendar-daylight-savings-ends-time
.... 363
calendar-daylight-savings-starts
.... 362
calendar-daylight-time-offset 363
calendar-daylight-time-zone-name
.... 349
calendar-latitude 349
calendar-location-name 349
calendar-longitude 349
calendar-standard-time-zone-name
.... 349
calendar-time-zone 349
calendar-week-start-day 344
case-fold-search 94
case-replace 96
change-major-mode-with-file-name
.... 193
coding 183
colon-double-space 206
comint-completion-addsuffix 375
comint-completion-autolist 375
comint-completion-fignore 370
comint-completion-recexact 375
comint-input-autoexpand 374
comint-input-ignoredups 375
comint-prompt-regexp 374
comint-scroll-show-maximum-output
.... 375
comint-scroll-to-bottom-on-input
.... 375
comint-scroll-to-bottom-on-output
.... 375
command-history 48
command-line-args 442
comment-column 246
comment-end 246
comment-indent-function 246
comment-line-start 273
comment-line-start-skip 273

comment-multi-line 246
comment-padding 245
comment-start 246
comment-start-skip 246
compare-ignore-case 139
compilation-scroll-output 278
compile-command 277
completion-auto-help 46
completion-ignored-extensions 45
ctl-arrow 83
ctl-x-4-map 410
ctl-x-map 410
current-input-method 179

D

dabbrev-abbrev-char-regexp 295
dabbrev-abbrev-skip-leading-regexp
    295
dabbrev-case-fold-search 294
dabbrev-case-replace 294
dabbrev-check-all-buffers 294
dabbrev-limit 293
dbx-mode-hook 283
default-buffer-file-coding-system
    185
default-directory 107
default-enable-multibyte-characters
    176
default-input-method 179
default-justification 225
default-major-mode 193
delete-auto-save-files 118
delete-old-versions 114
desktop-enable 385
desktop-files-not-to-save 385
diary-file 357
diary-hook 361
diary-mail-days 357
diff-switches 139
dired-chown-program 335
dired-copy-preserve-time 334
dired-garbage-files-regexp 330
dired-kept-versions 331
dired-listing-switches 329

dired-listing-switches (MS-DOS)
    472
display-time-24hr-format 82
dos-codepage 470
dos-display-scancodes 464
dos-hyper-key 463
dos-keypad-mode 463
dos-printer 469
dos-ps-printer 469
dos-super-key 463
dos-unsupported-character-glyph .. 471
double-click-time 417

E

echo-keystrokes 83
emacs-lisp-mode-hook 228
emerge-combine-versions-template
    262
emerge-startup-hook 263
enable-multibyte-characters .. 176, 188
enable-recursive-minibuffers 43
enriched-fill-after-visiting 220
enriched-translations 220
eol-mnemonic-dos 19
eol-mnemonic-mac 19
eol-mnemonic-undecided 19
eol-mnemonic-unix 19
esc-map 410
european-calendar-style 358
exit-language-environment-hook ... 177
explicit-shell-file-name 369

F

fast-lock-cache-directories 170
fast-lock-minimum-size 170
fast-lock-save-others 170
file-coding-system-alist 182
file-name-buffer-file-type-alist
    467
file-name-coding-system 186
file-name-handler-alist 141
fill-column 205
fill-prefix 207
find-file-existing-other-name 120

find-file-hooks 111
find-file-not-found-hooks 111
find-file-run-dired 110
find-file-visit-truename 120
find-ls-option 341
find-tag-marker-ring-length 256
font-lock-beginning-of-syntax-
    function 169
font-lock-mark-block-function 168
font-lock-maximum-decoration 169
font-lock-maximum-size 169
font-lock-support-mode 172
fortran-analyze-depth 270
fortran-break-before-delimiters .. 273
fortran-check-all-num 271
fortran-column-ruler 274
fortran-comment-indent-char 273
fortran-comment-indent-style 272
fortran-comment-line-extra-indent
    272
fortran-comment-region 273
fortran-continuation-indent 271
fortran-continuation-string 269
fortran-do-indent 271
fortran-electric-line-number 270
fortran-if-indent 271
fortran-line-number-indent 270
fortran-minimum-statement-indent ...
    271
fortran-structure-indent 271
fortran-tab-mode-default 270

G

gdb-mode-hook 283
gud-xdb-directories 280

H

help-map 410
highlight-nonselected-windows 61
highlight-wrong-size-font 187
history-length 47

I

indent-tabs-mode 197
indent-tabs-mode (Fortran mode)... 269
inferior-lisp-program 287
inhibit-eol-conversion 182
initial-major-mode 25
input-method-highlight-flag 178
input-method-verbose-flag 178
insert-default-directory 107
interpreter-mode-alist 192
inverse-video 83
isearch-mode-map 87
ispell-dictionary 105

J

jdb-mode-hook 283

K

kept-new-versions 114
kept-old-versions 114
kill-buffer-hook 146
kill-ring 70
kill-ring-max 69
kill-whole-line 66

L

latex-block-names 216
latex-mode-hook 218
latex-run-command 217
lazy-lock-defer-contextually 171
lazy-lock-defer-on-scrolling 171
lazy-lock-defer-time 170
lazy-lock-minimum-size 170
lazy-lock-stealth-lines 171
lazy-lock-stealth-time 171
lazy-lock-stealth-verbose 171
line-number-display-limit 82
lisp-body-indent 233
lisp-indent-offset 233
lisp-interaction-mode-hook 228
lisp-mode-hook 228
lisp-mode-map 410
list-directory-brief-switches 138

list-directory-verbose-switches .. 138
load-path 285
lpr-add-switches 378
lpr-command (MS-DOS) 469
lpr-commands 378
lpr-headers-switches 378
lpr-headers-switches (MS-DOS) ... 468
lpr-switches 378
lpr-switches (MS-DOS) 469

M

mail-abbrevs 305
mail-aliases 304
mail-archive-file-name 303
mail-default-reply-to 303
mail-from-style 304
mail-mode-hook 309
mail-personal-alias-file 304
mail-self-blind 302
mail-setup-hook 309
mail-signature 308
mail-user-agent 309
mail-yank-prefix 307
make-backup-files 113
Man-fontify-manpage-flag 249
mark-even-if-inactive 61
mark-ring 63
mark-ring-max 63
message-log-max 17
midnight-hook 146
midnight-mode 146
minibuffer-local-completion-map .. 411
minibuffer-local-map 411
minibuffer-local-must-match-map .. 411
minibuffer-local-ns-map 411
minibuffer-scroll-overlap 43
mode-line-inverse-video 83
mode-specific-map 410
mouse-scroll-min-lines 157
mouse-yank-at-point 159
muddle-mode-hook 228

N

next-line-add-newlines 31
next-screen-context-lines 79
no-redraw-on-reenter 83
nroff-mode-hook 219

O

outline-level 211
outline-minor-mode-prefix 210
outline-mode-hook 210
outline-regexp 211

P

page-delimiter 203
paragraph-separate 202
paragraph-start 202
parens-require-spaces 247
pdb-mode-hook 283
perldb-mode-hook 283
picture-mode-hook 297
picture-tab-chars 299
plain-tex-mode-hook 218
print-region-function (MS-DOS) .. 469
printer-name 378
printer-name (MS-DOS) 468
ps-font-family 380
ps-font-info-database 380
ps-font-size 380
ps-landscape-mode 379
ps-lpr-command 379
ps-lpr-command (MS-DOS) 469
ps-lpr-switches 379
ps-lpr-switches (MS-DOS) 469
ps-number-of-columns 379
ps-page-dimensions-database 379
ps-paper-type 379
ps-print-color-p 379
ps-print-header 379
ps-printer-name 379
ps-printer-name (MS-DOS) 469

R

read-quoted-char-radix............. 30
require-final-newline............. 113
revert-without-query.............. 117
rlogin-explicit-args.............. 376
rmail-decode-mime-charset 183
rmail-delete-after-output 317
rmail-delete-message-hook 314
rmail-dont-reply-to-names 320
rmail-edit-mode-hook.............. 326
rmail-file-coding-system 183
rmail-file-name................... 311
rmail-highlighted-headers 325
rmail-ignored-headers............. 325
rmail-mail-new-frame.............. 321
rmail-mode-hook................... 311
rmail-movemail-flags.............. 327
rmail-output-file-alist 317
rmail-pop-password................ 327
rmail-pop-password-required 327
rmail-preserve-inbox.............. 327
rmail-primary-inbox-list 314
rmail-redisplay-summary 323
rmail-retry-ignored-headers 320
rmail-secondary-file-directory ... 316
rmail-secondary-file-regexp 316
rmail-summary-line-count-flag 323
rmail-summary-window-size 323

S

same-window-buffer-names 154
same-window-regexps............... 154
save-abbrevs 293
scheme-mode-hook.................. 228
scroll-conservatively............. 80
scroll-margin 80
scroll-preserve-screen-position ... 80
sdb-mode-hook 283
search-slow-speed................. 87
search-slow-window-lines 88
selective-display-ellipses 82
sendmail-coding-system 183, 306
sentence-end 201
sentence-end-double-space 205
server-temp-file-regexp 377

server-window 377
set-language-environment-hook 177
shell-cd-regexp 369
shell-command-default-error-buffer
.... 368
shell-command-execonly 375
shell-command-regexp.............. 371
shell-completion-fignore 370
shell-file-name 368
shell-input-ring-file-name 374
shell-popd-regexp 369
shell-prompt-pattern.............. 374
shell-pushd-regexp................ 369
shell-set-directory-error-hook ... 369
slitex-mode-hook 218
slitex-run-command................ 217
sort-fold-case 382
special-display-buffer-names 163
special-display-frame-alist 164
special-display-regexps 164
split-window-keep-point 152
standard-fontset-spec............. 187
standard-indent 224
suggest-key-bindings.............. 49

T

tab-stop-list 197
tab-width......................... 84
tags-file-name 254
tags-table-list 254
term-file-prefix 423
term-setup-hook 423
tex-bibtex-command 218
tex-default-mode 214
tex-directory 217
tex-dvi-print-command............. 217
tex-dvi-view-command.............. 217
tex-main-file 218
tex-mode-hook 218
tex-run-command 217
tex-shell-hook 218
tex-show-queue-command 217
tex-start-options-string 218
text-mode-hook 209
track-eol......................... 31

truncate-lines 35
truncate-partial-width-windows ... 152

U

undo-limit 33
undo-strong-limit 33
unibyte-display-via-language-
    environment 189
user-mail-address 421

V

vc-command-messages 138
vc-comment-alist 135
vc-consult-headers 137
vc-default-back-end 125
vc-default-init-version 126
vc-directory-exclusion-list 128
vc-dired-recurse 127
vc-dired-terse-display 127
vc-follow-symlinks 137
vc-handle-cvs 136

vc-header-alist 135
vc-initial-comment 126
vc-keep-workfiles 137
vc-log-mode-hook 124
vc-make-backup-files 113, 137
vc-mistrust-permissions 137
vc-path 138
vc-static-header-alist 135
vc-suppress-confirm 138
version-control 114
visible-bell 83

W

w32-pass-alt-to-system 474
which-func-modes 248
window-min-height 155
window-min-width 155

X

x-cut-buffer-max 159
xdb-mode-hook 283

Concept Index

*

'*Messages*' buffer 17

.

'.mailrc' file 304

/

// in file name..................... 42

8

8-bit display....................... 189

A

A and B buffers (Emerge) 258
Abbrev mode..................... 289
abbrevs 289
aborting recursive edit 426
accented characters 188
accessible portion 382
accumulating scattered text.......... 70
action options (command line) 441
active fields (customization buffer) ... 395
adaptive filling 207
againformation 388
alarm clock........................ 362
ange-ftp........................... 141
appending kills in the ring........... 68
appointment notification 361
apropos 54
arguments (command line) 441
arguments, numeric 37
arguments, prefix 37
arrow keys 30
ASCII 21
Asm mode 275
astronomical day numbers 351
attribute (Rmail) 318
Auto Compression mode 140
Auto Fill mode 204
Auto Save mode 117
Auto-Lower mode.................. 164

B

Auto-Raise mode 164
autoload 285
Awk mode 227

back end (version control) 121
backend options (VC) 136
backtrace for bug reports 435
backup file 113
backup file names on MS-DOS 466
base buffer 149
batch mode 443
binding 23
blank lines 34
blank lines in programs.............. 245
body lines (Outline mode) 210
bold font 398
bookmarks 77
borders (X Windows) 452
boredom 388
branch (version control) 128
buffer menu 147
buffers 143
buggestion 388
bugs 430
building programs 277
button down events 416
byte code 285

C

C editing.......................... 227
c indentation styles 242
C mode 263
C-................................ 21
C++ mode......................... 263
calendar 343
calendar and LaTeX 346
calendar, first day of week 344
capitalizing words.................. 208
case conversion 208
centering.......................... 205
change buffers 143
change log......................... 249
Change Log mode 250

changes, undoing 32
character set (keyboard) 21
characters (in text) 24, 82
checking out files 121
checking spelling 103
Chinese 175
Chinese calendar 351
choosing a major mode 191
citing mail 307
click events 416
codepage, MS-DOS 470
coding systems 180
collision 116
color of window (X Windows) 450
colors 164
Column Number mode 82
columns (and rectangles) 71
columns (indentation) 195
columns, splitting 383
Comint mode 372
command 23
command history 47
command line arguments 441
comments 244
comparing files 139
compilation errors 277
Compilation mode 278
compilation under MS-DOS 472
complete 46
complete key 22
completion 43
completion (symbol names) 247
completion in Lisp 247
completion using tags 247
compression 140
conflicts 130
connecting to remote host 375
continuation line 35
Control 21
control characters 21
Control-Meta 228
converting text to upper or lower case
     208
Coptic calendar 351
copying files 140
copying text 67

CORBA IDL mode 263
correcting spelling 103
CPerl mode 227
crashes 117
creating files 109
creating frames 161
current buffer 143
cursor 15
cursor location 36
cursor location, under MS-DOS 467
cursor motion 30
customization 391
customization buffer 394
customization groups 395
customizing faces 398
customizing Lisp indentation 233
cut buffer 159
cutting and X 159
cutting text 65
CVS 121
cvs watch feature 136
CVSREAD environment variable (CVS)
     136

D

day of year 346
daylight savings time 362
DBX 280
debuggers 280
default argument 41
default-frame-alist 162
defining keyboard macros 405
defuns 230
deleting blank lines 34
deleting characters and lines 32
deleting files (in Dired) 329
deletion 65
deletion (of files) 140
deletion (Rmail) 313
desktop 385
Devanagari 175
developediment 388
diary 355
diary file 357
digest message 326

directory header lines 338
directory listing..................... 138
directory listing on MS-DOS 472
Dired 329
Dired sorting 340
disabled command 418
DISPLAY environment variable........ 448
display name (X Windows) 448
doctor 430
DOS codepages..................... 470
double clicks 416
double slash in file name 42
down events 416
drag events......................... 416
drastic changes 117
dribble file 433

E

echo area........................... 16
editable fields (customization buffer).. 395
editing binary files 384
editing in Picture mode 297
editing level, recursive............... 385
EDITOR environment variable........ 376
EDT............................... 386
Eldoc mode 248
Eliza.............................. 430
Emacs as a server................... 376
Emacs initialization file 419
Emacs-Lisp mode.................. 286
emacsclient........................ 376
Emerge 257
emulating other editors.............. 386
encoding of characters............... 175
end-of-line conversion 180, 181
end-of-line conversion on
          MS-DOS/MS-Windows 466
end-of-line conversion, mode-line
          indication 19
Enriched mode 219
entering Emacs 25
environment........................ 368
environment variables 444
erasing characters and lines........... 32
error log 277

error message in the echo area 16
(ESC) replacing (META) key 21
ESHELL environment variable........ 369
etags program 252
Ethiopian 175
Ethiopic calendar 351
European character sets 188
exiting 25
exiting recursive edit 385
expanding subdirectories in Dired 338
expansion (of abbrevs) 289
expansion of C macros 267
expression.......................... 228
expunging (Dired) 330
expunging (Rmail) 313

F

faces 166
faces under MS-DOS 464
Fast Lock mode 170
file dates 115
file directory....................... 138
file local variables.................. 403
file names 107
file names under MS-DOS 465
file names under Windows 95/NT 466
file truenames 120
files............................... 107
files, visiting and saving 109
fill prefix 206
filling text......................... 203
find and Dired 340
finding strings within text 85
flagging files (in Dired) 329
flow control 428
Flyspell mode 103
Follow mode....................... 81
font (default) 162
font (principal) 165
Font Lock mode 168
font name (X Windows) 449
fonts and faces 398
fonts, emulating under MS-DOS 464
fontsets 186
formatted text..................... 219

formfeed 202
Fortran continuation lines 269
Fortran mode 268
forwarding a message 321
frame size under MS-DOS 465
frames 157
frames on MS-DOS 464
French Revolutionary calendar 351
FTP 141
function 23
function definition 23
function key 409

G

GDB 280
geometry (X Windows) 451
getting help with keys 34
global keymap 408
global mark ring 63
global substitution 95
Gnus 365
Go Moku 388
graphic characters 29
Greek 175
Gregorian calendar 350
growing minibuffer 42
GUD library 280
gzip 140

H

hard newline 220
hardcopy 377
head version 129
header (TEX mode) 217
header line (Dired) 338
headers (of mail message) 302
heading lines (Outline mode) 210
Hebrew calendar 351
height of minibuffer 42
help 51
Hexl mode 384
hiding in Dired (Dired) 339
highlighting region 60
Hindi 175

history of commands 47
history of minibuffer input 46
history reference 374
holidays 347
HOME directory under MS-DOS 466
hook 400
horizontal scrolling 80
Hscroll mode 81
Hyper (under MS-DOS) 463

I

Icomplete mode 46
Icon mode 227
icons (X Windows) 453
IDL mode 263
ignoriginal 388
in-situ subdirectory (Dired) 338
inbox file 314
incremental search 85
indentation 195
Indentation Calculation 236
indentation for comments 244
indentation for programs 231
indirect buffer 149
indirect buffers and outlines 214
inferior process 277
inferior processes under MS-DOS 472
Info 57
Info index completion 247
init file 419
init file, default name under MS-DOS
        465
initial options (command line) 441
initial-frame-alist 162
input event 22
input methods 177
input with the keyboard 21
inserted subdirectory (Dired) 338
inserting blank lines 34
insertion 29
international scripts 175
international support (MS-DOS) 470
interval operator (in regexps) 253
invisible lines 210
IPA 175

Islamic calendar 351
ISO commercial calendar 351
ISO Latin character sets 188
iso-ascii library 189
iso-transl library 189
ispell program 105
italic font 398

J

Japanese 175
Java mode 263
JDB 280
Julian calendar 351
Julian day numbers 351
justification 205

K

Kerberos POP authentication 328
key 22
key bindings........................ 408
key rebinding, permanent 419
key rebinding, this session 411
key sequence 22
keyboard input 21
keyboard macro 405
keyboard translations 418
keymap 408
kill ring 67
killing buffers..................... 146
killing characters and lines 32
killing Emacs 25
killing rectangular areas of text 71
killing text 65
Korean........................... 175

L

label (Rmail) 318
language environment, automatic selection
    on MS-DOS 470
language environments 176
Lao 175
LaTeX mode 214
Lazy Lock mode 170

leaving Emacs 25
libraries........................... 285
line number commands 36
Line Number mode 82
line wrapping...................... 35
Lisp editing 227
Lisp string syntax.................. 420
Lisp symbol completion 247
list 228
listing current buffers 144
loading Lisp code 285
local keymap 410
local variables 401
local variables in files 403
location of point 36
locking (CVS) 136
locking and version control 122
locking files 116
locking under version control 136
locking, non-strict (RCS) 136
long file names in DOS box under
    Windows 95/NT 466
lpr usage under MS-DOS 469
Lucid Widget X Resources 456

M

M-................................. 21
Macintosh end-of-line conversion 181
macro expansion in C 267
mail 301
mail (on mode line) 82
mail aliases........................ 304
MAIL environment variable........... 314
Mail mode 305
mail-composition methods 309
MAILHOST environment variable 327
mailrc file 304
major modes 191
make 277
Makefile mode..................... 227
making pictures out of text characters
    297
manipulating paragraphs 201
manipulating sentences............. 200
manipulating text 199

manuals, on-line 57
Marathi........................... 175
mark.............................. 59
mark ring 63
marking in Dired 332
marking sections of text 62
Markov chain...................... 388
master file........................ 121
matching parentheses 243
Mayan calendar.................... 351
Mayan calendar round 355
Mayan haab calendar 354
Mayan long count.................. 354
Mayan tzolkin calendar............. 354
memory full 428
menu bar.......................... 19
Menu Bar mode 166
Menu X Resources (Lucid widgets)... 456
Menu X Resources (Motif widgets)... 457
merge buffer (Emerge) 258
merging changes 130
merging files....................... 257
message........................... 301
message number 311
messages saved from echo area........ 17
Meta.............................. 21
Meta (under MS-DOS).............. 463
Meta commands and words.......... 199
Midnight mode 146
minibuffer......................... 41
minibuffer history.................. 46
minibuffer keymaps 411
minor mode keymap 410
minor modes 391
mistakes, correcting................ 101
mode hook 228
mode line 17
mode line (MS-DOS)................ 471
mode, Abbrev 289
mode, Auto Compression 140
mode, Auto Fill 204
mode, Auto Save 117
mode, C 263
mode, Column Number.............. 82
mode, Comint 372
mode, Compilation................. 278

mode, CORBA IDL................. 263
mode, Emacs-Lisp 286
mode, Enriched.................... 219
mode, Fast Lock 170
mode, Follow 81
mode, Font Lock................... 168
mode, Fortran 268
mode, Hexl........................ 384
mode, Hscroll...................... 81
mode, Java........................ 263
mode, LaTeX...................... 214
mode, Lazy Lock 170
mode, Line Number................ 82
mode, Mail........................ 305
mode, major 191
mode, Menu Bar................... 166
mode, minor...................... 391
mode, Objective C................. 263
mode, Outline 210
mode, Overwrite................... 392
mode, Paragraph-Indent Text........ 209
mode, Pike........................ 263
mode, Resize-Minibuffer 42
mode, Scroll Bar................... 165
mode, Shell 370
mode, SliTEX...................... 214
mode, TEX 214
mode, Text 209
mode, Transient Mark............... 60
mode, View 139
modes for programming languages ... 227
modified (buffer)................... 109
moon, phases of 350
Motif Widget X Resources........... 457
mouse 409
mouse button events 416
mouse buttons (what they do) 157
mouse support under MS-DOS....... 463
movemail 327
movemail program 327
movement......................... 30
moving inside the calendar 343
moving point 30
moving text 67
moving the cursor.................. 30
MS-DOG 463

MS-DOS end-of-line conversion 181
MS-DOS peculiarities 463
MULE 175
multibyte characters 175
multiple displays 163
multiple views of outline 214
multiple windows in Emacs 151
mustatement 388

N

named configurations (RCS) 132
narrowing 382
newline 29
newlines, hard and soft 220
NFS and quitting 426
non-strict locking (RCS) 136
non-window terminals 172
nonincremental search 88
nroff 219
NSA 309
numeric arguments 37

O

Objective C mode 263
on-line manuals 57
operating on files in Dired 334
operations on a marked region 61
option, user 393
options (command line) 441
other editors 386
out of memory 428
Outline mode 210
outline with multiple views 214
outragedy 388
Overwrite mode 392

P

pages 202
Paragraph-Indent Text mode 209
paragraphs 201
parentheses 243
parts of the screen 15
pasting 67

pasting and X 159
patches, sending 437
PDB 280
per-buffer variables 401
Perl mode 227
Perldb 280
Persian calendar 351
phases of the moon 350
Picture mode and rectangles 299
pictures 297
Pike mode 263
point 15
point location 36
point location, under MS-DOS 467
POP inboxes 327
POP inboxes in reverse order 328
prefix arguments 37
prefix key 22
preprocessor highlighting 267
presidentagon 388
primary Rmail file 311
primary selection 159
printing under MS-DOS 472
program building 277
program editing 227
prompt 41
properbose 388
puzzles 388

Q

query replace 96
quitting 425
quitting (in search) 86
quitting Emacs 25
quitting on MS-DOS 463
quoting 29
quoting file names 141

R

RCS 121
read-only buffer 145
reading mail 311
reading netnews 365
rebinding keys, permanently 419
rebinding keys, this session 411
rebinding major mode keys 411
rebinding mouse buttons 416
rectangle 71
rectangles and Picture mode 299
recursive editing level 385
regexp 89
regexp syntax 90
region 59
region face 167
region highlighting 60
registered file 121
registers 75
regular expression 89
remote file access 141
remote host 375
repeating a command 39
replacement 95
reply to a message 320
REPLYTO environment variable 303
reporting bugs 432
Resize-Minibuffer mode 42
resolving conflicts 130
resources 453
restriction 382
retrying a failed message 320
Rlogin 375
Rmail 311
rot13 code 326
running Lisp functions 277
Russian 175

S

saved echo area messages 17
saving files 109
saving keyboard macros 407
saving option value 397
saving sessions 385
SCCS 121
screen 15
Scroll Bar mode 165
scrolling 79
scrolling in the calendar 345
SDB 280
search-and-replace commands 95
searching 85
searching in Rmail 313
secondary selection 159
selected buffer 143
selected window 151
selecting buffers in other windows 153
selection, primary 159
selective display 210
selective undo 32
self-documentation 51
sending mail 301
sending patches for GNU Emacs 437
sentences 200
server, using Emacs as 376
setting a mark 59
setting option value 396
setting variables 394
sexp 228
shell commands 367
shell commands, Dired 336
SHELL environment variable 369
Shell mode 370
Show Paren mode 243
simultaneous editing 115
single-frame terminals 172
size of minibuffer 42
slashes repeated in file name 42
SliTeX mode 214
snapshots and version control 131
soft newline 220
sorting 380
sorting Dired buffer 340
speedbar 162
spelling, checking and correcting 103
splitting columns 383
standard fontset 187
starting Emacs 25
startup (command line arguments) ... 441
startup (init file) 419
startup fontset 187

stealth fontification 171
string substitution 95
string syntax 420
subdirectories in Dired 338
subscribe groups 366
subshell 367
subtree (Outline mode) 213
summary (Rmail) 322
sunrise and sunset 349
Super (under MS-DOS) 463
suspending 25
switch buffers 143
switches (command line) 441
syntactic analysis 235
syntactic component 236
syntactic symbol 236
syntax highlighting 168
syntax table 419

T

tab stops 196
tables, indentation for 196
tags completion 247
tags table 250
Tcl mode 227
techniquitous 388
television 68
Telnet 375
TERM environment variable 433
termscript file 433
TEX mode 214
TEXEDIT environment variable 376
TEXINPUTS environment variable 217
text 199
text and binary files on
    MS-DOS/MS-Windows 466
Text mode 209
Thai 175
Tibetan 175
time (on mode line) 82
top level 17
tower of Hanoi 388
Transient Mark mode 60
transposition 230
triple clicks 416

truenames of files 120
truncation.......................... 35
trunk (version control) 128
two-column editing 383
typos, fixing 101

U

uncompression 140
undeletion (Rmail) 314
undigestify 326
undo.............................. 32
undo limit 33
unibyte operation 443, 445
Unibyte operation 188
unibyte operation (MS-DOS) 470
unsubscribe groups 366
untranslated file system 467
user option 393
userenced 388
using tab stops in making tables 196

V

variable 393
vc-resolve-conflicts 131
version control 120
VERSION_CONTROL environment variable
    114
vi................................ 386
Vietnamese........................ 175
View mode 139
viewing 139
views of an outline................ 214
visiting files.................. 108, 109

W

watching files (CVS) 136
weeks, which day they start on....... 344
widening 382
Windows clipboard support.......... 464
windows in Emacs 151
word processing 219
word search 88
word wrap 204

words................................. 199
words, case conversion 208
work file 121
wrapping........................... 35
WYSIWYG 219

X

X cutting and pasting.............. 159
XDB............................ 280
xon-xoff......................... 428

Y

yahrzeits......................... 353
yanking 67
yanking previous kills 69

Z

Zippy............................ 389
Zmacs mode....................... 61

Available from the Free Software Foundation...

This is a list of items available from the Free Software Foundation as of the publication of this manual. New items may not yet appear on this list. Please consult our web site at http://www.gnu.org/order/orders.html for current information and pricing, or call our distribution office at +1-617-542-5942.

BOOKS:

- **GNU Emacs Manual** - Just an editor? It's a lifestyle! 542 pp. $30
- **GNU Emacs Lisp Reference Manual** - 2 volumes, 948 pp. $60
- **Programming in Emacs Lisp: An Introduction** - 257 pp. $20
- **Using and Porting GNU CC** - Compilers for C, C++, etc. 574 pp. $35
- **Debugging with GDB** - How to use the GNU Debugger. 314 pp. $20
- **GNU Make** - Extensions, writing makefiles, reference. 174 pp. $20
- **Bison Manual** - YACC-compatible parser generator. 102 pp. $20
- **GAWK: GNU Awk User's Guide** - Easy text processing. 324 pp. $25
- **Texinfo** - Producing printed and online documentation. 244 pp. $25
- **C Library Reference Manual** - Revised for V.2. 2 vol., 1080 pp. $60
- **Flex: The Lexical Scanner Generator** - An improved lex. 120 pp. $20
- **Termcap Manual** - Display terminal data base library. 64 pp. $15
- **Calc Manual** - Numeric math and algebra in GNU Emacs. 572 pp. $50

OTHER ITEMS:

- **GNU Source Code CD-ROM** All the GNU project source code - 4 discs.
- **GNU Compiler Tools Binaries CD-ROM** Directly installable compiler executables for various systems (see *www.gnu.org/order/binaries.html*).
- **GNU Software for MS-Windows and MS-DOS and Compatible Systems** - the GNU compiler, tools, and utilities for various Microsoft OSes and compatible systems. This CD-ROM comes with a printed guide to installation. See *www.gnu.org/order/windows.html* for more info.
- **Reference cards** - available for Emacs, Calc, GDB, Flex, and Bison.
- **GNU t-shirts**

All purchases made from the FSF help support the development of more free software and documentation. The Free Software Foundation is a 501 (c) 3 not-for-profit corporation, and donations are tax-deductible in the U.S.

Free Software Foundation, 59 Temple Place, Suite 330, Boston, MA 02111
+1-617-542-5942 Fax: +1-617-542-2652 gnu@gnu.org http://www.gnu.org